THE PLATES
OF MORMON

THE PLATES OF MORMON

A BOOK OF MORMON STUDY EDITION

Based on Textual and Narrative Structures in the English Translation

EDITED BY
BRANT A. GARDNER

Greg Kofford Books
Salt Lake City, 2023

Copyright © 2023 Brant A. Gardner
Cover design copyright © 2023 Greg Kofford Books, Inc.
Cover design by Loyd Isao Ericson

Published in the USA.

All rights reserved. No part of this volume may be reproduced in any form without written permission from the publisher, Greg Kofford Books. The views expressed herein are the responsibility of the author and do not necessarily represent the position of Greg Kofford Books.

ISBN: 978-1-58958-776-2
Also available in ebook.

Greg Kofford Books
P.O. Box 1362
Draper, UT 84020
www.gregkofford.com
facebook.com/gkbooks
twitter.com/gkbooks

Library of Congress Control Number: 2023949919

For Royal Skousen,
whose important work on the Book of Mormon
manuscripts made this edition possible.

Contents

Introduction	ix

The Book of Mormon

Title Page	1
[The Book of Lehi]	3
The Book of Mosiah	5
The Book of Alma, the Son of Alma	69
The Book of Helaman	237
The Book of Nephi, the Son of Nephi	277
The Book of Nephi, One of the Disciples of Jesus Christ	339
The Book of Mormon	343
The Book of Ether	363
The Book of Moroni	397

The Small Plates of Nephi

The Words of Mormon	417
The Book of Nephi: His Reign and Ministry	419
The Book of Nephi	473
The Book of Jacob, the Brother of Nephi	551
The Book of Enos	569
The Book of Jarom	571
The Book of Omni	573

Introduction

In 2015, The Joseph Smith Papers Project published the Printer's Manuscript of the Book of Mormon.[1] Six years later, in 2021, the extant pages and fragments of the Original Manuscript followed.[2] Both of these publications present a photograph of a manuscript page on the left with the transcription (and notes) on the right. The transcription is faithful to the manuscript, meaning that there is no punctuation or paragraphing.

When the Printer's Manuscript was given to John H. Gilbert, the compositor and typesetter for Grandin Press, he had to create or delineate the sentences and paragraphs that would make the text more accessible. Although Gilbert's paragraphs have changed through versification and modern formatting, the sentences have persisted much as he punctuated them. This edition returns to the problem presented to Gilbert. As then, the challenge is to take the straight dictation copied onto the Printer's Manuscript and add punctuation and paragraph formatting to make the text easier to read.

The main source for this study edition is the electronic version of the Joseph Smith Paper's published transcript of the Printer's Manuscript. This was then compared to the printed transcript and accompanying images, which resulted in the discovery of a few errors that have been silently corrected. It should be noted that the printed transcript does not contain those errors.

Editorial Decisions

The following describes the features, organizational logic, and some of the added paratextual information in this edition. Many of these concepts are discussed more fully in the companion volume, *Engraven Upon Plates, Printed Upon Paper: Textual and Narrative Structures of the Book of Mormon*.[3] Reading the two books together provides the undergirding principles for the editorial decisions that are embodied here. Each book is also able to stand alone.

Mormon's Plates and the Small Plates

A reader's first experience with the Book of Mormon is not with the record that its ancient author and namesake originally intended. Instead, since its first edition in 1830, the Book of Mormon has opened with a replacement text containing records from earlier ancient authors who had different reasons for writing. The set of plates known as the small plates replaced the beginning of Mormon's record that disappeared when the so-called "lost 116 pages" containing the book of Lehi and the opening chapters of the

---

1. The Printer's Manuscript is almost completely intact. Wear on the bottom of the first page has resulted in the loss of one sentence on the recto and a line and some words from the line above it on the verso. In the published version, the missing text is supplied from the 1830 edition and grayed out to indicate that it has been restored. *Printer's Manuscript of the Book of Mormon*, xii.

2. "Of the nearly 500 pages that were placed in the Nauvoo House cornerstone, portions of 232 pages survive, amounting to roughly 28 percent of the text. Some of what remains is badly faded, obscured, or otherwise damaged." *Original Manuscript of the Book of Mormon*, xi.

3. Brant A. Gardner, *Engraven Upon Plates, Printed Upon Paper: Textual and Narrative Structures of the Book of Mormon* (Salt Lake City: Greg Kofford Books, 2013); hereafter cited as *Engraven Upon Plates*.

book of Mosiah were stolen.⁴ The Book of Nephi: His Reign and Ministry (also known as First Nephi) was the first book of those small plates that restored the Nephite history and stories that were on those pages. While the small plates offer a parallel history to the narrative that Mormon had written, he did not intend them to be a part of his account (W of M 1:1–7), and they do not reflect the way he compiled and framed his record.

Because of those lost pages, the great mind that conceived the Book of Mormon does not appear in the standard published text until The Words of Mormon. Like the books of the small plates, this short explanation was not part of Mormon's intended record. It was rather written as an introduction to that small set to explain why they were appended to his history. Although they were an introduction, evidence suggests that it was placed at the end of the small plates.

This edition has thus elected to begin with what has been retained of Mormon's planned Book of Mormon, opening with a placeholder for the lost book of Lehi as well as the unknown number of lost chapters from the beginning of the book of Mosiah. Those are followed by the books of Mosiah through Moroni. The small plates books (1 Nephi through Omni) are then included as an appendix of sorts, with The Words of Mormon acting as their introduction.⁵ Similarly, the Title Page was the last text on Mormon and Moroni's plates.⁶ Although physically at the end, it has always been moved to the beginning. This edition follows that convention.

Revision of Spelling and Grammar

The Book of Mormon was dictated during an age when English spelling was yet to be standardized, with each of Joseph Smith's scribes having an idiosyncratic way of spelling some words. This edition corrects spelling to modern expectations. However, there are some cases where the spelling might affect how the passage is understood. In those cases, a particular meaning has been selected for the text with a note discussing the reason for the decision.

The general standardization of spelling does not extend to the standardization of grammar. At times, a plural noun was written where a singular noun would be expected. For example, several times the text indicates that one would do something with their "mights." There are also many cases where there are problems with subject-verb agreement, and these are retained as written. For example, "they was" has not been changed to "they were."

There are several places where the text has some version of "had eat" rather than "had eaten." This may represent the dialectical pronunciation "had et." It has been retained as a possible representation of the dialect.

Both the Original and Printer's Manuscripts have random capitalizations, which have been regularized here. In some cases, capitalization has been removed to conform to modern usage. Thus, there are places where words such as "heaven," "hell," and "church" are capitalized in the manuscripts but not in this edition. The capitalized versions too easily recall modern definitions that may or may not match the concept conveyed in the text.

---

4. For a history and investigation into this loss, see Don Bradley, *The Lost 116 Pages: Reconstructing the Book of Momron's Missing Pages* (Salt Lake City: Greg Kofford Books, 2019), 57–82.

5. The reasons for this are explored in detail in Chapter 15 of *Engraven Upon Plates*.

6. "History, circa June–October 1839 [Draft 1]," 9, The Joseph Smith Papers, accessed September 29, 2023, https://www.josephsmithpapers.org/paper-summary/history-circa-june-october-1839-draft-1/9.

Finally, the manuscripts often use the abbreviation "&C" rather than write out "etcetera." These have silently been expanded to the full form. Similarly, "&" has been silently replaced with "and."

Altered Text and Deletions

This edition uses square brackets to indicate places where a word has been added that differs from that in the Printer's Manuscript. For example, 1 Nephi 1:7 reads: "And it came to pass [that] in the which rebellion, they were desirous to return unto the land of Jerusalem." The word "that" in square brackets was taken from the Original and is missing in the Printer's Manuscript. Each entry in brackets is explained in a footnote.

There is a special case where the text is quoting passages from the King James Bible and an italicized word has been removed. Empty square brackets mark the missing word or words, with a footnote providing the information on what was removed. For example, 2 Nephi 13:14 reads: "The Lord will enter into judgment with the ancients of his people, and the princes thereof. For ye have eaten up the vineyard and the spoil of the poor [ ] your houses." The empty brackets mark the removal of the words "is in" from the King James Bible.

The Logic for the Punctuation of Sentences

There is no single correct way to punctuate the text. John Gilbert's punctuation allowed for much longer sentences than modern readers prefer. It is possible that the longer sentences better reflect the dictated nature of the text. Despite that, this edition intentionally attempts to create shorter sentences where possible to make reading easier. With longer ones, parentheses are often added to assist the reader in comprehending some of the complex sentences.

There are also a significant number of incomplete sentences in the manuscripts, only some of which have been corrected in subsequent editions. These have been punctuated as best as they can be. Footnotes indicate the existence of the incomplete sentence and at times discuss the reason the sentence remains as is.

In general, Gilbert did an excellent job of demarcating and punctuating sentences. Nevertheless, there have been a few cases where the sentence construction here differ. In at least one case, the difference is significant. The following replicates Gilbert's sentences for Ether 12:6–9 that are still in the current edition:

> And now, I, Moroni, would speak somewhat concerning these things; I would show unto the world that faith is things which are hoped for and not seen; wherefore, dispute not because ye see not, for ye receive no witness until after the trial of your faith.
>
> For it was by faith that Christ showed himself unto our fathers, after he had risen from the dead; and he showed not himself unto them until after they had faith in him; wherefore, *it must needs be that some had faith in him, for he showed himself not unto the world.*
>
> But because of the faith of men he has shown himself unto the world, and glorified the name of the Father, and prepared a way that thereby others might be partakers of the heavenly gift, that they might hope for those things which they have not seen.
>
> Wherefore, ye may also have hope, and be partakers of the gift, if ye will but have faith.

As punctuated, we have the confusing claim that Jesus did not show himself unto the world, even though it appears clear that the purpose of the passage is to indicate that he did. Because "but" often begins new sentences, in verse 8 Gilbert created a logical sentence beginning with that word. The problem in this case is that "but" also often takes a slightly different meaning in the manuscripts. In this case, it should be read as "except." A change in punctuation restores that intent:

> And now I, Moroni, would speak somewhat concerning these things. I would show unto the world that faith is things which are hoped for and not seen. Wherefore, dispute not because ye see not. For ye receive no witness—not until after the trial of your faith. For it was by faith that Christ showed himself unto our fathers, after that he had risen from the dead. And he showed [not] himself unto them until after they had faith in him. Wherefore, it must needs be that some had faith in him. *For he showed himself not unto the world but because of the faith of men.*
>
> He has shown himself unto the world and glorified the name of the Father, and prepared a way that thereby others might be partakers of the heavenly gift, that they might hope for those things which they have not seen. Wherefore, ye may also have hope and be partakers of the gift—if ye will but have faith.

It is a small change, but it makes sense of the otherwise confusing claim.

The Logic for the Creation of Paragraphs

Modern written English has conventions for what constitutes a paragraph. This edition intentionally uses an entirely different concept for creating them.[7] In ancient texts written prior to the invention of punctuation, the function of separating ideas or events relied upon textual markers rather than visual indications. For example, the ubiquitous "and it came to pass" functions as a textual flow marker. It marks the movement of the text and events through time (and is therefore almost exclusively appearing in historical narrative rather than doctrinal exposition). Based on that function, this edition typically uses the phrase as the basis for a new paragraph, even when the resulting one is rather short.

Where "and it came to pass" moves the text through time, "and now" marks new information that is associated with the same timeframe as the previous information.[8] They function similarly to the English markers "after" and "with." It is also used as a basis for beginning a new paragraph.

Other words that have been used in various editions of the Book of Mormon to introduce a paragraph do not have that function in this formatting. For example, in this

---

7. The details of the Book of Mormon constructions behind these decisions are found in Chapter 6 of *Engraven Upon Plates*.

8. According to John Gee, "An analysis of the original Book of Mormon chapter division shows that the phrase 'and now' serves as verbal punctuation marking a major break in the text both between and within chapters. The Book of Mormon phrase is a literal translation of the Hebrew expression $w't(h)$, which is used both in the Hebrew Bible and in Epigraphic Hebrew to mark a transition between major sections of text." John Gee, "Verbal Punctuation in the Book of Mormon I: (And) Now," *Interpreter: A Journal of Latter-day Saint Faint and Scholarship* 50 (2022): 48. While I agree that "and now" marks divisions, my reading of the function in the Book of Mormon text comes from the text itself rather than comparison to any ancient language.

edition, "therefore" does not begin a new paragraph. It is a conclusion to the argument that begins earlier and is thus left associated with the argument.

Finally, there are some cases where this edition separates lines to represent an intentional repetition of elements. These were likely literary elements that were intended for the reader to understand. They may be seen as poetic forms, although many are not and instead are simply the result of the literary competence of the writer.

The Logic for Chapters and Headers

The chapters in this formatting follow those of the manuscripts and the pre-1879 editions of the Book of Mormon. However, since most readers will be more familiar with the modern chapter and verse numbering, those have been retained. Modern chapters are noted in bold square brackets. Sentences do not always conform to verses, but the verse numbers have been inserted in the familiar locations in superscript.

The Original and Printer's Manuscripts have book headers and chapter headers that are translations from Mormon's golden plates and were thus original to the text. These have been augmented with chapter synopses in modern editions. As these synopses were not part of the translation of Mormon's writings, they are not included here. There are some cases where this edition makes a different decision on the division between a header and the text. In most cases, the manuscripts provided Gilbert with no indication for where the header ended and the main text began. He did an excellent job in making the divisions in most cases. When this edition has relocated the division, an explanation is provided in a footnote.

Asides and Insertions

When Mormon or another author or editor inserts information that is tangential to the initial purpose of their writing, the aside is set off with arrow brackets (> <). They are typically footnoted to explain the nature of the aside or insertion. Where the insertion is long, it is also indented.

Long Isaiah (and Other) Quotations

Isaiah was a poet prophet whose writings are considered excellent poetry. His and other poetic texts have been formatted as such. The formatting herein has interacted with that in Grant Hardy's *The Book of Mormon: Maxwell Institute Study Edition*.[9] Sometimes it follows Hardy, other times it is arranged differently.

In some cases, Hardy elected to format some of Isaiah in prose. Robert Alter's translation of the Hebrew Bible[10] was consulted for those passages, and this edition instead follows Alter's poetic formatting.

This edition also follows Hardy in using boldface to mark the locations where words have been added to what we have in the King James Bible passages. There are no footnotes to explain the added text. Nevertheless, there are differences between the bolded text in this edition compared to Hardy's edition. The *Maxwell Institute Study*

---

9. Grant Hardy, ed., *The Book of Mormon: Maxwell Institute Study Edition* (Provo, UT: Neal A. Maxwell Institute, 2018).

10. Robert Alter, *The Hebrew Bible: The Prophets*, vols. 2–3 (New York and London: W. W. Norton & Company, 2019).

Edition is based on the most recent edition of the Book of Mormon, and this edition relies upon the Printer's Manuscript. Some of the entries Hardy highlighted were the result of editorial changes made after the Book of Mormon was initially published. One place where that makes a difference is 1 Nephi 20:1, where Joseph Smith added the phrase "or out of the waters of baptism" for the 1840 edition. As it was not in the Printer's Manuscript, the phrase is not included here.

As a last comment on editing, I wish to reprise Moroni's statement: "And now, if there are faults they are the mistakes of men" (Title Page). There are numerous edits on the Printer's Manuscript, and the attempt here was made to keep those relevant to the first printing; however, the errors of men (this editor) are inevitable.

Quotations, Allusions, and Echoes

The Book of Mormon's language not only echoes the language of the King James Bible, but specific verses are often directly quoted as they appear in that text. This edition provides footnotes to the quoted or alluded passages. It is not exhaustive but should represent the majority—and most important—of those quotations or allusions. These footnotes rely heavily on the work of Nicholas J. Frederick.[11] For the Old Testament quotations, an unpublished paper created by Dave Larsen for Book of Mormon Central was used with permission.

Finally, three important resources should be noted that are invaluable to this and any in depth study of the text of the Book of Mormon:

- Royal Skousen and Robin Scott Jensen, eds., *Revelations and Translations, Volume 3: Printer's Manuscript of the Book of Mormon*. Facsimile edition. Part 1 and 2 of vol. 3 of the Revelations and Translations series of The Joseph Smith Papers, edited by Ronald J. Esplin and Matthew J. Grow. (Salt Lake City: Church Historian's Press, 2015)
- Royal Skousen and Robin Scott Jensen, eds., *Revelations and Translations, Volume 5: Original Manuscript of the Book of Mormon*. Facsimile edition. Vol. 5 of the Revelations and Translations series of *The Joseph Smith Papers*, edited by Matthew C. Godfrey, R. Eric Smith, Matthew J. Grow, and Ronald J. Esplin. (Salt Lake City: Church Historian's Press, 2021)
- Royal Skousen, *Analysis of Textual Variants of the Book of Mormon*. Parts 1–6 of the Critical Text of the Book of Mormon, 1st ed. (Provo, UT: Foundation for Ancient Research & Mormon Studies and Neal A. Maxwell Institute for Religious Scholarship, 2004–2009)

These are referenced throughout this study edition as *Printer's Manuscript of the Book of Mormon*, *Original Manuscript of the Book of Mormon*, and Skousen, *Analysis of Textual Variants*.

---

11. Nicholas J. Frederick, "The Book of Mormon and Its Redaction of the King James New Testament: A Further Evaluation of the Interaction between the New Testament and the Book of Mormon," *Journal of Book of Mormon Studies* 27 (2018): 44–87.

The Book of Mormon

An account written by the hand of Mormon upon plates. Taken from the plates of Nephi.[a] Wherefore, it is an abridgment of the record of the people of Nephi, and also of the Lamanites.

> Written to the Lamanites (which are a remnant of the house of Israel).
>   And also to Jew and Gentile.
> Written by way of commandment.
>   And also by the spirit of prophesy and of revelation.
> Written and sealed up, and hid up, unto the Lord.
>   That they might not be destroyed.
> To come forth by the gift and power of God, unto the interpretation thereof.
>
> Sealed by the hand of Moroni
> and hid up unto the Lord
>   to come forth in due time,
>   by the way of Gentile.
> The interpretation thereof by the gift of God.[b]

(>An abridgment taken from the book of Ether also, which is a record of the people of Jared which were scattered at the time the Lord confounded the language of the people when they were building a tower to get to heaven.[c]<)

---

a. Beginning with the 1830 edition, these sentences were formatted as a subtitle. They are an essential part of the message and have therefore been moved to the text. In addition, they have been separated into two sentences to better indicate that the Book of Mormon is written upon plates and that it is the text of the Book of Mormon that is taken from the plates of Nephi, not that the plates themselves which were taken from the plates of Nephi.

b. These sentences have been formatted to highlight the repeated concepts. Although repetition and parallelism may be defined as poetry, the Book of Mormon rarely uses them as formal poetry. In these sentences, the various repetitions serve to highlight the message through the repetition even though they do not conform to a particular poetic structure.

c. This sentence is somewhat problematic. It comes immediately before the statement: "which is to show unto the remnant of the house of Israel how great things the Lord hath done for their fathers." If these sentences are read in sequence, then this purpose statement would refer to the book of Ether and not to the entirely of the Book of Mormon. The statement should apply to the whole and not just to the book of Ether. Therefore, it is placed in parentheses to set it off as an insertion rather than a continual thought.

Moroni is the author of the Title Page and editor of the book of Ether. Although this is the Title Page for his father's work, he wanted to make certain to note his own contribution. Thus, it is an inserted afterthought. It would be convenient to suppose that there was an original draft of the Title Page that Moroni copied and inserted this sentence as he copied. That would conform with practices we will see throughout the Book of Mormon. However, there is no evidence for an earlier draft. It is also possible that Moroni included this statement here at the time it occurred to him. It clearly interrupts the flow of the text.

Which is to show unto the remnant of the House of Israel
> how great things the Lord
> hath done for their fathers.

And that they may know the covenants of the Lord—
> that they are not cast off forever.

And also to the convincing of the Jew and Gentile
> that Jesus is the Christ,
> the Eternal God—
> manifesting himself unto all nations.

And now if there be fault, it be the mistake of men. Wherefore, condemn not the things of God, that ye may be found spotless at the Judgment Seat of Christ.

[The Book of Lehi]

[The following by Joseph Smith was included in the first edition of the published Book of Mormon as a preface to explain the absence of the original book of Lehi that was lost among the earliest translated pages of the golden plates.]

To the Reader——

As many false reports have been circulated respecting this, the following, work and also many unlawful measures taken by evil designing persons to destroy me, and also the work, I would inform you that I translated by the gift & power of God and caused to be written, one hundred and sixteen pages, the which I took from the Book of Lehi (which was an account abridged from the plates of Lehi by the hand of Mormon), which said account some person, or persons, have stolen and kept from me—notwithstanding my utmost exertion to recover it again.

And being commanded of the Lord that I should not translate the same over again (for Satan had put it into their hearts to tempt the Lord their God by altering the words that they did read—contrary from that which I translated and caused to be written)—and if I should bring forth the same words again—or in other words if I should translate the same over again—they would publish that which they had stolen. And Satan would stir up the hearts of this generation that they might not receive this work.

But behold, the Lord said unto me: "I will not suffer that Satan shall accomplish his evil design in this thing. Therefore, thou shalt translate from the plates of Nephi until ye come to that which ye have translated, which ye have retained. And behold, ye shall publish it as the record of Nephi. And thus, I will confound those who have altered my words. I will not suffer that they shall destroy my work. Yea, I will shew unto them that my wisdom is greater than the cunning of the Devil."

Wherefore, to be obedient unto the commandments of God, I have—through his grace and mercy, accomplished that which he hath commanded me respecting this thing.

I would also inform you that the plates of which hath been spoken was found in the township of Manchester, Ontario County, New York.

The Author

The Book of Mosiah

[Mosiah – Unknown number of missing chapters]

Two clues in the Printer's Manuscript indicate that some early chapters of the book of Mosiah were lost along with the book of Lehi. The first is the absence of a book header following the book title, which is something that all other individual abridged books in the Book of Mormon begin with.[a]

The second is that when preparing the Printer's Manuscript, Oliver Cowdery initially labeled the opening chapter of Mosiah as "Chapter III," which was later changed to "Chapter I" by crossing out two of the Roman numeral Is. Because of this some have assumed that the original number reflected the chapter count before Martin Harris lost the early manuscript, and have thus concluded that two chapters had been lost. However, there seems to be a better explanation for the chapter numbering, which was added later as the manuscript was being prepared for publication—sometimes skipping a number or accidentally continuing the chapter count from the previous book.[b]

It seems that this latter type of mistake is the best explanation for the "Chapter III." In the Printer's Manuscript Cowdery originally assigned the book of Omni as "Chapter I," and The Words of Mormon was mistakenly numbered "Chapter 2.d." The opening extant chapter of Mosiah was likely assigned "III" as a logical continuation of that numbering.[c]

Although we cannot know the number of chapters that were lost, we can identify some of its narrative history. With book titles named after initial dynastic leaders,[d] the book of Mosiah was likely named for Mosiah (the father of king Benjamin, and the first Nephite king not directly of Nephi's lineage) and would have thus contained at least the story of him becoming the new king of the Nephites and meeting with the people of Zarahemla, if not also the departure from the land of Nephi. The transition from Mosiah to Benjamin is also missing, as well as the description of the wars that led up to the current chapter 1 of the book of Mosiah. Some of that information is available at the end of the book of Omni and the end of The Words of Mormon.[e] Based on the lengths of Mormon's abridged accounts of Nephite history throughout his record, it is likely that the missing history of the first Mosiah covered multiple chapters.

---

a. For more on the headers see Chapter 6 of *Engraven Upon Plates*.

b. Royal Skousen, "Critical Methodology and the Text of the Book of Mormon," *FARMS Review* 6, no. 1 (1994): 138.

c. For an extended analysis, see Brant A. Gardner, "When Hypotheses Collide: Responding to Lyon and Monson's 'When Pages Collide,'" *Interpreter: A Journal of Mormon Scripture* 5 (2013): 110–13.

d. See Chapter 12 of *Engraven Upon Plates*.

e. For an in-depth exploration of this lost history, see Don Bradley, *The Lost 116 Pages: Reconstructing the Book of Momron's Missing Pages* (Salt Lake City: Greg Kofford Books, 2019), 241–84.

Chapter I [Mosiah 1–3]

[1] ¹And now, there was no more contention in all the land of Zarahemla, among all the people which belonged to King Benjamin, so that King Benjamin had continual peace all the remainder of his days.

²And it came to pass that he had three sons. And he called their names Mosiah, and Helorum, and Helaman. And he caused that they should be taught in all the language of his fathers, that thereby they might become men of understanding, and that they might know concerning the prophesies which had been spoken by the mouths of their fathers (which was delivered them by the hand of the Lord). ³And he also taught them concerning the records which were engraven on the plates of brass, saying:

My sons, I would that ye should remember that were it not for these plates (which contain these records and these commandments) we must have suffered in ignorance even at this present time, not knowing the mysteries of God.[a] ⁴For it were not possible that our father Lehi could have remembered all these things to have taught them to his children, except it were for the help of these plates. For he, having been taught in the language of the Egyptians—therefore he could read these engravings and teach them to his children, that thereby they could teach them to their children.

And so, fulfilling the commandments of the Lord God, even down to this present time, ⁵I say unto you, my sons, were it not for these things which have been kept and preserved by the hand of the Lord God (that we might read and understand of his mysteries and have his commandments always before our eyes), that even our fathers would have dwindled in unbelief. And we should have been like unto our brethren the Lamanites, which know nothing concerning these things, or even do not believe them when they are taught them, because of the tradition of their fathers, which are not correct.

⁶O my sons! I would that ye should remember that these sayings are true. And also that these records are true. And behold, also the plates of Nephi which contain the records and the sayings of our fathers from the time they left Jerusalem until now—and they are true. And we can know of their surety because we have them before our eyes.

⁷And now my sons, I would that ye should remember to search them diligently, that ye may profit thereby. And I would that ye should keep the commandments of God, that ye may prosper in the land, according to the promises which the Lord made unto our fathers.

⁸And many more things did King Benjamin teach his sons which are not written in this book.

⁹And it came to pass that after King Benjamin had made an end of teaching his sons that he waxed old. And he saw that he must very soon go the way of all the earth.[b] ¹⁰Therefore, he thought it expedient that he should confer the kingdom upon one of his sons. Therefore, he had Mosiah brought before him. And these are the words which he spake unto him, saying:

---

a. The phrase "mystery of God" appears in 1 Corinthians 4:1, Colossians 2:2, and Revelation 10:7.
b. See 1 Kings 2:2: "I go the way of all the earth."

My son, I would that ye should make a proclamation throughout all this land among all this people (or the people of Zarahemla, and the people of Mosiah, which dwell in this land), that thereby they may be gathered together. For on the morrow I shall proclaim unto them, this my people, out of mine own mouth, that thou art a king and a ruler over this people which the Lord our God hath given us.

[11] And moreover, I shall give this people a name, that thereby they may be distinguished above all the people which the Lord God hath brought out of the land of Jerusalem. And this I do because they have been a diligent people in keeping the commandments of the Lord. [12] And I give unto them a name that never shall be blotted out, except it be through transgression.

[13] Yea, and moreover I say unto you, that if this highly favored people of the Lord should fall into transgression, and become a wicked and an adulterous people, that the Lord will deliver them up, that thereby they become weak like unto their brethren. And he will no more preserve them by his matchless and marvelous power as he hath hitherto preserved our fathers. [14] For I say unto you, that if he had not extended his arm in the preservation of our fathers, they must have fallen into the hands of the Lamanites and become victims to their hatred.

[15] And it came to pass that after King Benjamin had made an end of these sayings to his son, that he gave him charge concerning all the affairs of the kingdom. [16] And moreover, he also gave him charge concerning the records which were engraven on the plates of brass. And also the plates of Nephi. And also the sword of Laban. And the ball (or director, which led our fathers through the wilderness, which was prepared by the hand of the Lord, that thereby they might be lead, every one, according to the heed and diligence which they gave unto him). [17] Therefore, as they were unfaithful, they did not prosper nor progress in their journey, but were driven back and incurred the displeasure of God upon them. And therefore, they were smitten with famine and sore afflictions to stir them up in remembrance of their duty.

[18] And now it came to pass that Mosiah went and did as his father had commanded him. And proclaimed unto all the people which were in the land of Zarahemla, that thereby they might gather themselves together, to go up to the temple to hear the words which his father should speak unto them.

[2] [1] And it came to pass that after Mosiah had done as his father had commanded him, and had made a proclamation throughout all the land, that the people gathered themselves together throughout all the land, that they might go up to the temple to hear the words which King Benjamin should speak unto them. [2] And there were a great number, even so many that they did not number them. For they had multiplied exceedingly and waxed great in the land.

[3] And they also took of the firstlings of their flocks, that they might offer sacrifice and burnt offerings according to the law of Moses. [4] And also, that they might give thanks to the Lord, their God, who had brought them out of the land of Jerusalem. And who had delivered them out of the hands of their enemies. And had appointed just men to be their teachers. And also a just man to be their king—who had established peace in the land of Zarahemla, and who had taught them to keep the commandments of God—that thereby they might rejoice and be filled with love towards God and all men.

[5] And it came to pass that when they came up to the temple, they pitched their tents

round about—every man according to his family (consisting of his wife, and his sons, and his daughters, and their sons, and their daughters, from the eldest down to the youngest). Every family being separate one from another. ⁶And they pitched their tents round about the temple, every man having his tent with the door thereof towards the temple, that thereby they might remain in their tents and hear the words which King Benjamin should speak unto them. ⁷For the multitude being so great that King Benjamin could not teach them all within the walls of the temple. Therefore, he caused a tower to be erected, that thereby his people might hear the words which he should speak unto them.

⁸And it came to pass that he began to speak to his people from the tower. And they could not all hear his words because of the greatness of the multitude. Therefore, he caused that the words which he spake should be written and sent forth among those that were not under the sound of his voice, that they might also receive his words. ⁹And these are the words which he spake, and caused to be written, saying:

> My brethren, all ye that have assembled yourselves together, you that can hear my words which I shall speak unto you this day. For I have not commanded you to come up hither to trifle with the words which I shall speak. But that you should hearken unto [me[a]]—and open your ears, that ye may hear—and your hearts, that ye may understand—and your minds, that the mysteries of God[b] may be unfolded to your view.
>
> ¹⁰I have not commanded you to come up hither that ye should fear me, or that ye should think that I, of myself, am more than a mortal man. ¹¹But I am (like as yourselves) subject to all manner of infirmities in body and mind. Yet, as I have been chosen by this people, and was consecrated by my father, and was suffered by the hand of the Lord that I should be a ruler and a king over this people.[c] And have been kept and preserved by his matchless power to serve thee with all the might, mind, and strength, which the Lord hath granted unto me. ¹²I say unto you, that as I have been suffered to spend my days in your service (even up to this time).[d] And have not sought gold, nor silver, nor no manner of riches of you. ¹³Neither have I suffered that ye should be confined in dungeons. Nor that ye should make slaves one [of[e]] another. Or that ye should murder. Or plunder or steal. Or commit adultery. Or even I have not suffered that ye should commit any manner of wickedness—and have taught you that ye should keep the commandments of the Lord in all things which he hath commanded you.
>
> ¹⁴And even I, myself, have labored with mine own hands that I might serve you, and that ye should not be laden with taxes, and that there should nothing come upon you which was grievous to be borne. And of all these things (which I have spoken), ye yourselves are witnesses this day. ¹⁵Yet, my brethren, I have not done these things that I might boast. Neither do I tell these things that thereby I

---

a. The Printer's Manuscript has "you." This has a superlinear insertion of "me," which is the intended meaning. It was probably corrected during the proofreading.

b. The phrase "mystery of God" appears in 1 Corinthians 4:1, Colossians 2:2, and Revelation 10:7.

c. The sentence appears to run through the end of verse 13. It is never complete. To make it easier to read, it has been broken up with the understanding that this highlights the incompleteness.

d. The text continues to have a hanging verb: "as I have been." It is not resolved.

e. The Printer's Manuscript has "with." Oliver Cowdery changed it to the more appropriate "of."

might accuse you. But I tell you these things that ye may know that I [can^a] answer a [clean^b] conscience before God this day.

¹⁶Behold I say unto you, that because I said unto you that I had spent my days in your service, I do not desire to boast. For I have only been in the service of God. ¹⁷And behold, I tell you these things that ye may learn wisdom—that ye may learn that when ye are in the service of your fellow beings, ye are only in the service of your God.

¹⁸Behold, ye have called me your king. And if I, whom ye call your king, do labor to serve you, then had not ye ought to labor to serve one another?

¹⁹And behold also, if I, who ye call your king, who has spent his days in your service (and yet hath been in the service of God), doth merit any thanks from you, O how had you ought to thank your heavenly king! ²⁰I say unto you, my brethren, that if you should render all the thanks and praise which your whole souls hath power to possess to that God who hath created you, and hath kept and preserved you, and hath caused that ye should rejoice, and hath granted that ye should live in peace one with another—²¹I say unto you, that if ye should serve him, who hath created you from the beginning, and art preserving you from day to day by lending you breath (that ye may live, and move, and do according to your own will, and even supporting you, from one moment to another)—I say, if ye should serve him with all your whole soul—and yet ye would be unprofitable servants.

²²And behold, all that he requires of you is to keep his commandments. And he hath promised you that if ye would keep his commandments, ye should prosper in the land. And he never doth vary from that which he hath said. Therefore, if ye do keep his commandments, he doth bless you and prosper you.

²³And now, in the first place he hath created you and granted unto you your lives. For which ye are indebted unto him. ²⁴And secondly, he doth require that ye should do as he hath commanded you. For which, if ye do, he doth immediately bless you. And therefore, he hath paid you. And ye are still indebted unto him—and are, and will be forever and ever. Therefore, of what have ye to boast?

²⁵And now I ask, can ye say ought of yourselves? I answer you, nay. Ye cannot say that thou art even as much as the dust of the earth. Yet thou wast created of the dust of the earth. But behold, it belongeth to him who created you.

²⁶And I, even I, whom ye call your king, am no better than ye yourselves are. For I am also of the dust. And thou beholdest that I am old and am about to yield up this mortal frame to its mother earth. ⁷Therefore, as I said unto you—that I had served you, walking with a clear conscience before God—even so I, at this time, have caused that ye should assemble yourselves together, that I might be found blameless and that your blood should not come up on me when I shall stand to be judged of God of the things whereof he hath commanded me concerning you.

²⁸I say unto you that I have caused that ye should assemble yourselves together,

---

a. Probably added during proofreading.

b. Skousen, *Analysis of the Textual Variants*, 2:1148: "Here in the printer's manuscript, Cowdery initially wrote 'a clear conscience', which is what we expect. He virtually immediately overwrote the final *r* of *clear* with an *n* . . . , thus ending up with 'a clean conscience', which is also possible (but not what we expect)." Skousen continues to note that Cowdery had other instances where an "r" in the original was copied as an "n" in the Printer's Manuscript. It was typeset as "clear" in the 1830 printed version.

that I might rid my garments of your blood at this period of time, when I am about to go down to my grave, that I might go down in peace. And my immortal spirit may join the choirs above in singing the praises of a just God.

²⁹And moreover, I say unto you that I have caused that ye should assemble yourselves together that I might declare unto you that I can no longer be your teacher nor your king. ³⁰For even at this time, my whole frame doth tremble exceedingly while attempting to speak unto you. But the Lord God doth support me, and hath suffered me that I should speak unto you. And hath commanded me that I should declare unto you this day that my son Mosiah is a king and a ruler over you.

³¹And now, my brethren, I would that ye should do as ye hath hitherto done. As ye have kept my commandments, and also the commandments of my father, and have prospered and have been kept from falling into the hands of your enemies—even so, if ye shall keep the commandments of my son (or the commandments of God which shall be delivered unto you by him[a]), ye shall prosper in the land. And your enemies shall have no power over you.

³²But, O my people! Beware lest there shall arise contentions among you, and ye list to obey the evil spirit (which was spoken of by my father Mosiah). ³³For behold, there is a wo pronounced upon him who listeth to obey that spirit. For if he listeth to obey him, and remaineth, and dieth in his sins—the same drinketh damnation to his own soul. For he receiveth for his wages an everlasting punishment, having transgressed the law of God contrary to his own knowledge.

³⁴I say unto you, that there are not one among you, except it be your little children, that have not been taught concerning these things—but what knoweth that ye are eternally indebted to your heavenly Father—to render to him all that you have and are—and also have been taught concerning the records (which contain the prophesies which hath been spoken by the holy prophets, even down to the time our father Lehi left Jerusalem)—³⁵and also all that hath been spoken by our fathers until now. And behold, also they spake that which was commanded them of the Lord, therefore they are just and true.

³⁶And now I say unto you my brethren, that after ye have known and have been taught all these things, if ye should transgress and go contrary to that which hath been spoken, that ye do withdraw yourselves from the spirit of the Lord, that it may have no place in you—to guide you in wisdom's paths, that ye may be blessed, prospered, and preserved. ³⁷I say unto you, that the man that doeth this, the same cometh out in open rebellion against God. Therefore, he listeth to obey the evil spirit and becometh an enemy to all righteousness. Therefore, the Lord hath no place in him, for he dwelleth not in unholy temples.[b] ³⁸Therefore, if that man repenteth not, and remaineth, and dieth, an enemy to God, the demands of divine justice doth awaken his immortal soul to a lively sense of his own guilt, which doth cause him to shrink from the presence of the Lord, and doth fill his

---

a. Before correction, this phrase was "shall be delivered unto him by you." This was clearly incorrect and therefore changed with superlinear insertions.

b. Amulek provides a quotation in Alma 34:36, but it is not present outside of the Book of Mormon. The reference to temples suggests that it was on the brass plates.

breast with guilt, and pain, and anguish, which is like an unquenchable fire whose flames ascendeth up forever, and ever.[a]

[39]And now, I say unto you that mercy hath no claim on that man. Therefore, his final doom is to endure a never-ending torment.

[40]O all ye old men! And also ye young men! And you little children (which can understand my words)! For I have spoken plain unto you, that ye might understand. I pray that ye should awake to a remembrance of the awful situation of those that have fallen into transgression. [41]And moreover, I would desire that ye should consider on the blessed and happy state of those that keep the commandments of God. For behold, they are blessed in all things, both temporal and spiritual. And if they hold out faithful to the end, they are received into heaven, that thereby they may dwell with God in a state of never-ending happiness.

O remember, remember that these things are true! For the Lord God hath spoken it.

[3] [1]And again, my brethren, I would call your attention. For I have somewhat more to speak unto you. For behold, I have things to tell you concerning that which is to come. [2]And the things which I shall tell you are made known unto me by an angel from God.

[3]And he said unto me: "Awake!"

And I awoke. And behold, he stood before me. And he said unto me:

Awake! And hear the words which I shall tell thee! For behold, I am come to declare unto thee glad tidings of great joy.[b] [4]For the Lord hath heard thy prayers. And hath judged of thy righteousness. And hath sent me to declare unto thee, that thou mayest rejoice. And that thou mayest declare unto thy people that they also may also be filled with joy.

[5]For behold, the time cometh, and is not far distant, that with power the Lord Omnipotent (who reigneth, which was, and is, from all eternity to all eternity) shall come down from heaven among the children of men and shall dwell in a tabernacle of clay—and shall go forth amongst men, working mighty miracles—such as healing the sick, raising the dead, causing the lame to walk, the blind to receive their sight, and the deaf to hear, and curing all manner of diseases. [6]And he shall cast out devils (or the evil spirits which dwelleth in the hearts of the children of men). [7]And lo, he shall suffer temptations and pain of body—hunger, thirst, and fatigue. Even more than man can suffer, except it be unto death. For behold, blood cometh from every pore, so great shall be his anguish for the wickedness and the abominations of his people.

[8]And he shall be called Jesus Christ, the Son of God, the Father of Heaven and of Earth, the Creator of all things from the beginning. And his mother shall be called Mary. [9]And lo, he cometh unto his own, that salvation might come unto the children of men, even through faith on his name.

And even after all this, they shall consider him as a man, and say that he hath a devil—and shall scourge him and shall crucify him. [10]And he shall rise the third day from the dead.

And behold, he standeth to judge the world.

---

a. See Revelation 14:11: "And the smoke of their torment ascendeth up for ever and ever."
b. See Luke 2:10: "Fear not: for, behold, I bring you good tidings of great joy."

And behold all these things are done that a righteous judgment might come upon the children of men.

¹¹For behold, and also his blood atoneth for the sins of those who have fallen by the transgression of Adam who hath died not knowing the will of God concerning them, and who have ignorantly sinned. ¹²But wo! Wo unto him who knoweth that he rebelleth against God! For salvation cometh to none such, except it be through repentance, and faith on the Lord Jesus Christ.

¹³And the Lord God hath sent his holy prophets among all the children of men to declare these things to every kindred, nation, and tongue—that thereby, whosoever should believe that Christ should come, the same might receive remission of their sins and rejoice with exceeding great joy, even as though he had already come among them.

¹⁴Yet, the Lord God saw that his people were a stiff-necked people. And he appointed unto them a law, even the law of Moses. ¹⁵And many signs, and wonders, and types, and shadows, showed he unto them concerning his coming. And also holy prophets spake unto them concerning his coming. And yet, they hardened their hearts, and understood not, that the law of Moses availeth nothing, except it were through the atonement of his blood.

¹⁶And even if it were possible that little children could sin, they could not be saved. But I say unto you, they are blessed. For behold, as in Adam (or by nature) they fall, even so the blood of Christ atoneth for their sins. ¹⁷And moreover, I say unto you that there shall be no other name given, nor no other way, nor means, whereby salvation can come unto the children of men. Only in and through the name of Christ, the Lord Omnipotent. ¹⁸For behold, he judgeth. And his judgment is just. And the infant perisheth not that dieth in his infancy.

But men drinketh damnation to their own souls, except they humble themselves and become as little children and believeth that salvation was, and is, and is to come—in and through the atoning blood of Christ the Lord Omnipotent. ¹⁹For the natural man is an enemy to God, and has been from the fall of Adam. And will be forever, and ever, but if[a] he yieldeth to the enticings of the Holy Spirit and putteth off the natural man and he becometh a Saint through the atonement of Christ the Lord—and becometh as a child: submissive, meek, humble, patient, full of love, willing to submit to all things which the Lord seeth fit to inflict upon him, even as a child doth submit to his father.

²⁰And moreover, I say unto you, that the time shall come when the knowledge of a Savior shall spread throughout every nation, kindred, tongue, and people.[b] ²¹And behold, when that time cometh, none shall be found blameless before God (except it be little children), only through repentance, and faith on the name of the Lord God Omnipotent.

²²And even at this time, when thou shalt have taught thy people the things

---

a. The 1920 edition of the Book of Mormon changed this to "unless." The phrase "but if" was once used with that meaning but is now obsolete. In current usage, "but if" would lead to an incomplete sentence. See Skousen, *Analysis of the Textual Variants*, 2:1173.

b. See Revelation 14:6: "And I saw another angel fly in the midst of heaven, having the everlasting gospel to preach unto them that dwell on the earth, and to every nation, and kindred, and tongue, and people."

which the Lord thy God hath commanded thee, even then are they found no more blameless in the sight of God, only according to the words which I have spoken unto thee.

²³And now, I have spoken the words which the Lord God hath commanded me. ²⁴And thus saith the Lord:

> They shall stand as a bright testimony against this people at the judgment day, whereof they shall be judged—every man according to his works, whether they be good, or whether they be evil. ²⁵And if they be evil, they are consigned to an awful view of their own guilt, and abominations, which doth cause them to shrink from the presence of the Lord into a state of misery and endless torment, from whence they can no more return. ²⁶Therefore, they have drunk damnation to their own souls. Therefore, they have drunk out of the cup of the wrath of God, which justice could no more deny unto them than it could deny that Adam should fall because of his partaking of the forbidden fruit. Therefore, mercy could have claim on them no more, forever. ²⁷And their torment is as a lake of fire and brimstone,[a] whose flames are unquenchable, and whose smoke ascendeth up forever.[b]

And ever thus hath the Lord commanded me. Amen.

---

a. See Revelation 20:14: "And death and hell were cast into the lake of fire. This is the second death."
b. See Revelation 14:11: "And the smoke of their torment ascendeth up for ever and ever."

Chapter II [Mosiah 4]

[4] ¹And now it came to pass that when King Benjamin had made an end of speaking the words which had been delivered unto him by the angel of the Lord, that he cast his eyes round about on the multitude. And behold, they had fell to the earth, for the fear of the Lord had come upon them. ²And they had viewed themselves in their own carnal states, even less then the dust of the earth.

And they all cried aloud with one voice, saying: "O, have mercy, and apply the atoning blood [a] Christ, that we may receive forgiveness of our sins, and our hearts may be purified. For we believe in Jesus Christ, the Son of God, who created heaven and earth, and all things—who shall come down among the children of men."

³And it came to pass that after they had spoken these words, the spirit of the Lord came upon them. And they were filled with joy, having received a remission of their sins, and having peace of conscience because of the exceeding faith which they had in Jesus Christ (which should come, according to the words which King Benjamin had spoken unto them).

⁴And King Benjamin again opened his mouth, and began to speak unto them, saying:

My friends, and my brethren, my kindred, and my people! I would again call your attention, that ye may hear and understand the remainder of my words which I shall speak unto you. ⁵For behold, that if the knowledge of the goodness of God at this time hath awakened you to a sense of your nothingness and your worthlessness and fallen state—

⁶I say unto you, that if ye have come to a knowledge of the goodness of God, and his matchless power, and his wisdom, and his patience, and his glory, long-suffering towards the children of men, and also the atonement, which hath been prepared from the foundation of the world that thereby salvation might come to him that should put his trust in the Lord, and should be diligent in keeping his commandments, and continue in the faith, even unto the end of his life (I mean the life of the mortal body)—

⁷I say, that this is the man that receiveth salvation through the atonement which was prepared from the foundation of the world for all mankind, which ever was, ever since the fall of Adam, or which is or which ever shall be, even unto the end of the world.[b] ⁸And this is the means whereby salvation cometh. And there is none other salvation, save this, which hath been spoken of. Neither is there any conditions whereby man can be saved, except the conditions which I have told you.

⁹Believe in [God[c]]. Believe that he is, and that he created all things, both in heaven and in earth. Believe that he hath all wisdom, and all power, both in heaven and in earth. Believe that man doth not comprehend all the things which the Lord can comprehend.

---

a. The Printer's Manuscript has "that we," which is clearly a copy error. Oliver Cowdery discovered the error and corrected it to "of."

b. This is a very long sentence, beginning in verse 5 and only ending here. Although it is a single sentence, it is separated into paragraphs to assist the reader in following the multiple internal clauses.

c. The word "God" had been left out of the Printer's Manuscript. It was restored superlinearly and appears in the 1830 edition. It was probably missed while copying and restored upon proofreading.

Chapter II [Mosiah 4]

[10] And again, believe that ye must repent of your sins, and forsake them—and humble yourselves before God, and ask in sincerity of heart that he would forgive you. And now, if you believe all these things—see that ye do them.

[11] And again I say unto you (as I have said before), that as ye have come to the knowledge of the glory of God (or if ye have known of his goodness and have tasted of his love), and have received a remission of your sins (which causeth such exceeding great joy in your souls), even so, I would that ye should remember, and always retain in remembrance, the greatness of God, and your own nothingness—and his goodness and long-suffering towards you unworthy creatures—and humble yourselves even in the depths of humility, calling on the name of the Lord daily—and standing steadfastly in the faith of that which is to come, which was spoken by the mouth of the angel.

[12] And behold I say unto you, that if ye do this, ye shall always rejoice and be filled with the love of God—and always retain a remission of your sins, and ye shall grow in the knowledge of the glory of him who created you (or in the knowledge of that which is just and true). [13] And ye will not have a mind to injure one another, but to live peaceably and to render to every man according to that which is his due. [14] And ye will not suffer your children that they go hungry or naked. Neither will you suffer that they transgress the laws of God, and fight and quarrel one with another—and [serve[a]] the devil (which is the master of sin, or which is the evil spirit which hath been spoken of by our fathers, he being an enemy to all righteousness). [15] But ye will teach them to walk in the ways of truth, and soberness. Ye will teach them to love one another, and to serve one another.

[16] And also ye, yourselves, will succor those that stand in need of your succor. Ye will administer of your substance unto him that standeth in need. And ye will not suffer that the beggar putteth up his petition to you in vain and turn him out to perish.

[17] Perhaps thou shalt say: "The man hath brought upon himself his misery, therefore I will stay my hand and will not give unto him of my food, nor impart unto him of my substance (that he may not suffer). For his punishments are just." [18] But I say unto you, O man! Whosoever doeth this, the same hath great cause to repent. And except he repenteth of that which he hath done, he perisheth forever and hath no interest in the kingdom of God. [19] For behold, are we not all beggars? Do we not all depend upon the same being, even God, for all the substance which we have, for both food and raiment, and for gold, and for silver, and for all the riches which we have of every kind?

[20] And behold, even at this time ye have been calling on his name and begging for a remission of your sins. And hath he suffered that ye have begged in vain? Nay, he hath poured out his spirit upon you, and hath caused that your hearts should be filled with joy, and hath caused that your mouths should be stopped that ye could not find utterance—so so exceeding great was your joy!

[21] And now, if God (who hath created you, on whom you are dependent for your lives, and for all that ye have, and are), doth grant unto you whatsoever ye ask

---

a. The Printer's Manuscript has "save," which is clearly incorrect. The correction to "serve" was done later, probably during proofreading. Skousen, *Analysis of the Textual Variants,* 2:1187.

(that is right) in faith, believing that ye shall receive[a]—O then how had ye ought to impart of the substance that ye have one to another!

²²And if ye judge the man who putteth up his petition to you for your substance (that he perish not) and condemn him—how much more just will be your condemnation for withholding your substance, which doth not belong to you—but to God, to whom also your life belongeth! And yet, ye put up no petition or repenteth not of the thing which thou hast done. ²³I say unto you, wo be unto that man! For his substance shall perish with him. And now, I say these things unto those which are rich as pertaining to the things of this world.

²⁴And again, I say unto the poor, ye that have not and yet hath sufficient that ye remain from day to day—I mean all you that deny the beggar because ye have not—I would that ye say in your hearts that I give not because I have not. But if I had, I would give. ²⁵And now, if ye say this in your hearts, ye remain guiltless. Otherwise, ye are condemned, and your condemnation is just. For ye covet that which ye have not received.

²⁶And now, for the sake of these things which I have spoken unto you, that is, for the sake of retaining a remission of your sins from day to day (that ye may walk guiltless before God), I would that ye should impart of your substance to the poor—every man according to that which he hath. Such as feeding the hungry. Clothing the naked. Visiting the sick and administering to their relief, both spiritually and temporally, according to their wants.

²⁷And see that all these things are done in wisdom and order. For it is not requisite that a man should run faster than what he hath strength. And again, it is expedient that he should be diligent, that thereby he might win the prize. Therefore, all things must be done in order.

²⁸And I would that ye should remember that whosoever among you that borroweth of his neighbor should return the thing that he borroweth, according as he doth agree, or else thou shalt commit sin—and perhaps thou shalt cause thy neighbor to commit sin also.

²⁹And finally, I cannot tell you all the things whereby ye may commit sin. For there are divers ways and means, even so many that I cannot number them. ³⁰But this much I can tell you—that if ye do not watch yourselves, and your thoughts, and your words, and your deeds, and observe to keep the commandments of God, and continue in the faith of what ye have heard concerning the coming of our Lord, even unto the end of your lives—ye must perish.

And now, remember, O man! Remember, and perish not!

---

a. Echoes Matthew 21:22: "And all things, whatsoever ye shall ask in prayer, believing, ye shall receive."

Chapter III [Mosiah 5]

[5] ¹And now it came to pass that when King Benjamin had thus spoken to his people, he sent among them, desiring to know of his people if they believed the words which he had spoken unto them. ²And they all cried with one voice, saying:

Yea, we believe all the words which thou hast spoken unto us. And also we know of their surety and truth because of the spirit of the Lord Omnipotent, which hath wrought a mighty change in us (or in our hearts)—that we have no more disposition to do evil, but to do good continually. ³And we ourselves, also, through the infinite goodness of God and the manifestations of his spirit, have great views of that which is to come. And were it expedient, we could prophesy of all things.

⁴And it is the faith which we have had on the things, which our king hath spoken unto us, and hath brought us to this great knowledge, whereby we do rejoice with such exceeding great joy. ⁵And we are willing to enter into a covenant with our God, to do his will, and to be obedient to his commandments in all things that he shall command us all the remainder of our days, that we may not bring upon ourselves a never-ending torment, as has been spoken by the angel, that we may not drink out of the cup of the wrath of God.

⁶And now, these are the words which King Benjamin desired of them. And therefore, he said unto them:

Ye have spoken the words that I desired. And the covenant which ye have made is a righteous covenant.

⁷And now, because of the covenant which ye have made, ye shall be called the children of Christ—his sons, and his daughters. For behold, this day he hath spiritually begotten you.[a] For ye say that your hearts are changed through faith on his name. Therefore, ye are born of him, and have become his sons and his daughters. ⁸And under this head, ye are made free. And there is no other head, whereby ye can be made free. There is no other name given whereby salvation cometh. Therefore, I would that ye should take upon you the name of Christ, all you that have entered into the covenant with God—that ye should be obedient unto the end of your lives.

⁹And it shall come to pass that whosoever doeth this shall be found at the right hand of God. For he shall know the name by which he is called. For he shall be called by the name of Christ. ¹⁰And now, it shall come to pass that whosoever shall not take upon them the name of Christ must be called by some other name. Therefore, he findeth himself on the left hand of God.

¹¹And I would that ye should remember also, that this is the name that I said I should give unto you, that never should be blotted out except it be through transgression. Therefore, take heed that ye do not transgress, that the name be not blotted out of your hearts.

¹²I say unto you, I would that ye should remember to retain the name written always in your hearts, that ye are not found on the left hand of God—but that ye hear, and know, the voice by which ye shall be called, and also the name by which he

---

a. Perhaps an allusion to Psalm 2:7: "Thou art my Son; this day have I begotten thee."

shall call you. ¹³For how knoweth a man the master which he hath not served, and which is a stranger unto him, and is far from the thoughts and intents of his heart?

¹⁴And again, doth a man take an ass which belongeth to his neighbor, and keep him? I say unto you nay. He will not even suffer that he shall feed among his flocks, but will drive him away, and cast him out. I say unto you, that even so shall it be among you, if ye know not the name by which ye are called. ¹⁵Therefore, I would that ye should be steadfast, and immovable—always abounding in good works[a]—that Christ, the Lord God Omnipotent, may seal you his—that you may be brought to heaven, that ye may have everlasting salvation and eternal life through the wisdom, and power, and justice, and mercy of him who created all things in heaven and in earth. Who is God above all. Amen.

---

a. See 1 Corinthians 15:58: "Therefore, my beloved brethren, be ye steadfast, unmoveable, always abounding in the work of the Lord."

Chapter IV [Mosiah 6]

[6] ¹And now King Benjamin thought it was expedient, after having finished speaking to the people, that he should take the names of all those who had entered into a covenant with God, to keep his commandments.

²And it came to pass that there was not one soul, save it were little children, but what had entered into the covenant, and had taken upon them the name of Christ.

³And again, it came to pass that when King Benjamin had made an end of all these things, and had consecrated his son Mosiah to be a ruler and a king over his people, and had given him all the charges concerning the kingdom, and also had appointed priests to teach the people (that thereby they might hear and know the commandments of God, and to stir them up in remembrance of the oath which they had made)—he dismissed the multitude. And they returned (every one according to their families) to their own houses.

⁴And Mosiah began to reign in his father's stead. And he began to reign in the thirtieth year of his age, making (in the whole) about four hundred and seventy six years from the time that Lehi left Jerusalem.

⁵And King Benjamin lived three years. And he died.

⁶And it came to pass that King Mosiah did walk in the ways of the Lord. And did observe his judgments, and his statutes. And did keep his commandments in all things, whatsoever he commanded him. ⁷And King Mosiah did cause his people, that they should till the earth. And he also himself did till the earth, that thereby he might not become burdensome to his people, that he might do according to that which his father had done in all things. And there was no contention among all his people for the space of three years.

Chapter V [Mosiah 7–8]

[7] ¹And now it came to pass that after King Mosiah had had continual peace for the space of three years, he was desirous to know concerning the people which went up to dwell in the land of Lehi-Nephi (or in the city of Lehi-Nephi). For his people had heard nothing from them from the time they left the land of Zarahemla. Therefore, they wearied him with their teasings.

²And it came to pass that King Mosiah granted that sixteen of their strong men might go up to the land of Lehi-Nephi, to enquire concerning their brethren.

³And it came to pass that on the morrow they started to go up, having with them one Ammon, he being a strong and mighty man, and a descendent of Zarahemla. And he was also their leader.

⁴And now, they knew not the course they should travel in the wilderness to go up to the land of Lehi-Nephi. Therefore, they wandered many days in the wilderness, even forty days did they wander. ⁵And when they had wandered forty days, they came to a hill which is north of the land of Shilom. And there they pitched their tents.

⁶And Ammon took three of his brethren (and their names were Amaleki, Helem, and Hem) and they went down into the land of Nephi. ⁷And behold, they met the king of the people which was in the land of Nephi and in the land of Shilom. And they were surrounded by the king's guard, and was taken, and was bound, and was committed to prison.

⁸And it came to pass, when they had been in prison two days, they were again brought before the king. And their bands were loosed. And they stood before the king and was permitted (or rather commanded) that they should answer the questions which he should ask them. ⁹And he saith unto them:

> Behold, I am Limhi, the son of Noah, which was the son of Zeniff, which came up out of the land of Zarahemla to inherit this land, which was the land of their fathers, which was made a king by the voice of the people. ¹⁰And now, I desire to know the cause whereby ye were so bold as to come near the walls of the city when I, myself, was with my guards without the gate.
>
> ¹¹And now, for this cause have I suffered that ye should be preserved, that I might enquire of you. Or else I should have caused that my guards should have put you to death.
>
> Ye are permitted to speak.

¹²And now, when Ammon saw that he was permitted to speak, he went forth and bowed himself before the king. And rising again, he said:

> O king! I am very thankful before God this day that I am yet alive and am permitted to speak. And I will endeavor to speak with boldness. ¹³For I am assured that if ye had known me, ye would not have suffered that I should have wore these bands. For I am Ammon, and am a descendant of Zarahemla, and have come up out of the land of Zarahemla to enquire concerning our brethren which Zeniff brought up out of that land.

¹⁴And now it came to pass that after Limhi had heard the words of Ammon, he was exceeding glad. And said:

Now, I know of a surety that my brethren (which was in the land of Zarahemla) are yet alive! And now I will rejoice! And on the morrow, I will cause that my people shall rejoice also. ¹⁵For behold, we are in bondage to the Lamanites, and are taxed with a tax which is grievous to be borne.

And now behold, our brethren will deliver us out of our bondage (or out of the hands of the Lamanites). And we will be their slaves. For it is better that we be slaves to the Nephites then to pay tribute to the king of the Lamanites.

¹⁶And now, King Limhi commanded his guards, that they should no more bind Ammon nor his brethren—but caused that they should go to the hill which was north of Shilom, and bring their brethren into the city, that thereby they might eat, and drink, and rest, themselves from the labors of their journey. For they had suffered many things. They had suffered hunger, thirst, and fatigue.

¹⁷And now it came to pass on the morrow, that King Limhi sent a proclamation among all his people, that thereby they might gather themselves together to the temple to hear the words which he should speak unto them.

¹⁸And it came to pass that when they had gathered themselves together, that he spake unto them in this wise, saying:

O ye my people! Lift up your heads! And be comforted! For behold, the time is at hand (or is not far distant) when we shall no longer be in subjection to our enemies, notwithstanding our many strugglings (which have been in vain). Yet, I trust there remaineth an effectual struggle to be made. ¹⁹Therefore, lift up your heads, and rejoice! And put your trust in God—in that God who was the God of Abraham, and Isaac, and Jacob. And also that God who brought the children of Israel out of the land of Egypt and caused that they should walk through the Red Sea on dry ground—and fed them with manna, that they might not perish in the wilderness. And many more things did he do for them. ²⁰And again, that same God hath brought our fathers out of the land of Jerusalem, and hath kept and preserved his people, even until now.

And behold, it is because of our iniquities and abominations that has brought us into bondage. ²¹And ye all are witnesses this day, that Zeniff[a] (who was made king over this people), he being over-zealous to inherit the land of his fathers, therefore being deceived by the cunning and craftiness of King Laman—who, having entered into a treaty with King Zeniff and having yielded up into his hands the possessions of a part of the land (or even the city of Lehi-Nephi, and the city of Shilom, and the land round about)—²²and all this he done for the sole purpose of bringing this people into subjection, or into bondage.[b]

And behold, we, at this time, do pay tribute to the king of the Lamanites—to the amount of one half of our corn, and our barley, and even all our grain of every kind—and one half of the increase of our flocks, and our herds. And even one half of all we have or possess, the king of the Lamanites doth exact of us—or our lives!

²³And now, is not this grievous to be borne? Is not this, our afflictions, great?

---

a. Oliver Cowdery originally wrote Zenith and corrected it to Zeniff.

b. The verbal phrase "having yielded up" is not grammatically resolved. A slightly different rendering of verse 22 would have completed the verb. This suggests that verse 22 is the intended result and that the intervening clauses caused the sentence to drift in the dictation.

Now behold, how great reason have we to mourn. ²⁴Yea, I say unto you, great are the reasons which we have to mourn! For behold, how many of our brethren have been slain, and their blood hath been spilt in vain? And all because of iniquity. ²⁵For if this people had not fallen into transgression, the Lord would not have suffered that this great evil should come upon them. But behold, they would not hearken unto his words. But there arose contentions among them, even so much that they did shed blood among themselves.

²⁶And a prophet of the Lord have they slain, yea, a chosen man of God, who told them of their wickedness and abominations, and prophesied of many things which is to come, yea, even the coming of Christ—²⁷and because he saith unto them that Christ was the God, the father of all things. And saith that he should take upon him the image of man. And it should be the image after which man was created in the beginning (or, in other words, he said that man was created after the image of God). And that God should come down among the children of men. And take upon him flesh and blood. And go forth upon the face of the earth. ²⁸And now, because he said this, they did put him to death.

And many more things did they do which brought down the wrath of God upon them. Therefore, who wondereth that they are in bondage, and that they are smitten with sore afflictions? ²⁹For behold, the Lord hath said: "I will not succor my people in the day of their transgression, but I will hedge up their ways, that they prosper not. And their doings shall be as a stumbling block before them."

³⁰And again, he saith: "If my people shall sow filthiness, they shall reap the chaff thereof in the whirlwind. And the effects thereof is poison."

³¹And again, he saith: "If my people shall sow filthiness, they shall reap the east wind, which bringeth immediate destruction."

³²And now behold, the promise of the Lord is fulfilled. And ye are smitten and afflicted, ³³but if[a] ye will turn to the Lord with full purpose of heart and put your trust in him and serve him with all diligence of mind. And if ye do this, he will, according to his own will and pleasure, deliver you out of bondage.

[8] ¹And it came to pass that after King Limhi had made an end of speaking to his people (for he spake many things unto them, and only a few of them have I written in this book), he told his people all the things concerning their brethren which were in the land of Zarahemla. ²And he caused that Ammon should stand up before the multitude and rehearse unto them all that had happened unto their brethren from the time that Zeniff went up out of the land even until the time that he himself came up out of the land. ³And he also rehearsed unto them the last words which King Benjamin had taught them, and explained them to the people of King Limhi so that they might understand all the words which he spake.

⁴And it came to pass that after he had done all this, that King Limhi dismissed the multitude. And caused that they should return, every one unto his own house.

⁵And it came to pass that he caused that the plates which contained the record of his people, from the time that they left the land of Zarahemla, should be brought before Ammon, that he might read them.

⁶Now, as soon as Ammon had read the record, the king inquired of him to know if

---

a. Should be read with the meaning of "unless."

Chapter V [Mosiah 7–8]

he could interpret languages. And Ammon told him that he could not. ⁷And the king saith unto him:

I, being grieved for the afflictions of my people, I caused that forty and three of my people should take a journey into the wilderness that thereby they might find the land of Zarahemla, that we might appeal unto our brethren to deliver us out of bondage. ⁸And they were lost in the wilderness for the space of many days. Yet, they were diligent and found not the land of Zarahemla—but returned to this land having traveled in a land among many waters, having discovered a land which was covered with bones of men and of beasts. And was also covered with ruins of buildings of every kind. Having discovered a land which had been peopled with a people which were a numerous as the hosts of Israel.

⁹And for a testimony that the things that they have said is true, they have brought twenty-four plates which are filled with engravings. And they are of pure gold. ¹⁰And behold, also they have brought breastplates, which are large. And they are of brass and of copper and are perfectly sound.

¹¹And again, they have brought swords. The hilts thereof hath perished, and the blades thereof were cankered with rust. And there is no one in the land that is able to interpret the language, or the engravings, that are on the plates. Therefore, I said unto thee, canst thou translate?

¹²And I say unto thee again, knowest thou of anyone that can translate? For I am desirous that these records should be translated into our language. For perhaps they will give us a knowledge of a remnant of the people which have been destroyed, from whence these records came. Or perhaps they will give us a knowledge of this very people, which hath been destroyed. And I am desirous to know the cause of their destruction.

¹³Now, Ammon saith unto him:

I can assuredly tell thee, O king, of a man that can translate the records. For he hath wherewith that he can look, and translate all records that are of ancient date. And it is a gift from God. And the things are called interpreters. And no man can look in them, except he be commanded, lest he should look for that he had not ought, and he should perish.

And whosoever is commanded to look in them, the same is called seer. ¹⁴And behold, the king of the people, which is in the land of Zarahemla, is the man that is commanded to do these things, and which hath this high gift from God.

¹⁵And the king saith that: "A seer is greater than a prophet."
¹⁶And Ammon saith that:

A seer is a revelator, and a prophet also. And a gift which is greater can no man have, except he should possess the power of God.[a] ¹⁷But a seer can know of things which has past, and also of things which is to come. And by them shall all things be revealed, or rather, shall secret things be made manifest, and hidden things shall come to light. And things which is not known, shall be made known by them. And

---

a. Oliver Cowdery later altered the sentence to read "And a gift which is greater can no man have, except he should possess the power of God, [which no man can, yet a man may have great power given him from God.]" That is the reading in the 1830 edition.

also things shall be made known by them which otherwise could not be known. ⁱ⁸Thus, God hath provided a means that man, through faith, might work mighty miracles. Therefore, he becometh a great benefit to his fellow beings.

¹⁹And now, when Ammon had made an end of speaking these words, the king rejoiced exceedingly and gave thanks to God, saying:

> Doubtless a great mystery is contained within these plates. And these interpreters was doubtless prepared for the purpose of unfolding all such mysteries to the children of men.
>
> ²⁰O how marvelous are the works of Lord! And how long doth he suffer with his people! Yea, and how blind, and impenetrable are the understandings of the children of men! For they will not seek wisdom. Neither do they desire that she should rule over them. ²¹Yea, they are as a wild flock, which fleeth from the shepherd, and scattereth, and are driven and are devoured by the beasts of the forest.

Chapter VI [Mosiah 9–10]

[9] *The record of Zeniff. An account of his people from the time they left the land of Zarahemla until the time that they were delivered out of the hands of the Lamanites.*

¹I, Zeniff, having been taught in all the language of the Nephites—and having had a knowledge of the land of Nephi (or of the land of our fathers first inheritance)—and I having been sent as a spy among the Lamanites, that I might spy out their forces, that our army might come upon them and destroy them—but when I saw that which was good among them, I was desirous that they should not be destroyed.[a] ²Therefore, I contended with my brethren in the wilderness. For I would that our ruler should make a treaty with them. But he, being an austere and a bloodthirsty man, commanded that I should be slain. But I was rescued by the shedding of much blood. For father fought against father, and brother against brother, until the greatest number of our army was slain—destroyed in the wilderness.

And we returned (those of us that were spared) to the land of Zarahemla, to relate that tale to their wives and their children. ³And yet I, being overzealous to inherit the land of our fathers, collected as many as were desirous to go up to possess the land and started again on our journey into the wilderness, to go up to the land. But we were smitten with famine, and sore affliction. For we were slow to remember the Lord our God. ⁴Nevertheless, after many days wandering in the wilderness, we pitched our tents in the place where our brethren were slain, which was near to the land of our fathers.

⁵And it came to pass that I went again (with four of my men) into the city, in unto the king—that I might know of the disposition of the king. And that I might know if I might go in (with my people) and possess the land in peace. ⁶And I went in unto the king. And he covenanted with me that I might possess the land of Lehi-Nephi and the land of Shilom. ⁷And he also commanded that his people should depart out of that land.

And I and my people went into the land, that we might possess it. ⁸And we began to build buildings and to repair the walls of the city, yea, even the walls of the city of Lehi-Nephi, and the city of Shilom. ⁹And we began to till the ground, yea, even with all manner of seeds—with seeds of corn, and of wheat, and of barley, and with neas, and with sheum, and with seeds of all manner of fruits. And we did begin to multiply and prosper in the land.

¹⁰Now, it was the cunning and the craftiness of King Laman to bring my people into bondage, that he yielded up the land that we might possess it. ¹¹Therefore, it came to pass that after we had dwelt in the land for the space of twelve years, that King Laman began to grow uneasy—lest by any means my people should wax strong in the land. And that they could not overpower them and bring them into bondage.

¹²Now, they were a lazy and an idolatrous people. Therefore, they were desirous to bring us into bondage, that they might glut themselves with the labors of our hands. Yea, that they might feast themselves upon the flocks of our fields. ¹³Therefore, it came to pass that King Laman began to stir up his people, that they should contend with my people. Therefore, there began to be wars and contentions in the land. ¹⁴For in the thirteenth year of my reign, in the land of Nephi (away on the south of the land of Shilom), when my people were watering and feeding their flocks and tilling their

---

a. It is difficult to parse this sentence due to the clauses with the verb "having," which appear to be resolved only in the "but when I saw" phrase. This formatting shows the "having" phrases as intentional repetitions, and then uses the final phrase as the conclusion.

lands—a numerous host of Lamanites came upon them and began to slay them, and to take of their flocks and the corn of their fields.

¹⁵Yea, and it came to pass that they fled, all that were not overtaken, even into the city of Nephi. And did call upon me for protection.

¹⁶And it came to pass that I did arm them with bows, and with arrows, with swords, and with cimiters, and with clubs, and with slings, and with all manner of weapons of war (which we could invent). And I and my people did go forth against the Lamanites to battle. ¹⁷Yea, in the strength of the Lord did we go forth to battle against the Lamanites. For I and my people did cry mightily to the Lord, that he would deliver us out of the hands of our enemies. For we were awakened to a remembrance of the deliverance of our fathers.

¹⁸And God did hear our cries and did answer our prayers. And we did go forth in his might. Yea, we did go forth against the Lamanites. And in one day and a night we did slay three thousand and forty-three. We did slay them, even until we had driven them out of our land. ¹⁹And I, myself, with mine own hands did help bury their dead. And behold, to our great sorrow and lamentation, two hundred and seventy-nine of our brethren were slain.

[10] ¹And it came to pass that we again began to establish the kingdom. And we again began to possess the land in peace. And I caused that there should be weapons of war made of every kind, that thereby I might have weapons for my people against the time the Lamanites should come up again to war against my people. ²And I set guards round about the land, that the Lamanites might not come upon us again unawares and destroy us. And thus I did guard my people and my flocks, and keep them from falling into the hands of our enemies.

³And it came to pass that we did inherit the land of our fathers for many years, yea, for the space of twenty and two years. ⁴And I did cause that the men should till the ground. And raise all manner of grain. And all manner of fruit of every kind. ⁵And I did cause that the women should spin, and toil, and work. And work[a] all manner of fine linen. Yea, and cloth of every kind, that we might clothe our nakedness. And thus we did prosper in the land. Thus we did have continual peace in the land for the space of twenty and two years.

⁶And it came to pass that King Laman died. And his son began to reign in his stead. And he began to stir his people up in rebellion against my people. Therefore, they began to prepare for war, and to come up to battle against my people. ⁷But I, having sent my spies out round about the land of Shemlon that I might discover their preparations, that I might guard against them, that they might not come upon my people and destroy them.[b]

⁸And it came to pass that they came up upon the north of the land of Shilom with their numerous hosts. Men armed with bows, and with arrows, and with swords, and with cimiters, and with stones, and with slings. And they had their heads shaved, that

---

a. The doubled "and work" is uncorrected in the Printer's Manuscript. Skousen suggests that it is an error and that a parallel passage in Helaman 6:13 strongly suggests that the second *and work* is in error. Skousen, *Analysis of the Textual Variants*, 2:1247–48. It has been retained and punctuated to make sense, as it is in the Printer's Manuscript and continues into the current edition.

b. An incomplete sentence. This is not unusual when the sentence begins with the construction "having." Joseph Smith noticed this and changed it to "I had" for the 1937 edition. That change has been preserved in subsequent editions. Skousen, *Analysis of the Textual Variants*, 2:1252.

Chapter VI [Mosiah 9-10]

they were naked. And they were girded about with a leathern girdle about their loins.

⁹And it came to pass that I caused that the women and children of my people should be hid in the wilderness. And I also caused that all my old men that could bear arms, and also all my young men that were able to bear arms, should gather themselves together to go to battle against the Lamanites. And I did place them in their ranks, every man according to his age.

¹⁰And it came to pass that we did go up to battle against the Lamanites. And I, even I in my old age, did go up to battle against the Lamanites.

And it came to pass that we did go up in the strength of the Lord to battle.

¹¹Now, the Lamanites knew nothing concerning the Lord, nor the strength of the Lord. Therefore, they depended upon their own strength. Yet they were a strong people, as to the strength of men.

¹²They were a wild, and ferocious, and a bloodthirsty people, believing in the tradition of their fathers, which is this—believing that they were driven out of the land of Jerusalem because of the iniquities of their fathers, and that they were wronged in the wilderness by their brethren, and they were also wronged while crossing the sea. ¹³And again, that they were wronged while in the land of their first inheritance after they had crossed the sea.

And all this because that Nephi was more faithful in keeping the commandments of the Lord. Therefore, he was favored of the Lord. For the Lord heard his prayers and answered them. And he took the lead of their journey in the wilderness.

¹⁴And his brethren was wroth with him, because they understood not the dealings of the Lord. They was also wroth with him upon the waters, because they hardened their hearts against the Lord.

¹⁵And again, they were wroth with him when they had arriven to the promised land. Because they said that he had taken the ruling of the people out of their hands. And they sought to kill him.

¹⁶And again, they were wroth with him because he departed into the wilderness (as the Lord had commanded him). And took the records, which were engraven on the plates of brass. For they said that he robbed them.

¹⁷And thus, they have taught their children that they should hate them—and that they should murder them, and that they should rob and plunder them, and do all they could to destroy them. Therefore, they have an eternal hatred towards the children of Nephi. ¹⁸For this very cause hath King Laman, by his cunning and lying craftiness, and his fair promises, hath deceived me—that I have brought this my people up into this land that they may destroy them. Yea, and we have suffered this many years in the land.

¹⁹And now I, Zeniff, after having told all these things unto my people concerning the Lamanites, I did stimulate them to go to battle with their might, putting their trust in the Lord. Therefore, we did contend with them face to face.

²⁰And it came to pass that we did drive them again out of our land. And we slew them with a great slaughter, even so many that we did not number them.

²¹And it came to pass that we returned again to our own land. And my people [again[a]] began to tend their flocks and to till their ground.

²²And now, I, being old, did confer the kingdom upon one of my sons. Therefore, I say no more. And may the Lord bless my people. Amen.

---

a. Oliver Cowdery added this word, probably during proofreading.

Chapter VII [Mosiah 11–13:24]

[11] ¹And now it came to pass that Zeniff conferred the kingdom upon Noah, one of his sons. Therefore, Noah began to reign in his stead. And he did not walk in the ways of his father. ²For behold, he did not keep the commandments of God. But he did walk after the desires of his own heart. And he had many wives and concubines. And he did cause his people to commit sin and do that which was abominable in the sight of the Lord. Yea, and they did commit whoredoms and all manner of wickedness.

³And he laid a tax of one fifth part of all they possessed: and a fifth part of their gold, and of their silver, and a fifth part of their ziff, and of their copper, and of their brass, and their iron—and a fifth part of their fatlings. And also a fifth part of all their grain. ⁴And all this did he take to support himself, and his wives, and his concubines, and also his priests and their wives, and their concubines. Thus, he had changed the affairs of the kingdom. ⁵For he put down all the priests that had been consecrated by his father, and consecrated new ones in their stead—such as were lifted up in the pride of their hearts. ⁶Yea, and thus were they supported in their laziness and in their idolatry, and in their whoredoms, by the taxes which King Noah had put upon his people. Thus did the people labor exceedingly to support iniquity. ⁷Yea, and they also became idolatrous, because they were deceived by the vain and flattering words of the king and priests. For they did speak flattering things unto them.

⁸And it came to pass that King Noah built many elegant and spacious buildings. And he ornamented them with fine work of wood, and of all manner of precious things—of gold, and of silver, and of iron, and of brass, and of Ziff, and of copper. ⁹And he also built him a spacious palace, and a throne in the midst thereof—all of which was of fine wood, and was ornamented with gold and silver, and with precious things.

¹⁰And he also caused that his workman should work all manner of fine work within the walls of the temple, of fine wood, and of copper, and of brass. ¹¹And the seats which was sat apart for the high priests (which was above all the other seats), he did ornament with [pure[a]] gold. And he caused a breastwork to be built before them, that they might rest their bodies and their arms upon while they should speak lying and vain words to his people.

¹²And it came to pass that he built a tower near the temple, yea, a very high tower, even so high that he could stand upon the top thereof and overlook the land of Shilom, and also the land of Shemlon, which was possessed by the Lamanites. And he could even look over all the land round about.

¹³And it came to pass that he caused many buildings to be built in the land Shilom.[b] And he caused a great tower to be built on the hill north of the land Shilom, which had been a resort for the children of Nephi at the time they fled out of the land. And thus he did do with the riches which he obtained by the taxation of his people.

¹⁴And it came to pass that he placed his heart upon his riches. And he spent his time in riotous living with his wives and his concubines. And so did also his priests spend their time with harlots.

---

a. Oliver Cowdery originally wrote "fine." He crossed it out and inserted "pure." It is not certain when this occurred. It might have been immediate or upon proofreading. The 1830 and subsequent editions all read "pure." Skousen, *Analysis of the Textual Variants*, 2:1270.

b. Oliver Cowdery originally copied "Shemlon" but almost immediately corrected it to "Shilom." Skousen, *Analysis of the Textual Variants*, 2:1272.

¹⁵And it came to pass that he planted a vineyards round about in the land. And he built wine presses and made wine in abundance. And therefore, he became a winebibber—and also his people.

¹⁶And it came to pass that the Lamanites began to come in upon his people, upon small numbers, and to slay them in their fields and while they were tending their flocks. ¹⁷And King Noah sent guards round about the land to keep them off, but he did not send a sufficient number. And the Lamanites come[a] upon them and killed them and drove many of their flocks out of the land. Thus the Lamanites began to destroy them, and to exercise their hatred upon them.

¹⁸And it came to pass that King Noah sent his armies against them. And they were driven back, or they drive[b] them back for a time. Therefore, they returned rejoicing in their spoil. ¹⁹And now, because of this great victory, they were lifted up in the pride of their hearts. They did boast in their own strength, saying that their fifty could stand against thousands of the Lamanites. And thus they did boast and did delight in blood, and the shedding of the blood of their brethren. And this because of the wickedness of their king and priests.

²⁰And it came to pass that there was a man among them whose name was Abinadi. And he went forth among them and began to prophesy, saying:

> Behold, thus saith the Lord! And thus hath he commanded me, saying: "Go forth. And say unto this people, thus saith the Lord! Wo be unto this people! For I have seen their abominations, and their wickedness, and their whoredoms. ²¹And except they repent, I will visit them in mine anger. And except they repent, and turn to the Lord, their God—behold I will deliver them into[c] the hands of their enemies. Yea, and they shall be brought into bondage and they shall be afflicted by the hand of their enemies.
>
> ²²And it shall come to pass that they shall know that I am the Lord, their God—and am a jealous God, visiting the iniquities of my people.
>
> ²³And it shall come to pass that except this people repent and turn unto[d] the Lord, their God, they shall be brought into bondage. And none shall deliver them, except it be the Lord, the Almighty God.
>
> ²⁴Yea, and it shall come to pass that when they shall cry unto me, I will be slow to hear their cries.[e] Yea, and I will suffer them that they be smitten by their enemies. ²⁵And except they repent in sackcloth and ashes, and cry mightily to the Lord, their God, I will not hear their prayers. Neither will I deliver them out of their afflictions."

And thus saith the Lord. And thus hath he commanded me.

---

a. Skousen suggests that it was possible that the Original Manuscript might have had the simple past or perhaps "did come." The compositor changed it to "came." I have left it as in the Printer's Manuscript. Skousen, *Analysis of the Textual Variants*, 2:1274.

b. Skousen suggests that it was possible that the original manuscript might have had the simple past, or perhaps "did drive." The compositor changed it to "drove." It has been retained as in the Printer's Manuscript. Skousen, *Analysis of the Textual Variants*, 2:1274.

c. Originally there was only the word "in." The word "to" was probably added during proofreading. They are combined according to modern usage.

d. Probably added during proofreading.

e. Perhaps an allusion to Jeremiah 11:11: "Though they shall cry unto me, I will not hearken unto them."

²⁶Now it came to pass that when Abinadi had spoke these words unto them, they were wroth with him, and sought to take away his life. But the Lord delivered him out of their hands.

²⁷Now, when King Noah had heard of the words which Abinadi had spake unto the people, he was also wroth. And saith:

> Who is Abinadi that I, and my people, should be judged of him? Or who is the Lord, that shall bring upon my people such great affliction? ²⁸I command you to bring Abinadi hither, that I may slay him. For he hath said these things that he might stir up my people to anger, one with another, and to raise contentions among my people. Therefore, I will slay him.

²⁹Now, the eyes of the people were blinded. Therefore, they hardened their hearts against the words of Abinadi and they sought from that time forward to take him. And King Noah hardened his heart against the word of the Lord. And he did not repent of his evil doings.

[12] ¹And it came to pass that after the space of two years, that Abinadi came among them in disguise—that they knew him not. And began again to prophesy among them, saying:

> Thus hath the Lord commanded me, saying: "Abinadi! Go and prophesy unto this, my people. For they have hardened their hearts against my words. They have repented not of their evil doings. Therefore, I will visit them in my anger. Yea, in my fierce anger will I visit them in their iniquities and abominations. ²Yea, wo be unto this generation!"
>
> And the Lord said unto me: "Stretch forth thy hand. And prophesying—saying: Thus saith the Lord. It shall come to pass that this generation, because of their iniquities, shall be brought into bondage. And shall be smitten on the cheek. Yea, and shall be driven by men. And shall be slain. And the vultures of the air and the dogs, yea, and the wild beasts, shall devour their flesh.
>
> ³And it shall come to pass that the life of King Noah shall be valued even as a garment in a hot furnace. For he shall know that I am the Lord.
>
> ⁴And it shall come to pass that I will smite this my people with sore afflictions. Yea, with famine and with pestilence. And I will cause that they shall howl all the day long. ⁵Yea, and I will cause that they shall have burdens lashed upon their backs. And they shall be driven before like a dumb ass.
>
> ⁶And it shall come to pass that I will send forth hail among them. And it shall smite them. And they shall also be smitten with the east wind. And insects shall pester their land also, and devour their grain. ⁷And they shall be smitten with a great pestilence. And all this will I do because of their iniquities, and abominations.
>
> ⁸And it shall come to pass that except they repent, I will utterly destroy them from off the face of the earth. Yet, they shall leave a record behind them. And I will preserve them for other nations which shall possess the land. Yea, even this will I do, that I may discover the abominations of this people to other nations."

And many things did Abinadi prophesy against this people.

⁹And it came to pass that they were angry with him. And they took him and carried him bound before the king. And saith unto the king:

Behold, we have brought a man before thee, which has prophesied evil concerning thy people. And saith that God will destroy them. ¹⁰And he also prophesieth evil concerning thy life. And saith that thy life shall be as a garment in a furnace of fire.

¹¹And again, he saith that thou shall be as a stalk, even as a dry stalk of the field, which is ran over by the beasts and trodden under foot.

¹²And again, he saith thou shalt be as the blossoms of a thistle, which (when it is fully ripe), if the wind bloweth, it is driven forth upon the face of the land. And he pretendeth the Lord hath spoken it. And he saith all this shall come upon thee, except thou repent—and this because of thine iniquities.

¹³And now, O king! What great evil hast thou done? Or what great sins has thy people committed, that we should be condemned of God, or judged of this man?

¹⁴And now, O king! Behold, we are guiltless. And thou, O king, hast not sinned. Therefore, this man hast lied concerning you. And he hath prophesied in vain. ¹⁵And behold, we are strong. We shall not come into bondage or be taken captive by our enemies. Yea, and thou hast prospered in the land. And thou shalt also prosper.

¹⁶Behold, here is the man. We deliver him into thy hands. Thou mayest do with him as seemeth thee good.

¹⁷And it came to pass that King Noah caused that Abinadi should be cast into prison. And he commanded that the priests should gather themselves together, that he might hold a council with them—what he should do with him.

¹⁸And it came to pass that they saith unto the king: "Bring him hither, that we may question him."

And the king commanded that he should be brought before them. ¹⁹And they began to question him, that they might cross him, that thereby they might have wherewith to accuse him. But he answered them boldly and withstood all their questions. Yea, to their astonishment. For he did withstand them in all their questions and did confound them in all their words.

²⁰And it came to pass that one of them saith unto him:

What meaneth the words which are written, and which have been taught by our fathers, saying:

²¹How beautiful upon the mountains are the feet of him that bringeth good tidings, that publisheth peace, that bringeth good tidings of good, that publisheth salvation—that saith unto Zion, thy God reigneth?

²²Thy watchmen shall lift up the voice. Together shall they sing. For they shall see eye to eye when the Lord shall bring again Zion.

²³Break forth into joy. Sing together, ye waste places of Jerusalem! For the Lord hath comforted his people. He hath redeemed Jerusalem. ²⁴The Lord hath made bare his holy arm in the eyes of all the nations, and all the ends of the earth shall see the salvation of our God.[a]

²⁵And now Abinadi saith unto them:

Are you priests? And pretend to teach this people? And to understand the

---

a. Quoting Isaiah 52:7–10.

spirit of prophesying? And yet desireth to know of me what these things mean?

²⁶I say unto you, wo be unto you for perverting the ways of the Lord! For if ye understand these things, ye have not taught them. Therefore, ye have perverted the ways of the Lord. ²⁷Ye have not applied your hearts to understanding. Therefore, ye have not been wise. Therefore, what teachest thou this people?

²⁸And they said: "We teach the law of Moses."

²⁹And again he saith unto them:

If ye teach the law of Moses, why do ye not keep it? Why do ye set your hearts upon riches? Why do ye commit whoredoms. And spend your strength with harlots? Yea, and cause this people to commit sin—that the Lord hath sent me to prophesy against this people—yea, even a great evil against this people? ³⁰Knowest thou not that I speak the truth? Yea, thou knowest that I speak the truth. And you had ought to tremble before God.

³¹And it shall come to pass that ye shall be smitten for thine iniquities. For ye have said that ye teach the law of Moses. And what knowest thou concerning the law of Moses? Doth salvation come by the law of Moses? What sayest thou?

³²And they answered and said that salvation did come by the law of Moses. ³³And Abinadi saith unto them:

I know if ye keep the commandments of God, ye shall be saved. Yea, if ye keep the commandments which the Lord delivered unto Moses in the mount of Sinai, saying:

³⁴"I am the Lord thy God, which have brought thee out of the land of Egypt. Out of the house of bondage. ³⁵Thou shalt have no other God before me. ³⁶Thou shalt not make unto thee any graven image. Or any likeness of any thing in the heaven above, or things which is in the earth beneath."[a]

³⁷Now, Abinadi saith unto them: "Have ye done all this? I say unto you, nay. Ye have not. And have ye taught this people that they should do all these things? I say unto you, nay. Ye have not."

[13] ¹And now, when the king had heard these words, he said unto his priests: "Away with this fellow! And slay him! For what have we to do with him? For he is mad."

²And they stood forth and attempted to lay their hands on him. But he withstood them, and said unto them:

³Touch me not! For God shall smite you if ye lay your hands upon me! For I have not delivered the message which the Lord sent me to deliver. Neither have I told you that which ye requested that I should tell. Therefore, God will not suffer that I shall be destroyed at this time. ⁴But I must fulfill the commandments wherewith God hath commanded me. And because I have told you the truth, ye are angry with me.

And again, because I have spoken the word of God, ye have judged me, that I am mad.

⁵Now it came to pass after Abinadi had spoken these words that the people of King Noah durst not lay their hands on him. For the spirit of the Lord was upon him. And

---

a. Quoting Exodus 20:2–4.

Chapter VII [Mosiah 11–13:24]

his face shone with exceeding luster, even as Moses' did while in the Mount of Sinai (while speaking with the Lord). ⁶And he spake with power and authority from God. And he continued his words, saying:

⁷Ye see that ye have not power to slay me. Therefore, I finish my message. Yea, and I perceive that it cuts you to your hearts, because I tell you the truth concerning your iniquities. ⁸Yea, and my words fill you with wonder and amazement, and with anger! ⁹But I finish my message. And then it mattereth not whither I go, if it so be that I am saved. ¹⁰But this much I tell you. What you do with me after this shall be as a type and a shadow of things which is to come.

¹¹And now, I read unto you the remainder of the commandments of God. For I perceive that they are not written in your hearts. I perceive that ye have studied, and taught iniquity the most part of your lives.

¹²And now, ye remember that I said unto you:

Thou shalt not make unto thee any graven image. Or any likeness of things which is in heaven above, or which is in the earth beneath, or which is in the water under the earth.

¹³And again, thou shalt not bow down thyself unto them. Nor serve them. For I, the Lord thy God, am a jealous God—visiting the iniquities of the fathers upon the children unto the third and fourth generation of them that hate me. ¹⁴And showing mercy unto thousands of them that love me and keep my commandments.

¹⁵Thou shalt not take the name of the Lord, thy God, in vain. For the Lord will not hold him guiltless that taketh his name in vain.

¹⁶Remember the sabbath day, to keep it holy. ¹⁷Six days shalt thou labor and do all thy work. ¹⁸But the seventh day, the sabbath of the Lord, thy God, thou shalt not do any work—thou nor thy son, nor thy daughter, thy manservant, nor thy maidservant, nor thy cattle, nor thy stranger that is within thy gates. ¹⁹For in six days the Lord made heaven and earth, and the sea, and all that in them is. Wherefore, the Lord blessed the sabbath day and hallowed it.

²⁰Honor thy father and thy mother, that thy days may be long upon the land which the Lord, thy God, giveth thee.

²¹Thou shalt not kill.

²²Thou shalt not commit adultery.

Thou shalt not steal.

²³Thou shalt not bare false witness against thy neighbor.

²⁴Thou shalt not covet thy neighbor's house.

Thou shalt not covet thy neighbor's wife, nor his manservant, nor his maidservant, nor his ox, nor his ass, nor any thing that is thy neighbor's.[a]

---

a. Abinadi repeats Exodus 20:4, then continues quoting Exodus 20:5–17.

Chapter VIII [Mosiah 13:25–16:15]

[**13 continued**]²⁵And it came to pass that after Abinadi had made an end of these sayings, that he said unto them:

Have ye taught this people that they should observe to do all these things—for to keep these commandments?^a ²⁶I say unto you, nay. For, if ye had, the Lord would not have caused me to come forth and to prophesy evil concerning this people.

²⁷And now, ye have said that salvation cometh by the law of Moses. I say unto you that it is expedient that ye should keep the law of Moses as yet. But I say unto you, that the time shall come when it shall no more be expedient to keep the law of Moses. ²⁸And moreover I say unto you, that salvation doth not come by the law alone.^b And were it not for the atonement (which God himself shall make for the sins and iniquities of his people) that they must unavoidably perish, notwithstanding the law of Moses.

²⁹And now I say unto you, that it was expedient that there should be a law given to the children of Israel. Yea, even a very strict law. For they were a stiff-necked people, quick to do iniquity, and slow to remember the Lord, their God. ³⁰Therefore, there was a law given them. Yea, a law of performances and of ordinances. A law which they were to observe strictly from day to day. To keep them in remembrance of God and their duty towards him. ³¹But behold, I say unto you, that all these things were types of things to come.

³²And now, did they understand the law? I say unto you, nay. They did not all understand the law. And this, because of the hardness of their hearts. For they understood not that there could not any man be saved, except it were through the redemption of God. ³³For behold, did not Moses prophesy unto them concerning the coming of the Messiah? And that God should redeem his people? Yea, and even all the prophets which have prophesied even since the world began—have they not spoken (more or less) concerning these things? ³⁴Have they not said that God himself should come down among the children of men? And take upon him the form of man? And go forth in mighty power upon the face of the earth? ³⁵Yea, and have they not said also that he should bring to pass the resurrection of the dead? And that he himself should be oppressed and afflicted?

[**14**] ¹Yea, even doth not Isaiah say:

> Who hath believed our report?
>> And to whom is the arm of the Lord revealed?
>
> ²For he shall grow up before him as a tender plant,
>> and as a root out of dry ground.
>
> He hath no form nor comeliness.
>> And when we shall see him,
>> there is no beauty
>> that we should desire him.
>
> ³He is despised and rejected of men.

---

a. Perhaps alluding to Deuteronomy 15:5: "Only if thou carefully hearken unto the voice of the Lord thy God, to observe to do all these commandments which I command thee this day."

b. Perhaps an allusion to Romans 3:20, which was more directly used in 2 Nephi 2:5.

Chapter VIII [Mosiah 13:25–16:15]

A man of sorrows and acquainted with grief.
And we hid (as it were) our faces from him.
 He was despised. And we esteemed him not.
⁴Surely, he hath borne our griefs,
 and carried our sorrows.
Yet, we did esteem him stricken,
 smitten of God,
 and afflicted.
⁵But he was wounded for our transgressions.
 He was bruised for our iniquities.
The chastisement of our peace was upon him.
 And with his stripes we are healed.
⁶All we, like sheep, have gone astray.
 We have turned every one to his own way.
 And the Lord hath laid on him the iniquities of us all.

⁷He was oppressed.
And he was afflicted.
 Yet, he opened not his mouth.
He is brought as a lamb to the slaughter.
 And, as a sheep before her shearers is dumb,
  so he **opened** not his mouth.
⁸He was taken from prison and from judgment.
 And who shall declare his generation?
For he was cut off out of the land of the living.
 For the **transgressions** of my people was he stricken.
⁹And he made his grave with the wicked
 and with the rich in his death
because he had done no **evil**,
 neither was any deceit in his mouth.

¹⁰Yet, it pleased the Lord to bruise him.
 He hath put him to grief.
When thou shalt make his soul an offering for sin,
 he shall see his seed.
He shall prolong his days.
 And the pleasure of the Lord shall prosper in his hand.
¹¹He shall see of the [travail[a]] of his soul—
 and shall be satisfied.
By his knowledge shall my righteous servant justify many.
 For he shall bear their iniquities.
¹²Therefore, will I divide him a portion with the great.
 And he shall divide the spoil with the strong,
because he hath poured out his soul unto death.

---

a. The Printer's Manuscript has "travel." Oliver Cowdery spelled both travel and travail as "travel." Skousen, *Analysis of the Textual Variants,* 2:1323.

> And he was numbered with the transgressors.
> And he bear the **sins** of many,
>   and made intercession for the transgressors.[a]

[15] ¹And now Abinadi saith unto them:

I would that ye should understand that God himself shall come down among the children of men. And shall redeem his people. ²And because he dwelleth in flesh, he shall be called the Son of God. And having subjected the flesh to the will of the Father—being the Father and the Son. ³The Father because he was conceived by the power of God. And the Son because of the flesh—thus becoming the Father and Son. ⁴And they are one God. Yea, the very eternal Father of Heaven and of Earth.

⁵And thus, the flesh becoming subject to the spirit (or the Son to the Father, being one God) suffereth temptation. And yieldeth not to the temptation. But suffereth himself to be mocked, and scourged, and cast out, and disowned by his people.

⁶And after all this, and after working many mighty miracles among the children of men, he shall be led. Yea, even as Isaiah said: "As a sheep before the shearer is dumb, so he opened not his mouth.[b]"

⁷Yea, even so he shall be led, crucified, and slain. The flesh becoming subject even unto death. The will of the Son being swallowed up in the will of the Father.

⁸And thus, God breaketh the bands of death. Having gained the victory over death—giving the Son power to make intersession for the children of men—⁹having ascended into heaven—having the bowels of mercy being filled with compassion toward the children of men—standing betwixt them and justice, having broken the bands of death—taken[c] upon himself their iniquity and their transgressions, having redeemed them and satisfied the demands of justice.

¹⁰And now I say unto you, who shall declare his generation?[d]

Behold, I say unto you that "when his soul has been made an offering for sin, he shall see his seed."[e] And now, what say ye? And who shall be his seed?

¹¹Behold, I say unto you that whosoever hath heard the words of the prophets, yea, all the holy prophets which have prophesied concerning the coming of the Lord.

I say unto you, that all those who hath hearkened unto their words, and believed that the Lord would redeem his people, and have looked forward to that day for a remission of their sins—I say unto you, that these are his seed (or they are heirs of the kingdom of God). ¹²For these are they whose sins he hath borne. These are they for whom he hath died, to redeem them from their transgressions. And now, are they not his seed? ¹³Yea, and are not the prophets, every one that has opened his mouth to prophesy (that has not fallen into transgression)?[f] I mean all the holy prophets ever since the world began. I say unto you that they are his seed.

---

a. Compare Isaiah 53:1–12.

b. Quotes Isaiah 53:7: "He was oppressed, and he was afflicted, yet he opened not his mouth: he is brought as a lamb to the slaughter, and as a sheep before her shearers is dumb, so he openeth not his mouth."

c. The grammatical parallelism suggests that this should be understood as "taking."

d. Quoting Isaiah 53:8: "He was taken from prison and from judgment: and who shall declare his generation? for he was cut off out of the land of the living: for the transgression of my people was he stricken."

e. See Isaiah 53:10: "Yet it pleased the Lord to bruise him; he hath put him to grief: when thou shalt make his soul an offering for sin, he shall see his seed."

f. Incomplete sentence.

Chapter VIII [Mosiah 13:25–16:15]

¹⁴And these are they which hath published peace,
    that hath brought good tidings of good,
that hath published salvation—
    that saith unto Zion, thy God reigneth!
¹⁵And O how beautiful upon the mountains were their feet?[a]
    ¹⁶And again how beautiful upon the mountains
        are the feet of those that art still publishing peace?
    ¹⁷And again, how beautiful upon the mountains
        are the feet of those who shall hereafter publish peace?
    Yea, from this time henceforth, and forever.

¹⁸And behold, I say unto you this is not all.

    For, O how beautiful upon the mountains
        are the feet of him that bringeth good tidings,
    that is the founder of peace?
        Yea, even the Lord, who hath redeemed his people.
        Yea, him who hath granted salvation unto his people.[b]

¹⁹For were it not for the redemption which he hath made for his people, which was prepared from the foundation of the world—I say unto you, were it not for this, that all mankind must have perished.

²⁰But behold, the bands of death shall be broken. And the son reigneth, and hath power over the dead. Therefore, he bringeth to pass the resurrection of the dead. ²¹And there cometh a resurrection, even a first resurrection. Yea, even a resurrection of those that have been, and which are, and which shall be, even until the resurrection of Christ (for so shall he be called).

²²And now, the resurrection of all the prophets and all those that have believed in their words (or all those that have kept the commandments of God), these shall come forth in the first resurrection. Therefore, they are the first resurrection. ²³They are raised to dwell with God who hath redeemed them. Thus, they have eternal life through Christ, who hath broken the bands of death. ²⁴And there are those who have part in the first resurrection. And these are they that have died before Christ came (in their ignorance, not having salvation declared unto them). And thus the Lord bringeth about the restoration of these. And they have a part in the first resurrection (or hath eternal life), being redeemed by the Lord. ²⁵And little children also hath eternal life.

²⁶But behold, and fear and tremble before God! For ye had ought to tremble. For the Lord redeemeth none such that rebelleth against him, and dieth in their sins. Yea, even all those that have perished in their sins, ever since the world began—that have willfully rebelled against God, that have known the commandments of God, and would not keep them. These are they that have no part in the first resurrection. ²⁷Therefore, had ye not ought to tremble? For salvation cometh to none such. For the Lord hath redeemed none such, yea, neither can the Lord redeem such. For he cannot deny himself. For he cannot deny justice when it hath its claim.

---

a. There is an intentional echo of Isaiah 52:7.

b. Verses 14–18 interweave phrases from Isaiah 52 with Abinadi's exposition. It appears that he created a response that not only used the words of the question, but also the Isaianic style of the verses of the question.

²⁸And now I say unto you, that the time shall come that the salvation of the Lord shall be declared to every nation, kindred, tongue, and people.ᵃ ²⁹Yea, Lord:

> Thy watchmen shall lift up their voice.
> With the voice together shall they sing.
> For they shall see eye to eye
> when the Lord shall bring again Zion.
> ³⁰Break forth into joy.
> Sing together, ye waste places of Jerusalem.
> For the Lord hath comforted his people.
> He hath redeemed Jerusalem.
> ³¹The Lord hath made bare his holy arm
> in the eyes of all the nations,
> and all the ends of the earth
> shall see the salvation of our God.ᵇ

[16] ¹And now it came to pass that after Abinadi had spoken these words, he stretched forth his hands and said:

The time shall come when all shall see the salvation of the Lord!ᶜ When every nation, kindred, tongue, and peopleᵈ shall see eye to eye, and shall confess before God that his judgments are just! ²And then shall the wicked be cast out. And they shall have cause to howl, and weep, and wail, and gnash their teeth. And this because they would not hearken unto the voice of the Lord. Therefore, the Lord redeemeth them not. ³For they are carnal, and devilish, and the devil hath power over them. Yea, even that old serpent that did beguile our first parents—which was the cause of their fall, which was the cause of all mankind's becoming carnal, sensual, devilish—knowing evil from good, subjecting themselves to the devil. ⁴Thus, all mankind were lost.

And behold, they would have been endlessly lost, were it not that God redeemed his people from their lost and fallen state. ⁵But remember, that he that persists in his own carnal nature and goes on in the ways of sin and rebellion against God, he remaineth in his fallen state. And the devil hath all power over him. Therefore, he is as though there was no redemption made, being an enemy to God. And also is the devil an enemy to God.

⁶And now, if Christ had not come into the world (speaking of things to come as though they had already come) there could have been no redemption.ᵉ ⁷And if Christ had not risen from the dead, or broken the bands of death—that the grave

---

a. See Revelation 14:6: "And I saw another angel fly in the midst of heaven, having the everlasting gospel to preach unto them that dwell on the earth, and to every nation, and kindred, and tongue, and people."

b. Quoting Isaiah 52:10.

c. See Isaiah 52:4: "The Lord hath made bare his holy arm in the eyes of all the nations; and all the ends of the earth shall see the salvation of our God."

d. See Revelation 14:6: "And I saw another angel fly in the midst of heaven, having the everlasting gospel to preach unto them that dwell on the earth, and to every nation, and kindred, and tongue, and people."

e. This verse has its own internal explanation. It begins in the past tense and then adds the disclaimer that Abinadi is speaking "as though" it had happened, knowing it was yet to come. While that is a good description of the "prophetic present," it is also possible that this is an immediate correction of a tense error in the translation dictation.

Chapter VIII [Mosiah 13:25–16:15]

should have no victory, and that death should have no sting—there could have been no resurrection. ⁸But there is a resurrection. Therefore, the grave hath no victory. And the sting of death^a is swallowed up in Christ.

⁹He is the light and the life of the world.^b Yea, a light that is endless—that can never be darkened. Yea, and also a life which is endless, that there can be no more death.

¹⁰Even this mortal shall put on immortality. And this corruption shall put on incorruption.^c And shall be brought to stand before the bar of God, to be judged of him according to their works (whether they be good, or whether they be evil). ¹¹If they be good, to the resurrection of endless life and happiness. And if they be evil, to the resurrection of endless damnation.^d Being delivered up to the devil (who hath subtly subjected them, which is damnation). ¹²Having gone according to their own carnal wills and desires. Having never called upon the Lord while the arms of mercy was extended towards them. For the arms of mercy was extended towards them, and they would not. They being warned of their iniquities, and yet they would not repent and depart from them. And they were commanded to repent. And yet they would not repent.

¹³And now, had ye not ought to tremble, and repent of your sins, and remember—only in and through Christ ye can be saved. ¹⁴Therefore, if ye teach the law of Moses, also teach that it is a shadow of those things which are to come. ¹⁵Teach them that redemption cometh through Christ the Lord, which is the very eternal Father. And shall come forth; they that have done good, unto the resurrection of life; and they that have done evil, unto the resurrection of damnation. Amen.

---

a. The phrase "sting of death" appears in 1 Corinthians 15:56.
b. Allusion to John 1:4: "In him was life; and the life was the light of men."
c. See 1 Corinthians 15:54 for the use of "corruption and incorruption."
d. See John 5:29: "And shall come forth; they that have done good, unto the resurrection of life; and they that have done evil, unto the resurrection of damnation."

Chapter IX [Mosiah 17–21]

[17] ¹And now it came to pass that when Abinadi had finished these sayings, that the king commanded that the priests should take him, and cause that he should be put to death. ²But there was one among them, whose name was Alma—[he also, being a descendant of Nephi. And he was a young man.][a] And he believed the words which Abinadi had spoken. For he knew concerning the iniquity which Abinadi had testified against them. Therefore, he began to plead with the king, that he would not be angry with Abinadi. But suffer that he might depart in peace. ³But the king was more wroth and caused that Alma should be cast out from among them. And sent his servants after him, that they might slay him. ⁴But he fled from before them and hid himself, that they found him not. And he, being concealed for many days, did write all the words which Abinadi had spoken.

⁵And it came to pass that the king caused that his guards should surround Abinadi, and take him. And they bound him and cast him into prison. ⁶And after three days, having counseled with his priests, he caused that he should again be brought before him. ⁷And he said unto him:

> Abinadi. We have found an [accusation[b]] against thee. And thou art worthy of death. ⁸For thou hast said that God himself should come down among the children of men. And now, for this cause thou shalt be put to death, unless thou wilt recall all the words which thou hast spoken evil concerning me, and my people.

⁹Now, Abinadi saith unto him:

> I say unto you, I will not recall the words which I have spoken unto you concerning this people. For they are true. And that ye may know of their surety, I have suffered myself that I have fallen unto your hands. ¹⁰Yea, and will suffer even until death. And I will not recall my words. And they shall stand as a testimony against you. And if ye slay me, ye will shed innocent blood. And this shall also stand as a testimony against you at the last day.

¹¹And now, King Noah was about to release him for he feared his word. For he feared that the judgments of God would come upon him. ¹²But the priests lifted up their voices against him and began to accuse him, saying: "He hath reviled the king!" Therefore, the king was stirred up in anger against him and he delivered him up, that he might be slain.

¹³And it came to pass that they took him, and bound him, and scourged his skin with faggots. Yea, even unto death. ¹⁴And now when the flames began to scorch him, he cried unto them, saying:

> ¹⁵Behold! Even as ye have done unto me, so shall it come to pass that thy seed shall cause that many shall suffer the pains that I do suffer, even the pains of death by fire. And this, because they believe in the salvation of the Lord, their God.
> ¹⁶And it will come to pass that ye shall be afflicted with all manner of diseases

---

a. Oliver Cowdery apparently missed much of a line in the original copy. The Printer's Manuscript has a superlinear addition of "he also being a descendant of Nephi . . . and he was a young man".

b. The Printer's Manuscript has "acquisition," which is clearly incorrect. The compositor corrected it to "accusation," which is the intent. Skousen, *Analysis of the Textual Variants*, 3:1356.

Chapter IX [Mosiah 17–21]

because of your iniquities. ¹⁷Yea, and ye shall be smitten on every hand, and shall be driven and scattered to and fro, even as a wild flock is driven by wild and ferocious beasts. ¹⁸And in that day ye shall be hunted. And ye shall be taken by the hand of your enemies. And then ye shall suffer as I suffer the pains of death by fire. ¹⁹Thus, God executeth vengeance upon those that destroy his people.

O God! Receive my soul!

²⁰And now, when Abinadi had said these words, he fell, having suffered death by fire. Yea, having been put to death because he would not deny the commandments of God. Having sealed the truth of his words by death.

[18]¹And now it came to pass that Alma (who had fled from the servants of King Noah) repented of his sins and iniquities and went about privately among the people. And began to teach the words of Abinadi, ²yea, concerning that which was to come. And also concerning the resurrection of the dead. And the redemption of the people which was to be brought to pass through the power and sufferings and death of Christ. And his resurrection and ascension into heaven. ³And as many as would hear his word he did teach. And he taught them privately, that it might not come to the knowledge of the king. And many did believe his words.

⁴And it came to pass that as many as did believe him did go forth to a place which was called Mormon, having received its name from the king, being in the borders of the land, having been infested by times (or at seasons) by wild beasts.

⁵Now, there was in Mormon a fountain of pure water. And Alma resorted thither, there being (near the water) a thicket of small trees, where he did hide himself in the daytime from the searches of the king.

⁶And it came to pass that as many as believed him went forth thither to hear his words.

⁷And it came to pass after many day,[a] there were a goodly number gathered together to the place of Mormon to hear the words of Alma. Yea, all were gathered together that believed on his word, to hear him. And he did teach them. And did preach unto them repentance, and redemption, and faith, on the Lord.

⁸And it came to pass that he said unto them:

> Behold, here is the waters of Mormon (for thus were they called).
> And now, as ye are desirous to come into the fold of God—
> And to be called his people.
> And are willing to bear one another's burdens (that they may be light).
> ⁹Yea, and are willing to mourn with those that mourn.
> Yea, and comfort those that stand in need of comfort.
> And to stand as witnesses of God at all times, and in all things, and in all places that ye may be in, even until death,
>   that ye may be redeemed of God
> And be numbered with those of the first resurrection,
>   that ye may have eternal life.
> ¹⁰Now, I say unto you, if this be the desire of your hearts, what have you against being baptized in the name of the Lord?
> As a witness before him that ye have entered into a covenant with him,

---

a. The compositor changed this to the expected "days."

> that ye will serve him and keep his commandments,
> that he may pour out his spirit more abundantly upon you?[a]

¹¹And now, when the people had heard these words, they clapped their hands for joy and exclaimed: "This is the desires of our hearts!"

¹²And now it came to pass that Alma took [Helam[b]], he being one of the first, and went and stood forth in the water. And cried, saying: "O Lord! Pour out thy spirit upon thy servant, that he may do this work with holiness of heart!"

¹³And when he had said these words, the spirit of the Lord was upon him, and he said:

> [Helam[c]], I baptize thee having authority[d] from the Almighty God. As a testimony that ye have entered into a covenant to serve him until you are dead as to the mortal body. And may the spirit of the Lord be poured out upon you. And may he grant unto you eternal life, through the redemption of Christ (which he hath prepared from the foundation of the world).

¹⁴And after Alma had said these words, both Alma and [Helam[e]] was buried in the water. And they arose and came forth out of the water rejoicing. Being filled with the spirit.

¹⁵And again, Alma took another, and went forth a second time into the water. And baptized him according to the first (only, he did not bury himself again in the water). ¹⁶And after this manner he did baptize every one that went forth to the place of Mormon. And they were in number about two hundred and four souls. Yea, and they were baptized in the waters of Mormon and were filled with the grace of God. ¹⁷And they were called the church of God (or the church of Christ) from that time forward.

¹⁸And it came to pass that whosoever was baptized by the power and authority of God, they was added to his church.

And it came to pass that Alma, having authority from God, ordained priests—even one priest to every fifty of their number did he ordain to preach unto them, and to teach them concerning the things pertaining to the kingdom of God.

¹⁹And he commanded them that they should teach nothing save it were the things which he had taught, and which had been spoken by the mouth of the holy prophets.

²⁰Yea, even he commanded them that they should preach nothing save it were repentance and faith on the Lord who hath redeemed his people.

²¹And he commanded them that there should be no contention one with another, but that they should look forward with one eye, having one faith and one baptism.[f] Having their hearts knit together in unity and in love one towards another.

²²And thus, he commandeth them to preach. And thus, they became the children of God.

---

a. The shorter phrases emphasize the specifics of the covenant Alma offered.

b. Oliver Cowdery mistakenly wrote Helaman, and it was later corrected. As Skousen notes, by the time Cowdery copied this part of the manuscript, he had more often seen the name Helaman. This is the case for many of the instances of Helam. See Skousen, *Analysis of the Textual Variants*, 3:1370.

c. The Printer's Manuscript has Helaman. See Skousen, *Analysis of the Textual Variants*, 3:1370.

d. Probably added during proofreading.

e. The Printer's Manuscript has Helaman. See Skousen, *Analysis of the Textual Variants*, 3:1370.

f. Uses language from Ephesians 4:3: "One Lord, one faith, one baptism."

Chapter IX [Mosiah 17–21]

²³And he commanded them, that they should observe the sabbath day and keep it holy. And also, every day they should give thanks to the Lord, their God.

²⁴And he also commanded them that the priests which he had ordained should labor with their own hands for their support.

²⁵And there was one day in every week that was set apart that they should gather themselves together to teach the people, and to worship the Lord, their God. And also, as often as it was in their power, to assemble themselves together. ²⁶And the priests was not to depend upon the people for their support, but for their labor they were to receive the grace of God, that they might wax strong in the spirit. Having the knowledge of God—that they might teach with power and authority from God.

²⁷And again, Alma commanded that the people of the church should impart of their substance, every one according to that which he hath. If he have more abundantly, he should impart more abundantly. And he that hath but little, but little should be required. And to him that hath not—should be given. ²⁸And thus they should impart of their substance of their own free will, and good desires towards God, [to those priests that stood in need, yea, and to every needy, naked soul.]ᵃ ²⁹And this he said unto them, having been commanded of God. And they did walk uprightly before God, imparting to one another both temporally and spiritually, according to their needs and their wants.

³⁰And now it came to pass that all this was done in Mormon. Yea, by the waters of Mormon, in the forest that was near the waters of Mormon. Yea, the place of Mormon. The waters of Mormon. The forest of Mormon. How beautiful are they to the eyes of them who there came to the knowledge of their redeemer! Yea, and how blessed are they! For they shall sing to his praise forever. ³¹And these things were done in the borders of the land, that they might not come to the knowledge of the king.

³²But behold, it came to pass that the king, [havingᵇ] discovered a movement among the people, sent his servants to watch them. Therefore, on the day that they were assembling themselves together to hear the word of the Lord, they were discovered unto the king.

³³And now, the king saith that Alma was a-stirring up the people to a rebellion against him. Therefore, he sent his army to destroy them.

³⁴And it came to pass that Alma and the people of the Lord were apprised of the coming of the king's army. Therefore, they took their tents and their families, and departed into the wilderness. ³⁵And they were in number about four hundred and fifty souls.

[19] ¹And it came to pass that the army of the king returned, having searched in vain for the people of the Lord.

²And now, behold, the forces of the king were small, having been reduced. And there began to be a division among the remainder of the people. ³And the lesser part began to breathe out threatenings against the king. And there began to be a great contention among them.

---

a. When Oliver Cowdery first copied this section, he skipped a phrase that was later added. He inserted: "to those priests that stood in need—yea, and to every needy, naked soul." This was probably added as he proofread. Interestingly, the punctuation was included as well. The punctuation has been retained as Cowdery entered it. Skousen notes that the compositor added "and" before "to those priests that stood in need." That change persists in the modern edition. It has been left it out, as it was an addition by the compositor, not Cowdery. Skousen, *Analysis of the Textual Variants*, 3:1375.

b. Probably added during proofreading.

⁴And now, there was a man among them whose name was Gideon. And he, being a strong man and an enemy to the king, therefore, he drew his sword, and swore in his wrath that he would slay the king.

⁵And now it came to pass that he fought with the king. And when the king saw that he was about to over-[power^a] him, he fled—and ran, and got upon the tower (which was near the temple). ⁶And Gideon pursued after him and was about to get up on the tower to slay the king, and the king cast his eyes round about towards the land of Shemlon. And behold, the army of the Lamanites were within the borders of the land.

⁷And now, the king cried out in the anguish of his soul, saying: "Gideon! Spare me! For the Lamanites are upon us, and they will destroy them! Yea, they will destroy my people!" ⁸And now, the king was not so much concerned about his people as he was about his own life. Nevertheless, Gideon did spare his life.

⁹And the king commanded the people, that they should flee before the Lamanites. And he, himself, did go before them. And they did flee into the wilderness with their women and their children.

¹⁰And it came to pass that the Lamanites did pursue them, and did overtake them, and began to slay them.

¹¹Now it came to pass that the king commanded them, that all the men should leave their wives, and their children, and flee before the Lamanites. ¹²Now, there were many that would not leave them. But had rather stay and perish with them. And the rest left their wives and their children, and fled.

¹³And it came to pass that those that tarried with their wives and their children, caused that their fair daughters should stand forth and plead with the Lamanites, that they would not slay them.

¹⁴And it came to pass that the Lamanites had compassion on them, for they were charmed with the beauty of their women. ¹⁵Therefore, the Lamanites did spare their lives. And took them captives. And carried them back to the land of Nephi. And granted unto them that they might possess the land, under the conditions—tat they would deliver up the King Noah into the hands of the Lamanites, and deliver up their property, even one-half of all they possessed. One half of their gold. And their silver. And all their precious things. And thus, they should pay tribute to the king of the Lamanites from year to year.

¹⁶And now, there was one of the sons of the king among those that was taken captive whose name was Limhi.

¹⁷And now, Limhi was desirous that his father should not be destroyed. Nevertheless, Limhi was not ignorant of the iniquities of his father, he himself being a just man.

¹⁸And it came to pass that Gideon sent men into the wilderness secretly, to search for the king and those that was with him.

And it came to pass that they met the people in the wilderness, all save the king and his priests. ¹⁹Now, they had sworn in their hearts that they would return to the land of Nephi. And if their wives and their children were slain (and also those that had tarried with them), that they would seek revenge and also perish with them. ²⁰And the king commanded them, that they should not return. And they were angry with the king and caused that he should suffer, even unto death by fire. ²¹And they were about to take the priests also, to put them to death. And they fled before them.

---

a. Probably added during proofreading.

Chapter IX [Mosiah 17–21]

²²And it came to pass that they were about to return to the land of Nephi and they met the men of Gideon. And the men of Gideon told them of all that had happened to their wives and their children. And that the Lamanites had granted unto them that they might possess the land by paying a tribute to the Lamanites of one-half of all they possessed. ²³And the people told the men of Gideon that they had slain the king, and his priests had fled from them, farther into the wilderness.

²⁴And it came to pass that after they had ended the cerimony[a], that they returned to the land of Nephi, rejoicing because their wives, and their children, were not slain. And they told Gideon what they had done to the king.

²⁵And it came to pass that the king of the Lamanites made an oath unto them, that his people should not slay them. ²⁶And also Limhi (being the son of the king, having the kingdom conferred upon him by the people) made oath unto the king of the Lamanites, that his people should pay tribute unto him, even one-half of all they possessed.

²⁷And it came to pass that Limhi began to establish the kingdom and to establish peace among his people. ²⁸And the king of the Lamanites set guards round about the land that he might keep the people of Limhi in the land, that they might not depart into the wilderness. And he did support his guards out of the tribute which he did receive from the Nephites.

²⁹And now, King Limhi did have continual peace in his kingdom for the space of two years, that the Lamanites did not molest them nor seek to destroy them.

[20] ¹Now, there was a place in Shemlon where the daughters of the Lamanites did gather themselves together, for to sing, and to dance, and to make themselves merry.

²And it came to pass that there was, one day, a small number of them gathered together to sing and to dance. ³And now, the priests of King Noah, being ashamed to return to the city of Nephi. Yea, and also fearing that the people would slay them—therefore, they durst not return to their wives, and their children. ⁴And, having tarried in the wilderness and having discovered the daughters of the Lamanites, they laid and watched them. ⁵And when there were but few of them gathered together to dance, they came forth out of their secret places and took them and carried them into the wilderness. Yea, twenty and four of the daughters of the Lamanites they carried into the wilderness.

⁶And it came to pass that when the Lamanites found that their daughters had been missing, they were angry with the people of Limhi, for they thought it was the people of Limhi. ⁷Therefore, they sent their armies forth. Yea, even the king himself went before his people. And they went up to the land of Nephi to destroy the people of Limhi.

⁸And now, Limhi had discovered them from the tower, even all their preparations for war did he discover. Therefore, he gathered his people together and laid wait for them in the fields and in the forests.

⁹And it came to pass that when the Lamanites had come up, that the people of Limhi began to fall upon them from their waiting places and began to slay them.

¹⁰And it came to pass that the battle became exceeding sore, for they fought like lions for their prey.

---

a. This is clearly the word in the Printer's Manuscript. The spelling is corrected in the printed versions to "ceremony." It is retained here as it is a somewhat awkward word in this context. It is not clear what is meant, as the description does not really indicate a ceremony. Skousen, *Analysis of the Textual Variants*, 3:1395, suggests that "ceremony" be emended to "sermon." While that fits a little better, it is still an awkward fit for the context.

¹¹And it came to pass that the people of Limhi began to drive the Lamanites before them, yet they were not half so numerous as the Lamanites. But they fought for their lives, and for their wives, and for their children. Therefore, they exerted themselves. And like dragons did they fight.

¹²And it came to pass that they found the king of the Lamanites among the number of their dead. Yet, he was not dead, having been wounded and left upon the ground (so speedy was the flight of his people). ¹³And they took him and bound up his wounds, and brought him before Limhi, and said: "Behold, here is the king of the Lamanites. He, having received a wound, hath fallen among their dead. And they have left him. And behold, we have brought him before you. And now, let us slay him."

¹⁴But Limhi saith unto them: "Ye shall not slay him, but bring him hither, that I may see him."

And they brought him. And Limhi saith unto him: "What cause have ye to come up to war against my people? Behold, my people have not broken the oath that I made unto you. Therefore, why should ye break the oath which ye made unto my people?"

¹⁵And now the king said: "I have broken the oath because thy people did carry away the daughters of my people. Therefore, in my anger I did cause my people to come up to war against thy people."

¹⁶Now, Limhi had heard nothing concerning this matter. Therefore, he saith: "I will search among my people. And whosoever hath done this thing shall perish." Therefore, he caused a search to be made among his people.

¹⁷Now, when Gideon had heard these things (he being the king's captain), he went forth and said unto the king:

> I pray thee, forbear, and do not search this people, and lay not this thing to their charge. ¹⁸For do ye not remember the priests of thy father, which this people sought to destroy? And are they not in the wilderness? And is it not they which have stolen the daughters of the Lamanites? ¹⁹And now, behold, and tell the king of these things, that he may tell his people, that they may be pacified towards us.
>
> For behold, they are already preparing to come against us. And behold, also there are but few of us. ²⁰And behold, they come with their numerous hosts. And except the king doth pacify them towards us, we must perish. ²¹For are not the words of Abinadi fulfilled (which he prophesied against us)? And all this, because we would not hearken unto the word of the Lord and turn from our iniquities.
>
> ²²And now, let us pacify the king. And we fulfil the oath which we have made unto him. For it is better that we should be in bondage than that we should lose our lives.[a] Therefore, let us put a stop to the shedding of so much blood.

²³And now, Limhi told the king all the things concerning his father and the priests that had fled into the wilderness. And attributed the carrying away of their daughters to them.

²⁴And it came to pass that the king was pacified towards his people. And he said unto them: "Let us go forth to meet my people, without arms. And I swear unto you with an oath that my people shall not slay thy people."

---

[a]. See the similar sentiment in Exodus 14:12: "Is not this the word that we did tell thee in Egypt, saying, Let us alone, that we may serve the Egyptians? For it had been better for us to serve the Egyptians, than that we should die in the wilderness."

Chapter IX [Mosiah 17–21]

²⁵And it came to pass that they followed the king and went forth without arms to meet the Lamanites.

And it came to pass that they did meet the Lamanites. And the king of the Lamanites did bow himself down before them, and did plead in behalf of the people of Limhi. ²⁶And when the Lamanites saw the people of Limhi (that they were without arms), that they had compassion on them, and were pacified towards them—and returned with their king in peace to their own land.

[21] ¹And it came to pass that Limhi and his people returned to the city of Nephi and began to dwell in the land again in peace.

²And it came to pass that after many days, the Lamanites began again to be stirred up in anger against the Nephites. And they began to come into the borders of the land round about. ³Now, they durst not slay them because of the oath which their king had made unto Limhi. But they would smite them on their cheeks, and exercise authority over them—and began to put heavy burdens upon their backs, and drive them as they would a dumb ass. ⁴Yea, all this was done that the word of the Lord might be fulfilled. And now, the afflictions of the Nephites was great. And there was no way that they could deliver themselves out of their hands. For the Lamanites had surrounded them on every side.

⁶And it came to pass that the people began to murmur with the king because of their afflictions. And they began to be desirous to go against them to battle. And they did afflict the king sorely with their complaints. Therefore, he granted unto them that they should do according to their desires. ⁷And they gathered themselves together again, and put on their armor, and went forth against the Lamanites to drive them out of their land.

⁸And it came to pass that the Lamanites did beat them, and drove them back, and slew many of them.

⁹And now, there was a great mourning and lamentation among the people of Limhi. The widow a mourning for her husband. The son and the daughter mourning for their father. And the brothers for their brethren. ¹⁰Now, there were a great many widows in the land and they did cry mightily from day to day, for a great fear of the Lamanites had come upon them.

¹¹And it came to pass that their continual cries did stir up the remainder of the people of Limhi to anger against the Lamanites. And they went again to battle. But they were driven back again, suffering much loss. ¹²Yea, they went again, even the third time, and suffered in the like manner. And those that were not slain returned again to the city of Nephi. ¹³And they did humble themselves, even to the dust, subjecting themselves to the yoke of bondage, submitting themselves to be smitten, and to be driven to and fro, and burdened according to the desires of their enemies. ¹⁴And they did humble themselves, even in the depths of humility. And they did cry mightily to God. Yea, even all the day long did they cry unto their God, that he would deliver them out of their afflictions.

¹⁵And now, the Lord was slow to hear their cry because of their iniquities. Nevertheless, the Lord did hear their cries, and began to soften the hearts of the Lamanites, that they began to ease their burdens. Yet, the Lord did not see fit to deliver them out of bondage.

¹⁶And it came to pass that they began to prosper by degrees in the land—and began to raise grain more abundantly, and flocks, and herds, that they did not suffer with hunger. ¹⁷Now, there was a great number of women, more than there was of men.

Therefore, King Limhi commanded that every man should impart to the support of the widows, and their children, that they might not perish with hunger. And this they did because of the greatness of their number that had been slain.

¹⁸Now, the people of Limhi kept together in a body (as much as it was possible), and secure their grain, and their flocks.ᵃ ¹⁹And the king, himself, did not trust his person without the walls of the city, unless he took his guards with him—fearing that he might (by some means) fall into the hands of the Lamanites.

²⁰And he caused that his people should watch the land round about, that by some means they might take those priests that fled into the wilderness, which had stolen the daughters of the Lamanites and that had caused such a great destruction to come upon them. ²¹For they were desirous to take them, that they might punish them. For they had come into the land of Nephi by night and carried off of their grain and many of their precious things. Therefore, they laid wait for them.

²²And it came to pass that there was no more disturbance between the Lamanites and the people of Limhi, even until the time that Ammon and his brethren came into the land. ²³And the king, having been without the gates of the city with his guard, he discovered Ammon and his brethren. And supposing them to be priests of Noah, therefore he caused that they should be taken, and bound, and cast into prison. And had they been the priests of Noah, he would have caused that they should be put to death. ²⁴But when he found that they were not, but that they were his brethren and had come from the land of Zarahemla, he was filled with exceeding great joy.

²⁵Now, King Limhi had sent (previous to the coming of Ammon) a small number of men to search for the land of Zarahemla. But they could not find it. And they were lost in the wilderness. ²⁶Nevertheless, they did find a land which had been peopled. Yea, a land which was covered with dry bones. Yea, a land which had been peopled and which had been destroyed. And they, having supposed it to be the land of Zarahemla, returned to the land of Nephi, having arrived in the borders of the land not many days before the coming of Ammon. ²⁷And they brought a record with them, even a record of the people whoseᵇ bones they had found. And they were engraven on plates of ore.

²⁸And now, Limhi was again filled with joy on learning from the mouth of Ammon that King Benjamin had a gift from God whereby he could interpret such engravings. Yea, and Ammon also did rejoice. ²⁹Yet, Ammon and his brethren were filled with sorrow because so many of their brethren had been slain. ³⁰And also that King Noah and his priests had caused the people to commit so many sins and iniquities against God. And they also did mourn for the death of Abinadi—and also for the departure of Alma and the people that went with him, who had formed a church of God through the strength and power of God, and faith on the words which had been spoken by Abinadi. ³¹Yea, they did mourn for their departure. For they knew not whither they had fled.

Now, they would have gladly joined with them. For they themselves had entered into a covenant with God, to serve him and keep his commandments. ³²And now, since the coming of Ammon, King Limhi had also entered into a covenant with God (and also many of his people), to serve him and keep his commandments.

³³And it came to pass that King Limhi, and many of his people, was desirous to be baptized. But there was none in the land that had authority from God. And Ammon

---

a. An awkward sentence. Perhaps it would make better sense if it were "and [did] secure their grain."
b. Probably added during proofreading.

declined doing this thing, considering himself an unworthy servant. ³⁴Therefore, they did not, at that time, form themselves into a church—waiting upon the spirit of the Lord. Now, they were desirous to become even as Alma and his brethren, which had fled into the wilderness. ³⁵They were desirous to be baptized as a witness and a testimony that they were willing to serve God, with all their hearts. Nevertheless, they did prolong the time. And an account of their baptism shall be given hereafter.

³⁶And now, all the study of Ammon and his people, and King Limhi and his people, was to deliver themselves out of the hands of the Lamanites, and from bondage.

Chapter X [Mosiah 22]

[22]¹And now it came to pass that Ammon and King Limhi began to consult with the people, how they should deliver themselves out of bondage. And even they did cause that all the people should gather themselves together. And this they did that they might have the voice of the people concerning the matter.

²And it came to pass that they could find no way to deliver themselves out of bondage, except it were to take their women, and children, and their flocks, and their herds, and their tents, and depart into the wilderness. For the Lamanites, being so numerous—that it was impossible for the people of Limhi to contend with them (thinking to deliver themselves out of bondage by the sword).

³Now it came to pass that Gideon went forth and stood before the king, and said unto him:

⁴Now, O king! Thou hast hitherto hearkened unto my words many times when we have been contending with our brethren the Lamanites. And now, O king, if thou hast not found me to be an unprofitable servant, or if thou hast hitherto listened to my word in any degree and they have been of service to thee, even so, I desire that thou wouldst listen to my words at this time. And I will be thy servant and deliver this people out of bondage.

⁵And the king granted unto him that he might speak. And Gideon saith unto him:

⁶Behold[a] the back pass through the back wall, on the back side of the city. The Lamanites (or the guards of the Lamanites) by night are drunken. Therefore, let us send a proclamation among all this people that they gather together their flocks, and herds, that they may drive them into the wilderness by night. ⁷And I will go, according to thy command, and pay the last tribute of wine to the Lamanites. And they will be drunken. And we will pass through the secret pass on the left of their camp when they are drunken and asleep. ⁸Thus, we will depart with our women, and our children, our flocks, and our herds—into the wilderness. And we will travel around the land of Shilom.

⁹And it came to pass that the king hearkened unto the words of Gideon.

¹⁰And it came to pass that King Limhi caused that his people should gather their flocks together. And he sent the tribute of wine to the Lamanites. And he also sent more wine as a present unto them. And they did drink freely of the wine which King Limhi did send unto them.

¹¹And it came to pass that the people of King Limhi did depart by night into the wilderness, with their flocks, and their herds. And they went round about the land of Shilom, in the wilderness, and bent their course towards the land of Zarahemla, being led by Ammon and his brethren. ¹²And they had taken all their gold, and silver, and their precious things which they could carry, and also their provisions with them, into the wilderness. And they pursued their journey. ¹³And after being many days in the wilderness, they arrived in the land of Zarahemla and joined [his[b]] people and became his subjects.

---

a. This is one of the rare times that "behold" appears to function in its historical definition of looking or recognizing something.

b. The word "his" is in the Printer's Manuscript and was kept in the text until the 1920 Latter-day

¹⁴And it came to pass that Mosiah received them with joy. And he also received their records—and also the records which had been found by the people of Limhi.

¹⁵And now it came to pass when the Lamanites had found that the people of Limhi had departed out of the land by night, that they sent an army into the wilderness to pursue them. ¹⁶And after they had pursued them two days, they could no longer follow their tracks. Therefore, they were lost in the wilderness.

Saint edition. At that time, it was changed to "Mosiah's" which is clearly the intent. Skousen, *Analysis of the Textual Variants*, 3:1428.

Chapter XI [Mosiah 23–27]

[23] *An account of Alma and the people of the Lord, which was driven into the wilderness by the people of King Noah.*

¹Now Alma, having been warned of the Lord that the armies of King Noah would come upon them, and had made it known to his people—therefore, they gathered together their flocks, and took of their grain, and departed into the wilderness before the armies of King Noah. ²And the Lord did strengthen them, that the people of King Noah could not overtake them, to destroy them.

³And it came to pass that they fled eight days journey into the wilderness. ⁴And they came to a land, yea, even a very beautiful and pleasant land. A land of pure water. ⁵And it came to pass that they pitched their tents, and began to till the ground, and began to build buildings, etc. Yea, they were industrious and did labor exceedingly.

⁶And it came to pass that the people were desirous that Alma should be their king, for he was beloved by his people. ⁷But he saith unto them:

> Behold, it is not expedient that we should have a king. For thus saith the Lord: "Ye shall not esteem one flesh above another, or one man shall not think himself above another.ᵃ" Therefore, I say unto you, it is not expedient that ye should have a king. ⁸Nevertheless, if it were possible that ye could always have a just man to be your kings, it would be well for you to have a king. ⁹But remember the iniquity of King Noah, and his priests.
>
> And I, myself, was caught in a snare, and did many things which was abominable in the sight of God, the Lord, which caused me sore repentance. ¹⁰Nevertheless, after much tribulation, the Lord did hear my cries and did answer my prayers, and hath made me an instrument in his hands in bringing so many of you to a knowledge of his truth. ¹¹Nevertheless, in this I do not glory, for I am unworthy to glory of myself.
>
> ¹²And now I say unto you: As you have been oppressed by King Noah and have been in bondage to him and his priests, and have been brought into iniquity by them, therefore, ye were bound with the bands of iniquity.
>
> ¹³And now, as ye have been delivered by the power of God out of these bonds, yea, out of the hands of King Noah and his people, and also from the bonds of iniquityᵇ—even so, I desire that ye should stand fast in this liberty, wherewith ye have been made free. And that ye trust no man to be a king over you. ¹⁴And also, trusting no one to be your teachers, nor your ministers, except he be a man of God—walking in his ways, and keeping his commandments.ᶜ

¹⁵Thus did Alma teach his people—that every man should love his neighbor as

---

a. There is no obvious biblical reference. This type of statement usually indicates a quotation from scripture, which in the Nephite world was the brass plates. It either represents a lost text from the brass plates or an oral rephrasing of a command that was well known. We do see a similar text from Nephi: "Behold, the Lord esteemeth all flesh in one" (1 Ne. 17:35). Nephi may be referring to the same brass plates text.

b. This part of the verse is separated from the sentence beginning "Even so" in order to highlight the intentional reverse parallelism of the two previous verses.

c. See Deuteronomy 30:16: "In that I command thee this day to love the Lord thy God, to walk in his ways, and to keep his commandments."

Chapter XI [Mosiah 23–27]

himself, that there should be no contention among them. ¹⁶And now, Alma was their high priest. He being the founder of their church.

¹⁷And it came to pass that none received authority to preach or to teach, except it were by him—from God. Therefore, he consecrated all their priests, and all their teachers. And none were consecrated except it were just men. ¹⁸Therefore, they did watch over their people, and did nourish them with things pertaining to righteousness.

¹⁹And it came to pass that they began to prosper exceedingly in the land. And they called the land [Helam^a].

²⁰And it came to pass that they did multiply and prosper exceedingly in the land of [Helam^b]. And they built a city, which they called the city of [Helam^c].

>²¹Nevertheless, the Lord seeth fit to chasten his people. Yea, he trieth their patience and their faith. ²²Nevertheless, whosoever putteth his trust in Him, the same shall be lifted up at the last day. Yea, and thus it was with this people. ²³For behold, I will show unto you that they were brought into bondage. And none could deliver them but the Lord, their God, yea, even the God of Abraham, and of Isaac, and of Jacob.

²⁴And it came to pass that he did deliver them. And he did show forth his mighty power unto them, and great was their rejoicings.^{d}<

²⁵For behold, it came to pass that while they were in the land of [Helam^e] (yea, in the city of [Helam^f]), while tilling the land round about—behold, an army of the Lamanites were in the borders of the land.

²⁶Now it came to pass that the brethren of Alma fled from their fields and gathered themselves together into the city of [Helam^g]. And they were much frightened because of the appearance of the Lamanites. ²⁷But Alma went forth and stood among them, and exhorted them that they should not be frightened but that they should remember the Lord, their God—and he would deliver them. ²⁸Therefore, they hushed their fears, and began to cry unto the Lord that he would soften the hearts of the Lamanites, that they would spare them, and their wives, and children.

²⁹And it came to pass that the Lord did soften the hearts of the Lamanites. And Alma and his brethren went forth and delivered themselves up into their hands. And the Lamanites took possession of the Land of [Helam^h].

³⁰Now, the armies of the Lamanites (which had followed after the people of King Limhi) had been lost in the wilderness for many days. ³¹And behold, they had found those priests of King Noah in a place which they called Amulon. And they had began to posess the land of Amulon. And had began to till the ground. ³²Now, the name of the leader of those priests was Amulon.

---

    a. The Printer's Manuscript has Helaman. See Skousen, *Analysis of the Textual Variants*, 3:1370.
    b. The Printer's Manuscript has Helaman. See Skousen, *Analysis of the Textual Variants*, 3:1370.
    c. The Printer's Manuscript has Helaman. See Skousen, *Analysis of the Textual Variants*, 3:1370.
    d. Verses 21–24 are Mormon's inserted foreshadowing of what is coming, as well as Mormon's reason that such difficulties might befall the righteous. Verse 24 shows what the conclusion of the event would be, but it is chronologically out of place here.
    e. The Printer's Manuscript has Helaman. See Skousen, *Analysis of the Textual Variants*, 3:1370.
    f. The Printer's Manuscript has Helaman. See Skousen, *Analysis of the Textual Variants*, 3:1370.
    g. The Printer's Manuscript has Helaman. See Skousen, *Analysis of the Textual Variants*, 3:1370.
    h. The Printer's Manuscript has Helaman. See Skousen, *Analysis of the Textual Variants*, 3:1370.

³³And it came to pass that Amulon did plead with the Lamanites. And he also sent forth their wives, which was the daughters of the Lamanites, to plead with their brethren, that they should not destroy their husbands.

³⁴And it came to pass that the Lamanites had compassion on Amulon, and his brethren, and did not destroy them, because of their wives. And Amulon and his brethren did join the Lamanites. And they were traveling in the wilderness in search of the land of Nephi when they discovered the land of [Helam^a], which was possessed by Alma and his brethren.

³⁶And it came to pass that the Lamanites promised unto Alma and his brethren, that if they would show them the way which led to the land of Nephi, that they would grant unto them their lives, and their liberty. ³⁷But it came to pass that after Alma had shown them the way that led to the land of Nephi, the Lamanites would not keep their promise. But they set guards round about the land of [Helam^b], over Alma and his brethren. ³⁸And the remainder of them went to the land of Nephi. And a part of them returned to the land of [Helam^c], and also brought with them the wives and the children of the guards which had been left in the land. ³⁹And the king of the Lamanites had granted unto Amulon that he should be a king and a ruler over his people, which was in the land of [Helam^d]. Nevertheless, he should have no power to do anything contrary to the will of the king of the Lamanites.

[24] ¹And it came to pass that Amulon did gain favor in the eyes of the king of the Lamanites. Therefore, the king of the Lamanites granted unto him and his brethren, that they should be appointed teachers over his people. Yea, even over the people which was in the land of Shemlon, and the land of Shilom, and in the land of Amulon. ²For the Lamanites had taken possession of all these lands. Therefore, the king of the Lamanites had appointed kings over all these lands.

³And now, the name of the king of the Lamanites was Laman, being called after the name of his father, and therefore, he was called King Laman. And he was king over a numerous people. ⁴And he appointed teachers of the brethren of Amulon in every land which was possessed by his people. And thus, the language of Nephi began to be taught among all the people of the Lamanites. ⁵And they were a people friendly one with another. Nevertheless, they knew not God. Neither did the brethren of Amulon teach them anything concerning the Lord, their God. Neither the law of Moses, nor did they teach them the words of Abinadi. ⁶But they taught them that they should keep their record and that they might write one to another. ⁷And thus the Lamanites began to increase in riches: and began to trade one with another and wax great—and began to be a cunning and a wise people (as to the wisdom of the world). Yea, a very cunning people—delighting in all manner of wickedness and plunder, except it were among their own brethren.

⁸And now it came to pass that Amulon began to exercise authority over Alma and his brethren, and began to persecute him, and cause that his children should persecute their children. ⁹For Amulon knew Alma, that he had been one of the king's priests, and that it was he that believed the words of Abinadi and was driven out before the king.

---

a. The Printer's Manuscript has Helaman. See Skousen, *Analysis of the Textual Variants*, 3:1370.
b. The Printer's Manuscript has Helaman. See Skousen, *Analysis of the Textual Variants*, 3:1370.
c. The Printer's Manuscript has Helaman. See Skousen, *Analysis of the Textual Variants*, 3:1370.
d. The Printer's Manuscript has Helaman. See Skousen, *Analysis of the Textual Variants*, 3:1370.

Chapter XI [Mosiah 23–27]

And therefore he was wroth with him (for he was subject to King Laman). Yet, he exercised authority over them. And put tasks upon them. And put taskmasters over them.

[10] And it came to pass that so great was their afflictions, that they began to cry mightily to God.

[11] And it came to pass that Amulon commanded them that they should stop their cries. And put guards over them to watch them, that whosoever should be found calling upon God should be put to death.

[12] And it came to pass that Alma and his people did not raise their voices to the Lord, their God, but did pour out their hearts to him. And he did know the thoughts of their hearts.

[13] And it came to pass that the voice of the Lord came to them in their afflictions, saying:

> Lift up your heads and be of good comfort! For I know of the covenant which ye have made unto me. And I will covenant with this, my people, and deliver them out of bondage. [14] And I will also ease their burdens, which is put upon your shoulders, that even you cannot feel them upon your backs, even while you are in bondage. And this will I do, that ye may stand as witnesses for me hereafter—and that ye may know of a surety, that I, the Lord God, do visit my people in their afflictions.

[15] And now it came to pass that the burdens which was laid upon Alma and his brethren were made light. Yea, the Lord did strengthen them, that they could bear up their burdens with ease. And they did submit cheerfully, and with patience, to all the will of the Lord.

[16] And it came to pass that so great was their faith, and their patience, that the voice of the Lord came unto them again, saying: "Be of good comfort! For on the morrow I will deliver thee out of bondage."

[17] And he saith unto Alma: "Thou shalt go before this people. And I will go with thee and deliver this people out of bondage."

[18] Now it came to pass that Alma and his people, in the nighttime, gathered their flocks together, and also of their grain. Yea, even all the nighttime were they gathering their flocks together. [19] And in the morning the Lord caused a deep sleep to come upon the Lamanites. Yea, and all their taskmasters were in a profound sleep.

[20] And it came to pass that Alma and his people departed into the wilderness. And when they had traveled all day, they pitched their tents in a valley. And they called the name of the valley Alma, because he led their way in the wilderness. [21] Yea, and in the valley of Alma they poured out their thanks to God, because he had been merciful unto them, and eased their burdens, and had delivered them out of bondage. For they were in bondage, and none could deliver them except it were the Lord, their God. [22] And they gave thanks to God. Yea, all their men, and all their women, and all their children that could speak, lifted their voices in the praises of their God.

[23] And now, the Lord said unto Alma: "Haste thee, and get thou and this people out of this land. For the Lamanites have awoke and doth pursue thee. Therefore, get thee out of this land. And I will stop the Lamanites in this valley, that they come no further in pursuit of this people."

[24] And it came to pass that they departed out of the valley and took their journey into the wilderness.

²⁵And it came to pass that after they had been in the wilderness twelve days, they arrived to the land of Zarahemla. And King Mosiah did also receive them with joy.

[25] ¹And now, King Mosiah caused that all the people should be gathered together. ²Now, there were not so many of the children of Nephi (or so many of those which were descendants of Nephi) as there were of the people of Zarahemla (which was a descendant of [Muloch[a]] and those which came with him into the wilderness). ³And there were not so many of the people of Nephi, and of the people of Zarahemla, as there was of the Lamanites. Yea, they were not half so numerous.

⁴And now, all the people of Nephi was assembled together, and also all the people of Zarahemla. And they were gathered together in two bodies.

⁵And it came to pass that Mosiah did read (and caused to be read) the records of Zeniff to his people. Yea, he read the records of the people of Zeniff from the time they left the land of Zarahemla until the time they returned again, ⁶and he also read the account of Alma and his brethren. And all their afflictions from the time they left the land of Zarahemla until the time they returned again.

⁷And now, when Mosiah had made an end of reading the records, his people which tarried in the land were struck with wonder and amazement, ⁸for they knew not what to think.

For when they beheld those that had been delivered out of bondage—they were filled with exceeding great joy.[b]

⁹And again, when they thought of their brethren which had been slain by the Lamanites—they were filled with sorrow, and even shed many tears of sorrow.

¹⁰And again, when they thought of the immediate goodness of God and his power in delivering Alma and his brethren out of the hands of the Lamanites and of bondage—they did raise their voices and gave thanks to God.

¹¹And again, when they thought upon the Lamanites (which was their brethren)—of their sinful and polluted state—they were filled with pain and anguish for the welfare of their souls.

¹²And it came to pass that when[c] those which were the children of Amulon and his brethren (which had taken to wife the daughters of the Lamanites)—they were displeased with the conduct of their fathers. And they would no longer be called by the names of their fathers. Therefore, they took upon themselves the name of Nephi, that they might be called the children of Nephi and be numbered among those which were called Nephites.

¹³And now, all the people of Zarahemla were numbered with the Nephites. And this because the kingdom had been conferred upon none but those which were descendants of Nephi.

¹⁴And now it came to pass that when Mosiah had made an end of speaking and reading to the people, he desired that Alma should also speak to the people.

---

a. It is supposed that this is a variant spelling for Mulek, and it was changed to Mulek in 1879. Skousen notes that it is possible that it refers to a different person. Skousen, *Analysis of the Textual Variants*, 3:1464.

b. From here to verse 12, the "and again" sentences are separated to emphasize the parallels. This sentence would typically fit with the previous paragraph because the "for" is an explanation of what came before. In this case it is the introduction to the "and again" sentences.

c. The Printer's Manuscript originally had "when," which was crossed out in heavier ink typical of the editing of the 1837 edition. The 1830 edition retained "when," but it was removed in 1837. The removal recognized that it created an incomplete sentence.

¹⁵And it came to pass that Alma did speak unto them when they were assembled together in large bodies. And he went from one body to another, preaching unto the people repentance and faith on the Lord. ¹⁶And he did exhort the people of Limhi and his brethren (all those that had been delivered out of bondage), that [they[a]]should remember that it was the Lord that did deliver them.

¹⁷And it came to pass that after Alma had taught the people many things, and had made an end of speaking to them, that King Limhi was desirous that he might be baptized. And all his people were desirous that they might be baptized also. ¹⁸Therefore, Alma did go forth into the water and did baptize him. Yea, he did baptize them after the manner he did his brethren in the waters of Mormon. Yea, and as many as he did baptize did belong to the church of God. And this because of their belief on the words of Alma.

¹⁹And it came to pass that King Mosiah granted unto Alma that he might establish churches throughout all the land of Zarahemla. And gave him power to ordain priests and teachers over every church. ²⁰Now, this was done because there was so many people that they could not be all governed by one teacher. Neither could they all hear the word of God in one assembly. ²¹Therefore, they did assemble themselves together in different bodies, being called churches—every church having their priests and their teachers, and every priest preaching the word according as it was delivered to him by the mouth of Alma. ²²And thus, notwithstanding there being many churches, they [were[b]]all one church, yea, even the church of God. For there was nothing preached in all the churches except it were repentance and faith in God.

²³And now, there was seven churches in the land of Zarahemla.

And it came to pass that whosoever was desirous to take upon them the name of Christ, or of God, they did join the churches of God. ²⁴And they were called the people of God. And the Lord did pour out his spirit upon them. And they were blessed, and prospered in the land.

[26] ¹Now it came to pass that there was many of the rising generation that could not understand the words of King Benjamin, being little children at the time he spake unto his people. And they did not believe the tradition of their fathers. ²They did not believe what had been said concerning the resurrection of the dead. Neither did they believe concerning the coming of Christ.

³And now, because of their unbelief, they could not understand the word of God. And their hearts were hardened, ⁴and they would not be baptized. Neither would they join the church. And they were a separate people as to their faith, and remained so ever after, even in their carnal and sinful state. For they would not call upon the Lord, their God.

⁵And now, in the reign of Mosiah they were not half so numerous as the people of God. But because of the dissentions among the brethren, they became more numerous. ⁶For it came to pass that they did deceive many (with their flattering words) which were in the church. And did cause them to commit many sins. Therefore, it became expedient that those who committed sin, that was in the church, should be admonished by the church.

⁷And it came to pass that they were brought before the priests and delivered up unto the priests by the teachers. And the priests brought them before Alma, which was the high priest. ⁸Now, King Mosiah had given Alma the authority over the church.

⁹And it came to pass that Alma did not know concerning them, for there were many

---

a. Probably added during proofreading.
b. Probably added during proofreading.

witnesses against them. Yea, the people stood and testified of their iniquity in abundance. ¹⁰Now, there had not any such thing happened before in the church. Therefore, Alma was troubled in his spirit. And he caused that they should be brought before the king. ¹¹And he saith unto the king: "Behold, here are many which we have brought before thee, which are accused of their brethren. Yea, and they have been taken in divers iniquities and they do not repent of their iniquities. Therefore, we have brought them before thee, that thou may judge them according to their crimes."

¹²But King Mosiah saith unto Alma: "Behold, I judge them not. Therefore, I deliver them into thy hands to be judged."

¹³And now, the spirit of Alma was again troubled. And he went and enquired of the Lord what he should do concerning this matter. For he feared that he should do wrong in the sight of God.

¹⁴And it came to pass that after he had poured out his whole soul to God, the voice of the Lord came to him, saying:

> ¹⁵Blessed art thou, Alma! And blessed are they which were baptized in the waters of Mormon. Thou art blessed because of thy exceeding faith in the words alone of my servant Abinadi. ¹⁶And blessed are they, because of their exceeding faith in the words alone which thou hast spoken unto them. ¹⁷And blessed art thou because thou hast established a church among this people. And they shall be established. And they shall be my people.ᵃ ¹⁸Yea, blessed is this people, which is willing to bear my name. For in my [nameᵇ] shall they [beᶜ] called. And they are mine.
>
> ¹⁹And because thou hast enquired of me concerning the transgressor, thou art blessed. ²⁰Thou art my servant. And I covenant with thee that thou shalt have eternal life. And thou shalt serve me, and go forth in my name, and shall gather together my sheep. ²¹And he that will hear my voice shall be my sheep. And him shall ye receive into the church. And him will I also receive.
>
> ²²For behold, this is my church. Whosoever that is baptized, shall be baptized unto repentance. And whosoever ye receive, shall believe in my name. And him will I freely forgive. ²³For it is I that taketh upon me the sins of the world. For it is I that hath created them. And it is I that granteth unto him that believeth, in the end, a place at my right hand. ²⁴For behold, in my name are they called. And if they know me, they shall come forth, and shall have a place eternally at my right hand.
>
> ²⁵And it shall come to pass that when the second trump shall sound, then shall they that never knew me come forth and shall stand before me. ²⁶And then shall they know that I am the Lord, their God, that I am their Redeemer. But they would not be redeemed. ²⁷And then will I confess into unto them that I never knew them.ᵈ And they shall depart into everlasting fire, prepared for the devil and his angels. ²⁸Therefore, I say unto you, that he that will not hear my voice, the same shall ye not receive into my church. For him I will not receive at the last day. ²⁹Therefore, I say unto you, go.

---

  a. It is not entirely who "they" is referring to. This edition reads it as referring to churches. Thus, the "churches shall be established—and the churches shall be my people."

  b. Probably added during proofreading.

  c. Probably added during proofreading.

  d. See Matthew 7:23: "And then will I profess unto them, I never knew you: depart from me, ye that work iniquity."

And whosoever transgresseth against me, him shall ye judge according to the sins which he hath committed. And if he confess his sins before thee and me, and repenteth in the sincerity of his heart, him shall ye forgive. And I will forgive him also. ³⁰Yea, and as often as my people repent will I forgive them their trespasses against me.

³¹And ye shall also forgive one another your trespasses. For verily I say unto you, he that forgiveth not his neighbor's trespasses (when he saith that he repenteth), the same hath brought himself under condemnation. ³²Now, I say unto you, go.

And whosoever will not repent of his sins, the same shall not be numbered among my people. And this shall be observed from this time forward.

³³And it came to pass when Alma had heard these words he wrote them down, that he might have them—and that he might judge the people of that church according to the commandments of God.

³⁴And it came to pass that Alma went and judged those that had been taken in iniquity, according to the word of the Lord. ³⁵And whosoever repented of their sins and did confess them, them he did number among the people of the church. ³⁶And them that would not confess their sins and repent of their iniquity, the same were not numbered among the people of the church. And their names were blotted out.

³⁷And it came to pass that Alma did regulate all the affairs of the church. And they began again to have peace and to prosper exceedingly in the affairs of the church. Walking circumspectly before God: receiving many and baptizing many.

³⁸And now, all these things did Alma and his fellow laborers do (which were over the church). Walking in all diligence. Teaching the word of God in all things. Suffering[a] all manner of afflictions. Being persecuted by all those who did not belong to the church of God. ³⁹And they did admonish their brethren. And they were also admonished, every one, by the word of God, according to his sins (or to the sins which he had committed)—being commanded of God to pray without ceasing, and to give thanks in all things.

[27] ¹And now it came to pass that the persecutions which was inflicted on the church by the unbelievers became so great that the church began to murmur and complain to their leaders concerning the matter. And they did complain to Alma. And Alma laid the case before their King Mosiah. And Mosiah consulted with his priests.

²And it came to pass that King Mosiah sent a proclamation throughout the land round about, that there should not any unbeliever persecute any of those which belonged to the church of God. ³And there was a strict command throughout all the churches—that there should be no persecutions among them, that there should be an equality among all men—⁴that they should let no pride nor haughtiness disturb their peace—that every man should esteem his neighbor as himself, laboring with their own hands for their support. ⁵Yea, and all their priests and teachers should labor with their own hands for their support in all cases, save it were in sickness, or in much want. And doing these things, they did abound in the grace of God.

⁶And there began to be much peace again in the land. And the people began to be very numerous and began to scatter abroad upon the face of the earth. Yea, on the

---

a. The Printer's Manuscript has "sufferings," which is clearly incorrect. It is treated as a spelling error and corrected.

north, and on the south, on the east, and on the west—building large cities and villages in all quarters of the land. ⁷And the Lord did visit them and prosper them. And they became a large and a wealthy people.

⁸Now, the sons of Mosiah was numbered among the unbelievers. And also one of the sons of Alma was numbered among them (he being called Alma, after his father). Nevertheless, he became a very wicked, and an idolatrous man. And he was a man of many words and did speak much flattery to the people. Therefore, he led many of the people to do after the manner of his iniquities. ⁹And he became a great hinderment to the prosperity of the church of God. Stealing away the hearts of the people. Causing much dissention among the people. Giving a chance for the enemy of God to[a] exercise his power over them.

¹⁰And now it came to pass that while he was going about to destroy the church of God (for he did go about secretly, with the sons of Mosiah, seeking to destroy the church and to lead astray the people of the Lord, contrary to the commandments of God, or even the king)—¹¹and, as I said unto you, as they were going about rebelling against God—behold, the angel of the Lord appeared unto them.[b] And he descended as it were in a cloud. And he spake as it were with a voice of thunder which caused the earth [to[c]] shake upon which they stood. ¹²And so great was their astonishment that they fell to the earth and understood not the words which he spake unto them. ¹³Nevertheless, he cried again, saying:

> Alma! Arise and stand forth! For why persecuteth thou the church of God? For the Lord hath said: "This is my church and I will establish it—and nothing shall overthrow it, save it is the transgressions of my people."

¹⁴And again, the angel saith:

> Behold, the Lord hath heard the prayers of his people, and also the prayers of his servant Alma (which is thy father). For he hath prayed with much faith concerning thee, that thou mightest be brought to the knowledge of the truth. Therefore, for this purpose have I come to convince thee of the power and authority of God—that the prayers of his servants might be answered, according to their faith.

> ¹⁵And now behold, can ye dispute the power of God? For behold, doth not my voice shake the earth? And can ye not also behold me before you? And I am sent from God.

> ¹⁶Now, I say unto thee, go! And remember the captivity of thy fathers in the land of [Helam[d]], and in the land of Nephi. And remember how great things he hath done for them.[e] For they were in bondage and he hath delivered them.

> And now I say unto thee: Alma, go thy way. And seek to destroy the church

---

a. Probably added during proofreading.

b. The original intent of the sentence was derailed with the explanatory information about what they did to lead the church astray. Repetitive resumption comes after the "and, and I said unto you."

c. Probably added during proofreading.

d. This instance was not originally Helaman. However, it was spelled Helem. I have corrected it to what has become standard.

e. Perhaps an allusion to 1 Samuel 12:24: "Only fear the Lord, and serve him in truth with all your heart: for consider how great *things* he hath done for you."

Chapter XI [Mosiah 23–27]

no more, that their prayers may [be[a]] answered—and this, even if thou wilt, of thyself, be cast off.

[17]And now it came to pass that these were the last[b] words which the angel spake unto Alma. And he departed.

[18]And now Alma, and those that were with him, fell again to the earth. For great was their astonishment. For with their own eyes they had beheld an angel of the Lord. And his voice was as thunder which shook the earth. And they knew that there was nothing, save the power of God, that could shake the earth and cause it to tremble as though it would part asunder.

[19]And now, the astonishment of Alma was so great that he became dumb, that he could not open his mouth. Yea, and he became weak, even that he could not move his hands. Therefore, he was taken by those that were with him, and carried helpless, even until [he[c]] was laid before his father. [20]And they rehearsed unto his father all that had happened unto them. And his father rejoiced. For he knew that it was the power of God.

[21]And he caused that a multitude should be gathered together, that they might witness what the Lord had done for his son, and also for those that were with him. [22]And he caused that the priests should assemble themselves together. And they began to fast, and to pray to their Lord, their God, that he would open the mouth of Alma, that he might speak. And also, that his limbs might receive their strength, that the eyes of the people might be opened to see, and know, of the goodness and glory of God.

[23]And it came to pass, after they had fasted and prayed for the space of two days and two nights, the limbs of Alma received their strength. And he stood up. And began to speak unto them, bidding them to be of good comfort. [24]For, said he:

> I have repented of my sins and have been redeemed of the Lord. Behold, I am born of the spirit. [25]And the Lord [said[d]] unto me: "Marvel not that all mankind—yea, men and women, all nations, kindreds, tongues, and people—must be born again.[e] Yea, born of God. Changed [from[f]] their carnal and fallen state to a state of righteousness. Being redeemed of God. Becoming his sons and daughters. [26]And thus, they become new creatures. And unless they do this, they can in nowise inherit the kingdom of God."

[27]I say unto you, unless this be the case, they must be cast off. And this I know because I was like to be cast off. [28]Nevertheless, after wading through much tribulation, repenting nigh unto death—the Lord, in mercy, hath seen fit to snatch me out of an everlasting burning. And I am born of God. [29]My soul hath been redeemed from the gall of bitterness and bonds of iniquity.

I was in the darkest abyss, but now I behold the marvelous light of God. My

---

a. Inadvertently left out. The scribe had written "understood," then immediately crossed it out to enter the correct word, "answered." In doing so, the verb "be" was missed. The compositor added it for the 1830 edition. Skousen, *Analysis of the Textual Variants*, 3:1509.

b. The Printer's Manuscript has "lost." The 1830 edition corrected it to "last," which is used here. The original is not extant.

c. Probably added during proofreading.

d. Probably added during proofreading.

e. See John 3:7: "Marvel not that I said unto thee, Ye must be born again."

f. Probably added during proofreading.

soul was wrecked[a] with eternal torment, but I am snatched. And my soul is pained no more.

[30]I rejected my redeemer and denied that which had been spoken of by our fathers. But now, that they may foresee that he will come, and that he remembereth every creature of his creating—and[b] he will make himself manifest unto all. [31]Yea, every knee shall bow,[c] and every tongue confess before him, yea, even at the last day when all men shall stand to be judged of him. Then shall they confess that he is God. Then shall they confess (who live without God in the world) that the judgment of an everlasting punishment is just upon them. And they shall quake, and tremble, and shrink beneath the glance of his all-searching eye.

[32]And now it came to pass that Alma began, from this time forward, to teach the people—and those which were with Alma at the time the angel appeared unto them—traveling round about through all the land, publishing to all the people the things which they had heard and seen—and preaching the word of God in much tribulation, being greatly persecuted by those which were unbelievers. Being smitten by many of them. [33]But, notwithstanding all this, they did impart much consolation to the church. Confirming their faith and exhorting them (with long suffering, and much travail) to keep the commandments of God.

[34]And [four[d]]of them were the sons of Mosiah. And their names were Ammon, and Aaron, and Omner, and Himni. These were the names of the sons of Mosiah. [35]And after they had traveled throughout all the land of Zarahemla, and among all the people which was under the reign of King Mosiah—zealously striving to repair all the injuries which they had done to the church: confessing all their sins, and publishing all the things which they had seen, and explaining the prophecies and the scriptures to all who desired to hear them. [36]And thus they were instruments in the hands of God, in bringing many to the knowledge of the truth. Yea, to the knowledge of their redeemer.

> [37]And how blessed are they!
> For they did publish peace.
>> They did publish good tidings of good.
> And they did declare unto the people
>> that the Lord reigneth.[e]

---

a. This was not changed to "racked" in LDS editions until 1879. Skousen sees this as a scribal error, substituting the similar sounding word for the intended "racked." Skousen, *Analysis of the Textual Variants*, 3:1514.

b. The "and" was removed by Joseph Smith for the 1837 edition. That removal fixed the otherwise incomplete sentence. However, it is probable that the "and" was intended to be read as "therefore," which completes the sentence.

c. Uses language from Philippians 2:10: "At the name of Jesus every knee should bow." Philippians is using language from Isaiah 45:21: "Unto me every knee shall bow, every tongue shall swear." Given the preponderance of quotations and allusions to the New Testament, the language is most likely based on Philippians.

d. Probably added in proofreading.

e. An intentional echo of Isaiah 52:7: "How beautiful upon the mountains are the feet of him that bringeth good tidings, that publisheth peace; that bringeth good tidings of good, that publisheth salvation; that saith unto Zion, Thy God reigneth!"

Chapter XII [Mosiah 28:1–28:19]

[28] ¹Now it came to pass that after the sons of Mosiah had done all these things, they took a small number with them and returned to their father (the king), and desired of him that he would grant unto them that they might (with those whom they had selected) go up to the land of Nephi—that they might preach the things which they had heard—and that they might impart the word of God to their brethren, the Lamanites. ²That they perhaps they might bring them to the knowledge of the Lord, their God, and convince them of the iniquity of their fathers. And that perhaps they might cure them of their hatred towards the Nephites, that they might also be brought to rejoice in their Lord, their God, that they might become friendly to one another. And that there should be no more contentions in all the land, which the Lord, their God, hath given them.

³Now, they were desirous that salvation should be declared to every creature. For they could not bear that any human soul should perish. Yea, even the very thoughts that any soul should endure endless torment did cause them to quake and tremble. ⁴And thus did the spirit of the Lord work upon them. For they were the very vilest of sinners, And the Lord saw fit (in his infinite mercy) to spare them. Nevertheless, they suffered much anguish of soul because of their iniquities and suffering, much fearing that they should be cast off forever.

⁵And it came to pass that they did plead with their father many days, that they might go up to the land of Nephi.

⁶And it came to pass that King Mosiah went and enquired of the Lord if he should let his sons go up among the Lamanites to preach the word. ⁷And the Lord said unto Mosiah: "Let them go up. For many shall believe on their words, and they shall have eternal life. And I will deliver thy sons out of the hands of the Lamanites."

⁸And it came to pass that Mosiah granted that they might go and do according to their request. ⁹And they took their journey into the wilderness, to go up to preach the word among the Lamanites. And I shall give an account of their proceedings hereafter.

¹⁰Now, King Mosiah had no one to confer the kingdom upon, for there was not any of his sons which would accept of the kingdom. ¹¹Therefore, he took the records which were engraven upon the plates of brass, and also the plates of Nephi, and all the things which he had kept, and preserved, according to the commandments of God.[a]

> And after having translated, and caused to be written, the records which were on the plates of gold (which had been found by the people of Limhi) which was delivered to him by the hand of Limhi—¹²and this he done because of the great anxiety of his people.[b] For they were desirous beyond measure to know concerning those people which had been destroyed.

¹³And now, he translated them by the means of those two stones which was

---

a. There is a grammatical expectation that we should have some action occur that resolves "he took the records." We don't get it here. It comes at the beginning of the next original chapter, or Mosiah 28:20 in the modern versification. The mention of the records moves to an important subtheme in Mormon's writing, but it apparently was not one that was planned at this point. Mosiah 28:20 serves as a repetitive resumption. The inserted account was sufficiently important, however, that Mormon created a chapter break to separate it from the following information.

b. This is another example of a sentence with an early participle that is never really resolved, resulting in an incomplete sentence.

fastened into the two rims of a bow. ¹⁴Now, these things was prepared from the beginning, and was handed down from generation to generation for the purpose of interpreting languages. ¹⁵And they have been kept, and preserved, by the hand of the Lord, that he should discover to every creature which should possess the land, the iniquities and abominations of his people. ¹⁶And whosoever has the things is called seer, after the manner of old times.[a]

¹⁷Now, after Mosiah had finished translating these records, behold, it gave an account of the people which was destroyed from the time that they were destroyed, back to the building of the great tower at the time the Lord confounded the languages of the people, and they were scattered abroad upon the face of all the earth. Yea, and even from that time until the creation of Adam.

¹⁸Now, this account did cause the people of Mosiah to mourn exceedingly. Yea, they were filled with sorrow. Nevertheless, it gave them much knowledge, in the which they did rejoice. ¹⁹And this account shall be written hereafter, for behold, it is expedient that all people should know the things which are written in this account.<[b]

---

a. See 1 Samuel 9:9: "Beforetime in Israel, when a man went to inquire of God, thus he spake, Come, and let us go to the seer: for he that is now called a Prophet was beforetime called a Seer."

b. The repetitive resumption comes in the next verse, which was originally a different chapter.

Chapter XIII [Mosiah 28:20–29:46]

[**28 continued**] ²⁰And now, as I said unto you,[a] that after King Mosiah had done these things, he took the plates of brass, and all the things which he had kept, and conferred them upon Alma, which was the son of Alma. Yea, all the records, and also the interpreters, and conferred them upon him—and commanding him that he should keep and preserve them.[b] And also keep a record of the people. Handing them down from one generation to another, even as they had been handed down from the times that Lehi left Jerusalem.

[**29**] ¹Now, when Mosiah had done this, he sent out through all the land, among all the people, desiring to know their will concerning who should be their king.

²And it came pass that the voice of the people came, saying: "We are desirous that Aaron, thy son, should be our king, and our ruler."

³Now, Aaron had gone up to the land of Nephi. Therefore, the king could not confer the kingdom upon him, [neither would Aaron take upon him the kingdom.[c]] Neither was any of the sons of Mosiah willing to take upon them the kingdom. ⁴Therefore, King Mosiah sent again among the people, yea, even a written word sent he among the people. And these were the words that were written, saying:

⁵Behold, O ye my people (or my brethren, for I esteem you as such). For I desire that ye should consider the cause which [ye[d]] are called to consider. For ye are desirous to have a king. ⁶Now, I declare unto you, that he to whom that the kingdom doth rightly belong hath declared—and will not take upon him the kingdom.

⁷And now, if there should be another appointed in his stead, behold, I fear there would rise contentions among you. And who knoweth but what my sons (to whom the kingdom doth belong) should turn to be angry and draw away a part of this people after him, which will cause wars and contentions among you, which would be the cause of shedding much blood, and perverting the way of the Lord, Yea, and destroy the souls of much[e] people.

⁸Now, I say unto you: Let us be wise and consider these things. For we have no right to destroy my son. Neither should we have any right to destroy another if he should be appointed in his stead. ⁹And if my son should turn again to his pride and vain things, he would recall[f] the things which he had said, and claim his right to the kingdom, which would cause him (and also this people) to commit much sin.

---

a. This is Mormon's recognition that he has inserted an aside and must return. The following information is the repetitive resumption that confirms the interruption and continuation.

b. Even though there are two verbs of different tenses, it seems to be a translator error. The intent of the sentence feels like it should speak both of having the items conferred, and then commanded to be preserved.

c. The phrase was probably added during proofreading.

d. The Printer's Manuscript has "yea," which is clearly incorrect and intended to be "ye." The compositor changed this to the expected "ye" for the 1830 edition.

e. The word is "mtch." The compositor originally crossed it out and inserted "many." Nevertheless, it was set as "much" in 1830. The 1837 edition changed it to "many," which has remained to the current edition. Skousen, *Analysis of the Textual Variants*, 3:1541. Hyrum Smith (the scribe at this point) earlier wrote "mutch," suggesting that "much" is the intended word in the Original Manuscript.

f. The sense of "recall" is to take back, not remember.

¹⁰And now, let us be wise. And look forward to these things, and do that which will make for the peace of this people. ¹¹Therefore, I will be your king the remainder of my days. Nevertheless, let us appoint judges to judge this people, according to our law. And we will newly arrange the affairs of this people. For we will appoint wise men to be judges, that will judge this people according to the commandments of God.

¹²Now, it is better that a man should be judged of God than of man. For the judgments of God are always just, but the judgments of man are not always just. ¹³Therefore, if it was possible that ye could have just men to be your kings, which would establish the laws of God and judge this people according to his commandments—yea, if ye could have men for your kings which would do even as my father Benjamin did for this people—I say unto you if this could always be the case, then it would be expedient that ye should always have kings to rule over you.

¹⁴And even I, myself, have labored with all the power and facilities which I have possessed to teach you the commandments of God and to establish peace throughout the land, that there should be no wars, nor contentions, no stealing, nor plundering, nor murdering, nor no manner of iniquity. ¹⁵And whosoever hath committed iniquity, him have I punished according to the crime which he hath committed, according to the law which hath been given to us by our fathers.

¹⁶Now, I say unto you, that because all men are not just, it is not expedient that ye should have a king (or kings) to rule over you. ¹⁷For behold, how much iniquity doth one wicked king cause to be committed? Yea, and what great destruction? ¹⁸Yea, remembering [King[a]] Noah—his wickedness, and his abominations—and also the wickedness and abominations of his people.[b] Behold[c] what great destruction did come upon them. And also because of their iniquities they were brought into bondage. ¹⁹And were it not for the interposition of their all-wise Creator (and this because of their sincere repentance) they must unavoidably remain in bondage until now.

²⁰But behold, he did deliver them because they did humble themselves before him. And [because[d]] they cried mightily unto him, he did deliver them out of bondage. And thus doth the Lord work with his power in all cases among the children of men, extending the arm of mercy towards them that put their trust in him.

²¹And behold, now I say unto you, ye cannot dethrone[e] an iniquitous king, save it be through much contention and the shedding of much blood. ²²For behold, he hath his friends in iniquity. And he keepeth his guards about him. And he teareth up the laws of those which have reigned in righteousness before him. And he trampleth under his feet the commandments of God. ²³And he enacteth laws, and sendeth them forth among his people—yea, laws after the manner of his own

---

a. Probably added during proofreading. Perhaps this was inserted according to the Original Manuscript, or perhaps to disambiguate the name Noah.
b. Incomplete sentence. The verb "remembering" is not resolved.
c. In the sense of seeing or recognizing.
d. Probably added during proofreading.
e. The scribe first wrote "death" (perhaps misreading "dethrone" in the Original). The scribe realized that it was incorrect and wrote "remove," which is the correct intent but not the original word. Oliver Cowdery inserted "dethrone," probably during proofreading. Skousen, *Analysis of the Textual Variants*, 3:1554.

Chapter XIII [Mosiah 28:20–29:46]

wickedness. And whosoever doth not obey his laws, he causeth to be destroyed. And whosoever doth rebel against him, he will send his armies against them to war. And if he can, he will destroy them. And thus, an unrighteous king doth pervert the ways of all righteousness.

²⁴And now behold, I say unto you: It is not expedient that such abominations should come upon you! ²⁵Therefore, choose you (by the voice of the people) judges, that ye may be judged according to the laws which hath been given you by our fathers, which are correct, and which was given them by the hand of the Lord.

²⁶Now, it is not common that the voice of the people desireth anything contrary to that which is right. But it is common for the lesser part of the people to desire that which is not right. Therefore, this shall ye observe and make it your law, to do your business by the voice of the people. ²⁷And if the time cometh that the voice of the people doth choose iniquity, then is the time that the judgments of God will come upon you. Yea, then is the time he will visit you with great destruction, even as he hath hitherto visited this land.

²⁸And now, if ye have judges and they do not judge you according to the law which has been given, ye can cause that he may be judged of a higher judge. ²⁹If your higher judges doth not judge righteous judgments, ye shall cause that a small number of your lower judges should be gathered together. And they shall judge your higher judges according to the voice of the people.

³⁰And I commanded you to do these things in the fear of the Lord. And I commanded you to do these things. And that ye have no king--that if these people commit sins and iniquities, they shall be answered upon their own heads. ³¹For behold, I say unto you: The sins of many people have been caused by the iniquities of their kings. Therefore, their iniquities are answered upon the heads of their kings.

³²And now, I desire that this inequality should be no more in this land—especially among this, my people. But I desire that this land be a land of liberty. And every man may enjoy his rights and privileges alike, so long as the Lord sees fit that we may live and inherit the land. Yea, even as long as any of our posterity remaineth upon the face of the land.

³³And many more things did King Mosiah write unto them—unfolding unto them all the trials and troubles [ᵃ] a righteous king. Yea, all the travails of soul for their people. And also all the murmurings of the people to their king. And he explained it all unto them. ³⁴And he told them that these things had not ought to be, but that the burden should come upon all the people, that every man might bear his part.

³⁵And he also unfolded unto them all the disadvantages they labored under by having an unrighteous king to rule over them. ³⁶Yea, all his iniquities and abominations: and all the wars and contentions, and bloodshed, and the stealing, and the plundering, and the committing of whoredoms, and all manner of iniquities which cannot be enumerated—telling them that these things ought not to be, that they was expressly repugnant to the commandments of God.

³⁷And now it came to pass after King Mosiah had sent these things forth among the people, they were convinced of the truth of his words. ³⁸Therefore, they relinquished their desires for a king and became exceedingly anxious that every man should have an

---

a. The needed "of" was added by the compositor for the 1830 edition.

equal chance, throughout all the land. Yea, and every man expressed a willingness to answer for his own sins. ³⁹Therefore, it came to pass that they assembled themselves together in bodies throughout the land, to cast in their voices concerning who should be their judges, to judge them according to the law which had been given them. And they were exceedingly rejoiced because of the liberty which had been granted unto them.

⁴⁰And they did wax strong in love towards Mosiah. Yea, they did esteem him more than any other man. For they did not look upon him as a tyrant who was seeking for gain, yea, for that lucre which doth corrupt the soul. For he had not exacted riches of them, neither had he delighted in [the[a]] shedding of blood. But he had established peace in the land. And he had granted unto his people, that they should be delivered from all manner of bondage. Therefore, they did esteem him. Yea, exceedingly beyond measure.

⁴¹And it came to pass that they did appoint judges to rule over them (or to judge them), according to the law. And this they done throughout all the land.

⁴²And it came to pass that Alma was appointed to be the Chief Judge—he being also the high priest, his father having conferred the office upon him, and had given him the charge concerning all the affairs of the church.

⁴³And now it came to pass that that Alma did walk in the ways of the Lord and he did keep his commandments. And he did judge righteous judgments. And there was continual peace through the land. ⁴⁴And thus commenced the reign of the judges throughout all the land of Zarahemla, among all the people which was called the Nephites. And Alma was the first and chief judge.[b]

⁴⁵And now it came to pass that his father died, being eighty and two years old, having lived to fulfill the commandments of God.

And it came to pass that that Mosiah died also, in the thirty and third year of his reign—being sixty and three years. Making, in the whole, five hundred and nine years from the time Lehi left Jerusalem.

⁴⁶And thus ended the reign of the kings over the people of Nephi. And thus ended the days of Alma, who was the founder of their church.

---

a. Probably added during proofreading.

b. Although Chief Judge is treated as a position in most of the text, in this case (and in the header for the book of Alma), the term "chief" is descriptive rather than part of a proper noun.

The Book of Alma, the Son of Alma[a]

The account of Alma, who was the son of Alma. The first and chief[b] judge over the people of Nephi and also the high priest over the church. An account of the reign of the judges and the wars and contentions among the people—and also, an account of a war between the Nephites and the Lamanites, according to the record of Alma, the first and chief judge.

Chapter I [Alma 1–3]

[1] ¹Now it came to pass that in the first year of the reign of the judges over the people of Nephi, from this time forward—

>King Mosiah, having gone the way of all the earth[c]—having warred a good warfare,[d] walking uprightly before God, leaving no one to reign in his stead—nevertheless, he established laws.[e] And they were acknowledged by the people. Therefore, they were obliged to abide by the laws which he had made.[f]<

²And it came to pass that in the first year of the reign of Alma in the Judgment Seat, there was as man brought before him to be judged—a man which was large and was noted for his much strength. ³And he had gone about among the people, preaching to them that which he termed to be the word of God, bearing down against the church, declaring unto the people that every priest and teacher had ought to become popular, and they ought not to labor with their own hands. But that they had ought to be supported by the people.

⁴And he also testified unto the people that all mankind should be saved at the last day—and that they need not fear, nor tremble. But that they might lift up their heads and rejoice. For the Lord had created all men and had also redeemed all men. And in the end, all men should have eternal life.

⁵And it came to pass that he did teach these things so much that many did believe on his words, even so many that they began to support him and give him money. ⁶And he began to be lifted up in the pride of his heart, and to wear very costly apparel, yea, and even began to establish a church after the manner of his preaching.

---

a. The scribe originally left out the title of the book, and it was added later. Skousen suggests that it was an error based on the similarity to the header that immediately follows. Skousen, *Analysis of the Textual Variants*, 3:1574.

b. This is a description and therefore left in lower case. See also Mosiah 29:44.

c. See 1 Kings 2:2: "I go the way of all the earth."

d. The phrase "warred a good warfare" echoes language in 1 Timothy 1:18.

e. An incomplete sentence. The intent was to speak of the events of the first year, but Mormon realized that in order to tell the story of Nehor he had to establish the rule of law. Thus, there is an interruption that is resolved with repetitive resumption in verse 2.

f. Starting in the book of Alma, the marking of years becomes important. This contrasts to the very sporadic marking of years seen in the book of Mosiah, so this is not due to Mormon's editing. That change makes Mormon begin with the year, but Mormon interjects some concluding thoughts on Mosiah$_2$, even though he had noted his death in Mosiah 29:46. When verse 2 begins again with noting the first year of the reign of Alma, we have the repetitive resumption that marks the end of the aside.

⁷And it came to pass, as he was going to preach to those who believed on his word, he met a man which belonged to the church of God, yea, even one of their teachers. And he began to contend with him sharply, that he might lead away the people of the church. But the man withstood him, admonishing him with the words of God.

⁸Now, the name of the man was Gideon. And it was him that was an instrument in the hands of God in delivering the people of Limhi out of bondage.

⁹Now, because Gideon withstood him with the words of God, he was wroth with Gideon, and drew his sword and began to smite him. Now, Gideon, being stricken with many years. therefore he was not able to withstand his blows. Therefore, he was slain by the sword. ¹⁰And the man who slew him was taken by the people of the church and was brought before Alma to be judged according to the crime which he had committed.

¹¹And it came to pass that he stood before Alma and pled for himself with much boldness. ¹²But Alma said unto him:

> Behold, this is the first time that priestcraft has been introduced among this people. And behold, thou art not only guilty of priestcraft, but hast endeavored to enforce it by the sword. And were priestcraft to be enforced among this people, it would prove their entire destruction.
>
> ¹³And thou hast shed the blood of a righteous man, yea, a man which has done much good among this people. And were we to spare thee, his blood would come upon us for vengeance. ¹⁴Therefore, thou art condemned to die, according to the law which has been given us by Mosiah, our last king. And they have been acknowledged by this people. Therefore, this people must abide by the law.

¹⁵And it came to pass that they took him. And his name was Nehor. And they carried him upon the top of the hill Manti. And there he was caused, or rather, did acknowledge between the heavens and the earth, that what he had taught to the people was contrary to the word of God. And there he suffered an ignominious death. ¹⁶Nevertheless, this did not put an end to the spreading of priestcraft through the land. For there were many which loved the vain things of the world. And they went forth, preaching false doctrines. And this they did for the sake of riches and honor. ¹⁷Nevertheless, they durst not lie (if it were known) for fear of the law. For liars were punished. Therefore, they pretended to preach according to their belief.

And now, the law could have no power on any man for their belief. ¹⁸And they durst not steal, for fear of the law. For such were punished. Neither durst they rob, nor murder. For he that murdereth was punished unto death.

¹⁹But, it came to pass that whosoever did not belong to the church of God began to persecute those that did belong to the church of God, and had taken upon them the name of Christ. ²⁰Yea, they did persecute them, and afflict them with all manner of words. And this, because of their humility. Because they were not proud in their own eyes. And because they did impart the word of God, one with another—without money and without price.[a]

²¹Now, there was a strict law among the people of the church, that there should not any man belonging to the church arise and persecute those that did not belong to the church and that there should be no persecution among themselves. ²²Nevertheless, there

---

a. An allusion to Isaiah 55:1: "Ho, every one that thirsteth, come ye to the waters, and he that hath no money; come ye, buy, and eat; yea, come, buy wine and milk without money and without price."

were many among them who began to be proud and began to contend warmly with their adversaries, even unto blows. Yea, they would smite one another with their fists.

²³Now, this was in the second year of the reign of Alma. And it was a cause of much affliction to the church. Yea, it was the cause of much trial with the church, ²⁴for the hearts of many were hardened. And their names were blotted out, that they were remembered no more among the people of God—and also, many withdrew themselves from among them.

²⁵Now, this was a great trial to those that did stand fast in the in the faith. Nevertheless, the[y^a] were steadfast and immovable in keeping the commandments of God.^b And they bore with patience the persecution which was heaped upon them. ²⁶And when their priests left their labor to impart the word of God unto the people, the people also left their labors to hear the word of God. And when the priest had imparted unto them the word of God, they all returned again diligently unto their labors—and the priest not esteeming himself above his hearers. For the preacher was no better than the hearer, neither was the teacher any better than the learner. And thus, they were all equal. And they did all labor, every man according to his strength. ²⁷And they did impart of their substance (every man according to that which he had) to the poor, and the needy, and the sick, and the afflicted. And they did not wear costly apparel. Yet, they were neat and comely. ²⁸And thus, they did establish the affairs of the church. And thus, they began to have continual peace again, notwithstanding all their persecutions.

²⁹And now, because of the steadiness of the church, they began to [be[c]] exceeding rich—having abundance of all things, whatsoever they stood in need: abundance of flocks and herds, and fatlings of every kind, and also abundance of grain, and of gold, and of silver, and of precious things, and abundance [of[d]] silk, and fine twined linen, and all manner of good homely cloth. ³⁰And thus, in their prosperous circumstances, they did not send away [any[e]] which was naked, that was hungry, or that was athirst, or that was sick, or that had not been nourished. And they did not set their hearts upon riches. Therefore, they were liberal to all—both old and young, both bond and free, both male and female[f]—whether out of the church, or in the church—having no respects to persons, as to those who stood in need. ³¹And thus, they did prosper and become far more wealthy than those who did not belong to their church.

³²For those who did not belong to their church did indulge themselves in sorceries, and in idolatry, or idleness, and in babblings, and in envyings, and strife, and wearing costly apparel—being lifted up in the pride of their own eyes—persecuting, lying, thieving, robbing, committing whoredoms, and murdering, and all manner of wickedness. Nevertheless, the law was put in force upon all those who did transgress it, inasmuch as it were possible.

³³And it came to pass that by thus exercising the law upon them, every man suffer-

---

a. The word "they" is clearly meant. The inadvertently omitted "y" is supplied.
b. Uses language from 1 Corinthians 15:58: "Therefore, my beloved brethren, be ye steadfast, unmoveable, always abounding in the work of the Lord."
c. Probably added during proofreading.
d. Probably added during proofreading.
e. Probably added during proofreading.
f. See Galatians 3:28: "There is neither Jew nor Greek, there is neither bond nor free, there is neither male nor female: for ye are all one in Christ Jesus."

ing according to that which he had done, they became more still and durst not commit any wickedness (if it were known). Therefore, there was much peace among the people of Nephi until the fifth year of the reign of the judges.

[2] ¹And it came to pass in the commencement of the fifth year of their reign, there began to be a contention among the people. For a certain man (being called Amlici), he being a very cunning man, yea, a wise man as to the wisdom of the world—he being after the order of the man that slew Gideon by the sword, who was executed according to the law.[a]

²Now, this Amlici had (by his cunning) drawn away much people after him, even so much that they began to be very powerful. And they began to endeavor to establish Amlici to be a king over the people.

³Now, this was alarming to the people of the church, and also to all those who had not been drawn away after the persuasions of Amlici. For they knew that, according to their law, that such things must be established by the voice of the people. ⁴Therefore, if it were possible that Amlici should gain the voice of the people, he (being a wicked man) would deprive them of their rights and privileges of the church, etcetera[b]. For it was his intent to destroy the church of God.

⁵And it came to pass that the people assembled themselves together throughout all the land, every man according to his mind (whether it were for or against Amlici)—in separate bodies—having much dispute and wonderful contentions one with another. ⁶And thus, they did assemble themselves together to cast in their voices concerning the matter. And they were laid before the judges.

⁷And it came to pass that the voice of the people came against Amlici, that he was not made king over the people. ⁸Now, this did cause much joy in the hearts of those which were against him. But Amlici did stir up those which were in his favor to anger against those which were not in his favor.

⁹And it came to pass that they gathered themselves together and did consecrate Amlici to be their king. ¹⁰Now, when Amlici was made king over them, he commanded them that they should take up arms against their brethren. And this he done that he might subject them to him.

¹¹Now, the people of Amlici were distinguished by the name of Amlici, being called Amlikites.[c] And the remainder were called Nephites, or the people of God. ¹²Therefore, the people of the Nephites was aware of the intent of the Amlikites, and therefore they did prepare for to meet them. Yea, they did arm themselves with swords, and with scimitars, and with bows, and with arrows, and with stones, and with slings, and with all manner of weapons of war of every kind. ¹³And thus they were prepared to meet the Amlicites at the time of their coming. And there was appointed captains, and higher captains, and chief captains, according to their numbers.

¹⁴And it came to pass that Amlici did arm his men with all manner of weapons

---

a. The verbs are never reconciled, creating a grammatically incomplete sentence.

b. The text reads "&c". It was removed in the 1920 edition. Skousen, *Analysis of the Textual Variants*, 3:1603.

c. Skousen suggests that the presence of /k/ here probably indicated that it was /k/ in the original manuscript. This also suggests that it would have been "Amliki" instead of "Amlici." Since Skousen thinks this was the original, it has not been changed. Skousen, *Analysis of the Textual Variants*, 3:1605. Nevertheless, the length of time between the dictation of the Original and the copying of the Printer's Manuscript suggests that Oliver Cowdery may not have remembered the oral pronunciation and been influenced by the names Amaleki (Omni 1:12), Amalekite (Alma 21:5), and Amalickiah (Alma 46:3).

of war of every kind. And he also appointed rulers and leaders over his people, to lead them to war against their brethren.

¹⁵And it came to pass that the Amlicites came up upon the hill Amnihu, which was east of the river Sidon, which ran by the land of Zarahemla. And there they began to make war with the Nephites.

¹⁶Now Alma, he being the Chief Judge and the Governor of the people of Nephi—therefore, he went up with his people—yea, with his captains and chief captains, yea, at the heads of his armies—against the Amlicites to battle. ¹⁷And they began to slay the Amlicites upon the hill east of Sidon. And the Amlicites did contend with the Nephites with great strength, insomuch that many of the Nephites did fall before the Amlicites. ¹⁸Nevertheless, the Lord did strengthen the hand of the Nephites, that they slew the Amlicites with a great slaughter, that they began to flee before them.

¹⁹And it came to pass that the Nephites did pursue the Amlicites all that day, and did slay them with much slaughter, insomuch that there was slain of the Amlicites twelve thousand five hundred thirty and two souls. And there was slain of the Nephites six thousand five hundred sixty and two souls.

²⁰And it came to pass that when Alma could pursue the Amlicites no longer, he caused that his people should pitch their tents in the valley of Gideon (the valley being called after that Gideon which was slain by the hand of Nehor with the sword). And in this valley the Nephites did pitch their tents for the night. ²¹And Alma sent spies to follow the remnant of the Amlicites, that he might know of their plans and their plots, whereby he might guard himself against them—that he might preserve his people from being destroyed.

²²Now, those which he had sent out to watch the camp of the Amlicites were called Zeram, and Amnor, and Manti, and Limher. These were they which went out with their men to watch camp of the Amlicites.

²³And it came to pass that on the morrow they returned into the camp of the Nephites in great haste, being greatly astonished, and struck with much fear, saying:

> ²⁴Behold, we followed the camp of the Amlicites. And to our great astonishment, in the land of Minon, above the land of Zarahemla, in the course of the land of Nephi—we saw a numerous host of the Lamanites. And behold, the Amlicites have joined them. ²⁵And they are upon our brethren in that land. And they are fleeing before them with their flocks, and their wives, and their children, towards our city. And except we make haste, they obtain possession of our city, and our fathers, and our wives, and our children, be slain.

²⁶And it came to pass that the people of Nephi took their tents and departed out of the valley of Gideon towards their city, which was the city of Zarahemla. ²⁷And behold, as they were crossing the river Sidon, the Lamanites and the Amlicites (being as numerous almost as it were as the sands of the sea) [came[a]] upon them to destroy them. ²⁸Nevertheless, the Nephites, being strengthened by the hand of the Lord, having prayed mightily to him that he would deliver them out of the hands of their enemies—therefore, the Lord did hear their cries and did strengthen them. And the Lamanites and the Amlicites did fall before them.

---

a. The manuscript has "coming," perhaps following the previous "being." Oliver Cowdery changed it to "came," which makes a complete sentence.

²⁹And it came to pass that Alma fought with Amlici with the sword, face to face. And they did contend mightily one with another.

³⁰And it came to pass that Alma, he being a man of God, being exercised with much faith, and[a] he cried, saying: "O Lord, have mercy. And spare my life, that I may be an instrument in thy hands to save and protect this people."

³¹Now, when Alma had said these words, he contended again [with[b]] Amlici. And he was strengthened, insomuch that he slew Amlici with the sword. ³²And he also contended with the king of the Lamanites. But the king of the Lamanites fled back from before Alma and sent his guards to contend with Alma. ³³But Alma, with his guards, contended with the guards of the king of the Lamanites until he slew and drove them back. ³⁴And thus he cleared the ground (or rather the bank), which was on the west of the river Sidon, throwing the bodies of the Lamanites which had been slain into the waters of the river Sidon, that thereby his people might have room to cross and contend with the Lamanites and the Amlicites on the west side of the river Sidon.

³⁵And it came to pass that when they had all crossed the river Sidon that the Lamanites and the Amlicites began to flee before them, notwithstanding they were so numerous that they could not be numbered. ³⁶And they fled before the Nephites towards the wilderness, which was west and north, away beyond the borders of the land. And the Nephites did pursue them with their might and did slay them. ³⁷Yea, they were met on every hand, and slain, and driven, until they were scattered on the west and on the north, until they had reached the wilderness which was called Hermounts. And it was that part of the wilderness which was infested by wild beasts, and ravenous beasts.

³⁸And it came to pass that many died in the wilderness of their wounds and were devoured by those beasts, and also the vultures of the air. And their bones have been found and have been heaped up on the earth.

[3] ¹And it came to pass that the Nephites (which were not slain by the weapons of war), after having buried those which had been slain.[c] >Now, the number of the slain were not numbered, because of the greatness of their number.[d]< And after they had finished burying their [dead[e]], they all returned to their lands, and to their houses, and their wives, and their children.

²Now, many women and children had been slain with the sword. And also, many of their flocks and their herds. And also, many of their fields of grain were destroyed, for they were trodden down by the hosts of men.

³And now, as many of the Lamanites and the Amlicites which had been slain (upon the bank of the river Sidon) were cast into the waters of Sidon. And behold, their bones are in the depths of the sea. And they are many.

⁴And the Amlicites were distinguished from the Nephites. For they had marked themselves with red in their foreheads, after the manner of the Lamanites. Nevertheless, they had not shorn their heads like unto the Lamanites.

---

a. Another case where this "and" serves as "therefore."

b. Probably added during proofreading.

c. Incomplete sentence. The next sentence uses repetitive resumption to return to what was done after burying the dead.

d. This sentence interrupts the main idea. It leaves the previous sentence grammatically unresolved, and the thread of the text is picked up in the next verse with repetitive resumption.

e. Probably added during proofreading.

⁵Now, the heads of the Lamanites were shorn. And they were naked, save it were skin which was girded about their loins, and also their armor, which was girded about them—and their bows, and their arrows, and their stones, and their slings.

>⁶And the skins of the Lamanites were dark, according to the mark which was set upon their fathers, which was a curse upon them because of their transgressions and their rebellion against their brethren—which consisted of Nephi, Jacob, and Joseph, and Sam, which were just and holy men. ⁷And their brethren sought to destroy them. Therefore, they [were^a] cursed. And the Lord God set a mark upon them, yea, upon Laman, and Lemuel, and also the sons of Ishmael, and the Ishmaelitish women. ⁸And this was done that their seed might be distinguished from the seed of their brethren—that thereby the Lord God might preserve his people—that they might not mix and believe in incorrect traditions, which would prove their destruction.

⁹And it came to pass that whosoever did mingle his seed with that of the Lamanites did bring the same curse upon his seed. ¹⁰Therefore, whomsoever suffered himself to be led away by the Lamanites were called under that head. And there was a mark set upon him.

¹¹And it came to pass that whosoever would not believe in the tradition of the Lamanites, but believed those records which were brought out of the land of Jerusalem, and also in the tradition of their fathers (which were correct), which believed in the commandments of God, and kept them—were called the Nephites (or the people of Nephi) from that time forth. ¹²And it is they which have kept the records (which are true) of their people, and also of the people of the Lamanites.[b]<

¹³Now, we will return again to the Amlicites. For they also had a mark set upon them. Yea, [even[c]] they set the mark upon themselves, yea, over a mark of red upon their foreheads. ¹⁴Thus the word of God is fulfilled, for these are the words which he saith to Nephi:

> Behold, the Lamanites have I cursed. And I will set a mark upon them, that they and their seed may be separated from thee and thy seed, from this time henceforth, and forever, except they repent of their wickedness and turn to me, that I may have mercy upon them.
>
> ¹⁵And again, I will set a mark upon him that mingleth his seed with thy brethren, that they may be cursed also.
>
> ¹⁶And again will I set a mark upon him that fighteth against thee, and thy seed.
>
> ¹⁷And again, I say: He that departeth from thee shall no more be called thy seed. And I will bless thee, etcetera, and whomsoever shall be called thy seed, henceforth and forever.[d]

---

a. Probably added during proofreading.

b. The mention of the physical description of the Lamanites led Mormon to expound on the spiritual "appearance." Thus, Mormon discusses the mark placed upon them. The language here is very similar to 2 Nephi 5:21–23, which Mormon had likely read by the time he wrote this (W of M 1:3). It is also possible that this was a well-known statement about the Lamanites that Mormon was recounting. Because it comes as an aside, it is something from his memory rather than the source text in front of him. Mormon repeats the ideas with different words in verses 14–17. The next verse makes it clear that Mormon understands that this was an aside.

c. Probably added during proofreading.

d. This is clearly a quotation, but not to an extant text in our current Book of Mormon. The quotation

And these were the promises of the Lord unto Nephi and to his seed.

>¹⁸Now, the Amlicites knew not that they were fulfilling the words of God when they began to mark themselves in their foreheads. Nevertheless, as they had come out in open rebellion against God. Therefore, it was expedient that the curse should fall upon them. ¹⁹Now, I would that ye should see that they brought upon themselves the curse, and even so doeth every man that is cursed bringeth upon himself his own condemnation.ᵃ<

²⁰Now it came to pass that not many days after the battle which was fought in the land of Zarahemla by the Lamanites and the Amlicites, that there was another army of the Lamanites came in upon the people of Nephi, in the same place where the first army met the Amlicites.

²¹And it came to pass that there was an army sent to drive them out of their land. ²²Now, Alma himself, being afflicted with a wound, did not go up to battle at this time against the Lamanites. ²³But he sent up a numerous army against them. And they went up, and slew many of the Lamanites, and drove the remainder of them out of the borders of their land. ²⁴And then they returned again and began to establish peace in the land—being troubled no more (for a time) with their enemies.

²⁵Now, all these things were done, yea, all those wars and contentions was commenced, and ended, in the fifth year of the reign of the judges. ²⁶And in one year was thousands, and tens of thousands, of souls were sent to the eternal world, that they might reap their rewards according to their works, whether they were good, or whether they were bad—to reap eternal happiness or eternal misery, according to the spirit which he listed to obey (whether it be a good spirit, or a bad one). >²⁷For every man receiveth wages of him who he listeth to obey, and this according to the words of the spirit of prophecy. Therefore, let it be according to the truth.ᵇ<

And thus ended the fifth year of the reign of the judges.

---

would have been on the large plates, and we have only the small plates text. Nephi's description of the Lamanite curse comes in 2 Nephi 5:21–23, which includes the cursing and the prohibition against "mixing seed." It is interesting that this version of the cursing comes more in line with the flow of the text, where the previous one was an interjection. It seems that Mormon got a little ahead of himself.

a. Mormon provides the moral with this insertion.
b. Mormon provides the moral.

Chapter II [Alma 4]

[4] ¹Now it came to pass in the sixth year of the reign of the judges over the people of Nephi there was no contentions nor wars in the land of Zarahemla. ²And the people, being afflicted, yea greatly afflicted for the loss of their brethren, and also for the loss of their flocks and herds, and also for the loss of their fields of grain which was trodden under foot and destroyed by the Lamanites—³and so great was their affliction[s[a]] that every soul had cause to mourn.[b] And they believed that it was the judgments of God sent upon them because of their wickedness and their abominations. Therefore, they were awakened to a remembrance of their duty. ⁴And they began to establish the church more fully. Yea, and many were baptized in the waters of Sidon and were joined to the church of God. Yea, they were baptized by the hand of Alma, who had been consecrated the High Priest over the people of the church by the hand of his father, Alma.

⁵And it came to pass in the seventh year of the reign of the judges there was about three thousand five hundred souls that united themselves to the church of God and were baptized. And thus ended the seventh year of the reign of the judges over the people of Nephi. And there was continual peace in all that time.

⁶And it came to pass in the eighth year of the reign of the judges that the people of the church began to wax proud because of their exceeding riches, and their fine silks, and their fine twined linen, and because of their many flocks and herds, and their gold and their silver, and all manner of precious things, which they had obtained by their industry. And in all these things were they lifted up in the pride of their eyes. For they began to wear very costly apparel.

⁷Now this was the cause of much affliction to Alma, yea, and to many of the people which Alma had consecrated to be teachers, and priests, and elders, over the church. Yea, many of them were sorely grieved for the wickedness which they saw had begun to be among their people. ⁸For they saw, and beheld with great sorrow, that the people of the church began to be lifted up in the pride of their eyes and to set their hearts upon riches, and upon the vain things of the world—that they began to be scornful one towards another. And they began to persecute those that did not believe according to their own will and pleasure. ⁹And thus, in this eighth year of the reign of the judges, there began to be great contentions among the [people of the[c]] church. Yea, there was envyings, and strifes, and malice, and persecutions, and pride, even to exceed the pride of those who did not belong to the church of God. ¹⁰And thus ended the eighth year of the reign of the judges. And the wickedness of the church was a great stumbling block to those who did not belong to the church. And thus, the church began to fail in its progress.

¹¹And it came to pass in the commencement of the ninth year, Alma, seeing the wickedness of the church, and also that the example of the church began to lead those who were unbelievers on from one piece of iniquity to another (thus bringing on the destruction of the people)—¹²yea, seeing great inequality among the people—some

---

a. The "s" was added during proofreading.

b. This sentence could have been easily resolved into a logical sentence by removing the internal clauses to yield: "And the people. . . had cause to mourn." As with many sentences with multiple clauses, this sentence loses its way. It uses "and so great was their afflictions that every soul" as a type of repetitive resumption to return to the meaning of the sentence.

c. Probably added during proofreading.

lifting themselves up with their pride—despising others, turning their backs upon the needy, and the naked, and those which were hungry, and those which were athirst, and those which were sick and afflicted—[a]

[13]Now, this was a great cause for lamentations among the people—while others were abasing themselves, succoring those who stood in need of their succor, such as imparting their substance to the poor, and the needy, feeding the hungry, and suffering all manner of afflictions for Christ's sake (which should come according to the spirit of prophecy), [14]looking forward to that day, thus retaining a remission of their sins—being filled with great joy because of the resurrection of the dead, according to the will, and power, and deliverance, of Jesus Christ from the [bands[b]] of death.

[15]And now it come to pass that Alma, having seen the afflictions of the humble followers of God, and the persecutions which was heaped upon them by the remainder of his people, and seeing all their inequality—he began to be very sorrowful. Nevertheless, the spirit of the Lord did not fail him.

[16]And he selected a wise man which was among the elders of the church and gave him power, according to the voice of the people, that he might have power to enact laws according to the laws which had been given, and to put them in force according to the wickedness and the crimes of the people.

[17]Now, this man's name was [Nephihah[c]], and he was appointed Chief Judge. And he sat upon in the Judgment Seat, to judge and to govern the people.

[18]Now, Alma did not grant unto him the office of being High Priest over the church, but the retained the office of High Priest unto himself. But he delivered the Judgment Seat unto Nephihah. [19]And this he did that he, himself, might go forth among his people (or among the people of Nephi), that he might preach the word of God unto them, to stir them up in remembrance of their duty, and that he might pull down, by the word of God, all the pride, and craftiness, and all the contentions which was among his people (seeing no way that he might reclaim them, save it were in bearing down in pure testimony against them). [20]And thus, in the commencement of the ninth year of the reign of the judges over the people of Nephi, Alma delivered up the Judgment Seat to Nephihah, and confined himself, wholly, to the high priesthood of the holy order of God—to the testimony of the word, according to the spirit of revelation and prophesy.

---

a. The two phrases with "seeing" want a resolution that never comes. The intended contrast is between unbelievers who did not care for others versus those of the church who did care for the needy. Verse 13 is the turning point, but verses 11 and 12 are never grammatically resolved.

b. The scribe originally wrote "pains of death." This was apparently changed in proofreading, with "pains" being crossed out and "bands" being written superlinearly.

c. The name was "Nephiah" in the Printer's Manuscript. Skousen notes that this is a consistent spelling for this particular scribe. The name has been regularized to Nephihah, as seen in other parts of the manuscript and from other scribes. Skousen, *Analysis of the Textual Variants*, 3:1662.

Chapter III [Alma 5]

[5] *The words which Alma, the High Priest (according to the holy order of God), delivered to the people in their cities and villages throughout the land.*

¹Now it came to pass that Alma began to declare the word of God unto the people—first in the land of Zarahemla, and from thence throughout all the land. ²And these are the words which he spake to the people in the church which was established in the city of Zarahemla, according to his own record, saying:[a]

³I, Alma, having been consecrated by my father, Alma, to be a high priest over the church of God (he having power and authority from [God[b]] to do these things), behold I say unto you that he began to establish church in the land which was in the borders of Nephi, yea, the land was called the land of Mormon. Yea, and he did baptize his brethren in the waters of Mormon.

⁴And behold, I say unto you, they were delivered out of the hand of the people of King Noah by the mercy and power of God.

⁵And behold, after that they were brought into bondage by the hands of the Lamanites in the wilderness, yea, I say unto you, they were in captivity. And again, the Lord did deliver them out of bondage by the power of his word. And we were brought into this land. And here we began to establish the church of God throughout this land also.

⁶And now behold, I say unto you, my brethren (you that belong to this church), have you sufficiently retained in remembrance the captivity of your fathers? Yea, and have you sufficiently retained in remembrance his mercy and long suffering towards them? And moreover, have ye sufficiently retained in remembrance that he hath delivered their souls from hell?

⁷Behold, he changed their hearts. Yea, he awaked them out of a deep sleep. And they awake unto God. Behold, they were in the midst of darkness. Nevertheless, their souls were illuminated by the light of the everlasting word.

Yea, they were encircled about by the bands of death and the chains of hell, and an everlasting destruction did await them. ⁸And now, I ask of you, my brethren, were they destroyed? Behold, I say unto you, nay, they were not. ⁹And again I ask, was the bands of death broken? And the chains of hell (which encircled them about), were they loosed? I say unto you, yea, they were loosed! And their souls did expand. And they did sing redeeming love. And I say unto you that they are saved.

¹⁰And now, I ask of you—on what conditions are they saved? Yea, what grounds had they to hope for salvation? What is the cause of there being loosed from the bands of death, yea, and also the chains of hell? ¹¹Behold, I can tell you. Did not my father, Alma, believe in the words which was delivered by the mouth of Abinadi? And was he not a holy prophet? Did he not speak the word of God? And my father, Alma, believed them. ¹²And, according to his faith, there was a mighty change wrought in his heart.

Behold, I say unto you that this is all true.

¹³And behold, he preached the word unto your fathers. And a mighty change was also wrought in their hearts. And they humbled themselves and put their trust in the true

---

a. This chapter is Mormon copying text from Alma's personal record. Because it is a whole chapter, it is not set as a quotation to save that visual marker for internal quotations.

b. Probably added during proofreading.

and living God. And behold, they were faithful until the end. Therefore, they were saved.

¹⁴And now behold, I ask of you, my brethren of the church—

have ye spiritually been born of God?ᵃ

Have ye received his image in your own countenances?

Have ye experienced this mighty change in *your*ᵇ hearts?

¹⁵Do ye exercise faith in the redemption of him who created you?ᶜ

Do you look forward with an eye of faith, and view this mortal body raised in immortality, and this corruption raised in incorruption,ᵈ to stand before God to be judged, according to the deeds which hath been done in the mortal body?

¹⁶I say unto you: Can you imagine to yourselves that ye hear the voice of the Lord saying unto you in that day: "Come unto me ye blessed! For behold, your works have been the works of righteousness upon the face of the earth."

¹⁷Or, do you imagine to yourselves that ye can lie unto the Lord at that day, and say: "Lord, our works have been righteous works upon the face of the earth"—and that he will save you?

¹⁸Or otherwise, can ye imagine yourselves brought before the tribunal of God, with your souls filled with guilt, and remorse, having a remembrance of all your guilt—yea, a perfect remembrance of all your wickedness, yea, remembrance that ye have set at defiance the commandments of God?

¹⁹I say unto you: Can ye look up to God at that day with a pure heart and clean hands?ᵉ

I say unto you: Can you look up. having the image of God engraven upon your countenances?

²⁰I say unto you: Can ye think of being saved when you have yielded yourselves to become subjects to the devil?

²¹I say unto you: Ye will know, at that day, that ye cannot be saved! For there can no man be saved, except his garments are washed white. Yea, his garments must be purified until they are cleansed from all stain through the blood of him (of whom it hath been spoken by our fathers) which should come to redeem his people from their sins.

²²And now, I ask of you, my brethren: How will any of you feel if ye shall stand before the bar of God, having your garments stained with blood and all manner of filthiness?

Behold, what will these things testify against you? ²³Behold, will they not testify that ye are murderers? Yea, and also that ye are guilty of all manner of wickedness?

²⁴Behold my brethren, do ye suppose that such an one can have a place to sit down in the kingdom of God, with Abraham, with Isaac, and with Jacob,ᶠ and also all the holy

---

a. Separated to highlight the parallels.

b. Italics have been added to emphasize the shift from the mighty change that Alma the Elder's people experienced to the new emphasis on the people of Zarahemla.

c. The two sentences beginning with "do" have been separated in order to better see the parallelism. The length of the second suggests that this is not a true poetic parallel, but rather a rhetorical parallel. Alma is making great use of short phrases and repetition. In this section, he utilizes questions that emphasize his point.

d. See 1 Corinthians 15:54 for the use of "corruption and incorruption."

e. The phrase "pure heart and clean hands" alludes to Psalm 24:4: "He that hath clean hands, and a pure heart; who hath not lifted up his soul unto vanity, nor sworn deceitfully."

f. Compare Matthew 8:11: "Many shall come from the east and west, and shall sit down with Abraham, and Isaac, and Jacob, in the kingdom of heaven."

prophets (whose garments are cleansed, and are spotless, pure, and white)?

²⁵I say unto you, nay, except ye make our Lord Creator a liar from the beginning (or suppose that he is a liar from the beginning). Or also, ye cannot suppose that such an one can have place in the kingdom of heaven. But they shall be cast out. For they are the children of the kingdom of the devil.

²⁶And now behold, I say unto you my brethren—if ye have experienced a change of heart and if ye have felt to sing the song of redeeming love, I would ask—can ye feel so now? ²⁷Have ye walked, keeping yourselves blameless before God? Could ye say (if ye were called to die at this time) within yourselves, that ye have been sufficiently humble—that your garments have been cleansed and made white through the blood of Christ (which will come to redeem his people from their sins)?

²⁸Behold, are ye stripped of pride? I say unto you, if ye are not, [ye are not^a] prepared to meet God. (Behold, ye must prepare quickly, for the kingdom of heaven is soon at hand^b).^c And such an one hath not Eternal life.

²⁹Behold, I say: Is there one among you who is not stripped of envy? I say unto you that such an one is not prepared. And I would that he should prepare quickly. For the hour is close at hand. And he knoweth not when the time shall come. For such an one is not found guiltless.

³⁰And again, I say unto you: Is there one among you that doth make a mock of his brother? Or that heapeth upon him persecutions? ³¹Wo unto such an one! For he is not prepared. And the time is at hand that he must repent, or he cannot be saved. ³²Yea, even wo unto all ye workers of iniquity.

Repent, repent, for the Lord God hath spoken it. ³³Behold, he sendeth an invitation unto all men. For the arms of mercy is extended towards them. And he saith: "Repent! And I will receive you." ³⁴Yea, he saith:

> Come unto me! And ye shall partake of the fruit of the tree of life, yea, ye shall eat and drink of the bread and the waters of life freely. ³⁵Yea, come unto me! And bring forth works of righteousness. And ye shall not be put down and cast into the fire. ³⁶For behold, the time is at hand that whosoever bringeth forth not good fruit, or whosoever doeth not the works of righteousness, the same hath cause to wail and mourn.

³⁷O ye workers of iniquity! Ye that are puffed up in the vain things of the world! Ye that have professed to have known the ways of righteousness!^d

Nevertheless, ye have gone astray, as sheep having no shepherd, notwithstanding a shepherd hath called after you. And art still calling after you. But ye will not hearken unto his voice.

---

a. Probably added during proofreading.

b. See Matthew 3:2: "Repent ye: for the kingdom of heaven is at hand."

c. This sentence is set in parentheses to help the reader understand that the next sentence refers to those who are not prepared to meet God in the previous sentence. Without them, it might be supposed that those who are preparing for the kingdom of heaven would not have eternal life, which is contrary to the meaning.

d. This is not a known quotation from any of our scriptures outside of the Book of Mormon. Typically, Book of Mormon prophets quote from the brass plates rather than previous Nephite prophets, although this is certainly a theme that would be comfortable in Nephi's records.

³⁸Behold, I say unto you that the good shepherd[a] doth call you, yea, and in his own name he doth call you (which is the name of Christ). And if ye will not hearken unto the voice of the good shepherd[b]—to the name by which ye are called—behold, ye are not the sheep of the good shepherd.[c] ³⁹And now, if ye are not the sheep of the good shepherd,[d] of what fold are ye?

Behold, I say unto you, that the devil is your shepherd. And ye are of his fold. And now, who can deny this? Behold, I say unto you: Whosoever denieth this is a liar, and a child of the devil. ⁴⁰For I say unto you, that whatsoever is good cometh from God, and whatsoever is evil cometh from the devil. ⁴¹Therefore, if a man bringeth forth good works, [he[e]] harkeneth unto the voice of the good shepherd,[f] and he doth follow him. But whosoever bringeth forth evil works, the same becometh a child of the devil. For he harkeneth unto *his*[g] voice, and doth follow him. ⁴²And whosoever doeth this must receive his wages of him. Therefore, for his wages he receiveth death as to things pertaining unto righteousness—being dead unto all good works.

⁴³And now my brethren, I say unto you: Would that ye should hear me! For I speak in the energy of my soul. For behold, I have spoken unto you plain, that ye cannot err (or, have spoken according to the commandments of God). ⁴⁴For I am called to speak after this manner, according to the holy order of God, which is in Christ Jesus. Yea, I am commanded to stand and testify unto this people the things which have been spoken by our fathers concerning the things which is to come.

⁴⁵And this is not all. Do ye suppose that I know not of these things myself? Behold, I testify unto you that I do know that these things whereof I have spoken are true. And how do ye suppose that I know of their surety?

⁴⁶Behold, I say unto you—they are made known unto me by the Holy Spirit of God. Behold, I have fasted, and prayed many days, that I might know these things of myself.

And now, I do know of myself that they are true. For the Lord God hath made them manifest unto me by his Holy Spirit. And this is the spirit of revelation which is in me.

⁴⁷And moreover I say unto you, that as it has thus been revealed unto me that the words which have been spoken by our fathers are true, even so (according to the spirit of prophecy which is in me, which is also by the manifestations of the spirit of God), ⁴⁸I say unto you that I know of myself that whatsoever I shall say unto you concerning that which is to come, is true.

And I say unto you, that I know that Jesus Christ shall come—yea, the son of[h] the only begotten of the Father—full of grace, and mercy, and truth.[i] And behold, it

---

a. See John 10:11: "I am the good shepherd."
b. See John 10:11: "I am the good shepherd."
c. See John 10:11: "I am the good shepherd."
d. See John 10:11: "I am the good shepherd."
e. Probably added during proofreading.
f. See John 10:11: "I am the good shepherd."
g. Italics added to emphasize the shift in the entity to whom "his" refers. The first is the good shepherd, the second the devil.
h. Removed in 1837. A comma was added to make it "the Son, the Only Begotten of the Father." The original "of" (left in the text because it is in the Printer's Manuscript) was probably the result of the more common phrase "son of the father."
i. See John 1:4 for the phrase "full of grace and truth."

is he that cometh to take away the sins of the world, yea, the sins of every man which steadfastly believeth on his name.

⁴⁹And now I say unto you that this is the order after which I am called—yea, to [preach^a] unto my beloved brethren, yea, and everyone that dwelleth in the land—yea, to preach unto all, both old and young, both bond and free.^b Yea, I say unto you—the aged, and also the middle aged, and the rising generation—yea, to cry unto them that they must repent and be born again. ⁵⁰Yea, thus saith the spirit: "Repent all the ends of the earth! For the kingdom of heaven is soon at hand! Yea, the Son of God cometh in his glory—in his might, majesty, power, and dominion."

Yea, my beloved brethren, I say unto you that the spirit saith: "Behold the glory of the king of all the earth! And also, the king of heaven shall very soon shine forth among all the children of men!"

⁵¹And also the spirit saith unto me, yea crieth unto me with a mighty voice, saying: "Go forth and say unto this people—repent! For except ye repent, ye can in no wise inherit the kingdom of heaven."

⁵²And again I say unto you, the spirit saith: "Behold! The axe is laid at the root of the tree. Therefore, every tree that bringeth not forth good fruit shall be hewn down and cast into the fire,^c yea, a fire which cannot be consumed, even an unquenchable fire. Behold, and remember! The Holy One hath spoken it."

⁵³And now, my beloved brethren, I say unto you: Can ye withstand these sayings?

Yea, can ye lay aside these things, and trample the Holy One under your feet?

Yea, can ye be puffed up in the pride of your hearts?

Yea, will ye still persist in the wearing of costly apparel and setting your hearts upon the vain things of the world—upon your riches?

Yea, will ye persist in supposing that ye are better one than another?

⁵⁴Yea, will ye persist in the persecutions of your brethren, who humble themselves and do walk after the holy order of God, wherewith they have been brought into this church, having been sanctified by the Holy Spirit? And they do bring forth works which is meet for repentance.^d

⁵⁵Yea, and will you persist in turning your backs upon the poor, and the needy, and withholding your substance from them?

⁵⁶And finally, all ye that will persist in your wickedness, I say unto you that these are they which shall be hewn down and cast into the fire, except they speedily repent.

⁵⁷And now I say unto you, all you that are desirous to follow the voice of the good shepherd^e: Come ye out from the wicked and be ye separate! And touch not their unclean things. And [behold^f], their names shall be blotted out, that the names of the wicked shall not be numbered among the names of the righteous—that the word of God may be fulfilled which saith: "The names of the wicked shall not be mingled with

---

a. Originally had "speak." Probably changed in proofreading.
b. See Galatians 3:28: "There is neither Jew nor Greek, there is neither bond nor free, there is neither male nor female: for ye are all one in Christ Jesus."
c. Quoting Matthew 3:10, Luke 3:9.
d. See Matthew 3:8: "Bring forth therefore fruits meet for repentance."
e. See John 10:11: "I am the good shepherd."
f. Probably added during proofreading.

the names of my people. ⁵⁸For the names of the righteous shall be written in the Book of Life. And unto them will I grant an inheritance at my right hand."ᵃ

And now, my brethren, what have ye to say against this? I say unto you, if ye speak against it, it matters not. For the word of God must be fulfilled. ⁵⁹For what shepherd is there among you, having many sheep, doth not watch over them that the wolves enter not, and devour his flock? And behold, if a wolf enter his flock, doth he not drive him out? Yea, and at the last, if he can, he will destroy him.

⁶⁰And now I say unto you, that the good shepherdᵇ doth call after you. And, if you will hearken unto his voice, he will bring you into his fold. And ye are his sheep. And he commandeth you that ye suffer no ravenous wolf to enter among you, that ye may not be destroyed.

⁶¹And now I, Alma, do command you in the language of him who hath commanded me, that ye observe to do the words which I have spoken unto you. ⁶²I speak by way of command unto you that belong to the church. And unto those which do not belong to the church, I speak by way of invitation, saying: Come, and [beᶜ] baptized unto repentance, that ye also may be partakers of the [fruitᵈ] of the tree of life.

---

a. This quotation is not in our extant scriptures outside of the Book of Mormon.
b. See John 10:11: "I am the good shepherd."
c. Probably added during proofreading.
d. The scribe originally wrote "spirit," doubtless influenced by the phrase "partake of the spirit." However, it was corrected during proofreading to be the more logical "partake of the *fruit* of the tree of life."

Chapter IV [Alma 6]

[6] ¹And now it came to pass that after Alma had made an end of speaking unto the people of the church which was established in the city of Zarahemla, he ordained priests and elders by laying on his hands, according to the order of God, [to^a] preside and watch over the church.

²And it came to pass that whomsoever did not belong to the church, who repented of their sins, was baptized unto repentance and was received into the church.

³And it also came to pass that whomsoever did belong to the church, that did not repent of their wickedness, and humble themselves before God (I mean, those which were lifted up in the pride of their hearts), the same were rejected. And their names were blotted out—that their names were not numbered among those of the righteous. ⁴And thus they began to establish the order of the church in the city of Zarahemla.

⁵Now, I would that ye should understand that the word of God was liberal unto all, that no one was deprived of the privilege of assembling themselves together to hear the word of God. ⁶Nevertheless, the children of God were commanded that they should gather themselves together oft and join in fasting and mighty prayer in behalf of the welfare of the souls of those who knew not God.

⁷And now it came to pass that when Alma had made these regulations, he departed from them (yea, from the church which was in the city of Zarahemla) and went over upon the east of the river Sidon into the valley of Gideon >(there having been a city built which was called the city of Gideon, which was in the valley that was called Gideon, being called after the man which was slain by the hand of Nehor with the sword).<^b

⁸And Alma went, and began to declare the word of God unto the church which was established in the valley of Gideon, according to the revelation of the truth of the word which had been spake by his fathers—and according to the spirit of prophecy which was in him, according to the testimony of Jesus Christ, the Son of God, which should come for to redeem his people from their sins—and the holy order by which he was called. And thus it is written. Amen.

---

a. Probably added during proofreading.
b. This is a short aside. Verse 8 picks up with the repetitive resumption of the original intent to indicate that Alma had traveled to the valley of Gideon.

Chapter V [Alma 7]

[7] *The words of Alma, which he delivered to the people in Gideon, according to his own record.*

¹Behold, my beloved brethren—seeing that I have been permitted to come unto you, therefore, I attempt to address you in my language, yea, by my own mouth—seeing that it is the first time that I have spoken unto you by the words of my mouth—I, having been wholly confined to the Judgment Seat, having had much business that I could not come unto you. ²And even I could not have come now at this time, were it not that the Judgment Seat hath been given to another, to reign in my stead. And the Lord in much mercy hath granted that I should come unto you.

³And behold, I have come having great hopes and much desire that I should find that ye had humbled yourselves before God. And that ye had continued in the supplicating of his grace, that I should find that ye were blameless before him—that I should find that ye were not in the awful dilemma that our brethren were in at Zarahemla.

⁴But, blessed be the name of God, that he hath given unto me to know, yea, hath given unto me the exceeding great joy of knowing, that they are established again in the way of his righteousness.

⁵And I trust, according to the spirit of God which is in me, that I shall also have joy over you. Nevertheless, I do not desire that my joy over you should come by the cause of so much afflictions and sorrow, which I have had for the brethren at Zarahemla. For behold, my joy cometh over them after wading through much afflictions and sorrow.

⁶But behold, I trust that ye are not in a state of so much unbelief as were your brethren.

I trust that ye are not lifted up in the pride of your hearts.

Yea, I trust that ye have not set your hearts upon riches, and the vain things of the world.

Yea, I trust that you do not worship idols, but that ye do worship the true and the living God. And that ye look forward for the remission of your sins (with an everlasting faith), which is to come.

⁷For behold, I say unto you: There be many things to come. And behold, there is one thing which is of more importance than they all. For behold, the time is not far distant that the Redeemer liveth, and cometh among his people.

⁸Behold, I do not say that he will come among us at the time of his dwelling in his mortal tabernacle, for behold the spirit hath not said unto me this that this should be the case. Now, as to this thing I do not know. But this much I [do[a]] know, that the Lord God hath power to do all things which is according to his word.

⁹But behold, the spirit hath said this much unto me, saying:

> Cry unto this people, saying: Repent ye, repent ye! And prepare the way of the Lord! And walk in his paths, which are strait![b] For behold, the kingdom of heaven is at hand, and the Son of God cometh upon the face of the earth.

---

a. The Printer's Manuscript has only the letter "d". The word "do" is written above the line, probably during proofreading.

b. Oliver Cowdery used the same spelling for both "strait" and "straight." I have left the spelling as in the Printer's Manuscript, although an argument can be made that "straight" is intended here.

¹⁰And behold, he shall be born of Mary at Jerusalem (which is the land of our forefathers), she being a virgin—a precious and chosen vessel who shall be overshadowed and conceive by the power of the Holy Ghost, and bring forth a son. Yea, even the Son of God.

¹¹And he shall go forth—suffering pain and affliction, and temptation of every kind. And this, that the word might be fulfilled which saith:

He will take upon him the pains and the sicknesses of his people. ¹²And he will take upon him death, that he may loose the bands of death which bind his people. And he will take upon him their infirmities, that his bowels may be filled with mercy, according to the flesh, that he may know, according to the flesh, how to suffer his people according to their infirmities.[a]

¹³Now, the spirit knoweth all things. Nevertheless, the Son of God suffereth according to the flesh that he might take upon him the sins of his people, that he might blot out their transgressions, according to the power of his deliverance. And now behold, this is the testimony which is in me.

¹⁴Now, I say unto you, that ye must repent and and be born again. For the spirit saith: "If ye are not born again ye cannot inherit the kingdom of heaven."[b] Therefore, come, and be baptized unto repentance—that ye may be washed from your sins, that ye may have faith on the Lamb of God[c], which taketh away the sins of the world, which is mighty to save, and to cleanse from all unrighteousness.

¹⁵Yea, I say unto you come, and fear not. And lay aside every sin which easily doth beset you, which doth bind you down to destruction. Yea, come, and go forth, and show unto your God that ye are willing to repent of your sins and enter into a covenant with him to keep his commandments. And witness it unto him this day by going into the waters of baptism.

¹⁶And whosoever doeth this, and keepeth the commandments of God from thenceforth, the same will remember that I say unto him. Yea, he will remember that I have said unto him—he shall have eternal life, according to the testimony of the Holy Spirit, which testifieth in me.

¹⁷And now, my beloved brethren. do you believe these things? Behold, I say unto you—yea, I know that you believe them. And the way I know that ye believe them is by the manifestation of the spirit, which is in me.

And now, because your faith is strong concerning that (yea, concerning the things which I have spoken), great is my joy. ¹⁸For as I said unto you from the beginning, that I had much desire that ye was not in the state of dilemma like your brethren. Even so, I have found that my desires have been gratified.

¹⁹For I perceive that ye are in the paths of righteousness.[d]

I perceive that ye are in the paths which to leads to the kingdom of God.

Yea, I perceive that ye are making his paths strait.[e]

---

a. Not a reference to extant scriptures outside of the Book of Mormon.

b. The closest extant scripture is John 3:3: "Except a man be born again, he cannot see the kingdom of God."

c. The phrase "Lamb of God" is from John 1:29.

d. See Psalm 23:3: "He restoreth my soul: he leadeth me in the paths of righteousness for his name's sake."

e. The Printer's Manuscript has "strait," the spelling of which could represent both "strait" and "straight."

²⁰I perceive that it hath been made known unto you by the testimony of his word, that he cannot walk in crooked paths. Neither doth he vary from that which he hath said. Neither hath he a shadow of turning from the right to the left, or from that which is right to that which is wrong. Therefore, his course is one eternal round.

²¹He doth not dwell in unholy temples.[a] Neither can filthiness, or anything which is unclean be received into the kingdom of God. Therefore, I say unto you: The time shall come, yea, and it shall be at the last day, that he which is filthy shall remain in his filthiness.

²²And now, my beloved brethren, I have said these things unto you, that I might awaken you to a sense of your duty to God, that ye may walk blameless before him, that ye may walk after the holy [order[b]] of God (after which ye have been received).

²³And now, I would that ye should be humble, and be submissive, and gentle, easy to be entreated, full of patience and long suffering—being temperate in all things, being diligent in keeping the commandments of God at all times—asking for whatsoever things ye stand in need (both spiritual and temporal), always returning thanks unto God for whatsoever things ye do receive.

²⁴And see that ye have faith, hope, and charity.[c] And then ye will always abound in good works. ²⁵And may the Lord bless you and keep your garments spotless, that ye may at last be brought to sit down with Abraham, Isaac, and Jacob,[d] and the holy prophets which have been ever since the world began (having your garments spotless, even as their garments are spotless) in the kingdom of heaven, to go no more out.

²⁶And now my beloved brethren, I have spoken these [words[e]] unto you, according to the spirit which testifieth in me. And my soul doth exceedingly rejoice, because of the exceeding diligence and heed which ye have given unto my word.

²⁷And now, may the peace of God rest upon you, and upon your houses, and lands, and upon your flocks, and herds, and all that you possess—your women and your children, according to your [faith[f]] and good works from this time forth, and forever. And thus, I have spoken. Amen.

---

a. Amulek provides a quotation in Alma 34:36, but it is not present outside of the Book of Mormon. The reference to temples suggests that this reference was on the brass plates.

b. Probably added during proofreading.

c. Faith, hope, and charity echo 1 Corinthians 13:13: "And now abideth faith, hope, charity, these three; but the greatest of these *is* charity."

d. Compare Matthew 8:11: "Many shall come from the east and west, and shall sit down with Abraham, and Isaac, and Jacob, in the kingdom of heaven."

e. Probably added during proofreading.

f. Probably added during proofreading.

Chapter VI [Alma 8]

·¹And [now^a] it came to pass that Alma returned from the land of Gideon, after having taught the people of Gideon many things which cannot be written—having established the order of the church, according as he had before done in the land of Zarahemla. Yea, he returned to his own house at Zarahemla to rest himself from the labors which he had performed. ²And thus ended the ninth year of the reign of the judges over the people of Nephi.

³And it came to pass in the commencement of the tenth year of the reign of the judges over the people of Nephi, that Alma departed from thence and took his journey over into the land of Melek, on the west of the river Sidon (on the west by the borders of the wilderness). ⁴And he began to teach the people in the land of Melek, according to the holy order of God (by which he had been called). And he began to teach [the^b] people throughout all the land of Melek.

⁵And it came to pass that the people came to him [throughout^c] all the borders of the land, which was by the wilderness side.

And it came to pass that they were baptized throughout all the land, ⁶so that when he had finished his work at Melek, he departed thence and traveled three days journey on the north of the land of Melek. And he came to a city which was called Ammonihah^d.

> ⁷Now, it was the custom of the people of Nephi to call their lands and their cities and their villages, yea, even all their small villages, after the name of him who first possessed them. And thus it was with the land of Ammonihah.^e<

⁸And it came to pass that when Alma had came to the city of Ammonihah, he began to peach the word of God unto them. ⁹Now, Satan had got great hold upon the hearts of the people of the city of Ammonihah. Therefore, they would not hearken unto the words of Alma. ¹⁰Nevertheless, Alma labored much in the spirit, wrestling with God in mighty prayer that he would pour out his spirit upon the people which was in the city, that he would also grant that he might baptize them unto repentance. ¹¹Nevertheless, they hardened their hearts, saying unto him:

Behold, we know that thou art Alma. ¹²And we know that thou [art^f] High Priest over the church which thou hast established in many parts of the land, according to your tradition. And we are not of thy church.^g And we do not believe in such foolish traditions.

And now, we know that because we are not of thy church, we know that

---

a. Probably added during proofreading.
b. Probably added during proofreading.
c. Probably added during proofreading.
d. The Printer's Manuscript has "Ammonidah" consistently in this section. Skousen notes that we do not havee the Original for this part of the text, and that this particular scribe appears to have misread the Original while copying from it to the Printer's Manuscript. Oliver Cowdery made the corrections in the Printer's Manuscript. Thus, this and subsequent appearances of "Ammonidah" have been silently changed to "Ammonihah." See Skousen, *Analysis of the Textual Variants,* 3:1735.
e. This aside seems to have little to do with the subject. It appears that it occurred to Mormon and was not planned. Verse 8 is the repetitive resumption.
f. Probably entered during proofreading.
g. The scribe's eye skipped to the repetition that the Ammonihahites were not of Alma$_2$'s church and

thou hast no power over us. And thou hast delivered up the Judgment Seat unto Nephihah. Therefore, thou art not the Chief Judge over us now.

¹³When the people had said this, and had withstood all his words, and reviled him, and spit upon him, and [caused^a] that he should be cast of out of their city.^b And he departed thence and took his journey towards the city which was called Aaron.

¹⁴And it came to pass that while he was journeying thither, being weighed down with sorrow, wading through much tribulation and anguish of soul because of the wickedness of the people which was in the city of Ammonihah—and it came to pass^c that while Alma was thus weighed down with sorrow, behold, an angel of the Lord appeared unto him, saying:

¹⁵Blessed art thou Alma. Therefore, lift up thy head and rejoice! For thou hast great cause to rejoice. For thou hast been faithful in keeping the commandments of God from the time which thou received thy first message from him. Behold, I am he that delivered it unto thee.

¹⁶And behold, I am sent to command thee that thou return to the city of Ammonihah and preach again unto the people of the city. Yea, preach unto them, yea, say unto them—except they repent, the Lord God will destroy them. ¹⁷For behold, they do study at this time that they may destroy the liberty of the thy people (for thus saith the Lord), which is contrary to the statutes, and judgments, and commandments, which he hath given unto his people.

¹⁸Now it came to pass that after Alma had received his message from the angel of the Lord, he returned speedily to the land of Ammonihah.

And it came to pass that he entered the city by another way, yea, by the way which was on the south of the city Ammonihah.

¹⁹And it came to pass that as he entered the city, he was an hungered and he saith to a man: "Will ye give to an humble servant of God something to eat?

²⁰And the man saith unto him: "I am a Nephite, and I know that thou art a holy prophet of God. For thou art the man which an angel saith in a vision—'thou shalt receive.' Therefore, go with me into my house. And I will impart unto thee of my [food^d]. And I know that thou will be a blessing unto me and my house."

²¹And it came to pass that the man received him into his house. And the man was called Amulek. And he brought bread and meat and sat before Alma.

²²And it came to pass that Alma ate bread and was filled. And he blessed Amulek and his house. And he gave thanks unto God. ²³And after he had eat, and was filled, he saith unto Amulek:

---

erroneously added "we know that thou hast no power over us." This was removed prior to printing the first edition. See Skousen, *Analysis of the Textual Variants*, 3:1737.

a. The scribe for this part of the Printer's Manuscript wrote "cursed." Oliver Cowdery changed it to "caused" during proofreading. See Skousen, *Analysis of the Textual Variants*, 3:1739.

b. The beginning "when" is never resolved. It could have been resolved if "and caused that he should" were "the people caused that he should."

c. Although this edition usually creates a new paragraph with "and it came to pass," in this case it is the repetitive resumption to try to complete the sentence that began with "while he was journeying."

d. The scribe had misread the word, and the Printer's Manuscript originally had "favor." Oliver Cowdery corrected it during proofreading.

Chapter VI [Alma 8]

I am Alma, and am the High Priest over the churches of God throughout the land. ²⁴And behold, I have been called to preach the word of God among all this people, according to the spirit of revelation and prophecy.

And I was in this land, and they would not receive me. But they cast me out. And I was about to set my back towards this land forever. ²⁵But behold, I have been commanded that I should turn again and prophecy unto this people, yea, and to testify against them concerning their iniquities.

²⁶And now Amulek, because thou hast fed me and took me in, thou art blessed. For I was an hungered, for I had fasted many days.

²⁷And it came to pass that Alma tarried many days with Amulek before he began to preach unto the people.

²⁸And it came to pass that the people did wax more gross in their iniquities. ²⁹And the word came to Alma saying: "Go, and also say unto my servant Amulek—'go forth'. Prophesy unto this people, saying: Repent ye! For thus saith the Lord, except ye repent, I will visit this people in mine anger. Yea, and I will not turn my fierce anger away."

³⁰And it came to pass that Alma went forth, and also Amulek, among the people to declare the words of God unto them. And they were filled with the Holy Ghost. ³¹And they had power given unto them, insomuch that they could not be confined in dungeons, neither were it possible that any man could slay them. Nevertheless, they did not exercise their power until they were bound in bands and cast into prison. Now, this was done that the Lord might show forth his power in them.

³²And it came to pass that they went forth, and began to preach, and to prophesy unto the people, according to the spirit and power which the Lord had given them.

Chapter VII [Alma 9]

[9] *The words of Alma, and also the words of Amulek—which was declared unto the people which was in the land of Ammonihah. And also, they are cast into prison, and delivered by the miraculous power of God which was in them. According to the record of Alma.*

¹And again, I Alma, having been commanded of God that I should take Amulek, and go forth and preach again unto this people (or the people which was in the city of Ammonihah)ᵃ—

And it came to pass as I began to preach unto them, they began to contend with me saying: ²"Who art thou? Suppose ye that we shall believe the testimony of one man, although he should preach unto us that the earth should pass away?" ³Now, they understood not the words which they spake. For they knew not that the earth should pass away.

⁴And they saith also: "We will not believe thy words if thou shouldst prophecy that this great city should be destroyed in one day!" ⁵Now, they knew not that God could do such marvelous works. For they were a hard-hearted and a stiffnecked people.

⁶And they saith: "Who is God, that sendeth no more authority than one man among this people to declare unto them the truth of such great and marvelous things?" ⁷And they stood forth to lay their hands on me. But behold, they did not.

And I stood with boldness to declare unto them. Yea, I did boldly testify unto them, saying:

⁸Behold! O ye wicked and perverse generation! How have ye forgotten the tradition of your fathers? Yea, how soon ye have forgotten the commandments of God!

⁹Do ye not remember that our father Lehi was brought out of Jerusalem by the hand of God?

Do ye not remember that they were all led by him through the wilderness?

¹⁰And have ye forgotten so soon how many times he delivered our fathers out of the hands of their enemies, and preserved them from being destroyed, even by the hands of their own brethren?

¹¹Yea, and if it had not been for his matchless power, and his mercy, and his long-suffering towards us, we should unavoidably have been cut off from the face of the earth long before this period of time, and perhaps been consigned to a state of endless misery and woe.

¹²Behold, now I say unto you, that he commandeth you to repent. And except ye repent, ye can in no wise inherit the kingdom of God. But behold, this is not all. He hath commanded you to repent, or he will utterly destroy you from off the face of the earth. Yea, he will visit you in his anger. And in his fierce anger he will not turn away.

¹³Behold, do ye not remember the words which he spake unto Lehi, saying that: "Inasmuch as ye shall keep my commandments ye shall prosper in the land"?

---

a. This has been left as an incomplete sentence. It is probable that it was orally linked to the next sentence (beginning with "and it came to pass"). Nevertheless, the second sentence starts a new idea. They have been separated to make reading easier.

Chapter VII [Alma 9]

And again, it is said that: "Inasmuch as ye will not keep my commandments, ye shall be cut off from the presence of the Lord."ª

¹⁴Now, I would that ye should remember that inasmuch as the Lamanites have not kept the commandments of God, they have been cut off from the presence of the Lord.ᵇ Now, we see that the word of the Lord hath been verified in this thing. And the Lamanites have been cut off from his presenceᶜ from the beginning of their transgressions in the land. ¹⁵Nevertheless, I say unto you that it shall be more tolerable for them in the day of judgment than for you, if ye remain in your sins. Yea, and even more tolerable for them in this life than for you, except ye repent. For there are many promises which is extended to the Lamanites. ¹⁶For it is because of the traditions of their fathers that [causethᵈ] them to remain in their state of ignorance. Therefore, the Lord will be merciful unto them, and prolong their existence in the land. ¹⁷And at some period of time they will be brought to believe in his word, and to know of the incorrectness of the traditions of their fathers. And many of them will be saved. For the Lord will be merciful unto all who call on his name.

¹⁸But behold, I say unto you, that if ye persist in your wickedness, that your days shall not be prolonged in the land. For the Lamanites shall be sent upon you. And if ye repent not, they shall come in a time when you know not. And ye shall be visited with utter destruction. And it shall be according to the fierce anger of the Lord. ¹⁹For he will not suffer you that ye shall live in your iniquities to destroy his people.

I [sayᵉ] unto you, nay—he would rather suffer that the Lamanites might destroy all this people (which is called the people of Nephi), if it were possible that they could fall into sins and transgressions after having had so much light, and so much knowledge given unto them of their Lord, their God.

²⁰Yea, after having been such a highly favored people of the Lord. Yea, after having been favored above every other nation, kindred, tongue, or people.ᶠ After having had all things made known unto them (according to their desires, and their faith, and prayers) of that which has been, and which is, and which is to come—²¹having been visited by the Spirit of God, having conversed with angels. and having been spoken unto by the voice of the Lord—and having the spirit of prophesy and the spirit of revelation—

And also many gifts—the gift of speaking with tongues, and the gift of preaching, and the gift of the Holy Ghost, and the gift of translation.

²²Yea, and after having been delivered of God out of the land of Jerusalem by the hand of the Lord--having been saved from famine, and from sicknesses, and all manner of diseases of every kind.

---

a. The basic promise and curse is found in 2 Nephi 1:20. The language is not the same. This suggests that either Alma is getting his quotation from the large plates, which had a different version, or he is paraphrasing rather than quoting from memory. The statement "it is said" suggests the latter. The phrase "cut off from my presence" is found in Leviticus 22:3.

b. The phrase "cut off from my presence" is found in Leviticus 22:3.

c. The phrase "cut off from my presence" is found in Leviticus 22:3.

d. The scribe wrote "causes," and Oliver Cowdery corrected it to "causeth" during proofreading.

e. Added during proofreading.

f. See Revelation 14:6: "And I saw another angel fly in the midst of heaven, having the everlasting gospel to preach unto them that dwell on the earth, and to every nation, and kindred, and tongue, and people."

And they, having been[a] waxed strong in battle, that they might not be destroyed—having been brought out of bondage, time after time, and having been kept and preserved, until now.[b]

And they have been prospered, until they are rich in all manner of things.

[23] And now behold, I say unto you that if this people (who have received so many blessings from the hand of the Lord) should transgress contrary to the light and knowledge which they do have, I say unto you that if this be the case that if they should fall into transgressions, that it would be far more tolerable for the Lamanites than for them. [24] For behold, the promises of the Lord are extended to the Lamanites, but they are not unto you if ye transgress. For, hath not the Lord expressly promised, and firmly decreed, that if ye will rebel against him that ye shall utterly be destroyed from off the face of the earth?

[25] And now, for this this cause, that ye may not be destroyed, the Lord hath sent his angel to visit many of his people, declaring unto them that they must go forth, and cry mightily unto this people, saying:

Repent ye, repent ye! For the kingdom of heaven is nigh at hand. [26] And not many days hence, the Son of God shall come in his glory. And his glory shall be the glory of the only begotten of the Father, full of grace, equity, and truth[c]—full of patience, mercy, and long-suffering—quick to hear the cries of his people, and to answer their payers. [27] And behold, he cometh to redeem those who will be baptized unto repentance, through faith on his name. [28] Therefore, prepare ye the way of the Lord! For the time is at hand that every man shall reap a reward of their works, according to that which they have been—if they have been righteous, they shall reap the salvation of their souls, according to the power and deliverance of Jesus Christ. And if they have been evil, they shall reap the damnation of their souls, according to the power and captivation of the devil.

[29] Now behold, this is the voice of the angel, crying unto the people.

[30] And now, my beloved brethren, for ye are my brethren and ye had ought to be beloved, and ye had ought to bring forth works which is mete for repentance,[d] seeing that your hearts have been grossly hardened against the word of God, and seeing that ye are a lost, and a fallen people.

[31] Now it came to pass that when I, Alma had, spoken these words, behold, the people were wroth with me because I said unto them that they was a hard-hearted and a stiffnecked people. [32] And also, because I said unto them that they were a lost and a fallen people—they was angry with me and sought to lay their hands upon [me[e]], that they might cast me into prison. [33] But it came to pass that the Lord did not suffer them that they should take me (at that time) and cast me into prison.

And it came to pass that Amulek went, and stood forth, and began to preach unto them also. And now, the words of Amulek are not all written. Nevertheless, a part of his words are written in this book.

---

a. Removed for the 1920 edition. Skousen, *Analysis of the Textual Variants*, 3:1765.

b. From the beginning of the third sentence of verse 20 to here is a single long sentence. It has been separated it out to make it easier to follow.

c. See John 1:4 for the phrase "full of grace and truth."

d. See Matthew 3:8: "Bring forth therefore fruits meet for repentance."

e. Added during proofreading.

Chapter VIII [Alma 10–11]

[10] ¹Now, these are the words which Amulek preached unto the people which was in the land of Ammonihah, saying:

²I am Amulek. I am the son of Gidanah[a], who was the son of Ishmael, who was a descendant of Aminadi. And it was that same Aminadi which interpreted the writing which was upon the wall of the temple, which was written by the finger of God. ³And Aminadi was a descendant of Nephi, who was the son of Lehi, who came out of the land of Jerusalem, who was a descendant Manasseh, who was the son of Joseph, which was sold into Egypt by the hands of his brethren.

⁴And behold, I am also a man of no small reputation among all those who know me. Yea, and behold, I have many kindred and friends. And I have also acquired much riches by the hand of my industry. ⁵Nevertheless, after all this, I never have known much of the ways of the Lord, and his mysteries, and marvelous power. I said, I never had known much of these things. But behold, I mistake. For I have seen much of his mysteries, and his miraculous power, yea, even in the preservation of the lives of this people. ⁶Nevertheless, I did harden my heart. For I was called many times, and I would not hear. Therefore, [I[b]] knew concerning these things. Yet, I would not know. Therefore, I went on rebelling against God in the wickedness of my heart, even until the fourth day of this seventh month, which is in the tenth year of the reign of our Judges.

⁷As I was a-journeying to see a very near kindred, behold an angel of the Lord appeared unto me, and said:

> Amulek, return to thine own house. For thou shalt feed a prophet of the Lord, yea, a holy man which art a chosen man of God. For he hath fasted many days because of the sins of this people. And he is an hungered. And thou shall receive him into thy house and feed him. And he shall bless thee, and thy house. [And the blessing of the Lord shall rest upon thee and thy house.][c]

⁸And it came to pass that I obeyed the voice of the angel and returned towards my house. And as I was a going thither, I found the man which the angel said unto me—thou shalt receive into thy house. And behold, it was this same man which hath been speaking unto you concerning the things of God. ⁹And the angel said unto me: "He is a holy man." Wherefore, I know he is a holy man, because it was said by an angel of God.

¹⁰And again, I know that the things whereof he hath testified are true. For behold I say unto you, that as the Lord liveth, even so, he hath sent his angel to make these things manifest unto me. And this he hath done while this Alma hath dwelt at my house. ¹¹For behold, he hath blessed mine house. He hath blessed me, and my women, and my children, and my father, and my kinsfolks. Yea, even all

---

a. The 1830 edition has Giddonah, probably based on the later occurrence of that name. Skousen sees them as different names and suggests that the spelling in the Printer's Manuscript should be preserved. Skousen, *Analysis of the Textual Variants*, 3:1774.

b. Added during proofreading.

c. Added during proofreading.

my kindred hath he blessed. And the blessing of the Lord hath rested upon us, according to the words which he spake.

¹²And now, when Amulek had spoken these words, the people began to be astonished, seeing there was more than one witness which testified of the things whereof they were accused, and also of the things which was to come (according to the spirit of prophesy which was in them). ¹³Nevertheless, there were some among them which thought to question them, that by their cunning devices they might catch them in their words, that they might find witness against them, that they might deliver them to the judges, that they might be judged according to the law—and that they might be slain, or cast into prison, according to the crime which they could make appear on witness against them.

¹⁴Now, it was those men (which sought to destroy them) which were lawyers, which were hired, or appointed by the people, to administer the law at their times of trials, or at the trials of the crimes of the people before the judges. ¹⁵Now, these lawyers were learned in all the arts and cunning of the people. And this was to enable them, that they might be skillful in their profession.

¹⁶And it came to pass that they began to question Amulek, that thereby they might make him cross his words, or contradict the words which he should speak. ¹⁷Now, they knew not that Amulek could know of their design. But it came to pass as they began to question him, he perceived their thoughts. And he saith unto them:

> O, ye wicked and perverse generation! Ye lawyers and hypocrites! For ye are laying the foundations of the devil. For ye are laying traps and snares to catch the holy ones of God. ¹⁸Ye are laying plans to pervert the ways of the righteous, and to bring down the wrath of God upon your heads, even to the utter destruction of this people. ¹⁹Yea, well did Mosiah say (who was our last king)—when he was about to deliver up the kingdom (having no one to confer it upon, causing that this people should be governed by their own voices)—yea, well did he say that if the time should come that the voice of this people should cause iniquity, that is, if the time should come that this people should fall into transgression, they would be ripe for destruction.
>
> ²⁰And now, I say unto you, that well doth the Lord judge of your iniquities! Well doth he cry unto this people by the voice of his angels: "Repent ye, repent ye! For the kingdom of heaven is at hand!" ²¹Yea, well doth he cry by the voice of his angels that: "I will come down among my people—with equity, and justice in my hands."
>
> ²²Yea, and I say unto you, that if it were not for the prayers of the righteous which are now in the land, that ye would, even now, be visited with utter destruction. Yet, it would not be by flood as were the people in the days of Noah—but it would be by famine, and by pestilence, and the sword. ²³But it is by the prayers of the righteous that ye are spared.
>
> Now therefore, if ye will cast out the righteous from among you, then will not the Lord stay his hand,[a] but in his fierce anger he will come out against you. Then ye shall be smitten by famine, and by pestilence, and by the sword. And the time is soon at hand, except ye repent.

²⁴And now it came to pass that the people were more angry with Amulek. And they

---

a. The "then will not the Lord stay his hand" is intended to mean "then the Lord will not stay his hand." The use is correct, and readers should not attempt to read it as a question.

cried out, saying: "This man doth revile against our laws, which are just—and our wise lawyers, which we have selected."

²⁵But Amulek stretched forth his hand, and cried the mightier unto them saying:

O ye wicked and perverse generation! Why hath Satan got such great hold upon your hearts? Why will ye yield yourselves unto him, that he may have power over you, to blind your eyes, that ye will not understand [the[a]] words which are spoken, according [to[b]] their truth. ²⁶For behold, have I testified against your law? Ye do not understand. Ye say that I have spoken against your law, but I have not. But I have spoken in favor of your law, to your condemnation.

²⁷And now behold, I say unto you that the foundation of the destruction of this people is beginning to be laid by the unrighteousness of your lawyers, and your judges

²⁸And now it came to pass that when Amulek had spoken these words, the people cried out against him, [saying[c]]: "Now, we know that this man is a child of the devil! For he hath lied unto us. For he hath spoken against our law. And now he saith that he hath not spoken it! ²⁹And again, he hath reviled against our lawyers, and our judges!"

³⁰And it come to pass that the lawyers put it into their hearts that they should remember these things against him.

³¹And it came to pass that there was one among them whose name was Zeezrom. Now, he being[d] the foremost to accuse Amulek and Alma, he being one of the most expert among them, having much business to do among the people.[e] ³²Now, the object of these lawyers were to get gain. And they got gain according to their employ.

>[11] ¹Now, it was in the law of Mosiah that every man which was a judge of the law, or which was appointed to be judges, should receive wages according to the time which they labored to judge those which were brought before them to be judged.

²Now, if a man oweth another and he would not pay that which he did owe, he was complained of to the judge, and the judge executed authority and sent forth officers that the man should be brought before him, and [he[f]] judgeth the man, according to the law and the [evidences[g]] which are brought against him. And thus, the man is compelled to pay that which he oweth, or be striped, or be cast out from among the people as a thief, and a robber.

³And the judge receiveth for his wages according to his time: a [senine[h]] of gold for a day, or a senum of silver (which is equal to a senine of gold). And this is according to the law which was given.

⁴Now, these are the names of the different pieces of their gold, and of their silver, according to their value. And the names are given by the Nephites. For they did

---

a. Added during proofreading.
b. Added during proofreading.
c. Added during proofreading.
d. Joseph Smith changed this to "was" for the 1837 edition, allowing for the completion of the sentence.
e. Incomplete sentence.
f. Added during proofreading.
g. The scribe wrote "witnesses," which Oliver Cowdery corrected to "evidences" during proofreading.
h. The scribe wrote "senire," which Oliver Cowdery corrected to "senine" during proofreading.

not reckon after the manner of the Jews which were at Jerusalem, neither did they measure after the manner of the Jews. But they altered their reckoning and their measure according to the minds and the circumstances of the people in every generation until the reign of the judges, they having been established by King Mosiah.

⁵Now, the reckoning is thus:

⁶A senine of gold.
A sean of gold.
A shum of gold,
and a limnah of gold.

⁷A senum of silver.
An amnor of silver.
An ezrum of silver.
And an onti[a] of silver.

A senum of silver was equal to a senine of gold, an[d] either for a measure of barley, and also for a measure of every kind of grain.

⁸Now, the amount of a [seon[b]] of gold was twice the value of a senine.
⁹And a shum of gold was twice the value of a sean.
¹⁰And a limnah of gold was the value of them all.
¹¹And an amnor of silver was as great as two senums.
¹²And an ezrum of silver was as great as four senums.
¹³And [onti[c]] was as great as them all.

¹⁴Now, this is the value of the lesser numbers of their reckoning:
¹⁵A shiblon is half of a senum. Therefore, a shiblon for half a measure of barley.
¹⁶And a shilum is a half of a shiblon.
¹⁷And a leah is the half of the shilum.
¹⁹Now, an antion of gold is equal to three shiblons.[d]

¹⁸Now, this is their number, according to their reckoning.[e]<

²⁰Now, it was for the sole purpose for to get gain, because they received their wages according to their employ.[f] Therefore, they did stir up the people to riotings, and all

---

a. The scribe wrote "onthi," which Oliver Cowdery corrected to "onti" during proofreading.

b. The scribe wrote "sean," which Oliver Cowdery corrected to "seon" during proofreading.

c. The scribe wrote "anti," which Oliver Cowdery corrected to "onti" during proofreading. However, Cowdery did not include the article "an onti" as it reads in modern editions. The article is expected and might have been intended when the scribe wrote "anti," perhaps conflating "an onti" into a single word as he copied.

d. The 1830 typesetter reversed the order of these two sentences (verses 18 and 19.) Both the Original and the Printer's Manuscript have them as reproduced. This has required that the verse numbers appear out of order.

e. This is a very long insertion that has two functions. The immediate function is to allow the reader to understand the extent of the offered bribes. It is secondarily used as a source, or at least a touchpoint, for some names we see in the text. We have Ze-ezrom, where ezom is listed. Later we will see Antion-ah, and antion is in the list. See Gordon C. Thomasson, "What's in a Name? Book of Mormon Language, Names, and [Metonymic] Naming," *Journal of Book of Mormon Studies* 1 (1994):1–27.

f. This sentence is the repetitive resumption to return to the text after the interruption. See Alma 10:32.

manner of disturbances, and wickedness—that they might have more employ, that they might get money, according to the suits which was brought before them. Therefore, they did stir up the people against Alma and Amulek.

²¹And this Zeezrom began to question Amulek saying: "Will ye answer me a few questions which I shall ask you?" >Now, Zeezrom was a man which was expert in the devices of the devil, that he might destroy that which was good. Therefore, he saith unto Amulek: "Will ye answer the questions which I shall put unto you?"<

²² And Amulek saith unto him: "Yea, I will, if it be according to the spirit of the Lord which is in me. For I shall say nothing which is contrary to the spirit of the Lord."

And Zeezrom saith unto him: "Behold, here is six onties of silver. And all these will I give unto thee, if thou wilt deny the existence of a supreme being."

²³Now, Amulek saith:

O, thou child of hell! Why tempt ye me? Knoweth thou that the righteous yieldeth to no such temptations? ²⁴Believest thou that there is no God? I say unto you, nay, thou knowest thot there is a God. But thou lovest that lucre more than him! ²⁵And now, thou hast lied before God unto me. For thou saidest unto me, "behold these six onties which are of great worth, I will give unto thee," when thou had it in thy heart to retain them from me. And it was only thy desires that I should deny the true and living God, that thou mightest have cause to destroy me. And now behold, for this great evil thou shalt have thy reward.

²⁶And Zeezrom saith unto him: "Thou sayest there is a true and a living God."
²⁷And Amulek saith: "Yea, there is a true and a living God."
²⁸Now, Zeezrom saith: "Is there more than one God?"
²⁹And he answereth: "No."
³⁰Now, Zeezrom saith unto him again: "How knowest thou these things?"
³¹And he saith: "An angel hath made them known unto me."
³²And Zeezrom saith again: "Who is he that shall come? Is it the Son of God?"
³³And he said unto him: "Yea."
³⁴And Zeezrom saith again: "Shall he save his people in their sins?"
And Amulek answered and said unto him: "I say unto you he shall not! For it is impossible for him to deny his word.

³⁵Now, Zeezrom saith unto the people: "See that ye remember these things! For he saith there is but one God, yet he saith that the Son of God shall come but he shall not save his people, as though he had authority to command God."

³⁶Now, Amulek said again unto him: "Behold, thou hast lied! For thou sayest that I spake as though I had authority to command God because I said he shall not save his people in their sins. ³⁷And I say unto you again, that he cannot save them in their sins. For I cannot deny his word. And he hath said that no unclean thing can inherit the kingdom of heaven.[a] Therefore, how can ye be saved except ye inherit the kingdom of heaven? Therefore, ye cannot be saved in your sins."

³⁸Now, Zeezrom saith again unto him: "Is it the Son of God, the very Eternal Father?"

---

a. Some of the themes appear in Ephesians 5:5: "For this ye know, that no whoremonger, nor unclean person, nor covetous man, who is an idolater, hath any inheritance in the kingdom of Christ and of God."

³⁹And Amulek saith unto him:

Yea, he is the very Eternal Father of Heaven and Earth, and all things which in them is. He is the beginning and the end. The first and the last.ᵃ ⁴⁰And he shall come into the world to redeem his people. And he shall take upon him the transgressions of those who believe on his name. And these are they that shall have eternal life. And salvation cometh to none else. ⁴¹Therefore, the wicked remain as though there had been no redemption made, except it be the loosing of the bands of death. For behold, the day cometh that all shall rise from the dead and stand before God and be judged according to [theirᵇ] works.

⁴²Now, there is a death which is called temporal death, and the death of Christ shall loose the bands of this temporal death, that all shall be raised from this temporal death. ⁴³The spirit and the body shall be reunited again in its perfect form. Both limb and joint shall be restored to its proper frame, even as we now are at this time. And we shall be brought to stand before God, knowing even as we know now, and have a bright recollection of all our guilt.

⁴⁴Now, this restoration shall come to all: both old and young, both bond and free, both male and female,ᶜ both the wicked and the righteous. And [evenᵈ] there shall not so much as a hair of their heads be lost. But all things shall be restored to its perfect frame as it is now ([orᵉ] in the body), and shall be brought, and be [arraignedᶠ] before the bar of Christ the Son, and God the Father, and the Holy Spirit, which [isᵍ] one Eternal God, to be judged according to their works, whether they be good or whether they be evil.

⁴⁵Now behold, I have spoken unto to you concerning the death of the mortal body, and also concerning the resurrection of the mortal body. I say unto you that this mortal body is raised to an immortal body (that is, from death), even from the first death unto life, that they can die no more—their spirits uniting with their bodies, never to be divided. Thus, the whole becoming spiritual and immortal, that they can no more see corruption.

⁴⁶Now, when Amulek had finished these words, the people began again to be astonished. And also Zeezrom began to tremble. And thus ended the words of Amulek. Or, this is all that I have written.

---

a. See Revelation 22:13: "I am Alpha and Omega, the beginning and the end, the first and the last."
b. The text had "his," which Oliver Cowdery corrected during proofreading.
c. See Galatians 3:28: "There is neither Jew nor Greek, there is neither bond nor free, there is neither male nor female: for ye are all one in Christ Jesus."
d. Added during proofreading.
e. The scribe had written "on and," which is confusing. Oliver Cowdery changed it to "or" during proofreading.
f. The word in the Printer's Manuscript is "reigned," which does not make sense. The compositor changed it to "arraigned," which is the logical intent. I have kept "arraigned," assuming "reigned" to have been a spelling error.
g. This word is missing in the Printer's Manuscript, and Oliver Cowdery did not catch it during proofreading. It was added by the compositor and is clearly required.

Chapter IX [Alma 12–13:9]

[12] ¹Now Alma, seeing that the words of Amulek had silenced Zeezrom (for he beheld that Amulek had caught him in his lying and deceiving,[a] to destroy him), and seeing that he began to tremble under a consciousness of his guilt—he opened his mouth and began to speak unto him and to establish the words of Amulek, and to explain thing[b] beyond—or to unfold the scriptures beyond that which Amulek had done.

²Now, the words that Alma spake unto Zeezrom was heard by the people round about, for the multitude was great. And he spake on this wise:

³Now Zeezrom, seeing that thou hast been taken in thy lyings and craftiness (for thou hast not lied unto men only, but thou hast lied unto God, for behold, he knows all thy thoughts)—⁴and thou seest that thy thoughts are made known unto us by this spirit—and thou seest that we know that thy plan was a very subtle plan (as to the subtlety of the devil), for to lie and to deceive this people, that thou mightest set them against us, to revile us and to cast us out—[c]

⁵Now, this was a plan of thine Adversary[d] and he hath exercised his power in thee (now, I would that ye should remember that what I say unto thee, I say unto all). ⁶And behold, I say unto you all that this was a snare of the Adversary, which he hath laid to catch this people—that he might bring you into subjection unto him, that he might encircle you about with his chains, that he might chain you down to everlasting destruction, according to the power of his captivity.

⁷Now, when Alma had spoken these words, Zeezrom began to tremble more exceedingly. For he was convinced more and more of the power of God. And he was also convinced that Alma and Amulek had a knowledge of him, for he was convinced that they knew the thoughts and intents of his hearts. For power was given unto them, that they might know of these things, according to the spirit of prophesy.

⁸And[e] Zeezrom began to enquire of them diligently, that he might know more concerning the kingdom of God. And he saith unto Alma: "What does this mean, which Amulek hath spoken, concerning the resurrection of the dead, that all shall rise from the dead, both the just and the unjust, and are brought to stand before God to be judged according to their works?"

⁹And now, Alma began to expound these things unto him, saying:

---

 a. The Printer's Manuscript has the singular, and an "s" has been erased. All printed versions have the plural "lyings and deceivings." See Skousen, *Analysis of Textual Variants*, 3:1839.

 b. The Printer's Manuscript has the singular. The intention is certainly the plural "to explain things beyond," and that is how it has appeared in printed editions. Skousen, *The Earliest Text*, 320, has "things" in the plural.

 c. None of the "seeing" participial phrases are grammatically resolved.

 d. As written, "thine adversary" would appear to reference someone who is Zeezrom's adversary. The context is clearly to indicate Satan, the Adversary. It might be simpler to change "thine" to "the," but the text is preserved as it is in the Printer's Manuscript, and as it continues to appear in our current edition. However, by capitalizing "Adversary," the reader can see it as a name rather than a description. It makes the sentence parallel to "this was a plan of thy devil." To continue the emphasis, it is also capitalized "Adversary" in verse 6.

 e. Inserted during proofreading as "&".

It is given unto many to know the mysteries of God.[a] Nevertheless, they are laid under a strict command that they shall not impart, only according to the portion of his word which he doth grant unto the children of men, according to the heed and diligence which they give unto him. [10]Therefore, he that will harden his heart, the same receiveth the lesser portion of the word. And he that will not harden his heart, to him is given the greater portion of the word—until it is given unto him to know the mysteries of God,[b] until they knew them in full.

[11]And he that will harden his heart, to him is given the lesser portion of the word, until they know nothing concerning his mysteries. And then they are taken captive by the devil and led by his will down to destruction. Now, this is what is meant by the chains of hell.

[12]And Amulek hath spoken plainly concerning death and being raised from this mortality to a state of immortality and being brought before the bar of God to be judged according to are our works.

[13]Then, if our hearts have been hardened, yea, if we have hardened our hearts against the word (insomuch that it hath not been found in us)—then will our state be awful.

For then we shall be condemned. [14]For our words[c] will condemn us. Yea, all our work will condemn us. We shall not be found spotless. And our thoughts will also condemn us.

And in this awful state we shall not durst look up to our God, and would fane be glad if we could command the rocks and the mountains to fall upon us, to hide us from his presence.[d] [15]But this cannot be.

We must come forth and stand before him in his glory, and in his power, and in his might, majesty, and dominion—and acknowledge to their everlasting shame that all his judgments are just, that he is just in all his works. And that he is merciful unto the children of men. And that he hath all power to save every man that believeth on his name and bringeth forth fruit mete for repentance.

[16]And now behold, I say unto you, then cometh a death, even a second death, which is a spiritual death. [17]Then is a time that whosoever dieth in his sins (as to the temporal death) shall also die a spiritual death. Yea, he shall die as to things pertaining unto righteousness. Then is the time when their torment shall be as a lake of fire and brimstone,[e] whose flames ascendeth up forever and ever.[f]

And then is the time that thy shall be chained down to an everlasting destruction, according to the power and captivity of Satan, having subjected them according to his will. [18]Then (I say unto you) they shall be as though there had been no

---

a. The phrase "mystery of God" appears in 1 Corinthians 4:1, Colossians 2:2, and Revelation 10:7.
b. The phrase "mystery of God" appears in 1 Corinthians 4:1, Colossians 2:2, and Revelation 10:7.
c. The scribe originally attempted to write "works" but mistakenly wrote "words." That is how it continues to read. However, Skousen suggests that even though the Original might have read "words" at this point, it should have been "works." Skousen, *Analysis of the Textual Variants,* 3:1851. "Works" makes more sense when the following clause appears to clarify that it is all our works, rather than some of them, that will condemn us. That clause does not work well when the reference amplifies "words."
d. Allusion to Revelation 6:16: "And said to the mountains and rocks, Fall on us, and hide us from the face of him that sitteth on the throne, and from the wrath of the Lamb."
e. See Revelation 20:14: "And death and hell were cast into the lake of fire. This is the second death."
f. See Revelation 14:11: "And the smoke of their torment ascendeth up for ever and ever."

redemption made. For they cannot be redeemed, according to God's justice. And they cannot die, seeing there is no more corruption.

[19]Now it came to pass that when Alma had made an end of speaking these words, the people began to be more astonished. [20]But there was one Antionah (who was a chief ruler among them) came forth and said unto him:

> What is this that thou hast said, that man should rise from the dead, and be changed from this mortal to an immortal state, that the soul can never die? [21]What does this scripture mean, which saith that God placed cherubims[a] and a flaming sword on the east of the Garden of Eden, lest our first parents should enter and partake of the fruit of the tree of life, and live forever? And thus, we see that there was no possible chance that they should live forever.

[22]Now, Alma saith unto him:

> This is the thing which I was about to explain. Now, we see that Adam did fall by partaking of the forbidden fruit, according to the word of God. And thus we see that by his fall, that all mankind became a lost and a fallen people.
>
> [23]And now behold, I say unto you, that if it had been possible for Adam for to have partaken of the fruit of the tree of life at that time, that there would have been no death. And the word would have been void, making God a liar. For he said: "If thou eat thereof, thou shalt surely die."
>
> [24]And we see that death comes upon mankind. Yea, the death which has been spoken of by Amulek, which is the temporal death. Nevertheless, there was a space granted unto man in which he might repent. Therefore, this life became a probationary state. A time to prepare to meet God. A time to prepare for that endless state which has been spoken of by us, which is after the resurrection of the dead.
>
> [25]Now, if it had not been for the plan of redemption (which was laid from the foundation of the world), there could have been no resurrection of the dead. But there was a plan of redemption laid, which shall bring to pass the resurrection of the dead, of which has been spoken.
>
> [26]And now behold, if it were possible that our first parents could have went forth and partaken of the tree of life, they would have been forever miserable, having no preparatory state. And thus, the plan of redemption would have been frustrated, and the word of God would have been void, taking none effect. [27]But behold, it was not so. But it was appointed unto man, that they must die.[b] And after death, they must come to judgment, even that same judgment of which we have spoken, which is the end.
>
> [28]And after God had appointed that these [things[c]] should come unto man, behold, then he saw that it was expedient that man should know concerning the things whereof he had appointed unto them. [29]Therefore, he sent angels to converse with them, which caused men to behold of his Glory. [30]And they began, from

---

a. The scribe originally wrote "Cherabs" and immediately overwrote the "s" with "i" and added "ims." That created the double plural "Cherubims," which has both the Hebrew plural "-im" and the English plural "-s." Joseph Smith later crossed out the final "s," but the double plural reflects the way it appears at times in the King James Version.

b. See Hebrews 9:27: "And as it is appointed unto men once to die, but after this the judgment."

c. Added during proofreading.

that time forth, to call on his name. Therefore, God conversed with men and made known unto them the plan of redemption, which had been prepared from the foundation of the world.

And this he made known unto them, according to their faith, and repentance, and their holy works. ³¹Wherefore, he gave commandments unto men (they having first transgressed the first commandments as to things which were temporal). And, becoming as Gods (knowing good from evil)[a], placing themselves in a state to act (or being placed in a state to act according to their wills and pleasures, whether to do evil or to do good)—³²therefore, God gave unto them commandments (after having made known unto them the plan of redemption) that they should not do evil, the penalty thereof being a second death (which was an everlasting death as to things pertaining unto righteousness).[b] For on such, the plan of redemption could have no power. For the works of justice could not be destroyed, according to the supreme goodness of God. ³³But God did call on men, in the name of his Son, this being the plan of redemption which was laid, saying:

> If ye will repent, and harden not your hearts, then will I have mercy upon you through mine only begotten Son. ³⁴Therefore, whosoever repenteth, and hardeneth not his heart, he shall have claim on mercy through mine only begotten Son unto a remission of their sins. And these shall enter into my rest.[c] ³⁵And whosoever will harden his heart and will do iniquity, behold, I swear in my wrath that they shall not enter into my rest.[d]

³⁶And now my brethren, behold I say unto you, that if ye will harden your hearts ye shall not enter into the rest of the Lord. Therefore, your iniquity provoketh him, that he sendeth down his wrath upon you, as in the first provocation—yea (according to his word), in the last provocation as well as in the first, to the everlasting destruction of your souls. Therefore, according to his word, [unto[e]] the last death as well as the first.

³⁷And now my brethren, seeing we know these things, and they are true—let us repent and harden not our hearts, that we provoke not the Lord our God to pull down his wrath upon us in these, his second commandments, which he hath given unto us. But let us enter into the rest of God which is prepared according to his word.

[13] ¹And again, my brethren, I would cite your minds forwards[f] to the time which the Lord God gave these commandments unto his children. And I would that ye should remember that the Lord God ordained priests after his holy order (which was after the order of his Son) to teach these things unto the people. ²And

---

a. Alludes to Genesis 3:5: "For God doth know that in the day ye eat thereof, then your eyes shall be opened, and ye shall be as gods, knowing good and evil."

b. Although this sentence is much longer than modern preferences would allow, it needs to be read as a complete thought. This is an argument that is set up with the first set of clauses, and then leading to "therefore," which signals the logical conclusion to the problem of the first part.

c. The phrase "enter into my rest" comes from Psalm 95:11.

d. The phrase "enter into my rest" comes from Psalm 95:11.

e. The scribe wrote "until," and Oliver Cowdery changed it to "unto" during proofreading.

f. A modern reader wants this to have been "look back to" rather than "forwards."

those priests were ordained after the order of his Son in a manner that thereby the people might know in what manner to look forward to his Son for redemption.

³And this is the manner after which they were ordained, being called and prepared from the foundation of the world, according to the foreknowledge of God, on account of their exceeding faith and good works in the first place—being left to choose good or evil. Therefore, they (having chosen good [and[a]] exercising exceeding great faith) are called with a holy calling, yea, with that holy calling which was prepared with, and according to, a preparatory redemption for such.

⁴And thus they, having been called to this holy calling on account of their faith--.[b] While others would reject the spirit of God on account of the hardness of their hearts, and blindness of their minds—while if it had not been for this, they might had as great privilege as their brethren (⁵or in fine, in the first place, they were on the same standing with their brethren).

Thus, this holy calling (being prepared from the foundation of the world for such as would not harden their hearts), being in and through the atonement of the only begotten Son (which was prepared)—⁶and thus, being called by this holy calling,[c] and ordained unto the high priesthood of the holy order of God to teach his commandments unto the children of men—that they also might enter into his rest.[d] ⁷This high priesthood, being after the order of his Son, which order was from the foundation of the world (or in other words, being without beginning of days or end of years[e]), being prepared from eternity to all eternity, according to his foreknowledge of all things.[f]

⁸Now, they were ordained after this manner. Being called with a holy calling and ordained with a holy ordinance, and taking upon themselves the high priesthood of the holy order—which calling, and ordinance, and high priesthood, is without beginning or end. ⁹Thus, they become high priests forever, after the order of the Son of[g] the only begotten of the Father, which is without beginning of days or end of years[h]—which is full of grace, equity, and truth.[i] And thus it is. Amen.

---

a. Added as "&" during proofreading.

b. This is a difficult sentence. The beginning has been left as an incomplete sentence because the next two phrases beginning with "while" change the focus of the sentence.

c. Repetitive resumption to return to the original idea.

d. Even after the repetitive resumption, the sentence is never grammatically resolved.

e. See Hebrews 7:3: "Without father, without mother, without descent, having neither beginning of days, nor end of life; but made like unto the Son of God; abideth a priest continually."

f. An incomplete sentence.

g. This same phrase occurred in Alma 5:49. It is crossed out in the Printer's Manuscript but appears to be from the changes Joseph Smith did for the 1837 edition. It was set as "Son of the only begotten" in the 1830 edition.

h. See Hebrews 7:3: "Without father, without mother, without descent, having neither beginning of days, nor end of life; but made like unto the Son of God; abideth a priest continually."

i. See John 1:4 for the phrase "full of grace and truth."

Chapter X [Alma 13:10–15:19]

[**13 continued**] ¹⁰Now, as I said concerning the holy order (or this high priesthood), there were many which were ordained and became high priests of God. And it was on account of the exceeding faith and repentance, and their righteousness before God—they, choosing to repent and work righteousness rather than to perish. ¹¹Therefore, they were called after this holy order and were sanctified. And their garments were washed white through the blood of the Lamb.

¹²Now they, after being sanctified by the Holy Ghost, having their garments made white, being pure and spotless before God—could not look upon sin save it were with abhorrence. And there were many, an exceeding great many, which were made pure and entered into the rest of the Lord, their God.

¹³And now, my brethren, I would that ye should humble yourselves before God and bring forth fruit mete for repentance, that ye may also enter into that rest. ¹⁴Yea, humble yourselves, even as the people in the days of Melchizedek, who was also a high priest after this same order which I have spoken, who also took upon him the high priesthood forever. ¹⁵And it was this same Melchizedek to whom Abraham paid tithes.ᵃ Yea, even our Father Abraham paid tithes of one tenth part of all he possessed.

¹⁶Now, [theseᵇ] ordinances were given after this manner, that thereby the people might look forward on the Son of God—it being a type of his order (or it being his order)—and this that they might look forward to him for a remission of their sins, that they might enter into their rest of the Lord.

¹⁷Now, this Melchisedek was a king over the land of Salem. And his people had waxed strong in iniquity and abominations. Yea, they had all gone astray. They were full of all manner of wickedness. ¹⁸But Melchisedek, having exercised mighty faith, and received the office of the high priesthood (according to the holy order of God), did preach repentance unto his people.

And behold, they did repent. And Melchisedek did establish peace in the land in his days. Therefore, he was called the prince of peace, for he was the King of Salem. And he did reign under his father.

¹⁹Now, there were many before him and also there were many afterwards. But none were greater. Therefore, of him they have more particularly made mention.

²⁰Now, I need not rehearse the matter. What I have said may suffice. Behold, the scriptures are before you. If ye will wrest them, it shall be to your own destruction.ᶜ

---

a. See Hebrews 7: 1–2: "For this Melchisedec, king of Salem, priest of the most high God, who met Abraham returning from the slaughter of the kings, and blessed him; To whom also Abraham gave a tenth part of all; first being by interpretation King of righteousness, and after that also King of Salem, which is, King of peace." This is a condensation of Genesis 14:18–20: "And Melchizedek king of Salem brought forth bread and wine: and he *was* the priest of the most high God. And he blessed him, and said, Blessed *be* Abram of the most high God, possessor of heaven and earth: And blessed be the most high God, which hath delivered thine enemies into thy hand. And he gave him tithes of all."

b. The Printer's Manuscript has "their," but the typesetter changed it to "these" for the 1830 edition. Joseph Smith corrected the Printer's Manuscript to "these" in 1837. That matches the 1830 edition, but the original is not extant at this point, so it is uncertain what the original was. It has been changed it to "these," assuming Joseph was returning the word to the original meaning. See Skousen, *Analysis of the Textual Variants*, 3:1895–96.

c. See 2 Peter 3:16: "They that are unlearned and unstable wrest, as they do also the other scriptures, unto their own destruction."

²¹And now it came to pass that when Alma had said these words unto them, he stretched forth his hand unto them and cried with a mighty voice, saying:

Now is the time to repent. For the day of salvation draweth nigh.

²²Yea, and the voice of the Lord, by the mouth of angels, doth declare it unto all nations.

Yea, doth declare it that they may have glad tidings of great joy.[a]

Yea, and he doth sound these glad tidings among all his people.

Yea, even to them that are scattered abroad upon the face of the earth.

Wherefore, they have come unto us. ²⁴And they are made known unto us in plain terms that we may understand, that we cannot err. And this because of our being wanderers in a strange land. Therefore, we are thus highly favored, for we have these glad tidings declared unto us in all parts of our vineyard. For behold, angels are declaring it unto many at this time in our land. And this is for the purpose of preparing the hearts of the children of men for to receive his word at the time of his coming in his glory.

²⁵And now, we only wait to hear the joyful news declared unto us by the mouth of angels of his coming. For the time cometh, we know not how soon. Would to God that it might be in my day. But, let it be sooner or later, in it I will rejoice. ²⁶And it shall be made known unto just and holy men by the mouth of angels at the time of his coming, that the words of our fathers might be fulfilled according to that which they have spoken concerning him, which was according to the spirit of prophesy which was in them.

²⁷And now, my brethren, I wish from the inmost part of my heart, yea, with great anxiety even unto pain, that ye would hearken unto my words—and cast off your sins and not procrastinate the day of your repentance. ²⁸But that ye would humble yourselves before the Lord, and call on his holy name, and watch and pray continually, that ye may not be tempted above that which ye can bear. And thus be led by the Holy Spirit, becoming humble, meek, submissive, patient, full of love, and all long-suffering—²⁹having faith on the Lord, having a hope that ye shall receive eternal life, having the love of God always in your hearts—that ye may be lifted up at the last day, and enter into his rest. ³⁰And may the Lord grant unto you repentance, that ye may not bring down his wrath upon you, that ye may not be bound down by the chains of hell, that ye may not suffer the second death.

³¹And it came to pass that Alma spake many more words unto the people which are not written in this book.

[14] ¹And it came to pass that after he had made an end of speaking unto the people, many of them did believe on his words, and began to repent, and to search the scriptures. ²But the more part of them were desirous that they might destroy Alma and Amulek, for they were angry with Alma because of the plainness of his words unto Zeezrom. And they also said that Amulek had lied unto them, and had reviled against their law, and also against their lawyers and judges. ³And they were also angry with Alma and Amulek because they had testified so plainly against their wickedness.

They sought to put them away privily,[b] ⁴but it came to pass that they did not. But

---

a. See Luke 2:10: "Fear not: for, behold, I bring you good tidings of great joy."
b. Uses language from Matthew 1:19: "Then Joseph her husband, being a just man, and not willing

they took them, and bound them with strong cords, and took them before the Chief Judge of the land. ⁵And the people went forth and witnessed against them, testifying that they had reviled against their law, and their lawyers, and judges of the land, and also all the people that were in the land—and also testified that there was but one God, and that he should send his Son among the people, but he should not save them. And many such things did the people testify against Alma and Amulek.

And it came to pass that it was done before the Chief Judge of the land.

⁶And it also came to pass that Zeezrom was astonished at the words which had been spoken. And he also knew concerning the blindness of the minds which he had caused among the people by his lying words. And his soul began to be harrowed up under a consciousness of his own guilt. Yea, he began to be encircled about by the pains of hell.

⁷And it came to pass that he began to cry unto the people, saying: "Behold! I am guilty! And these men are spotless before God!"

And it came to pass that he began to plead for them from that time forth. But they reviled him, saying: "Art thou also possessed with the devil?"

And it came to pass that they spit upon him, and cast him out from among them, and also all those who believed in the words which had been spoken by Alma and Amulek. And they cast them out and sent men to cast stones at them. ⁸And they brought their wives and children together. And whosoever had believed (or had been taught to believe) in the word of God, they caused that they should be cast into the fire. And they also brought forth their records which contained the holy scriptures, and cast them into the fire also, that they might be burned and destroyed by fire.

⁹And it came to pass that they took Alma and Amulek and carried them forth to the place of martyrdom, that they might witness the destruction of those which were consumed by fire.

¹⁰And it came to pass that when Amulek saw the pains of the women and children which were consuming in the fire, he was also pained. And he saith unto Alma: "How can we witness this awful scene? Therefore, let us stretch forth our hands and exercise the power of God, which is in us, and save them from the flames!"

¹¹But Alma saith unto him:

> The spirit constraineth me, that I must not stretch forth mine hand. For behold, the Lord receiveth them up unto himself in glory. And he doth suffer that they may do this thing (or that the people may do this thing unto them, according to the hardness of their hearts), that the judgments which he shall exercise upon them in his wrath may be just. And the blood of the innocent shall stand as a witness against them, yea, and cry mightily against them at the last day.

¹²Now, Amulek saith unto Alma: "Behold, perhaps they will burn us also!"

¹³And Alma saith: "Be it according to the will of God, the Lord. But behold, our work is not finished. Therefore, they burn us not now."

¹⁴It came to pass that when the bodies of those which had been cast into the fire were consumed, and also the records which were cast in with them, the Chief Judge of the land came and stood before Alma and Amulek as they were bound. And he smote them with his hand upon their cheeks, and saith unto them:

---

to make her a publick example, was minded to put her away privily."

Chapter X [Alma 13:10–15:19]

After what ye have seen, will ye preach again unto this people, that they shall be cast into a lake of fire and brimstone?[a] ¹⁵Behold, ye see that ye had not power to save them which had been cast into the fire. Neither hath God saved them because they were of thy faith.

And the judge smote them again upon their cheeks and asked: "What say ye for yourselves?" >¹⁶Now, this judge was after the order and faith of Nehor, which slew Gideon.<

¹⁷And it came to pass that Alma and Amulek answered him nothing. And he smote them again, and delivered them to the officers to be cast into prison.

¹⁸And it came to pass that when they had been cast into prison three days, there came many lawyers, and judges, and priests, and teachers, which were of the profession of Nehor. And they came in unto the prison to see them. And they questioned them about many words. But they answered them nothing.

¹⁹And it came to pass that the judge stood before them, and saith: "Why do ye not answer the words of this people? Know ye not that I have power to deliver ye up unto the flames?" And he commanded them to speak. But they answered nothing.

²⁰And it came to pass that they departed and went their ways, but came again on the morrow. And the judge also smote them again on their cheeks. And many came forth also, and smote them, saying: "Will ye stand again and judge this people, and condemn our law? If ye have such great power, why do ye not deliver yourselves?"

²¹And many such things did they say unto them, gnashing their teeth upon them, and spitting upon them, and saying: "How shall we look when we are damned?"—²²and many such things. Yea, all manner of such things did they say unto them. And thus they did mock them for many days.

And they did withhold food from them, that they might hunger—and water that they might thirst. And they also did take from them their clothes, that they were naked. And thus they were bound with strong cords and confined in prison.

²³And it came to pass, after they had thus suffered for many days (and it was on the twelfth day in the tenth month in the tenth year of the reign of the judges over the people of Nephi), that the Chief Judge over the land of Ammonihah, and many of their teachers, and their lawyers, went in unto the prison where Alma and Amulek was bound with cords. ²⁴And the Chief Judge stood before them and smote them again, and saith unto them: "If ye have the power of God, deliver yourselves from these bands! And then we will believe that the Lord will destroy this people, according to your words."

²⁵And it came to pass that they all went forth and smote them, saying the same words, even until the last. And when the last had spoken unto them, the power of God was upon Alma and Amulek. And they arose and stood upon their feet. ²⁶And Alma cried, saying: "How long shall we suffer these great afflictions, O Lord? O Lord, give us strength, according to our faith which is in Christ, even unto deliverance!" And they brake the cords with which they were bound. And when the people saw this, they began to flee, for the fear of destruction had come upon them.

²⁷And it came to pass that so great was their fear, that they fell to the earth and did not obtain the outer door of the prison. And the earth shook mightily. And the walls of the prison were rent in twain, so that they fell to the earth. And the Chief Judge, and the lawyers, and priests, and teachers, which smote upon Alma and Amulek, were slain by

---

a. See Revelation 20:14: "And death and hell were cast into the lake of fire. This is the second death."

the fall thereof. ²⁸And Alma and Amulek came forth out of the prison and they were not hurt. For the Lord had granted unto them power, according to their faith, which was in Christ. And they straightway came forth out of the prison. And they were loosed from their bands. And the prison had fallen to the earth. And every soul which was within the walls thereof, save it were Alma and Amulek, were slain. And they straightway came forth into the city.

²⁹Now, the people, having heard a great noise, came running together by multitudes, to know the cause of it. And when they saw Alma and Amulek coming forth out of the prison, and the walls thereof had fallen to the earth, they were struck with great fear, and fled from the presence of Alma and Amulek, even as a goat fleeth with her young from two lions. And thus they did flee from the presence of Alma and Amulek.

[15] ¹And it came to pass that Alma and Amulek were commanded to depart out of that city. And they departed, and came out even into the land of Sidom.

And behold, there they found all the people which had departed out of the land of Ammonihah, who had been cast out and stoned, because they believed in the words of Alma. ²And they related unto them all that had happened unto their wives and children, and also concerning themselves, and of their power of deliverance.

³And also, Zeezrom lay sick at Sidom, with a burning fever, which was caused by the great tribulations of his mind on account of his wickedness. For he supposed that Alma and Amulek was no more. And he supposed that they had been slain by the cause of his iniquity. And by this great sin, and his many other sins, did harrow up his mind until it did become exceeding sore, having no deliverance. Therefore, he began to be scorched with a burning heat.

⁴Now, when he heard that Alma and Amulek was in the land of Sidom, his heart began to take courage. And he sent a message immediately unto them, desiring them to come unto him.

⁵And it came to pass that they went immediately, obeying the message which he had sent unto them. And they went in unto the house unto Zeezrom. And they found him upon his bed, sick—being very low with a burning fever. And his mind also was exceeding sore because of his iniquities. And when he saw them, he stretched forth his hand, and besought them, that they would heal him.

⁶And it came to pass that Alma said unto him, taking him by the hand: "Believest thou in the power of Christ unto salvation?"

⁷And he answered, and said: "Yea, I believe all the words that thou hast taught."

⁸And Alma saith: "If thou believest in the redemption of Christ, thou canst be healed."

⁹And he saith: "Yea, I believe, according to thy words."

¹⁰And then Alma cried unto the Lord, saying: "O Lord, our God! Have mercy on this man. And heal him, according to his faith, which is in Christ!"

¹¹And it came to pass that when Alma had said these words, that Zeezrom leaped upon his feet and began to walk. And this was done to the great astonishment of all the people. And the knowledge of this went forth throughout all the land of Sidom. ¹²And Alma baptized Zeezrom unto the Lord. And he began from that time forth, to preach unto the people. ¹³And Alma established a church in the land of Sidom, and consecrated priests and teachers in the land, to baptize unto the Lord whosoever were desirous to be baptized.

¹⁴And it came to pass that they were many. For they did flock in from all the region

round about Sidom and were baptized. ¹⁵But as to the people that were in the land of Ammonihah, they yet remained a hardhearted and a stiffnecked people. And they repented not of their sins, ascribing all the power of Alma and Amulek to the devil. For they were of the profession of Nehor and did not believe in the repentance of their sins.

¹⁶And it came to pass that Alma and Amulek—Amulek having forsaken all his gold, and his silver, and his precious things (which was in the land of Ammonihah) for the word of God—he being rejected by those which were once his friends, and also by his father, and his kindred—¹⁷therefore, after Alma having established the church at Sidom, seeing a great check, yea, seeing that the people were checked as to the pride of their hearts and began to humble themselves before God, and began to assemble themselves together at their sanctuaries to worship God before the altar—watching and praying continually, that they might be delivered from Satan, and from death, and from destruction— ᵃ

¹⁸Now, as I said, Alma having seen all these things—therefore, he took Amulek and came over to the land of Zarahemla. And took him to his own house, and did administer unto him in his tribulations, and strengthened him in the Lord.

¹⁹And thus ended the tenth year of the reign of the judges over the people of Nephi.

---

a. This is a run-on sentence. There are so many internal clauses that the subject changes from Amulek to Alma without either set of phrases having any resolution. The solution in this edition is the same that the compositor used. Verse 18 is an attempt to start over, but it still focuses on Alma rather than Amulek, who was the original subject.

Chapter XI [Alma 16]

[16] ¹And it came to pass in the eleventh year of the reign of the judges over the people of Nephi, on the fifth day of the second month (there having been much peace in the land of Zarahemla—there having been no wars nor contentions for a certain number of years even until the fifth day of the second month in the eleventh year), there was a cry of war heard throughout the land. ²For behold, the armies of the Lamanites had come in on the wilderness side into the borders of the land, even into the city of Ammonihah and began to slay the people and to destroy the city.

³And now it came to pass, before the Nephites could raise a sufficient army to drive them out of the land, they had destroyed the people which were in the city of Ammonihah, and also some around the borders of Noah, and taking others captive into the wilderness.[a]

⁴Now it came to pass that the Nephites were desirous to obtain those which had been carried away captive into the wilderness. ⁵Therefore, he that had been appointed chief captain over the armies of the Nephites (and his name was Zoram, and he had two sons, Lehi and Aha)[b]— Now, Zoram and his two sons, knowing that Alma was High Priest over the church, and having heard that he had the spirit of prophesy, therefore they went unto him, and desired of him to know whither the Lord would that they should go into the wilderness in search of their brethren who had been taken captive by the Lamanites.

⁶And it came to pass that Alma enquired of the Lord concerning the matter. And Alma returned and said unto them:

> Behold, the Lamanites will cross the river Sidon in the south wilderness, away up beyond the borders of the land of Manti. And behold, and there shall ye meet them, on the east of the river Sidon. And there the Lord will deliver unto thee thy brethren which have been taken captive by the Lamanites.

⁷And it came to pass that Zoram and his sons crossed over the river Sidon with their armies, and marched away beyond the borders of Manti into the south wilderness, which was on the east side of the river Sidon. ⁸And they came upon the armies of the Lamanites. And the Lamanites were scattered and driven into the wilderness.

And they took their brethren which had been taken captive by the Lamanites. And there was not one soul of them which had been lost that were taken captive. And they were brought by their brethren to possess their own lands. ⁹And thus ended the eleventh year of the judges, the Lamanites having been driven out of the land.

And the people of Ammonihah were destroyed. Yea, every living soul of the Ammonihahites were destroyed, and also their great city which they said God could not destroy because of its greatness.

---

a. The word "taking" was changed to "taken" in the 1852 LDS edition. See Skousen, *Analysis of the Textual Variants*, 3:1936. That change matched the verb tense of "had destroyed." The verb "taking" is perfectly understandable but would suggest that "had destroyed" would have needed to change to "having destroyed" to keep the tenses the same.

b. Similar to the end of our current Alma 15:17, there is a transition between a hanging sentence and the beginning with a repetition of the beginning of the verse prior to the time it was slightly derailed. It appears that this is a feature of the dictation of the text.

Chapter XI [Alma 16]

¹⁰But behold, in one day it was left desolate. And their carcasses were mangled by dogs and by wild beasts of the wilderness. ¹¹Nevertheless, after many days their dead bodies were heaped up upon the face of the earth, and they were covered with a shallow covering.

And now, so great was the scent thereof, that the people did not go in to possess the land of Ammonihah for many years. And it was called desolation of Nehors, for they were of the profession of Nehor which were slain. And their lands remained desolate.

¹²And it came to pass that the Lamanites did not come again to war against the Nephites until the fourteenth year of the reign of the judges over the people of Nephi. And thus for three years did the people of Nephi have continual peace in all the land.

¹³And Alma and Amulek went forth, preaching repentance unto the people in their temples, and in their sanctuaries, and also in their synagogues, which was built after the manner of the Jews. ¹⁴And as many as would hear their words unto them—they did impart the word of God without any respects of persons, continually.[a]

¹⁵And thus did Alma and Amulek go forth (and also many more which had been chosen for the work) to preach the word throughout all the land. And the establishment of the church became general throughout the land, in all the region round, about among all the people of the Nephites. ¹⁶And there was no inequality among them. For the Lord did pour out his spirit on all the face of the land, for to prepare the minds of the children of men (or to prepare their hearts) to receive the word which should be taught among them at the time of his coming, ¹⁷that they might not be hardened against the word, that they might not be unbelieving, and go on to destruction—but that they might receive the word with joy—and, as a branch, be grafted into the true vine[b], that they might enter into the rest of the Lord, their God.

¹⁸Now, those priests which did go forth among the people, did preach against all lyings, and deceivings, and envyings, and strifes, and malice, and revilings—and stealing, robbing, plundering, murdering, committing adultery, and all manner of lasciviousness—crying that these things ought not so, to be holding forth things which must shortly come, yea, ¹⁹holding forth the coming of the Son of God—his sufferings, and death, and the resurrection of the dead. ²⁰And many of the people did enquire concerning the place where the Son of God should come. And they were taught that he would appear unto them after his resurrection. And this the people did hear with great joy and gladness.

²¹And now, after the church, having been established throughout all the land, having got the victory over the devil, and the word of God being preached in its purity in all the land, and the Lord pouring out his blessings upon the people—[c] And thus ended the fourteenth year of the reign of the judges over the people of Nephi.

---

a. Modern sensibilities would add a word to this sentence to have it read more smoothly: "And [to] as many as would hear their words unto them—they did impart the word of God without any respects of persons, continually."

b. Echoes language from John 1:15: "I am the true vine, and my Father is the husbandman."

c. Another run-on sentence where verbs such as "having" are never resolved.

Chapter XII [Alma 17–20]

[17] *An account of the sons of Mosiah, which rejected their rights to the kingdom for the word of God and went up to the land of Nephi to preach to the Lamanites. Their sufferings and deliverance. According to the record of Alma.*

¹And now it came to pass that as Alma was a-journeying from the land of Gideon southward, away to the land of Manti—behold, to his astonishment, he met the sons of Mosiah a-journeying towards the land of Zarahemla. ²Now, these sons of Mosiah were with Alma at the time the angel first appeared unto him. Therefore, Alma did rejoice exceedingly to see his brethren. And what added more to his joy, they were still his brethren in the Lord. Yea, and they had waxed strong in the knowledge of the truth. For they were men of a sound understanding, and they had searched the scriptures diligently, that they might know the word of God. ³But this is not all. They had given themselves to much prayer and fasting. Therefore, they had the spirit of prophesy and the spirit of revelation. And when they taught, they taught with power and authority, even as with the power and authority of God.

⁴And they had been teaching the word of God for the space of fourteen years among the Lamanites, having had much success in bringing many to the knowledge of the truth. Yea, by the power of their words many were brought before the altar of God, to call on his name and confess their sins before him.

⁵Now, these are the circumstances which attended them in their journeyings. For they had many afflictions. They did suffer much, both in body and in mind (such as hunger, thirst, and fatigue), and also much labor in the spirit.

⁶Now, these were their journeyings. Having taken leave of their father Mosiah in the first year of the reign of the judges, having refused the kingdom which their father was desirous to confer upon them (and also this was the minds of the people), ⁷nevertheless, they departed out of the land of Zarahemla, and took their swords, and their spears, and their bows, and their arrows, and their slings. And this they done that they might provide food for themselves while in the wilderness. ⁸And thus, they departed into the wilderness, with their numbers, which they had selected to go up to the land of Nephi to preach the word unto the Lamanites.

⁹And it came to pass that they journeyed many days in the wilderness. And they fasted much and prayed much, that the Lord would grant unto them a portion of his spirit to go with them, and abide with them, that they might be an instrument in the hands of God to bring (if it were possible) their brethren the Lamanites to the knowledge of the truth, to the knowledge of the baseness of the traditions of their fathers, which were not correct.

¹⁰And it came to pass that the Lord did visit them with his spirit. And said unto them: "Be comforted." And they were comforted. ¹¹And the Lord said unto them also: "Go forth among the Lamanites, thy brethren, and establish my word. Yet, ye shall be patient in long suffering and afflictions, that ye may show forth good examples unto them in me. And I will make an instrument of thee in my hands, unto the salvation of many souls."

¹²And it came to pass that the hearts of the sons of Mosiah, and also those which were with them, took courage to go forth unto the Lamanites to declare unto them the word of God.

Chapter XII [Alma 17-20]

¹³And it came to pass when they had arriven[a] in the borders of the land of the Lamanites, that they separated themselves, and departed one from another—trusting in the Lord that they should meet again at the close of their harvest.

>For they supposed that great was the work which they had undertaken. ¹⁴And assuredly it was great. For they had undertaken to preach the word of God to a wild, and a hardened, and a ferocious people—a people which delighted in the murdering the Nephites, and robbing and plundering them. And their hearts were set upon riches, or upon gold and silver, and precious stones. Yet, they sought to obtain these things by murdering and plundering, that they might not labor for them with their own hands. ¹⁵Thus, they were a very indolent people, many of whom did worship idols.

And the curse of God had fell upon them because of the traditions of their fathers. Notwithstanding, the promises of the Lord were extended unto them, on the conditions of repentance. ¹⁶Therefore, this was the cause for which the sons of Mosiah had undertaken the work, that perhaps they might bring them unto repentance, that perhaps they might bring them to know of the plan of redemption.[b]<

¹⁷Therefore they, separated themselves, one from another, and went forth among them. Every man alone, according to the word and power of God which was given unto him.

¹⁸Now, Ammon, being the chief among them (or rather he did minister unto them), he departed from them after having blessed them according to their several stations, having imparted the word of God unto them (or administered unto them) before his departure. And thus they took their several journeys throughout the land.

¹⁹And Ammon went to the land of Ishmael, the land being called after the sons of Ishmael (which also became Lamanites). ²⁰And, as Ammon entered the land of Ishmael, the Lamanites took him and bound him (as was their custom to bind all the Nephites which fell into their hands) and carry them before the king. And thus it was left to the pleasure of the king to slay them, or to retain them in captivity, or to cast them into prison, or to cast them out of his land, according to his will and pleasure.

²¹And thus, Ammon was carried before the king which was over the land of Ishmael. And his name was Lamoni. And he was a descendant of Ishmael. ²²And the king enquired of Ammon if it were his desires to dwell in the land among the Lamaintes, or among his people.[c]

²³And Ammon said unto him: "Yea, I desire to dwell among this people for a time. Yea, and perhaps until the day I die."

²⁴And it came to pass that King Lamoni was much pleased with Ammon and caused that his bands should be loosed. And he would that Ammon should take one of

---

a. The Printer's Manuscript had "arrived," but it was changed in proofreading to "arriven."

b. This section could either be an aside or simply part of the description. It follows the theme of the brothers' journey, but the specific language of murdering, plundering, and being a "very indolent people" is Mormon's inserted opinion based on similar statements he makes in his record. The fact that we get a repetitive resumption in verse 17 would further suggest that it is an insertion. In this case, it is not so much an insertion into the planned text but rather Mormon's insertion of his opinions into the record of the sons of Mosiah as found in Alma's personal record.

c. It seems that "or among his people" is a qualifier of "Lamanites" rather than a choice between Lamoni's people or a different city of the Lamanites.

his daughters to wife. ²⁵But Ammon saith unto him: "Nay, but I will be thy servant." Therefore, Ammon became a servant to King Lamoni.

And it came to pass that he was set among other servants to watch the flocks of Lamoni, according to the custom of the Lamanites.

²⁶And it came to pass that after he had been in the service of the king three days, that as he was with the Lamanitish servants a-going forth with their flocks to the place of water, which was called the water of Sebus (and all the Lamanites drive their flocks hither that they might have water).ᵃ ²⁷Therefore, as Ammon and the servants of the king were driving forth their flocks to this place of water, behold, a certain number of the Lamanites who had been with their flocks to water stood and scattered the flock of Ammon and the servants of the king. And they scattered them, insomuch that they fled many ways.

²⁸Now, the servants of the king began to murmur, saying: "Now the king will slay us, as he has our brethren, because their flocks were scattered by the wickedness of these men." And they began to weep exceedingly, saying: "Behold, our flocks are scattered already." ²⁹Now, they wept because of the fear of being slain.

Now, when Ammon saw this, his heart was swollen within him with joy. For said he: "I will show forth my power unto these my fellow servants (or the power which is in me) in restoring these flocks unto the king, that I may win the hearts of these my fellow servants, that I may lead them to believe in my words." ³⁰Now, these were the thoughts of Ammon when he saw the affliction of those which he termed to be his brethren.

³¹And it came to pass that he flattered them by his words, saying: "My brethren! Be of good cheer! And let us go in search of the flocks. And we will gather them together and bring them back unto the place of water. And thus we will reserve the flocks unto the king, and he will not slay us."

³²And it came to pass that they went in search of the flocks. And they did follow Ammon. And they rushed forth with much swiftness, and did head the flocks of the king, and did gather them together again to the place of water.

³³And those men again stood to scatter their flocks. But Ammon saith unto his brethren: "Encircle the flocks round about, that they flee not. And I go and contend with these men, which do scatter our flocks." ³⁴Therefore, they did as Ammon had commanded them. And he went forth and stood to contend with those which stood by the waters of Sebus. And they were not in number a very few. ³⁵Therefore, they did not fear Ammon. For they supposed that one of their men could slay him according to their pleasure. For they knew not that the Lord had promised Mosiah that he would deliver his sons out of their hands. Neither did they know anything concerning the Lord. Therefore, they delighted in the destruction of their brethren. And for this cause they stood to scatter the flocks of the king.

³⁶But Ammon stood forth and began to cast stones at them with his sling, yea, with mighty power he did sling stones amongst them. And thus he slew a certain number of them, insomuch that they began to be astonished at his power. Nevertheless, they were angry because of the slain of their brethren, and they were determined that he should fall. Therefore, seeing that they could not hit him with their stones, they came forth with clubs to slay him.

³⁷But behold, every man that lifted his club to smite Ammon, he smote off their arms

---

a. This sentence is difficult to parse. It could perhaps be resolved by having the next sentence attached to it, but it feels more like the run-on sentences that are seen in other locations.

with his sword. For he did withstand their blows by smiting their arms with the edge of his sword, insomuch that they began to be astonished, and began to flee before him. Yea, and they were not few in number. And he caused them to flee by the strength of his arm.

³⁸Now, six of them had fallen by the sling, but he slew none save it were their leader.[a] And he smote off as many of their arms as was lifted against him. And they were not a few. ³⁹And when he had driven them afar off, he returned. And they watered their flocks, and returned them to the pastures of the king. And then went in unto the king bearing the arms (which had been smote off by the sword of Ammon) of those who sought to slay him. And they were carried in unto the king for a testimony of the things which they had done.

[18] ¹And it came to pass that King Lamoni caused that his servants should stand forth and testify to all the things which they had seen concerning the matter. ²And when they had all testified to the things which they had seen and he had learned of the faithfulness of Ammon in preserving his flocks, and also of his great power in contending against those who sought to slay him—he was astonished exceedingly, and saith: "Surely this is more than a man! Behold! Is not this the Great Spirit, which doth send such great punishments upon this people because of their murders?"

³And they answered the king and said: "Whether he be the Great Spirit, or a man, we know not but this much—we do know that he cannot be slain by the enemies of the king. Neither can they scatter the king's flocks when he is with us, because of his expertness and great strength. Therefore, we know that he is a friend to the king. And now, O king, we do not believe that a man hath such great power. For we know that he cannot be slain."

⁴And now, when the king heard these words, he said unto them: "Now I know that it is the Great Spirit. And he hath come down at this time to preserve your lives, that I might not slay you as I did your brethren. Now, this is the Great Spirit of which our fathers have spoken."

>⁵Now, this was the tradition of Lamoni, which he had received from his father, that there was a Great Spirit. Notwithstanding they believed in a Great Spirit, they supposed that whatsoever they did was right. Nevertheless, Lamoni began to fear exceedingly with fear least he had done wrong in slaying his servants. ⁶For he had slew many of them because their brethren had scattered their flocks at the place of water. And thus, because they had had their flocks scattered, they were slain.

⁷Now, it was the practice of these Lamanites to stand by the waters of Sebus to scatter the flocks of the people, that thereby they might drive away many that were scattered unto their own land—it being a practice of plunder among them.[b]<

---

a. The phrase "with his sword" was added at the end of the sentence in 1837. Skousen notes that without that phrase it would suggest that only the leader had been killed, but other texts indicate that more were slain. Skousen, *Analysis of the Textual Variants*, 3:1972.

b. Mormon inserts information for his readers so they understand the reference to the Great Spirit. He appears to assume that his readers (at least at this point in his record) are familiar with Yahweh (or Jehovah), but he understands that they might not know much about Lamanite religion. Thus, this information is inserted.

The second part of the insertion is the explanation for slaying the servants. The servants had noted this fear earlier when it could have come from Alma's record. In this case, it is Mormon reiterating that information to make the current part of Alma's record more clear. Interestingly, while Mormon understands that the event happened, he does not appear to fully understand the causes or implications of the scattering of the flocks.

⁸And it came to pass that King Lamoni inquired of his servants, saying: "Where is this man that hath such great power?"

⁹And they saith unto him: "Behold, he is feeding thy horses."

>Now, the king had commanded his servants, previous to the time of the watering of their flocks, that they should prepare his horses and his chariots, and conduct him forth to the land of Nephi. For there had been a great feast appointed at the land of Nephi by the father of Lamoni (who was king over all the land).ᵃ<

¹⁰Now, when King Lamoni heard that Ammon was preparing his horses and his chariots, he was more astonished because of the faithfulness of Ammon, saying: "Surely there has not been any servant among all my servants that has been so faithful as this man. For even he doth remember all my commandments, to execute them. ¹¹Now, I surely know that is the Great Spirit. And I would desire him that he come in unto me. But I durst not."

¹²And it came to pass that when Ammon had made ready the horses and the chariots for the king and his servants, he went in unto the king. And he saw that the countenance of the King was changed. Therefore, he was about to return out of his presence. ¹³And one of the king's servants said unto him: "Rabbanah!" >(which is, being interpreted, powerful or great kingᵇ—considering their kings to be powerful)<. And thus, he said unto him: "Rabbanah! The king desireth thee to stay."

¹⁴Therefore, Ammon turned himself unto the king, and saith unto him: "What wilt thou that I should do for thee, O king?" And the king answered him not for the space of an hour, according to their time. For he knew not what he should say unto him.

¹⁵And it came to pass that Ammon said unto him again: "What desirest thou of me?" But the king answered him not.

¹⁶And it came to pass that Ammon, being filled with the spirit of God—therefore, he perceived the thoughts of the king. And he saith unto him: "Is it because that thou hast heard that I defended thy servants and thy flocks, and slew seven of their brethren with the sling and with the sword, and smote off the arms of others in order to defend thy flocks and thy servants? Behold, is it this that causeth thy marvelings? ¹⁷I say unto you, what is it,ᶜ that thy marvelings are so great? Behold, I am a man, and am thy servant. Therefore, whatsoever thou desirest, which is right, that I will do."

¹⁸Now, when the king had heard these words, he marveled again. For he beheld that Ammon could discern his thoughts. But notwithstanding this, King Lamoni did open his mouth, and said unto him: "Who art thou? Art thou that Great Spirit, which knows all things?"

¹⁹Ammon answered, and said unto him: "I am not."

²⁰And the king saith: "How knowest thou the thoughts of my heart? Thou mayest speak boldly and tell me concerning these things. And also, tell me by what power ye slew, and smote off the arms of my brethren that scattered my flocks. ²¹And now, if thou wilt tell me concerning these things, whatsoever thou desirest, I will give unto thee. And if it

---

a. This is not information that would have been part of this quoted section. Mormon may have known it from Alma's record, but it is an aside during this quotation of the exchange between Lamoni and his servants.

b. Uses language from John 1:38: "They said unto him, Rabbi, (which is to say, being interpreted, Master)."

c. The word "what" is retained from the Printer's Manuscript through to our present editions, but it seems awkward. The context suggests that it should be emended to "why." The compositor's comma after "what is it" has been retained as the best way to make sense of the sentence.

Chapter XII [Alma 17–20]

were needed, I would guard thee with my armies. But I know that thou art more powerful than all they. Nevertheless, whatsoever thou desirest of me, I will grant it unto thee."

²²Now, Ammon, being wise yet harmless, he saith unto Lamoni: "Wilt thou hearken unto my words if I tell thee by what power I do these things? And this is the thing that I desire of thee."

²³And the king answered him, and said: "Yea, I will believe all thy words." And thus he was caught with guile.

²⁴And Ammon began to speak unto him with boldness, and said unto him: "Believest thou that there is a God?"

²⁵And he answered unto him: "I do not know what that meaneth."

²⁶And then Ammon saith: "Believest thou that there is a Great Spirit?"

²⁷And he saith: "Yea."

²⁸And Ammon saith: "This is God." And Ammon saith unto him again: "Believest thou that this Great Spirit, which is God, created all things which is in heaven and in the earth?"

²⁹And he saith: "Yea, I believe that he created all things which is in the earth. But I do not know the heavens."

³⁰And Ammon saith unto him: "The heavens is a place where God dwells, and all his holy angels."

³¹And King Lamoni saith: "Is it above the earth?"

³²And Ammon saith: "Yea, and he looketh down upon all the children of men. And he knows all the thoughts and intents of the heart. For by his hand were they all created from the beginning."

³³And King Lamoni saith: "I believe all these things which thou hast spoken. Art thou sent from God?"

³⁴Ammon saith unto him: "I am a man. And man, in the beginning, was created after the image of God. And I am called by his holy spirit to teach these things unto this people, that they may be brought to a knowledge of that which is just and true. ³⁵And a portion of that spirit dwelleth in me, which giveth me knowledge, and also power, according to my faith and desires, which is in God."

³⁶Now, when Ammon had said these words, he began to[a] the creation of the world, and also to the creation of Adam, and told him all the things concerning the fall of man, and rehearsed and laid before him the records of the holy scriptures of the people, and which had been spoken by the prophets, even down to the time that their father Lehi left Jerusalem. ³⁷And he also rehearsed unto them (for it was unto the king and to his servants) all the journeyings of their fathers in the wilderness, and all their sufferings with hunger and thirst, and their travel, etcetera.

³⁸And he also rehearsed unto them concerning the rebellions of Laman and Lemuel, and the sons of Ishmael. Yea, all their rebellions did he relate unto them. And he expounded unto them all the records and scriptures from the time that Lehi left Jerusalem down to the present time. ³⁹But this is not all. For he expounded unto them the plan of redemption, which was prepared from the foundation of the world. And he also made known unto them concerning the coming of Christ. And all the works of the Lord did he make known unto them.

---

a. Although this does not make easy sense, it was left unchanged in printed editions until 1852, when it was changed to "at." Skousen, *Analysis of the Textual Variants,* 3:1990.

⁴⁰And it came to pass that after he had said all these things, and expounded them to the king, that the king believed all his words. ⁴¹And he began to cry unto the Lord, saying: "O Lord! Have mercy, according to thy abundant mercy which thou hast had upon the people of Nephi—have upon me, and my people!"

⁴²And now, when he had said this, he fell unto the earth as if he were dead.

⁴³And it came to pass that his servants took him and carried him in unto his wife, and laid him upon a bed. And he lay as if he were dead for the space of two days and two nights. And his wife, and his sons, and his daughters, mourned over him after the manner of the Lamanites, greatly lamenting his loss.

[19] ¹And it came to pass that after two days and two nights, they were about to take his body and lay it into a sepulcher which they had made for the purpose of burying their dead. ²Now, the queen, having heard of the fame of Ammon, therefore she sent and desired that he should come in unto her.

³And it came to pass that Ammon did as he was commanded and went in unto the queen and desired to know what she would that he should do. ⁴And she saith unto him: "The servants of my husband have made it known unto me that thou art a prophet of a holy god[a], and that thou hast power to do many mighty works in his name. ⁵Therefore, if this is the case, I would that ye should go in and see my husband. For he has been laid upon his bed for the space of two days and two nights. And some say that he is not dead. But others say that he is dead, and that he stinketh, and that he ought to be placed in the sepulcher. But as for myself, to me he doth not stink."

⁶Now, this was what Ammon desired. For he knew that King Lamoni was under the power of God. He knew that the dark veil of unbelief, [b] being cast away from his mind, and the light which did light up his mind (which was the light of the glory of God, which was a marvelous light of his goodness, yea, this light had infused such joy into his soul)—the cloud of darkness having been dispelled, and the light of everlasting light was lit up in his soul. Yea, he knew that this had overcome his natural frame, and he was carried away in God. ⁷Therefore, what the queen desired of him was his only desire. Therefore, he went in to see the king, according as the queen had desired him.

⁸And he saw the king, and he knew that he was not dead. And he saith unto the queen: "He is not dead, but he sleepeth in God. And on the morrow he shall rise again. Therefore, bury him not." ⁹And Ammon saith unto her: "Believest thou this?"

And she said unto him: "I have had no witness save thy word and the word of our servants. Nevertheless, I believe that it shall be according as thou hast said."

¹⁰And Ammon said unto her: "Blessed art thou, because of thy exceeding faith. I say unto thee: Woman, there has not been such great faith among all the people of the Nephites."

¹¹And it came to pass that she watched over the bed of her husband from that time even until that time on the morrow which Ammon had appointed that he should rise.

---

a. This is a Lamanite queen speaking who likely does not yet even know the Nephite God. Therefore, her comment indicates a generic god rather than Yahweh (or Jehovah).

b. The Original Manuscript is extant at this point, and the Printer's Manuscript copied this sentence just as it appeared in the Original. The verb "was" seems required to make sense, but it was not added until the 1906 edition. See Skousen, *Analysis of the Textual Variants*, 3:1999. Based on similar expressions, the phrase "yea, this light had infused" is the intended follow up to "the dark veil of unbelief." The rest are inserted clauses that make it more difficult to parse this as a sentence.

Chapter XII [Alma 17–20]

¹²And it came to pass that he arose, according to the words of Ammon. And as he arose, he stretched forth his hand unto the woman, and said: "Blessed be the name of God, and blessed art thou! ¹³For, as sure as thou livest, behold I have seen my redeemer and he shall come forth and be born of a woman. And he shall redeem all mankind who believe on his name."

Now, when he had said these words, his heart was swollen within him. And he sunk again with joy. And the queen also sunk down, being overpowered by the spirit.

¹⁴Now Ammon, seeing the spirit of the Lord poured out according to his prayers upon the Lamanites, his brethren, which had been the cause of so much mourning among the Nephites (or among all the people of God), because of their iniquities and their traditions.[a] And Ammon fell upon his knees, and began to pour out his soul in prayer, and thanksgiving to God for what he had done for his brethren. And he also was overpowered with joy. And thus, they all three had sunk to the earth.

¹⁵Now, when the servants of the king had saw that they had fallen, they also began to cry unto God. For the fear of the Lord had come upon them also. For it was they which had stood before the king and testified unto him concerning the great power of Ammon.

¹⁶And it came to pass that they did call on the name of the Lord in their might, even until they had all fallen to the earth, save it were one of the Lamanitish women whose name was Abish (she having been converted unto the Lord for many years on account of a remarkable vision of her father—¹⁷thus having been converted to the Lord—never had made it known). Therefore, when she saw that all the servants of Lamoni had fallen to the earth, and also her mistress the queen, and the king, and Ammon, lay prostrate upon the earth, she knew that it was the power of God. And supposing that this opportunity, by making known unto the people what had happened among them—that by beholding this scene it would cause them to believe in the power of God. Therefore, she ran forth from house to house making it known unto the people.

¹⁸And they began to assemble themselves together unto the house of the king. And there came a multitude. And to their astonishment they beheld the king, and the queen, and their servants prostrate upon the earth. And they all lay there as though they were dead. And they also saw Ammon. And behold, he was a Nephite.

¹⁹And now, the people began to murmur among themselves—some saying that it was a great evil that had come upon them (or upon the king and his house) because he had suffered that the Nephite should remain in the land. ²⁰But others rebuked them, saying: "The king hath brought this evil upon his house because he slew his servants who had had their flocks scattered at the waters of Sebus."

²¹And they were also rebuked by those men which had stood at the waters of Sebus, and scattered the flocks which belonged to the king. For they were angry with Ammon because of the number which he had slain of their brethren at the waters of Sebus, while defending the flocks of the king.

²²Now, one of them (whose brother had been slain with the sword of Ammon), being exceeding angry with Ammon, drew his sword and went forth that he might let it fall upon Ammon, to slay him. And as he lifted the sword to smite him, behold, he fell dead.

---

a. It is possible to resolve this sentence if the "and Ammon" is read as intending "therefore Ammon" in the same sentence. As it stands, it is another run-on sentence such as others that appear to follow the pattern of an unresolved -ing verb.

>²³Now, we see that Ammon could not be slain. For the Lord had said unto Mosiah, his father: "I will spare him. And it shall be unto him according to thy faith." Therefore, Mosiah trusted him unto the Lord.[a]<

²⁴And it came to pass that when the multitude beheld that the man had fell dead who lifted the sword to slay Ammon, fear came upon them all, and they durst not put forth their hands to touch him, or any of those which had fallen. And they began to marvel again among themselves—what could be the cause of this great power, or what all these things could mean.

²⁵And it came to pass that there was many among them who said that Ammon was the Great Spirit, and others said that he was sent by the Great Spirit. ²⁶But others rebuked them, all saying that he was a monster which hath been sent from the Nephites to torment us. ²⁷And there were some which said that Ammon was sent by the Great Spirit to afflict them, because of their iniquities, and that it was the Great Spirit that had always attended the Nephites, which had ever delivered them out of their hands. And they said that it was this Great Spirit which had destroyed so many of their brethren, the Lamanites. ²⁸And thus, the contention began to be exceeding sharp among them.

And while they were thus contending, the woman servant (which had caused the multitude to be gathered together) came. And when she saw the contention which was among the multitude, she was exceeding sorrowful, even unto tears.

²⁹And it came to pass that she went and took the queen by the hand, that perhaps she might raise her from the ground. And as soon as she touched her hand, she arose and stood upon her feet, and cried with a loud voice, saying: "O blessed Jesus, who has saved me from an awful hell! O blessed God, have mercy on this people!"

³⁰And when she had said this, she clapped her hands, being filled with joy, speaking many words which were not understood. And when she had done this, she took the King Lamoni by the hand. And behold, he arose, and stood upon his feet. ³¹And he, immediately seeing the contention among his people, went forth and began to rebuke them, and to teach them the words which he had heard from the mouth of Ammon. And as many as heard his words believed, and were converted unto the Lord. ³²But there was many among them who would not hear his words. Therefore, they went their way.

³³And it came to pass that when Ammon arose, he also administered unto them, and also did all the servants of Lamoni. And they did all declare unto the people the selfsame thing, that their hearts had been changed, that they had no more desire to do evil. ³⁴And behold, many did declare unto the people that they had seen angels and had conversed with them. And thus they had told them things of God, and of his righteousness.

³⁵And it came to pass that there was many that did believe in their words. And as many as did believe, were baptized. And they became a righteous people. And they did establish a church among them. ³⁶And thus, the work of the Lord did commence among the Lamanites. Thus, the Lord did begin to pour out his spirit upon them. >And we see that his arm is extended to all people who will repent and believe on his name.[b]<

---

a. This is Mormon's insertion of information that was probably not on the plates. We cannot know whether the sons of Mosiah knew of the Lord's promise to Mosiah, but Mormon knew, and he mentioned it at the time the promise was given and twice now in his recounting of Alma's record.

b. After creating the narrative of the events based on Alma's record, Mormon steps away from his role as narrator of history and shows his overarching interests in the history he is recording. The history serves a theological purpose.

Chapter XII [Alma 17–20]

[20] ¹And it came to pass that when they had established a church in that land, that King Lamoni desired that Ammon should go with him to the land of Nephi, that he might show him unto his father.

²And it came to pass that the voice of the Lord came to Ammon, saying: "Thou shalt not go up to the land of Nephi. For behold, the king will seek thy life. But thou shalt go to the land of Middoni. For behold, thy brother Aaron, and also Muloki, and Ammah, are in prison."

³Now it came to pass that when Ammon had heard this, he saith unto Lamoni: "Behold, my brother, and brethren, are in prison at Middoni. And I go, that I may deliver them."

⁴Now, Lamoni saith unto Ammon: "I know in the strength of the Lord thou canst do all things. But behold, I will go with thee to the land of Middoni, for the king of the land of Middoni (whose name is Antiomno) is a friend unto me. Therefore, I go to the land of Middoni, that I may flatter the king of the land. And he will cast thy brethren out of prison."

Now, Lamoni saith unto him: "Who told thee thy that thy brethren were in prison?"

⁵And Ammon saith unto him: "No one hath told me, save it be God. And he said unto me: 'Go and deliver thy brethren, for they are in prison in the land of Middoni.'"

⁶Now, when Lamoni had heard this, he caused that his servants should make ready his horses and his chariots. ⁷And he saith unto Ammon: "Come. I will go with thee down to the land of Middoni. And there I will plead with the king, that he will cast thy brethren out of prison."

⁸And it came to pass that as Ammon and Lamoni was a-journeying thither, that they met the father of Lamoni, who was king over all the land. ⁹And behold, the father of Lamoni saith unto him: "Why did ye not come to the feast on that great day, when I made a feast unto my sons, and unto my people." ¹⁰And he also saith: "Whither art thou going with this Nephite, which is one of the children of a liar?"

¹¹And it came to pass that Lamoni rehearsed unto him whither he was going. For he feared to offend him. ¹²And he also told him all the cause of his tarrying in his own kingdom, that he did not go unto his father, to the feast which he had prepared.

¹³And now, when Lamoni had rehearsed unto him all these things, behold, to his astonishment his father was angry with him, and saith: "Lamoni. Thou art going to deliver these Nephites, which are sons of liar? Behold, he robbed our fathers, and now his children also are come amongst us, that they may, by their cunning and their lyings, deceive us—that they again may rob us of our property."

¹⁴Now, the father of Lamoni commanded him that he should slay Ammon with the sword. And he also commanded him that he should not go to the land of Middoni, but that he should return with him to the land of Ishmael.

¹⁵But Lamoni saith unto him: "I will not slay Ammon. Neither will I return to the land of Ishmael. But I go to the land of Middoni, that I may release the brethren of Ammon. For I know that they are just men and holy prophets of the true God."

¹⁶Now, when his father heard these words, he was angry with him. And he drew his sword that he might smite him to the earth. ¹⁷But Ammon stood forth, and saith unto him: "Behold, thou shalt not slay thy son. Nevertheless, it were better that he should fall than thee. For behold, he hath repented of his sins. But if thou shouldst fall at this time, in thine anger, thy soul could not be saved. ¹⁸And again, it is expedient that thou

shouldst forbear. For if thou shouldst slay thy son, he being an innocent man, his blood would cry from the ground to the Lord his God for vengeance to come upon thee. And perhaps thou wouldst lose thy soul."

[19] Now, when Ammon had said these words unto him, he answered him, saying: "I know that if I should slay my son that I should shed innocent blood. For it is thou that hast sought to destroy him."

[20] And he stretched forth his hand to slay Ammon. But Ammon withstood his blows, and also smote his arm, that he could not use it.

[21] Now, when the king saw that Ammon could slay him, he began to plead with Ammon, that he would spare his life. [22] But Ammon raised his sword, and said unto him: "Behold, I will smite thee, except thou wilt grant unto me that my brethren may be cast out of prison."

[23] Now the king, fearing that he should lose his life, said: "If thou wilt spare me, I will grant unto thee whatsoever thou wilt ask, even to the half of the kingdom."

[24] Now, when Ammon saw that he had wrought upon the old king according to his desire, he saith unto him: "If thou wilt grant that my brethren may be cast out of prison, and also that Lamoni may retain his kingdom, and that ye be not displeased with him, but grant that he may do according to his own desires in whatsoever thing he thinketh—and then will I spare thee. Otherwise, I will smite thee to the earth."

[25] Now, when Ammon had said these words, the king began to rejoice because of his life. [26] And when he saw that Ammon had no desires to destroy him, and when he also saw the great love he had for his son Lamoni, he was astonished exceedingly, and saith: "Because this is all that thou hast desired, that I would release thy brethren and suffer that my son Lamoni should retain his kingdom, behold, I will grant unto you that my son may retain his kingdom from this time and forever. And I will govern him no more. [27] And I will also grant unto thee, that thy brethren may be cast out of prison. And thou and thy brethren may come unto me in my kingdom. For I shall greatly desire to see thee." For the king was greatly astonished at the words which he had spoken, and also at the words which had been spoken by his son Lamoni. Therefore, he was desirous to learn them.

[28] And it came to pass that Ammon and Lamoni proceeded on their journey towards the land of Middoni.

And it came to pass that Lamoni found favor in the eyes of the king of the land. Therefore, the brethren of Ammon was brought forth out of prison. [29] And when Ammon did meet them, he was exceeding sorrowful. For behold, they were naked, and their skins were worn exceedingly because of being bound with strong cords. And they also had suffered hunger thirst, and all kind of affliction. Nevertheless, they were patient in all their sufferings.

[30] And as it happened, it was their lot to have fallen into the hands of a more hardened and a more stiffnecked people. Therefore, they would not hearken unto their words. And they had cast them out, and had smote them, and had driven them from house to house, and from place to place, even until they had arrived to the land of Middoni. And there they were taken and cast into prison, and bound with strong cords, and kept in prison for many days. And were delivered by Lamoni and Ammon.

Chapter XIII [Alma 21–22]

[21] *An account of the preaching of Aaron and Muloki (and their brethren) to the Lamanites*

¹Now, when Ammon and his brethren separated themselves in the borders of the land of the Lamanites, behold, Aaron took his journey towards the land which was called by the Lamanites Jerusalem, calling it after the land of their fathers' nativity. And it was away, joining the borders of Mormon.

²Now, the Lamanites, and the Amalekites, and the people of Amulon, had built a great city which was called Jerusalem.

³Now, the Lamanites, of themselves, were sufficiently hardened. But the Amalekites and the Amulonites were still harder. Therefore, they did cause the Lamanites that they should harden their hearts, that they should wax stronger in wickedness and their abominations.

⁴And it came to pass that Aaron came to the city of Jerusalem, and firstly began to preach to the Amalekites. And he began to preach to them in their synagogues. For they had built synagogues after the order of the Nehors, for many of the Amalekites and the Amulonites were after the order of the Nehors. ⁵Therefore, as Aaron entered into one of their synagogues to preach unto the people. And, as he was speaking unto them, behold, there arose an Amalekites, and began to contend with him, saying:

> What is that, that thou hast testified? Hast thou seen an angel? Why do not angels appear unto us? Behold, are not this people as good as thy people? ⁶Thou also sayest, except we repent we shall perish. How knowest thou the thought and intent of our heart? How knowest thou that we have cause to repent? How knowest thou that we are not a righteous people? Behold, we have built sanctuaries and we do assemble ourselves together to worship God. We do believe that God will save all men.

⁷Now, Aaron said unto him: "Believest thou that the Son of God shall come to redeem mankind from their sins?"

⁸And the man saith unto him: "We do not believe that thou knowest any such thing. We do not believe in these foolish traditions. We do not believe that thou knowest of things to come, neither do we believe that thy fathers (and also that our fathers) did know concerning the things which they spake of that which is to come."

⁹Now, Aaron began to open the scriptures unto them, concerning the coming of Christ, and also concerning the resurrection of the dead, and that there could be no redemption for mankind, save it were through the death and sufferings of Christ, and the atonement of his blood.

¹⁰And it came to pass that as he began to expound these things unto them, they were angry with him, and began to mock him. And they would not hear the words which he spake. ¹¹Therefore, when he saw that they would not hear his words, he departed out of the synagogue, and came over to a village which was called Ani Anti. And there he found Muloki a-preaching the word unto them, and also Ammah and his brethren. And they contended with many about the word.

¹²And it came to pass that they saw that the people would harden their hearts. Therefore, they departed and came over into the land of Middoni. And they did preach

the word unto many. And few believed on the words which they taught. ¹³Nevertheless, Aaron and a certain number of his brethren were taken and cast into prison. And the remainder of them fled out of the land of Middoni unto the regions round about.

¹⁴And those which were cast into prison suffered many things. And they were delivered by the hand of Lamoni and Ammon. And they were fed and clothed. ¹⁵And they went forth again to declare the word. And thus, they were delivered for the first time out of prison, and thus they had suffered. ¹⁶And they went forth, whithersoever they were led by the spirit of the Lord, preaching the word of God in every synagogue of the Amalekites, or in every assembly of the Lamanites where they could be admitted.

¹⁷And it came to pass that the Lord began to bless them, insomuch that they brought many to the knowledge of the truth. Yea, they did convince many of their sins, and of the tradition of their fathers which were not correct.

> ¹⁸And it came to pass that Ammon and Lamoni returned from the land of Middoni to the land of Ishmael, which was the land of their inheritance. ¹⁹And King Lamoni would not suffer that Ammon should serve him or be his servant. ²⁰But he caused that there should be synagogues built in the land of Ishmael.
>
> And he caused that his people (or the people which was under his reign) should assemble themselves together. ²¹And he did rejoice over them, and he did teach them many things. And he did also declare unto them that they were a people which was under him, and that they were a free people, that they were free from the oppressions of the king, his father—for that his father had granted unto him, that he might reign over the people (which were in the land of Ishmael and in all the land round about). ²²And he also declared unto them that they might have the liberty of worshiping the Lord, their God according to their desires, in whatsoever place they were in—if it were in the land which was under the reign of King Lamoni. ²³And Ammon did preach unto the people of King Lamoni.
>
> And it came to pass that he did teach them all things, concerning things pertaining to righteousness. And he did exhort them daily, with all diligence. And they gave heed unto his word, and they were zealous for keeping the commandments of God.[a]<

[22] ²Now, as Ammon was thus teaching the people of Lamoni continually, we will return to the account of Aaron and his other brethren. For after he departed from the land of Middoni, he was led by the spirit to the land of Nephi, even to the house of the king which was over all the land (save it were the land of Ishmael). And he was the father of Lamoni.

²And it came to pass that he went in unto him (into the king's palace) with his brethren, and bowed himself before the king, and said unto him: "Behold, O king. We are the brethren of Ammon, whom thou hast delivered out of prison. ³And now, O king, if thou wilt spare our lives, we will be thy servants."

And the king saith unto them: "Arise! For I will grant unto you your lives. And I will not suffer that ye shall be my servants, but I will insist that ye shall administer

---

a. At this point, Mormon returns to the story of Ammon and Lamoni. The chapter headings suggest that the different brother's stories were in different sections of Alma's records. Assuming that to be true (and it would be a logical division), this information comes from Ammon's record. Therefore, it is an insertion into the current source from a different one. This is made clear in the following verse, where Mormon explicitly states that he is returning to the account of Aaron and his brethren.

unto me. For I have been somewhat troubled in mind because of the generosity and the greatness of the words of thy brother Ammon. And I desire to know the cause why he has not come up out of Middoni with thee."

⁴And and Aaron saith unto the king: "Behold, the spirit of the Lord hath called him another way. He hath gone to the land of Ishmael to teach the people of Lamoni."

⁵Now, the king saith unto them: "What is this that ye have said concerning the spirit of the Lord? Behold, this is the thing which doth trouble me. ⁶And also, what is this that Ammon said: "If ye will repent ye shall be saved? And if ye will not repent ye shall be cast off at the last day?"

⁷And Aaron answered him, and said unto him: "Believest thou that there is a God?"

And the king saith: "I know that the Amalekites say that there is a God, and I have granted unto them that they should build sanctuaries, that they might assemble themselves together to worship him. And if now thou sayest there is a God, behold, I will believe."

⁸And now, when Aaron heard this, his heart began to rejoice. And he saith: "Behold, assuredly as thou livest, O king, there is a God."

⁹And the king saith: "Is God that Great Spirit that brought our fathers out of the land of Jerusalem?"

¹⁰And Aaron said unto him: "Yea, he is that Great Spirit. And he created all things, both in heaven and in earth. Believest thou this?"

¹¹And he saith: "Yea, I believe that the Great Spirit created all things. And I desire that ye should tell me concerning all these things. And I will believe thy words."

¹²And it came to pass that when Aaron saw that the king would believe his words, he began from the creation of Adam. Reading the scriptures unto the king. How God created man after his own image, and that God gave him commandments, and that because of transgression, man had fallen. ¹³And Aaron did expound unto him the scriptures from the creation of Adam, laying the fall of man before him—and their carnal state, and also the plan of redemption which was prepared from the foundation of the world through Christ for all whosoever would believe on his name. ¹⁴And since man had fallen he could not merit anything of himself, but the sufferings and death of Christ atoneth for their sins through faith and repentance, etcetera—and that he breaketh the bands of death, that the grave shall have no victory, and that the sting of death[a] should be swallowed up in the hopes of glory. And Aaron did expound all these things unto the king.

¹⁵And it came to pass that after Aaron had expounded these things unto him, the king saith: "What shall I do, that I may have this Eternal Life of which thou hast spoken? Yea, what shall I do, that I may be born of God, having this wicked spirit rooted out of my breast, and receive his spirit that I may be filled with joy, that I may not be cast off at the last day?" "Behold," saith he, "I will give up all that I possess, yea, I will forsake my kingdom, that I may receive this great joy."

¹⁶But Aaron saith unto him: "If thou desirest this thing, if thou will bow down before God, yea, if thou repent of all thy sins and will bow down before God, and call on his name in faith, believing that ye shall receive—then shalt thou receive the hope which thou desirest."

¹⁷And it came to pass that when Aaron had said these words, the king did bow

---

a. The phrase "sting of death" appears in 1 Corinthians 15:56.

down before the Lord, upon his knees. Yea, even he did prostrate himself upon the earth. And cried mightily, saying: [18]"O God! Aaron hath told me that there is a God. And if there is a God, and if thou art God, wilt thou make thyself known unto me? And I will give away all my sins to know thee--and, that I may be raised from the dead and be saved at the last day."

And now, when the king had said these words, he was struck as if he were dead.

[19]And it came to pass that his servants ran and told the queen all that had happened unto the king. And she came in unto the king. And when she saw him lay as if he were dead, and also Aaron and his brethren standing as though they had been the cause of his fall, she was angry with them and commanded that her servants (or the servants of the king) should take them and slay them.

[20]Now, the servants had seen the cause of the king's fall. Therefore, they durst not lay their hands on Aaron and his brethren. And they [pled[a]] with the queen, saying: "Why commandest thou that we should slay these men, when behold, one of them is mightier than us all? Therefore, we shall fall before them."

[21]Now, when the queen saw the fear of the servants, she also began to fear exceedingly, lest there should some evil come upon her. And she commanded her servants that they should go and call the people, that they might slay Aaron and his brethren.

[22]Now, when Aaron saw the determination of the queen (and he also knowing the hardness of the hearts of the people), feared lest that a multitude should assemble themselves together, and there should be a great contention and a disturbance among them. Therefore, he put forth his hand and raised the king from the earth and said unto him: "Stand!" And he stood upon his feet, receiving his strength.

[23]Now, this was done in the presence of the queen and many of the servants. And when they saw it, they greatly marveled and began to fear. And the king stood forth and began to minister unto them. And he did minister unto them, insomuch that his whole household were converted unto the Lord.

[24]Now, there was a multitude gathered together, because of the commandment of the queen. And there began to be great murmurings among them, because of Aaron and his brethren. [25]But the king stood forth among them, and administered unto them.

And it came to pass that they were pacified towards Aaron and those which were with him.

[26]And it came to pass that when the king saw that the people were pacified, he caused that Aaron and his brethren should stand forth in the midst of the multitude, and that they should preach the word unto them.

[27]And it came to pass that the king sent a proclamation throughout all the land, among all his people which was in all his land—

> which was in all the regions round about, which was bordering even to the sea on the east and on the west, and which was divided from the land of Zarahemla by a narrow strip of wilderness which ran from the sea east even to the sea west— and round about on the borders of the seashore, and the borders of the wilderness (which was on the north, by the land of Zarahemla, through the borders of Manti

---

a. The transcript of the Printer's Manuscript shows "[f/p]led." The page itself shows that the first letter is formed a little unusually and could be read as /f/. However, there is a loop that would make it /p/, and "pled" is the only word that makes sense.

Chapter XIII [Alma 21–22]

by the head of the river Sidon), running from the east towards the west. And thus were the Lamanites and the Nephites divided.

²⁸Now, the more idle part of the Lamanites lived in the wilderness and dwelt in tents. And they were spread through the wilderness on the west in the land of Nephi, yea, and also on the west of the land of Zarahemla, in the borders by the seashore—and on the west in the land of Nephi in the place of their fathers first inheritance, and thus bordering along by the seashore.

²⁹And also, there was many Lamanites on the east, by the seashore, whither the Nephites had driven them. And thus, the Nephites were nearly surrounded by the Lamanites. Nevertheless, the Nephites had taken possession of all the northern parts of the land, bordering on the wilderness at the head of the river Sidon, from the east to the west, round about on the wilderness sides—on the north, even until they came to the land which they called Bountiful. ³⁰And it bordered upon the land which they called Desolation, it being so far northward that it came into the land which had been peopled, and had been destroyed, of whose bones we have spoken, which was discovered by the people of Zarahemla—it being the place of their first landing.

³¹And they came from there up into the south wilderness. Thus, the land on the northward was called Desolation, and the land on the southward was called Bountiful (it being the wilderness which was filled with all manner of wild animals of every kind), a part of which had come from the land northward for food.

³²And now, it was only the distance of a day and a half's journey for a Nephites on the line Bountiful and the land Desolation, from the east to the west sea. And thus, the land of Nephi, and the land of Zarahemla, was nearly surrounded by water, there being a small neck of land between the land northward and the land southward.

³³And it came to pass that the Nephites had inhabited the land Bountiful, even from the east unto the west sea. And thus, the Nephites, in their wisdom, with their guards and their armies, had hemmed in the Lamanites on the south, that thereby they should have no more possession on the north, that they might not overrun the land northward. ³⁴Therefore, the Lamanites could have no more possessions—only in the land of Nephi and the wilderness round about.

Now, this was wisdom in the Nephites. As the Lamanites were an enemy to them, they would not suffer their afflictions on every hand, and also that they might have a country whither they might flee, according to their desires.ᵃ<

³⁵And now, I after having said this, return again to the account of Ammon, Aaron, Omner, and Himni, and their brethren.

---

a. This aside is triggered by the mention of the whole of the Lamanite lands. Mormon perhaps realized that his future readers would not automatically understand this, so he described the extent of those lands. Being a Nephite, Mormon also wanted to show the division between Lamanite and Nephite lands. Thus, we have a long insertion of geographic information that was not on Mormon's sources. This also means that Mormon is describing conditions from long before his time. He may have had access to accurate records, or these directions may have been his best distillation of the historical information available to him.

Mormon understands that he has wandered far afield, and notes that he will return to the intended story. Apparently, the shift from copying or editing a source to his own long insertion was a sufficient that the re-entry into the story required a new chapter to begin. There is no other discernible reason for this chapter break.

Chapter XIV [Alma 23–26]

[23] ¹Behold, now it came to pass that the king of the Lamanites sent a proclamation among all his people that they should not lay their hands on Ammon, or Aaron, or Omner, or Himni. Nor neither of their brethren which should go forth preaching the word of God, in whatsoever place they should be, in any part of their land. ²Yea, he sent a decree among them, that they should not lay their hands on them to bind them, or to cast them into prison. Neither should they spit upon them, nor smite them, nor cast them out of their synagogues, nor scourge them. Neither should they cast stones at them. But that they should have free access to their houses, and also their temples, and their sanctuaries. ³And thus, they might go forth and preach the word, according to their desires. For the king had been converted unto the Lord, and all his household. Therefore, he sent this proclamation throughout the land unto his people, that the word of God might have no obstruction, but that it might go forth throughout all the land—that his people might be convinced concerning the wicked traditions of their fathers, and that they might be convinced that they were all brethren, and that they had not ought to murder, nor to plunder, nor to steal, nor to commit adultery, nor to commit any manner of wickedness.

⁴And now it came to pass that when the king had sent forth this proclamation, that Aaron and his brethren went forth from city to city, and from one house of worship to another—establishing churches and consecrating priests and teachers throughout the land among the Lamanites—to preach and to teach the word of God among them. And thus, they began to have great success. ⁵And thousands were brought to the knowledge of the Lord. Yea, thousands were brought to believe in the traditions of the Nephites. And they were taught the records and the prophecies which were handed down, even to the present time.

⁶And, as sure as the Lord liveth, so sure as many as believed (or as many as were brought to the knowledge of the truth) through the preaching of Ammon and his brethren, according to the spirit of revelation and of prophecy, and the power of God working miracles in them—yea, I say unto you, as the Lord liveth, as many of the Lamanites as believed in their preaching and were converted unto the Lord, never did fall away.[a] ⁷For they became a righteous people. They did lay down their weapons of their rebellion, that they did not fight against God no more, neither against any of their brethren.

⁸Now, these are they which were converted unto the Lord: ⁹the people of the Lamanites which were in the land of Ishmael, ¹⁰and also of the people of the Lamanites which were in the land of Middoni, ¹¹and also of the people of the Lamanites which were in the city of Nephi, ¹²and also of the people of the Lamanites which were in the land of Shilom, and which were in the land of Shemlon, and in the city of Lemuel, and in the city of Shimnilom. ¹³And these are the names of the cities of the Lamanites which were converted unto the Lord. And these are they that laid down the weapons of their rebellion, yea, all their weapons of war. And they were all Lamanites.

¹⁴And the Amalekites were not converted, save only one. Neither was any of Amulonites. But they did harden their hearts, and also the hearts of the Lamanites in that part of the land, whithersoever they dwelt. Yea, and all their villages, and all their

---

a. This sentence required repetitive resumption to get back on track and complete the idea and the sentence.

cities. ¹⁵Therefore, we have named all the cities of the Lamanites in which they did repent, and come to the knowledge of the truth, and were converted.

¹⁶And now it came to pass that the king, and those people which were converted, were desirous that they might have a name, that thereby they might be distinguished from their brethren. Therefore, the king consulted with Aaron and many of their priests, concerning the name that they should take upon them, that they might be distinguished.

¹⁷And it came to pass that they called their name Anti-Nephi-Lehies.[a] And they were called by this name and were no more called Lamanites. ¹⁸And they began to be a very industrious people. Yea, and they were friendly with the Nephites. Therefore, they did open a correspondence with them. And the curse of God did no more follow them.

[24] ¹And it came to pass that the Amalekites, and the Amulonites, and the Lamanites which were in the land of Amulon, and also in the land of [Helam[b]], and which was in the land of Jerusalem—and in fine, in all the land round about (which had not been converted, and had not taken upon them the name of Anti-Nephi-Lehi)—were stirred up by the Amalekites and by the Amulonites to anger against their brethren. ²And their hatred became exceeding sore against them, even insomuch that they began to rebel against their king, insomuch that they would not that he should be their king. Therefore, they took up arms against the people of Anti-Nephi-Lehi.

³Now, the king conferred the kingdom upon his son. And he called his name Anti-Nephi-Lehi. ⁴And the king died in that self-same year that the Lamanites began to make preparations for war against the people of God.

⁵Now, when Ammon and his brethren (and all those which had come up with him) saw the preparations of the Lamanites to destroy their brethren, they came forth to the land of Midian. And there Ammon met all his brethren. And from thence they came to the land of Ishmael, that they might hold a council with Lamoni, and also with his brother Anti-Nephi-Lehi, what they should do to defend themselves against the Lamanites.

⁷Now, there was not one soul among all the people which had been converted unto the Lord that would take up arms against their brethren. Nay, they would not even make any preparations for war. Yea, and also their king commanded them that they should not.

Now, these are the words which he said unto the people concerning the matter:

I thank my God, my beloved people, that our great God has, in goodness, sent these our brethren (the Nephites) to us, to preach unto us. And to convince us of the traditions of our wicked fathers. ⁸And behold, I thank my great God that he has given us a portion of his spirit to soften our hearts, that we have opened a correspondence with these brethren the Nephites. ⁹And behold, I also thank my God that by opening this correspondence we have been convinced of our sins, and of the many murders which we have committed. ¹⁰And I also thank my God, yea, my great God, that he hath granted unto us that we might repent of these things. And also, that he hath forgiven us of these our many sins and murders which we have committed, and took away the guilt from our hearts through the merits of his Son.

¹¹And now, behold my brethren, since it has been all that we could do (as we were the most lost of all mankind) to repent of all our sins—the many murders which

---

a. The Printer's Manuscript does not have hyphens, rendering this AntiNephiLehies, with the capitalization as indicated. The hyphens have been added according to typical usage.

b. The Printer's Manuscript has "Helaman." See Skousen, *Analysis of the Textual Variants*, 3:1370.

we have committed—and to get God to take them away from our hearts.ᵃ For it was all we could do to repent sufficiently before God, that he would take away our stain.

¹²Now, my best beloved brethren, since God hath taken away our stains, and our swords have become bright—then let us stain our swords no more with the blood of our brethren. ¹³Behold I say unto you, nay, let us retain our swords, that they be not stained with the blood of our brethren! For perhaps, if we should stain our swords again, they can no more be washed bright through the blood of the Son of our great God, which shall be shed for the atonement of our sins. ¹⁴And the great God has had mercy on us, and made these things known unto us, that we might not perish. Yea, and he hath made these things known unto us beforehand, because he loveth our souls as well as he loveth our children. Therefore, in his mercy he doth visit us by his angels, that the plan of salvation might be made known unto us, as well as unto future generations. ¹⁵O, how merciful is our God!

And now behold, since it has been as much as we could do to get our stains taken away from us, and our swords are made bright, let us hide them away, that they may be kept brightᵇ as a testimony to our God at the last day (or at the day that we shall be brought to stand before him, to be judged), that we have not stained our swords in the blood of our brethren since he imparted his word unto us. And has made us clean thereby.

¹⁶And now my brethren, if our brethren seek to destroy us, behold we will hide away our swords, yea, even we will bury them deep in the earth, that they may be kept bright as a testimony that we have never used them, at the last day. And if our brethren destroy us, behold, we shall go to our God and shall be saved.

¹⁷And now it came to pass that when the king had made an end of these sayings, and all the people were assembled together, they took their swords, and all the weapons which were used for the shedding of man's blood, and they did bury them up deep in the earth. And this they did (it being in their view a testimony to God, and also to men) that they never use weapons again for the shedding of man's blood. ¹⁸And this they did (vouching and covenanting with God) that rather than to shed the blood of their brethren, they would give up their own lives. And rather than to take away from a brother, they would give unto him. And rather than to spend their days in idleness, they would labor abundantly with their hands.

>¹⁹And thus we see, that when these Lamanites were brought to believe, and to know the truth, that they were firm, and would suffer even unto death rather than to commit sin. And thus, we see that they buried the weapons of peace (or they buried the weapons of war, for peace).ᶜ<

---

a. The sentence is awkward and does not easily resolve. The "since it has been all that we could do" might have been resolved with "for it was all we could do," but that still seems rather awkward. The first sentence has been left grammatically incomplete to keep the power of the second sentence.

b. The Printer's Manuscript had "kept as bright," but the "as" was crossed out. Compared with another cross-out on the page that has a superlinear replacement, it would appear that this correction occurred during transcription. Therefore, the word "as" has been removed. This also replicates the phrase as it appears in the following verse, confirming that the "as" should be removed.

c. Not only is this an insertion, but it is an important declaration that Mormon will use this incident as a hallmark of true Lamanite conversion. The idea of laying down weapons will be seen again in Mormon's future descriptions of converted Lamanites.

Chapter XIV [Alma 23–26]

²⁰And it came to pass that their brethren, the Lamanites, made preparations for war, and came up to the land of Nephi for the purpose of destroying the king, and to place another in his stead. And also, of destroying the people of Anti-Nephi-Lehi out of the land.

²¹And it came to pass that when the people saw that they were coming against them, they went out to meet them, and prostrated themselves before them to the earth, and began to call on the name of the Lord. And thus, they were in this attitude when the Lamanites began to fall upon them and began to slay them with the sword. ²²And thus, without meeting any resistance, they did slay a thousand and five of them. And we know that they are blessed. For they have gone to dwell with their God.

²³Now, when the Lamanites saw that their brethren would not flee from the sword, neither would they turn aside to the right hand or to the left, but that they would lay down and perish—and praised God, even in the very act of perishing under the sword[a]—²⁴Now, when the Lamanites saw this, they did forbear from slaying them. And there were many whose hearts had swollen in them for those of their brethren who had fallen under the sword. For they repented of the thing which they had done.

²⁵And it came to pass that they threw down their weapons of war and they would not take them again. For they were stung for the murders which they had committed. And they came down, even as their brethren—relying upon the mercies of those whose arms were lifted to slay them.

²⁶And it came to pass that the people of God were joined that day by more than the number which had been slain. And those which had been slain were righteous people. Therefore, we have no reason to doubt but what they are saved. ²⁷And there was not a wicked man slain among them. But there were more than a thousand brought to the knowledge of the truth.

>Thus we see that the Lord worketh in many ways to the salvation of his people.

²⁸Now, the greatest number of those of the Lamanites which slew so many of their brethren were Amalekites, and Amulonites—the greatest number of whom were after the order of the Nehors.

²⁹Now, among those which joined the people of the Lord, there were none which were Amalekites, or Amulonites, or which were of the order of Nehor—but they were actual descendants of Laman and Lemuel. ³⁰And thus, we can plainly discern that after a people has been once enlightened by the spirit of God, and hath had great knowledge of things pertaining to righteousness, and then have fallen away into sin and transgression—they become more hardened. And thus, their state becometh worse than as though they had never known these things.[b]<

---

a. This sentence loses its way and appears to require repetitive resumption to return to the point, which was that the Lamanites "did forbear from slaying them," but the inclusion of the descriptions of the actions of the Anti-Nephi-Lehies caused the derailment of the train of thought.

b. It cannot be known if the accusation that most of those who were doing the killing were Amalekites and Amulonites. However, even if that information were on Alma's record, it is very much in Mormon's interest to highlight their culpability. Mormon makes it explicit that the worst enemies of the Nephites were those who had apostatized from them. It is a theme he will emphasis in his writing. Thus, his inclusion of his moralizing "thus, we can plainly discern" confirms his interest in this aspect—again, whether or not it was information specifically available on the source records.

[25] ¹And behold, Now it came to pass that those Lamanites were more angry because they had slain their brethren. Therefore, they swore vengeance upon the Nephites. And they did no more attempt to slay the people of Anti-Nephi-Lehi at that time—²but they took their armies and went over into the borders of the land of Zarahemla, and fell upon the people which were in the land of Ammonihah and destroyed them.

³And after that they had many battles with the Nephites in the which they were driven and slain—[a] ⁴And among the Lamanites which were slain were most all the seed of Amulon, and his brethren, which were the priests of Noah. And they were slain by the hands of the Nephites. ⁵And the remainder, having fled into the east wilderness, and having usurped the power and authority over the Lamanites—caused that many of the Lamanites should perish by fire, because of their belief—⁶for many of them, after having suffered much loss, and so many afflictions, they began to be stirred up in remembrance of the words which Aaron and his brethren had preached to them in their land. Therefore, they began to disbelieve the traditions of their fathers, and to believe in the Lord and that he gave great power unto the Nephites. And thus, there were many of them converted in the wilderness.

⁷And it came to pass that those rulers which were the remnant of the children of Amulon caused that they should be put to death, yea, all those that believed in these things. ⁸Now, this martyrdom caused that many of their brethren should be stirred up to anger. And there began to be contention in the wilderness. And the Lamanites began to hunt the seed of Amulon and his brethren, and began to slay them. And they fled into the east wilderness. ⁹And behold, they are hunted at this day by the Lamanites.[b] Thus the word of Abinadi was brought to pass which he said concerning the seed of the priests which caused that he should suffer death by fire. ¹⁰For he said unto them: "what ye shall do unto me shall be a type of things to come."

¹¹And now, Abinadi was the first that suffered death by fire because of his belief in God. Now, this is what he meant, that many should suffer death by fire, according as he had suffered. ¹²And he said unto the priests of Noah, that their seed should cause many to be put to death in the like manner as he was, and that they should be scattered abroad, and slain, even as a sheep (having no shepherd) is driven and slain by wild beasts. And now behold, these words were verified. For they were driven by the Lamanites. And they were hunted. And they were smitten.

¹³And it came to pass that when the Lamanites saw that they could not overpower the Nephites, they returned again to their own land. And many of them came over to dwell in the land of Ishmael, and the land of Nephi, and did join themselves to the people of God, which was the people of Anti-Nephi-Lehi. ¹⁴And they did also bury their weapons of war, according as their brethren had. And they began to be a righteous people. And they did walk in the ways of the Lord, and did observe to keep his commandments, and his statutes. ¹⁵Yea, and they did keep the law of Moses. For it was expedient that they should keep the law of Moses as yet, for it was not all fulfilled. But, notwithstanding the law of Moses, they did look forward to the coming of Christ—considering that the law

---

a. The phrase "after that they had many battles" is not resolved.

b. When we have narrative in the text, it is difficult to know if Mormon is copying the narrative or if he is creating it from his source. In this case, however, this sentence must have been copied as it would have been impossible for that condition to be true in Mormon's time. This may suggest that most of this narrative was copied rather than rewritten.

of Moses was a type of his coming—and believing that they must keep those outward performances until the time that he should be revealed unto them.

[16] Now, they did not suppose that salvation came by the law of Moses. But the law of Moses did serve to strengthen their faith in Christ. And thus they did retain a hope, through faith, unto eternal salvation—relying upon the spirit of prophecy which spake of those things to come.

[17] And now behold, Ammon, and Aaron, and Omner, and Himni, and their brethren, did rejoice exceedingly for the success which they had had among the Lamanites—seeing that the Lord had granted unto them according to their prayers, and that he had also verified his word unto them in every particular.

[26] [1] And now, these are the words of Ammon to his brethren, which saith thus:

> My brothers and my brethren! Behold, I say unto you: How great reason have we to rejoice! For, could we have supposed, when we started from the land of Zarahemla, that God would have granted unto us such great blessings?
>
> [2] And now, I ask—what great blessings hath he bestowed upon us? Can ye tell?
>
> [3] Behold! I answer for you. For our brethren, the Lamanites, were in darkness. Yea, even in the darkest abyss. But behold how many of them are brought to behold the marvelous light of God! And this is the blessing which hath been bestowed upon us, that we have been made instruments in the hands of God, to bring about this great work.
>
> [4] Behold, thousands of them do rejoice, and have been brought into the fold of God. [5] Behold, the field was[a] ripe. And blessed are ye. For ye did thrust in the sickle and did reap with your mights.[b] Yea, all the day long did ye labor. And behold the number of your sheaves! And they shall be gathered into the garners, that they are not wasted.
>
> [6] Yea, they shall not be beaten down by the storm at the last day. Yea, neither shall they be harrowed up by the whirlwinds. But, when the storm cometh, they shall be gathered together in their place, that the storm cannot penetrate to them.
>
> Yea, neither shall they be driven with fierce winds whithersoever the enemy listeth to carry them. [7] But behold, they are in the hands of the Lord of the harvest. And they are his. And he will raise them up at the last day.
>
> [8] Blessed be the name of our God! Let us sing to his praise! Yea, let us give thanks to his holy name! For he doth work righteousness forever. [9] For, if we had not come up out of the land of Zarahemla, these our dearly beloved brethren (which have so dearly beloved us) would still have been racked with hatred against us. Yea, and they would also have been strangers to God.

[10] And it came to pass that when Ammon had said these word, his brother Aaron rebuked him, saying: "Ammon! I fear that thy joy doth carry thee away unto boasting!"

[11] But Ammon saith unto him:

> I do not boast in my own strength, or in my own wisdom. But behold, my joy is full.

---

a. The Printer's Manuscript had "is," which was corrected to "was" during proofreading. The Original is extant here and has "was." Skousen, *Analysis of the Textual Variants*, 4:2137.

b. The language alludes to Revelation 14:15. This represents Joseph using language familiar to him, as the specific quotation was not on the plates.

Yea, my heart is brim with joy. And I will rejoice in my God! ¹²Yea, I know that I am nothing as to my strength. I am weak. Therefore, I will not boast of myself. But I will boast of my God! For in his strength, I can do all things.

Yea behold, many mighty miracles we have wrought in this land. For which we will praise his name forever. ¹³Behold how many thousands of our brethren hath he loosed from the pains of hell! And they are brought to sing redeeming love—and this because of the power of his word, which is in us. Therefore, have we not great reason to rejoice?

¹⁴Yea, we have reason to praise him forever. For he is the Most High God, and has loosed our brethren from the chains of hell. ¹⁵Yea, they were encircled about with everlasting darkness and destruction. But behold, he hath brought them into his everlasting light, yea, into everlasting salvation. And they are encircled about with the matchless bounty of his love.

Yea, and we have been instruments in his hands—of doing this great and marvelous work.ª ¹⁶Therefore, let us glory! Yea, we will glory in the Lord! Yea, we will rejoice! For our joy is full. Yea, we will praise our God forever.

Behold, who can glory too much in the Lord? Yea, who can say too much of his great power, and of his mercy—of his long suffering towards the children of men?

Behold, I say unto you, I cannot say the smallest part which I feel. ¹⁷Who could have supposed that our God would have been so merciful as to have snatched us from our awful sinful and polluted state? ¹⁸Behold, we went forth, even in wrath, with mighty threatenings, to destroy his church.

¹⁹O then, why did he not consign us to an awful destruction? Yea, why did he not let the sword of his justice fall upon us, and doom us to eternal despair? ²⁰O! My soul almost (as it were) fleeth at the thought! Behold, he did not exercise his justice upon us—but in his great mercy, hath brought us over that everlasting gulf of death and misery, even to the salvation of our souls.

²¹And now behold, my brethren! What natural man is there that knoweth these things? I say unto you, there is none that knoweth these things, save it be the penitent. ²²Yea, he that repenteth, and exerciseth faith, and bringeth forth good works, and prayeth continually (without ceasing)—unto such it is given to know the mysteries of God.ᵇ Yea, unto such it shall be given to reveal things which never have been revealed. Yea, and it shall be given unto such, to bring thousands of souls to repentance, even as it hath been given unto us to bring these, our brethren, to repentance.

²³Now, do ye remember, my brethren that we said unto our brethren in the land of Zarahemla: "We go up to the land of Nephi, to preach unto our brethren the Lamanites?" And they laughed us to scorn.ᶜ ²⁴For they said unto us: "Do ye suppose that ye can bring the Lamanites to the knowledge of the truth? Do ye suppose that ye can convince the Lamanites of the incorrectness of theᵈ traditions of

---

a. See Isaiah 29:14: "Therefore, behold, I will proceed to do a marvellous work among this people, even a marvellous work and a wonder."

b. The phrase "mystery of God" appears in 1 Corinthians 4:1, Colossians 2:2, and Revelation 10:7.

c. Echoes language from Psalm 22:7: "All they that see me laugh me to scorn."

d. The Printer's Manuscript had "convince the Lamanites of the traditions of their fathers." Oliver Cowdery later added "incorrectness of the." Skousen suggests that the correction was made when Cowdery read the text back to Joseph Smith as part of proofing. Royal Skousen, *Analysis of the Textual Variants*, 4:2142.

Chapter XIV [Alma 23–26]

their fathers—as stiffnecked a people as they are—whose hearts delighteth in the shedding of blood, whose days have been spent in the grossest iniquity, whose ways have been the ways of a transgressor from the beginning?"

Now my brethren, ye remember that this was their language. ^{25}And moreover, they did say: "Let us take up arms against them, that we destroy them and their iniquity out of the land, lest they overrun us and destroy us." ^{26}But behold, my beloved brethren, we came into the wilderness—not with the intent to destroy our brethren—but with the intent that perhaps we might save some few of their souls.

^{27}Now, when our hearts were depressed and we were about to turn back, behold, the Lord comforted us, and said: "Go amongst thy brethren, the Lamanites, and bear with patience thine afflictions. And I will give unto thee success."

^{28}And now behold, we have come, and been forth amongst them! And we have been patient in our sufferings. And we have suffered every privation.

Yea, we have traveled from house to house, relying upon the mercies of the world—not upon the mercies of the world alone, but upon the mercies of God.^{a} ^{29}And we have entered into their houses and taught them. And we have taught them in their streets. Yea, and we have taught them upon their hills. And we have also entered into their temples and their synagogues, and taught them.

And we have been cast out, and mocked, and spit upon, and smote upon our cheeks. And we have been stoned, and taken and bound with strong cords, and cast into prison. And through and the power and wisdom of God, we have been delivered again. ^{30}And we have suffered all manner of afflictions.

And all this, that perhaps we might be the means of saving some soul. And we supposed that our joy would be full, if perhaps we could be the means of saving some.

^{31}Now behold, we can look forth and see the fruits of our labors. And are they few? I say unto you, nay, they are many! Yea, and we can witness of their sincerity because of their love towards their brethren, and also towards us. ^{32}For behold, they had rather sacrifice their lives than even to take the life of their enemy. And they have buried their weapons of war deep in the earth because of their love towards their brethren.

^{33}And now behold, I say unto you: Has there been so great love in all the land? Behold, I say unto you, nay! There has not, even among the Nephites—^{34}for behold, *they* would take up arms against their brethren. *They* would not suffer themselves to be slain. But behold, how many of *these* have laid down their lives!^{b} And we know that they have gone to their God, because of their love, and of their hatred to sin.

^{35}Now, have we not reason to rejoice? Yea, I say unto you: There never was men that had so great reason to rejoice as we since the world began! Yea, and my joy is carried away, even unto boasting in my God. For he has all power, all wisdom, and all understanding. He comprehendeth all things, and he is a merciful being, even unto salvation to those who will repent and believe on his name.

^{36}Now, if this is boasting, even so will I boast! For this is my life and my light—my joy and my salvation, and my redemption from everlasting wo.

---

a. This sentence doesn't use the corrective "or," but it does have a phrase that was intended to correct an imprecise phrase just prior.

b. Italics have been added to "they" and "these" to help clarify the people referred to. "They" are the Nephites, and "these" are the Anti-Nephi-Lehies.

Yea, blessed is the name of my God who hath been mindful of this people (which are a branch of the tree of Israel) and hath been lost from its body in a strange land.

Yea, I say blessed be the name of my God, who hath been mindful of us wanderers in a strange land. ³⁷Now my brethren, we see that God is mindful of every people, in whatsoever land they may be in.

Yea, he numbereth his people. And his bowels of mercy is over all the earth. Now, this is my joy, and my great thanksgiving.

Yea, and I will give thanks unto my God forever. Amen.

Chapter XV [Alma 27–29]

[27] ¹Now it came to pass that when the Lamanites which had gone to war against the Nephites had found, after their many struggles for to destroy them—that it was in vain to seek their destruction, they returned again to the land of Nephi.

²And it came to pass that the Amalekites, because of their loss, were exceeding angry. And when they saw that they could not seek revenge from the Nephites, they began to stir up the people in anger against their brethren, the people of Anti-Nephi-Lehi. Therefore, they began again to destroy them.

³Now, this people again refused to take their arms. And they suffered themselves to be slain, according to the desires of their enemies.

⁴Now, when Ammon and his brethren saw this work of destruction among those who they so dearly beloved, and among those who had so dearly beloved them (for they were treated as though they were the angels sent from God to save them from everlasting destruction)—therefore, when Ammon and his brethren saw this great work of destruction, they were moved with compassion.[a] And they said unto the king: ⁵"Let us gather together this people of the Lord. And let us go down to the land of Zarahemla, to our brethren the Nephites, and flee out of the hands of our enemies, that we be not destroyed."

⁶But the king saith unto them: "Behold, the Nephites will destroy us, because of the many murders and sins we have committed against them."

⁷And Ammon saith: "I will go and enquire of the Lord. And if he saith unto us: 'go down unto our brethren.' Will ye go?"

⁸And the king saith unto him: "Yea, if the Lord saith unto us 'go,' we will go down unto our brethren. And we will be their slaves until we repair unto them the many murders and sins which we have committed against them."

⁹But Ammon saith unto him: "It is against the law of our brethren, which was established by my father, that there should be any slaves among them. Therefore, let us go down and rely upon the mercies of our brethren."

¹⁰But the king saith unto him: "Inquire of the Lord. And if he saith unto us 'go,' we will go. Otherwise, we will perish in the land."

¹¹And it came to pass that Ammon went, and inquired of the Lord. And the Lord said unto him: ¹²"Get this people out of this land, that they perish not! For Satan hath great hold on the hearts of the Amalekites, which do stir up the Lamanites to anger against their brethren, to slay them. Therefore, get thee out of this land! And blessed art this people, in this generation. For I will preserve them."

¹³And now it came to pass that Ammon went, and told the king all the words which the Lord had said unto him.

¹⁴And it came to pass that they gathered together all their people, yea, all the people of the Lord—and did gather together all their flocks, and herds, and departed out of the land, and came into the wilderness[b] which divided the land of Nephi from the land of Zarahemla, and came over near the borders of the land.

¹⁵And it came to pass that Ammon saith unto them: "Behold, I and my brethren will

---

a. This is an interesting sentence. It appears to fit the nature of a run-on sentence, but apparently either the writer or the translator realized this and used repetitive resumption to start the idea over again.

b. The scribe originally copied "and it came to pass," but words were crossed out to put the correct phrase in place. Certainly, the frequency of "and it came to pass" led to that particular error. Since there

go forth into the land of Zarahemla, and ye shall remain here until we return. And we will try the hearts of our brethren, whether they will that ye shall come into their land."

[16]And it came to pass that as Ammon was going forth into the land, that he and his brethren met Alma, over in the place of which has been spoken. And behold, this was a joyful meeting.

[17]Now, the joy of Ammon was so great, even that he was full. Yea, he was swallowed up in the joy of his God, even to the exhausting of his strength. And he fell again to the earth.

[18]Now, was not this exceeding joy? Behold! This is joy which none receiveth, save it be the truly penitent and humble seeker of happiness.

[19]Now, the joy of Alma in meeting his brethren was truly great. And also the joy of Aaron, of Omner, and Himni. But behold, their joy was not that to exceed their strength.

[20]And now it came to pass that Alma conducted his brethren back to the land of Zarahemla, even to his own house.

[21]And it came to pass that they went and told the Chief Judge all the things which had happened unto them in the land of Nephi, among their brethren the Lamanites.

[22]And it came to pass that the Chief Judge sent a proclamation throughout all the land, desiring the voice of the people concerning the admitting their brethren, which were the people of Anti-Nephi-Lehi.

And it came to pass that the voice of the people came saying:

> Behold, we will give up the land of Jershon (which is on the east by the sea, which joins the land Bountiful, which is on the south of the land Bountiful). And this land Jershon is the land which we will give unto our brethren for an inheritance. [23]And behold, we will set our armies between the land Jershon and the land Nephi, that we may protect our brethren in the land of Jershon. And this we do for our brethren, on account of their fear to take up arms against their brethren, lest they should commit sin. And this, their great fear, came because of their sore repentance, which they had on account of the many murders and their awful wickedness.
>
> [24]And now behold, this will we do unto our brethren, that they may inherit the land Jershon. And we will guard them from their enemies by our armies on conditions that they will give us a portion of their substance, to assist us, that we may maintain our armies.

[25]Now it came to pass that when Ammon had heard this, he returned to the people of Anti-Nephi-Lehi (and also Alma with him), into the wilderness where they had pitched their tents, and made known unto them all these things. And Alma also related unto them his conversion, with Ammon, and Aaron, and his brethren.

And it came to pass that it did cause great joy among them.

[26]And it came to pass that they went down into the land of Jershon and took possession of the land of Jershon. And they were called by the Nephites the people of Ammon. Therefore, they were distinguished by that name ever after.

>[27]And they were among the people of Nephi, and also numbered among the

---

were no punctuation marks, it would have been an assumed new sentence, rather than a continuation which the correct phrase was.

Chapter XV [Alma 27–29]

people which were of the church of God. And they were also distinguished for their zeal towards God, and also towards men. For they were perfectly honest and upright in all things. And they were firm in the faith of Christ, even unto the end. ²⁸And they did look upon shedding the blood of their brethren with the greatest abhorrence. And they never could be prevailed upon to take up arms against their brethren. And they never did look upon death with any degree of terror. For their hope, and views of Christ, and the resurrection.ᵃ Therefore, death was swallowed up to them by the victory of Christ over it.ᵇ ²⁹Therefore, they would suffer death in the most aggravating and distressing manner which could be inflicted by their brethren before they would take the sword or the cimeter to smite them. ³⁰And thus, they were a zealous, and beloved people—a highly favored people of the Lord.ᶜ<

[28] ¹And now it came to pass that after the people of Ammon were established in the land of Jershon, and a church also established in the land of Jershon, and the armies of the Nephites were set round about the land of Jershon, yea, in all the borders round about the land of Zarahemla—behold, the armies of the Lamanites had followed their brethren into the wilderness. ²And thus, [tᵈ] a tremendous battle, yea, even such an one as never had been known among all the people in the land from the time Lehi left Jerusalem. Yea, and tens of thousands of the Lamanites were slain and scattered abroad. ³Yea, and also there was a tremendous slaughter among the people of Nephi. Nevertheless, the Lamanites were driven, and scattered, and the people of Nephi returned again to their land.

⁴And now, this was a time that there was a great mourning and lamentation heard throughout all the land, among all the people of Nephi. ⁵Yea, the cry of widows mourning for their husbands—and also of fathers mourning for their sons—and the daughter for the brother, yea, the brother for the father. And thus, the cry of mourning was heard among every one of them, a-mourning for their kindred which had been slain.

⁶And now, surely this was a sorrowful day. Yea, a time of solemnity, and a time of much fasting and prayer. ⁷And thus ended the fifteenth year of the reign of the judges over the people of Nephi.

⁸And this is the account of Ammon and his brethren their journeyings into the land of Nephi, their sufferings in the land—their sorrows and their afflictions, and their incomprehensible joy—and the reception and safety of the brethren in the land of Jershon. And now may the Lord, the redeemer of all men, bless their souls forever.

⁹And this is the account of the wars and contentions among the Nephites, and also the wars between the Nephites and the Lamanites. And the fifteenth year of the reign of the judges is ended.

>¹⁰And from the first year to the fifteenth has brought to pass the destruction of many thousand lives. Yea, it has brought to pass an awful scene of bloodshed. ¹¹And the bodies of many thousands are laid low in the earth, while the bodies

---

a. The phrase "for their hope" appears to have the meaning "because of their hope."
b. Uses language from Isaiah 25:8: "He will swallow up death in victory."
c. This is Mormon's moralizing conclusion more than an aside. It has been set apart because it is his own insights and not necessarily taken from his source text.
d. Joseph Smith added "there was" for the 1837 edition. Without those two words, the sentence would be incomplete. Nevertheless, those words were not in the original, which is extant at this point. Skousen, *Analysis of the Textual Variants*, 4:2182.

of many thousands are moldering in heaps upon the face of the earth. Yea, and many thousands are mourning for the loss of their kindred, because they have reason to fear (according to the promises of the Lord), that they are consigned to a state of endless wo—¹²while many thousands of others truly mourn for the loss of their kindred, yet they rejoice, and exult in the hope, yea, and even know (according to the promises of the Lord), that they are raised to dwell at the right hand of God, in a state of never-ending happiness. ¹³And thus we see how great the inequality of man is, because of sin and transgression—and the power of the devil, which comes by the cunning plans which he hath devised to ensnare the hearts of men. And thus, we see the great call of the diligence of men to labor in the vineyards of the Lord. ¹⁴And thus, we see the great reason of sorrow, and also of rejoicing—sorrow because of death and destruction among men—and joy because of the Light of Christ unto life.[a]

[29] ¹O that I were an angel and could have the wish of mine heart—that I might go forth and speak with the trump of God, with a voice to shake the earth, and cry repentance unto every people! ²Yea, I would declare unto every soul, as with the voice of thunder, repentance and the plan of redemption—that they should repent and come unto our God, that there might be no more sorrow upon all the face of the earth.

³But behold, I am a man and do sin in my wish. For I had ought to be content with the things which the Lord hath allotted unto me. ⁴I had not ought to harrow up in my desires the firm decree of a just God. For I know that he granteth unto men according to their desires, whether it be unto death or unto life. Yea, I know that he allotteth unto men, yea, decreeth unto them—decrees which are unalterable, according to their wills—whether it be unto salvation or unto destruction. ⁵Yea, and I know that good and evil hath come before all men, or he that knoweth not good from evil is blameless. But he that knoweth good and evil, to him it is given according to his desires—whether he desireth good or evil, life or death, joy or sorrow, or remorse of conscience.

⁶Now, seeing that I know these things, why should I desire more than to perform the work to which I have been called? ⁷Why should I desire that I was an angel, that I could speak unto all the ends of the earth? ⁸For behold, the Lord doth grant unto all nations—of their own nation and tongue, to teach his word. Yea, in wisdom, all that he seeth fit that they should have. Therefore, we see that the Lord doth counsel in his wisdom, according to that which is just and true.

⁹I know that which the Lord hath commanded me, and I glory in it. I do not glory of myself, but I glory in that which the Lord hath commanded me. Yea, and this is my glory, that perhaps I may be an instrument in the hands of God, to bring some soul to repentance. And thus, this is my joy.

¹⁰And behold, when I see many of my brethren truly penitent and coming to

---

a. The closing of the fifteenth year would have been the end of the chapter, but Mormon feels moved to elaborate on the contrast between the misery of the wars of men compared to the goodness of God. There is no original chapter ending at this point because what follows is Mormon's elaboration on that theme of goodness. All of the modern chapter 29 is Mormon's reaction to the end of the war, even though he has given little detail for that war.

Chapter XV [Alma 27–29]

the Lord, their God, then is my soul filled with joy. Then do I remember what the Lord has done for me.

Yea, even that he hath heard my prayer.

Yea, then do I remember his merciful arm, which he extended towards me.

[11]Yea, and I also remember the captivity of my fathers. For I surely do know that the Lord did deliver them out of bondage, and by this did establish his church.

Yea, the Lord God—the God of Abraham, the God of Isaac, and the God of Jacob—did deliver them out of bondage.

[12]Yea, I have always remembered the captivity of my fathers. And that same God who delivered them out of the hands of the Egyptians, did deliver them out of bondage.

[13]Yea, and that same God did establish his church among them.

Yea, and that same God hath called me by a holy calling, to preach the word unto this people. And hath given me much success, in the which my joy is full. [14]But I do not joy in my own success alone.ut my joy is more full because of the success of my brethren, which have been up to the land of Nephi.

[15]Behold, they have labored exceedingly, and have brought forth much fruit. And how great shall be their reward!

[16]Now, when I think of the success of these my brethren, my soul is carried away, even to the separation of it from the body (as it were)—so great is my joy!

[17]And now, may God grant unto these, my brethren, that they may sit down in the kingdom of God. Yea, and also all those which are the fruit of their labors, that they may go no more out, but that they may praise him forever. And may God grant that it may be done, according to my words, even as I have spoken. Amen.<

Chapter XVI [Alma 30–35]

[30] ¹Behold, now it came to pass that after the people of Ammon were established in the land of Jershon, yea, and also after the Lamanites were driven out of the land, and their dead were buried by the people of the land—(²now, their dead were not numbered because of the greatness of their numbers neither were the dead of the Nephites numbered)—but it came to pass that after they had buried their dead,[a] and also after the days of fasting and mourning and prayer—[b]

And it was in the sixteenth year of the reign of the judges over the people of Nephi, there began to be continual peace throughout all the land. ³Yea, and the people did observe to keep the commandments of the Lord. And they were strict in observing the ordinances of God, according to the law of Moses. For they were taught to keep the law of Moses until it should be fulfilled. ⁴And thus the people did have no disturbance in all the sixteenth year of the reign of the judges over the people of Nephi.

⁵And it came to pass in the seventeenth year of the reign of the judges, there was continual peace.

⁶But, it came to pass in the latter end of the seventeenth year, there came a man into the land of Zarahemla. And he was anti Christ,[c] for he began to preach unto the people against the prophecies which had been spoken by the prophets concerning the coming of Christ.

⁷Now, there was no law against a man's belief. For it was strictly contrary to the commands of God that there should be a law which would bring men on to unequal grounds. ⁸For thus saith the scripture: "Chose ye this day whom ye will serve."[d] ⁹Now, if a man desired to serve God it was his privilege (or rather if he believed in God it was his privilege), to serve him. But if he did not believe in him, there was no law to punish him. ¹⁰But, if he murdered, he was punished unto death. And if he robbed, he was also punished. And if he stole, he was also punished. And if he committed adultery, he was also punished. Yea, for all this wickedness they were punished. ¹¹For there was a law that men should be judged according to their crimes. Nevertheless, there was no law against a man's belief. Therefore, a man was punished only for the crimes which he had done. Therefore, all men were on equal grounds.

¹²And this anti Christ, whose name was Korihor (and the law could have no hold upon him)[e] —and he began to preach unto the people that there should be no Christ. And after this manner did he preach, saying:

---

a. An example of sentence-level repetitive resumption.

b. This sentence might feel completed with the second half of the next sentence. Nevertheless, it has been left unresolved because the statement of the year and then the information that there was peace is a standard set. They are typically separate sentences, so they are left as such here. All of verse 1 and the first half of verse 2 are a repetitive resumption to recover from the long insertion that ended with Alma's soliloquy.

c. This is usually rendered Anti-Christ, after the biblical usage. That is not the meaning in the Book of Mormon. These are not titles, but descriptions. Each person so indicated is simply preaching against the idea of Christ. It is a theological argument, not a theological entity.

d. See Joshua 24:15.

e. Parentheses are added to the Printer's Manuscript as part of the editing for the 1837 edition. They remove the final "and" that I have placed after the last parenthesis. See *Printer's Manuscript of the Book of Mormon*, 1:509.

¹³O ye that are bound down under a foolish and a vain hope! Why do ye yoke yourselves with such foolish things? Why do ye look for a Christ? For no man can know of anything which is to come. ¹⁴Behold, these things which ye call prophecies, which ye say are handed down by holy prophets—behold, they are foolish traditions of your fathers. ¹⁵How do ye know of their surety? Behold, ye cannot know of things which ye do not see. Therefore, ye cannot know that there shall be a Christ.

¹⁶Ye look forward, and say that ye see a remission of your sins. But behold, it is the effects of a frenzied mind. And this derangement of your minds comes because of the tradition of your fathers, which lead you away into a belief of things which are not so.

¹⁷And many more such things did he say unto them, telling them that there could be no atonement made for the [sins of men[a]]. But every man faired in this life according to the management of the creature. Therefore, every man prospered, according to his genius, and that every man conquered according to his strength. And whatsoever a man did was no crime. ¹⁸And thus, he did preach unto them—leading away the hearts of many, causing them to lift up their heads in their wickedness. Yea, leading away many women, and also men, to commit whoredoms—telling them that when a man was dead, that was the end thereof.

¹⁹Now, this man went over to the land of Jershon also, to preach these things among the people of Ammon (which were once the people of the Lamanites). ²⁰But behold, they were more wise then many of the Nephites. For they took him, and bound him, and carried him before Ammon (which was a High Priest over that people).

²¹And it came to pass that he caused that he should be carried out of the land.

²²And it came to pass that he came over into the land of Gideon and began to preach unto them also. And here he did not have much success. For he was taken, and bound, and carried before the High Priest, and also the Chief Judge over the land.

And it came to pass that the High Priest saith unto him: "Why do ye go about perverting the ways of the Lord? Why do ye teach this people that there shall be no Christ—to interrupt their rejoicings? Why do ye speak against all the prophecies of the holy prophets?"

²³Now, the High Priest's name was Giddonah. And Korihor saith unto him:

> Because I do not teach the foolish traditions of your fathers, and because I do not teach this people to bind themselves down under the foolish ordinances and performances, which are laid down by ancient priests to usurp power and authority over them, to keep them in ignorance, that they may not lift up their heads, but be brought down, according to thy words.

²⁴Ye say that this people is a free people. Behold, I say they are in bondage.

Ye say that those ancient prophecies are true. Behold, I say that ye do not know that they are true.

²⁵Ye say that this people is a guilty and a fallen people because of the transgression of a parent. Behold, I say that a child is not guilty because of its parents.

²⁶And ye also say that Christ shall come. But behold, I say that ye do not know that there shall be a Christ. And ye say also that he shall be slain for the sins of the world.

---

a. The Printer's Manuscript has "sins of the world," but the original was "sins of men." There is a superlinear correction, which is the text in all printed editions.

²⁷And thus, ye lead away this people after the foolish traditions of your fathers, and according to your own desires. And ye keep them down, even as it were in bondage, that ye may glut yourselves with the labors of their hands, that they durst not look up with boldness—and that they durst not enjoy their rights and privileges. ²⁸Yea, they durst not make use of that which is their own, lest they should offend their priests which do yoke them according to their desires, and hath brought them to believe (by their traditions and their dreams, and their whims, and their visions, and their pretended mysteries), that they should (if they did not do according to their words) offend some unknown being, which they say is God—a being which never hath been seen, nor known, which never was, nor never will be.

²⁹Now, when the High Priest and the Chief Judge saw the hardness of his heart, yea, when they saw that he would revile even against God, they would not make any reply to his words. But they caused that he should be bound. And they delivered him up into the hands of the officers. And sent him to the land of Zarahemla, that he might be brought before Alma and the Chief Judge which was Governor over all the land.

³⁰And it came to pass that when he was brought before Alma and the Chief Judge, that he did go on in the same manner as he did in the land of Gideon. Yea, he went on to blasphemy.[a] ³¹And he did rise up in great swelling words before Alma, and did revile against the priests and teachers, accusing them of leading away the people after the silly traditions of their fathers for the sake of glutting in the labors of the people.

³²Now, Alma saith unto him:

Thou knowest that we do not glut ourselves upon the labors of this people. For behold, I have labored, even from the commencement of the reign of the judges until now, with mine own hands for my support—notwithstanding my many travels round about the land to declare the word of God unto my people. ³³And notwithstanding the many labors which I have performed in the church, I have never received so much as even one senine for my labor. Neither hath any of my brethren, save it were in the Judgment Seat. And then we have received only according to law for our time.

³⁴And now, if we do not receive any thing[b] for our labor in the church, what doth it profit us to labor in the church, save it were to declare the truth, that we may have rejoicings in the joy of our brethren? ³⁵Then why sayest thou that we preach unto this people to get gain, when thou of thyself knowest that we receive no gain? And now, believest thou that we deceive this people, that causeth such joy in their hearts?

³⁶ And Korihor answered him: "Yea."

³⁷And then Alma saith unto him: "Believest thou that there is a God?"

³⁸And he answered: "Nay."

³⁹Now, Alma saith unto him:

If[c] ye deny again that there is a God and also deny the Christ.[d] For behold I say unto you, I know there is a God, and also that Christ shall come. ⁴⁰And now what

---

a. "Blasphemy" was changed to "blaspheme" in the 1830 edition. The original is not extant.

b. This is left as it appears in the Printer's Manuscript rather than closing up the space to "anything."

c. Joseph Smith changed "if" to "will" in the 1837 edition. That change makes much better sense. Skousen, *Analysis of the Textual Variants*, 4:2231–32. It has been left as another awkward sentence.

d. This is an example of an *if>and* construction that has the meaning of *if>then* in expected English.

evidence have ye that there is no God? Or that Christ cometh not? I say unto you that ye have none, save it be your word only.

⁴¹But behold, I have all things as a testimony that these things are true. And ye also have all things as a testimony unto you, that they are true. And will ye deny them?

Believest thou that these things are true? ⁴²Behold, I know that thou believest. But thou art possessed with a lying spirit, and ye have put off the spirit of God, that it may have no place in you. But the devil hath power over you, and he doth carry you about—working devices that he may destroy the children of God.

⁴³And now Korihor saith unto Alma: "If thou wilt show me a sign, that I may be convinced that there is a God, yea, show unto me that he hath power—and then will I be convinced of the truth of thy words."

⁴⁴But Alma saith unto him:

Thou hast had signs enough. Will ye tempt your God? Will ye say, "show unto me a sign" when ye have the testimony of all these, thy brethren, and also all the holy prophets? The scriptures are laid before thee. Yea, and all things denote there is a God. Yea, even the earth, and all things that is upon the face of it. Yea, and its motion, yea, and also all the planets which move in their regular form doth witness that there is a supreme creator. ⁴⁵And yet do ye go about leading away the hearts of this people, testifying unto them there is no God. And yet will ye deny against all these witnesses?

And he said: "Yea, I will deny, except ye shall show me a sign."

⁴⁶And now it came to pass that Alma said unto him:

Behold, I am grieved because of the hardness of your heart (yea, that ye will still resist the spirit of the truth)—that thy soul may be destroyed.

⁴⁷But behold, it is better that thy soul should be lost than that thou shouldst be the means of bringing many souls down to destruction by thy lying and by thy flattering words. Therefore, if thou shalt deny again, behold, God shall smites[a] thee that thou shalt become dumb, that thou shalt never open thy mouth any more, that thou shalt not deceive this people any more.

⁴⁸Now, Korihor saith unto him: "I do not deny the existence of a God, but I do not believe that there is a God. And I say also, that ye do not know that there is a God. And except ye show me a sign, I will not believe."

⁴⁹Now, Alma saith unto him: "This will I give unto thee for a sign, that thou shalt be struck dumb, according to my words. And I say that, in the name of God, that ye shall be struck dumb, that ye shall no more have utterance."

⁵⁰Now, when Alma had said these words, Korihor was struck dumb, that he could not have utterance, according to the words of Alma.

⁵¹And now, when the Chief Judge [saw[b]] this, he put forth his hand, and wrote unto Korihor saying: "Art thou convinced of the power of a God, in whom did ye desire that Alma should show forth his sign? Would ye, that he should afflict others, to show unto thee a sign? [Behold][c], he hath showed unto you a sign. And now, will ye dispute more?"

---

a. The Printer's Manuscript does have "smites" here, as indicated. Clearly, it should be "smite."

b. Apparently added in proofreading against the Original Manuscript. Required for meaning.

c. Apparently corrected in proofreading. The Printer's Manuscript had "would," which was crossed out; "behold" was written above the line.

⁵²And Korihor put forth his hand, [and[a]] wrote, saying:

> I know that I am dumb. For I cannot speak. And I know that nothing, save it were the power of God, could bring this upon me. Yea, and I also knew that there was a God.
>
> ⁵³But behold, the devil hath deceived me. For he appeared unto me in the form of an angel and said unto me: "Go and reclaim this people. For they have all gone astray after an unknown God." And he saith unto me: "There is no God." Yea, and he taught me that which I should say. And I have taught his words. And I taught them because they were pleasing unto the carnal mind. And I taught them, even until I had much success, insomuch that I verily believed that they were true. And for this cause, I withstood the truth, even until I have brought this great curse upon me.

⁵⁴Now, when he had said this, he besought that Alma should pray unto God, that the curse might be taken from him. ⁵⁵But Alma said unto him: "If this curse should be taken from thee, thou wouldst again lead away the hearts of this people. Therefore, it shall be unto thee, even as the Lord will."

⁵⁶And it came to pass that the curse was not taken off of Korihor. But he was cast out, and went about from house to house, a-begging for his food.

⁵⁷Now, the knowledge of what had happened unto Korihor was immediately published throughout all the land. Yea, the proclamation was sent forth by the Chief Judge to all the people in the land—declaring unto those who had believed in the words of Korihor that they must speedily repent, lest the same judgments would come unto them.

⁵⁸And it came to pass that they were all convinced of the wickedness of Korihor. Therefore, they were all converted again unto the Lord. And thus, this put an end to the iniquity after the manner of Korihor. And Korihor did go about from house to house a-begging food for his support.

⁵⁹And it came to pass that as he went forth among the people, yea, among a people which had separated themselves from the Nephites and called themselves Zoramites (being led by a man whose name was Zoram)—and as he went forth amongst them, behold, he was ran upon, and trodden down, even until he was dead.[b] >⁶⁰And thus we see the end of him, who perverteth the ways of the Lord. And thus we see that the devil will not support his children at the last day, but doth speedily drag them down to hell.[c]<

[31] ¹Now it came to pass that after the end of Korihor, Alma—having received tidings that the Zoramites were perverting the ways of the Lord, and that Zoram (which was their leader) was leading the hearts of the people to bow down to dumb idols, etcetera—his heart again began to sicken because of the iniquity of the people. ²For it was the cause of great sorrow to Alma, to know of iniquity among his people. Therefore, his heart was exceeding sorrowful because of the separation of the Zoramites from the Nephites.

³Now, the Zoramites had gathered themselves together in a land which they called Antionum, which was east of the land of Zarahemla, which lay nearly bordering upon the seashore, which was south of the land Jershon, which also bordered upon the wilderness south, which wilderness was full of the Lamanites. ⁴Now, the Nephites greatly

---

a. Apparently added during proofreading.

b. Repetitive resumption is used to recover from the inserted phrase.

c. Mormon steps out of his narrator role and provides his moral lesson from the experience with Korihor. This conclusion hints at the reason that Mormon elected to include this event.

Chapter XVI [Alma 30–35]

feared that the Zoramites would enter into a correspondence with the Lamanites, and that it would be the means of great loss on the part of the Nephites.

⁵And now, as the preaching of the word had had[a] a greater tendency to lead the people to do that which was just, yea, it had had more powerful effect upon the minds of the people than the sword, or anything else which had happened unto them. ⁶Therefore, Alma thought it was expedient that they should try the virtue of the word of God. Therefore, he took Ammon, and Aaron, and Omner. And Himni he did leave in the church in Zarahemla. But the former three he took with him—and also Amulek and Zeezrom (which were at Melek). And he also took two of his sons. ⁷Now, the eldest of his sons he took not with him (and his name was Helaman). But the names of those which he took with him were Shiblon and Corianton. And these are the names of those which went with him among the Zoramites, to preach unto them the word.

⁸Now, the Zoramites were dissenters from the Nephites. Therefore, they had the word of God preached unto them, ⁹but they had fell into great errors. For they would not observe to keep the commandments of God and his statutes (according to the law of Moses). ¹⁰Neither would they observe the performances of the church, to continue in prayer and supplication to God daily, that they might not enter into temptation. ¹¹Yea, in fine, they did pervert the ways of the Lord in very many instances. Therefore, for this cause Alma and his brethren went into the land to preach the word unto them.

¹²Now, when they had come into the land, behold, to their astonishment, they found that the Zoramites had built synagogues, and that they did gather themselves together on one day of the week (which day they did call the day of the Lord). And they did worship after a manner which Alma and his brethren had never beheld. ¹³For they had a place built up in the center of their synagogue, a place of standing, which was high above the head. And the top thereof would only admit one person. ¹⁴Therefore, whosoever desired to worship must go forth and stand upon the top thereof, and stretch forth his hands towards heaven, and cry with a loud voice, saying:

> ¹⁵Holy, Holy God! We believe that thou art God. And we believe that thou art holy, and that thou wast a spirit, and that thou art a spirit, and that thou wilt be a spirit forever. ¹⁶Holy God! We believe that thou hast separated us from our brethren.
>
> And we do not believe in the traditions of our brethren, which was handed down to them by the childishness of their fathers. But we believe that thou hast elected us to be thy holy children. And also, thou hast made it known unto us, that there shall be no Christ. ¹⁷But thou art the same yesterday, today, and forever.[b]
>
> And thou hast elected us that we shall be saved, whilst all around us are elected to be cast by thy wrath down to hell. For the which holiness, O God, we thank thee. And we also thank thee that thou hast elected us, that we may not be led away after the foolish traditions of our brethren, which doth bind them down to a belief of Christ, which doth lead their hearts to wander far from thee, our God. ¹⁸And again, we thank thee, O God, that we are a chosen, and a holy people. Amen.

¹⁹Now it came to pass that after Alma, and his brethren, and his sons, had heard

---

a. The compositor removed the second "had" for the 1830 edition. It has been kept that way since. Note that he did not similarly remove the second "had" later in the same sentence.
b. See Hebrews 13:8: "Jesus Christ the same yesterday, and to day, and for ever.".

these prayers, they were astonished beyond all measure. ²⁰For behold, every man did go forth and offer up these same prayers.

²¹Now, the place was called by them *rameumptom* (which, being interpreted, is the holy stand). ²²Now, from this stand they did offer up, every man, the selfsame prayer unto God—thanking their God that they were chosen of him, and that he [had^a] not led them away after the tradition of their brethren, and that their hearts were not stolen away to believe in things to come, which they knew nothing about.

²³Now, [when^b] the people had all offered up thanks after their manner, they returned to their homes—never speaking of their God again until they had assembled themselves together again to the holy stand, to offer up thanks after their manner.

²⁴Now, when Alma saw this, his heart was grieved. For he saw that they were a wicked and a perverse people. Yea, he saw that their hearts were set upon gold, and upon silver, and upon all manner of fine goods. ²⁵Yea, and he also saw that their hearts were lifted up unto great boasting in their pride. ²⁶And he lifted up his voice to heaven, and cried saying:

> O! How long, O Lord, wilt thou suffer
> > that thy servants shall dwell here below in the flesh,
> > to behold such gross wickedness among the children of men?
>
> ²⁷Behold, O God, they cry unto thee—
> > and yet their hearts are swallowed up in their pride.
>
> ²⁸Behold, O God! They cry unto thee with their mouths,
> > while they are puffed up, even to greatness—
> > with the vain things of the world.
>
> Behold, O my God—their costly apparel,
> > and their ringlets,
> > and their bracelets,
> > and their ornaments of gold,
> > and all their precious things,
> > which they are ornamented with!
>
> And behold, their hearts are set upon them.
> > And yet they cry unto thee, and say:
>
> "We thank thee, O God, for we are a chosen people unto thee,"
> > while others shall perish.
>
> ²⁹Yea, and they say that thou hast made it known unto them
> > that there shall be no Christ.
>
> ³⁰O Lord God! How long wilt thou suffer
> > that such wickedness and [infidelity^c] shall be among this people?
>
> O Lord! Wilt thou give me strength,
> > that I may bear with mine infirmities!

---

a. Restored from the Original Manuscript. The Printer's Manuscript and current printed verse have "did." Skousen, *Analysis of the Textual Variants*, 4:2254–55.

b. Restored from the Original Manuscript. The Printer's Manuscript and current printed verse have "after". Skousen, *Analysis of the Textual Variants*, 4:2255.

c. Restored from the Original Manuscript. The Printer's Manuscript and current printed verse have "iniquity." *Printer's Manuscript of the Book of Mormon*, 1:521.

Chapter XVI [Alma 30–35]

For I am infirm.
    And such wickedness among this people doth pain my soul!
³¹O Lord! My heart is exceeding sorrowful.
    Wilt thou comfort my soul in Christ?
O Lord, wilt thou grant unto me,
    that I may have strength,
    that I may suffer with patience these afflictions,
    which shall come upon me because of the iniquity of this people?
³²O Lord! Wilt thou comfort my soul and give unto me success—
    and also my fellow laborers, which are with me,
yea, Ammon, and Aaron, and Omner,
    and also Amulek and Zeezrom, and also my two sons.
Yea, even all these wilt thou comfort, O Lord?
    Yea, wilt thou comfort their souls in Christ?
³³Wilt thou grant unto them, that they may have strength,
    that they may bear their afflictions which shall come upon them,
    because of the iniquities of this people?
³⁴O Lord! Wilt thou grant unto us
    that we may have success
    in bringing them again unto thee, in Christ? ³⁵
³⁵Behold, O Lord, their souls are precious.
    And many of them are our near brethren.
Therefore, give unto us, O Lord, power and wisdom,
    that we may bring these, our brethren, again unto thee!

³⁶Now it came to pass that when Alma had said these words, that he clapped his hands upon all they which were with him. And behold, as he clapped his hands upon them, they were filled with the Holy Spirit. ³⁷And after that, they did separate themselves, one from another, taking no thought for themselves—what they should eat, or what they should drink, or what they should put on.ᵃ ³⁸And the Lord provided for them, that they should hunger not, neither should they thirst. Yea, and he also gave them strength, that they should suffer no manner of afflictions save it were swallowed up in the joys of Christ. Now, this was according to the prayer of Alma. And this because he prayed in faith.

[32] ¹And it came to pass that they did go forth and began to preach the word of God unto the people, entering into their synagogues and into their houses. Yea, and even they did preach the word in their streets.

²And it came to pass that after much labor among them, they began to have success among the [poorer class of the peopleᵇ]. For behold, they were cast out of the synagogues because of the coarseness of their apparel. ⁴³Therefore, they were not permitted to enter into their synagogues to worship God, being esteemed as filthiness. Therefore, they were poor. Yea, they were esteemed by their brethren as dross. Therefore, they were poor as to things of the world. And also, they were poor in heart.

⁴Now, as Alma was teaching and speaking unto the people upon the hill Onidah,

---

a. An allusion to Matthew 6:25.
b. Changed to agree with the Original Manuscript. The Printer's Manuscript had "poor class of people," which has been retained in published editions.

there came a great multitude unto him, which were those of which have been speaking of, which were poor in heart because of their poverty as to things of the world. ⁵And they came unto Alma. And the one which wa[s^a] the most foremost among them, saith unto him:

Behold. What shall these, my brethren, do? For they are despised of all men because of their poverty, yea, and more especially by our priests. For they have cast us out of our synagogues, which we have labored abundantly to build with our own hands. And they have cast us out because of this, our exceeding poverty, that we have no place to worship our God. And behold, what shall we do?

⁶And now, when Alma heard this, he turned him about, his face immediately towards him, and he beheld with great joy. For he beheld that their afflictions had truly humbled them, and that they were in a preparation to hear the word. ⁷Therefore, he did say no more to the other multitude. But he stretched forth his hand, and cried unto those which he beheld which were truly penitent, and saith unto them:

⁸I behold that ye are lowly in heart. And if so, blessed are ye.

⁹Behold, thy brother hath said: "What shall we do, for we are cast out of our synagogues, that we cannot worship our God?"

¹⁰Behold, I say unto you: Do ye suppose that ye cannot worship God, save it be in your synagogues only? ¹¹And moreover, I would ask—do ye suppose that ye must not worship God only once in a week?

¹²I say unto you: It is well that ye are cast out of your synagogues, that ye may be humble and that ye may learn wisdom. For it is necessary that ye should learn wisdom. For it is because that ye are cast out that ye are despised of your brethren (because of your exceeding poverty), that ye are brought to a lowliness of heart. For ye are necessarily brought to be humble.

¹³And now, because ye are compelled to be humble, blessed are ye. For a man, sometimes if he is compelled to be humble, seeketh repentance. And now, surely whosoever repenteth shall find mercy. And he that findeth mercy and endureth to the end, the same shall be saved.^b

¹⁴And now, as I said unto you, that because ye were compelled to be humble, ye were blessed. Do ye not suppose that they are more blessed who truly humble themselves because of the word? ¹⁵Yea, he that truly humbleth himself, and repenteth of his sins, and endureth to the end, the same shall be blessed^c—yea, much more blessed than they who art compelled to be humble because of their exceeding poverty. ¹⁶Therefore, blessed are they who humbleth themselves without being compelled to be humble. Or rather in other words, blessed is he that believeth in the word of God and is baptized without stubbornness of heart—yea, without being brought to know the word (or even compelled to know) before they will believe.

¹⁷Yea, there are many which do say: "If thou wilt show unto us a sign from heaven, then we shall know of a surety—then we shall believe." ¹⁸Now I ask: Is this

---

a. Supplied by the editors of the *Printer's Manuscript of the Book of Mormon*. The word ran to the edge of the page and is difficult to read.

b. See Matthew 10:22: "he that endureth to the end shall be saved."

c. See Matthew 10:22: "he that endureth to the end shall be saved."

faith? Behold, I say unto you, nay. For if a man knoweth a thing he hath no cause to believe. For he knoweth it.

[19]And now, how much more cursed is he that knoweth the will of God and doeth it not, than he that only believeth (or only hath cause to believe) and falleth into transgression? [20]Now, of this thing ye must judge. Behold, I say unto you that it is on the one hand even as it is on the other. And it shall be unto every man, according to his work.

[21]And now, as I said concerning faith, faith is not to have a perfect knowledge of things. Therefore, if ye have faith, ye hope for things which is not seen which are true.[a]

[22]And now behold, I say unto you (and I would that ye should remember that God is merciful unto all who believe on his name)—therefore, he desireth (in the first place) that ye should believe, yea, even on his word.[b] [23]And now, he imparteth his word by angels unto men, yea, not only men but women also. Now, this is not all. Little children doth have words given unto them many times, which confound the wise and the learned.

[24]And now, my beloved brethren, as ye have desired to know of me what ye shall do (because ye are afflicted and cast out), now, I do not desire that ye should suppose that I mean to judge you—only according to that which is true.[c] [25]For I do not mean that ye, all of you, have been compelled to humble yourselves. For I verily believe there are some among you which would humble themselves, let them be in whatsoever circumstances he might.

[26]Now, as I said concerning faith, that it was not a perfect knowledge, even so it is with my words. Ye cannot know of their surety at first (unto perfection) any more than faith is a perfect knowledge. [27]But behold, if ye will awake and arouse your faculties, even to an experiment upon my words, and exercise a particle of faith—yea, even if ye can no more than desire to believe—let this desire work in you, even until ye believe in a manner that ye can give place for a portion of my words.

[28]Now, we will compare the word unto a seed. Now, if ye give place that a seed may be planted in your heart—behold, if it be a true seed (or a good seed)—if ye do not cast it out by your unbelief (that ye will resist the spirit of the Lord)—behold, it will begin to swell within your breasts. And when you feel these swellings motions, ye will begin to say within yourselves—it must needs be that this is a good seed (or that the word is good). For it beginneth to enlarge my soul. Yea, it beginneth to enlighten my understanding. Yea, and it beginneth to be delicious to me.

[29]Now behold, would not this increase your faith? I say unto you, yea. Nevertheless, it hath not grown up to a perfect knowledge. [30]But behold, as the seed swelleth, and sprouteth, and beginneth to grow—and then ye must needs say that the seed is good. For behold, it swelleth, and sprouteth, and beginneth to grow.

And now behold, will not this strengthen your faith? Yea, it will strengthen

---

a. Uses language from Hebrews 11:1: "Now faith is the substance of things hoped for, the evidence of things not seen."

b. This sentence shifts from intending to describe what Alma said to God's mercy. It is plausible that the intention was to describe the way Alma taught that principle, but the sentence shifts its focus.

c. An incomplete sentence. The "as ye have desired" requires some action to finish the idea. It is never completed. When the discourse returns to the topic in verse 26, it returns to verse 21.

your faith. For ye will say, I know that this is a good seed. For behold, it sprouteth, and beginneth to grow.[a]

[31] And now behold, are ye sure that this is a good seed? I say unto you, yea. For every seed bringeth forth unto its own likeness. [32] Therefore, if a seed groweth, it is good. But if it groweth not, behold, it is not good. Therefore, it is cast away.

[33] And now behold, because ye have tried the experiment, and planted the seed, and it swelled, and sprouteth, and beginneth to grow—ye must needs know that the seed is good.

[34] And now behold, is your knowledge perfect? Yea, your knowledge is perfect in that thing, and your faith is dormant. And this, because you know. For ye know that the word hath swelled your souls. And ye also know that it hath sprouted up, that your understanding doth begin to be enlightened and your mind doth begin to expand. [35] O then, is not this real? I say unto you, yea! Because it is light. And whatsoever is light is good. Because it is discernible. Therefore, ye must know that it is good.

And now behold, after ye have tasted this light, is your knowledge perfect? [36] Behold, I say unto you, nay. Neither must ye lay aside your faith. For ye have only exercised your faith to plant the seed, that ye might try the experiment, to know if the seed was good.

[37] And behold, as the tree beginneth to grow, ye will say: Let us nourish it with great care, that it may get root, that it may grow up and bring forth fruit unto us. And now behold, if ye nourish it with much care, it will get root, and grow up, and bring forth fruit. [38] But, if ye neglect the tree, and take no thought for its nourishment, behold it will not get any root. And when the heat of the sun cometh, and scorcheth it—and because it hath no root, it withereth away,[b] and ye pluck it up and cast it out.[c]

[39] Now, this is not because the seed was not good. Neither is it because the fruit thereof would not be desirable. But it is because your ground is barren and ye will not nourish the tree. Therefore, ye cannot have the fruit thereof. [40] And thus it is. If ye will not nourish the word, looking forward with an eye of faith to the fruit thereof, ye can never pluck of the fruit of the tree of life. [41] But if ye will nourish the word, yea, nourish the tree as it beginneth to grow by your faith—with great diligence and with patience, looking forward to the fruit thereof—and[d] it shall take root.

And behold, it shall be a tree, springing up unto everlasting life.[e] [42] And because of your diligence, and your faith, and your patience, with the word in nourishing it that it may take root in you—behold by and by, ye shall pluck the fruit thereof, which is most precious, which is sweet above all that is sweet and which is white above all that is whites—yea, and pure above all that is pure. And ye shall feast

---

a. The phrase "and now behold will not this strengthen your faith, yea, it will strengthen your faith for ye will say I know that this is a good seed for behold it sproutest and begineth to grow" was left out of the 1830 edition. It was restored in the 1908 RLDS edition and later in the 1981 LDS edition. Skousen, *Analysis of the Textual Variants*, 4:2278.

b. See Matthew 13:6: "And when the sun was up, they were scorched; and because they had no root, they withered away."

c. The "and because" appears to be the same meaning as "then because" in order to resolve the "when" in the first part of the verse.

d. This is an *if>and* construction which modern readers expect to be *if>then*.

e. See John 4:14: "shall be in him a well of water springing up into everlasting life."

upon this fruit, even until ye are filled, that ye hunger not, neither shall ye thirst. ⁴²Then, my brethren, ye shall reap the rewards of your faith, and your diligence, and patience, and long suffering—waiting for the tree to bring forth fruit unto you.

[33] ¹Now, after Alma had spoken these words, they sent forth unto him, desiring to know whether they should believe in one God, that they might obtain this fruit of which he had spoken—or how they should plant the seed (or the word) of which he had spoken (which he said must be planted in their hearts)—or in what manner they should begin to exercise their faith. ²And Alma saith unto them:

Behold, ye have said that ye could not worship your God because ye are cast out of your synagogues. But behold, I say unto you, if ye suppose that ye cannot worship your God ye do greatly err—and ye had ought to search the scriptures. For, if ye suppose that they have taught you this, ye do not understand them. ³Do ye remember to have read what Zenos (the prophet of old) hath said concerning prayer, or worship? ⁴For he saith:

> Thou art merciful, O God!
> > For thou hast heard my prayer,
> > > even when I was in the wilderness.
> Yea, thou wast merciful
> > when I prayed concerning those which were mine enemies.
> > And thou didst turn them to me.
> ⁵Yea, O God, and thou wast merciful unto me
> > when I did cry unto thee in my field,
> when I did cry unto thee in my prayer.
> > And thou didst hear me.
> ⁶And again, O God, when I did turn to my house
> > thou didst hear me in my prayer.
> ⁷And when I did turn unto my closet, O Lord,
> > and prayed unto thee,
> > thou didst hear me.
> ⁸Yea, thou art merciful unto thy children
> > when they cry unto thee,
> to be heard of thee (and not of men).
> > And thou wilt hear them.
> ⁹Yea, O God, thou hast been merciful unto me,
> > and heard my cries in the midst of thy congregations.
> ¹⁰Yea, and thou hast also heard me
> > when I have been cast out and have been despised by mine enemies.
> ¹¹Yea, thou didst hear my cries,
> > and wast angry with mine enemies.
> And thou didst visit them, in thine anger,
> > with speedy destruction.
> And thou didst hear me
> > because of mine afflictions and my sincerity.
> And it is because of thy Son
> > that thou hast been thus merciful unto me.

> Therefore, I will cry unto thee in all mine afflictions.
> For in thee is my joy.
> For thou hast turned thy judgments away from me—
> because of thy Son.

¹²And now, Alma saith unto them:

Do ye believe those scriptures which have been written by them of old? ¹³Behold, if ye do—ye must believe what Zenos saith. For behold, he saith: "Thou hast turned away thy judgments because of thy Son."

¹⁴Now behold, my brethren, I would ask if ye have read these scriptures? If ye have, how can ye disbelieve on the Son of God? ¹⁵For it is not written that Zenos alone spake of these things—but Zenock also spake of these things. ¹⁶For behold, he saith: "Thou art angry, O Lord, with this people because they will not understand of thy mercies, which thou hast bestowed upon them because of thy Son."

¹⁷And now my brethren, ye see that a second prophet of old has testified of the Son of God. And because the people would not understand his words, they stoned him to death.

¹⁸But behold, this is not all. These are not the only ones which have spoken concerning the Son of God. ¹⁹Behold, he was spoken of by Moses. Yea, and behold, a type was raised up in the wilderness, that whosoever would look upon it might live. And many did look, and live. ²⁰But few understood the meaning of those things, and this because of the hardness of their hearts. But there were many which were so hardened that they would not look. Therefore, they perished. Now, the reason that they would not look is because they did not believe that it would heal them.

²¹O my brethren! If ye could be healed by merely casting about your eyes, that ye might be healed! Would ye not behold quickly? Or would ye rather harden your hearts in unbelief, and be slothful, that ye would not cast about your eyes, that ye might perish? ²²If so, wo shall come upon you. But if not so, then cast about your eyes, and begin to believe in the Son of God, that he will come to redeem his people, and that he shall suffer and die to atone for their sins. And that he shall rise again from the dead, which shall bring to pass the resurrection that all men shall stand before him be to be judged at the last and judgment day, according to their works.

²³And now my brethren, I desire that ye should plant this word in your hearts. And as it beginneth to swell, even so, nourish it by your faith. And behold, it will become a tree, springing up in you unto everlasting life. And then may God grant unto you that your burdens may be light, through the joy of his Son. And even all this can ye do, if ye will. Amen.

[34] ¹And now it came to pass that after Alma had spoken these words unto them, he sat down upon the ground. And Amulek arose and began to teach them, saying:

²My brethren! I think that is it is impossible that ye should be ignorant of the things which have been spoken concerning the coming of Christ, who is taught by us to be the Son of God. Yea, I know that these things were taught unto you bountifully, before your dissension from among us.

³And, as ye have desired of my beloved brother that he should make known

Chapter XVI [Alma 30–35]

unto you what ye should do because of your afflictions—and[a] he hath spoken somewhat unto you to prepare your minds. Yea, and he hath exhorted you unto faith, and to patience. ⁴Yea, even that ye would have so much faith as even to plant the word in your heart, that ye may try the experiment of its goodness.

⁵And we have beheld that the great question which is in your minds, is whether the word be in the Son of God—or whether there shall be no Christ. ⁶And ye also [behold[b]] that my brother hath proven unto you, in many instances, that the word is in Christ unto salvation. ⁷My brother hath called upon the words of Zenos, that redemption cometh through the Son of God. And also upon the words of Zenock. And also he hath appealed unto Moses, to prove that these things are true.

⁸And now behold, I will testify unto you, of myself, that these things are true. Behold, I say unto you that I do know that Christ shall come among the children of men, to take upon him the transgressions of his people—and that he shall atone for the sins of the world. For the Lord God hath spoken it. ⁹For it is expedient that an atonement should be made. For according to the great [plans[c]] of the eternal God, there must be an atonement made—or else all mankind must unavoidably perish. Yea, all are hardened. Yea, all are fallen and are lost and must perish, except it be through the atonement, which it is expedient should be made.

¹⁰For it is expedient that there should be a great and last sacrifice. Yea, not a sacrifice of man, neither of beast, neither of any manner of fowl. For it shall not be a human sacrifice. But it must be an infinite, and an eternal sacrifice. ¹¹Now, there is not any man that can sacrifice his own blood, which will atone for the sins of another.

Now, if a man murdereth, behold, will our law (which is just) take the life of his brother? I say unto you, nay. ¹²But the law requireth the life of him who hath murdered. Therefore, there [can be[d]] nothing which is short of an infinite atonement which will suffice for the sins of the world. ¹³Therefore, it is expedient that there should be a great, and last, sacrifice. And then shall there be (or it is expedient there should be) a stop to the shedding of blood. Then shall the law of Moses be fulfilled. Yea, it shall all be fulfilled every jot and tittle. And none shall have passed away.[e]

¹⁴And behold, this is the whole meaning of the law—every whit a-pointing to that great and last sacrifice. And that great and last sacrifice will be the Son of God, yea, infinite and eternal. ¹⁵And thus, he shall bring salvation to all those who shall believe on his name, this being the intent of this last sacrifice—to bring about the bowels of mercy, which overpowereth justice, and bringeth about means unto men that they may have faith unto repentance. ¹⁶And thus, mercy can satisfy the demands of justice, and encircles them in the arms [of[f]] safety, while he that exer-

---

a. This "and" functions as "therefore."

b. Restored per original, as indicated in *Original Manuscript of the Book of Mormon*, 5:289. The current printed edition follows the Printer's Manuscript which has "beheld."

c. Restored per original, as indicated in *Original Manuscript of the Book of Mormon*, 5:289. The current printed edition follows the Printer's Manuscript, which has "plan."

d. Restored per original. The Printer's Manuscript has "can." The "be" was added in 1837. Skousen, *Analysis of the Textual Variants*, 4:2301.

e. See Matthew 5:18: "For verily I say unto you, Till heaven and earth pass, one jot or one tittle shall in no wise pass from the law, till all be fulfilled."

f. Probably added during proofreading.

ciseth no faith [unto[a]] repentance is exposed to the whole law of the demands of justice. Therefore, only unto him that hath faith unto repentance is brought about the great and eternal plan of redemption. [17]Therefore, may God grant unto you, my brethren, that ye might begin to exercise your faith unto repentance, that ye begin to call upon his holy name, that he would have mercy upon you.

> [18]Yea, cry unto him for mercy!
>> For he is mighty to save.
> [19]Yea, humble yourselves,
>> and continue in prayer unto him.
> [20]Cry unto him when ye are in your fields.
>> Yea, over all your flocks.
> [21]Cry unto him in your houses.
>> Yea, over all your household, both morning, midday, and evening.
> [22]Yea, cry unto him
>> against the power of your enemies.
> [23]Yea, cry unto him
>> against the devil, which is an enemy to all righteousness.
> [24]Cry unto him over the crops of your fields,
>> that ye may prosper in them.
> [25]Cry over the flocks of your fields,
>> that they may increase.

[26]But this is not all. Ye must pour out your souls in your closets, and your secret places, and in your wilderness. [27]Yea, and when you do not cry unto the Lord, let your hearts be full—drawn out in prayer unto him, continually, for your welfare, and also for the welfare of those which are around you.[b]

[28]And now, behold my brethren, I say unto you: Do not suppose that this is all. For after ye have done all these things, if ye turn away the needy, and the naked, and visit not the sick and afflicted, and impart of your substance (if ye have) to those which stand in need—I say unto you, if ye do not any of these things, behold your prayer is vain and availeth you nothing, and ye are as hypocrites which do deny the faith. [29]Therefore, if ye do not remember to be charitable, ye are as dross which the refiners do cast out (it being of no worth) and is trodden underfoot of men.[c]

[30]And now, my brethren, I would that after ye have received so many witnesses (seeing that the Holy Scriptures testifies of these things)—come forth and bring fruit unto repentance.[d] [31]Yea, I would that ye would come forth and harden not your hearts any longer. [32]For behold, now is the time, and the day, of your salva-

---

a. The Printer's Manuscript has "is left." That was crossed out and "unto" was written superlinearly, probably during proofreading.

b. This is a set of parallels where the sentences are paralleled in their beginnings and most often in a form where there is an initial phrase and a conclusion. They clearly reference Zenos (without attribution), as we have Alma citing Zenos about prayer in Alma 33:3–11. Some of the phrases are similar. This is possibly a quotation from something in Zenos or Amulek's spontaneous elaboration on the phrases that Alma has so recently preached. When the next paragraph begins with "and now," it feels like Amulek has punctuated the end of his quotation.

c. The phrase "trodden underfoot of men" occurs in Matthew 5:13.

d. See Matthew 3:8: "Bring forth therefore fruits meet for repentance."

Chapter XVI [Alma 30–35]

tion. And therefore, if ye will repent and harden not your hearts—immediately shall the great plan of redemption be brought about unto you. For behold, this life is the time for men to prepare to meet God. Yea behold, the day of this life is the day for men to perform their labors.

³³And now, as I said unto you before, as ye have had so many witnesses, therefore I beseech of you that ye do not procrastinate the day of your repentance until the end.ᵃ For after this day of life (which is given us to prepare for eternity)—behold, if we do not improve our time while in this life—then cometh the night of darkness wherein there can be no labor performed. ³⁴Ye cannot say, when ye are brought to that awful crisis, that I will repent, that I will return to my God. Nay, ye cannot say this. For that same spirit which doth possess your bodies at the time that ye go out of this life, that same spirit will have power to possess your body in that eternal world. ³⁵For behold, if ye have procrastinated the day of your repentance even until death, behold, ye have become subjected to the spirit of the devil. And he doth seal you his. Therefore, the spirit of the Lord hath withdrawn from you, and hath no place in you. And the devil hath all power over you. And this is the final state of the wicked. ³⁶And this I know, because the Lord hath said: "he dwelleth not in unholy temples, but in the hearts of the righteous doth he dwell."ᵇ Yea, and he hath also said that the righteous should sit down in his kingdom, to go no more out. But their garments should be made whites through the blood of the Lamb.

³⁷And now, my beloved brethren, I desire that ye should remember these things, and that ye should work out your salvation with fearᶜ before God, and that ye should no more deny the coming of Christ—³⁸that ye contend no more against the Holy Ghost. But that ye receive it, and take upon you the name of Christ—that ye humble yourselves, even to the dust and worship God (in whatsoever place ye may be in) in spirit and in truth.ᵈ And that ye live in thanksgiving daily for the many mercies and blessings which he doth bestow upon you. ³⁹Yea, and I also exhort you my brethren, that ye be watchful unto prayer continually, that ye may not be led away by the temptations of the devil, that he may not overpower you, that ye may not become his subjects at the last day. For behold, he rewardeth you no good thing.

⁴⁰And now, my beloved brethren, I would exhort you to have patience, and that ye bear with all manner of afflictions—that ye do not revile against those who do cast you out because of your exceeding poverty, lest ye become sinners like unto them. ⁴¹But that ye have patience, and bear with those afflictions with a firm hope that ye shall one day rest from all your afflictions.

[35] ¹Now it came to pass that after Amulek had made an end of these words, they withdrew themselves from the multitude and came over into the land of Jershon. ²Yea, and the rest of the brethren (after they had preached the word unto the Zoramites) also came over into the land of Jershon.

---

a. Although this sentence begins as though it were a repetitive resumption, Amulek is rather summarizing what he had said. It was not an interruption but a repetition for emphasis and expansion.

b. Clearly given as a quotation but to an unknown scripture. The context of temples suggests that it was on the brass plates.

c. See Philippians 2:12: "Wherefore, my beloved, as ye have always obeyed, not as in my presence only, but now much more in my absence, work out your own salvation with fear and trembling."

d. The phrase "worship . . . in spirit and truth" is found in John 4:23.

³And it came to pass that after the more popular part of the Zoramites had consulted together concerning the words which had been preached unto them—they were angry because of the word. For it did destroy their craft. Therefore, they would not hearken unto the words. ⁴And they sent, and gathered together (throughout all the land) all the people—and consulted with them concerning the words which had been spoken.

⁵Now, their rulers, and their priests, and their teachers, did not let the people know concerning their desires. Therefore, they found out privily the minds of all the people.

⁶And it came to pass that after they had found out the minds of all the people—those which were in favor of the words which had been spoken by Alma and his brethren, were cast out of the land. And they were many. And they came over also into the land of Jershon.

⁷And it came to pass that Alma and his brethren did minister unto them.

⁸Now, the people of the Zoramites were angry with the people of Ammon (which were in Jershon). And the chief ruler of the Zoramites (being a very wicked man) sent over unto the people of Ammon—desiring them, that they should cast out of their land all those which came over from them into their land. ⁹And he breathed out many threatenings against them.

And now the people of Ammon did not fear their words. Therefore, they did not cast them out—but they did receive all the poor of the Zoramites that came over unto them. And they did nourish them, and did clothe them, and did give unto them lands for their inheritance. And they did administer unto them, according to their wants.

¹⁰Now, this did stir up the Zoramites to anger against the people of Ammon. And they began to mix with the Lamanites and to stir them up also to anger against them. ¹¹And thus, the Zoramites and the Lamanites began to make preparations for war against the people of Ammon, and also against the Nephites. ¹²And thus ended the seventeenth year of the reign of the judges over the people of Nephi.

¹³And the people of Ammon departed out of the land of Jershon and came over into the land of Melek, and gave place in the land of Jershon for the armies of the Nephites, that they might contend with the armies of the Lamanites and the armies of the Zoramites. And thus commenced a war between betwixt the Lamanites and the Nephites in the eighteenth year of the reign of the judges. And an account shall be given of their wars hereafter.[a]

¹⁴And Alma, and Ammon, and their brethren, and also the two sons of Alma, returned to the land of Zarahemla after having been instruments in the hands of God of bringing many of the Zoramites to repentance. And as many as were brought to repentance were driven out of their land. But they have lands for their inheritance in the land of Jershon. And they have taken up arms to defend themselves, and their wives, and their children, and their lands.

¹⁵Now, Alma, being grieved for the iniquity of his people, yea, for the wars, and the bloodsheds, and the contentions, which were among them—and having been to declare the word (or sent to declare the word) among all the people in every city—and seeing that the hearts of the people began to wax hard, and that they began to be offended because of the strictness of the word—his heart was exceeding sorrowful. ¹⁶Therefore, he caused that his sons should be gathered together, that he might give unto them, every one, his charge (separately) concerning the things pertaining unto righteousness. And we have an account of his commandments which he gave unto them, according to his own record.

---

a. This story picks up in Alma 43.

Chapter XVII [Alma 36–37]

[36] *The commandment of Alma to his son, Helaman.*

¹My son, give ear to my words. For I swear unto you, that inasmuch as ye shall keep the commandments of God ye shall prosper in the land. ²I would that ye should do as I have done in remembering the captivity of our fathers. For they were in bondage. And none could deliver them, except it were the God of Abraham, and the God of Isaac, and the God of Jacob. And he surely did deliver them in their afflictions.

³And now, O my son Helaman—behold, thou art in thy youth. And therefore I beseech of thee, that thou wilt hear my words, and learn of me. For I do know that whomsoever shall put his trust in God shall be supported in their trials, and their troubles, and their afflictions, and shall be lifted up at the last day. ⁴And I would not that ye think that I know of myself—not of the temporal, but of the spiritual—not of the carnal mind, but of God.

⁵Now behold, I say unto you: If I had not been born of God I should not have known these things. But God hath, by the mouth of his holy angel, made these things known unto me—not of any worthiness of myself. ⁶For I went about with the sons of Mosiah—seeking to destroy the church of God. But behold, God sent his holy angel to stop us by the way. ⁷And behold, he spake unto us—as it were the voice of thunder. And the whole earth did tremble beneath our feet. And we all fell to the earth, for the fear of the Lord came upon us.

⁸But behold, the voice said unto me: "Arise!" And I arose—and stood up—and beheld the angel. ⁹And he said unto me: "If[a] thou wilt, of thyself, be destroyed—seek no more to destroy the church of God."

¹⁰And it came to pass that I fell to the earth. And it was for the space of three days and three nights that I could not open my mouth—neither had I the use of my limbs. ¹¹And the angel spake more things unto me, which were heard by my brethren—but I did not hear them. For, when I heard the words: "If[b] thou wilt be destroyed of thyself, seek no more to destroy the church of God," I was struck with such great fear and amazement (lest perhaps that I should be destroyed) that I fell to the earth, and I did hear no more.

²But I was racked with eternal torment, for my soul was harrowed up to the greatest degree and racked with all my sins. [c]

> ¹³Yea, I did remember all my sins and iniquities,
> for which I was tormented with the pains of hell.
> Yea, I saw that I had rebelled against my God,
> and that I had not kept his holy commandments.
> ¹⁴Yea, and I had murdered many of his children,
> or rather, led them away unto destruction.

---

   a. The word "if" at the beginning of the sentence might be used in the sense of "unless." The first clause needs something to indicate a negation, since Alma is told *not* to persecute the church. This quotation is probably more accurately rendered as in Alma 36:11.

   b. As in the statement being quoted, the beginning "if" should be read as "unless."

   c. This sentence is separated to a new paragraph to parallel verse 19. Both verses appear to function as transitions from the prose to the poetic.

>   Yea, and in fine,
>   so great had been my iniquities
>   that the very thoughts of coming into the presence of my God
>   did rack my soul with inexpressible horror.
> ¹⁵O thought I,
>   that I could be banished—
>   and become extinct,
>   both soul and body—
>   that I might not be brought to stand in the presence of my God,
>   to be judged of my deeds!ᵃ

¹⁶And now, for three days and for three nights was I racked, even with the pains of a damned soul.

¹⁷And it came to pass that as I was thus racked with torment—while I was harrowed up by the memory of my many sins—behold, I remembered also to have heard my father prophesy unto the people concerning the coming of one Jesus Christ, a Son of God, to atone for the sins of the world. ¹⁸Now, as my mind caught hold upon this thought, I cried within my heart: "O Jesus! Thou Son of God! Have mercy on me, who art in the gall of bitterness,ᵇ and art encircled about by the everlasting chains of death!"

¹⁹And now behold, when I thought this—I could remember my pains no more!

>   Yea, I was harrowed up by the memory of my sins no more!
>   ²⁰And, O! what joy, and what marvelous light I did behold!
>   Yea, my soul was filled with joy,
>   as exceeding as was my pain.
>   ²¹Yea, I say unto you, my son,
>   that there could be nothing so exquisite—
>   and so bitter—
>   as was my pains.
>   Yea, and again, I say unto you, my son,
>   that on the other hand—
>   there can be nothing so exquisite and sweet
>   as was my joy.
>   ²²Yea, and methought I saw,
>   even as our father Lehi saw—
>   God sitting upon his throne—
>   surrounded with numberless concourses of angels,
>   in the attitude of singing,
>   and praising their God.
>   Yea, and my soul did long to be there.

²³But behold, my limbs did receive their strength again, and I stood upon my feet—and did manifest unto the people that I had been born of God. ²⁴Yea, and from that time, even until now, I have labored without ceasing, that I might bring souls unto

---

a. This is a set of poetic parallels. The beginning phrases are similar, and the construction has a short sentence followed by a conclusion. This format is reprised beginning in verse 19.

b. The phrase "gall of bitterness" is found in Acts 6:23.

Chapter XVII [Alma 36–37]

repentance, that I might bring them to taste of the exceeding joy of which I did taste, that they might also be born of God and be filled with the Holy Ghost.

²⁵Yea, and now behold, O my son, the Lord doth give me exceeding great joy in the fruit of my labors. ²⁶For because of the word which he hath imparted unto me, behold, many hath been born of God—and hath tasted as I have tasted—and hath seen eye to eye, as I have seen. Therefore, they do know of these things of which I have spoken, as I do know. And the knowledge which I have is of God. ²⁷And I have been supported under trials and troubles of every kind, yea, and in all manner of afflictions.

>Yea, God hath delivered me
>>from prisons,
>>and from bonds,
>>and from death.
>Yea, and I do put my trust in him,
>>and he will still deliver me. ²
>⁸And I know that he will raise me up at the last day,
>>to dwell with him in glory.
>Yea, and I will praise him forever.
>>For he hath brought our fathers out of Egypt,
>>and he hath swallowed up the Egyptians in the Red Sea,
>>and he led them by his power into the promised land.
>Yea, and he hath delivered them out of bondage,
>>and captivity (from time to time).
>Yea, and he hath also brought our fathers out of the land of Jerusalem.
>And he hath also,
>>by his everlasting power,
>>delivered them out of bondage and captivity (from time to time),
>>even down to the present day.
>And I have always retained in remembrance their captivity.
>²⁹Yea, and ye also had ought to retain in remembrance (as I have done)
>>their captivity.^a

³⁰But behold, my son, this is not all. For ye had ought to know (as I do know) that inasmuch as ye shall keep the commandments of God, ye shall prosper in the land. And ye had ought to know also, that inasmuch as ye will not keep the commandments of God, ye shall be cut off from his presence.^b Now, this is according to his word.^c

[37] ¹And now, my son Helaman, I command you, that ye take the records which have been entrusted with me. ²And I also command you, that ye shall keep a record of this people (according as I have done) upon the plates of Nephi—and keep all these things sacred which I have kept, even as I have kept them. For it is for a wise purpose that they are kept.

---

a. Alma reprises the form but shifts the use. The first set described his need for, and process of, repentance. The second set elaborates the result of his transformative experience.

b. The phrase "cut off from my presence" is found in Leviticus 22:3.

c. Alma brackets his explanation of his conversion with the promise of preservation in the land upon keeping God's commandments. That was the opening in verse 1, and it closes this section. Although it is the end of a chapter in the modern version, it was not originally. Nevertheless, it is a section change. Not only do the bracketed statements set it off, but the next verse shifts topics.

³And these plates of brass, which contain these engravings (which have the records of the Holy Scriptures upon them, which have the genealogy of our forefathers, even from the beginning)—⁴and behold, it hath been prophesied by our fathers, that they should be kept, and handed down, from one generation to another—and be kept, and preserved, by the hand of the Lord, until they should go forth unto every nation, kindred, tongue, and people[a]—that they shall know of the mysteries contained thereon.[b]

⁵And now behold, if they are kept, they must retain their brightness. Yea, and they will retain their brightness. Yea, and also shall all the plates which do contain that which is holy writ.

⁶Now, ye may suppose that this is foolishness in me. But behold, I say unto you, that by small and simple things are great things brought to pass. And small means, in many instances, doth confound the wise. ⁷And the Lord God doth work by [c] means, to bring about his great and eternal purposes—and by very small means the Lord doth confound the wise and bringeth about the salvation of many souls.

⁸And now, it hath hitherto been wisdom in God that these things should be preserved. For behold, they have enlarged the memory of this people, yea, and convinced many of the error of their ways, and brought them to the knowledge of their God—unto the salvation of their souls. ⁹Yea, I say unto you, were it not for these things that these records do contain (which are on these plates), Ammon and his brethren could not have convinced so many thousands of the Lamanites of the incorrect tradition of their fathers. Yea, these records, and their words, brought them unto repentance—that is, they brought them to the knowledge of the Lord, their God, and to rejoice in Jesus Christ, their Redeemer. ¹⁰And who knoweth but what they will be the means of bringing many thousands of them, yea, and also many thousands of our stiffnecked brethren, the Nephites (which are now hardening their hearts in sins, and iniquities), to the knowledge of their Redeemer.

¹¹Now, these mysteries are not yet fully made known unto me. Therefore, I shall forbear. ¹²And it may suffice if I only say they are preserved for a wise purpose, which purpose is known unto God, for he doth counsel in wisdom over all his works. And his paths are straight, and his course is one eternal round.

¹³O remember! Remember, my son Helaman, how strict is[d] the commandments of God! And he saith:

> If ye will keep my commandments,
> ye shall prosper in the land.

---

a. See Revelation 14:6: "And I saw another angel fly in the midst of heaven, having the everlasting gospel to preach unto them that dwell on the earth, and to every nation, and kindred, and tongue, and people."

b. This is a difficult sentence to parse because it seems to be incomplete. The original idea would appear to have been: "And these plates of brass . . . should be kept." The various added phrases seem to have made it so that the grammatical requirements of the beginning were lost.

c. This sentence is as it appears in the Printer's Manuscript, and it has not been altered in the modern edition. Nevertheless, there seems to be a missing word that may or may not have been in the Original but appears to be required by the logic of the sentence. Perhaps "small" should have been here. The context is for small means, and by having "small" here, the "very small means" in the next phrase would be a logical and literary intensification. Skousen notes that this is a possible emendation. Skousen, *Analysis of the Textual Variants*, 4:2348–50.

d. Corrected to "are" during proofreading. Both the Original and Printer's Manuscripts had "is," so it is left without correction. Skousen, *Analysis of the Textual Variants*, 4:2352.

Chapter XVII [Alma 36–37]

But if ye keep not his commandments,
ye shall be cut off from^a his presence.^b

¹⁴And now remember, my son, that God hath entrusted you with these things, which are sacred, which he hath kept sacred—and also which he will keep and preserve (for a wise purpose in him) that he may show forth his power unto future generations.

¹⁵And now behold, I tell you by the spirit of prophesy that if ye transgress the commandments of God—behold, these things which are sacred shall be taken away from you, by the power of God. And ye shall be delivered up unto Satan, that he may sift you as chaff before the wind.^c ¹⁶But if ye keep the commandments of God, and do with these things which are sacred, according to that which the Lord doth command you (for you must appeal unto the Lord for all things whatsoever ye must do with them)—behold, no power of earth of or hell can take them from you.

For God is powerful to the fulfilling of all his words.
¹⁷For he will fulfill all his promises which he shall make unto you.
For he hath fulfilled his promise which he hath made unto our fathers.
¹⁸For he promised unto them that he would reserve these things
for a wise purpose in him,
that he might show forth his power unto future generations.^d

¹⁹And now behold, one purpose hath he fulfilled, even to the restoration of many of thousands of the Lamanites to the knowledge of the truth. And he hath shown forth his power in them. And he will also still show forth his power in them, unto future generations. Therefore, they shall be preserved. ²⁰Therefore, I command you, my son Helaman, [that^e] ye be diligent in fulfilling all my words and that ye be diligent in keeping the commandments of God as they are written.

²¹And now, I will speak unto you concerning those twenty-four plates—that ye keep them, that the mysteries, and the works of darkness, and their secret works (or the secret works of those people which have been destroyed) may be made manifest unto this people. Yea, all their murders, and robbings, and their plunderings, and all their wickedness, and abominations, may be made manifest unto this people.

Yea, and that ye preserve these directors. ²²For behold the Lord saw that his people began to work in darkness, yea, work secret murders, and abominations—therefore, the Lord said: "If they did not repent, they should be destroyed from off the face of the earth." ²³And the Lord said: "I will prepare unto my servant Gazelem, a stone, which shall shine forth in darkness, unto light, that I may discover unto my people (which

---

a. The phrase "cut off from my presence" is found in Leviticus 22:3.

b. This is the third time this command is quoted. The other two bracketed our modern chapter 36. This use does not appear to mark a change in topic as Helaman is tasked with remembering the sacred things in the next verse, and the previous verses spoke of those sacred things. Perhaps there is an intent with the emphasis on remembering that the promise of prospering or destruction would be implied as also pertaining to Helaman's charge to keep the sacred relics—that their preservation was included in the commandments that were to be kept that would bring prosperity, or destruction were they not followed.

c. See Luke 22:31: "And the Lord said, Simon, Simon, behold, Satan hath desired to have you, that he may sift you as wheat." See also Psalm 35:5: "Let them be as chaff before the wind."

d. These lines form a chiasm: ABBA. Thanks to Kerry Hull for pointing this out.

e. Restored from *Original Manuscript of the Book of Mormon*, 5:305. The Printer's Manuscript has "the," which is clearly in error. It was corrected for the 1830 edition.

serve me), that I may discover unto them the works of their brethren, yea, their secret works—their works of darkness, and their wickedness, and abominations."

²⁴And now, my son, these directors were prepared that the word of the Lord God might be fulfilled which he spake, saying: ²⁵"I will bring forth out of darkness, unto light—all their secret works, and their abominations. And except they repent, I will destroy them from off the face of the earth. And I will bring to light all their secrets, and abominations—unto every nation that shall hereafter possess the land."

²⁶And now, my son, we see that they did not repent. Therefore, they have been destroyed. And thus far, the word of God hath been fulfilled. Yea, their secret abominations have been brought out of darkness, and made known unto us.

²⁷And now, my son, I command you, that ye retain all their oaths, and their covenants, and their agreements in their secret abominations, yea, and all their signs, and their wonders—ye shall retain from this people that they know them not, lest peradventure they should fall into darkness also and be destroyed. ²⁸For behold, there is a curse upon all this land, that destruction shall come upon all those workers of darkness, according to the power of God, when they are fully ripe. Therefore, I desire that this people might not be destroyed. ²⁹Therefore, ye shall keep these secret plans of their oaths, and their covenants, from this people—and only their wickedness, and their murders, and their abominations, shall ye make known unto them. And ye shall teach them to abhor such wickedness, and abominations, and murders. And ye shall also teach them that these people were destroyed on account of their wickedness, and abominations, and their murders.

³⁰For behold, they murdered all the prophets of the Lord which came among them to declare unto them concerning their iniquities. And the blood of those which they murdered did cry unto the Lord, their God, for vengeance upon those which were their murderers. And thus, the judgments of God did come upon them workers of darkness and secret combinations. ³¹Yea, and cursed be the land forever and ever unto those workers of darkness, and secret combinations, even unto destruction—except they repent before they are fully ripe.

³²And now my son, remember the words which I have spoken unto you.

> Trust not those secret plans unto this people,
>   but teach them an everlasting hatred
>   against sin and iniquity.
> ³³Preach unto them repentance and faith
>   on the Lord Jesus Christ.
> Teach them to humble themselves,
>   and to be meek and lowly in heart.
> Teach them to withstand every temptation of the devil—
>   with their faith on the Lord Jesus Christ.
> ³⁴Teach them to never be weary of good works,
>   but to be meek and lowly in heart.
> For such shall find rest to their souls.

³⁵O remember, my son, and learn wisdom in thy youth. Yea, learn in thy youth to keep the commandments of God.[a]

---

a. Although Alma is still commanding Helaman, these two sentences act as a transition from what Helaman is to do for others to what he should do for his own spirituality.

Chapter XVII [Alma 36–37]

³⁶Yea, and cry unto God for all thy support.
    Yea, let all thy doings be unto the Lord,
    and whithersoever thou goest, let it be in the Lord.
Yea, let thy thoughts
    be directed unto the Lord.
Yea, let the affections of thy heart
    be placed upon the Lord forever.
³⁷Counsel [ᵃ] the Lord in all thy doings,
    and he will direct thee for good.
Yea, when thou liest down at night,
    lie down unto the Lord,
    that he may watch over you in your sleep.
And when thou risest in the morning,
    let thy heart be full of thanks unto God.
And if ye always do these things,
    ye shall be lifted up at the last day.

³⁸And now, my son, I have somewhat to say concerning the thing which our fathers call a ball, or director, or our fathers called it *liahona* (which is, being interpreted, a compass). And the Lord prepared it—³⁹and behold, there cannot any man work after the manner of so curious a workmanship.

And behold, it was prepared to show unto our fathers the course which they should travelᵇ in the wilderness. ⁴⁰And it did work for them, according to their faith in God. Therefore, if they had faith to believe that God could cause that those spindles should point the way they should go—behold, it was done. Therefore, they had this miracle (and also many other miracles wrought by the power of God), day by day. ⁴¹Nevertheless, because those miracles were worked by small means (nevertheless it did show unto them marvelous works)—they were slothful and forgot to exercise their faith and diligence. And then those marvelous works ceased, and they did not progress in their journey. ⁴²Therefore, they tarried in the wilderness (or did not travelᶜ a direct course) and were afflicted with hunger and thirst—because of their transgressions.

⁴³And now, my son, I would that ye should understand that these things are not without a shadow. For, as our fathers were slothful to give heed to this compass (now these things were temporal)—they did not prosper. Even so it is with things which are spiritual. ⁴⁴For behold, it is as easy to give heed to the word of Christ which will point to you a strait course to eternal bliss as it was for our fathers to give heed to this compass, which would point unto them a straight course to the promised land.

⁴⁵And now I say, is there not a type in this thing? For just as suredly as this director did bring our fathers (by following its course) to the promised land—shall the word of Christ, if we follow its course, carry us beyond this vale of [sorrowᵈ] into a far better land of promise.

---

    a. The intent is surely to counsel with, rather than to counsel God. Nevertheless, this word is not attested in the Printer's Manuscript. The word "with" was added in the 1920 edition. See Skousen, *Analysis of the Textual Variants*, 4:2367–69.

    b. The Printer's Manuscript has "travail," but the intent is clearly "travel." They are often interchanged in the Printer's Manuscript.

    c. Another instance of travail that clearly should be travel.

    d. The Printer's Manuscript originally had "tears." The correction was probably made during

⁴⁶O, my son, do not let us be slothful[a] because of the easiness of the way! For so was it with our fathers. For so was it prepared for them, that if they would look, they might live. Even so it is with us. The way is prepared, and if we will look, we may live forever.

⁴⁷And now, my son, see that ye take care of these sacred things. Yea, see that ye look to God and live. Go unto this people, and declare the word, and be sober. My son, farewell.

---

proofreading. Skousen, *Analysis of the Textual Variants*, 4:2378.

a. An awkward sentence in modern English. More modern phrasing would be "let us not be slothful."

Chapter XVIII [Alma 38]

[38] *The commandments of Alma to his son, Shiblon.*

¹My son, give ear to my words. For I say unto you even as I said unto Helaman,

> that inasmuch as ye shall keep the commandments of God,
> ye shall prosper in the land.
> And inasmuch as ye will not keep the commandments of God,
> ye shall be cut off from his presence.[a]

²And now, my son, I trust that I shall have great joy in you because of your steadiness and your faithfulness unto God. For as you have commenced in your youth to look to the Lord, your God, even so I hope that you will continue in keeping his commandments. For blessed is he that endureth to the end.[b]

³I say unto you, my son, that I have had great joy in thee already, because of thy faithfulness, and thy diligence, and thy patience, and thy long suffering, among the people of the Zoramites. ⁴For I knew that thou wast in bonds. Yea, and I also knew that thou wast stoned for the word's sake. And thou didst bear all these things with patience because the Lord was with thee. And now, thou knowest that the Lord did deliver thee. ⁵And now my son, Shiblon, I would that ye should remember that as much as ye shall put your trust in God, even so much ye shall be delivered out of your trials, and your troubles, and your afflictions. And ye shall be lifted up, as at the last day.

⁶Now, my son, I would not that ye should think that I know these things of myself. But it is the Spirit of God which is in me which maketh these things known unto me. For if I had not been born of God, I should not have known these things. ⁷But behold, the Lord in his great mercy sent his angel to declare unto me that I must stop the work of destruction among his people. Yea, and I have seen a angel face to face. And he spake with me. And his voice was as thunder. And it shook the whole earth.

⁸And it came to pass that I was three days and three nights in the most bitter pain and anguish of soul. And never, until I did cry out unto the Lord Jesus Christ for mercy, did I receive a remission of my sins. But behold, I did cry unto him! And I did find peace to my soul.

⁹And now, my son, I have told you this that ye may learn wisdom, that ye may learn of me that there is no other way, nor means, whereby man can be saved—only in and through Christ. Behold, he is the life and the light of the world.[c] Behold, he is the word of truth and righteousness.[d]

¹⁰And now, as ye have begun to teach the word, even so I would that ye should continue to teach. And I would that ye would be diligent, and temperate, in all things.

¹¹See that ye are not lifted up unto pride.

> Yea, see that ye do not boast
> in your own wisdom,
> nor of your much strength.

---

a. The phrase "cut off from my presence" is found in Leviticus 22:3.
b. See Matthew 10:22: "he that endureth to the end shall be saved."
c. See John 8:12: "Then spake Jesus again unto them, saying, I am the light of the world." Also, John 1:4: "In him was life; and the life was the light of men."
d. Uses language from John 1:1, 4.

¹²Use boldness, but not overbearance.
>And also see that ye bridle all your passions,
>>that ye may be filled with love.

See that ye refrain from idleness.

¹³Do not pray as the Zoramites do,
>for ye have seen that they pray to be heard of men
>and to be praised for their wisdom.

¹⁴Do not say:
>"O God, I thank thee that we are better than our brethren."

But rather say:
>"O Lord, forgive my unworthiness, and remember my brethren in mercy."

Yea, acknowledge your unworthiness before God
>at all times.

¹⁵And may the Lord bless your soul
>and receive you at the last day into his kingdom,
>>to sit down in peace.[a]

Now go, my son, and teach the word unto this people. Be sober. My son, farewell.

---

a. These sentences have similar command structures. They are not necessarily poetic, but the paralleling does emphasize the commands.

Chapter XIX [Alma 39–42]

[39] *The commandments of Alma to his son, Corianton.*

¹And now, my son, I have somewhat more to say unto thee than what I said unto thy brother. For behold, have ye not observed the steadiness of thy brother—his faithfulness and his diligence in keeping the commandments of God? Behold, has he not set a good example for thee? ²For thou didst not give so much heed unto my words as did thy brother among the people of the Zoramites.

Now, this is what I have against thee. Thou didst go on unto boasting in thy strength, and thy wisdom. ³And this is not all, my son, thou didst do that which was grievous unto me. For thou didst forsake the ministry and did go over into the land of Siron among the borders of the Lamanites, after the harlot Isabel. ⁴Yea, she did steal away the hearts of many. But this was no excuse for thee, my son. Thou shouldst have tended to the ministry wherewith thou wast entrusted.

⁵Know ye not, my son, that these things are an abomination in the sight of the Lord?, yea, most abominable above all sins save it be the shedding of innocent blood or denying the Holy Ghost? ⁶For behold, if ye deny the Holy Ghost when it one[a] hath had place in you, and ye know that ye deny it—behold, this is a sin which is unpardonable. Yea, and whosoever murdereth against the light and knowledge of God—it is not easy for him to obtain forgiveness. Yea, I say unto you, my son, that it is not easy for him to obtain a forgiveness.

⁷And now, my son, I would that ye had not been guilty of so great a crime. I would not dwell upon your crimes, to harrow up your soul—if it were not for your good. ⁸But behold, ye cannot hide your crimes from God. And except ye repent, they will stand as a testimony against you at the last day.

⁹Now, my son, I would to God that ye should repent and forsake your sins, and go no more after the lusts of your eyes—but cross yourself in all these things. For except ye do this, ye can in no wise inherit the kingdom of God. O remember, and take it upon you, and cross yourself in these things!

¹⁰And I command you to take it upon you to counsel [b] your elder brothers in your undertakings. For behold, thou art in thy youth, and ye stand in need to be nourished by your brothers and give heed to their counsel. ¹¹Suffer not yourself to be led away by any vain or foolish thing. Suffer not that the devil lead away your heart again after those wicked harlots. Behold, O my son, how great iniquity ye brought upon the Zoramites! For when they saw your conduct they would not believe in my words.

¹²And now, the Spirit of the Lord doth say unto me: "Command thy children to do good, lest they lead away the hearts of many people to destruction." Therefore, I command you, my son, in the fear of God, that ye refrain from your iniquities—¹³that ye turn to the Lord with all your mind, might, and strength, that ye lead away the hearts of no more[c] to do wickedly, but rather—return unto them and acknowledge your faults,

---

a. The sense is clearly "once," and it has been changed in the 1830 edition.

b. The context requires "with" at this point, but it is not present in the Printer's Manuscript nor in early editions of the Book of Mormon. It was eventually added in 1920. Skousen, *Analysis of the Textual Variants*, 4:2393.

c. This is a somewhat awkward phrase for modern readers. There is an assumed [people] in the

and [retain*a*] that wrong which ye have done. ¹⁴Seek not after riches nor the vain things of this world. For behold, you cannot carry them with you.

¹⁵And now, my son, I would say somewhat unto you concerning the coming of Christ. Behold, I say unto you, that it is him that surely shall come to take away the sins of the world. Yea, he cometh to declare glad tidings of salvation unto his people.

¹⁶And now, my son, this was the ministry unto which ye were called, to declare these glad tidings unto this people, to prepare their minds (or rather that salvation might come unto them), that they may prepare the minds of their children to hear the word at the time of his coming.

¹⁷And now, I will ease your mind somewhat on this subject. Behold, you marvel why these things should be known so long beforehand. Behold, I say unto you, is not a soul at this time as precious unto God as a soul will be at the time of his coming? ¹⁸Is it not as necessary that the plan of redemption should be made known unto this people as well as unto their children? ¹⁹Is it not as easy at this time for the Lord to send his angel to declare those glad tidings unto us, as unto our children, or as after the time of his coming?

[40] ¹Now, my son, here is somewhat more I would say unto thee. For I perceive that thy mind is worried concerning the resurrection of the dead. ²Behold, I say unto you, that there is no resurrection (or I would say, in other words), that this mortal does not put on immortality—this corruption does not put on incorruption*b*—until after the coming of Christ. ³Behold, he bringeth to pass the resurrection of the dead. But behold, my son—the resurrection is not yet.

Now, I unfold unto you a mystery (nevertheless, there are many mysteries which are kept, that no one knoweth them save God himself). But I show unto you one thing, which I have inquired diligently of God that I might know, that is, concerning the resurrection. ⁴Behold, there is a time appointed that all shall come forth from the dead.

Now, when this time cometh, no one knows. But God knoweth the time which is appointed.

⁵Now, whether there shall be one time, or a second time, or a third time, that men shall come forth from the dead—it mattereth not. For God knoweth all these things. And it sufficeth me to know that this is the case, that there is a time appointed [when*c*] all shall rise from the dead.

⁶Now, there must needs be a space betwixt the time of death and the time of the resurrection.

⁷And now, I would inquire what becometh of the souls of men from the time of death to the time appointed for the resurrection?

⁸Now, whether there is more than one time appointed for men to rise, it mattereth not. For all do not die at once. And this mattereth not. All is as one day with God, and time only is measured unto man. ⁹Therefore, there is a time appointed unto men that they shall

---

phrase "lead away the hearts of no more [people]." It is possible that the inflection of the dictation would have made this more understandable to the scribe while writing it down.

a. The Original Manuscript here is difficult to read. Skousen suggests that it might have been "repair," though "retain" is also possible. See *Printer's Manuscript of the Book of Mormon*, 2:17. The current printed version has "refrain from." The intent is perhaps closer to recover, as the idea was to undo the damage Corianton had done.

b. See 1 Corinthians 15:54 for the use of "corruption and incorruption."

c. Restored per the Original Manuscript. The Printer's Manuscript and later printed editions have "that." *Printer's Manuscript of the Book of Mormon*, 2:19.

rise from the dead. And there is a space between the time of death and the resurrection.

And now, concerning this space of time—what becometh of the souls of men is the thing which I have inquired diligently of the Lord to know. And this is the thing of which I do know. ¹⁰And when the time cometh when all shall rise—then shall they know that God knoweth all the times which are appointed unto man.

¹¹Now, concerning the state of the soul between death and the resurrection—behold, it hath been made known unto me by an angel that the spirits of all men, as soon as they are departed from this mortal body—yea, the spirits of all men, whether they be good or evil—are taken home to that God who gave them life.

¹²And then shall it come to pass that the spirits of those which are righteous are received into a state of happiness which is called paradise—a state of rest—a state of peace—where they shall rest from all their troubles, and from all care, and sorrow, etcetera.

¹³And then shall it come to pass that the spirits of the wicked—(yea, which are evil, for behold they have no part nor portion of the spirit of the Lord, for behold they chose evil works rather than good—therefore, the spirit of the devil did enter into them, and take possession of their house)—and these shall be cast out into outer darkness.[a] There shall be weeping, and wailing, and gnashing of teeth[b]—and this because of their own iniquity—being led captive by the will of the devil.

¹⁴Now, this is the state of the souls of the wicked, yea, in darkness, and a state of awful, fearful looking for of the fiery indignation of the wrath of God upon them.[c] Thus, they remain in this state—as well as the righteous in paradise, until the time of their resurrection.

¹⁵Now, there are some that have understood that this state of happiness, and this state of misery of the soul (before the resurrection)—was a first resurrection. Yea, I admit it may be termed a resurrection—the raising the spirit (or the soul) and their consignation to happiness or misery, according to the words which have been spoken.

¹⁶And behold, again it hath been spoken that there is a first resurrection—a resurrection of all those which have been, or which are, or which shall be—down to the resurrection of Christ from the dead. ¹⁷Now, we do not suppose that this first resurrection, which is spoken of in this manner, can be the resurrection of the souls and their consignation to happiness or misery. Ye cannot suppose that this is what it meaneth. ¹⁸Behold, I say unto you, nay! But it meaneth the reuniting of the soul with the body of those from the days of Adam down to the resurrection of Christ.

¹⁹Now, whether the souls and the bodies of those of which have been spoken shall all be reunited at once, the wicked as well as the righteous, I do not say. Let it suffice that I say that they all come forth (or in other words, their resurrection cometh to pass), before the resurrection of those which die after the resurrection of Christ.

²⁰Now, my son, I do not say that their resurrection cometh at the resurrection of Christ. But behold, I give it as my opinion, that the souls and the bodies are reunited of the righteous at the resurrection of Christ, and his ascension into heaven. ²¹But, whether it be at his resurrection or after, I do not say. But this much I say, that there is

---

a. This is a difficult sentence. The phrases set in parentheses are a long aside. The shorter sentence would be "the spirits of the wicked . . . shall be cast out."

b. See Matthew 8:11: "But the children of the kingdom shall be cast out into outer darkness: there shall be weeping and gnashing of teeth."

c. See Hebrews 10:27: "But a certain fearful looking for of judgment and fiery indignation."

a space betwixt between death and the resurrection of the body—and a state of the soul in happiness or in misery, until the time which is appointed of God that the dead shall come forth and be reunited—both soul and body—and be brought to stand before God, and be judged according to their works. ²²Yea, this bringeth about the restoration of those things of which have been spoken by the mouths of the prophets. ²³The soul shall be restored to the body and the body to the soul. Yea, and every limb and joint shall be restored to its body. Yea, even a hair of their heads shall not be lost. But all things shall be restored to its proper and perfect frame.

²⁴And now, my son, this is the restoration of which has been spoken by the mouths of the prophets—²⁵and then shall the righteous shine forth in the kingdom of God.[a]

²⁶But behold, an awful death cometh upon the wicked. For they die as to things pertaining to things of righteousness. For they are unclean, and no unclean thing can inherit the kingdom of God.[b] But they are cast out and consigned to partake of the fruits of their labors (or their works), which have been evil. And they drink the drugs[c] of a bitter cup.

[41] ¹And now, my son, I have somewhat to say concerning the restoration of which has been spoken. For behold, some have a-wrested the scriptures,[d] and have gone far astray because of this thing. And I perceive that thy mind hath been worried also, concerning this thing. But behold, I will explain it unto thee.

²I say unto thee, my son, that the plan of restoration is requisites with the justice of God. For it is requisite that all things should be restored to their proper order. Behold, it is requisite and just, according to the power and resurrection of Christ, that the soul of man should be restored to its body—and that every part of the body should be restored to itself.

³And it is requisite with the justice of God, that men should be judged according to their works. And if their works were good in this life, and the desires of their hearts were good, that they should also (at the last day) be restored unto that which is good. ⁴And if their works are evil, they shall be restored unto him for evil. Therefore, all things shall be restored to their proper order—everything to its natural frame (mortality raised to immortality—corruption to incorruption[e])—raised to endless happiness to inherit the kingdom of God, or to endless misery, to inherit the kingdom of the devil—the one on one hand, the other on the other. ⁵The one [restored[f]] to happiness, according to his desires of happiness or good, according to his desires of good—and the other to evil, according to his desires of evil. For, as he has desired to do evil all the day long, even so shall he have his reward of evil when the night cometh.

⁶And so it is on the other hand. If he hath repented of his sins and desired righ-

---

a. See Matthew 13:43: "Then shall the righteous shine forth as the sun in the kingdom of their Father."

b. Some of the themes appear in Ephesians 5:5: "For this ye know, that no whoremonger, nor unclean person, nor covetous man, who is an idolater, hath any inheritance in the kingdom of Christ and of God."

c. Both the Original and Printer's Manuscript have "drugs." The compositor changed it to "dregs," which is clearly the intended word. Skousen explains that both Joseph Smith and Oliver Cowdery at times used a more common word in the place of a less common one. See Skousen, *Analysis of the Textual Variants*, 4:2418.

d. See 2 Peter 3:16: "They that are unlearned and unstable wrest, as *they do* also the other scriptures, unto their own destruction."

e. See 1 Corinthians 15:54 for the use of "corruption and incorruption."

f. Restored per the Original Manuscript. The Printer's Manuscript and subsequent printed editions have "raised." Skousen, *Analysis of the Textual Variants*, 4:2422.

teousness until the end of his days, even so shall he be rewarded unto righteousness. ⁷These are they that are redeemed of the Lord. Yea, these are they that are taken out, that are delivered from that endless night of darkness. And thus they stand or fall, for behold, they are their own judges—whether to do good or do evil. ⁸Now, the decrees of God are unalterable. Therefore, the way is prepared, that whosoever will, may walk therein, and be saved.

⁹And now behold, my son, do not risk one more offence against your God upon those points of doctrine, which ye hath hitherto risked to commit sin. ¹⁰Do not suppose, because it hath been spoken concerning restoration, that ye shall be restored from sin to happiness. Behold, I say unto you: Wickedness never was happiness.

¹¹And now, my son, all men that are in a state of nature (or, I would say, in a carnal state) are in the gall of bitterness and in the bonds of iniquity.ª They are without God in the world, and they have gone contrary to the nature of God.ᵇ Therefore, they are in a state contrary to the nature of happiness.

¹²And now, behold, is the meaning of the word restoration to take a thing of a natural state, and place it in an unnatural state, or to place it in a state opposite to its nature? ¹³O, my son, this is not the case! But the meaning of the word restoration is to bring back again—evil for evil, or carnal for carnal, or devilish for devilish—good for that which is good, righteous for that which is righteous, just for that which is just, merciful for that which is merciful. ¹⁴Therefore, my son, see that ye are merciful unto your brethren.

Deal justly. Judge righteously. And do good continually. And if ye do all these things, then shall ye receive your reward. Yea, ye shall have mercy restored unto you again. Ye shall have justice restored unto you again. Ye shall have a righteous judgment restored unto you again—and ye shall have good rewarded unto you again. ¹⁵For that which ye doth send out, shall return unto you again and be restored. Therefore, the word restoration more fully condemneth the sinner, and justifieth him not at all.

[42] ¹And now, my son, I perceive there is somewhat more which doth worry your mind which ye cannot understand, which is concerning the justice of God in the punishment of the sinner. For ye do try to suppose that it is injustice that the sinner should be consigned to a state of misery.

²Now behold, my son, I will explain this thing unto thee. For behold, after the Lord God sent our first parents forth from the garden of Eden to till the ground (from whence he was taken), yea, he [droveᶜ] out the man, and he placed at the east end of the garden of Eden, cherubimsᵈ and flaming sword, which turned every way, to keep the tree of life.

³Now, we see that the man had become as God, knowing good and evil. And, lest he should put forth his hand and take also of the tree of life, and eat, and live forever—that the Lord God placed [cherubims,ᵉ] and the flaming sword, that he should not partake

a. See Acts 8:23: "For I perceive that thou art in the gall of bitterness, and in the bond of iniquity."
b. See Ephesians 2:12: "That at that time ye were without Christ, being aliens from the commonwealth of Israel, and strangers from the covenants of promise, having no hope, and without God in the world."
c. Restored per the Original Manuscript. The reference is to Genesis 3:24: "So he drove out the man; and he placed at the east of the garden of Eden Cherubims, and a flaming sword which turned every way, to keep the way of the tree of life." Skousen, *Analysis of the Textual Variants*, 4:2430.
d. Cherubims is a double plural, with the *-s* from English added to the *-im* of the Hebrew. However, since the reference is to Genesis 3:24 where the word is also cherubims, It has been left as the double plural.
e. The corrected Printer's Manuscript transcript has "cherubim," but the unedited Printer's Manuscript

of the fruit. ⁴And thus we see that there was a time granted unto man to repent, yea, probationary time—a time to repent, and serve God. ⁵For behold, if Adam had put forth his hand immediately and partook of the tree of life, he would have lived forever (according to the word of God)—having no space for repentance. Yea, and also the word of God would have been void, and the great plan of salvation would have been frustrated.

⁶But behold, it was appointed unto man to die. Therefore, as they were cut off from the tree of life, therefore they should be cut off from the face of the earth. And man became lost forever. Yea, they became fallen man.

⁷And now, we see by this, that our first parents were cut off, both temporally and spiritually, from the presence of the Lord. And thus, we see they became subjects, to follow after their own will. ⁸Now behold, it was not expedient that man should be reclaimed from this temporal death. For that would destroy the great plan of happiness. ⁹Therefore, as the soul could never die, and the fall had brought upon all mankind a spiritual death as well as a temporal—that is, they were cut off from the presence of the Lord[a]—therefore it was expedient that mankind should be reclaimed from this spiritual death. ¹⁰Therefore, as they had become carnal, sensual, and devilish by nature, this probationary state became a state for them to prepare. It became a [preparatory[b]] state.

¹¹And now, remember, my son! If it were not for the plan of redemption (laying it aside)—as soon as they were dead, their souls were miserable—being cut off from the presence of the Lord.[c]

¹²And now, there was no means to reclaim men from this fallen state, which man had brought upon himself, because of his own disobedience. ¹³Therefore, according to justice—the plan of redemption could not be brought about—only on conditions of repentance of men in this probationary state, yea, this preparatory state. For except it were for these conditions, mercy could not take effect except it should destroy the work of justice.

Now, the work of justice could not be destroyed. If so, God would cease to be God. ¹⁴And thus, we see that all mankind were fallen, and they were in the grasp of justice, yea, the justice of God, which consigned them forever to be cut off from his presence.

¹⁵And now, the plan of mercy could not be brought about, except an atonement should be made. Therefore, God himself atoneth for the sins of the world, to bring about the plan of mercy—to appease the demands of justice, that God might be a perfect, just God—and a merciful God.

¹⁶Also now, repentance could not come unto men except there were a punishment (which also was as eternal as the life of the soul)—should be affixed, opposite to the plan of happiness (which was as eternal also), as the life of the soul.

¹⁷Now, how could a man repent, except he should sin? How could he sin, if there was no law? How could there be a law, save there was a punishment?

¹⁸Now, there was a punishment affixed, and a just law given, which brought remorse of conscience unto man.

---

appears to have "cherubims," Skousen appears to see this instance in the Printer's Manuscript as that text's original reading. The manuscript page clearly shows a cross out with the heavier ink that was used for Joseph Smith's 1837 corrections. Skousen, *Analysis of the Textual Variants*, 4:2431.

 a. The phrase "cut off from my presence" is found in Leviticus 22:3.

 b. The Printer's Manuscript has "probationary," but the Original Manuscript and all printed editions have the correct "preparatory." Skousen, *Analysis of the Textual Variants*, 4:2435.

 c. The phrase "cut off from my presence" is found in Leviticus 22:3.

Chapter XIX [Alma 39–42]

¹⁹Now, if there was no law given—if a man murdered [ᵃ] he should die—would he be afraid he should die if he should murder? ²⁰And also, if there was no law given against sin, men would not be afraid to sin. ²¹And if there was no law given, if men sinned, what could justice do, or mercy either? For they would have no claim upon the creature. ²²But there is a law given, and a punishment affixed, and repentance granted, which repentance mercy claimeth. Otherwise, justice claimeth the creature, and executeth the law—and the law inflicteth the punishment. If not so, the works of justice would be destroyed, and God would cease to be God.

²³But God ceaseth not to be God! And mercy claimeth the penitent. And mercy cometh because of the atonement. And the atonement bringeth to pass the resurrection of the dead. And the resurrection of the dead bringing back men into the presence of God. And thus, they are restored into his presence, to be judged according to their works, according to the law and justice. ²⁴For behold, justice exerciseth all his demands. And also mercy claimeth all which is her own. And thus, none but the truly penitent are saved.

²⁵What? Do ye suppose that mercy can rob justice? I say unto you, nay—not one whit! If so, God would cease to be God. ²⁶And thus, God bringeth about his great and eternal purposes, which was prepared from the foundation of the world. And thus cometh about the salvation and the redemption of men—and also their destruction, and misery. ²⁷Therefore, O my son, whosoever will come—may come and partake of the waters of life freely.[ᵇ] And whosoever will not come—the same is not compelled to come. But in the last day, it shall be restored unto him according to his deeds. ²⁸If he hath desired to do evil, and hath not repented in his days—behold, evil shall be done unto him, according to the restoration of God.

²⁹And now, my son I desire that ye should let these things trouble you no more, and only let your sins trouble you with that trouble which shall bring you down unto repentance.

³⁰O my son! I desire that ye should deny the justice of God no more. Do not endeavor to excuse yourself in the least point because of your sins by denying the justice of God! But do you let the justice of God, and his mercy, and his long suffering, have full sway in your heart—but let it bring you down to the dust in humility.

³¹And now, my son, ye are called of God to preach the word unto this people. And now, my son, go thy way. Declare the word with truth and soberness, that thou mayest bring souls unto repentance, that the great plan of mercy may have claim upon them. And may God grant unto you, even according to my word. Amen.

---

a. It is possible that the word "and" is missing at this point. It appears to be required for the sense of the sentence. The Original Manuscript is not extant at this point. Modern editions do not emend the sentence.

b. See Revelation 22:17: "And whosoever will, let him take the water of life freely."

Chapter XX [Alma 43–44]

[43] ¹And now it came to pass that the sons of Alma did go forth among the people to declare the word unto them. And Alma also, himself, could not rest. And he also went forth. ²Now, we shall say no more concerning their preaching, except that they preached the word and the truth, according to the spirit of prophecy and revelation. And they preached after the holy order of God—by which they were called.

³And now, I return to an account of the wars between the Nephites and the Lamanites in the eighteenth year of the reign of the judges.[a] ⁴For behold, it [came to pass that[b]] the Zoramites became Lamanites. Therefore, in the commencement of the eighteenth year the people of the Nephites saw that the Lamanites were coming upon them. Therefore, they made preparations for war. Yea, they gathered together their armies in the land of Jershon.

⁵And it came to pass that the Lamanites came with their thousands. And they came into the land of Antionum, which was the land of the Zoramites. And a man by the name of Zerahemnah was their leader.

⁶And now, as the Amalekites were of a more wicked and a murderous disposition than the Lamanites were (in and of themselves)—therefore, Zerahemnah appointed chief captains over the Lamanites, and they were all the Amalekites and the Zoramites. ⁷Now, this he done that he might preserve their hatred towards the Nephites, that he might bring them into subjection, to the accomplishment of his designs. ⁸For behold, his designs were to stir up the Lamanites to anger against the Nephites. And this he done that he might usurp great power over them, and also that he might gain power over the Nephites by bringing them into bondage, etcetera.

⁹And now, the design of the Nephites were to support their lands, and their houses, and their wives, and their children, that they might preserve them from the hands of their enemies. And also, that they might preserve their rights, and their privileges, yea, and also their liberty—that they might worship God according to their desires. ¹⁰For they knew that if they should fall into the hands of the Lamanites, that whosoever should worship God in spirit and in truth[c] the true and the living God[d]—the Lamanites would destroy.

¹¹Yea, and they also knew the extreme hatred of the Lamanites towards their brethren, which were the people of Anti-Nephi-Lehi, which were called the people of Ammon. And they would not take up arms. Yea, they had entered into a covenant, and they would not break it. Therefore, if they should fall into the hands of the Lamanites, they would be destroyed. ¹²And the Nephites would not suffer that they should be destroyed. Therefore, they gave them lands for their inheritance. ¹³And the people of Ammon did give unto the Nephites a large portion of their substance to support their armies. And thus, the Nephites were compelled alone to withstand against the

---

a. Mormon treats the insertion of Alma's instructions to his sons as a diversion in his text. This is conceptual repetitive resumption that returns the reader to the end of Alma 35:13 and the beginnings of the war that will occupy most of the rest of the book of Alma.

b. Restored per the The Original Manuscript. The Printer's Manuscript has "it came that."

c. See John 4:23: "But the hour cometh, and now is, when the true worshippers shall worship the Father in spirit and in truth: for the Father seeketh such to worship him."

d. The phrase "the true and living God is found in 1 Thessalonians 1:9.

Chapter XX [Alma 43–44]

Lamanites, which were a compound of Laman, and Lemuel, and the sons of Ishmael, and all those which had dissented from the Nephites, which were Amalekites, and Zoramites, and the descendants of the priests of Noah. ¹⁴Now, those [dissenters[a]] were as numerous, nearly, as were the Nephites. And thus, the Nephites were obliged to contend with their brethren, even unto bloodshed.

¹⁵And it came to pass, as the armies of the Lamanites had gathered together in the land of Antionum—behold, the armies of the Nephites were prepared to meet them in the land of Jershon.

¹⁶Now, the leader of the Nephites (or the man which had been appointed to be the chief captain over the Nephites)—now the chief captain took the command of all the armies of the Nephites—and his name was Moroni.[b] ¹⁷And Moroni took all the command and the governments of their wars. And he was only twenty and five years old when he was appointed chief [commander[c]] over the armies of the Nephites.

¹⁸And it came to pass that he met the Lamanites in the borders of Jershon. And his people were armed with swords, and with scimitars, and all manner of weapons of war.

¹⁹And it came to pass that when the armies of the Lamanites saw that the people of Nephi—or that Moroni—had prepared his people with breastplates, and with arm shields, yea, and also shields to defend their heads.[d] And also, they were dressed with thick clothing.

²⁰Now, the army of Zerahemnah was not prepared with any such thing. They had only their swords, and their scimitars, their bows and their arrows, their stones and their slings—but they were naked, save it were a skin which was girded about their loins. Yea, all were naked, save it were the Zoramites and the Amalekites ²¹(but they were not armed with breastplates, nor shields). Therefore, they were exceeding afraid of the armies of the Nephites because of their armor—notwithstanding their number being so much greater than the Nephites.

²²Behold, now it came to pass that they durst not come against the Nephites in the borders of Jershon. Therefore, they departed out of the land of Antionum into the wilderness and took their journey round about in the wilderness, away by the head of the river Sidon, that they might come into the land of Manti and take possession of the land. For they did not suppose that the armies of Moroni would know whither they had gone. ²³But it came to pass as soon as they had departed into the wilderness, Moroni sent spies into the wilderness, to watch their camp. And Moroni, also knowing of the prophecies of Alma, sent certain men unto him, [desiring him that[e]] he should inquire of the Lord whither the armies of the Nephites should go to defend themselves against the Lamanites.

---

a. Restored per the Original Manuscript, which had "desenters." That was the spelling used earlier for "dissented," spelled "desented." The Printer's Manuscript has "desendants," probably influenced by "descendants of the priests of Noah" in the previous verse. Skousen, *Analysis of the Textual Variants,* 4:2463–64.

b. The clarification of the appointment of the chief captain was enough of a diversion that the sentence uses repetitive resumption to return to the original idea.

c. Restored per the Original Manuscript. The Printer's Manuscript has "captain," which corresponded to the title listed in the previous verse. Skousen, *Analysis of the Textual Variants,* 4:2466.

d. The sentence is grammatically unresolved. The "when" never has a concluding clause.

e. Restored per the Original Manuscript. The Printer's Manuscript has "unto him that," leaving out "desiring him." Skousen, *Analysis of the Textual Variants,* 4:2470.

²⁴And it came to pass that the word of the Lord came unto Alma. And Alma informed the messengers of Moroni that the armies of the Lamanites were marching round about in the wilderness, that they might come over into the land of Manti, that they might commence an attack upon the more weak part of the people. And those messengers went and delivered the message unto Moroni.

²⁵Now, Moroni, leaving a part of his army in the land of Jershon (lest by any means a part of the Lamanites should come into that land and take possession of the city), and Moroni took the remainder part of his army and marched over into the land of Manti.ᵃ

²⁶And he caused that all the people in that quarter of the land should gather themselves together to battle against the Lamanites, to defend their lands, and their country, their rights, and their liberties. Therefore, they were prepared against the time of the coming of the Lamanites.

²⁷And it came to pass that Moroni caused that his army should be secreted in the valley which was near the bank of the river Sidon (which was on the west of the river Sidon), in the wilderness. ²⁸And Moroni placed spies round about, that he might know when the camp of the Lamanites should come.

²⁹And now, as Moroni knew the intention of the Lamanites, that it was their intention to destroy their brethren, or to subject them and bring them into bondage (that they might establish a kingdom unto themselves over all the land)—³⁰and he also knowing that it was the only desire of the Nephites to preserve their lands, their liberty, and their church—therefore he thought it no sin that he should defend them by stratagem. Therefore, he found (by his spies) which course the Lamanites were to take. ³¹Therefore, he divided his army and brought a part over into the valley, and concealed them on the east and on the south of the hill Riplah. ³²And the remainder he concealed in the west valley, on the west of the river Sidon, and so down into the borders of the land Manti. ³³And thus, having placed his army according to his desire—he was prepared to meet them.

³⁴And it came to pass that the Lamanites came up on the north of the hill where a part of the army of Moroni was concealed.

³⁵And it came to pass that as the Lamanites had passed the hill Riplah and came into the valley and began to cross the river Sidon—the army which was concealed on the south of the hill (who was led by a man whose name was Lehi)—and he led his army forth and encircled the Lamanites about on the east, in their rear.

³⁶And it came to pass that the Lamanites, when they saw the Nephites coming upon them in their rear, turned them about and began to contend with the army of Lehi. ³⁷And the work of death commenced on both sides. But it was more dreadful on the part of the Lamanites. For their nakedness was exposed to the heavy blows of the Nephites with their swords, and their scimitars, which brought death almost at every stroke. ³⁸While, on the other hand, there was now and then a man fell among the Nephites by their [woundsᵇ], and the loss of blood—they being shielded from the more vital parts of the body (or the more vital parts of the body being shielded)—from the strokes of the Lamanites by their breastplates, and their arm shields, and their head plates. And thus, the Nephites did carry on the work of death among the Lamanites.

---

a. This sentence feels as though "leaving a part of his army" is not completed. It is completed with "and Moroni took the remainder." It would be clearer without the conjunction "and."

b. Restored per the Original Manuscript. The Printer's Manuscript, and subsequent printed editions, had "swords." Skousen, *Analysis of the Textual Variants*, 4:2480.

Chapter XX [Alma 43–44]

³⁹And it came to pass that the Lamanites became frightened because of the great destruction among them, even until they began to flee towards the river Sidon. ⁴⁰And they were pursued by Lehi and his men. And they were driven by Lehi into the waters of Sidon. And they crossed the waters of Sidon. And Lehi retained his armies upon the banks of the river Sidon, that they should not cross.

⁴¹And it came to pass that Moroni and his army met the Lamanites in the valley on the other side of the river Sidon.

And it came to pass that Moroni and his army began to fall upon them, and to slay they them.

⁴²And it came to pass that the Lamanites did flee again before them, towards the land of Manti. And they were met again by the armies of Moroni. ⁴³Now, in this case the Lamanites did fight exceedingly. Yea, never had the Lamanites been known to have fought with such exceeding great strength and courage—no, not even from the beginning. ⁴⁴And they were inspired by the Zoramites and the Amalekites (which were their chief captains and leaders) and by Zerahemnah, who was their chief captain (or their chief leader and commander). Yea, they did fight like dragons. And many of the Nephites were slain by their hand. [Yea[a]], for they did smite in two many of their headplates—and they did pierce many of their breastplates. And they did smite off many of their arms. And thus, the Lamanites did smite in their fierce anger. ⁴⁵Nevertheless, the Nephites were inspired by a better cause. For they were not fighting for monarchy, nor power, but they were fighting for their homes, and their liberties, their wives, and their children, and their all, yea, for their [rights[b]] of worship, and their church.

⁴⁶And they were doing that which they felt it was the duty which they owed to their God. For the Lord had said unto them, and also unto their fathers, that "inasmuch as ye are not guilty of the first offence, neither the second—ye shall not suffer yourselves to be slain by the hands of your enemies." ⁴⁷And again the Lord hath said that "ye shall defend your families, even unto bloodshed." Therefore, for this cause were the Nephites contending with the Lamanites, to defend themselves, and their families, and their lands, their country, and their rights, and their religion.

⁴⁸And it came to pass that when the men of Moroni saw the fierceness and the anger of the Lamanites, they were about to shrink and flee from them. And Moroni, perceiving their intent, sent forth—and inspired their hearts with these thoughts, yea, the thoughts of their lands, their liberty, yea, their freedom from bondage.

⁴⁹And it came to pass that they turned upon the Lamanites. And they cried with one voice unto the Lord, their God, for their liberty and their freedom from bondage. ⁵⁰And they began to stand against the Lamanites with power. And in the selfsame hour that they cried unto the Lord for their freedom, the Lamanites began to flee before them. And they [fled[c]], even to the waters of Sidon.

---

a. Restored per the *Original Manuscript of the Book of Mormon*, 5:331. The transcript of the Printer's Manuscript has "you." The word is cramped on the page but could be read as "you." Clearly, "yea" is the intention as well as the word from the extant original manuscript.

b. Emended as a spelling error. The Printer's Manuscript has "rites," which Oliver Cowdery did use as a spelling for "rights." Skousen has a long analysis of this. Skousen, *Analysis of the Textual Variants*, 4:2485–89. This meaning is confirmed by "rights" in verse 47.

c. The Printer's Manuscript has "fed," which clearly was intended to be "fled," as occurs in the printed editions.

⁵¹Now, the Lamanites were more numerous, yea, by more than double the number of the Nephites. Nevertheless, they were driven, insomuch that they were gathered together in one body in the valley upon the bank by the river Sidon. ⁵²Therefore, the armies of Moroni encircled them about, yea, even on both sides of the river. For behold, on the east were the men of Lehi. ⁵³Therefore, when Zerahemnah saw the men of Lehi on the east of the river Sidon, and the armies of Moroni on the west of the river Sidon, that they were encircled about by the Nephites—they were struck with terror. ⁵⁴Now, Moroni, when he saw their terror—he commanded his men that they should stop shedding their blood.

[44] ¹And it came to pass that they did stop and withdrew a pace from them. And Moroni said unto Zerahemnah:

> Behold, Zerahemnah, that we do not desire to be men of blood! Ye know that ye are in our hands. Yet we do not desire to slay you.
>
> ²Behold, we have not come out to battle against you that we might shed your blood for power. Neither do we desire to bring anyone to the yoke of bondage. But this is the very cause for which ye have come against us. Yea, and ye are angry with us because of our religion. ³But now, ye behold that the Lord is with us, and ye behold that he hath delivered you into our hands.
>
> And now, I would that ye should understand that this is done unto us because of our religion and our faith in Christ.
>
> And now, ye see that ye cannot destroy this, our faith.
>
> ⁴Now, ye see that this is the true faith of God. Yea, ye see that God will support, and keep, and preserve us—so long as we are faithful unto him, and unto our faith, and our religion. And never will the Lord suffer that we shall be destroyed, except we should fall into transgression and deny our faith.
>
> ⁵And now, Zerahemnah, I command you in the name of that all-powerful God who hath strengthened our arms, that we have gained power over you—by our faith, by our religion, and by our [rights[a]] of worship, and by our church, and by the sacred support which we owe to our wives, and our children—by that liberty which binds us to our lands, and our country. Yea, and also by the maintenance of the sacred word of God, to which we owe all our happiness—and by all that is most dear unto us.
>
> ⁶Yea, and this is not all. I command you by all the desires which ye have for life, that ye deliver up your weapons of war unto us. And we will seek not your blood. But we will spare your lives—if ye will go your way and come not again to war against us.
>
> ⁷And now, if ye do not this—behold, ye are in our hands, and I will command my men that they shall fall upon you, and inflict the wounds of death in your bodies, that ye may become extinct. And then we will see who shall have power over this people. Yea, we will see who shall be brought into bondage.

⁸And now it came to pass that when Zerahemnah heard these sayings, he came forth and delivered up his sword, and his scimitar, and his bow, into the hands of Moroni, and saith unto him:

---

a. Emended as a spelling error. The Printer's Manuscript has "rites," which Oliver did use as a spelling for "rights." Skousen has a long analysis of this. Skousen, *Analysis of the Textual Variants*, 4:2485–89.

Chapter XX [Alma 43–44]

⁹Behold, here is our weapons of war. We will deliver them up unto you. And we will not suffer ourselves to take an oath unto you, which we know that we shall break (and also our children). But take our weapons of war and suffer that we may depart into the wilderness. Otherwise, we will retain our swords—and we will perish or conquer.

Behold, we are not of your faith. We do not believe that it is God that hath delivered us into your hands. But we believe it is your cunning that hath preserved you from our swords. Behold, it is your breastplates and your shields that hath preserved you.

¹⁰And now, when Zerahemnah had made an end of speaking these words, Moroni returned the sword and the weapons of war which he had received unto Zerahemnah, saying:

Behold, we will end the conflict.

¹¹Now, I cannot retain the words which I have spoken. Therefore, as the Lord liveth, ye shall not depart, except ye depart with an oath that ye will not return again against us to war.

Now, as ye are in our hands, we will spill your blood upon the ground—or ye shall submit to the conditions to which I have proposed.

¹²And now, when Moroni had said these words, Zerahemnah retained his sword. And he was angry with Moroni. And he rushed forward, that he might slay Moroni. But, as he raised his sword, behold, one of Moroni's soldiers smote it, even to the earth. And it broke by the hilt. And he also smote Zerahemnah, that he took off his scalp—and it fell to the earth. And Zerahemnah withdrew from before them, into the midst of his soldiers.

¹³And it came to pass that the soldier which stood by, which smote off the scalp of Zerahemnah, took up the scalp from off the ground by the hair and laid it upon the point of his sword, and stretched it forth unto them—saying unto them with a loud voice, saying: ¹⁴"Even as this scalp hath fallen to the earth, which is the scalp of your chief, so shall ye fall to the earth, except ye will deliver up your weapons of war and depart with a covenant of peace!"

¹⁵Now, there were many, when they heard these words, and saw the scalp which was upon the sword—they were struck with fear. And many came forth and threw down their weapon of war at the feet of Moroni and entered into a covenant of peace. And as many as entered into a covenant, they suffered to depart into the wilderness.

¹⁶Now it came to pass that Zerahemnah was exceeding wroth. And he did stir up the remainder of his soldiers to anger, to contend more powerfully against the Nephites.

¹⁷And now, Moroni was angry—because of the stubbornness of the Lamanites. Therefore, he commanded his people that they should fall upon them and slay them.

And it came to pass that they began to slay them. Yea, and the Lamanites did contend with their swords and their mights. ¹⁸But behold, their naked skins and their bare heads, were exposed to the sharp swords of the Nephites. Yea behold, they were pierced, and smitten, yea, and did fall exceeding fast before the swords of the Nephites. And they began to be swept down, even as the soldier of Moroni had prophesied.

¹⁹Now, Zerahemnah, when he saw that they were all about to be destroyed, [he[a]] cried mightily unto Moroni—promising that he would covenant, and also his people with them—if they would spare the remainder of their lives, that they never would come to war again against them.

²⁰And it came to pass that Moroni caused that the work of death should cease again among the people.

And it came to pass that he took the weapons of war from the Lamanites. And after they had entered into a covenant (with him) of peace, they were suffered to depart into the wilderness.

²¹Now, the number of their dead were not numbered, because of the greatness of the number. Yea, the number of their dead were exceeding great—both on the Nephites, and on the Lamanites.

²²And it came to pass that they did cast their dead into the waters of Sidon. And they have gone forth and are buried in the depths of the sea. ²³And the armies of the Nephites (or of Moroni) returned, and came to their houses, and their lands. And thus ended the eighteenth year of the reign of the judges over the people of Nephi. ²⁴And thus ended the record of Alma, which was wrote upon the plates of Nephi.

---

a. Emended per the Original Manuscript. There is an ink spot blotting out a space that could easily have had a two-letter word. Skousen, *Analysis of the Textual Variants*, 4:2509.

Chapter XXI [Alma 45–49]

[45] *The account of the people of Nephi and their wars and dissensions in the days of Helaman, according to the record of Helaman which he kept in his days.*

¹Behold, now it came to pass that the people of Nephi were exceedingly rejoiced because the Lord had again delivered them out of the hands of their enemies. Therefore, they gave thanks unto the Lord, their God. Yea, and they did fast much, and pray much, and they did worship God with exceeding great joy.

²And it came to pass in the nineteenth year of the reign of the judges over the people of Nephi that Alma came unto his son, Helaman, and saith unto him: "Believest thou the words which I spake unto thee concerning these records which have been kept?"

³And Helaman saith unto him: "Yea, I believe."

⁴And Alma saith again: "Believest thou in Jesus Christ, which shall come?"

⁵And he saith: "Yea, I believe all the words which thou hast spoken."

⁶And Alma saith unto him again: "Will ye keep my commandments?"

⁷And he [said[a]]: "Yea, I will keep thy commandments, with all my heart."

⁸Then Alma saith unto him:

Blessed art thou! [And the[b]] Lord shall prosper thee in this land. ⁹But behold, I have somewhat to prophesy unto thee—but what I prophesy unto thee, ye shall not make known. Yea, what I prophesy unto thee, shall not be made known even until the prophecy is fulfilled. Therefore, write the words which I shall say.

¹⁰And these are the words:

Behold! I perceive that this very people, the Nephites (according to the spirit of revelation which is in me)—in four hundred years from the time that Jesus Christ shall manifest himself unto them—shall dwindle in unbelief.

¹¹Yea, and then shall they see wars, and pestilences, yea, famines and bloodsheds, even until the people of Nephi shall become extinct.

¹²Yea, and this because they shall dwindle in unbelief, and fall into the works of darkness, and lasciviousness, and all manner of iniquities.

Yea, I say unto you, that because they shall sin against so great light and knowledge—

yea, I say unto you, that from that day, even the fourth generation shall not all pass away before this great iniquity shall come.

¹³And when that great day cometh, behold, the time very soon cometh that those which are now (or the seed of those which are now) numbered among the people of the Nephites, shall no more be numbered among the people of Nephi.

¹⁴But whosoever remaineth and is not destroyed in that great and dreadful day shall be numbered among the Lamanites, and shall become like unto them—all save it be a few (which shall be called the disciples of the Lord). And them shall the Lamanites pursue, even until they shall become extinct. And now, because of iniquity, this prophecy shall be fulfilled.

---

a. Restored per the Original Manuscript. The Printer's Manuscript has "saith." Skousen, *Analysis of the Textual Variants*, 4:2517.

b. Restored per the Original Manuscript. *Original Manuscript of the Book of Mormon*, 5:339.

¹⁵And now it came to pass that after Alma had said these things to Helaman—he blessed him, and also his other sons. And he also blessed the earth, for the righteous' sake. ¹⁶And he said—thus saith the Lord God: "Cursed shall be the land, yea, this land (unto every nation, kindred, tongue, and people[a])—unto destruction (which do wickedly—when they are fully ripe).[b] And as I have said, so shall it be. For this is the cursing, and the blessing, of God upon the land. For the Lord cannot look upon sin with the least degree of allowance."

¹⁷And now, when Alma had said these words, he blessed the church. Yea, all those which should stand fast in the faith from that time henceforth. ¹⁸And when Alma had done this, he departed out of the land of Zarahemla—as if to go into the land of Melek.

And it came to pass that he was never heard of more. As to his death or his burial—we know not of.[c] ¹⁹Behold, this we know--that he was a righteous man. And the saying went abroad in the church that he was taken up by the spirit, or buried by the hand of the Lord even as Moses. But behold, the scripture saith: "The Lord took Moses unto himself."[d] And we suppose that he hath also received Alma, in the spirit, unto himself. Therefore, for this cause—we know nothing concerning his death and burial.

²⁰And now it came to pass in the commencement of the nineteenth year of the reign of the judges over the people of Nephi, that Helaman went forth among the people, to declare the word unto them. ²¹For behold, because of their wars with the Lamanites and the many little dissensions and disturbances which had been among the people—it became expedient that the word of God should be declared among them, yea, and that a regulation should be made throughout the church. ²²Therefore, Helaman and his brethren went forth to establish the church again in all the land, yea, in every city throughout all the land, which was possessed by the people of Nephi.

And it came to pass that they did appoint priests, and teachers, throughout all the land, over all the churches.

²³And now it came to pass that after Helaman and his brethren had appointed priests and teachers over the churches, that there arose a dissension among them. And they would not give heed to the words of Helaman and his brethren. ²⁵But, they grew proud, being lifted up in their hearts—because of their exceeding great riches. Therefore, they grew rich in their own eyes, and would not give heed to their words, to walk uprightly before God.

[46] ¹And it came to pass that as many as would not hearken to the words of Helaman and his brethren were gathered together against their brethren. ²And now behold, they were exceeding wroth, insomuch that they were determined to slay them.

³Now, the leader of those which were wroth against their brethren was a large and a

---

a. See Revelation 14:6: "And I saw another angel fly in the midst of heaven, having the everlasting gospel to preach unto them that dwell on the earth, and to every nation, and kindred, and tongue, and people."

b. This is a complicated sentence that is made more understandable by using parentheses to show the thoughts that are subordinate to the main idea. It would make better sense if it were reorganized: "Cursed be the land, yea, this land—unto destruction—unto every nation, kindred, tongue, and people which do wickedly—when they are fully ripe."

c. Uses language from, and may be an allusion to, Deuteronomy 34:6: "And he buried him in a valley in the land of Moab, over against Beth-peor: but no man knoweth of his sepulchre unto this day."

d. Moses's death and burial is recorded in Deuteronomy 34, but this quotation is not present, and the references Helaman makes do not match the details of Deuteronomy, suggesting that the brass plates had at least another, different account.

strong man. And his name was Amalickiah. ⁴And Amalickiah was desirous to be a king. And those people which were wroth were also desirous that he should be their king. And they were (the greater part of them) the lower judges of the land. And they were seeking for power. ⁵And they had been led by the flatteries of Amalickiah, that if they would support him and establish him to be their king, that he would make them rulers over the people. ⁶Thus, they were led away by Amalickiah to dissensions, notwithstanding the preaching of Helaman and his brethren, yea, notwithstanding their exceeding great care over the church (for they were high priests over the church).

⁷And there were many in the church which believed in the flattering words of Amalickiah. Therefore, they dissented, even from the church. And thus were the affairs of the people of Nephi exceeding precarious, and dangerous, notwithstanding their great victory which they had had over the Lamanites, and their great rejoicings which they had had because of their delivery by the hands of the Lord.

>⁸Thus, we see how quick the children of men doth forget the Lord, their God, yea, how quick to do iniquity, and to be led away by the evil one. ⁹Yea, and we also see the great wickedness one very wicked man can cause to take place among the children of men. ¹⁰Yea, we see that Amalickiah—because he was a man of cunning devices, and a man of many flattering words, that he led away the hearts of many people to do wickedly, yea, and to seek to destroy the church of God, and to destroy the foundation of liberty (which God had granted unto them—or which blessing God had sent upon the face of the land for the righteous sake).ᵃ<

¹¹And now it came to pass that when Moroni (which was the chief commander of the armies of the Nephites) had heard of these dissensions, he was angry with Amalickiah.

¹²And it came to pass that he rent his coat. And he took a piece thereof and wrote upon it: "In memory of our God, our religion, and freedom, and our peace—our wives, and our children." ¹³And he fastened it upon the end of a pole thereof. And he fastened on his headplate, and his breast plate, and his shields—and girded on his armor about his loins. And he took the pole, which had on the end thereof his rent coat, and he called it the title of liberty. And he bowed himself to the earth. And he prayed mightily unto his God for the blessings of liberty to rest upon his brethren—so long as there should a band of Christians remain to possess the land >¹⁴for thus were all the true believers of Christ, which belonged to the church of God called by those who did not belong to the church.<ᵇ

¹⁵And those who did belong to the church were faithful. Yea, all those who were true believers in Christ took upon them gladly the name of Christ, or Christians >as they were called, because of their belief in Christ, which should come.< ¹⁶And therefore, at this time Moroni prayed that the cause of the Christians, and the freedom of the land, might be favored.

¹⁷And it came to pass that when he had poured out his soul to God, he gaveᶜ all the land which was south of the land Desolation, yea, and in fine—all the land (both on the

---

a. Mormon inserts his summary of what he wants his readers to take from what he had just written.

b. Mormon adds this information from his knowledge. It would be unlikely for it to have been on the large plates, as anyone who might read them would already know that information. Thus, this is an aside directed at Mormon's future readers.

c. The reading in the current text is "named." That change was made in 1920. That is the intent of "gave," although in an archaic meaning. Skousen, *Analysis of the Textual Variants*, 4:2539.

north and on the south)—a chosen land and the land of liberty. ¹⁸And he saith: "Surely God shall not suffer that we who are despised because we take upon us the name of Christ, shall be trodden down and destroyed, until we bring it upon us by our own transgressions!"

¹⁹And when Moroni had said these words, he went forth among the people—waving the rent of his garment in the air, that all might see the writing which he had wrote upon the rent—and crying with a loud voice, saying: ²⁰"Behold! Whosoever will maintain this title upon the land—let them come forth in the strength of the Lord, and enter into a covenant that they will maintain their rights, and their religion, that the Lord God may bless them!"

²¹And it came to pass that when Moroni had proclaimed these words, behold the people came running together with their armors girded about their loins—rending their garments in token (or as a covenant) that they would not forsake the Lord, their God—or, in other words, if they should transgress the commandments of God, or fall into transgression, and be ashamed to take upon them the name of Christ—the Lord should rend them, even as they had rent their garments.

²²Now, this was the covenant which they made. And they cast their garments at the feet of Moroni, saying: "We covenant with our God that we shall be destroyed, even as our brethren in the land northward, if we shall fall into transgression! Yea, he may cast us at the feet of our enemies, even as we have cast our garments at thy feet, to be trodden under foot, if we should fall into transgression."

²³Moroni saith unto them:

> Behold! We are a remnant of the seed of Jacob! Yea, we are a remnant of the seed of Joseph, whose coat was rent by his brethren into many pieces. Yea, and now behold, let us remember to keep the commandments of God—or our garments shall be rent by our brethren, and we be cast into [prisons[a]], or be sold, or be slain. ²⁴Yea, let us preserve our liberty as a remnant of Joseph. Yea, let us remember the words of Jacob, before his death. For behold, he saw that a part of the remnant of the coat of Joseph was preserved and had not decayed. And he saith:
>
> > Even as this remnant of garment of my son's hath been preserved—so shall a remnant of the seed of my son be preserved by the hand of God and be taken unto himself—while the remainder of the seed of Joseph shall perish, even as the remnant of his garment. ²⁵Now behold, this giveth my soul sorrow. Nevertheless, my soul hath joy in my son because that part of his seed which shall be taken unto God.
>
> ²⁶Now behold, this was the language of Jacob. ²⁷And now, who knoweth but what the remnant of the seed of Joseph, which shall perish as his garment are, those which have [dissented[b]] from us? Yea, and even it shall be us—if we do not stand fast in the faith of Christ.

---

a. Restored per the Original Manuscript. The Printer's Manuscript has the singular "prison." Skousen, *Analysis of the Textual Variants*, 4:2547.

b. The typescript in the *Printer's Manuscript of the Book of Mormon*, 2:49, has "dese[r/n]ted." The reason for the r/n is that the letter is unclear. The 1830 edition has "dissented," and that is the common designation. Therefore, "dissented" is used here, assuming that the manuscript had the standard misspelling for that word. The word "dissented" appears in verse 28 referring to the same people, confirming that this is the proper reading here.

Chapter XXI [Alma 45–49]

²⁸And now it came to pass that when Moroni had said these words, he went forth—and also sent forth—in all the parts of the land where there were dissensions—and gathered together all the people which were desirous to maintain their liberty, to stand against Amalickiah and those which had dissented, which were called Amalickiahites.

²⁹And it came to pass that when Amalickiah saw that the people of Moroni were more numerous than the Amalickiahites, and he also saw that his people were doubtful concerning the justice of the cause in which they had undertaken—therefore, fearing that he should not gain the point, he took those of his people which would and departed into the land of Nephi.

³⁰Now, Moroni thought it was not expedient that the Lamanites should have any more strength. Therefore, he thought to cut off the people of Amalickiah—or to take them and bring them back—and put Amalickiah to death. Yea, for he knew that they would stir up the Lamanites to anger against them and cause them to come [down[a]] to battle against them. And this he knew that Amalickiah would do, that he might obtain his purposes. ³¹Therefore, Moroni thought it was expedient that he should take his armies, which had gathered themselves together and armed themselves, and entered into a covenant to keep the peace.

And it came to pass that he took his army and marched out [with his tents[b]] into the wilderness, to cut off the course of Amalickiah in the wilderness.

³²And it came to pass that he did according to his desires—and marched forth into the wilderness and headed the armies of Amalickiah.

³³And it came to pass that Amalickiah fled with a small number of his men, and the remainder were delivered up into the hands of Moroni and were taken back into the land of Zarahemla.

³⁴Now, Moroni, being a man which was appointed by the Chief Judges and the voice of the people—therefore he had power [to do[c]] according to his will with the armies of the Nephites, to establish, and to exercise authority over them.

³⁵And it came to pass that whomsoever of the Amalickiahites that would not enter into a covenant to support the cause of freedom, that they might maintain a free government—he caused to be put to death. And there was but few which denied the covenant of freedom.

³⁶And it came to pass also that he caused the title of liberty to be hoisted upon every tower which was in all the land which was possessed by the Nephites. And thus, Moroni planted the standard of liberty among the Nephites. ³⁷And they began to have peace again in the land. And thus, they did maintain peace in the land until nearly the end of the nineteenth year of the reign of the judges. ³⁸And Helaman and the high priests did also maintain order in the church, yea, even for the space of four years did they have much peace and rejoicing in the church.

>³⁹And it came to pass that there were many who died—firmly believing that their souls were redeemed by the Lord, Jesus Christ. Thus, they went out of the world rejoicing. ⁴⁰And there were some who died with fevers, which at some seasons of the year was very frequent in the land—but not so much so with fevers,

---

a. Restored per the Original Manuscript. Skousen, *Analysis of the Textual Variants*, 4:2562.
b. Restored per the Original Manuscript. Skousen, *Analysis of the Textual Variants*, 4:2563.
c. Restored per the Original Manuscript. Skousen, *Analysis of the Textual Variants*, 4:2566.

because of the excellent qualities of the many plants and roots which God had prepared to remove the cause of diseases which was subsequent to man by the nature of the climate. ⁴¹But there were many who died with old age. And those who died in the faith of Christ are happy in him—as we must needs suppose.[a]<

[47] ¹Now, we will return in our record to Amalickiah and those which [fled[b]] with him into the wilderness. For behold, he had taken those which [were[c]] with him and went up into the land of Nephi (>among the Lamanites[d]<) and did stir up the Lamanites to anger against the people of Nephi, insomuch that the king of the Lamanites sent a proclamation throughout all his land, among all his people, that they should gather themselves together again, to go up to battle against the Nephites.

²And it came to pass that when the proclamation had gone forth among them, they were exceeding afraid. Yea, they feared to displease the king, and they also feared to go to battle against the Nephites, lest they should lose their lives.

And it came to pass that they would not (or the more part of them would not) obey the commandment of the king.

³And now it came to pass that the king was wroth because of their disobedience. Therefore, he gave Amalickiah the command of that part of his army which was obedient unto his commands, and commanded him, that he should go forth and compel them to arms. ⁴Now, behold, this was the desires of Amalickiah. For he being a very subtle man to do evil, therefore he laid the plan in his heart to dethrone the king of the Lamanites.

⁵And now, he had got the command of those parts of the Lamanites which were in favor of the king. And he sought to gain favor of those which were not obedient. Therefore, he went forward to the place which was called Onidah. For thither had all the Lamanites fled, for they discovered the army coming. And they, supposing that they were coming to destroy them—therefore they fled to Onidah, to the place of arms. ⁶And they had appointed a man to be a king and a leader over them—being fixed in their minds, with a determined resolution that they would not be subjected to go against the Nephites.

⁷And it came to pass that they had gathered themselves together upon the top of the mount which was called Antipas, in preparation to battle. ⁸Now, it was not Amalickiah's intention to give them battle according to the commandments of the king. But behold, it was his intention to gain favor with the armies of the Lamanites, that he might place himself at their head, and dethrone the king, and take possession of the kingdom.

⁹And behold, it came to pass that he caused his army to pitch their tents in the valley which was near the mount Antipas.

¹⁰And it came to pass that when it was night, he sent a secret embassy into the

---

a. Mormon steps back from narration and inserts a moralizing comment. The confirmation that this is an interruption comes in the next sentence.

b. Restored per the Original Manuscript. The Printer's Manuscript has "had fled." Skousen, *Analysis of the Textual Variants,* 4:2570–71.

c. Restored per the Original Manuscript. The Printer's Manuscript has "went." Skousen, *Analysis of the Textual Variants,* 4:2570–71.

d. Mormon adds this clarification for his readers. He understood that a future reader might think that the land of Nephi meant that there were Nephites there. That had not been the case for around three generations (from the time of Mosiah, the father of King Benjamin). A contemporary record would not have had that information, as it would have been part of common knowledge.

mount Antipas—desiring that the leader of those which were upon the mount (whose name was Lehonti), that he should come down to the foot of the mount, for he desired to speak with him.

¹¹And it came to pass that when Lehonti received the message, he durst not go down to the foot of the mount.

And it came to pass that Amalickiah sent again, the second time—desiring him to come down.

And it came to pass that Lehonti would not. And he sent again, the third time.

¹²And it came to pass that when Amalickiah found that he could not get Lehonti to come down off from the mount, he went up into the mount, nearly to Lehonti's camp. And he sent again, the fourth time, his message unto Lehonti—desiring that he would come down—and that he would bring his guards with him.

¹³And it came to pass that when Lehonti had come down with his guards to Amalickiah, that Amalickiah desired him to come down, with his army, in the night time—and surround those men in their [camp[a]] (over whom the king had gave him command)—and that he would deliver them up into Lehonti's hands, if he would make him (Amalickiah), [the[b]] second leader over the whole army.

¹⁴And it came to pass that Lehonti came down with his men and surrounded the men of Amalickiah—so that before they awoke at the dawn of the day they were surrounded by the armies of Lehonti.

¹⁵And it came to pass that when they saw that they were surrounded—they pled with Amalickiah that he would suffer them to fall in with their brethren, that they might not be destroyed. Now, this was the very thing which Amalickiah desired.

¹⁶And it came to pass that he delivered his men, contrary to the commands of the king. Now, this was the thing that Amalickiah desired, that he might accomplish his designs in dethroning the king.

>¹⁷Now, it was the custom among the Lamanites, if their chief leader was killed, to appoint the second leader to be their chief leader.[c]<

¹⁸And it came to pass that Amalickiah caused that one of his servants should administer poison, by degrees, to Lehonti, that he died. ¹⁹Now, when Lehonti was dead, the Lamanites appointed Amalickiah to be their leader and their chief commander.

²⁰And it came to pass that Amalickiah marched with his armies (for he had gained his desires) to the land of Nephi, to the city of Nephi, which was the chief city. ²¹And the king came out to meet him (with his guards) for he supposed that Amalickiah had fulfilled his commands, and that Amalickiah had gathered together so great an army for to go against the Nephites to battle.

²²But behold, as the king came out to meet him, Amalickiah caused that his servants should go forth to meet the king. And they went [forth[d]] and bowed themselves before the king, as if to reverence him because of his greatness.

---

a. Restored per the Original Manuscript. The Printer's Manuscript has the plural "camps." Skousen, *Analysis of the Textual Variants*, 4:2578.

b. Restored per the Original Manuscript. The Printer's Manuscript, and subsequent printed editions, have "a." Skousen, *Analysis of the Textual Variants*, 4:2578.

c. This is Mormon's explanation for his future audience. This would not be needed in a contemporary document.

d. Restored per the Original Manuscript. Skousen, *Analysis of the Textual Variants*, 4:2580–81.

²³And it came to pass that the king put forth his hand, to raise them, as was the custom with the Lamanites (>and a token of peace, which custom they had taken from the Nephites^a<).

²⁴And it came to pass that when he had raised the first from the ground—behold, he stabbed the king to the heart. And he fell to the earth.

²⁵Now, the servants of the king fled, and the servants of Amalickiah raised a cry, saying: ²⁶"Behold! The servants of the king have stabbed him to the heart! And he has fell—and they have fled. Behold! Come and see!"

²⁷And it came to pass that Amalickiah commanded that his armies should march forth and see what had happened unto the king. And when they had come to the spot, and found the king lying in his gore, Amalickiah pretended to be wroth, and said: "Whosoever loved the king—let him go forth and pursue his servants, that they may be slain!"

²⁸And it came to pass that when all they who loved the king—when they heard these words—came forth and pursued after the servants of the king.

²⁹Now, when the servants of the king saw an army pursuing after they them, they were frightened again, and fled into the wilderness and came over into the land of Zarahemla and joined the people of Ammon. ³⁰And the army which pursued after them returned, having pursued after them in vain. And thus Amalickiah, by his fraud, gained the hearts of the people.

³¹And it came to pass on the morrow, he entered the city Nephi with his armies and took possession of the city.

³²And now it came to pass that the queen, when she had heard that the king was slain (for Amalickiah had sent an embassy to the queen, informing her that the king had been slain by his servants, that he had pursued them, with his army, but it was in vain—and they had made their escape)—³³therefore, when the queen had received this message—she sent unto Amalickiah—desiring him that he would spare the people of the city. And she also desired him that he should come in unto her. And she also desired him that he should bring witnesses with him, to testify concerning the death of the king.

³⁴And it came to pass that Amalickiah took the same servant that slew the king, and also they which were with him, and went in unto the queen—unto the place where she sat. And they all testified unto her, that the king was slain by his own servants. And they said also: "They have fled. Does not this testify against them?" And thus, they satisfied the queen concerning the death of the king.

³⁵And it came to pass that Amalickiah sought the favor of the queen—and took her unto him to wife. And thus, by his fraud, and by the assistance of his cunning servants, he obtained the kingdom. Yea, he was acknowledged king throughout all the land, among all the people of the Lamanites, which was composed of the Lamanites, and the Lemuelites, and the Ishmaelites, and all the dissenters from the Nephites, from the reign of Nephi down to the present time.

³⁶Now, these dissenters—having the same instruction and the same information of the Nephites, yea, having been instructed in the same knowledge of the Lord—nev-

---

a. This is Mormon's explanation for his future audience. It describes what must have been a nearly universal gesture, but in the way of his ethnocentrism, he has the Lamanites learning it from Nephites. He similarly suggested that the priests of Noah had taught reading and writing to the Lamanites (Mosiah 24:6).

Chapter XXI [Alma 45–49]

ertheless (it is strange to relate)—not long after their dissensions they became more hardened, and impenitent, and more wild, wicked, and ferocious than the Lamanites—drinking in with the traditions of the Lamanites—giving way to indolence, and all manner of lasciviousness. Yea, entirely forgetting the Lord, their God.

[48] ¹And now it came to pass that as soon as Amalickiah had obtained the kingdom, he began to inspire the hearts of the Lamanites against the people of Nephi. Yea, he did appoint men to speak unto the Lamanites, from their towers, against the Nephites. ²And thus, he did inspire their hearts against the Nephites, insomuch that in the latter end of the nineteenth year of the reign of the judges—he having accomplished his designs—therefore (thus far, yea, he having been made king over the Lamanites)—he sought also to reign over all the land. Yea, and all the people which were in the land—the Nephites as well as the Lamanites. ³Therefore, he had accomplished his design. For he had hardened the hearts of the Lamanites, and blinded their minds, and stirred them up to anger, insomuch that he had gathered together a numerous host to go to battle against the Nephites. ⁴For he was determined, because of the greatness of the number of his people to overpower the Nephites and to bring them into bondage. ⁵Thus, he did appoint chief captains of the Zoramites—they being the most acquainted with the strength of the Nephites and their places of resort, and their weakest parts of their cities. Therefore, he appointed them to be chief captains over his armies.

⁶And it came to pass that they took their camp and moved forth towards the land of Zarahemla in the wilderness.

⁷Now it came to pass that while Amalickiah had thus been obtaining power by fraud, and deceit—Moroni (on the other hand) had been a-preparing the minds of the people to be faithful unto the Lord, their God. ⁸Yea, he had been strengthening the armies of the Nephites and erecting small forts (or places of resort)—throwing up banks of earth round about, to enclose his armies. And also building walls of stone to encircle them about round about their cities and the borders of their lands, yea, all round about the land. ⁹And in their weakest fortifications he did place the greater number of men. And thus, he did fortify and strengthen the land which was possessed by the Nephites. ¹⁰And thus he was preparing to support their liberty, their lands, their wives, and their children, and their peace—and that they might live unto the Lord, their God, and that they might maintain that which was called (by their enemies) the cause of Christians.

>¹¹And Moroni was a strong, and a mighty man. He was a man of a perfect understanding.

Yea, a man that did not delight in bloodshed. A man whose soul did joy in the liberty, and the freedom, of his country, and his brethren—from bondage, and slavery.

¹²Yea, a man whose heart did swell with thanksgiving to his God for the many privileges and blessings which he bestowed upon his people. A man who did labor exceedingly for the welfare and safety of his people.

¹³Yea, and he was a man who was firm in the faith of Christ. And he had sworn, with an oath, to defend his people, his rights, and his country, and his religion, even to the loss of his blood.

¹⁴Now, the Nephites were taught to defend themselves against their enemies, even to the shedding of blood if it were necessary. Yea, and they were also taught

never to give an offence. Yea, and never to raise the sword, except it were against an enemy, except it were to preserve their lives. ¹⁵And this was their faith, that by so doing God would prosper them in the land—or, in other words, if they were faithful in keeping the commandments of God that he would prosper them in the land, yea, warn them to flee or to prepare for war, according to their danger. ¹⁶And also, that God would make it known unto them whither they should go to defend themselves against their enemies. And by so doing, the Lord would deliver them.

And this was the faith of Moroni. And his heart did glory in it—not in the shedding of blood—but in doing good, in preserving his people, yea, in keeping the commandments of God, yea, and resisting iniquity. ¹⁷Yea, verily, verily, I say unto you, if all men had been, and were, and ever would be, like unto Moroni—behold, the very powers of hell would have been shaken forever! Yea, the devil would never have no power over the hearts of the children of men!

¹⁸Behold, he was a man like unto Ammon, the son of Mosiah, yea, and even the other sons of Mosiah. Yea, and also Alma and his sons. For they were all men of God.ᵃ

¹⁹Now behold, Helaman and his brethren were no less serviceable unto the people than was Moroni. For they did preach the word of God, and they did baptize unto repentance, all men—whosoever would hearken unto their words. ²⁰And thus they went forth. And the people did humble themselves because of their words, insomuch that they were highly favored of the Lord. And thus, they were free from wars and contentions among themselves, yea, even for the space of four years.ᵇ<

²¹But, as I have said, in the latter end of the nineteenth year, notwithstanding their peace amongst themselves, they were compelled (reluctantly) to contend with their brethren, the Lamanites. ²²Yea, and in fine—their wars never did cease for the space of many years (with the Lamanites)—notwithstanding their much reluctance.

>²³Now, they were sorry to take up arms against the Lamanites because they did not delight in the shedding of blood. Yea, and this was not all. They were sorry to be the means of sending so many of their brethren out of this world—into an eternal world—unprepared to meet their God. ²⁴Nevertheless, they could not suffer to lay down their lives, that their wives, and their children, should be massacred by the barbarous cruelty of those who was once their brethren, yea, and had dissented from their church, and had left them and had gone to destroy them—by joining the Lamanites. ²⁵Yea, they could not bear that their brethren should rejoice over the blood of the Nephites so long as there were any who should keep the commandments of God. For the promises of the Lord were: "If they should keep his commandments, they should prosper in the land."ᶜ<

---

a. This is not the type of information that would have been on the plates. It represents Mormon's opinion of Moroni, and it is not part of the flow of the story.

b. This is a separate interjection that serves to transition from the discussion of Moroni as a righteous man to the story of the wars. Mormon includes Helaman and his brothers as righteous men. The conclusion that they were free from contentions for four years finishes the aside and returns to the theme of the war, which was the topic prior to this departure.

c. Before completely returning to his story, Mormon inserts a description of Nephite motivations. These are Mormon's opinions and would not have been present on the source plates.

Chapter XXI [Alma 45–49]

[49] ²And now it came to pass in the eleventh month of the nineteenth year, on the tenth day of the month—the armies of the Lamanites were seen approaching towards the land of Ammonihah. ²And behold, the city had been rebuilt. And Moroni had stationed an army by the borders of the city. And they had cast up dirt round about to shield them from the arrows and the stones of the Lamanites. For behold, they fought with stones and with arrows. >³Behold, I said that the city of Ammonihah had been rebuilt. I say unto you, yea, that it was in part rebuilt. And because the Lamanites had destroyed it once (because of the iniquity of the people), they supposed that it would again become an easy prey for them.ᵃ<

⁴But behold, how great was their disappointment! For behold, the Nephites had dug up a ridge of earth round about them which was so high that the Lamanites could not cast their stones and their arrows at them, that they might take effect. Neither could they come upon them, save it was by their place of entrance.

⁵Now, at this time, the chief captains of the Lamanites were astonished exceedingly, because of the wisdom of the Nephites in [repairing]ᵇ their places of security.

⁶Now, the leaders of the Lamanites had supposed (because of the greatness of their numbers), yea, they supposed that they should be privileged to come upon them as they had hitherto done. Yea, and they had also prepared themselves with shields and with breastplates. And they had also prepared themselves with garments of skins, yea, very thick garments, to cover their nakedness. ⁷And being thus prepared, they supposed that they should easily overpower and subject their brethren to the yoke of bondage—or slay and massacre them, according to their pleasure. ⁸But behold, to their uttermost astonishment, they were prepared for them—in a manner which never had been known among all the children of Lehi. Now, they were prepared for the Lamanites to battle—after the manner of the instructions of Moroni.

⁹And it came to pass that the Lamanites (or the Amalickiahites) were exceedingly astonished at their manner of preparation for war.

¹⁰Now, if King Amalickiah had came down out of the land of Nephi at the head of his army, perhaps he would have caused the Lamanites to have attacked the Nephites at the city of Ammonihah, for behold, he did care not for the blood of his people. ¹¹But behold, Amalickiah did not come down himself to battle. And behold, his chief captains durst not attack the Nephites at the city of Ammonihah. For Moroni had altered the management of affairs among the Nephites insomuch that the Lamanites were disappointed in their places of retreat, and they could not come upon them. ¹²Therefore, they retreated into the wilderness, and took their camp, and marched towards the land of Noah—supposing that to be the next best place for them to come against the Nephites. ¹³For they knew not that Moroni had fortified, or had built forts of security, for every city in all the land round about. Therefore, they marched forward to the land of Noah with a firm determination. Yea, their chief captains came forward, and took an oath that they would destroy the people of that city. ¹⁴But behold, to their astonishment, the city of Noah (which had hitherto been a weak place) had now, by the means of Moroni, became strong—yea, even to exceed the strength of the city Ammonihah.

---

a. Mormon realized that he needed to clarify that Ammonihah had been rebuilt since he had written of the description of the desolation of its destruction.

b. Restored per the Original Manuscript. The Printer's Manuscript has "preparing." Skousen, *Analysis of the Textual Variants*, 4:2604.

¹⁵And now behold, this was wisdom in Moroni. For he had supposed that they would be frightened at the city Ammonihah. And as the city of Noah had hitherto been the weakest part of the land—therefore, they would march thither to battle. And thus it was, according to his desires.

¹⁶And behold, Moroni had appointed Lehi to be chief captain over the men of that city. And it was that same Lehi which fought with the Lamanites in the valley on the east of the river Sidon.

¹⁷And now behold, it came to pass that when the Lamanites had found that Lehi commanded the city—they were again disappointed, for they feared Lehi exceedingly. Nevertheless, their chief captains had sworn with an oath to attack the city. Therefore, they brought up their armies.

¹⁸Now behold, the Lamanites could not get into their forts of security by any other way, save by the entrance, because of the highness of the bank which had been thrown up, and the depth of the ditch which had been dug round about (save it were by the entrance).[a] ¹⁹And thus were the Nephites prepared to destroy all such as should attempt to climb up, to enter in the fort by any other way—by casting over stones and arrows at them. ²⁰Thus, they were prepared, yea, a body of their most strong men with their swords, and their slings, to smite down all who should attempt to come into their place of security by the place of entrance. And thus, were they prepared to defend themselves against the Lamanites.

²¹And it came to pass that the captains of the Lamanites brought up their armies before the place of entrance and began to contend with the Nephites, to get into their place of security. But behold, they were driven back from time to time, insomuch that they were slain with an immense slaughter.

²²Now, when they found that they could not obtain power over the Nephites by the pass, they began to dig down their banks of earth, that they might obtain a pass to their armies, that they might have an equal chance to fight. But behold, in these attempts they were swept off by the stones and the arrows which were thrown at them. And instead of filling up their ditches by pulling down the banks of earth—they were filled up (in a measure) with their dead and wounded bodies. ²³Thus, the Nephites had all power over their enemies. And thus, the Lamanites did attempt to destroy the Nephites until their chief captains were all slain. Yea, and more than a thousand of the Lamanites were slain—while, on the other hand, there was not a single soul of the Nephites which were slain. ²⁴There were about fifty which were wounded, which had been exposed to the arrows of the Lamanites through the pass, but they were shielded by their shields, and their breastplates, and their headplates, insomuch that their wounds were upon their legs, many of which was very severe.

²⁵And it came to pass that when the Lamanites saw that their chief captains were all slain, they fled into the wilderness.

²⁶And it came to pass that they returned to the land of Nephi, to inform their King Amalickiah (who was a Nephite by birth) concerning their great loss.

And it came to pass that he was exceeding angry with his people, because he had not obtained his desire over the Nephites—he had not subjected them to the yoke of

---

a. The ending "save it were by the entrance" echoes the beginning of the sentence. It would appear that the meaning of the sentence is that the earthen banks were built up—save it were by the entrance. This is a different meaning that that the Lamanites could not enter any way "save by the entrance."

bondage. ²⁷Yea, he was exceeding wroth. And he did curse God, and also Moroni—swearing with an oath that he would drink his blood. And this—because Moroni had kept the commandments of God in preparing for the safety of his people.

²⁸And it came to pass that on the other hand, the people of Nephi did thank the Lord, their God, because of his [marvelous[a]] power in delivering them from the hands of their enemies.

And thus ended the nineteenth year of the reign of the judges over the people of Nephi. ²⁸Yea, and there was continual peace among them, and exceeding great prosperity in the church—because of their heed and diligence which they gave unto the word of God, which was declared unto them by Helaman, and Shiblon, and Corianton, and Ammon, and his brethren, etcetera—yea, and by all those which had been ordained by the holy order of God—being baptized unto repentance and sent forth to preach among the people, etcetera.

---

a. Restored per the Original Manuscript. The Printer's Manuscript has "matchless." Skousen, *Analysis of the Textual Variants,* 4:2609.

Chapter XXII [Alma 50]

[22] ¹And now it came to pass that Moroni did not stop making preparations for war, or to defend themselves against the Lamanites. For he caused that his armies should commence, in the commencement of the twentieth year of the reign of the judges, that they should commence in digging up heaps of earth round about all the cities throughout all the land which was possessed by the Nephites. ²And upon the top of these those ridges of earth, he caused that there should be timbers (yea, works of timbers) built up to the height of a man round about the cities. ³And he caused that upon those works of timbers, that there should be a frame of pickets built upon the timbers round about. And they were strong, and high. ⁴And he caused towers to be erected that overlooked those works of pickets. And he caused places of security to be built upon those towers, that the stones and the arrows of the Lamanites could not hurt them. ⁵And they were prepared, that they could cast stones from the top thereof, according to their pleasure and their strength—and slay him which should attempt to approach near the walls of the city. ⁶Thus, Moroni did prepare strongholds against the coming of their enemies round about every city in all the land.

⁷And it came to pass that Moroni caused that his armies should go forth into the east wilderness. Yea, and they went forth and drove all the Lamanites which were in the east wilderness into their own lands, which were south of the land of Zarahemla. >⁸And the land of Nephi did run in a straight course from the east sea to the west.ᵃ<

⁹And it came to pass that when Moroni had driven all the Lamanites out of the east wilderness, which was north of the lands of their own possessions, he caused that the inhabitants which were in the land of Zarahemla and in the land round about, should go forth into the east wilderness, even to the borders by the seashore, and possess the land. ¹⁰And he also placed armies on the south, in the borders of their possessions, and caused them to erect fortifications, that they might secure their armies, and their people, from the hands of their enemies. ¹¹And thus, he cut off all the strongholds of the Lamanites in the east wilderness, yea, and also on the west—fortifying the line between the Nephites and the Lamanites, between the land of Zarahemla and the land of Nephi—>from the west sea, running by the head of the river Sidon—the Nephites possessing all the land northward, yea, even all the land which was northward of the land Bountiful, according to their pleasure.ᵇ< ¹²Thus Moroni, with his armies (which did increase daily because of the assurance of protection which his works did bring forth unto them)—therefore, they did seek to cut off the strength and the power of the Lamanites from off the lands of their possessions, that they should have no power upon the lands of their possessions.

¹³And it came to pass that the Nephites began the foundation of a city. And they called the name of the city Moroni. And it was by the east sea, and it was on the south by the line of the possessions of the Lamanites. ¹⁴And they also began a foundation for a city between the city of Moroni and the city of Aaron—joining the borders of Aaron and Moroni. And they called the name of the city (or the land) Nephihah. ¹⁵And they also began, in that same year, to build many cities. On the north one (in a particular

---

a. Mormon's addition to the geographic descriptions. This would not have been in the source, though the other directions likely were. This is an addition for the modern reader.

b. Mormon's addition to the geographic descriptions.

Chapter XXII [Alma 50]

manner) which they called Lehi, which was in the north by the borders of the seashore. ¹⁶And thus ended the twentieth year.

>¹⁷And in these prosperous circumstances were the people of Nephi in the commencement of the twenty and first year of the reign of the judges over the people of Nephi. ¹⁸And they did prosper exceedingly. And they became exceeding rich, yea, and they did multiply and wax strong in the land. ¹⁹And thus, we see how merciful and just are all the dealings of the Lord, to the fulfilling of all his words unto the children of men.

Yea, we can behold that his words are verified, even at this time, which he spake unto Lehi, saying: ²⁰"Blessed art thou and thy children! And they shall be blessed. Inasmuch as they shall keep my commandments, they shall prosper in the land. But remember! Inasmuch as they will not keep my commandments, they shall be cut off from the presence of the Lord.ᵃ"

²¹And we see that these promises have been verified to the people of Nephi. For it has been their quarrelings and their contention, yea, their murderings and their plunderings—their idolatry—their whoredoms and their abominations (which were among themselves) which brought upon them their wars and their destructions. ²²And those who were faithful in keeping the commandments of the Lord, were delivered at all times—whilst thousands of their wicked brethren have been consigned to bondage, or to perish by the sword, or to dwindle in unbelief—and mingle with the Lamanites.

²³But behold, there never was a happier time among the people of Nephi, since the day of Nephi, than in the days of Moroni. Yea, even at this time, in the twenty and first year of the reign of the judges. ᵇ<

²⁴And it came to pass that the twenty and second year of the reign of the judges also ended in peace. Yea, and also the twenty and third year.

²⁵And it came to pass that, in the commencement of the twenty and fourth year of the reign of the judges, there would also have been peace among the people of Nephi—had it not been for a contention which took place among them concerning the land of Lehi and the land of Morianton (>which joined upon the borders of Lehi, both of which were on the borders by the seashore<). ²⁶For behold, the people which possessed the land of Morianton did claim a part of the land of Lehi. Therefore, there began to be a warm contention between them, insomuch that the people of Morianton took up arms against their brethren. And they were determined—by the sword to slay them. ²⁷But behold, the people which possessed the land of Lehi fled to the camp of Moroni and appealed unto him for assistance. For behold, they were not in the wrong.

²⁸And it came to pass that the people of Morianton, which were led by a man whose name was Morianton, found that the people of Lehi had fled to the camp of Moroni, they were exceeding fearful lest the army of Moroni should come upon them and destroy them. ²⁹Therefore, Morianton put it into their hearts that they should flee to the land which was northward (>which was covered with large bodies of waterᶜ<)

---

a. The phrase "cut off from my presence" is found in Leviticus 22:3.
b. Mormon's moralizing comment on this part of the Nephite story. These deviations from narration provide evidence of the reasons why Mormon selects certain stories and relates them in the way he does.
c. Mormon inserts this information. It is not clear why this is important to his future readers. It

and take possession of the land which was northward. ³⁰And behold, they would have carried this plan into an effect, which would have been a cause to have been lamented. But behold, Morianton (being a man of much passion)—therefore he was angry with one of his maidservants, and he fell upon her and beat her much.

³¹And it came to pass that she fled, and came over to the camp of Moroni and told Moroni all things concerning the matter—and also concerning their intentions to flee into the land northward. ³²Now behold, the people which were in the land Bountiful (or rather, Moroni) feared that they would hearken to the words of Morianton and unite with his people. And thus, he would obtain possessions of those parts of the land, which would lay a foundation for serious consequences among the people of Nephi, yea, which consequences would lead to the overthrow of their liberty [a] ³³Therefore, Moroni sent an army (with their camp) to head the people of Morianton, to stop their flight into the land northward.

³⁴And it came to pass that they did not head them until they had came to the borders of the land Desolation. And there they did head them by the narrow pass (>which led by the sea into the land northward, yea, by the sea on the west, and on the east<).

³⁵And it came to pass that the army, which was sent by Moroni, which was led by a man whose name was Teancum, did meet the people of Morianton. And so stubborn were the people of Morianton—being inspired by his wickedness and his flattering words, that a battle commenced between them, in the which Teancum did slay Morianton and defeat his army and took them prisoners, and returned to the camp of Moroni. And thus ended the twenty and fourth year of the reign of the judges over the people of Nephi. ³⁶And thus was the people of Morianton brought back. And, upon their covenanting to keep the peace, they were restored to the land of Morianton. And a union took place between them and the people of Lehi. And they were also restored to their lands.

³⁷And it came to pass that in the same year, that the people of Nephi had peace restored unto them, that Nephihah (the second Chief Judge) died, having filled the Judgment Seat with perfect uprightness before God. ³⁸(>Nevertheless, he had refused Alma to take possession of those records and those things which were esteemed by Alma and his fathers to be most sacred. Therefore, Alma had conferred them upon his son, Helaman[b]<).

³⁹Behold, it came to pass that the son of Nephihah was appointed to fill the Judgment Seat in the stead of his father. Yea, he was appointed Chief Judge and Governor over the people—with an oath and sacred ordinance to judge righteously and to keep the peace and the freedom of the people, and to grant unto them their sacred privileges, to worship the Lord, their God, yea, to support and maintain the cause of God—all his days. And to bring the wicked to justice according to their crime.

⁴⁰Now behold, his name was Pahoran. And Pahoran did fill the seat of his father and did commence his reign in the end of the twenty and fourth year over the people of Nephi.

---

would have been part of common knowledge at the time. It is possible the Mormon intended to identify this land of many waters with the land Desolation and the location of the hill Cumorah, which is in a land of many waters.

a. Foreshadowing of the Nephite final demise.

b. Mormon must have realized that he had not previously explained why Alma had the official records after giving up the political position that should have had custody of those records. He takes this occasion to remedy that omission.

Chapter XXIII [Alma 51]

[51] ¹And now it came to pass in the commencement of the twenty and fifth year of the reign of the judges over the people of Nephi—they, having established peace between the people of Lehi and the people of Morianton concerning their lands, and having commenced the twenty and fifth year in peace—²nevertheless, they did not long maintain an entire peace in the land. For there began to be a contention among the people concerning the Chief Judge Pahoran. For behold, there were a part of the people which desired that a few particular points of the law should be altered.

³But behold, Pahoran would not alter nor suffer the law to be altered. Therefore, he did not hearken to those who had sent in their voices with their petitions concerning the altering of the law. ⁴Therefore, those which were desirous that the law should be altered were angry with him, and desired that he should no longer be Chief Judge over the land. Therefore, there arose a warm dispute concerning the matter—but not unto bloodshed.

⁵And it came to pass that those who were desirous that Pahoran should be dethroned from the Judgment Seat were called kingmen. For they were desirous that the law should be altered in a manner to overthrow the free government and to establish a king over the land.

⁶And those who were desirous that Pahoran should remain Chief Judge over the land took upon them the name of freemen. And thus was the division among them. For the freemen had sworn (or covenanted) to maintain their rights and their privileges of their religion by a free government.

⁷And it came to pass that this matter of their contention was settled by the voice of the people.

And it came to pass that the voice of the people came in the favor of the freemen and Pahoran retained the Judgment Seat, which caused much rejoicing among the brethren of Pahoran, and also [among[a]] the people of liberty—which also put the kingmen to silence, that they durst not oppose, but were obliged to maintain, the cause of freedom.

⁸Now, those which were in favor of kings were those of high birth. And they sought to be kings. And they were supported by those which sought power and authority over the people. ⁹But behold, this was a critical time for such contentions to be among the people of Nephi. For behold, Amalickiah had again stirred up the hearts of the people of the Lamanites against the people of the Nephites. And he was gathering together soldiers from all parts of his land and arming them and preparing for war with all diligence. For he had sworn to drink the blood of Moroni. >¹⁰But behold, we shall see that [this[b]] promise which he made was rash.[c]< Nevertheless, he did prepare himself and his armies, to come to battle against the Nephites.

¹¹Now, his armies were not so great as they had hitherto been because of the many thousands which had been slain by the hand of the Nephites. But notwithstanding their great loss, Amalickiah had gathered together a wonderful great army, insomuch that he

---

    a. Restored per the Original Manuscript. The Printer's Manuscript has "many." Skousen, *Analysis of the Textual Variants*, 4:2641.

    b. Restored per the Original Manuscript. The Printer's Manuscript has "his." Skousen, *Analysis of the Textual Variants*, 4:2641–42.

    c. Mormon inserts a foreshadowing. There isn't enough information here to speculate on the reason for this inserted foreshadowing.

feared not to come down to the land of Zarahemla. ¹²Yea, even Amalickiah did himself come down at the head of the Lamanites. And it was in the twenty and fifth year of the reign of the judges. And it was at the same time that they had began to settle the affairs of their contentions concerning the Chief Judge Pahoran.

¹³And it came to pass that when the men which were called kingmen had heard that the Lamanites were coming down to battle against them, they were glad in their hearts. And they refused to take up arms. For they were so wroth with the Chief Judge, and also with the people of liberty, that they would not take up arms to defend their country.

¹⁴And it came to pass that when Moroni saw this—and also saw that the Lamanites were coming into the borders of the land—he was exceeding wroth because of the stubbornness of those people of whom he had labored with so much diligence to preserve. Yea, he was exceeding wroth. His soul was filled with anger against them.

¹⁵And it came to pass that he sent a petition, with the voice of the people, unto the Chief Governor of the land—desiring that he should [heed[a]] it—and give him, Moroni, power to compel those dissenters to defend their country, or to put them to death. ¹⁶For it was his first care to put an end to such contentions and dissensions among the people. For behold, this had been hitherto a cause of all their destructions.

And it came to pass that it was granted, according to the voice of the people.

¹⁷And it came to pass that Moroni commanded that his army should go against those kingmen, to pull down their pride, and their nobility, and level them with the earth—or they should take up arms and support the cause of liberty.

¹⁸And it came to pass that the armies did march forth against them. And they did pull down their pride, and their nobility, insomuch that as they did lift their weapons of war to fight against the men of Moroni, they were hewn down and leveled to the earth.

¹⁹And it came to pass that there were four thousand of those dissenters which were hewn down by the sword. And those of their leaders which were not slain in battle were taken and cast into prison. For there was no time for their trials at this period. ²⁰And the remainder of those dissenters, rather than to be smote down to the earth by the sword, yielded to the standard of liberty and were compelled to hoist the title of liberty upon their towers, and in their cities, and to take up arms in defense of their country. ²¹And thus, Moroni put an end to those kingmen, that there were not any known by the appellation of kingmen. And thus, he put an end to the stubbornness and the pride of those people which professed the blood of nobility—but they were brought down to humble themselves, like unto their brethren, and to fight valiantly for their freedom from bondage.

²²Behold, it came to pass that while Moroni was thus breaking down the wars and contentions among his own people, and subjecting them to peace and civilization, and making regulations to prepare for war against the Lamanites—behold, the Lamanites had came into the land of Moroni (which was in the borders by the seashore).

²³And it came to pass that the Nephites were not sufficiently strong in the city of Moroni. Therefore, Amalickiah did drive them—slaying many.

And it came to pass that Amalickiah took possession of the city, yea, possession of all their fortifications. ²⁴And those which fled out of the city of Moroni came to the city

---

a. Restored per the Original Manuscript. The Printer's Manuscript has "head." The compositor changed "head" to "read," which has remained the word used in the printed versions. Skousen, *Analysis of the Textual Variants*, 4:2643.

Chapter XXIII [Alma 51]

of Nephihah. And also, the people of the city of Lehi gathered themselves together and made preparations, and were ready to receive the Lamanites to battle.

[25] But it came to pass that Amalickiah would not suffer the Lamanites to go against the city of Nephihah to battle, but kept them down by the seashore, leaving men in every city to maintain and defend it. [26] And thus he went on, taking possession of many cities—the city of Nephihah, and the city of Lehi, and the city of Morianton, and the city of Omner, and the city of Gid, and the city of Mulek—all of which were on the east borders, by the seashore. [27] And thus had the Lamanites obtained, by the cunning of Amalickiah, so many cities (by their numberless hosts)—all of which were strongly fortified (after the manner of the fortifications of Moroni)—all of which afforded strongholds for the Lamanites.

[28] And it came to pass that they marched to the borders of the land Bountiful, driving the Nephites before them and slaying many.

[29] But it came to pass that they were met by Teancum, who had slain Morianton, and had headed his people in his flight.

[30] And it came to pass that he headed Amalickiah also, as he was marching forth with his numerous army, that he might take possession of the land Bountiful and also the land northward. But behold, he met with a disappointment by being repulsed by Teancum and his men. For they were great warriors. For every man of Teancum did exceed the Lamanites in their strength and in their skill of war, insomuch that they did gain advantage over the Lamanites.

[32] And it came to pass that they did harass them, insomuch that they did slay them, even until it was dark.

And it came to pass that Teancum and his men did pitch their tents in the borders of the land Bountiful. And Amalickiah did pitch his tents in the borders, on the beach by the seashore. And after this manner were they driven.

[33] And it came to pass that when the night had come, Teancum and his servant stole forth and went out by night—and went into the camp of Amalickiah. And behold, sleep had overpowered them, because of their much fatigue, which was caused by the labors and heat of the day.

[34] And it came to pass that Teancum stole privily into the tent of the king and put a javelin to his heart. And he did cause the death of the king immediately, that he did not awake his servants. [35] And he returned again privily to his own camp. And behold, his men were asleep. And he awoke them and told them all the things that he had done. [36] And he caused that his armies should stand in readiness, lest the Lamanites had awoke and should come upon them.

[37] And thus ended the twenty and fifth year of the reign of the judges over the people of Nephi. And thus ended the days of Amalickiah.

Chapter XXIV [Alma 52–53]

[52] ¹And now it came to pass in the twenty and sixth year of the reign of the judges over the people of Nephi, behold, when the Lamanites awoke on the first morning of the first month—behold, they found Amalickiah was dead in his own tent. And they also saw that Teancum was ready to give them battle on that day. ²And now, when the Lamanites saw this they were affrighted, and they abandoned their design in marching into the land northward, and retreated (with all their army) into the city of Mulek and sought protection in their fortifications.

³And it came to pass that the brother of Amalickiah was appointed king over the people. And his name was Ammoron. Thus, King Ammoron (the brother of King Amalickiah) was appointed to reign in his stead.

⁴And it came to pass that he did command that his people should maintain those cities which they had taken by the shedding of blood. For they had not taken any cities save they had lost much blood.

⁵And now, Teancum saw that the Lamanites were determined to maintain those cities which they had taken, and those parts of the land which they had obtained possession of—and also seeing the enormity of their number—Teancum thought it was not expedient that he should attempt to attack them in their forts. ⁶But he kept his men round about, as if making preparations for war. Yea, and truly he was preparing to defend himself against them by casting up walls round about and preparing places of resort.

⁷And it came to pass that he kept thus preparing for war until Moroni had sent a large number of men to strengthen his army. ⁸And Moroni also sent orders unto him that he should retain all the prisoners which fell into his hands. For as the Lamanites had taken many prisoners, that he should retain all the prisoners of the Lamanites as a ransom for those which the Lamanites had taken. ⁹And he also sent orders unto him that he should fortify the land Bountiful, and secure the narrow pass (which led into the land northward), lest the Lamanites should obtain that point and should have power to harass them on every side. ¹⁰And Moroni also sent unto him, desiring him that he would be faithful in maintaining that quarter of the land. And that he would seek every opportunity to scourge the Lamanites in that quarter, as much as was in his power, that perhaps he might take again (by stratagem, or some other way) those cities which had been taken out of their hands. And that he also would fortify and strengthen the cities round about which had not fallen into the hands of the Lamanites. ¹¹And he also said unto him: "I would come unto you, but behold, the Lamanites are upon us in the borders of the land by the west sea. And behold, I go against them. Therefore, I cannot come unto you."

¹²Now, the king, Ammoron, had departed out of the land of Zarahemla, and had made known unto the queen concerning the death of his brother, and had gathered together a large number of men, and had marched forth against the Nephites on the borders by the west sea. ¹³And thus, he was endeavoring to harass the Nephites and to draw away a part of their forces to that part of the land—while he had commanded those which he had left to possess the cities which he had taken, that they should also harass the Nephites on the borders by the east sea, and should take possession of their lands as much as it were in their power, according to the power of their armies. ¹⁴And

Chapter XXIV [Alma 52–53]

thus were the Nephites in those dangerous circumstances in the ending of the twenty and sixth year of the reign of the judges over the people of Nephi.

¹⁵But behold, it came to pass in the twenty and seventh year of the reign of the judges, [that[a]] Teancum—by the command of Moroni, who had established armies to protect the south and the west borders of the land, had began his march towards the land of Bountiful, that he might assist Teancum with his men in retaking the cities which they had lost.[b] ¹⁶And it came to pass that Teancum had received orders to make an attack upon the city of Mulek, and retake it, if it were possible.

¹⁷And it came to pass that Teancum made preparations to make an attack upon the city of Mulek and march forth with his army against the Lamanites. But he saw that it was impossible that he could overpower them while they were in their fortifications. Therefore, he abandoned his designs and he returned again to the city Bountiful, to wait for the coming of Moroni, that he might receive strength to his army.

¹⁸And it came to pass that Moroni did arrive with his army to the land of Bountiful in the latter end of the twenty and seventh year of the reign of the judges over the people of Nephi. ¹⁹And in the commencement of the twenty and eighth year, Moroni, and Teancum, and many of the chief captains, held a council of war—what they should do to cause the Lamanites to come out against them to battle—or that they might, by some means, flatter them out of their strongholds, that they might gain advantage over them, and take again the city of Mulek.

²⁰And it came to pass that they sent embassies to the army of the Lamanites which protected the city of Mulek, to their leader whose name was Jacob, desiring him that he would come out with his armies to meet them upon the plains between the two cities. But behold, Jacob (which was a Zoramite) would not come out with his army to meet them upon the plains.

²¹And it came to pass that Moroni, having no hopes of meeting them upon fair grounds—therefore, he resolved upon a plan that he might decoy the Lamanites out of their strongholds. ²²Therefore, he caused that Teancum should take a small number of men and march down near the seashore. And Moroni and his army, by night, marched into the wilderness on the west of the city Mulek. And thus, on the morrow, when the guards of the Lamanites had discovered Teancum—they ran and told it unto Jacob, their leader.

²³And it came to pass that the armies of the Lamanites did march forth against Teancum—supposing, by their numbers, to overpower Teancum because of the smallness of his numbers. And as Teancum saw the armies of the Lamanites coming out against him, he began [a[c]] retreat—down by the seashore, northward.

²⁴And it came to pass that when the Lamanites saw that he began to flee, they took courage, and pursued them with vigor. And while Teancum was thus leading away the Lamanites which were pursuing them in vain—behold, Moroni commanded that a part of his army which were with him should march forth into the city and take possession

---

a. Restored per the Original Manuscript, *Original Manuscript of the Book of Mormon*, 5:379. The Printer's Manuscript has "the," which doesn't make sense. It was corrected to "that" for the 1830 edition.

b. The sentence is hijacked by the information about Mormon, requiring that it start over with repetitive resumption in verse 16.

c. Restored pe the Original Manuscript. The Printer's Manuscript has "to," which is continued in the printed editions. Skousen, *Analysis of the Textual Variants*, 4:2666–67.

of it. ²⁵And thus, they did—and slew all those who had been left to protect the city, yea, all those who would not yield up their weapons of war. ²⁶And thus Moroni had obtained a possession[a] of the city Mulek with a part of his army—while he marched with the remainder to meet the Lamanites when they should return from the pursuit of Teancum.

²⁷And it came to pass that the Lamanites did pursue Teancum until they came near the city Bountiful. And then they were met by Lehi and a small army, which had been left to protect the city Bountiful.

²⁸And now behold, when the chief captains of the Lamanites had beheld Lehi with his army coming against them, they fled in much confusion, lest perhaps they should not obtain the city Mulek before Lehi should overtake them. For they were wearied because of their march and the men of Lehi were fresh. ²⁹Now, the Lamanites did not know that Moroni had been in their rear with his army. And all they feared was Lehi and his men. ³⁰Now, Lehi was not desirous to overtake them till they should meet Moroni and his army.

³¹And it came to pass that before the Lamanites had retreated far, they were surrounded by the Nephites—by the men of Moroni on one hand, and the men of Lehi on the other—all of whom were fresh, and full of strength. But the Lamanites were wearied because of their long march. ³²And Moroni commanded his men that they should fall upon them until they had given up their weapons of war.

³³And it came to pass that Jacob, being their leader (being also a Zoramite and having an unconquerable spirit)—he led the Lamanites forth to battle with exceeding fury against Moroni, ³⁴Moroni being in their course of march. Therefore, Jacob was determined to slay them and cut his way through to the city of Mulek. But behold, Moroni and his men were more powerful. Therefore, they did not give way before the Lamanites.

³⁵And it came to pass that they fought on both hands with exceeding fury. And there were many slain on both sides, yea, and Moroni was wounded. And Jacob was killed. ³⁶And Lehi pressed upon their rear with such fury with his strong men, that the Lamanites in the rear delivered up their weapons of war. And the remainder of them, being much confused, knew not [whither[b]] to go or to strike. ³⁷Moroni, seeing their confusion, he said unto them: "If ye will bring forth your weapons of war, and deliver them up—behold, we will forbear shedding your blood."

³⁸And it came to pass that when the Lamanites had heard these words, their chief captains (all those which were not slain) came forth and threw down their weapons of war at the feet of Moroni, and also commanded their men that they should do the same.

³⁹But behold, there were many that would not. And those who would not deliver up their swords were taken, and bound, and their weapons of war were taken from them. And they were compelled to march with their brethren forth into the land Bountiful. ⁴⁰And now, the number of prisoners which were taken exceeded more than the number of those which had been slain, yea, more than those which had been slain on both sides.

[53] ¹And it came to pass that they did set guards over the prisoners of the

---

a. This is the reading in both the Original and Printer's Manuscripts. Skousen notes that there are other uses where the "a" is somewhat intrusive. See Skousen, *Analysis of the Textual Variants*, 4:2667–69.

b. Restored per the Original Manuscript. The Printer's Manuscript has crossed out the "re" of "where" and written "ther" in the line above, making it read "whether." Skousen, *Analysis of the Textual Variants*, 4:2670.

Chapter XXIV [Alma 52–53]

Lamanites and did compel them to go forth and bury their dead, yea, and also the dead of the Nephites which were slain. And Moroni placed men over them, to guard them while they should perform their labors. ²And Moroni went to the city Mulek with Lehi and took command of the city, and gave it unto Lehi.

Now behold, this Lehi was a man who had been with Moroni in the more part of all his battles. And he was a man like unto Moroni. And they rejoiced in each other's safety. Yea, they were beloved by each other, and also beloved by all the people of Nephi.

³And it came to pass that after the Lamanites had finished burying their dead, and also the dead of the Nephites, they were marched back into the land Bountiful. And Teancum, by the orders of Moroni, caused that they should commence in laboring in digging a ditch round about the land (or the city) Bountiful. ⁴And he caused that they should build a breastwork of timbers upon the inner bank of the ditch. And they cast up dirt out of the ditch against the breastwork of timbers. And thus, they did cause the Lamanites to labor until they had encircled the city of Bountiful round about with a strong wall of timbers and earth to an exceeding height. ⁵And this city became an exceeding stronghold ever after. And in this city they did guard the prisoners of the Lamanites, yea, even within a wall which they had caused them to build with their own hands. Now, Moroni was compelled to cause the Lamanites to labor because it were easy to guard them while at their labor and he desired all his forces when he should make an attack upon the Lamanites.

⁶And it came to pass that Moroni had thus gained a victory over one of the greatest of the armies of the Lamanites and had obtained possession of the city Mulek, which was one of the strongest holds of the Lamanites in the land of Nephi. And thus, he had also built a stronghold to retain his prisoners.

⁷And it came to pass that he did no more attempt a battle with the Lamanites in that year. But he did employ his men in preparing for war, yea, and in making fortifications to guard against the Lamanites, yea, and also delivering their women and their children from famine and affliction, and providing food for their armies.

⁸And now it came to pass that the armies of the Lamanites on the west sea, south (while in the absence of Moroni)—on account of some intrigue amongst the Nephites (which caused dissensions amongst them)—had gained some ground over them Nephites, yea, insomuch that they had obtained possession of a number of their cities in that part of the land. ⁹And thus, because of iniquity amongst themselves, yea, because of dissensions and intrigue among themselves, they were placed in the most dangerous circumstances.

¹⁰And now behold, I have somewhat to say concerning the people of Ammon, which in the beginning were Lamanites—but by Ammon and his brethren (or rather, by the power and word of God) they had been converted unto the Lord. And they had been brought down into the land of Zarahemla and had ever since been protected by the Nephites. ¹¹And because of their oath, they had been kept from taking up arms against their brethren. For they had taken an oath, that they never would shed blood more. And according to their oath they would have perished. Yea, they would have suffered themselves to have fallen into the hands of their brethren had it not been for the pity, and the exceeding love, which Ammon and his brethren had had for them. ¹²And for this cause they were brought down into the land of Zarahemla. And they ever had been protected by the Nephites.

¹³But it came to pass that when they saw the danger, and the many afflictions, and tribulations, which the Nephites bore for them, they were moved with compassion and were desirous to take up arms in the defense of their country. ⁴But behold, as they were about to take their weapons of war, they were overpowered by the persuasions of Helaman, and his brethren. For they were about to break the oath which they had made. ¹⁵And Helaman feared, lest by so doing they should lose their souls. Therefore, all those which had entered into this covenant were compelled to behold their brethren wade through their afflictions, in their dangerous circumstances, at this time.

¹⁶But behold, it came to pass they had many sons which had not entered into a covenant that they would not take their weapons of war to defend themselves against their enemies. Therefore, they did assemble themselves together at this time—as many as were able to take up arms. And they called themselves Nephites.

¹⁷And they entered into a covenant to fight for the liberty of the Nephites, yea, to protect the land unto the laying down of their lives. Yea, even they covenanted that they never would give up their liberty—but they would fight, in all cases, to protect the Nephites, and themselves, from bondage.

¹⁸Now behold, there were two thousand of those young men which entered into this covenant and took their weapons of war to defend their country. ¹⁹Now behold, as they never had hitherto been a disadvantage to the Nephites—they became now (at this period of time) also a great support, for they took their weapons of war. And they would that Helaman should be their leader. ²⁰And they were all young men. And they were exceeding valiant for courage, and also for strength, and activity. But behold, this was not all. They were men which were true at all times, in whatsoever thing they were entrusted. ²¹Yea, they were men of truth and soberness. For they had been taught to keep the commandments of God and to walk uprightly before him.

²²And now it came to pass that Helaman did march at the head of his two thousand stripling soldiers, to the support of the people in the borders of the land, on the south, by the west sea. ²³And thus ended the twenty and eighth year of the reign of the judges over the people of Nephi, etcetera.

Chapter XXV [Alma 54–55]

[54] ¹And now it came to pass in [the commencement of[a]] the twenty and ninth year of the [reign of the[b]] judges that Ammoron sent unto Moroni—desiring that he would exchange prisoners.

²And it came to pass that Moroni felt to rejoice exceedingly at this request, for he desired the provisions which was imparted for the support of the Lamanite prisoners for the support of his own people. And he also desired his own people, for the strengthening of his own army.

³Now, the Lamanites had taken many women and children. And there was not a woman, nor a child, among all the prisoners of Moroni (or the prisoners which Moroni had taken). Therefore, Moroni resolved upon a stratagem to obtain as many prisoners of the Nephites from the Lamanites as it were possible. ⁴Therefore, he wrote an epistle and sent it by the servant of Ammoron—the same who had brought an epistle to Moroni. Now, these are the words which he wrote unto Ammoron, saying:

⁵Behold, Ammoron. I have wrote unto you somewhat concerning this war which ye have waged against my people (or rather which thy brother hath waged against them) and which ye are still determined to carry on after his death.

⁶Behold, I would tell you something concerning the justice of God, and the sword of his almighty wrath which doth hang over you, except ye repent and withdraw your armies into your own lands (or the lands of your possessions, which is the land of Nephi). ⁷Yea, I would tell you these things, if ye were capable of harkening unto them. Yea, I would tell you concerning that awful hell that awaits to receive such murderers as thou and thy brother hath been, except ye repent and withdraw your murderous purposes, and return with your armies to your own lands. ⁸But, as ye have once rejected these things and have fought against the people of the Lord, even so, I may expect you will do it again.

⁹And now behold, we are prepared to receive you. Yea, and except you withdraw your purposes, behold, ye will pull down the wrath of that God whom you have rejected upon you, even to your utter destruction. ¹⁰But, as the Lord liveth, our armies shall come upon you, except ye withdraw. And ye shall soon be visited with death. For we will retain our cities and our lands. Yea, and we will maintain our religion and the cause of our God.

¹¹But behold, it supposeth me that I talk to you concerning these things in vain—or it supposeth me that thou art a child of hell. Therefore, I will close my epistle by telling you that I will not exchange prisons, save it be on conditions that ye will deliver up a man, and his wife, and his children, for one prisoner. If this be the case, that ye will do it—I will exchange.

¹²And behold, if ye do not this, I will come against you with my armies. Yea, even I will arm my women, and my children, and I will come against you. And I will follow you, even into your own land, which is the land of our first inheritance. Yea, and it shall be blood for blood, yea, life for life. And I will give you battle, even until you are destroyed from off the face of the earth.

---

a. Restored per the Original Manuscript. Skousen, *Analysis of the Textual Variants*, 4:2687–88.
b. Restored per the Original Manuscript. Skousen, *Analysis of the Textual Variants*, 4:2687–88.

¹³Behold, I am in my anger—and also my people. Ye have sought to murder us. And we have only sought to defend [our lives^a]. But behold, if ye seek to destroy us more, we will seek to destroy you. Yea, and we will seek our [lands^b], the lands of our first inheritance.

¹⁴Now, I close my epistle. I am Moroni. I am a leader of the people of the Nephites.

¹⁵Now it came to pass that Ammoron, when he had received this epistle, he was angry. And he wrote another epistle unto Moroni. And these are the [words^c] which he wrote, saying:

¹⁶I am Ammoron, the king of the Lamanites. I am the brother of Amalickiah, whom ye have murdered. Behold, I will avenge his blood upon you. Yea, and I will come upon you with my armies. For I fear not your threatenings. ¹⁷For behold, your fathers did wrong their brethren, insomuch that they did rob them of their right to the government when it [rightfully^d] belonged unto them.

¹⁸And now behold, if ye will lay down your arms and subject yourselves to be governed by those to whom the government doth rightly belong, then will I cause that my people shall lay down their weapons and shall be at war no more.

¹⁹Behold, ye have breathed out many threatenings against me, and my people. But behold, we fear not your threatenings. ²⁰Nevertheless, I will grant to exchange prisoners, according to your request, gladly, that I may preserve my food for my men of war. And we will wage a war, which shall be eternal—either to the subjecting the Nephites to our authority, or to their eternal extinction.

²¹And as concerning that God, whom ye say we have rejected—behold, we know not such a being—neither ye. But if it so be that there is such a being—we know not but that he hath made us as well as you. ²²And if it so be that there is a devil, and a hell—behold, will he not send you there to dwell with my brother, which ye have murdered, which ye have hinted that he hath gone to such a place? But behold, these things [matter^e] not.

²³I am Ammoron, and a descendant of Zoram, whom your fathers pressed and brought out of Jerusalem. ²⁴And behold, I am [now^f] a bold Lamanite. Behold, this war hath been waged to avenge their wrongs, and to maintain, and to obtain, their rights to the government.

And I close my epistle to Moroni.

---

a. Restored per the Original Manuscript. The Printer's Manuscript and subsequent published versions have "ourselves." Skousen, *Analysis of the Textual Variants*, 4:2695.

b. Restored per the Original Manuscript. The Printer's Manuscript and subsequent published versions have the singular "land." Skousen, *Analysis of the Textual Variants*, 4:2696.

c. Emended. There is an ink smear that covers the word on the Printer's Manuscript. The surrounding text and the space available make this the logical word intended. This is the how it appears in our current edition.

d. Restored per the Original Manuscript. The Printer's Manuscript and subsequent published versions have "rightly." Skousen, *Analysis of the Textual Variants*, 4:2697.

e. Restored per the Original Manuscript. The Printer's Manuscript and subsequent published versions have "mattereth." Skousen, *Analysis of the Textual Variants*, 4:2697–98.

f. Restored per the Original Manuscript. The Printer's Manuscript and subsequent published versions have "now I am." Skousen, *Analysis of the Textual Variants*, 4:2698.

[55] ¹Now it came to pass that when Moroni had received this epistle, he was more angry—because he knew that Ammoron had a perfect knowledge of his fraud. Yea, he knew that Ammoron knew that it was not a just cause that had caused him to wage a war against the people of Nephi. ²And he said:

> Behold. I will not exchange prisoners with Ammoron, save he will withdraw his purpose, as I have stated in my epistle. For I will not grant unto him that he shall have any more power than what he hath got. ³Behold, I know the place where the Lamanites doth guard my people which they have taken prisoners. And as Ammoron would not grant unto me mine epistle—behold, I will give unto him according to my words. Yea, I will seek death among them until they shall sue for peace.

⁴And now it came to pass that when Moroni had said these words, he caused that a search should be made among his men, that perhaps he might find a man which was a descendant of [Laman's[a]] among them.

⁵And it came to pass that they found one, whose name was Laman. And he was one of the servants of the king which was murdered by Amalickiah. ⁶Now, Moroni caused that Laman, and a small number of his men, should go forth unto the guards which were over the Nephites. >⁷Now, the Nephites were guarded in the city of Gid.[b]< Therefore, Moroni caused that Laman and a small number of men, which was appointed to go with him.[c]

⁸And it came to pass that when it was evening, Laman went to the guards which were over the Nephites. And behold, they saw him [a-coming[d]] and they hailed him. But he saith unto them: "Fear not! Behold, I am a Lamanite. Behold, we have escaped from the Nephites, and they sleepeth. And behold, we have took of their wine and brought with us."

⁹Now, when the Lamanites heard these words, they received him with joy. And they said unto him: "Give us of your wine, that we may drink! We are glad that ye have thus taken wine with you. For we are weary."

¹⁰But Laman saith unto them: "Let us keep of our wine till we go against the Nephites to battle."

But this saying only made them more desirous to drink of the wine—¹¹for, said they: "We are weary. Therefore, let us take of the wine, and by and by we shall receive wine for our rations, which will strengthen us to go against the Nephites."

¹²And Laman saith unto them: "You may do according to your desires."

¹³And it came to pass that they did take of the wine freely. And it was pleasant to the taste. Therefore, they took of it more freely. And it was strong, having been prepared in its strength.

¹⁴And it came to pass they did drink and were merry. And by and by they were all drunken.

---

    a. Restored per the Original Manuscript. The Printer's Manuscript and subsequent published versions have "Laman" without the possessive. Skousen, *Analysis of the Textual Variants,* 4:2699.

    b. This information must have been on the source plates, but not at this particular point. Mormon inserts it because he had not mentioned it before. The fact that this should be considered an interruption comes from the repetitive resumption right after.

    c. Not a complete sentence. There is no object to resolve "caused."

    d. Restored per the Original Manuscript. The Printer's Manuscript and subsequent published versions have "coming." Skousen, *Analysis of the Textual Variants,* 4:2702.

¹⁵And now, when Laman and his men saw that they were all drunken, and were in a deep sleep, they returned to Moroni and told him all the things that had happened.

¹⁶And now, this was according to the design of Moroni. And Moroni had prepared his men with weapons of war. And he went to the city Gid while the Lamanites were in a deep sleep, and drunken—and cast in the weapons of war in unto the prisoners, insomuch that they were all armed—¹⁷yea, even to their women, and all those of their children—as many as were able to use a weapon of war when Moroni had armed all those prisoners. And all those things were done in a profound silence, ¹⁸but had they awoke the Lamanites.ª Behold, they were drunken. And the Nephites could have slain them.

¹⁹But behold, this was not the desire of Moroni. He did not delight in murder or bloodshed, but he delighted in the saving [ᵇ] his people from destruction. And for this cause, [thatᶜ] he might not bring upon him injustice, he would not fall upon the Lamanites and destroy them in their drunkenness. ²⁰But he had obtained his desire, for he had armed those prisoners of the Nephites which were within the [wallsᵈ] of the city, and had gave them power to gain possession of those parts which were within the walls. ²¹And then he caused his men which were with him to withdraw a pace from them and surround the armies of the Lamanites.

²²Now behold, this was done in the nighttime—so that when the Lamanites awoke in the morning, they beheld that they were surrounded by the Nephites without, and that their prisoners were armed within. ²³And thus, they saw that the Nephites had power over them. And in these circumstances, they found that it [wereᵉ] not expedient that they should fight with the Nephites. Therefore, their chief captains demanded their weapons of war. And they brought them forth and cast them at the feet of the Nephites—pleading for mercy.

²⁴Now behold, this was the desire of Moroni. He took them prisoners of war, and took possession of the city, and caused that all the prisoners should be liberated (which were Nephites). And they did join the army of Moroni, and were a great strength to his army.

²⁵And it came to pass that he did cause the Lamanites, which he had taken prisoners, that they should commence a labor in strengthening the fortifications round about the city Gid.

²⁶And it came to pass that when he had fortified the city Gid, according to his desires, he caused that his prisoners should be taken to the city Bountiful. And he also guarded that city with an exceeding strong force.

²⁷And it came to pass that they did (notwithstanding all the intrigues of the Lamanites) keep and protect all the prisoners which they had taken, and also maintain all the ground and the advantage which they had retaken.

---

a. The phrase "but had they awoke the Lamanites" is to be read with the meaning "so that they would not awaken the Lamanites."

b. Restored per the Original Manuscript by removing "of," as it reads in the Printer's Manuscript. Skousen, *Analysis of the Textual Variants*, 4:2706–7.

c. Restored per the Original Manuscript. The Printer's Manuscript omitted the word "that." Skousen, *Analysis of the Textual Variants*, 4:2707.

d. Restored per the Original Manuscript. The Printer's Manuscript has "wall." Skousen, *Analysis of the Textual Variants*, 4:2608–9.

e. Restored per the Original Manuscript. The Printer's Manuscript has "was." Skousen, *Analysis of the Textual Variants*, 4:2710.

Chapter XXV [Alma 54–55]

[28]And it came to pass that the Nephites began again to be victorious, and to reclaim their rights and their privileges. [29]Many times did the Lamanites attempt to encircle them about by night. But in these attempts they did lose many prisoners. [30]And many times did they attempt to administer of their wine to the Nephites, that they might destroy them with poison, or with drunkenness. [31]But behold, the Nephites were not slow to remember the Lord, their God, in this, their times of affliction. They could not be taken in their snares. Yea, they would not partake of their wine. Yea, they would not take of wine, save they had firstly given to some of the Lamanite prisoners. [32]And they were thus cautious that no poison should be administered among them. For if their wine would poison a Lamanite, it would also poison a Nephite. And thus they did try all their liquors.

[33]And now it came to pass that it was expedient for Moroni to make preparations to attack the city Morianton. For behold, the Lamanites had, by their labors, fortified the city Morianton until it had become an exceeding stronghold. [34]And they were continually bringing new forces into that city and also new supplies of provisions. [35]And thus ended the twenty and ninth year of the reign of the judges over the people of Nephi.

Chapter XXVI [Alma 56–58]

[56] ¹And now it came to pass in the commencement of the thirtieth year of the reign of the judges, in the second day, on the first month—Moroni received an epistle from Helaman stating the affairs of the people in that quarter of the land. ²And these are the words which he wrote, saying:

My dearly beloved brother Moroni, as well in the Lord as in the tribulations of our warfare. Behold, my beloved brother, I have somewhat to tell you concerning our warfare in this part of the land.

³Behold, two thousand of the sons of those men which Ammon brought down out of the land of Nephi.[a] Now, ye have known that these were a descendant of Laman, which was the eldest son of our father, Lehi. ⁴Now, I need not rehearse unto you concerning their traditions or their unbelief, for thou knowest concerning all these things. ⁵Therefore, it supposeth me that I tell you that two thousand of these young men hath taken their weapons of war, and would that I should be their leader. And we have come forth to defend our country.

⁶And now, ye also know concerning the covenant which their fathers made, that they would not take up their weapons of war against their brethren, to shed blood. ⁷But in the twenty and sixth year, when they saw our afflictions and our tribulations for them, they were about to break the covenant which they had made, and take up their weapons of war in our defense. ⁸But I would not suffer them that they should break this covenant which they had made, supposing that God would strengthen us, insomuch that we should not suffer more because of the fulfilling the oath which they had taken.

⁹But behold, here is one thing in which we may have great joy. For behold, in the twenty and sixth year, I, Helaman, did march at the head of these two thousand young men to the city of Judea to assist Antipus, whom ye had appointed a leader over the people of that part of the land.

¹⁰And I did join my two thousand sons (for they are worthy to be called sons) to the army of Antipus—in the which strength Antipus did rejoice exceedingly. For behold, his army had been reduced by the Lamanites because of the numerority[b] of their forces—having slain a vast number of our men, for which cause we have to mourn. ¹¹Nevertheless, we may console ourselves in this point, that they have died in the cause of their country and of their God. Yea, and they are happy.

¹²And the Lamanites had also retained many prisoners—all of whom are chief captains, for none other have they spared alive. And we suppose that they are now, at this time, in the land of Nephi. It is so if they are not slain.

¹³And now, these are the cities which the Lamanites have obtained possession by the shedding of the blood of so many of our valiant men: ¹⁴the land of Manti (or the city of Manti), and the city of Zeezrom, and the city of Cumeni, and the

---

a. This is an incomplete sentence. Adding it to following clauses does not make it better, and therefore it seemed best to simply end the sentence and let the other clauses stand as complete sentences.

b. Skousen suggests that "numerority," which occurs in the Original and Printer's Manuscripts, should be emended to "enormity" based on apparently parallel phrases in the text. Skousen, *Analysis of the Textual Variants*, 5:2726–27. This edition keeps it as written.

Chapter XXVI [Alma 56–58]

city of Antiparah. ¹⁵And these are the cities which they possessed when I arrived at the city of Judea. And I found Antipus and his men toiling with their mights to fortify the city. ¹⁶Yea, and they were depressed in body as well as in spirit. For they had fought valiantly by day, and toiled by night, to maintain their cities. And thus, they had suffered great afflictions of every kind.

¹⁷And now, they were determined to conquer in this place, or die. Therefore, you may well suppose that this little force which I brought with me, yea, those sons of mine, gave them great hopes, and much joy.

¹⁸And now it came to pass that when the Lamanites saw that Antipus had received a greater strength to his army, they were compelled by the orders of Ammoron to not come against the city of Judea (or against us) to battle. ¹⁹And thus, were we favored of the Lord. For had they came upon us in this, our weakness, they might have perhaps destroyed our little army. But thus, were we preserved. ²⁰They were commanded by Ammoron to maintain those cities which they had taken. And thus ended the twenty and sixth year.

And in the commencement of the twenty and seventh year, we had prepared our city (and ourselves) for defense. ²¹Now, we were desirous that the Lamanites should come upon us. For we were not desirous to make an attack upon them in their strongholds.

²²And it came to pass that we kept spies out, round about, to watch the movements of the Lamanites, that they might not pass us by night nor by day to make an attack upon our other cities, which were on the northward. ²³For we knew—in those cities—they were not sufficiently strong to meet them. Therefore, we were desirous, if they should pass by us, to fall upon them in their rear—and thus bring them up in the rear at the same time they were met in the front. We supposed that we could overpower them. But behold, we were disappointed in this, our desire. ²⁴They durst not pass by us with their whole army, ²⁵neither durst they with a part, lest they should not be sufficiently strong, and they should fall. Neither durst they march down against the city of Zarahemla. Neither durst they cross the head of Sidon, over to the city of Nephihah. ²⁶And thus, with their forces, they were determined to maintain those cities which they had taken.

²⁷And now it came to pass in the second month of this year, there was brought unto us many provisions from the fathers of those, my two thousand sons. ²⁸And also, there was sent two thousand men unto us from the land of Zarahemla. And thus, we were prepared with ten thousand men, and provisions for them, and also for their wives, and their children.

²⁹And the Lamanites, thus seeing our forces increase daily, and provisions arrive for our support—they began to be fearful and began to sally forth—if it were possible, to put an end to our receiving provisions and strength.

³⁰Now, when we saw that the Lamanites began to grow uneasy on this wise, we were desirous to bring a stratagem into an effect upon them. Therefore, Antipus ordered that I should march forth with my little sons to a neighboring city—as if we were carrying provisions to a neighboring city. ³¹And we were to march near the city Antiparah as if we were going to the city beyond, on the borders by the seashore.

³²And it came to pass that we did march forth, as if with our provisions, to go to that city.

³³And it came to pass that Antipus did march forth with a part of his army, leaving the remainder to maintain the city. But he did not march forth until I had gone forth with my little army and came near the city Antiparah.

³⁴And now, in the city Antiparah were stationed the strongest army of the Lamanites, yea, the most numerous.

³⁵And it came to pass that when they had been informed by their spies, they came forth with their army and marched against us.

³⁶And it came to pass that we did flee before them, northward. And thus, we did lead away the most powerful army of the Lamanites—³⁷yea, even to a considerable distance, insomuch that when they saw the army of Antipus pursuing them with their mights, they did not turn to the right nor to the left—but pursued their march in a straight course after us, and, as we suppose, that it was their intent to slay us before Antipus should overtake them. And this, that they might not be surrounded by our people.

³⁸And now, Antipus—beholding our danger—did speed the march of his army. But behold, it was night. Therefore, they did not overtake us. Neither did Antipus overtake them. Therefore, we did camp for the night.

³⁹And it came to pass that before the dawn of the morning—behold, the Lamanites were pursuing us. Now, we were not sufficiently strong to contend with them. Yea, I would not suffer that my little sons should fall into their hands. Therefore, we did continue our march. And we took our march into the wilderness.

⁴⁰Now, they durst not turn to the right nor to the left, lest they should be surrounded. Neither would I turn to the right nor to the left, lest they should overtake me. And we could not stand against them—but be slain. And they would make their escape. And thus, we did flee all that day into the wilderness, even until it was dark.

⁴¹And it came to pass that again when the light of the morning came, we saw the Lamanites upon us. And we did flee before them. ⁴²But it came to pass that they did not pursue us far—before they halted. And it was in the morning of the third day, on the seventh month.

⁴³And now, whether they were overtaken by Antipus we knew not. But I said unto my men: "Behold, we know not but they have halted for the purpose that we should come against them, that they might catch us in their snare. ⁴⁴Therefore, what say ye, my sons? Will ye go against them to battle?"

⁴⁵And now, I say unto you, my beloved brother, Moroni, that never had I seen so great courage—nay, not amongst all the Nephites! ⁴⁶For, as I had ever called them my sons (for they were, all of them, very young), even so, they said unto me: "Father, behold, our God is with us! And he will not suffer that we shall fall. Then let us go forth. We would not slay our brethren, if they would let us alone. Therefore, let us go, lest they should overpower the army of Antipus."

⁴⁷Now, they never had fought. Yet, they did not fear death. And they did think more upon the liberty of their fathers than they did upon their lives. Yea, they had been taught by their mothers that if they did not doubt, that God would deliver them. ⁴⁸And they rehearsed unto me the words of their mothers, saying: "We do not doubt. Our mothers knew."[a]

---

a. This punctuation changes the meaning of the verse. This was the intended message. Helaman had just stated that their mothers had told them that "if they did not doubt, God would deliver them."

⁴⁹And it came to pass that I did return with my two thousand against these Lamanites, which had pursued us. And now, behold, the armies of Antipus had overtaken them. And a terrible battle had commenced. ⁵⁰The army of Antipus, being weary because of their long march in so short a space of time, were about to fall into the hands of the Lamanites. And had I not returned with my two thousand, they would have obtained their purpose, ⁵¹for Antipus had fallen by the sword, and many of his leaders—because of their weariness, which was occasioned by the speed of their march. Therefore, the men of Antipus, being confused because of the fall of their leaders—began to give way before the Lamanites.

⁵²And it came to pass that the Lamanites took courage and began to pursue them. And thus were the Lamanites pursuing them with great vigor when Helaman came upon their rear with his two thousand, and began to slay them exceedingly, insomuch that the whole army of the Lamanites halted and turned upon Helaman.

⁵³Now, when the people of Antipus saw that the Lamanites had turned them about, they gathered together their men and came again upon the rear of the Lamanites.

⁵⁴And now it came to pass that we—the people of Nephi, the people of Antipus, and I with my two thousand—did surround the Lamanites and did slay them, yea, insomuch that they were compelled to deliver up their weapons of war, and also themselves, as prisoners of war.

⁵⁵And now it came to pass that when they had surrendered themselves up unto us—behold, I numbered those young men which had fought with me—fearing lest there were many of them slain.

⁵⁶But behold, to my great joy there had not one soul of them fallen to the earth. Yea, and they had fought as if with the strength of God. Yea, never was men known to have fought with such miraculous strength. And with such mighty power did they fall upon the Lamanites, that they did frighten them. And for this cause did the Lamanites deliver themselves up as prisoners of war. ⁵⁷And as we had no place for our prisoners that we could guard them, to keep them from the armies of the Lamanites—therefore, we sent them to the land of Zarahemla, and a part of those men which were not slain of Antipus with them. And the remainder I took, and joined them to my stripling Ammonites, and took our march back to the city of Judea.

[57] ¹And now it came to pass that I received an epistle from Ammoron, the king, stating that if I would deliver up those prisoners of war which we had taken, that he would deliver up the city of Antiparah unto us. ²But I sent an epistle unto the king, that we were sure our forces were sufficient to take the city of Antiparah by our force. And by delivering up the prisoners for that city, we should suppose ourselves unwise. And that we would only deliver up our prisoners on exchange. ³And Ammoron refused mine epistle, for he would not exchange prisoners. Therefore, we began to make preparations to go against the city of Antiparah.

Helaman underscored that they did as they were taught, and that they did not doubt. The focus should be on the young men not doubting God, not that they did not doubt their mothers. Grant Hardy makes a similar recommendation in *The Book of Mormon: Maxwell Institute Study Edition* (Provo, UT: Neal A. Maxwell Institute, 2018). (See the footnote to verse 48). The compositor added "it" for the 1830 printing, making it "our mothers knew it" rather than "our mothers knew."

⁴But the people of Antiparah did leave the city and fled to their other cities which they had possessions of, to fortify them. And thus, the city of Antiparah fell into our hands. ⁵And thus ended the twenty and eighth year of the reign of the judges.

⁶And it came to pass that in the commencement of the twenty and ninth year, we received a supply of provisions, and also an addition to our army from the land of Zarahemla and from the land round about, to the number of six thousand men, besides sixty of the sons of the Ammonites, which had come to join their brethren, my little band of two thousand. And now behold, we were strong. Yea, and we had also a-plenty of provisions brought unto us.

⁷And it came to pass that it was our desire to wage a battle with the army which was placed to protect the city Cumeni. ⁸And now behold, I will show unto you that we soon accomplished our desire. Yea, with our strong force (or with a part of our strong force), we did surround, by night, the city Cumeni—a little before they were to receive a supply of provisions.

⁹And it came to pass that we did camp round about the city for many nights. But we did sleep upon our swords, and keep guards, that the Lamanites could not come upon us by night and slay us, which they attempted many times. But as many times as they attempted this, their blood was spilt. ¹⁰At length their provisions did arrive, and they were about to enter the city by night. And we, instead of being Lamanites, were Nephites—therefore, we did take them and their provisions. ¹¹And notwithstanding the Lamanites being cut off from their support after this manner, they were still determined to maintain the city. Therefore, it became expedient that we should take those provisions and send them to Judea—and our prisoners to the land of Zarahemla.

¹²And it came to pass that not many days had passed away before the Lamanites began to lose all hopes of succor. Therefore, they yielded up the city. And thus we had accomplished our designs in obtaining the city Cumeni. ¹³But it came to pass that our prisoners were so numerous that, notwithstanding the enormity of our numbers, we were obliged to employ all our force to keep them, or to put them to death. ¹⁴For behold, they would break out in great numbers, and would fight with stones, and with clubs, or whatsoever things they could get into their hands, insomuch that we did slay upwards of two thousand of them after they had surrendered themselves prisoners of war. ¹⁵Therefore, it became expedient for us that we should put an end to their lives, or guard them sword in hand, down to the land of Zarahemla. And also, our provisions were not any more than sufficient for our own people—notwithstanding that which we had taken from the Lamanites.

¹⁶And now, in those critical circumstances, it became a very serious matter to determine concerning these prisoners of war. Nevertheless, we did resolve to send them down to the land of Zarahemla. Therefore, we selected a part of our men, and gave them charge over our prisoners, to go down to the land of Zarahemla. ¹⁷But it came to pass that on the morrow they did return.

And now behold, we did not inquire of them concerning the prisoners, for behold, the Lamanites were upon us. And they returned in season to save us from falling into their hands. For behold, Ammoron had sent to their support a new supply of provision and also a numerous army of men.

¹⁸And it came to pass that those men which we sent with the prisoners did ar-

Chapter XXVI [Alma 56–58]

rive in season to check them as they were about to overpower us. ¹⁹But behold, my little band of two thousand and sixty fought most desperately. Yea, they were firm before the Lamanites, and did administer death unto all those who opposed them. ²⁰And as the remainder of our army were about to give way before the Lamanites, behold, those two thousand and sixty were firm and undaunted. ²¹Yea, and they did obey, and observe to perform, every word of command with exactness. Yea, and even according to their faith, it was done unto them. And I did remember the words which they said unto me that their mothers had taught them.

²²And now behold, it was these, my sons, and those men which had been selected to convey the prisoners, to whom we owe this great victory. For it was they who did beat the Lamanites. Therefore, they were driven back to the city of Manti. ²³And we retained our city Cumeni and were not all destroyed by the sword. Nevertheless, we had suffered great loss.

²⁴And it came to pass that after the Lamanites had fled, I immediately gave orders that my men, which had been wounded, should be taken from among the dead—and caused that their wounds should be dressed.

²⁵And it came to pass that there were two hundred, out of my two thousand and sixty, which had feinted because of the loss of blood. Nevertheless, according to the goodness of God, and to our great astonishment, and also the joy of our whole army—there was not one soul of them which did perish. Yea, and neither was there one soul among them which had not received many wounds. ²⁶And now, their preservation was astonishing to our whole army—yea, that they should be spared while there was a thousand of our brethren which were slain. And we do justly ascribe it to the miraculous power of God, because of their exceeding faith in that which they had been taught, to believe that there was a just God—and whosoever did not doubt, that they should be preserved by his marvelous power. ²⁷Now, this was the faith of these of which I have spoken. They are young, and their minds are firm. And they do put their trust in God continually.

²⁸And now it came to pass that after we had thus taken care of our wounded men, and had buried our dead, and also the dead of the Lamanites (which were many), behold, we did inquire of Gid concerning the prisoners which they had started to go down to the land of Zarahemla with. ²⁹Now, Gid was the chief captain over the band which was appointed to guide them down to that land of Zarahemla. ³⁰And now, these are the words which Gid said unto me:

> Behold, we did start to go down to the land of Zarahemla with our prisoners.
>
> And it came to pass that we did meet the spies of our armies, which had been sent out to watch the camp of the Lamanites. ³¹And they cried unto us, saying: "Behold! The armies of the Lamanites are a-marching towards the city of Cumeni! And behold, they will fall upon them, yea, and will destroy our people!"
>
> ³²And it came to pass that our prisoners did hear their cries, which caused them to take courage. And they did rise up in rebellion against us.
>
> ³³And it came to pass, because of their rebellion, we did cause that our swords should come upon them.
>
> And it came to pass that they did, in a body, run upon our swords—in

the which the greater number of them were slain. And the remainder of them broke through and fled from us.

³⁴And behold, when they had fled, and we could not overtake them, we took our march—with speed—towards the city Cumeni.

And behold, we did arrive in time, that we might assist our brethren in preserving the city.

³⁵And behold, we are again delivered out of the hands of our enemies. And blessed is the name of our God. For behold, it is he that hath delivered us—[yea[a]], that hath done this great thing for us.

³⁶Now it came to pass that when I, Helaman, had heard these words of Gid, I was filled with exceeding joy because of the goodness of God in preserving us, that we might not all perish. Yea, and I trust that the souls of them which has been slain have entered into the rest of their God.

[58] ¹And behold, now it came to pass that our next object was to obtain the city of Manti. But behold, there was no way that we could lead them out of the city by our small bands, for behold, they remembered that which we had hitherto done. Therefore, we could not decoy them away from their strongholds. ²And they were so exceeding more numerous than was our army, that we durst not of go forth and attack them in their strongholds. ³Yea, and it became expedient that we should employ our men to the maintaining those parts of the land of the which we had retained of our possessions. Therefore, it became expedient that we should wait, that we might receive more strength from the land of Zarahemla, and also a new supply of provisions.

⁴And it came to pass that I, thus, did send an embassy to the [great[b]] Governor of our land, to acquaint him concerning the affairs of our people.

And it came to pass that we did wait to receive provisions and strength from the land of Zarahemla. ⁵But behold, this did not[c] profit us but little, for the Lamanites were also receiving great strength from day to day, and also many provisions. And thus were our circumstances at this period of time. ⁶And the Lamanites were sallying forth against us from time to time, resolving by stratagem to destroy us. Nevertheless, we could not come to battle with them because of their retreats[d] and their strongholds.

⁷And it came to pass that we did wait in these difficult circumstances for the space of many months, even until we were about to perish for the want of food.

⁸But it came to pass that we did receive food (which was guarded to us by an army of two thousand men) to our assistance. And this is all the assistance which we did receive to defend ourselves and our country from falling into the hands of our enemies, yea, to contend with an enemy which was innumerable.

⁹And now, the cause of these, our embarrassments (or the cause why they did

---

a. Restored per *Original Manuscript of the Book of Mormon*, 5:411. The beginning "y" is missing, but the "ea" is present. The Printer's Manuscript has "ye."

b. Restored per the Original Manuscript. The word "great" was not copied from the Original into the Printer's Manuscript. Skousen, *Analysis of the Textual Variants*, 5:2775.

c. This forms a double negative, and it was removed in the 1920 edition. It is present in both the Original and Printer's Manuscripts. Skousen, *Analysis of the Textual Variants*, 5:2776.

d. "Retreats," in this case, is parallel to stronghold. It should not be read as a verb.

Chapter XXVI [Alma 56–58]

not send more strength unto us), we knew not. Therefore, we were grieved, and also filled with fear, lest by any means the judgments of God should come upon our land to our overthrow and utter destruction. ¹⁰Therefore, we did pour out our souls in prayer to God, that he would strengthen us and deliver us out of the hands of our enemies, yea, and also give us strength that we might retain our cities, and our lands, and our possessions, for the support of our people.

¹¹Yea, and it came to pass that the Lord, our God, did visit us with assurances that he would deliver us, yea, insomuch that he did speak peace to our souls—and did grant unto us great faith and did cause us that we should hope for our deliverance in him. ¹²And we did take courage with our small force, which we had received, and were fixed with a determination to conquer our enemies, and to maintain our lands, and our possessions, and our wives, and our children, and the cause of our liberty. ¹³And thus, we did go forth with all our mights against the Lamanites, which were in the city of Manti. And we did pitch our tents by the wilderness side, which was near to the city.

¹⁴And it came to pass on the morrow, that when the Lamanites saw that we were in the borders by the wilderness which was near the city, that they sent out their spies round about us, that they might discover the number and the strength of our army.

¹⁵And it came to pass that when they saw that we were not strong as according to our numbers—and fearing that we should cut them off from their support (except they should come out to battle against us, and kill us)—and also supposing that they could easily destroy us with their numerous hosts—therefore, they began to make preparations to come out against us to battle. ¹⁶And when we saw that they were making preparations to come out against us, behold, I caused that Gid, with a small number of men, should secrete himself in the wilderness. And also that Teomner should, with a small number of men, secrete himself also in the wilderness.

¹⁷Now, Gid and his men was on the right, and the other on the left. And when they had thus secreted themselves, behold, I remained with the remainder of my army in that same place where we had first pitched our tents against the time that the Lamanites should come out to battle.

¹⁸And it came to pass that the Lamanites did come out with their numerous army against us. And when they had come and were about to fall upon us with the sword—I caused that my men (those which were with me) should retreat into the wilderness.

¹⁹And it came to pass that the Lamanites did follow after us with great speed. For they were exceedingly desirous to overtake us, that they might slay us. Therefore, they did follow us into the wilderness. And we did pass by in the midst of Gid, and Teomner, insomuch that they were not discovered by the Lamanites.

²⁰And it came to pass that when the Lamanites had passed by (or when the army had passed by), Gid and Teomner did rise up from their secret places, and did cut off the spies of the Lamanites that they should not return to the city.

²¹And it came to pass that when they had cut them off, they ran to the city and fell upon the guards which were left to guard the city, insomuch that they destroy them and did take possession of the city. ²²Now, this was done because the

Lamanites did suffer their whole army, save a few guards only, to be led away into the wilderness.

²³And it came to pass that Gid and Teomner, by this means, had obtained possession of their city stronghold.

And it came to pass that we took our course after having traveled much in the wilderness towards the land of Zarahemla. ²⁴And when the Lamanites saw that they were marching towards the land of Zarahemla, they were exceeding afraid, lest there was a plan laid to lead them on to destruction. Therefore, they began to retreat back into the wilderness again, yea, even back by the same way which they had came. ²⁵And behold, it was night and they did pitch their tents. For the chief captains of the Lamanites [had supposed[a]] that the Nephites were weary, because of their march. And, supposing that they had driven their whole army—therefore, they took no thought concerning the city of Manti.

²⁶Now it came to pass that when it was night, that I caused that my men should not sleep, but that they should march forward, by another way, towards the land of Manti. ²⁷And because of this, our march in the nighttime—behold, on the morrow, we were beyond the Lamanites, insomuch that we did arrive before them to the city of Manti. ²⁸And thus, it came to pass that by this stratagem, we did take possession of the city of Manti without the shedding of blood.

²⁹And it came to pass that when the armies of the Lamanites did arrive near the city and saw that we were prepared to meet them—they were astonished exceedingly, and struck with great fear, insomuch that they did flee into the wilderness.

³⁰Yea, and it came to pass that the armies of the Lamanites did flee out of all this quarter of the land. But behold, they have carried with them many of our women, and children, out of the land. ³¹And the cities which had been taken by the Lamanites, all of them are, at this period of time, in our possession. And our fathers, and our women, and our children, are returning to their homes—all save it be those which have been taken prisoners and carried off by the Lamanites. ³²But behold, our armies are small to maintain so great a number of cities and so great possessions. ³³But behold, we trust that our God, who hath given us victory over those lands, insomuch that we have obtained those cities, and those lands which were our own.

³⁴Now, we do not know the cause that the government does not grant us more strength. Neither does those men, which came up unto us, know why we have not received greater strength. ³⁵Behold, we do not know but what ye are unsuccessful, and ye have drawn away the forces into that quarter of the land. If so, we do not desire to murmur. ³⁶And if it is not so—behold, we fear that there is some [fraction[b]] in the government, that they do not send more men to our assistance. For we know that they are more numerous than that which they have sent. ³⁷But behold, it mattereth not. We trust God will deliver us, notwithstanding the weakness of our armies, yea, and deliver us out of the hands of our enemies.

³⁸Behold, this is the twenty and ninth year, and in the latter end. And we are in the possession of our lands. And the Lamanites have fled to the land of Nephi.

---

a. Restored per the Original Manuscript. The Printer's Manuscript has "& supposing," which appears to have been a copying error. Skousen, *Analysis of the Textual Variants*, 5:2787.

b. Restored per the Original Manuscript. The Printer's Manuscript has "far<c>tion." Skousen, *Analysis of the Textual Variants*, 5:2795.

Chapter XXVI [Alma 56–58]

³⁹And those sons of the people of Ammon (of which I have so highly spoken) are with me in the city of Manti. And the Lord hath supported them, yea, and kept them from falling by the sword, insomuch that even one soul hath not been slain. ⁴⁰But behold, they have received many wounds. Nevertheless, they stand fast in that liberty wherewith God hath made them free. And they are strict to remember the Lord, their God, from day to day. Yea, they do observe to keep his statutes, and his judgments, and his commandments—continually. And their faith is strong in the prophecies concerning that which is to come.

⁴¹And now, my beloved brother Moroni—that the Lord our God, who hath redeemed us and made us free, may keep you continually in his presence. Yea, and that he may favor this people, even that ye may have success in obtaining the possession of all that which the Lamanites hath taken from us, which was for our support.

And now behold, I close mine epistle. I am Helaman, the son of Alma.

Chapter XXVII [Alma 59–60]

[59] ¹Now it came to pass in the thirtieth year of the reign of the judges over the people of Nephi—after Moroni had received, and had read, Helaman's epistle—he exceedingly rejoiced because of the welfare, yea, the exceeding success which Helaman had had in obtaining those lands which were lost. ²Yea, and he did make it known unto all his people in all the land round about, in that part where he was, that they might rejoice also.

³And it came to pass that he immediately sent an epistle to Pahoran, desiring that he should cause men to be gathered together to strengthen Helaman (or the armies of Helaman), insomuch that he might, with ease, maintain that part of the land which he had been so miraculously prospered in retaining.

⁴And it came to pass when Moroni had sent this epistle to the land of Zarahemla, he began again to lay a plan, that he might obtain the remainder of those possessions and cities which the Lamanites had taken from them.

⁵And it came to pass that while Moroni was thus making preparations to go against the Lamanites to battle, behold, the people of Nephihah, which were gathered together from the city of Moroni, and the city of Lehi, and the city of Morianton, were attacked by the Lamanites—⁶yea, even those which had been compelled to flee from the land of Manti and from the land round about—had came over and joined the Lamanites in this part of the land. ⁷And thus, being exceeding numerous (yea, and receiving strength from day to day)—by the command of Ammoron they came forth against the people of Nephihah and they did begin to slay them with an exceeding great slaughter. ⁸And their armies were so numerous that the remainder of the people of Nephihah were obliged to flee before them. And they came, even and joined the army of Moroni.

⁹And now, as Moroni had supposed that there should be men sent to the city of Nephihah to the assistance of the people to maintain that city—and knowing that it was easier to keep the city from falling into the hands of the Lamanites than to take it from them—he supposed that they would easily maintain that city. ¹⁰Therefore, he retained all his force to maintain those places which he had recovered.

¹¹And now, when Moroni saw that the city of Nephihah was lost, he was exceeding sorrowful—and began to doubt because of the wickedness of the people—whether they should not fall into the hands of their brethren. ¹²Now, this was the case with all his chief captains. They doubted and marveled also, because of the wickedness of the people. And this, because of the success of the Lamanites over them.

¹²And it came to pass that Moroni was angry with the government because of their indifference concerning the freedom of their country.

[60] ¹And it came to pass that he wrote again to the Governor of the land, which was Pahoran. And these are the words which he wrote, saying:

> Behold, I direct mine epistle to Pahoran in the city of Zarahemla, which is the Chief Judge and the Governor over the land—and also to all those who hath been chosen by this people to govern and manage the affairs of this war. ²For behold, I have somewhat to say unto them—by the way of condemnation! For behold, ye yourselves know that ye have been appointed to gather together men and arm them with swords, and with scimitars, and all manner of weapons of war of every

kind, and send forth against the Lamanites in whatsoever parts they should come into our land.

³And now, behold, I say unto you that myself, and also my men, and also Helaman and his men, have suffered exceeding great sufferings—yea, even hunger, thirst, and fatigue, and all manner of afflictions of every kind. ⁴But behold, were this all we had suffered, we would not murmur nor complain. ⁵But behold, great has been the slaughter among our people. Yea, thousands have fallen by the sword—while it might have otherwise been, if ye had rendered unto our armies sufficient strength and succor for them! Yea, great has been your neglect towards us!

⁶And now, behold, we desire to know the cause of this exceeding great neglect. Yea, we desire to know the cause of your thoughtless state. ⁷Can you think to sit upon your thrones in a state of thoughtless stupor, while your enemies are spreading the work of death around you?

Yea, while they are murdering thousands of your brethren?

⁸Yea, even they which have looked up to you for protection?

Yea, have placed you in a situation that ye might have succored them?

Yea, ye might have sent armies unto them to have strengthened them, and have saved thousands of them from falling by the sword?

⁹But behold, this is not all! Ye have withheld your provisions from them, insomuch that many have fought and bled out their lives because of their great desires which they had for the welfare of this people. Yea, and this they have done when they were about to perish with hunger because of your exceeding great neglect towards them.

¹⁰And now, my beloved brethren (for ye had ought to be beloved)—yea, and ye had ought to have stirred yourselves more diligently for the welfare and the freedom of this people. But behold, ye have neglected them, insomuch that the blood of thousands shall come upon your heads for vengeance, yea, for known unto God were all their cries and all their sufferings!

¹¹Behold, could ye suppose that ye could sit upon your thrones, and because of the exceeding goodness of God, ye could do nothing—and he would deliver you? Behold, if ye have supposed this, ye have supposed in vain! ¹²Do ye suppose that, because so many of your brethren have been killed—[ᵃ] because of their wickedness? I say unto you, if ye have supposed this, ye have supposed in vain! For I say unto you [ᵇ], there are many which have fallen by the sword. And behold, it is to your condemnation! ¹³For the Lord suffereth the righteous to be slain, that his justice and judgment may come upon the wicked. Therefore, ye need not suppose that the righteous are lost because they are slain. But behold, they do enter into the rest of the Lord, their God.

¹⁴And now, behold I say unto you, I fear exceedingly that the judgments of God will come upon this people because of their exceeding slothfulness, yea, even

---

a. In 1840 the phrase "it is" was added and has been retained in the modern edition. The addition clarifies the intended meaning of the sentence. *Printer's Manuscript of the Book of Mormon*, 123.

b. The Printer's Manuscript has "that." The original is not extant, but there is some surrounding text. Skousen suggests that the spacing of the lacuna would suggest that the word "that" was not in original. He elected to remove it, and this edition follows his suggestion. Skousen, *Analysis of the Textual Variants*, 5:2809.

the slothfulness of our government, and their exceeding great neglect towards their brethren, yea, towards those which have been slain. ¹⁵For, were it not for the wickedness which first commenced at our head, we could have withstood our enemies, that they could have gained no power over us.

¹⁶Yea, had it not been for the war which broke out among ourselves, yea, were it not for those kingmen which caused so much bloodshed among ourselves, yea, at the time we were contending among ourselves—if we had united our strength (as we had hitherto have done)—yea, had it not been for the desire of power and authority which those kingmen had over us—had they been true to the cause of our freedom and united with us, and gone forth against our enemies instead of taking up their swords against us (which was the cause of so much bloodshed among ourselves)—yea, if we had gone forth against them in the strength of the Lord—we should have dispersed our enemies. For it would have been done according to the fulfilling of his word.

¹⁷But behold. Now the Lamanites are coming upon us and they are murdering our people with the sword, yea, our women, and our children—taking possession of our lands, and also carrying them away captive, causing them that they should suffer all manner of afflictions—and this because of the great wickedness of those who are seeking for power, and authority, yea, even those kingmen!

¹⁸But why should I say much concerning this matter? For we know not but what ye, yourselves, are a seeking for authority! We know not but what ye are also traitors to your country! ¹⁹Or, is it that ye have neglected us because ye are in the heart of our country and ye are surrounded by security, that ye do not cause food to be sent unto us, and also men, to strengthen our armies?

²⁰Have ye forgat the commandments of the Lord, your God?

Yea, have ye forgat the captivity of our fathers?

Have ye forgat the many times we have been delivered out of the hands of our enemies?

²¹Or do ye suppose that the Lord will still deliver us—while we sit upon our thrones, and do not make use of the means which the Lord hath provided for us! ²²Yea, will ye sit in idleness, while ye are surrounded with thousands of those—yea, and tens of thousands of those, which do also sit in idleness—while there are thousands round about in the borders of the land which are falling by the sword, yea, wounded, and bleeding? ²³Do ye suppose that God will look upon you as guiltless while ye sit still and behold these things? Behold, I say unto you, nay!

Now, I would that ye should remember that God hath said that the inward vessel shall be cleansed first, and then shall the outer vessel be cleansed also.[a] ²⁴And now, except ye do repent of that which ye have done, and begin to be up and doing, and send forth food and men unto us—and also unto Helaman, that he may support those parts of our country which he hath retained, and that we may also recover the remainder of our possessions in these parts—behold, it will be expedient that we contend no more with the Lamanites until we have first cleansed our inner vessel. Yea, even the great head of our government!

²⁵And except ye grant mine epistle and come out, and show unto me a true spirit

---

[a]. See Matthew 23:25: "Thou blind Pharisee, cleanse first that which is within the cup and platter, that the outside of them may be clean also."

Chapter XXVII [Alma 59–60]

of freedom, and try to strengthen and fortify our armies—and grant unto them food for their support—behold, I will leave a part of my freemen to maintain this part of our land. And I will leave the strength of, and the blessings, of God upon them—that none other power can operate against them ²⁶(and this, because of their exceeding faith, and their patience, in their tribulations). ²⁷And I will come unto you. And if there be any among you that hath a desire for freedom, yea, if there be even a spark of freedom remaining—behold, I will stir up insurrections among you, even until those who hath desires to usurp power and authority shall become extinct.

²⁸Yea behold, I do not fear your power nor your authority. But it is my God whom I fear! And it is according to his commandments that I do take my sword to defend the cause of my country. And it is because of your iniquity that we have suffered so much loss.

²⁹Behold, it is time! Yea, the time is now at hand that except ye do bestir yourselves in the defense of your country and your little ones, the sword of justice doth hang over you. Yea, and it shall fall upon you and visit you, even to your utter destruction.

³⁰Behold, I wait for assistance from you. And except ye do administer unto our relief—behold, I come unto you, even into the land of Zarahemla—and smite you with the sword insomuch that ye can have no more power to impede the progress of this people in the cause of our freedom. ³¹For behold, the Lord will not suffer that ye shall live and wax strong in your iniquities, to destroy his righteous people.

³²Behold, can you suppose that the Lord will spare you and come out in judgment against the Lamanites—when it is the tradition of their fathers that hath caused their hatred? Yea, and it hath been redoubled by those which have dissented from us—while your iniquity is for the cause of your love of glory and the vain things of the world! ³³Ye know that ye do transgress the laws of God. And ye do know that ye do trample them under your feet.

Behold, the Lord saith unto me: "If those whom ye have appointed your governors do not repent of their sins, and iniquities—ye shall go up to battle against them!"[a]

³⁴And now behold, I, Moroni, am constrained (according to the covenant which I have made) to keep the commandments of my God. Therefore, I would that ye should adhere to the word of God, and send speedily unto me of your provisions and of your men—and also to Helaman.

³⁵And behold, if ye will not do this—I come unto you speedily! For behold, God will not suffer that we should perish with hunger. Therefore, he will give unto us of your food, even if it must be by the sword. Now, see that ye fulfil the word of God.

³⁶Behold, I am Moroni, your Chief Captain. I seek not for power, but to pull it down. I seek not for honor of the world, but for the glory of my God—and the freedom and welfare of my country.

And thus, I close mine epistle.

---

a. There is no known reference.

Chapter XXVIII [Alma 61]

[61] ¹Behold, now it came to pass that soon after Moroni had sent his epistle unto the Chief Governor, he received an epistle from Pahoran, the Chief Governor. And these are the words which he received:

²I, Pahoran, which art the Chief Governor of this land, do send these words unto Moroni, the Chief Captain over the army.

Behold, I say unto you, Moroni, that I do not joy in your great afflictions. Yea, it grieves my soul. ³But behold, there are those who do joy in your afflictions, yea, insomuch that they have risen up in rebellion against me, and also those of my people which are freemen. Yea, and those which have risen up are exceeding numerous. ⁴And it is those who have sought to take away the Judgment Seat from me that have been the cause of this great iniquity. For they have used great flattery, and they have led away the hearts of many people, which will be the cause of sore affliction among us. They have withheld our provisions and have daunted our freemen, that they have not come unto you.

⁵And behold, they have driven me out before them. And I have fled to the land of Gideon with as many men as it were possible that I could get. ⁶And behold, I have sent a proclamation throughout this part of the land. And behold, they are flocking to us daily—to their arms, in the defense of their country, and their freedom, and to avenge our wrongs. ⁷And they have come unto us, insomuch that those which have rose up in rebellion against us are set at defiance, yea, insomuch that they do fear us and durst not come out against us to battle.

⁸They have got possession of the land of the city of Zarahemla. They have appointed a king over them and he hath written unto the king of the Lamanites—in the which he hath joined an alliance with him—in the which alliance he hath agreed to maintain the city of Zarahemla—in the which maintenance he supposeth will enable the Lamanites to conquer the remainder of the land, and he shall be placed king over this people when they shall be conquered under the Lamanites.

⁹And now, in your epistle, ye hath censured me—but it mattereth not. I am not angry, but do rejoice in the greatness of your heart. I, Pahoran, do not seek for power, save only to retain my Judgment Seat that I may preserve the rights and the liberty of my people. My soul standeth fast in that liberty in the which God hath made me free.

¹⁰And now behold, we will resist wickedness, even unto bloodshed! We would not shed the blood of the Lamanites, if they would stay in their own land. ¹¹We would not shed the blood of our brethren, if they would not rise up in rebellion and take the sword against us. ¹²We would subject ourselves to the yoke of bondage, if it were requisite with the justice of God—or if he should command us so to do.

¹³But behold, he doth not command us that we shall subject ourselves to our enemies, but that we should put our trust in him. And he will deliver us. ¹⁴Therefore, my beloved brother, Moroni, let us resist evil! And whatsoever evil we cannot resist with our words –yea, such as rebellions, and dissensions—let us resist them with our swords, that we may retain our freedom, that we may rejoice in the great privilege of our church, and in the cause of our Redeemer, and our

God. ¹⁵Therefore, come unto me speedily with a few of your men. And leave the remainder in the charge of Lehi and Teancum. Give unto them power to conduct the war in that part of the land, according to the spirit of God, which is also the spirit of freedom, which is in them.

¹⁶Behold, I have sent a few provisions unto them that they may not perish, until ye can come unto me. ¹⁷Gather together whatsoever force ye can upon your march hither and we will go speedily against those dissenters in the strength of our God, according to the faith which is in us. ¹⁸And we will take possession of the city of Zarahemla, that we may obtain more food to send forth unto Lehi and Teancum. Yea, we will go forth against them in the strength of the Lord, and we will put an end to this great iniquity!

¹⁹And now, Moroni, I do joy in receiving your epistle, for I was somewhat worried concerning what we should do—whether it should be just in us to go against our brethren. ²⁰But ye have said, except they repent, the Lord hath commanded you that ye should go against them.

²¹See that ye strengthen Lehi and Teancum, in the Lord. Tell them to fear not, for God will deliver them, yea, and also all those who stand fast in that liberty wherewith God hath made them free.

And now, I close mine epistle to my beloved brother, Moroni.

Chapter XXIX [Alma 62]

[62] ¹And now it came to pass that when Moroni had received this epistle, his heart did take courage and was filled with exceeding great joy because of the faithfulness of Pahoran, that he was not also a traitor to the freedom and cause of his country. ²But he did also mourn exceedingly because of the iniquity of those who had driven Pahoran from the Judgment Seat—yea in fine, because of those who had rebelled against their country and also their God.

³And it came to pass that Moroni took a small number of men (according to the desire of Pahoran) and gave Lehi and Teancum command over the remainder of his army—and took his march towards the land of Gideon. ⁴And he did raise the standard of liberty in whatsoever place he did enter, and gained whatsoever force he could in all his march towards the land of Gideon.

⁵And it came to pass that thousands did flock unto his standard and did take up their swords in the defense of their freedom, that they might not come into bondage. ⁶And thus, when Moroni had gathered together whatsoever men he could, in all his march, he came to the land of Gideon. And uniting his forces with that of Pahoran's, they became exceeding strong, even stronger than the men of Pachus (>which was the king of those dissenters, which had driven out the freemen, out of the land of Zarahemla, and had taken possession of the land<ᵃ).

⁷And it came to pass that Moroni and Pahoran went down with their armies into the land of Zarahemla, and went forth against the city, and did meet the men of Pachus—insomuch that they did come to battle. ⁸And behold, Pachus was slain and his men were taken prisoners. And Pahoran was restored to his Judgment Seat. ⁹And the men of Pachus received their trial, according to the law—and also those kingmen which had been taken and cast into prison. And they were executed, according to the law. Yea, those men of Pachus and those kingmen—whosoever would not take up arms in the defense of their country, but would fight against it—were put to death. ¹⁰And thus, it became expedient that this law should be strictly observed for the safety of their country. Yea, and whosoever was found a-denying their freedom was speedily executed, according to the law.

¹¹And thus ended the thirtieth year of the reign of the judges over the people of Nephi, Moroni and Pahoran having restored peace to the land of Zarahemla, among their own people—having inflicted death upon all those who were not true to the cause of freedom.

¹²And it came to pass in the commencement of the thirty and first year of the reign of the judges over the people of Nephi, Moroni immediately caused that provisions should be sent—and also an army of six thousand men should be sent—unto Helaman, to assist him in preserving that part of the land. ¹³And he also caused that an army of six thousand men, with a sufficient quantity of food, should be sent to the armies of Lehi and Teancum.

And it came to pass that this was done to fortify the land against the Lamanites.

---

a. Mormon understands that he hasn't mentioned Pachus before, and he now adds enough information that his readers will know who he was. The point he had been making was that Moroni was traveling to aid Pahoran, and that picks up in the next sentence as a repetitive resumption.

Chapter XXIX [Alma 62]

¹⁴And it came to pass that Moroni, and Pahoran, leaving a large body of men in the land of Zarahemla, took their march (with a large body of men) towards the land of Nephihah—being determined to overthrow the Lamanites in that city.

¹⁵And it came to pass that as they were marching towards the land, they took a large body of men of the Lamanites and slew many of them. And took their provisions and their weapons of war.

¹⁶And it came to pass after they had took them, they caused them to enter into a covenant that they would no more take up their weapons of war against the Nephites. ¹⁷And when they had entered into this covenant, they sent them to dwell with the people of Ammon. And they were in number about four thousand which had not been slain.

¹⁸And it came to pass that when they had sent them away, they pursued their march towards the land of Nephihah.

And it came to pass that when they had come to the city Nephihah, they did pitch their tents in the plains of Nephihah, which is near the city Nephihah. ¹⁹Now, Moroni was desirous that the Lamanites should come out to battle against them upon the plains. But the Lamanites, knowing of their exceeding great courage, and beholding the greatness of their numbers—therefore, they durst not come out against them. Therefore, they did not come to battle in that day. ²⁰And when the night came, Moroni went forth in the darkness of the night and came upon the top of the wall, to spy out in what part of the city the Lamanites did camp with their army.

²¹And it came to pass that they were on the east, by the entrance. And they were all asleep. And now, Moroni returned to his army, and caused that they should prepare, in haste, strong cords and ladders to be let down from the top of the wall into the inner part of the wall.

²²And it came to pass that Moroni caused that his men should march forth and come up upon the top of the wall and let themselves down into that part of the city, yea, even on the west, where the Lamanites did not camp with their armies.

²³And it came to pass that they were all let down into the city by night, by the means of their strong cords and their ladders. Thus, when the morning came, they were all within the walls of the city. ²⁴And now, when the Lamanites awoke and saw that the armies of Moroni were within the walls—they were a-frightened exceedingly, insomuch that they did flee out by the pass. ²⁵And now, when Moroni saw that they were fleeing before him, he did cause that his men should march forth against them—and slew many, and surrounded many others and took them prisoners. And the remainder of them fled into the land of Moroni, which was in the borders by the seashore. ²⁶Thus had Moroni and Pahoran obtained the possession of the city of Nephihah without the loss of one soul. And there were many of the Lamanites which were slain.

²⁷Now it came to pass that, as many of the Lamanites (that were prisoners) were desirous to join the people of Ammon and become a free people—.[a] ²⁸And it came to pass that as many as were desirous, unto them it was granted according to their desires.

---

a. As it appears on the Printer's Manuscript, this is an incomplete sentence. The problem is "that as many as were desirous." The 1830 compositor solved the sentence by remove the "as," which solution continues. Skousen, *Analysis of the Textual Variants*, 5:2851. The next sentence uses repetitive resumption to restart the idea. Although this edition typically uses "and it came to pass" to begin a new paragraph, this case is seen as starting over and therefore part of the concept that was begun in the first incomplete sentence.

²⁹Therefore, all the prisoners of the Lamanites did join the people of Ammon and did begin to labor exceedingly—tilling the ground, raising all manner of grain, and flocks, and herds of every kind. And thus were the Nephites relieved from a great burden, yea, insomuch that they were thus relieved from all the prisoners of the Lamanites.

³⁰Now it came to pass that Moroni, after he had obtained possession of the city of Nephihah—

> (having taken many prisoners,
> > which did reduce the armies of the Lamanites exceedingly—
> and having retained many of the Nephites which had been taken prisoners,
> > which did strengthen the army of Moroni exceedingly)—ᵃ

therefore, Moroni went forth from the land of Nephihah to the land of Lehi.

³¹And it came to pass that when the Lamanites saw that Moroni was a-coming against them, they were again frightened and fled before the army of Moroni.

³²And it came to pass that Moroni and his army did pursue them from city to city until they were met by Lehi and Teancum. And the Lamanites fled from Lehi and Teancum, even down upon the borders by the seashore, until they came to the land of Moroni. ³³And the armies of the Lamanites were all gathered together, insomuch that they were all in one body in the land of Moroni. Now, Ammoron, the king of the Lamanites, was also with them.

³⁴And it came to pass that Moroni, and Lehi, and Teancum, did encamp with their armies round about in the borders of the land of Moroni, insomuch that the Lamanites were encircled about in the borders, by the wilderness on the south, and in the borders by the wilderness on the east. ³⁵And thus, they did encamp for the night. For behold, the Nephites (and the Lamanites also) were weary—because of the greatness of the march. Therefore, they did not resolve upon any stratagem in the nighttime, save it were Teancum. For he was exceeding angry with Ammoron, insomuch that he considered that Ammoron and Amalickiah (his brother) had been the cause of this great and lasting war between them and the Lamanites, which had been the cause of so much war and bloodshed, yea, and so much famine.

³⁶And it came to pass that Teancum, in his anger, did go forth into the camp of the Lamanites and did let himself down over the wills of the city. And he went forth, with a cord, from place to place, insomuch that he did find the king. And he did cast a javelin at him, which did pierce him near the heart. But behold, the king did awake his servant before he died, insomuch that they did pursue Teancum, and slew him.

³⁷Now it came to pass that when Lehi, and Moroni, knew that Teancum was dead—they were exceeding sorrowful. For behold, he had been a man which had fought valiantly for his country, yea, a true friend to liberty. And he had suffered very many exceeding sore afflictions. But behold, he was dead, and had gone the way of all the earth.ᵇ

³⁸Now it came to pass that Moroni marched forth on the morrow and came upon the Lamanites, insomuch that they did slay them with a great slaughter. And they did drive them out of the land. And they did flee, even that they did not return at that time against the Nephites. ³⁹And thus ended the thirty and first year of the reign of the judges

---

a. These two lines form a nice reversed parallel. They appear to have been spontaneous rather than a planned text. Nevertheless, they are set apart here to highlight the reversed parallel.

b. See 1 Kings 2:2: "I go the way of all the earth."

Chapter XXIX [Alma 62]

over the people of Nephi. And thus, they had had wars, and bloodsheds, and famine, and affliction, for the space of many years. ⁴⁰And there had been murders, and contentions, and dissensions, and all manner of iniquity among the people of Nephites. Nevertheless, for the righteous' sake, yea, because of the prayers of the righteous—they were spared.

⁴¹But behold, because of the exceeding great length of the war between the Nephites and the Lamanites, many had become hardened because of the exceeding great length of the war. And many were softened because of their afflictions, insomuch that they did humble themselves before God, even in the depth of humility.

⁴²And it came to pass that after Moroni had fortified those parts of the land which were most exposed to the Lamanites, until they were sufficiently strong—he returned to the city of Zarahemla. And also Helaman returned to the place of his inheritance. And there was once more peace established among the people of Nephi. ⁴³And Moroni yielded up the command of his armies into the hands of his son, whose name was Moronihah. And he retired to his own house that he might spend the remainder of his days in peace.

⁴⁴And Pahoran did return to his Judgment Seat. And Helaman did take upon him again to preach unto the people the word of God. For because of so many wars, and contentions, it had become expedient that a regulation should again be made again in the church. ⁴⁵Therefore, Helaman, and his brethren, went forth and did declare the word of God with much power—unto the convincing many of the people of their wickedness, which did cause them to repent of their sins and be baptized unto the Lord, their God.

⁴⁶And it came to pass that they did establish again the church of God throughout all the land. ⁴⁷Yea, and regulations were made concerning the law and their judges. And their Chief Judges were chosen. ⁴⁸And the people of Nephi began to prosper again in the land, and began to multiply, and to wax exceeding strong again in the land. And they began to grow exceeding rich. ⁴⁹But notwithstanding their riches, or their strength, or their prosperity—they were not lifted up in the pride of their eyes—neither were they slow to remember the Lord, their God. But, they did humble themselves exceedingly before him—⁵⁰yea, they did remember how great things he, the Lord, had done for them, that he had delivered them from death, and from bonds, and from prisons, and from all manner of afflictions. And he had delivered them out of the hands of their enemies. ⁵¹And they did pray unto the Lord, their God, continually, insomuch that the Lord did bless them according to his word, so that they did wax strong and prosper in the land.

⁵²And it came to pass that all these things were done. And Helaman died in the thirty and fifth year of the reign of the judges over the people of Nephi.

Chapter XXX [Alma 63]

[63] ¹And it came to pass in the commencement of the thirty and sixth year of the reign of the judges over the people of Nephi, that Shiblon took possession of those sacred things which had been delivered unto Helaman by Alma. ²And he was a just man. And he did walk uprightly before God. And he did observe to do good continually, to keep the commandments of the Lord, his God (and also did his brother).

³And it came to pass that Moroni died also. And thus ended the thirty and sixth year of the reign of the judges.

⁴And it came to pass that in the thirty and seventh year of the reign of the judges there was a large company of men, even to the amount of five thousand and four hundred men, with their wives, and their children, departed out of the land of Zarahemla into the land which was northward.

⁵And it came to pass that Hagoth, he being an exceeding curious[a] man—therefore, he went forth and built him an exceeding large ship on the borders of the land Bountiful, by the land Desolation—and launched it forth into the west sea, by the narrow neck which led into the land northward. ⁶And behold, there were many of the Nephites which did enter therein, and did sail forth with much provisions—and also many women, and children. And they took their course northward. And thus ended the thirty and seventh year. ⁷And in the thirty and eighth year, this man built other ships. And the first ship did also return. And many more people did enter into it. And they also took much provisions, and set out again to the land northward.

⁸And it came to pass that they were never heard of more. And we suppose that they [are[b]] drowned up in the depths of the sea.

And it came to pass that one other ship also did sail forth. And whither she did go, we know not.

⁹And it came to pass that in this year, there were many people which went forth into the land northward. And thus ended the thirty and eighth year.

¹⁰And it came to pass in the thirty and ninth year of the reign of the judges, Shiblon died also. And Corianton had gone forth to the land northward in a ship, to carry forth provisions unto those people which had gone forth into that land. ¹¹Therefore, it became expedient for Shiblon to confer those sacred things, before his death, upon the son of Helaman, [who was[c]] called Helaman—being called after the name of his father.

¹²Now behold, all those engravings which were in the possession of Helaman, were written, and sent forth among the children of men—throughout all the land, save it were those parts which had been commanded by Alma should not go forth. ¹³Nevertheless, these things were to be kept sacred, and handed down from one generation to another. Therefore, in this year, they had been conferred upon Helaman (before the death of Shiblon).

¹⁴And it came to pass also in this year that there were some dissenters which had gone forth unto the Lamanites. And they were stirred up again to anger against the

---

a. The more archaic meaning here would be skilled.

b. Restored per the Original Manuscript. The Printer's Manuscript has "were." Skousen, *Analysis of the Textual Variants*, 5:2866.

c. Restored per the Original Manuscript. The Printer's Manuscript has "whose name." Skousen, *Analysis of the Textual Variants*, 5:2869.

Nephites. ¹⁵And also in this same year they came down with a numerous army, to war against the people of Moronihah (or against the army of Moronihah)—in the which they were beaten and driven back again to their own lands—suffering great loss. ¹⁶And thus ended the thirty and ninth year of the reign of the judges over the people of Nephi. ¹⁷And thus ended the account of Alma, and Helaman, his son—and also Shiblon, which was his son.

The Book of Helaman

An account of the Nephites. Their wars, and contentions, and their dissentions. And also, the prophecies of many holy prophets before the coming of Christ, according to the record of Helaman (which was the son of Helaman)—and also according to the records of his sons, even down to the coming of Christ. And also, many of the Lamanites are converted. An account of their conversion. An account of the righteousness of the Lamanites and the wickedness and abominations of the Nephites, according to the record of Helaman and his sons, even down to the coming of Christ. Which is called the book of Helaman, etcetera.

Chapter I [Helaman 1–2]

[1] ¹And now behold, it came to pass in the commencement of the fortieth year of the reign of the judges over the people of Nephi, there began to be a serious difficulty among the people of the Nephites. ²For behold, Pahoran had died and gone the way of all the earth.[a] Therefore, there began to be a serious contention concerning who should have the Judgment Seat among the brethren which were the sons of Pahoran. ³Now, these are their names which did contend for the Judgment Seat, which did also cause the people to contend—Pahoran, Paanchi, and Pacumeni. ⁴Now, these are not all the sons of Pahoran, for he had many. But these are they which did contend for the Judgment Seat. Therefore, they did cause three divisions among the people. ⁵Nevertheless, it came to pass that Pahoran was appointed by the voice of the people to be a Chief Judge and a Governor over the people of Nephi.

⁶And it came to pass that Pacumeni, when he saw that he could not obtain the Judgment Seat, he did unite with the voice of the people. ⁷But behold, Paanchi (and that part of the people that were desirous that he should be their Governor) was exceeding wroth. Therefore, he was about to flatter away those people to rise up in rebellion against their brethren.

⁸And it came to pass as he was about to do this, behold, he was taken and was tried (according to the voice of the people) and condemned unto death. For he had raised up in rebellion and sought to destroy the liberty of the people.

⁹Now, when those people which were desirous that he should be their Governor saw that he was condemned unto death—therefore, they were angry. And behold, they sent forth one Kishcumen, even to the Judgment Seat of Pahoran—and murdered Pahoran as he sat upon the Judgment Seat. ¹⁰And he was pursued by the servants of Pahoran. But behold, so speedy was the flight of Kishcumen that no man could overtake him. ¹¹And he went unto those that sent him. And they all entered into a covenant, yea, swearing by their everlasting Maker, that they would tell no man that Kishcumen had murdered Pahoran. ¹²Therefore, Kishcumen was not known among the people of Nephi. For he was in disguise at the time that he murdered Pahoran. And Kishcumen and his band, which had covenanted with him, did mingle themselves among the people in a manner that they all could not be found. But, as many as were found were condemned unto death.

---

a. See 1 Kings 2:2: "I go the way of all the earth."

¹³And now behold, Pacumeni was appointed, according to the voice of the people, to be a Chief Judge and a Governor over the people, to reign in the stead of his brother Pahoran. And it was according to his right. And all this was done in the fortieth year of the reign of the judges. And it had an end.

¹⁴And it came to pass in the forty and first year of the reign of the judges that the Lamanites had gathered together an innumerable army of men, and armed them with swords, and with scimitars, and with bows, and with arrows, and with headplates, and with breastplates, and with all manner of shields of every kind. ¹⁵And they came down again, that they might pitch battle against the Nephites. And they were led by a man whose name was Coriantumr. And he was a descendant of Zarahemla. And he was a dissenter from among the Nephites. And he was a large and a mighty man. ¹⁶Therefore, the king of the Lamanites (whose name was Tubaloth, who was the son of Ammoron)—now Tubaloth, supposing that Coriantumr (he being a mighty man) could stand against the Nephites, insomuch with his strength and also with his great wisdom, that by sending him forth he should gain power over the Nephites. ¹⁷Therefore, he did stir them up to anger. And he did gather together his armies, and he did appoint Coriantumr to be their leader, and did cause that they should march down into the land of Zarahemla to battle against the Nephites.

¹⁸And it came to pass that because of so much contention and so much difficulty in the government, that they had not kept sufficient guards in the land of Zarahemla. For they had supposed that the Lamanites durst not come into the heart of their lands and attack that great city Zarahemla. ¹⁹But it came to pass that Coriantumr did march forth at the head of his numerous host and came upon the inhabitants of the city. And their march was with such exceeding great speed that there was no time for the Nephites to gather together their armies. ²⁰Therefore, Coriantumr did cut down the watch by the entrance of the city and did march forth with his whole army into the city. And they did slay everyone who did oppose them, insomuch that they did take possession of the whole city.

²¹And it came to pass that Pacumeni (which was the Chief Judge) did flee before Coriantumr, even to the walls of the city.

And it came to pass that Coriantumr did smite him against the wall, insomuch that he died. And thus ended the days of Pacumeni.

²²And now, when Coriantumr saw that he was in possession of the city of Zarahemla, and saw that the Nephites had fled before them, and were slain, and were taken, and were cast into prison, and that he had obtained the possession of the strongest hold in all the land—his heart took courage, insomuch that he was about to go forth against all the land.

²³And now, he did not tarry in the land of Zarahemla, but he did march forth with a large army, even towards the city of Bountiful. For it was his determination to go forth and cut his way through with the sword, that he might obtain the north parts of the land. ²⁴And, supposing that their greatest strength was in the center of the land, therefore he did march forth, giving them no time to assemble themselves together, save it were in small bodies. And in this manner they did fall upon them and cut them down to the earth.

²⁵But behold, this march of Coriantumr through the center of the land gave Moronihah great advantage over them—notwithstanding the greatness of the number

of the Nephites which were slain. ²⁶For behold, Moronihah had supposed that the Lamanites durst not come into the center of the land, but that they would attack the cities round about in the borders as they had hitherto done. Therefore, Moronihah had caused that their strong armies should maintain those parts round about by the borders.

²⁷But behold, the Lamanites were not frightened (according to his desire). But they had come into the center of the land and had taken the capital city, which was the city of Zarahemla, and were marching through the most capital parts of the land—slaying the people with a great slaughter—both men, women, and children—taking possession of many cities and of many strongholds. ²⁸But when Moronihah had discovered this, he immediately sent forth Lehi (with an army) round about to head them, before they should come to the land Bountiful. ²⁹And thus he did. And he did head them before they came to the land Bountiful. And gave unto them battle, insomuch that they began to retreat back towards the land of Zarahemla.

³⁰And it came to pass that Moronihah did head them in their retreat and did give unto them battle, insomuch that it became an exceeding bloody battle, yea, many were slain. And among the number which were slain, Coriantumr was also found.

³¹And now behold, the Lamanites could not retreat neither way—neither on the north, nor on the south, nor on the east, nor on the west. For they were surrounded on every hand by the Nephites. ³²And thus had Coriantumr plunged the Lamanites into the midst of the Nephites insomuch that they were in the power of the Nephites. And he himself was slain. And the Lamanites did yield themselves [up^a] into the hands of the Nephites.

³³And it came to pass that Moronihah took possession of the city of Zarahemla again and caused that the Lamanites which had been taken prisoners should depart out of the land in peace. ³⁴And thus ended the forty and first year of the reign of the judges.

[2] ¹And it came to pass in the forty and second year of the reign of the judges, after Moronihah had established again the peace between the Nephites and the Lamanites—behold, there was no one to fill the Judgment Seat. Therefore, there began to be a contention again among the people, concerning who should fill the Judgment Seat.

²And it came to pass that Helaman, which was the son of Helaman, was appointed to fill the Judgment Seat by the voice of the people. ³But behold, Kishcumen (who had murdered Pahoran) did lay wait to destroy Helaman also. And he was upheld by his band, which had entered into a covenant that no one should know his wickedness. ⁴For there was one Gaddianton[b], who was exceeding expert in many words, and also in his craft to carry on the secret work of murder and of robbery. Therefore, he became the leader of the band of Kishcumen. ⁵Therefore, he did flatter them, and also Kishcumen, that if they would place him in the Judgment Seat, he would grant unto those which belonged to his band that they should be placed in power and authority among the people. Therefore, Kishcumen sought to destroy Helaman.

⁶And it came to pass as he went forth towards the Judgment Seat to destroy Helaman, behold, one of the servants of Helaman (having been out by night and having obtained through disguise a knowledge of those plans which had been laid by this band to destroy

---

a. Restored per the Original Manuscript. Skousen, *Analysis of the Textual Variants*, 5:2892.

b. Spelling as in the Original Manuscript. Skousen notes that the Original Manuscript is consistent in spelling it with doubled "d." Skousen, *Analysis of the Textual Variants*, 5:2894–96.

Helaman)ᵃ—⁷and it came to pass that he met Kishcumen, and he gave unto him a sign. Therefore, Kishcumen made known unto him the object of his desire—desiring that he would conduct him to the Judgment Seat, that he might murder Helaman.

⁸And it came to pass that when the servant of Helaman had known all the heart of Kishcumen, and how that it was his object to murder, and also that it was the object of all those which belonged to his band to murder, and to rob, and to gain power (and this was their secret plan, and their combination)—the servant of Helaman saith unto Kishcumen: "Let us go forth unto the Judgment Seat."

⁹Now, this did please Kishcumen exceedingly, for he did suppose that he should accomplish his design. But behold, the servant of Helaman (as they were going forth unto the Judgment Seat) did stab Kishcumen, even to the heart, that he fell dead without a groan. And he ran and told Helaman all the things which he had seen, and heard, and done.

¹⁰And it came to pass that Helaman did send forth to take this band of robbers, and secret murderers, that they might be executed according to the law. ¹¹But behold, when Gaddianton had found that Kishcumen did not return, he feared lest that he should be destroyed. Therefore, he caused that his band should follow him. And they took their flight out of the land by a secret way, into the wilderness. And thus, when Helaman sent forth to take them, they could nowhere be found.

>¹²And more of this Gaddianton shall be spoken hereafter. And thus ended the forty and second year of the reign of the judges over the people of Nephi.

¹³And behold, in the end of this book ye shall see that this Gaddianton did prove the overthrow, yea, almost the entire destruction—of the people of Nephi.

¹⁴Behold, I do not mean the end of the book of Helaman, but I mean the end of the book of Nephi, from which I have taken all the account which I have written.ᵇ<

---

a. An example of repetitive resumption in a sentence. This sentence had such a long inserted phrase that it started over, repeating "and it came to pass."

b. Mormon steps away from narration to indicate that this is an important incident that will be discussed later. He also lets his readers know why it is important: "in the end of this book ye shall see that this Gaddianton did prove the overthrow—yea, almost the entire destruction—of the people of Nephi." It is Mormon's thesis that the demise of the Nephites can be laid at the feet of Gaddiantons.

Chapter II [Helaman 3–6]

[3] ¹And now it came to pass in the forty and third year of the reign of the judges, there was no contention among the people of Nephi, save it were a little pride which was in the church, which did cause some little dissensions among the people, which affairs were settled in the ending of the forty and third year. ²And there was no contention among the people in the forty and fourth year, neither was there much contention in the forty and fifth year.

³And it came to pass in the forty and sixth, yea, there were much contentions and many dissensions, in the which there were an exceeding great many which departed out of the land of Zarahemla, and went forth unto the land northward to inherit the land.

>⁴And they did travel to an exceeding great distance, insomuch that they came to large bodies of water, and many rivers—⁵yea, and even they did spread forth into all parts of the land—[in^a] whatsoever parts it had not been rendered desolate and without timber—because of the many inhabitants which had before inherited the land.

>⁶And now, no part of the land was desolate, save it were for timber, etcetera. But because of the greatness of the destruction of the people which had before inhabited the land, it was called desolate. ⁷And, there being but little timber upon the face of the land, nevertheless, the people which went forth became exceeding expert in the working of cement. Therefore, they did build houses of cement, in the which they did dwell.

⁸And it came to pass that they did multiply, and spread, and did go forth from the land southward to the land northward and did spread, insomuch that they began to cover the face of the whole earth, from the sea south to the sea north, from the sea west to the sea east. ⁹And the people which were in the land northward did dwell in tents, and in houses of cement. And they did suffer whatsoever tree should spring up upon the face of the land, that it should grow up, that in time they might have timber to build their houses, yea, their cities, and their temples, and their synagogues, and their sanctuaries, and all manner of their buildings.

¹⁰And it came to pass, as timber was exceeding scarce in the land northward, they did send forth much by the way of shipping. ¹¹And thus, they did enable the people in the land northward, that they might build many cities, both of wood and of cement.

¹²And it came to pass that there were many of the people of Ammon (which were Lamanites by birth) did also go forth into this land.

¹³And now, there are many records kept of the proceedings of this people (by many of this people) which are particular, and very large, concerning them. ¹⁴But behold, a hundreth part of the proceedings of this people, yea, the account of the Lamanites, and of the Nephites—and their wars, and contentions, and dissensions, and their preaching, and their prophecies, and their shipping, and their building of ships, and their building of temples, and of synagogues, and their sanctuaries, and their righteousness, and their wickedness, and their murders, and their robbings,

---

a. Restored per the Original Manuscript. The Printer's Manuscript has "into." *Printer's Manuscript of the Book of Mormon*, 3:149.

and their plunderings—and all manner of abominations and whoredoms—cannot be contained in this work. ¹⁵But behold, there are many books and many records of every kind. And they have been kept, chiefly by the Nephites. ¹⁶And they have been handed down from one generation to another by the Nephites, even until they have fallen into transgression, and have been murdered, plundered, and hunted, and driven forth, and slain, and scattered upon the face of the earth, and mixed with the Lamanites, until they are no more called the Nephites—becoming wicked, and wild, and ferocious, yea, even becoming Lamanites.ᵃ<

¹⁷And now, I return again to mine account. Therefore, what I have spoken had passed after there had been great contentions, and disturbances, and wars, and dissensions, among the people of Nephi. ¹⁸The forty and sixth year of the reign of the judges ended.

¹⁹And it came to pass that there was still great contentions in the land, yea, even in the forty and seventh year, and also in the forty and eighth year. ²⁰Nevertheless, Helaman did fill the Judgment Seat with justice and equity. Yea, he did observe to keep the statutes and the judgments and the commandments of God. And he did do that which was right in the sight of God continually. And he did walk after the ways of his father,ᵇ insomuch that he did prosper in the land.

²¹And it came to pass that he had two sons. He gave unto the eldest the name of Nephi, and unto the youngest, the name of Lehi. And they began to grow up unto the Lord.

²²And it came to pass that the wars and contentions began to cease in a small degree among the people of the Nephites in the latter end of the forty and eighth year of the reign of the judges over the people of Nephi.

²³And it came to pass in the forty and ninth year of the reign of the judges there was continual peace established in the land—all save it were the secret combinations which Gaddianton the robber had established in the more settled parts of the land—which at that time were not known unto those which were at the head of government. Therefore, they were not destroyed out of the land.

²⁴And it came to pass that in this same year, there was exceeding great prosperity in the church, insomuch that there were thousands who did join themselves unto the church and were baptized unto repentance. ²⁵And so great was the prosperity of the church, and so many the blessings which were poured out upon the people, that even the high priests and the teachers were themselves astonished beyond measure.

²⁶And it came to pass that the work of the Lord did prosper, unto the baptizing and the uniting unto the church of God many souls, yea, even tens of thousands.

>²⁷Thus, we may see that the Lord is merciful unto all who will, in the sincerity of their hearts, call upon his holy name. ²⁸Yea, thus we see that the gate of heavenᶜ is open unto all, even to those who will believe on the name of Jesus Christ, which is

---

a. Mormon gets sidetracked from his purpose by the mention of those who have gone north and spends time describing the people of the north. One of the reasons for this insertion is that Mormon will associate the Gaddiantons with the lands northward and therefore needed to show that Nephites (which might include the Gaddiantons) had gone north. The specific descriptions fit the specific people that Mormon would associate with the Gaddiantons. Verse 17 verifies that this was an aside.

b. The language of doing right continually and walking in the ways of his father echoes language found in 1 Kings 22:43 and 2 Chronicles 20:32.

c. The phrase "gate of heaven" is found in Genesis 28:17.

Chapter II [Helaman 3–6]

the Son of God. ²⁹Yea, we see that whosoever will^a lay hold upon the word of God, which is quick and powerful, which shall divide asunder all the cunning, and the snares, and the wiles, of the devil^b—and lead the man of Christ in a [straight]^c and narrow course across that everlasting gulf of misery (which is prepared to engulf the wicked) ³⁰and land their souls, yea, their immortal souls—at the right hand of God in the kingdom of heaven, to sit down with Abraham, and Isaac, and with Jacob,^d and with all our holy fathers, to go no more out.^e<

³¹And in this year, there were continual rejoicings in the land of Zarahemla, and in all the regions round about, even in all the land which was possessed by the Nephites.

³²And it came to pass that there was peace and exceeding great joy in the remainder of the forty and ninth year. Yea, and also there was continual peace and great joy in the fiftieth year of the reign of the judges. ³³And in the fifty and first year of the reign of the judges there was peace also, save it were the pride which began to enter into the church—(>not into the church of God, but into the hearts of the people who professed to belong to the church of God^f<). ³⁴And they were lifted up in pride, even to the persecution of many of their brethren.

>Now, this was a great evil, which did cause the more humble part of the people to suffer great persecutions, and to wade through much affliction. ³⁵Nevertheless, they did fast and pray oft, and did wax stronger and stronger in their humility, and firmer and firmer in the faith of Christ—unto the filling their souls with joy, and consolation, yea, even to the purifying and the sanctification of their hearts, which sanctification cometh because of their yielding their hearts unto God.^g<

³⁶And it came to pass that the fifty and second year ended in peace also, save it were the exceeding great pride which had got into the hearts of the people. >And it was because of their exceeding great riches, and their prosperity in the land. And it did grow upon them from day to day.^h<

---

a. This is a run-on sentence. In the 1920 edition, the editors made this read "whosoever may, will." That resolves the sentence. Skousen, *Analysis of the Textual Variants*, 5: 2924.

b. Uses language from Hebrews 4:12: "For the word of God is quick, and powerful, and sharper than any twoedged sword, piercing even to the dividing asunder of soul and spirit."

c. The Printer's Manuscript has "strait." Oliver Cowdery did not distinguish between spellings for the two homophones. This edition elects to treat it as a spelling error for straight, based on what would otherwise be an unnecessary duplication of meaning with the following "narrow." The problem with the phrase "strait and narrow" is that it condenses Matthew 7:14, which says that "strait is the gate, and narrow is the way." Because strait and narrow modify two different things, there is a parallelism of emphasis. By eliminating the objects, "strait and narrow" echoes the language but muddies the meaning.

d. Compare Matthew 8:11: "Many shall come from the east and west, and shall sit down with Abraham, and Isaac, and Jacob, in the kingdom of heaven."

e. Mormon steps back from narrating to tell his readers the lesson they should learn from the history he has just recounted.

f. Mormon makes a clarifying insertion to highlight that the problem was the people and not the church itself.

g. Mormon uses the concept of being lifted up in pride (and at times, the wearing of costly apparel) to signify times when the Nephites moved away from their core religion. The aside gives Mormon's opinion of the problem of pride. It is Mormon's lesson from the plates and certainly not a reference to any text on the source plates.

h. Mormon inserts his opinion. This information would not have been on his source plates.

³⁷And it came to pass in the fifty and third year of the reign of the judges, Helaman died. And his eldest son, Nephi, began to reign in his stead.

And it came to pass that he did fill the Judgment Seat with justice and equity. Yea, he did keep the commandments of God, and did walk in the ways of his father.

[4] ¹And it came to pass in the fifty and fourth year, there were many dissensions in the church. And there was also a contention among the people, insomuch that there was much bloodshed. ²And the rebellious part were slain and driven out of the land. And they did go unto the king of the Lamanites.

³And it came to pass that they did endeavor to stir up the Lamanites to war against the Nephites. But behold, the Lamanites were exceeding afraid, insomuch that they would not hearken to the words of those dissenters. ⁴But, it came to pass in the fifty and sixth year of the reign of the judges, there were dissenters which went up from the Nephites unto the Lamanites. And they succeeded (with those others) in stirring them up to anger against the Nephites. And they were, all that year, preparing for war.

⁵And in the fifty and seventh year, they did come down against the Nephites to battle. And they did commence the work of death, yea, insomuch that in the fifty and eighth year of the reign of the judges, they succeeded in obtaining possession of the land of Zarahemla, yea, and also all the lands even unto the land which was near the land Bountiful. ⁶And the Nephites, and the armies of Moronihah, were driven even into the land of Bountiful. ⁷And there they did fortify against the Lamanites (>from the west sea even unto the east—it being a day's journey for a Nephites on the line which they had fortifiedᵃ<), and stationed their armies to defend their north country. ⁸And thus, those dissenters of the Nephites, with the help of a numerous army of the Lamanites, had obtained all the possession of the Nephites which was in the land southward. And all this was done in the fifty and eight, and ninth years of the reign of the judges.

⁹And it came to pass in the sixtieth year of the reign of the judges, Moronihah did succeed (with his armies) in obtaining many parts of the land, yea, they retained many cities which had fallen into the hands of the Lamanites.

¹⁰And it came to pass in the sixty and first year of the reign of the judges they succeeded in retaining even the half of all their possessions.

> ¹¹Now, this great loss of the Nephites, and the great slaughter which was among them, would not have happened—had it not been for their wickedness and their abomination, which was among them. Yea, and it was among those also which professed to belong to the church of God. ¹²And it was because of the pride of their hearts—because of their exceeding riches. Yea, it was because of their oppression to the poor—withholding their food from the hungry, withholding their clothing from the naked—and smiting their humble brethren upon the cheeks—making a mock of that which was sacred—denying the spirit of prophecy, and of revelation—murdering, plundering, lying, stealing, committing adultery, raising up in great contentions, and [dissentingᵇ] away into the land of Nephi among the Lamanites. ¹³And because of this, their great wickedness and their boastings in their own strength—they were left in their own strength. Therefore, they did not

---

a. Mormon inserts geographic information that would not have been stated in that way in his source.
b. Restored per the Original Manuscript. Printed editions have "deserted." Skousen, *Analysis of the Textual Variants*, 5:2932.

Chapter II [Helaman 3–6]

prosper, but were afflicted, and smitten, and driven before the Lamanites until they had lost possession of almost all their lands.[a]<

[14]But behold, Moronihah did preach many things unto the people because of their iniquity—and also Nephi, and Lehi (which were the sons of Helaman) did preach many things unto the people, yea, and did prophesy many things unto them concerning their iniquities, and what should come unto them if they did not repent of their sins.

[15]And it came to pass that they did repent. And inasmuch as they did repent, they did begin to prosper. [16]For when Moronihah saw that they did repent, he did venture to lead them forth from place to place, and from city to city, even until they had retained the one half of their property, and the one half of all their lands. [17]And thus ended the sixty and first year of the reign of the judges.

[18]And it came to pass in the sixty and second year of the reign of the judges, that Moronihah could obtain no more possessions over the Lamanites. [19]Therefore, they did abandon their design to obtain the remainder of their lands—for, so numerous was the Lamanites that it became impossible for the Nephites to obtain more power over them. Therefore, Moronihah did employ all his armies in maintaining those parts which he had taken.

[20]And it came to pass because of the greatness of the number of the Lamanites, the Nephites were in great fear lest they should be overpowered, and slain—trodden down and slain, and destroyed. [21]Yea, they began to remember the prophecies of Alma, and also the words of Mosiah. And they saw that they had been a stiffnecked people, and that they had set at naught the commandments of God, [22]and that that they had altered (and trampled under their feet) the laws of Mosiah (or that which the Lord commanded him to give unto the people)—and thus seeing that their laws had become corrupt[ed[b]], and that they had become a wicked people, insomuch that they were wicked, even [like[c]] unto the Lamanites. [23]And because of their iniquity, the church had began to dwindle. And they began to disbelieve in the spirit of prophecy, and in the spirit of revelation. And the judgments of God did stare them in the face. [24]And they saw they had become weak like unto their brethren the Lamanites, and that the spirit of the Lord did no more preserve them—yea, it had withdrawn from them because the spirit of the Lord doth not dwell in unholy temples.[d] [25]Therefore, the Lord did cease to preserve them by his miraculous and matchless power. For they had fallen into a state of unbelief, and awful wickedness.

And they saw that the Lamanites were more exceeding numerous than they, and except they should cleave unto the Lord, their God, they must unavoidably perish. [26]For behold, they saw that the strength of the Lamanites was as great as their strength, even man for man. And thus had they fallen into this great transgression. Yea, thus had they become weak (because of their transgression) in the space of not many years.

[5] [1]And it came to pass that in this same year, behold, Nephi delivered up the Judgment Seat to a man whose name was Cezoram—[2]for as their laws and their governments were established by the voice of the people, and they which chose evil were more

---

a. Mormom highlights the lesson he wants his readers to understand about the section he just narrated.
b. Added by Hyrum Smith, probably during proofreading.
c. Added by Hyrum Smith, probably during proofreading.
d. Amulek provides a quotation in Alma 34:36, but it is not present outside of the Book of Mormon. The mention of temples suggests that this reference was on the brass plates.

numerous than they which chose good—therefore, they were ripening for destruction. For the laws had become corrupted. ³Yea, and this was not all. They were a stiffnecked people, insomuch that they could not be governed by the law, nor justice, save it were to their destruction.

⁴And it came to pass that Nephi had become weary because of their iniquity. And he yielded up the Judgment Seat and took it upon him to preach the word of God all the remainder of his days—and his brother Lehi also, all the remainder of his days. ⁵For they remembered the words which their father Helaman spake unto them. And these are the words which he spake:

⁶Behold, my sons. I desire that ye should remember to keep the commandments of God. And I would that ye should declare unto the people these words.

Behold, I have given unto you the names of our first parents, which came out of the land of Jerusalem. And this I have done that when you remember your names, that ye may remember them. And, when ye remember them, ye may remember their works. And, when ye remember their works, ye may know how that it is said, and also written, that they were good. ⁷Therefore, my sons, I would that ye should do that which is good, that it may be said of you, and also written (even as it has been said and written of them).

⁸And now, my sons, behold—I have somewhat more to desire of you, which desire is that ye may not do these things that ye may boast, but that ye may do these things to lay up for yourselves a treasure in heaven,[a] yea, which is eternal, and which fadeth not away, yea, that ye may have that precious gift of eternal life, which we have reason to suppose hath been given to our fathers.

⁹O remember! Remember, my sons, the words which King Benjamin spake unto his people. Yea, remember that there is no other way, nor means, whereby man can be saved—only through the atoning blood of Jesus Christ, which shall come. Yea, remember that he cometh to redeem the world.

¹⁰And remember also the words which Amulek spake unto Zeezrom in the city of Ammonihah. For he said unto him that the Lord surely should come to redeem his people, but that he should not come to redeem them in their sins, but to redeem them from their sins. ¹¹And he hath power given unto him, from the Father, to redeem them from their sins because of repentance. Therefore, he hath sent his angels to declare the tidings of the conditions of repentance, which bringeth unto the power of the Redeemer unto the salvation of their souls.

¹²And now, my sons, remember! Remember that it is upon the rock of our Redeemer (which is Christ, the Son of God) that ye must build your foundation, that when the devil shall send forth his mighty winds, yea, his shafts in the whirlwind, yea, when all his hail, and his mighty storm shall beat upon you—it shall have no power over you to drag you down to the gulf of misery and endless wo—because of the rock upon which ye are built, which is a sure foundation—a foundation whereon, if men built, they cannot fall.

¹³And it came to pass that these were the words which Helaman taught to his sons. Yea, he did teach them many things which are not written, and also many things

---

a. See Matthew 6:20: "But lay up for yourselves treasures in heaven, where neither moth nor rust doth corrupt, and where thieves do not break through nor steal."

which are written. ¹⁴And they did remember his words. And therefore, they went forth (keeping the commandments of God) to teach the word of God among all the people of Nephi—beginning at the city Bountiful. ¹⁵And from thence, forth to the city of Gid. And from the city of Gid, to the city Mulek. ¹⁶And even from one city to another, until they had gone forth among all the people of Nephi which were in the land southward. And from thence into the land of Zarahemla, among the Lamanites.

¹⁷And it came to pass that they did preach with great power, insomuch that they did confound many of those dissenters which had gone over from the Nephites, insomuch that they came forth and did confess their sin0, and were baptized unto repentance, and immediately returned to the Nephites to endeavor to repair unto them the wrongs which they had done.

¹⁸And it came to pass that Nephi and Lehi did preach unto the Lamanites with such great power and authority, for they had power and authority given unto them that they might speak, and they also had what they should speak given unto them.[a]

¹⁹Therefore, they did speak (unto the great astonishment of the Lamanites) to the convincing them, insomuch that there were eight thousand of the Lamanites which were in the land of Zarahemla and round about baptized unto repentance, and were convinced of the wickedness of the traditions of their fathers.

²⁰And it came to pass that Nephi and Lehi did proceed to go from thence—to go to the land of Nephi.

²¹And it came to pass that they were taken by an army of the Lamanites and cast into prison, yea, even in that same prison in which Ammon and his brethren were cast by the servants of Limhi. ²²And after they had been cast into prison many days without food, behold, they went forth into the prison to take them, that they might slay them.

²³And it came to pass that Nephi and Lehi were encircled about as if by fire, even insomuch that they durst not lay their hands upon them for fear lest they should be burned. Nevertheless, Nephi and Lehi were not burned. And they were as standing in the midst of fire. And they were not burned. ²⁴And when they saw that they were encircled about with a pillar of fire and that it burned them not—their hearts did take courage. For they saw that the Lamanites durst not lay their hands upon them, neither durst they come near unto them—but stood as if they were struck dumb with amazement.

²⁶And it came to pass that Nephi and Lehi did stand forth, and began to speak unto them, saying: "Fear not! For behold, it is God that hath shown unto you this marvelous thing—in the which is shown unto you that ye cannot lay your hands upon us, to slay us."

²⁷And behold, when they had said these words, the earth shook exceedingly and the walls of the prison did shake as if they were about to tumble to the earth. But behold, they did not fall. And behold, they that were in the prison were Lamanites, and Nephites which were dissenters.

²⁸And it came to pass that they were overshadowed with a cloud of darkness. And an awful, solemn fear came upon them.

²⁹And it came to pass that there came a voice as if it were above the cloud of darkness, saying: "Repent ye! Repent ye! And seek no more to destroy my servants which I have sent unto you to declare good tidings."

³⁰And it came to pass when they heard this voice, and beheld that it was not a

---

a. This sentence can be considered if the "for they had power" is read as "because they had power."

voice of thunder, neither was it a voice of a great tumultuous noise—but behold, it was a still voice of perfect mildness, as if it had been a whisper.ª And it did pierce, even to the very soul. ³¹And notwithstanding the mildness of the voice, behold the earth shook exceedingly. And the walls of the prison trembled again as if it were about to tumble to the earth.

³²And behold, the cloud of darkness which had overshadowed them did not disperse. And behold, the voice came again, saying: "Repent ye! Repent ye! For the kingdom of heaven is at hand! And seek no more to destroy my servants."

And it came to pass that the earth shook again. And the walls trembled. ³³And also again, the third time, the voice came—and did speak unto them marvelous words which cannot be uttered by man. And the walls did tremble again. And the earth shook as if it were about to divide asunder.

³⁴And it came to pass that the Lamanites could not flee because of the cloud of darkness which did overshadow them, yea, and also they were immovable because of the fear which did come upon them.

³⁵Now, there was one among them who was a Nephite by birth, who had once belonged to the church of God but had dissented from them.

³⁶And it came to pass that he turned him about, and behold, he saw through the cloud of darkness the faces of Nephi and Lehi. And behold, they did shine exceedingly, even as the face of angels.ᵇ And he beheld that they did lift their eyes to heaven. And they were in the attitude as if talking (or lifting their voices) to some being which they beheld.

³⁷And it came to pass that this man did cry unto the multitude, that they might turn, and look. And behold, there was power given unto them that they did turn and look. And they did behold the faces of Nephi and Lehi. ³⁸And they said unto the man: "Behold! What doth all these things mean? And who is it with whom these men do converse?"

³⁹Now, the man's name was Aminadab. And Aminadab saith unto them: "They do converse with the angels of God."

⁴⁰And it came to pass that the Lamanites said unto him: "What shall we do, that this cloud of darkness may be removed from overshadowing us?"

⁴¹And Aminadab saith unto them: "You must repent, and cry unto the voice, even until ye shall have faith in Christ, in which was taught unto you by Alma and Amulek, and by Zeezrom. And when ye shall do this, the cloud of darkness shall be removed from overshadowing you."

⁴²And it came to pass that they all did begin to cry unto the voice of him which had shook the earth. Yea, they did cry, even until the cloud of darkness was dispersed.

⁴³And it came to pass that when they cast their eyes about and saw that the cloud of darkness was dispersed from overshadowing them—and behold, they saw that they were encircled about, yea, every soul, by a pillar of fire. ⁴⁴And Nephi and Lehi was in the midst of them. Yea, they were encircled about. Yea, they were as if in the midst of a flaming fire—yet it did harm them not, neither did it take hold upon the walls of the

---

a. Echoes language from 1 Kings 19:11–12: "And he said, Go forth, and stand upon the mount before the Lord. And, behold, the Lord passed by, and a great and strong wind rent the mountains, and brake in pieces the rocks before the Lord; but the Lord was not in the wind: and after the wind an earthquake; but the Lord was not in the earthquake: And after the earthquake a fire; but the Lord was not in the fire: and after the fire a still small voice."

b. See Exodus 34:29, where Moses's face shines.

prison. And they were filled with that joy which is unspeakable, and full of glory.ª ⁴⁵And behold, the Holy Spirit of God did come down from heaven and did enter into their hearts. And they were filled as if with fire. And they could speak forth marvelous words. ⁴⁶And it came to pass that there came a voice unto them, yea, a pleasant voice, as if it were a whisper, saying: ⁴⁷"Peace, peace be unto you because of your faith in my well beloved, which was from the foundation of the world."

⁴⁸And now, when they heard this, they cast up their eyes as if to behold from whence the voice came. And behold, they saw the heavens open and angels came down out of heaven and ministered unto them. ⁴⁹And there were about three hundred souls which saw and heard these things. And they were bid to go forth, and marvel not, neither should they doubt.

⁵⁰And it came to pass that they did go forth and did minister unto the people—declaring throughout all the regions round about all the things which they had heard and seen, insomuch that the more part of the Lamanites were convinced of them—because of the greatness of the evidences which they had received. ⁵¹And as many as were convinced did lay down their weapons of war, and also their hatred, and the tradition of their fathers.

⁵²And it came to pass that they did yield up unto the Nephites the lands of their possession.

[6] ¹And it came to pass that when the sixty and second year of the reign of the judges had ended, all these things had happened. And the Lamanites had become (the more part of them) a righteous people, insomuch that their righteousness did exceed that of the Nephites—because of their firmness and their steadiness in the faith. ²For behold, there were many of the Nephites which had become hardened, and impenitent, and grossly wicked, insomuch that they did reject the word of God, and all the preaching, and the prophesying, which did come among them. ³Nevertheless, the people of the church did have great joy because of the conversion of the Lamanites, yea, because of the church of God which had been established among them. And they did fellowship one with another, and did rejoice one with another, and did have great joy.

⁴And it came to pass that many of the Lamanites did come down into the land of Zarahemla and did declare unto the people of the Nephites the manner of their conversion, and did exhort them to faith and repentance. ⁵Yea, and many did preach with exceeding great power and authority—unto the bringing down many of them into the depths of humility, to be the humble followers of God and of the Lamb.

⁶And it came to pass that many of the Lamanites did go into the land northward. And also Nephi and Lehi went into the land northward to preach unto the people. And thus ended the sixty and third year. ⁷And behold, there was peace in all the land, insomuch that the Nephites did go into whatsoever part of the land they would, whether among the Nephites or the Lamanites.

⁸And it came to pass that the Lamanites did also go whithersoever they would, whether it were among the Lamanites or among the Nephites. And thus, they did have free intercourse, one with another, for to buy and to sell, and to get gain, according to their desire.

⁹And it came to pass that they became exceeding rich—both the Lamanites and

---

a. See 1 Peter 1:8: "Ye rejoice with joy unspeakable and full of glory."

the Nephites. And they did have an exceeding plenty of gold, and of silver, and of all manner of precious [metals[a]], both in the land south and in the land north.

>[10]Now, the land south was called Lehi, and the land north was called Mulek, which was after the son of Zedekiah. For the Lord did bring Mulek into the land north, and Lehi into the land south.[b]< [11]And behold, there was all manner of gold in both these lands, and of silver, and of precious ore of every kind. And there was also curious workmen which did work all kinds of ore—and did refine it. And thus, they did become rich. [12]They did raise grain in abundance, both in the north and in the south. And they did flourish exceedingly, both in the north and in the south. And they did multiply, and wax exceeding strong in the land. And they did raise many flocks, and herds, yea, many fatlings. [13]Behold, their women did toil, and spin, and did make all manner of cloth—of fine twined linen—and cloth of every kind, to clothe their nakedness.

And thus, the sixty and forth fourth year did pass away in peace. [14]And in the sixty and fifth year they did also have great joy, and peace, yea, much preaching, and many prophecies concerning that which was to come. And thus passed away the sixty and fifth year.

[15]And it came to pass that in the sixty and sixth year of the reign of the judges, behold Cezoram was murdered by an unknown hand as he sat upon the Judgment Seat.

And it came to pass that in the same year, that his son (which had been appointed by the people in his stead) was also murdered. And thus ended the sixty and sixth year.

[16]And in the commencement of the sixty and seventh year, the people began to grow exceeding wicked again. [17]For behold, the Lord had blessed them so long with the riches of the world that they had not been stirred up to anger, to wars, nor to bloodsheds. Therefore, they began to set their hearts upon their riches. Yea, they began to seek to get gain, that they might be lifted up, one above another. Therefore, they began to commit secret murders, and to rob, and to plunder, that they might get gain. [18]And now behold, those murderers and plunderers were a band which had been formed by Kishcumen[c] and Gaddianton.

And now, it had came to pass that there were many, even among the Nephites, of Gaddianton's band. But behold, they were more numerous among the more wicked part of the Lamanites. And they were called Gaddianton's robbers and murderers. [19]And it was they which did murder the Chief Judge Cezoram, and his son, while in the Judgment Seat. And behold, they were not found.

[20]And now it came to pass that when the Lamanites found that there were robbers among them, they were exceeding sorrowful. And they did use every means, whatsoever was in their power, to destroy them off the face of the earth. [21]But behold, Satan did stir up the hearts of the more parts of the Nephites, insomuch that they did unite with those bands of robbers, and did enter into their covenants, and their oaths, that

---

a. The Printer's Manuscript has "petals." Hyrum Smith edited the text to say "metals." The original is not extant, but many of Hyrum's changes appear to come from a comparison to the Original Manuscript. The 1830 edition made the change to "metals."

b. This is the only time that Mormon refers to the land north as Mulek. The land northward appears to be different. This seems to be a reference to the original division between Nephite and Mulekite lands, but that would not have been the designations after the merger of the two peoples. This seems to be an insertion, although without an obvious reason for its inclusion.

c. Spelling as in the Original Manuscript. Skousen notes that the Original Manuscript is consistent in spelling it with a "c." Skousen, *Analysis of the Textual Variants*, 5:2881.

Chapter II [Helaman 3–6]

they would protect and preserve one another in whatsoever difficult circumstances they should be placed in, that they should not suffer for their murders, and their plunderings, and their stealings.

>²³And it came to pass that they did have their signs, yea, their secret signs and their secret words—and this, that they might distinguish a brother who had entered into the covenant, that whatsoever wickedness his brother should do, he should not be injured by his brother, nor by those who did belong to his band who had taken this covenant. And thus, they might murder, and plunder, and steal, and commit whoredoms, and all manner of wickedness—contrary to the laws of their country, and also the laws of their God. ²⁴And whosoever of those which belonged to their band should reveal unto the world of their wickedness, and their abominations, should be tried—not according to the laws of their country, but according to the laws of their wickedness which had been given by Gaddianton and Kishcumen.

²⁵Now behold, it is these secret oaths and covenants which Alma commanded his son should not go forth unto the world, lest they should be a means of bringing down the people unto destruction. ²⁶Now behold, those secret oaths and covenants did not come forth unto Gaddianton from the records which were delivered unto Helaman. But behold, they were put into the heart of Gaddianton by that same being who did entice our first parents to partake of the forbidden fruit—²⁷yea, that same being who did plot with Cain, that if he would murder his brother Abel it should not be known unto the world. And he did plot with Cain and his followers from that time forth. ²⁸And also, it is that same being who put it into the hearts of the people to build a tower sufficiently high that they might get to heaven. And it was that same being which led on the people which came from that tower into this land, which spread the works of darkness and abominations over all the face of the land, until he dragged the people down to an entire destruction, and to an everlasting hell. ²⁹Yea, it is that same being who put it into the heart of Gaddianton to still carry on the work of darkness, and of secret murder. And he hath brought it forth from the beginning of man, even down to this time. ³⁰And behold, it is he which is the author of all sin. And behold, he doth carry on his works of darkness, and secret murder, and doth hand down their plots, and their oaths, and their covenants, and their plans of awful wickedness—from generation to generation, according as he can get hold upon the hearts of the children of men.

³¹And now behold, he had got great hold upon the hearts of the Nephites, yea, insomuch that they had become exceeding wicked. Yea, the more part of them had turned out of the way of righteousness and did trample under their feet the commandments of God, and did turn unto their own ways, and did build up unto themselves idols of their gold, and of their silver.ᵃ<

³²And it came to pass that all these iniquities did come unto them in the space of not many years, insomuch that a more part of it had come unto them in the sixty and seventh year of the reign of the judges over the people of Nephi. ³³And they did grow

---

a. This is not an aside, but an intentional interruption of the narrative to highlight Mormon's point. Mormon is making the case that the Gaddiantons, with their secret combinations, caused the downfall of the Nephites. Here he makes sure that the reader can't blame Helaman₁ for divulging these secrets. Nevertheless, Mormon still explicitly ties them to the Jaredites.

in their iniquities in the sixty and eighth year also, to the great sorrow and lamentation of the righteous.

>³⁴And thus we see that the Nephites did begin to dwindle in unbelief, and grow in wickedness, and abominations—while the Lamanites began to grow exceedingly in the knowledge of their God, yea, they did begin to keep his statutes, and commandments, and to walk in truth and uprightness before him. ³⁵And thus, we see that the spirit of the Lord began to withdraw from the Nephites—because of the wickedness, and the hardness of their hearts. ³⁶And thus, we see that the Lord began to pour out his spirit upon the Lamanites—because of their easiness, and willingness to believe in his word.ᵃ<

³⁷And it came to pass that the Lamanites did hunt the band of robbers of Gaddianton. And they did preach the word of God among the more wicked part of them, insomuch that this band of robbers was utterly destroyed from among the Lamanites.

³⁸And it came to pass on the other hand, that the Nephites did build them up and support them—beginning at the more wicked part of them, until they had overspread all the land of the Nephites and had seduced the more part of the righteous until they had come down to believe in their works, and partake of their spoils, and to join with them in their secret murders, and combinations. ³⁹And thus, they did obtain the sole management of the government, insomuch that they did trample under their feet, and smite, and rend, and turn their backs upon the poor and the meek, and humble followers of God. ⁴⁰And thus, we see that they were in an awful state, and ripening for an everlasting destruction.

⁴¹And it came to pass that thus ended the sixty and eighth year of the reign of the judges over the people of Nephi.

---

a. Mormon inserts an "and we see" comment to highlight his message. In this case, it is important to note that it is both the righteousness of the Lamanites as well as the wickedness of the Nephites.

Chapter III [Helaman 7–10]

[7] *The prophecy of Nephi, the Son of Helaman.*[a] *God threatens the people of Nephi, that he will visit them in his anger to their utter destruction, except they repent of their wickedness. God smiteth the people of Nephi with pestilence. They repent and turn unto him. Samuel, a Lamanite, prophesies unto the Nephites.*

¹Behold, now it came to pass in the sixty and ninth year of the reign of the judges over the people of the Nephites that Nephi, the son of Helaman, returned to the land of Zarahemla from the land northward. ²For he had been forth among the people which was in the land northward, and did preach the word of God unto them, and did prophesy many things unto them. ³And they did reject all his words, insomuch that he could not stay among them—but returned again unto the land of his nativity. ⁴And, seeing the people in a state of such awful wickedness, and those Gaddianton robbers filling the Judgment Seats (having usurped the power and authority of the land—laying aside the commandments of God, and not in the least aright before him)—doing no justice unto the children of men—⁵condemning the righteous because of their righteousness—letting the guilty and the wicked go unpunished because of their money—and moreover, to be held in office at the head of government to rule, and to do according to their wills, that they might get gain, and glory of the world—and moreover, that they might more easy commit adultery, and steal, and kill, and do according to their own wills.

⁶Now, this great iniquity had come upon the Nephites in the space of not many years. And when Nephi saw it, his heart was swollen with sorrow within his breast. And he did exclaim in the agony of his soul:

⁷O that I could have had my days in the days of when my father Nephi first came out of the land of Jerusalem! That I could have joyed with him in the promised land! Then were his people easy to be entreated—firm to keep the commandments of God and slow to be led to do iniquity—and they were quick to hearken unto the words of the Lord. ⁸Yea, if my days could have been in them days—then would my soul have had joy in the righteousness of my brethren! ⁹But behold, I am consigned that these are my days, and that my soul shall be filled with sorrow because of this the wickedness of my brethren.

¹⁰And behold, now it came to pass that it was upon a tower (which was in the garden of Nephi, which was by the highway which led to the chief market, which was in the city of Zarahemla). Therefore, as Nephi had bowed himself upon the tower (which was in his garden, which tower was also near unto the garden gate which led by the highway)— ¹¹and it came to pass that there was certain men passing by, and saw Nephi as he was a-pouring out his soul unto God upon the tower.[b] And they ran and told

---

a. The Printer's Manuscript has "The prophecy of Nephi, the son of Helaman" as a title. This edition reads it as part of the header. If it were a title, it would be unique in the text. It also makes sense as the first description of the header. Grant Hardy also set it as the first line of the header in *The Book of Mormon: Maxwell Institute Study Edition* (Provo, UT: Neal A. Maxwell Institute, 2018).

b. Verse 11 is the repetitive resumption to recover from the incomplete sentence before it, caused by the long parenthetical phrase, which was in itself a continuation of the incomplete sentence that began "Therefore, as Nephi had bowed himself."

the people what they had seen. And the people came together in multitudes, that they might know the cause of so great mourning for the wickedness of the people.

¹²And now, when Nephi arose and he beheld the multitudes of people which had gathered together—¹³and it came to pass that he opened his mouth and said unto them:

> Behold, why have ye gathered yourselves together? That I may tell you of your iniquities? ¹⁴Yea, because I have got upon my tower that I might pour out my soul unto my God because of the exceeding sorrow of my heart, which is because of your iniquities?
>
> ¹⁵And because of my mourning and lamentation, ye have gathered yourselves together and do marvel. Yea, and ye have great need to marvel! Yea, ye had ought to marvel—because ye are given away, that the devil hath got so great hold upon your hearts. ¹⁶Yea, how could ye have given away to the enticing of him who art seeking to hurl away your souls down to everlasting misery and endless wo?
>
> ¹⁷O repent ye! Repent ye! Why will ye die?ᵃ Turn ye! Turn ye unto the Lord, your God!
>
> Why hath he forsaken you? ¹⁸It is because you have hardened your hearts. Yea, ye will not hearken unto the voice of the good shepherd.ᵇ Yea, ye have provoked him to anger against you.
>
> ¹⁹And behold, instead of gathering you—except ye will repent, behold, he shall scatter you forth, that ye shall become meat for dogs and wild beasts.
>
> ²⁰O! How could you have forgotten your God in the very day that he hath delivered you? ²¹But behold, it is to get gain, to be praised of men—yea, and that ye might get gold, and silver. And ye have set your hearts upon the riches, and the vain things of this world, for the which ye do murder, and plunder, and steal, and bear false witness against your neighbor, and do all manner of iniquity.
>
> ²²And for this cause wo shall come unto you, except ye shall repent. For if ye will not repent, behold this great city (and also all those great cities which are round about, which are in the land of our possession) shall be taken away, that ye shall have no place in them. For behold, the Lord will not grant unto you strength as he hath hitherto done to withstand against your enemies. ²³For behold, thus saith the Lord: "I will not show unto the wicked of my strength, to one more than the other, save it be unto those who repenteth of their sins, and hearken unto my words."ᶜ Now therefore, I would that ye should behold, my brethren, that it shall be better for the Lamanites than for you, except ye shall repent. ²⁴For behold, they are more righteous than you. For they have not sinned against that great knowledge which ye have received. Therefore, the Lord will be merciful unto them.
>
> Yea, he will lengthen out their days and increase their seed, even when thou shalt be utterly destroyed, except thou shalt repent.
>
> ²⁵Yea, wo be in unto you because of that great abomination which hath come among you! And ye have united yourselves unto it, yea, to that secret band which was established by Gaddianton.
>
> ²⁶Yea, wo shall come unto you because of that pride which ye have suffered to

---

a. The phrase "why will ye die" occurs in Jeremiah 27:13.
b. See John 10:11: "I am the good shepherd."
c. There is no extant referent.

Chapter III [Helaman 7–10]

enter your hearts, which hath lifted you up beyond that which is good—because of your exceeding great riches.

²⁷Yea, wo be unto you because of your wickedness and abominations! And except ye repent, ye shall perish. Yea, even your lands shall be taken from you. ²⁸And ye shall be destroyed from off the face of the earth.

²⁹Behold, I do not say that these things shall be, of myself—because it is not of myself that I know these things. But behold, I know that these things are true because the Lord God hath made them known unto me. Therefore, I testify that they shall be.

[8] ¹And now it came to pass that when Nephi had said these words, behold, there were men which were judges which also belonged to the secret band of Gaddianton. And they were angry. And they cried out against him, saying unto the people: "Why do ye not seize upon this man and bring him forth, that he may be condemned according to the crime which he hath done? ²Why seest thou this man, and hearest him revile against this people, and against our law?"

>³For behold, Nephi had spoken unto them concerning the corruptness of their law. Yea, many things did Nephi speak which cannot be written. And nothing did he speak which were contrary to the commandments of God.ᵃ<

⁴And those judges were angry with him, because he spake plain unto them concerning their secret works of darkness. Nevertheless, they durst not lay their own hands upon him for they feared the people, lest they should cry out against them. ⁵Therefore, they did cry unto the people, saying:

Why do ye suffer this man to revile against us? For behold, he doth condemn all this people, even unto destruction! Yea, and also that these, our great cities, shall be taken from us, that we shall have no place in them! ⁶And now, we know that this is impossible. For behold, we are powerful, and our cities great. Therefore, our enemies can have no power overpower us.

⁷And now it came to pass that thus they did stir up the people to anger against Nephi and raised contentions among them. For there were some which did cry out:

Let this man alone! For he a is a good man! And those things which he saith will surely come to pass, except we repent!

⁸Yea behold, all the judgments will come upon us which he hath testified unto us. For we know that he hath testified aright unto us concerning our iniquities—and behold, they are many! And he knoweth as well all things which shall befall us, as he knoweth of our iniquities.

⁹Yea, and behold, if he had not been a prophet he could not have testified concerning those things.

¹⁰And it came to pass that those people which sought to destroy Nephi were compelled (because of their fear), that they did not lay their hands on him. Therefore, he began again to speak unto them—seeing that he had gained favor in the eyes of some,

---

a. Mormon realized that the quotation he had selected had not covered the problems with the laws that the judges complained about. Therefore, he rectifies the information after the fact.

insomuch that the remainder of them did fear. ¹¹Therefore, he was constrained to speak more unto them, saying:

Behold my brethren! Have ye not read that God gave power unto one man, even Moses, to smite upon the waters of the Red Sea—and they departed hither and thither, insomuch that the Israelites (which were our fathers) came through upon dry ground? And the waters closed upon the armies of the Egyptians and swallowed them up. ¹²And now behold, if God gave unto this man such power, then why should ye dispute among yourselves, and say that he hath given unto me no power whereby I may know concerning the judgments that shall come upon you, except ye repent?

¹³But behold, ye not only deny my words, but ye also deny all the words which hath been spoken by our fathers—and also the words which was spoken by this man Moses, which has had such great power given unto him, yea, the words which he hath spoken concerning the coming of Messiah. ¹⁴Yea, did he not bear record that the Son of God should come? And as he lifted up the brazen serpent in the wilderness, even so should he be lifted up which[a] should come.[b] ¹⁵And as many as should look upon that serpent should live. Even so, as many as should look upon the Son of God, with faith, having a contrite spirit,[c] might live—even unto that life which is eternal.

¹⁶And now behold, Moses did not only testify of these things, but also all the holy prophets from his day, even to the days of Abraham. ¹⁷Yea, and behold, Abraham saw of his coming and was filled with gladness and did rejoice.

¹⁸Yea, and behold I say unto you, that Abraham not only knew of these things—but there were many before the days of Abraham which were called by the order of God, yea, even after the order of his Son. And this, that it should be shown unto the people a great many thousand years before his coming that even redemption should come unto them.

¹⁹And now I would that ye should know that even since the days of Abraham that there hath been many prophets that hath testified these things. Yea behold, the prophet Zenos did testify boldly. For the which he was slain. ²⁰And behold, also Zenock, and also Ezaias,[d] and also Isaiah, and Jeremiah—Jeremiah being that same prophet which testified of the destruction of Jerusalem.

²¹And now, we know that Jerusalem was destroyed, according to the words of Jeremiah. O then, why not the Son of God come, according to his prophecy?

And now, will ye dispute that Jerusalem was not destroyed? Will ye say that the sons of Zedekiah were not slain, all except it were Mulek? Yea, and do ye

---

a. In 1837, Joseph Smith changed this to "who," which is the intent of the original "which." The reference is to Christ, not the brazen serpent.

b. See John 3:15: "That whosoever believeth in him should not perish, but have eternal life."

c. See Psalm 34:18: "The Lord is nigh unto them that are of a broken heart; and saveth such as be of a contrite spirit."

d. The 1830 edition printed this name as "Ezias," and that change continues to the modern edition. This is not a prophet known from the Old Testament as we know it. However, Orson Pratt saw it as a name of a prophet from the time of Abraham, referencing Doctrine and Covenants 84:11–13: "And Gad under the hand of Esaias; And Esaias received it under the hand of God. Esaias also lived in the days of Abraham, and was blessed of him." See Skousen, *Analysis of the Textual Variants*, 5:3022–23.

Chapter III [Helaman 7–10]

not behold that the seed of Zedekiah are with us? And they were driven out of the land of Jerusalem. But behold, this is not all. ²²Our father, Lehi, was driven out of Jerusalem because he testified of these things. Nephi also testified of these things—and also almost all of our fathers, even down to this time. Yea, they have testified of the coming of Christ, and have looked forward, and have rejoiced in his day, which is to come.

²³And behold, he is God! And he is with them, and he did manifest himself unto them, that they were redeemed by him. And they gave unto him glory because of that which is to come.

²⁴And now, seeing ye know these things and cannot deny them (except ye shall lie)—therefore, in this ye have sinned! For ye have rejected all these things, notwithstanding so many evidences which ye have received. Yea, even ye have received all things, both things in heaven and all things which are in earth, as a witness that they are true.

²⁵But behold, ye have rejected the truth and rebelled against your Holy God. And even at this time, instead of laying up for yourselves treasures in heaven (where nothing doth corrupt, and where nothing can come which is unclean[a])—ye are heaping up for yourselves wrath against the day of judgment!

²⁶Yea, even at this time, ye are ripening (because of your murders, and your fornication, and wickedness) for everlasting destruction! Yea, and except ye repent—it will come unto you soon.

²⁷Yea behold, it is now even at your doors. Yea, go ye in unto the Judgment Seat, and search. ²⁸And behold, your Judge is murdered and he lieth in his blood. And he hath been murdered by his brother, who seeketh to sit in the Judgment Seat. And behold, they both belong to your secret band, whose author is Gaddianton and the evil one (which seeketh to destroy the souls of men).

[9] ¹Behold, now it came to pass that when Nephi had spoken these words, certain men which were among them ran to the Judgment Seat, yea, even there were five which went. And they said among themselves, as they went:

²Behold! Now we will know of a surety whether this man be a prophet, and God hath commanded him to prophesy such marvelous things unto us.

Behold, we do not believe that he hath. Yea, we do not believe that he is a prophet. Nevertheless, if this thing which he hath said concerning the Chief Judge be true, that he be dead, then will we believe that the other words which he hath spoken is true.

³And it came to pass that they ran in their might and came in unto the Judgment Seat. And behold, the Chief Judge had fallen to the earth and did lie in his blood.

⁴And now behold, when they saw this, they were astonished exceedingly, insomuch that they fell to the earth. For they had not believed the words which Nephi had spoken concerning the Chief Judge. ⁵But now, when they saw, they believed. And fear came upon them, lest all the judgments which Nephi had spoken should come upon the people. Therefore, they did quake and had fallen to the earth.

---

a. See Matthew 6:20: "But lay up for yourselves treasures in heaven, where neither moth nor rust doth corrupt, and where thieves do not break through nor steal."

⁶Now, immediately, when the Judge had been murdered (he being stabbed by his brother, by a garb of secrecy—and he fled)—and the servants ran and told the people, raising the cry of murder among them. ⁷And behold, the people did gather themselves together unto the place of the Judgment Seat. And behold, to their astonishment, they saw those five men which had fallen to the earth.

⁸And now behold, the people knew nothing concerning the multitude which had gathered together at the garden of Nephi. Therefore, they said among themselves: "These men are they which have murdered the Judge, and God hath smitten them, that they could not flee from us."

⁹And it came to pass that they laid hold on them, and bound them, and cast them into prison. And there was a proclamation sent abroad that the Judge was slain and that the murderers had been taken, and was cast into prison.

¹⁰And it came to pass that on the morrow the people did assemble themselves together to mourn, and to fast, at the burial of the great and Chief Judge which had been slain. ¹¹And thus were[a] also those judges which were at the garden of Nephi and heard his words—were also gathered together at the burial.[b]

¹²And it came to pass that they inquired among the people, saying: "Where are the five, which was sent to inquire concerning the Chief Judge—whether he was dead?"

And they answered and said: "Concerning this five which ye say ye have sent, we know not. But there are five which are the murderers, whom we have cast into prison."

¹³And it came to pass that the judges desired that they should be brought. And they were brought. And behold, they were the five which were sent. And behold, the judges inquired of them to know concerning the matter. And they told them all that they had done, saying:

¹⁴We ran, and came to the place of the Judgment Seat. And when we saw all things, even as Nephi had testified—we were astonished insomuch that we fell to the earth. And when we were recovered from our astonishment, behold they cast us into prison.

¹⁵Now, as for the murder of this man, we know not who hath done it. And only this much we know. We ran, and came according as ye desired. And behold he was dead, according to the words of Nephi.

¹⁶And now it came to pass that the judges did expound the matter unto the people, and did cry out against Nephi, saying:

Behold! We know that this Nephi must have agreed with someone to slay the Judge—and then he might declare it unto us, that he might convert us unto his faith, that he might raise himself to be a great man, chosen of God, and a prophet.

¹⁷And now behold, we will detect this man! And he shall confess his fault and make known unto us the true murderer of this Judge.

¹⁸And it came to pass that the five were liberated on the day of the burial. Nevertheless, they did rebuke the judges in the words which they had spoken against

---

a. Removed in the 1907 vest pocket edition, and again in current printed editions. This resolves the problematic grammar of the repeated "were also gathered" at the end of the sentence. Skousen, *Analysis of Textual Variants*, 5:3031.

b. The "were" in the final clause is extraneous. It may have been the result of repetitive resumption. See previous note on the removal of the first "were," which corrects this.

Nephi, and did contend with them, one by one, insomuch that they did confound them. ¹⁹Nevertheless, they caused that Nephi should be taken, and bound, and brought before the multitude. And they began to question him in divers ways, that they might cross him, that they might accuse him to death—²⁰saying unto him: "Thou art confederate. Who is this man that hath done this murder? Now tell us and acknowledge thy fault." Saying: "Behold, here is money! And also, we will grant unto thee thy life, if thou wilt tell us, and acknowledge the agreement which thou hast made with him."

²¹But Nephi saith unto them:

O ye fools! Ye uncircumcised of heart![a] Ye blind, and ye stiffnecked people! Do ye know how long the Lord your God will suffer you, that ye shall go on in this, your ways of sin?

²²O , ye had ought to begin to howl and mourn, because of the great destruction at this time that which doth await you, except ye shall repent.

²³Behold, ye say that I have agreed with a man that he should murder Cezoram, our Chief Judge. But behold, I say unto you that this is because I have testified unto you, that ye might know concerning this thing, yea, even for a witness unto you that I did know of the wickedness and abominations which is among you. ²⁴And because I have done this, ye say that I have agreed with a man that he should do this thing. Yea, because I showed unto ye you this sign, ye are angry with me and seek to destroy my life.

²⁵And now behold! I will show unto you another sign. And see if ye will (in this thing) seek to destroy me!

²⁶Behold, I say unto you: Go to the house of Seantum, which is the brother of Cezoram, and say unto him: ²⁷Hath Nephi the pretended prophet (which doth prophesy so much evil concerning this people) agreed with thee—in the which ye have murdered Cezoram, which is your brother?

²⁸And behold, he shall say unto you, nay.

²⁹And ye shall say unto him—have ye murdered your brother?

³⁰And he shall stand with fear and wist not what to say. And behold, he shall deny unto you. And he shall make as if he were astonished. Nevertheless, he shall declare unto you that he is innocent. ³¹But behold, ye shall examine him. And ye shall find blood upon the skirts of his cloak.[b] ³²And when ye have seen this, ye shall say: From whence cometh this blood? Do we not know that it is the blood of your brother?

³³And then shall he tremble and shall look pale, even as if death had come upon him.

³⁴And then shall ye say—because of this fear, and this paleness, which hath come upon your face—behold, we know that thou art guilty. ³⁵And then shall greater fear come upon him.

And then shall he confess unto you and deny no more that he hath done this murder.

³⁶And then shall he say unto you that I, Nephi, knew nothing concerning the matter, save it were given unto me by the power of God.

---

a. The phrase "uncircumcised in heart" appears in Acts 7:51.
b. Uses language from Jeremiah 2:34: "Also in thy skirts is found the blood of the souls of the poor innocents."

And then shall ye know that I am an honest man and that I am sent unto you from God.

³⁷And it came to pass that they went, and did, even according as Nephi had said unto them. And behold, the words which he had said were true. For according to the words—he did deny. And also according to the words—he did confess. ³⁸And he was brought to prove that he, himself, was the very murderer, insomuch that the five were set at liberty, and also was Nephi.

³⁹And there were some of the Nephites which did believe on the words of Nephi. And there were some also, which believed because of the testimony of the five. For they had been converted while they were in prison.

⁴⁰And now, there were some among the people which said that Nephi was a prophet. ⁴¹And there were others which said: "Behold, he is a god! For except he was a god, he could not know of all things. For behold, he hath told us the thoughts of our hearts, and also hath told us things—and even he hath brought unto our knowledge the true murderer of our Chief Judge."

[10] ¹And it came to pass that there arose a division among the people, insomuch that they divided hither and thither and went their ways, leaving Nephi alone as he was standing in the midst of them.

²And it came to pass that Nephi went his way, towards his own house, pondering upon the things which the Lord had shown unto him.

³And it came to pass as he was thus pondering—being much cast down because of the wickedness of the people of the Nephites—their secret works of darkness, and their murderings, and their plunderings, and all manner of iniquities—and it came to pass as he was thus pondering in his heart[a]—behold, a voice came unto him, saying:

⁴Blessed art thou Nephi for those things which thou hast done! For I have beheld how thou hast, with unwearyingness, declared the word which I have given unto thee—unto this people. And thou hast not feared them. And hast not sought thine own life, but hath sought my will, and to keep my commandments.

⁵And now, because thou hast done this with such unwearyingness, behold, I will bless thee forever. And I will make thee mighty in word and in deed, in faith and in works, yea, even that all things shall be done unto thee according to thy word. For thou shalt not ask that which is contrary to my will.

⁶Behold, thou art Nephi. And I am God. Behold, I declare it unto thee, in the presence of mine angels, that ye shall have power over this people—and shall smite the earth with famine, and with pestilence, and destruction, according to the wickedness of this people.

⁷Behold, I give unto you power that whatsoever ye shall seal on earth shall be sealed in heaven. And whatsoever ye shall loose on earth shall be loosed in heaven.[b]

⁸And thus shall ye have power among this people. And thus, if ye shall say unto this temple—it shall be rent in twain! And it shall be done. ⁹And if ye shall say unto this mountain—be thou cast down and become smooth! And it shall be done. ¹⁰And behold, if ye shall say that God shall smite this people, it shall come to pass.

---

a. The several internal clauses required that the sentence use repetitive resumption to recover the intent of the beginning of the sentence.

b. See similar language in Matthew 16:19 and 18:18.

Chapter III [Helaman 7–10]

¹¹And now behold, I command you that ye shall go and declare unto this people that thus saith the Lord God, who is the Almighty: Except ye repent, ye shall be smitten, even unto destruction!

¹²And behold, now it came to pass that when the Lord had spoken these words unto Nephi, he did stop—and did not go unto his own house—but did return unto the multitudes, which were scattered about upon the face of the land, and began to declare unto them the word of the Lord, which had been spoken unto him concerning their destruction if they did not repent.

¹³Now behold, notwithstanding that great miracle which Nephi had done in telling them concerning the death of the Chief Judge, they did harden their hearts and did not hearken unto the words of the Lord. ¹⁴Therefore, Nephi did declare unto them the word of the Lord, saying: "Except ye repent, thus saith the Lord, ye shall be smitten, even unto destruction!"

¹⁵And it came to pass that when Nephi had declared unto them the word, behold, they did still harden their hearts and would not hearken unto his words. Therefore, they did revile against him and did seek to lay their hands upon him, that they might cast him into prison. ¹⁶But behold, the power of God was with him. And they could not take him to cast him into prison, for he was taken by the spirit and conveyed away out of the midst of them.

¹⁷And it came to pass that thus he did go forth in the spirit, from multitude to multitude, declaring the word of God, even until he had declared it unto them all (or sent it forth among all the people).

¹⁸And it came to pass that they would not hearken unto his words. And there began to be contentions, insomuch that they were divided against themselves and began to slay one another with the sword. ¹⁹And thus ended the seventy and first year of the reign of the judges over the people of Nephi.

Chapter IV [Helaman 11–12]

[11] ¹And now it came to pass in the seventy and second year of the reign of the judges that the contentions did increase, insomuch that there were wars throughout all the land, among all the people of Nephi. ²And it was this secret band of robbers which did carry on this work of destruction and wickedness. And thus this war did last all that year. And in the seventy and third year, it did also last.

³And it came to pass that in this year, Nephi did cry unto the Lord, saying: ⁴"O Lord! Do not suffer that this people shall be destroyed by the sword. But, O Lord, rather let there be a famine in the land to stir them up in remembrance of the Lord, their God. And perhaps they will repent and turn unto thee."

⁵And so it was done according to the words of Nephi. And there was a great famine upon the land among all the people of Nephi. And thus, in the seventy and fourth year the famine did continue. And the work of destruction did cease by the sword, but became sore by famine. ⁶And this work of destruction did also continue in the seventy and fifth year. For the earth was smitten, that it was dry and did not yield forth grain in the season of grain. And the whole earth was smitten, even among the Lamanites (as well as among the Nephites)—so that they were smitten, that they did perish by thousands in the more wicked parts of the land.

⁷And it came to pass that the people saw that they were about to perish by famine. And they began to remember the Lord, their God. And they began to remember the words of Nephi. ⁸And the people began to plead with their Chief Judges and their leaders, that they would say unto Nephi: "Behold, we know that thou art a man of God. And therefore—cry unto the Lord, our God, that he turn away from us this famine, lest all the words which thou hast spoken concerning our destruction be fulfilled."

⁹And it came to pass that the judges did say unto Nephi according to the words which had been desired.

And it came to pass that when Nephi saw that the people had repented and did humble themselves in sack cloth, he cried again unto the Lord, saying:

¹⁰O Lord! Behold, this people repenteth. And they have swept away the band of Gaddianton from amongst them, insomuch that they have become extinct. And they have concealed their secret plans in the earth.

¹¹Now, O Lord, because of this their humility—wilt thou turn away thine anger? And let thine anger be appeased in the destruction of those wicked men whom thou hast already destroyed.

¹²O Lord! Wilt thou turn away thine anger, yea thy fierce anger, and cause that this famine may cease in this land?

¹³O Lord! Wilt thou hearken unto me and cause that it may be done, according to my words—and send forth rain upon the face of the earth, that she may bring forth her fruit, and her grain, in the season of grain?

¹⁴O Lord! Thou didst hearken unto my words when I said—let there be a famine, that the pestilence of the sword might cease. And I know that thou wilt, even at this time, hearken unto my words. For thou saidst that: "If this people repent, I will spare them."

¹⁵Yea, O Lord! And thou seest that they have repented because of the famine, and the pestilence, and destruction which has come unto them.

¹⁶And now, O Lord! Wilt thou turn away thine anger and try again—if they will serve thee?ᵃ And if so, O Lord, thou canst bless them according to thy word, which thou hast said.

¹⁷And it came to pass that in the seventy and sixth year, the Lord did turn away his anger from the people, and caused that rain should fall upon the earth, insomuch that it did bring forth her fruit in the season of her fruit.

And it came to pass that it did bring forth her grain in the season of her grain.

¹⁸And behold, the people did rejoice and glorify God. And the whole face of the land was filled with rejoicing. And they did no more seek to destroy Nephi, but they did esteem him as a great prophet and man of God—having great power and authority given unto him from God.

¹⁹And behold, Lehi (his brother) was not a whit behind him as to things pertaining to righteousness. ²⁰And thus, it did come to pass that the people of Nephi began to prosper again in the land, and began to build up their waste places, and began to multiply, and spread, even until they did cover the whole face of the land—both on the northward and on the southward, from the sea west to the sea east.

²¹And it came to pass that the seventy and sixth year did end in peace. And the seventy and seventh year began in peace, and the church did spread throughout the face of all the land. And the more part of the people, both the Nephites and the Lamanites, did belong to the church. And they did have exceeding great peace in the land. And thus ended the seventy and seventh year. ²²And also they had peace in the seventy and eighth year, save it were a few contentions concerning the points of doctrine which had been laid down by the prophets.

²³And in the seventy and ninth year there began to be much strife. But it came to pass that Nephi and Lehi (and many of their brethren), which knew concerning the true points of doctrine—having many revelations daily—therefore, they did preach unto the people, insomuch that they did put an end to their strife in that same year.

²⁴And it came to pass that in the eightieth year of the reign of the judges over the people of Nephi there were a certain number of the dissenters from the people of Nephi, which had some years before gone over unto the Lamanites (and took upon themselves the name of Lamanites), and also a certain number which were real descendants of the Lamanites—being stirred up to anger by them (or by those dissenters)—therefore, they commenced a war with their brethren. ²⁵And they did commit murder and plunder. And then they would retreat back into the mountains and into the wilderness and secret places—hiding themselves, that they could not be discovered—receiving daily an addition to their numbers, inasmuch as there were dissenters that went forth unto them. ²⁶And thus, in time, yea, even in the space of not many years—they became an exceeding great band of robbers. And they did search out all the secret plans of Gaddianton. And thus, they became robbers of Gaddianton. ²⁷Now behold, these robbers did make

---

a. The sense of this is not to make God's turning away His anger contingent upon them first serving Him, but rather for God to give them another chance to see if they would serve Him. Nephi has indicated that they have already repented, so he is now asking God to see if their repentance is sincere.

great havoc, yea, even great destruction—among the people of Nephi, and also among the people of the Lamanites.

²⁸And it came to pass that it was expedient that there should be a stop put to this work of destruction. Therefore, they sent an army of strong men into the wilderness and upon the mountains, to search out this band of robbers—and to destroy them.

²⁹But behold, it came to pass that in that same year they were driven back, even into their own lands. And thus ended the eightieth year of the reign of the judges over the people of Nephi.

³⁰And it came to pass in the commencement of the eighty and first year, they did go forth again against this band of robbers and did destroy many. And they were also visited with much destruction. ³¹And they were again obliged to return out of the wilderness and out of the mountains, unto their own lands—because of the exceeding greatness of the numbers of those robbers which infested the mountains and the wilderness.

³²And it came to pass that thus ended this year. And the robbers did still increase and wax strong, insomuch that they did defy the whole armies of the Nephites and also of the Lamanites. And they did cause great fear to come unto the people upon all the face of the land—³³yea, for they did visit many parts of the land, and did do great destruction unto them, yea, did kill many, and did carry away others captive into the wilderness, yea, and more especially their women and their children. ³⁴And now, this great evil (which come unto the people because of their iniquity) did stir them up again in remembrance of the Lord, their God.

³⁵And thus ended the eighty and first year of the reign of the judges.

³⁶And in the eighty and second year they began again to forget the Lord, their God.
And in the eighty and third year they began to wax strong in iniquity.
And in the eighty and fourth year they did not mend their ways.

³⁷And it came to pass in the eighty and fifth year, they did wax stronger and stronger in their pride, and in their wickedness. And thus, they were ripening again for destruction.

³⁸And thus ended the eighty and fifth year.

>[12] ¹And thus, we can behold how false, and also the unsteadiness, of the hearts of the children of men.
Yea, we can see that the Lord,
in his great infinite goodness,
doth bless and prosper those who put their trust in him.
²Yea, and we may see at the very time
when he doth prosper his people—
yea, in the increase of their fields their flocks and their herds,
and in gold,
and in silver,
and in all manner of precious things of every kind and art—
sparing their lives,
and delivering them out of the hands of their enemies—
softening the hearts of their enemies,
that they should not declare wars against them—

Chapter IV [Helaman 11–12]

yea, and in fine, doing all things for the welfare
    and happiness of his people—
yea—then is the time that they do harden their hearts
    and do forget the Lord, their God,
    and do trample under their feet the Holy One.
Yea, and this because of their ease
    and their exceeding great prosperity.
³And thus we see that except the Lord doth chasten his people
    with many afflictions,
yea, except he doth visit them with death,
    and with terror,
    and with famine,
    and with all manner of pestilences—
    they will not remember him.
⁴O, how foolish, and how vain,
    and how evil,
    and devilish—
    and how quick to do iniquity
    and how slow to do good—
    are the children of men!
Yea, how quick to hearken unto the words of the evil one
    and to set their hearts upon the vain things of the world!
⁵Yea, how quick to be lifted up in pride!
    Yea, how quick to boast,
    and do all manner of that which is iniquity—
and how slow are they to remember the Lord, their God,
    and to give ear unto his counsels!
    Yea, how slow to walk in wisdom's paths!
⁶Behold, they do not desire that the Lord, their God,
    who hath created them,
    should rule and reign over them.
Notwithstanding his great goodness,
    and his mercy, towards them.
They do set at naught his counsels,
    and they will not that he should be their guide.

⁷O! How great is the nothingness of the children of men!
    Yea, even they are less than the dust of the earth!
⁸For behold, the dust of the earth moveth hither and thither
    to the dividing asunder
    at the command of our great, and everlasting God.
⁹Yea behold, at his voice doth the hills and the mountains
    tremble, and quake!
¹⁰And by the power of his voice,
    they are broken up and become smooth, yea, even like unto a valley.

¹¹Yea, by the power of his voice
   doth the whole earth shake!
¹²Yea, by the power of his voice
   doth the foundations rock,
   even to the very center!
¹³Yea, and if he say saith unto the earth:
   "Move! "
   And it is moved.
¹⁴Yea, if he say unto the earth:
   "Thou shalt go back, that it lengthen out the day for many hours."
   And it is done.
(>¹⁵And thus, according to his word—the earth goeth back, and it appeareth unto man that the sun standeth still.[a] Yea, and behold—this is so, for sure it is the earth that moveth and not the sun.[b] <)
¹⁶And behold, also if he saith unto the waters of the great deep:
   "Be thou dried up!"
   And it is done.[c]
¹⁷Behold, if he saith unto this mountain:
   "Be thou raised up, and come over and fall upon that city, that it be buried up!"
   And behold, it is done.
¹⁸And behold, if a man hideth up a treasure in the earth, and the Lord shall say:
   "Let it be accursed because of the iniquity of him that hath had it up!"
   Behold, it shall be accursed.
¹⁹And if the Lord shall say:
   "Be thou accursed, that no man shall find thee from this time henceforth and forever!"
   And behold, no man geteth it henceforth and forever.
²⁰And behold! If the Lord shall say unto a man:
   "Because of thine iniquities, thou shalt be a cursed forever!"
   And it shall be done.
²¹And if the Lord shall say:
   "Because of thine iniquities, thou shalt be cut off from my presence!"[d]
   And he will cause that it shall be so.

²²And wo unto whom he shall say this. For it shall be unto him that will do iniquity—and he cannot be saved. Therefore, for this cause, that men might be saved—hath repentance been declared. ²³Therefore, blessed are they who will repent and hearken unto the voice of the Lord, their God. For these are they that shall be saved. ²⁴And may God grant (in his great fulness) that men might be

---

a. Possibly a reference to Joshua 10:12.
b. Mormon inserts his understanding of the reference to Joshua.
c. Possible reference to Isaiah 51:10: "Art thou not it which hath dried the sea, the waters of the great deep; that hath made the depths of the sea a way for the ransomed to pass over?"
d. The phrase "cut off from my presence" is found in Leviticus 22:3.

Chapter IV [Helaman 11–12]

brought unto repentance and good works, that they might be restored unto grace, for grace,[a] according to their works.

²⁵And I would that all men might be saved. But, we read that in that great and last day there are some which shall be cast out, yea, which shall be cast off from the presence of the Lord—²⁶yea, which shall be consigned to a state of endless misery—fulfilling the words which saith:

"They that have done good,
    shall have everlasting life.
And they that have done evil,
    shall have everlasting damnation."[b]

And thus it is. Amen.[c]<

---

a. The phrase "grace for grace" occurs in John 1:14.

b. Perhaps an allusion to John 5:29: "And shall come forth; they that have done good, unto the resurrection of life; and they that have done evil, unto the resurrection of damnation."

c. Mormon introduced the Gaddianton robbers as a danger to the people and their government. He showed that they were eliminated after the famine, but they arose again. At this point, Mormon inserts not only his moral of that story, but he expands the moralization into a more free-form lamentation based on what he has just written. The beginning of this insertion may have been planned, but the whole of it has the feel of an extemporaneous creation. The beginning of the next chapter returns to the count of years and the wickedness of the Nephites that begin this aside.

Chapter V [Helaman 13–16]

[13] *The prophecy of Samuel the Lamanite to the Nephites.*

¹And now it came to pass in the eighty and sixth year, the Nephites did still remain in wickedness, yea, in great wickedness—while the Lamanites did observe strictly to keep the commandments of God, according to the law of Moses.

²And it came to pass that in this year there was one Samuel, a Lamanite, came into the land of Zarahemla and began to preach unto the people.

And it came to pass that he did preach, many day[a], repentance unto the people. And they did cast him out. And he was about to return to his own land, ³but behold, the voice of the Lord came unto him, that he should return again and prophesy unto the people whatsoever things should come into his heart.

⁴And it came to pass that they would not suffer that he should enter into the city. Therefore, he went and got up on the wall thereof and stretched forth his hand, and cried with a loud voice—and prophesied unto the people whatsoever things the Lord put into his heart. ⁵And he said unto them:

> Behold! I, Samuel, a Lamanite, do speak the words of the Lord which he doth put into my heart! And behold, he hath put it into my heart to say unto this people that the sword of justice hangeth over this people! And four hundred years passeth not away, save the sword of justice falleth upon this people. ⁶Yea, heavy destruction awaiteth this people. And it surely cometh unto this people. And nothing can save this people, save it be repentance and faith on the Lord Jesus Christ, which surely shall come into the world—and shall suffer many things and shall be slain for his people.
>
> ⁷And behold, an angel of the Lord hath declared it unto me. [And he did bring glad tidings to my soul.[b]] And behold, I was sent unto you to declare it unto you also, that ye might have glad tidings. But behold, ye would not receive me. ⁸Therefore, thus saith the Lord:
>
> Because of the hardness of the hearts of the people of the Nephites (except they repent) I will take away my word from them. And I will withdraw my spirit from them. And I will suffer them no longer. And I will turn the hearts of their brethren against them. ⁹And four hundred years shall not pass away before I will cause that they shall be smitten.
>
> Yea, I will visit them with the sword, and with famine, and with pestilence. ¹⁰Yea, I will visit them in my fierce anger. And there shall be those of the fourth generation which shall live of your enemies[c] to behold your utter destruction. And

---

a. Changed to "many days" in the 1837 edition. Skousen, *Analysis of the Textual Variants,* 5:3076.

b. The Original Manuscript is not extant at this point, and the Printer's Manuscript is somewhat confusing. The scribe wrote "& he did bring glad-tidings to my soul." The hyphen in "glad-tidings" represents that the word appears on two lines. "Glad" is at the end of the line, and "tidings" is the first word of the next line. The confusion is that "& he did bring glad" is crossed out, but "tidings to my soul" is not. The compositor resolved this by removing the entire phrase. Royal Skousen includes the phrase in his *The Book of Mormon: The Earliest Text* (New Haven, CT: Yale Univesity Press, 2009), 550. The repetition of "glad tidings" at the end of the next sentence implies that it should be the fulfillment of the promise at the beginning, confirming that this phrase is intended.

c. The phrase "live of your enemies" is awkward but clearly attested. The intent appears to be "[survive] of your enemies."

Chapter V [Helaman 13–16]

this shall surely come, except ye repent (saith the Lord). And those of the fourth generation shall visit your destruction. ¹¹But, if ye will repent and return unto the Lord, your God, I will turn away mine anger (saith the Lord).

Yea, thus saith the Lord: Blessed are they who will repent and turn unto me. But wo unto him that repenteth not.

¹²Yea, wo unto this great city of Zarahemla! For behold, it is because of they which are righteous that it is saved.

Yea, wo unto this great city! For I perceive, saith the Lord, that there are many, yea, even the more part of this great city, that will harden their hearts against me, saith the Lord.

¹³But blessed are they who will repent, for them will I spare. But behold, if it were not for the righteous which are in this great city—behold, I would cause that fire should come down out of heaven and destroy it. ¹⁴But behold, it is for the righteous' sake that it is spared. But behold, the time cometh (saith the Lord) that when ye shall cast out the righteous from among you—then shall ye be ripe for destruction!

Yea, wo be unto this great city because of the wickedness and abominations which is in her.

¹⁵Yea, and wo be unto this, the city of Gideon. For the wickedness and abominations which is in her.

¹⁶Yea, and wo be unto all the cities which are in the land round about (which is possessed by the Nephites) because of the wickedness and the abominations which is in them.

¹⁷And behold, a curse shall come upon the land, saith the Lord of Hosts, because of the people's sake (which is upon the land), yea, because of their wickedness and their abomination.

¹⁸And it shall come to pass (saith the Lord of Hosts, yea, our great and true God) that whoso shall hide up treasures in the earth shall find them again no more because of the great curse of the land (save it be a righteous man and shall hide it up unto the Lord, ¹⁹for I will, saith the Lord, that they shall hide up their treasures unto me).

And cursed be they who hideth not up their treasures unto me. For none hideth up their treasures unto me, save it be the righteous. And he that hideth not up his treasure unto me—cursed is he, and also the treasure. And none shall redeem it because of the curse of the land.

²⁰And the day shall come that they shall hide up their treasures because they have set their hearts upon riches. And because they have set their hearts upon their riches (and will hide up their treasures when they shall flee before their enemies)—because they will not hide them up unto me—cursed be they, and also their treasures. In that day shall they be smitten (saith the Lord).

²¹Behold ye (the people of this great city) and hearken unto my words! Yea, hearken unto the words which the Lord saith. For behold, he saith that ye are cursed because of your riches! And also are your riches cursed because ye have set your hearts upon them, and hath not hearkened unto the words of him who gave them unto you. ²²Ye do not remember the Lord, your God, in the things which he hath blessed you. But ye do always remember your riches—not to thank the Lord,

your God for them (yea, your heart is not drawn out unto the Lord), but they do swell with great pride unto boasting, and unto great swelling envyings, strifes, malice, persecutions, and murders, and all manner of iniquities. ²³For this cause hath the Lord God caused that a curse should come upon the land, and also upon your riches—and this, because of your iniquities.

²⁴Yea, wo unto this people because of this time which has arriven, that ye do cast out the prophets, and do mock them, and cast stones at them, and do slay them, and do all manner of iniquity unto them, even as they did of old time. ²⁵And now, when ye talk, ye say: If our days had been in the days of our fathers of old ye[a] would not have slain the prophets—ye would not have stoned them and cast them out.

²⁶Behold! Ye are worse than they. For, as the Lord liveth, if a prophet come among you and declareth unto you the word of the Lord, which testifieth of your sins, and iniquities—ye are angry with him, and cast him out, and seek all manner of ways to destroy him. Yea, you will say that he is a false prophet, and that he is a sinner, and of the devil—because he testifieth that your deeds are evil.

²⁷But behold, if a man shall come among you and shall say, do this—and there is no iniquity! Do that—and ye shall not suffer! Yea, he will say—walk after the pride of your own hearts, yea, walk after the pride of your eyes, and do whatsoever your heart desireth—and if a man shall come among you, and say this—ye will receive him and ye will say that he is a prophet—²⁸yea, ye will lift him up! And ye will give unto him of your substance. Ye will give unto him of your gold, and of your silver, and ye will clothe him with costly apparel. And, because he speaketh flattering words unto you and he saith that all is well—and then ye will not find no fault with him!

²⁹O ye wicked and ye perverse generation! Ye hardened and ye stiffnecked people! How long will ye suppose that the Lord will suffer you?

Yea, how long will ye suffer yourselves to be led by foolish and blind guides? Yea, how long will ye chose darkness rather than light? ³⁰Yea behold, the anger of the Lord is already kindled against you. Behold, he hath cursed the land because of your iniquity.

³¹And behold, the time cometh that he curseth your riches, that it becometh slippery and that ye cannot hold them. ³²And in the days of your poverty ye cannot retain them. And in the days of your poverty ye shall cry unto the Lord. And in vain shall ye cry. For your desolation is already come upon you. And your destruction is made sure. And then shall ye weep and howl! And in that day, saith the Lord of Hosts, and then shall ye lament, and say: ³³O, that I had repented, and had not killed the prophets, and stoned them, and cast them out![b]

Yea, in that day shall ye say: O, that we had remembered the Lord our God in the day that he gave us our riches! And then they would not have become slippery, that we should lose them. For behold, our riches are gone from us. ³⁴Behold, we layeth a tool here and on the morrow it is gone. And behold, our swords are taken from

---

a. This has been changed to "we" in the current edition. That fits better than "our fathers," but "ye" also makes sense with Samuel speaking to the Nephites.

b. Uses language from Matthew 23:37: "O Jerusalem, Jerusalem, *thou* that killest the prophets, and stonest them which are sent unto thee."

Chapter V [Helaman 13–16]

us in the day we have sought them for battle. ³⁵Yea, we have hid up our treasures and they have slipped away from us—because of the curse of the land. ³⁶O, that we had repented in the day that the word of the Lord came unto us! For behold, the land is cursed, and all things are become slippery, and we cannot hold them.

³⁷Behold, we are surrounded by demons. Yea, we are encircled about by the angels of him who hath sought to destroy our souls! Behold, our iniquities are great, O Lord! Canst thou not turn away thine anger from us?

And this shall be your language in them days. ³⁸But behold, your days of probation is passed. Ye have procrastinated the day of your salvation until it is everlastingly too late, and your destruction is made sure. Yea, for ye have sought, all the days of your lives, for that which ye could not obtain. And ye have sought for happiness in doing iniquity, which thing is contrary to the nature of that righteousness which is in our great and eternal head.

³⁹O ye people of the land! That ye would hear my words! And I pray that the anger of the Lord be turned away from you, and that ye would repent, and be saved.

[14] ¹And now it came to pass that Samuel, the Lamanite, did prophesy a great many more things which cannot be written. ²And behold, he saith unto them:

Behold, I give unto you a sign! For five years more cometh, and behold, then cometh the Son of God to redeem all those who shall believe on his name! ³And behold, this will I give unto you for a sign at the time of his coming. For behold, there shall be great lights in heaven, insomuch that in the night before he cometh there shall be no darkness, insomuch that it shall appear unto man as if it was day. ⁴Therefore, there shall be one day, and a night, and a day—as if it were one day and there were no night.

And this shall be unto you for a sign. For ye shall know of the rising of the sun and also of its sitting.ᵃ Therefore, they shall know of a surety that there shall be two days and a night. Nevertheless, the night shall not be darkened. And it shall be the night before he is born. ⁵And behold, there shall be a new star arise—such an one as ye never have beheld. And this also shall be a sign unto you. ⁶And behold, this is not all. There shall be many signs and wonders in heaven.

⁷And it shall come to pass that ye shall all be amazed, and wonder, insomuch that ye shall fall to the earth.

⁸And it shall come to pass that whosoever shall believe on the Son of God, the same shall have everlasting life.

⁹And behold, thus hath the Lord commanded, me by his angel, that I should come and tell this thing unto you. Yea, he hath commanded that I should prophesy these things unto you. Yea, he hath said unto me: Cry unto this people: Repent, and prepare the way of the Lord!ᵇ

¹⁰And now, because I am a Lamanite and hath spoken unto you the word

---

a. The Original Manuscript is not extant at this point, and Skousen notes that the compositor was using the Original rather than the Printer's Manuscript at this point for the typesetting. The compositor used "setting" rather than "sitting." It is possible that Oliver Cowdery changed "setting" to "sitting" inadvertently as the Printer's Manuscript often mixes sit/set. Skousen, *Analysis of the Textual Variants*, 5:3112.

b. The phrase "prepare the way of the Lord" echoes Isaiah 40:3: "The voice of him that crieth in the wilderness, Prepare ye the way of the Lord, make straight in the desert a highway for our God."

which the Lord hath commanded me—and because it was hard against you—ye are angry with me, and do seek to destroy me, and have cast me out from among you.

¹¹And ye shall hear my words! For, for this intent I have come up on the walls of this city—that ye might hear, and know of the judgments of God which doth await you because of your iniquities. ¹²And also that ye might know the conditions of repentance. And also that ye might know of the coming of Jesus Christ, the Son of God, the Father of Heaven and of Earth, the Creator of all things from the beginning. And that ye might know of the signs of his coming, to the intent that ye might believe on his name. ¹³And if ye believe on his name, ye will repent of all your sins, that thereby ye may have remission of them (through his merits).

¹⁴And behold again! Another sign I give unto you, yea, a sign of his death.

>¹⁵For behold, he surely must die that salvation may come. Yea, it behooveth him, and becometh expedient, that he dieth to bring to pass the resurrection of the dead, that thereby men may be brought into the presence of the Lord.

¹⁶Yea behold, this death bringeth to pass the resurrection and redeemeth all mankind from the first death, that spiritual death. For all mankind (by the fall of Adam being cut off from the presence of the Lord[a]) are considered as dead—both as to things temporal, and to things spiritual.

¹⁷But behold, the resurrection of Christ redeemeth mankind, yea, even all mankind—and bringeth them back into the presence of the Lord. ¹⁸Yea, and it bringeth to pass the conditions of repentance, that whosoever repenteth, the same is not hewn down and cast into the fire. But whosoever repenteth not is hewn down and cast into the fire. And there cometh upon them again a spiritual death, yea, a second death, for they are cut off again as to things pertaining to righteousness. ¹⁹Therefore, repent ye! Repent ye! Lest by knowing these things and not doing them, ye shall suffer yourselves to come under condemnation and ye are brought down unto this second death.[b]<

²⁰But behold, as I said unto you concerning another sign—a sign of his death—behold, in the day that he shall suffer death the sun shall be darkened and refuse to give his light unto you, and also the moon and the stars. And there shall be no light upon the face of the land, even from the time that he shall suffer death (for the space of three days) to the time that he shall rise again from the dead.

²¹Yea, at the time that he shall yield up the ghost there shall be thunderings and lightnings[c] for the space of many hours. And the earth shall shake, and tremble. And the rocks (which is upon the face of the earth, which is both above the earth and beneath), which ye know at this time is solid (or the more part of it is one solid mass), shall be broken up. ²²Yea, they shall be rent in twain and shall ever after be found in seams and in cracks, and in broken fragments upon the face of the whole earth, yea, both above the earth and both beneath.

---

a. The phrase "cut off from my presence" is found in Leviticus 22:3.

b. This appears to be a spontaneous aside generated by the desire to explain. Verse 20 has "as I said," which serves to return to the intended discussion of the sign.

c. Uses language from Revelation 8:5: "And there were voices, and thunderings, and lightnings, and an earthquake."

Chapter V [Helaman 13–16]

²³And behold, there shall be great tempests, and there shall be many mountains laid low—like unto a valley. And there shall be many places which are now called valleys which shall become mountains, whose height thereof is great. ²⁴And many highways shall be broken up. And many cities shall become desolate. ²⁵And many graves shall be opened and shall yield up many of their dead. And many saints shall appear unto many.^a

²⁶And behold, thus hath the angel spoken unto me. For he said unto me that there should be thunderings and lightnings for the space of many hours. ²⁷And he said unto me that whilst the thunder and the lightning lasted, and the tempest, that these things should be. And that darkness should cover the face of the whole earth for the space of three days.

²⁸And the angel said unto me that many shall see greater things than these, to the intent that they might believe that these signs and these wonders should come to pass upon all the face of this land, to the intent that there should be no cause for unbelief among the children of men. ²⁹And this to the intent that whosoever will believe might be saved. And that whosoever will not believe, a righteous judgment might come upon them. And also, if they are condemned—they bring upon themselves their own condemnation.

³⁰And now, remember! Remember, my brethren, that whosoever perisheth, perisheth unto himself!

And whosever doeth iniquity, doeth it unto himself!

For behold, ye are free. Ye are permitted to act for yourselves.

For behold, God hath given unto you a knowledge, and he hath made you free. ³¹He hath given unto you that ye might know good from evil. And he hath given unto you that ye might chose life, or death.

And ye can do good, and be restored unto that which is good (or have that which is good restored unto you)—or ye can do evil (and have that which is evil restored unto you).

[15] ¹And now my beloved brethren, behold, I declare unto you that except ye shall repent, your houses shall be left unto you desolate.^b ²Yea, except ye repent, your women shall have great cause to mourn in the day that they shall give suck.^c For ye shall attempt to flee, and there shall be no place for refuge. ³Yea, and wo unto them which are with child. For they shall be heavy, and cannot flee. Therefore, they shall be trodden down and shall be left to perish.

Yea, wo unto this people, which are called the people of Nephi—except they shall repent when they shall see all those signs and wonders which shall be showed unto them! For behold, they have been a chosen people of the Lord. Yea, the people of Nephi hath he loved and also hath he chastened them, yea, in the days of their iniquities he hath he chastened them, because he loveth them.^d

⁴But behold, my brethren, the Lamanites hath he hated because their deeds

---

a. See Matthew 27:52–53: "And the graves were opened; and many bodies of the saints which slept arose, And came out of the graves after his resurrection."

b. See Isaiah 5:9: "Of a truth many houses shall be desolate." The phrase "your house is left unto you desolate" occurs in Matthew 23:38.

c. See Matthew 24:19: "And woe unto them that are with child, and to them that give suck in those days!"

d. Proverbs 13:24: "he that loveth him chasteneth him betimes."

have been evil continually, and this because of the iniquity of the tradition of their fathers. But behold, salvation hath come unto them through the preaching of the Nephites! And for this intent hath the Lord prolonged their days. ⁵And I would that ye should behold that the more part of them are in the path of their duty, and they do walk circumspectly before God. And they do observe to keep his commandments, and his statutes, and his judgments, according to the law of Moses.

⁶Yea, I say unto you that the more part of them are doing this. And they are striving with unwearied diligence, that they may bring the remainder of their brethren to the knowledge of the truth. Therefore, there are many which do add to their numbers daily. ⁷And behold, ye do know of yourselves (for ye have witnessed it), that as many of them as are brought to the knowledge of the truth, and to know of the wicked and abominable traditions of their fathers. and are led to believe the Holy Scriptures—yea, the prophecies of the holy prophets (which are written), which leadeth them to faith on the Lord—and unto repentance, which faith and repentance bringeth a change of heart unto them. ⁸Therefore, as many as have come to this (ye know of yourselves) are firm and steadfast in the faith and in the things wherewith they have been made free. ⁹And ye know also that they have buried their weapons of war. And they fear to take them up, lest by any means they shall sin. Yea, ye can see that they fear to sin. For behold, they will suffer themselves, that they be trodden down, and slain by their enemies, and will not lift their swords against them. And this, because of their faith in Christ.

¹⁰And now, because of their steadfastness, when they do believe in that thing (which they do believe)—for because of their firmness, when they are once enlightened—behold, the Lord shall bless them, and prolong their days, notwithstanding their iniquity.ᵃ ¹¹Yea, even if they should dwindle in unbelief, the Lord shall prolong their days until the time shall come which hath been spoken of by our fathers—and also by the prophet Zenos, and many other prophets, concerning the restoration of our brethren, the Lamanites, again to the knowledge of the truth.

¹²Yea, I say unto you that in the latter times the promises of the Lord hath been extended to our brethren, the Lamanites. And, notwithstanding the many afflictions which they shall have, and notwithstanding they shall be driven to and fro upon the face of the earth, and be hunted, and shall be smitten, and scattered abroad—having no place for refuge—the Lord shall be merciful unto them.ᵇ ¹³And this is according to the prophecy—that they shall again be brought to the true knowledge, which is the knowledge of their Redeemer, and their great and their true shepherd, and be numbered among his sheep. ¹⁴Therefore, I say unto you:

---

a. An awkward sentence. The "when they do believe" is not really resolved.

b. It cannot be known if this is intentional, but Samuel appears to parallel the Lamanite future to the future Jews as Jacob described them:

> And after they have hardened their hearts and stiffened their necks against the Holy One of Israel, behold, the judgments of the Holy One of Israel shall come upon them. And the day cometh that they shall be smitten and afflicted.
>
> Wherefore, after they are driven to and fro, for thus saith the angel, many shall be afflicted in the flesh, and shall not be suffered to perish, because of the prayers of the faithful; they shall be scattered, and smitten, and hated; nevertheless, the Lord will be merciful unto them, that when they shall come to the knowledge of their Redeemer, they shall be gathered together again to the lands of their inheritance. (2 Ne. 6:10–11)

It shall be better for them than for you, except ye repent. ¹⁵For behold, had the mighty works been shown unto them which have been shown unto you, yea, unto them which have dwindled in unbelief because of the traditions of their fathers—ye can see of yourselves that they never would again have dwindled in unbelief. ¹⁶Therefore, saith the Lord: "I will not utterly destroy them. But I will cause that in the days of my wisdom—they shall return again unto me," saith the Lord.ᵃ

¹⁷And now behold, saith the Lord concerning the people of the Nephites: "If they will not repent and observe to do my will—I will utterly destroy them" (saith the Lordᵇ) "because of their unbelief, notwithstanding the many mighty works which I have done among them. And as surely as the Lord liveth, shall these things be" (saith the Lord).

[16] ¹And now it came to pass that there were many which heard the words of Samuel, the Lamanite, which he spake upon the walls of the city. And as many as believed on his words went forth and sought for Nephi. And when they came forth and found him, they confessed unto him their sins, and denied not—desiring that they might be baptized unto the Lord. ²But as many as there were which did not believe in the words of Samuel were angry with him, and they cast stones at him upon the wall and also many shot arrows at him as he stood upon the wall. But the spirit of the Lord was with him, insomuch that they could not hit him with their stones, neither with their arrows.

³Now, when they saw that they could not hit him, there were many more which did believe on his words, insomuch that they went away unto Nephi to be baptized. ⁴For behold, Nephi was baptizing and a-prophesying, and preaching—crying repentance unto the people, showing signs and wonders, working miracles among the people, that they might know that the Christ must shortly come—⁵telling them of things which must shortly come, that they might know, and remember (at the time of their coming) that they had been made known unto them beforehand, to the intent that they might believe. Therefore, as many as believed on the words of Samuel went forth unto him to be baptized. For they came repenting and confessing their sins. ⁶But the more part of them did not believe in the words of Samuel. Therefore, when they saw that they could not hit him with their stones, and their arrows—they cried out unto their captains, saying: "Take this fellow, and bind him. For behold, he hath a devil. And because of the power of the devil which is in him, we cannot hit him with our stones and our arrows. Therefore, take him and bind him—and away with him."

⁷And as they went forth to lay their hands on him, behold, he did cast himself down from the wall and did flee out of their [landsᶜ], yea, even unto his own country—and began to preach and to prophesy among his own people. ⁸And behold, he was never heard of more among the Nephites. And thus were the affairs of the people.

⁹And thus ended the eighty and sixth year of the reign of the judges over the people of Nephi. ¹⁰And thus ended also the eighty and seventh year of the reign of the judges.

---

a. There is no function for the repeated "saith the Lord." This appears to be another case where the memory that it was stated at the beginning faded and was thus repeated. It is a sufficiently common phrase that it might have been added almost unthinkingly.

b. The repetition of the bracketing "saith the Lord" phrases may suggest that there is something else at play.

c. Restored per the Original Manuscript. The Printer's Manuscript has "hands," which Oliver Cowdery misread from "lands" as he copied onto the latter. See Skousen, *Analysis of the Textual Variants*, 5:3158–59.

And the more part of the people remaining in their pride, and wickedness.

And the lesser part walking more circumspectly before God.[a]

¹¹And thus were the conditions also in the eighty and eighth year of the reign of the judges. ¹²And there were but little alteration in the affairs of the people, save it were the people began to be more hardened in iniquity, and do more and more of that which was contrary to the commandments of God in the eighty and ninth year of the reign of the judges.

¹³But behold, it came to pass in the ninetieth year of the reign of the judges, there were great signs given unto the people, and wonders, and the words of the prophets began to be fulfilled. ¹⁴And angels did appear unto men—wise men—and did declare unto them glad tidings of great joy.[b] And thus, in this year the scriptures began to be fulfilled. ¹⁵Nevertheless, the people began to harden their hearts (all save it were the most believing part of them—both of the Nephites, and also of the Lamanites) and began to depend upon their own strength, and upon their own wisdom, saying: ¹⁶"Some things they may have guessed right, among so many. But behold, we know that all these great and marvelous works cannot come to pass which hath been spoken."

¹⁷And they began to reason and to contend among themselves—saying ¹⁸that:

> It is not reasonable that such a being as a Christ shall come. If so, and he be the Son of God, the Father of Heaven and of Earth (as it hath been spoken)—why will he not show himself unto us as well as unto they which shall be unto Jerusalem? ¹⁹Yea, why will he not show himself in this land, as well as in the land of Jerusalem? ²⁰But behold, we know that this is a wicked tradition which has been handed down unto us by our fathers, to cause us that we should believe in some great and marvelous thing which should come to pass. But not among us. But in a land which is far distant. A land which we know not. Therefore, they can keep us in ignorance. For we cannot witness with our own eyes that they are true. ²¹And they will, by the cunning and the mysterious arts of the evil one, work some great mystery which we cannot understand, which will keep us down, to be servants to their words and also servants unto them. For we depend upon them to teach us the word. And thus will they keep us in ignorance (if we will yield ourselves unto them) all the days of our lives.

²²And many more things did the people imagine up in their hearts, which were foolish, and vain. And they were much disturbed. For Satan did stir them up to do iniquity continually. Yea, he did go about spreading rumors and contentions upon all the face of the land that he might harden the hearts of the people against that which was good, and against that which should come. ²³And, notwithstanding the signs and the wonders which was wrought among the people of the Lord, and the many miracles which they did—Satan did get great hold upon the hearts of the people, upon all the face of the land. ²⁵And thus ended the ninetieth year of the reign of the judges over the people of Nephi.

²⁵And thus ended the book of Helaman, according to the record of Helaman and his sons.

---

a. Verses 9–12 would form a paragraph. These two sentences are pulled out to emphasize the nice reversed parallelism.

b. See Luke 2:10: 'Fear not: for, behold, I bring you good tidings of great joy."

The Book of Nephi, the Son of Nephi

Which was the son of Helaman. And Helaman was the son of Helaman, which was the son of Alma, which was the son of Alma—being a descendant of Nephi, which was the son of Lehi, which came out of Jerusalem in the first year of the reign of Zedekiah the King of Judah.[a]

Chapter I [3 Nephi 1–2]

[1] ¹Now it came to pass that the ninety and first year had passed away. And it was six hundred years from the time that Lehi left Jerusalem. And it was in the year that Lachoneus was the Chief Judge and the Governor over the land. ²[And[b]] Nephi, the son of Helaman, had departed out of the land of Zarahemla, giving charge unto his son, Nephi (which was his eldest son) concerning the plates of brass, and all the records which had been kept—and all those things which had been kept sacred from the departure of Lehi out of Jerusalem. ³Then he departed out of the land. And whither he went, no man knoweth. And his son, Nephi, did keep the record in his stead, yea, the record of this people.

⁴And it came to pass that in the commencement of the ninety and second year, behold the prophecies of the prophets began to be fulfilled more fully. For there began to be greater signs and greater miracles wrought among the people. ⁵But there were some which began to say that the time was past for the words to be fulfilled which was spoken by Samuel, the Lamanite. ⁶And they began to rejoice over their brethren, saying: "Behold, the time is past! And the words of Samuel are not fulfilled. Therefore, your joy, and your faith concerning this thing hath been vain."

⁷And it came to pass that they did make a great uproar throughout the land. And the people which believed began to be very sorrowful, lest by any means those things which had been spoken might not come to pass. ⁸But behold, they did watch steadfastly for that day and that night and that day, which should be as one day, as if there were no night, that they might know that their faith had not been vain.

⁹Now it came to pass that there was a day set apart by the unbelievers, that all those

---

a. This is a unique book header. Mormon previously used such headers to indicate a particular book on the large plates that he was abridging; however, this does not do that. The book that would become knows as Third Nephi was not an abridgement of the large plates; rather, it was based on the record of Nephi, the son of Nephi. Thus, this header is instead similar to the type of chapter headers in the book of Alma that indicated when Mormon was sourcing Alma's private record rather than the large plates. (For example, see the chapter header to Alma XII (17–20).) While those headers still gave descriptions, this header instead cites *authority*. It is possible that the whole header was intended as the title. The first "son of" clause has been left in the title. The rest has been moved to a header more for convention than surety that it was intended as such.

b. The Printer's Manuscript had "land of Nephi." That would be incorrect, as Lachoneus was the governor over the land of Zarahemla, not Nephi. This was recognized, and the "of" crossed out and replaced with "and." There was also a cross out of another "and" to make the phrase read correctly, "and Nephi and the son."

who believed in those traditions should be put to death, except the sign should come to pass, which had been given by Samuel, the prophet.

¹⁰Now it came to pass that when Nephi, the son of Nephi, saw this wickedness of his people, his heart was exceeding sorrowful.

¹¹And it came to pass that he went out, and bowed himself down upon the earth, and cried mightily to his God in behalf of his people, yea, those which were about to be destroyed because of their faith in the tradition of their fathers.

¹²And it came to pass that he cried mightily unto the Lord all that day. And behold, the voice of the Lord came unto him, saying:

> ¹³Lift up your head and be of good cheer! For behold, the time is at hand. And on this night shall the sign be given. And on the morrow come I into the world, to show unto the world that I will fulfil all that I have caused to be spoken by the mouth of my holy prophets.[a]
>
> ¹⁴Behold! I come unto my own, to fulfil all things which I have made known unto the children of men—from the foundation of the world—and to do the will both of the Father, and of the Son (—of the Father because of me—and of the Son, because of my flesh).
>
> And behold, the time is at hand. And this night shall the sign be given!

¹⁵And it came to pass that the words which came unto Nephi was fulfilled according as they had been spoken. For he beheld at the going down of the sun there was no darkness. And the people began to be astonished because there was no darkness when the night came.

¹⁶And there were many (which had not believed the words of the prophets)—fell to the earth and became as if they were dead. For they knew that the great plan of destruction which they had laid for those who had believed in the words of the prophets had been frustrated. For the sign which had been given was already at hand. ¹⁷And they began to know that the Son of God must shortly appear. Yea, and in fine, all the people upon the face of the whole earth, from the west to the east, both in the land north and in the land south—were so exceedingly astonished, that they fell to the earth. ¹⁸For they knew that the prophets had testified of these things for many years, and that the sign which had been given was already at hand. And they began to fear because of their iniquity and their unbelief.

¹⁹And it came to pass that there was no darkness in all that night, but it was [as[b]] light as though it was midday.

And it came to pass that the sun did rise in the morning again, according to its proper order. And they knew that it was the day that the Lord should be born because of the sign which had been given.

²⁰And it had come to pass, yea, all things, every whit, according to the words of the prophets.

---

a. See Acts 3:21: "Whom the heaven must receive until the times of restitution of all things, which God hath spoken by the mouth of all his holy prophets since the world began."

b. The Printer's Manuscript had "a light" and "a" was crossed out to be replaced with "as," written above the line. This certainly makes sense. It might also have been read "a-light" and still made sense. There are other occasions where the Printer's Manuscript (and presumably the Original Manuscript) had the form "a-verb."

Chapter I [3 Nephi 1–2]

²¹And it came to pass also that a new star did appear, according to the word.

²²And it came to pass from this time forth, there began to be lyings sent forth among the people (by Satan) to harden their hearts, to the intent that they might not believe in those signs and wonders which they had seen. But, notwithstanding those lyings and deceivings, the more part of the people did believe and were converted unto the Lord.

²³And it came to pass that Nephi went forth among the people (and also many others) baptizing unto repentance—in the which there were a great remission of sins. And thus, the people began again to have peace in the land. ²⁴And there were no contentions, save it were a few that began to preach—endeavoring to prove by the scriptures that it was no more expedient to observe the law of Moses. Now in this thing they did err, having not understood the scriptures. ²⁵But it came to pass that they soon became converted and were convinced of the error which they were in. For it was made known unto them that the law was not yet fulfilled and that it must be fulfilled in every whit. Yea, the word came unto them that it must be fulfilled, yea, that one jot nor tittle should not pass away—till it should all be fulfilled.ᵃ Therefore, in this same year were they brought to a knowledge of their error and did confess their faults. ²⁶And thus the ninety and second year did pass away—bringing glad tidings unto the people because of the signs which did come to pass (according to the words of the prophecy of all the holy prophets).

²⁷And it came to pass that the ninety and third year did also pass away in peace, save it were for the Gaddianton robbers (which did dwell upon the mountains) which did infest the land. For so strong were their holds and their secret places that the people could not overpower them. Therefore, they did commit many murders and did do much slaughter among the people.

²⁸And it came to pass that in the ninety and fourth year they began to increase in a great degree, because there were many dissenters of the Nephites which did flee unto them, which did cause much sorrow unto those Nephites which did remain in the land. ²⁹And there were also a cause of much sorrow among the Lamanites. For behold, they had many children which did grow up and began to wax strong in years, that they became for themselves, and were led away by some which were Zoramites—by their lyings, and their flattering words, to join those Gaddianton robbers. ³⁰And thus were the Lamanites afflicted also and began to decrease as to their faith and righteousness—because of the wickedness of the rising generation.

[2] ¹And it came to pass that thus passed away the ninety and fifth year also. And the people began to forget those signs and wonders which they had heard—and began to be less and less astonished at a sign or a wonder from heaven, insomuch that they began to be hard in their hearts and blind in their minds—and began to disbelieve all which they had heard and seen—²imagining up some vain thing in their hearts, that it was wrought by men and by the power of the devil to lead away and deceive the hearts of the people. And thus did Satan get possession of the hearts of the people again, insomuch that he did blind their eyes, and lead them away to believe that the doctrine of Christ was a foolish and a vain thing.

³And it came to pass that the people began to wax strong in wickedness and abomi-

---

a. See Matthew 5:18: "Till heaven and earth pass, one jot or one tittle shall in no wise pass from the law, till all be fulfilled."

nations. And they did not believe that there should be any more signs or wonders given. And Satan did go about leading away the hearts of the people—tempting them, and causing them that they should do great wickedness in the land.

⁴And thus did pass away the ninety and sixth year.

And also the ninety and seventh year.

And also the ninety and eighth year.

And also the ninety and ninth year.

⁵And unto also an hundred years had passed away, since the days of Mosiah, which was king over the people of the Nephites.

⁶And six hundred and nine years had passed away since Lehi left Jerusalem.

⁷And nine years had passed away from the time which the sign was given (which was spoken of by the prophets) that Christ should come into the world. ⁸Now, the Nephites began to reckon their time from this period which the sign was given, or from the coming of Christ. Therefore, nine years had passed away.ᵃ

⁹And Nephi, which was the father of Nephi (which had the charge of the records) did not return to the land of Zarahemla and could nowhere be found in all the land. ¹⁰And it came to pass that the people did still remain in wickedness—notwithstanding the much preaching and prophesying which was sent among them.

And thus passed away the tenth year also.

And the eleventh year also passed away in iniquity.

¹¹And it came to pass in the thirteenth year there began to be wars and contentions throughout all the land. And the Gaddianton robbers had become so numerous, and did slay so many of the people, and did lay waste so many cities, and did spread so much death and carnage throughout the land, that it became expedient that all the people, both the Nephites and the Lamanites, should take up arms against them. ¹²Therefore, all the Lamanites which had become converted unto the Lord did unite with their brethren, the Nephites—and were compelled (for the safety of their lives, and their women, and their children) to take up arms against those Gaddianton robbers. Yea, and also to maintain their rights and their privileges of their church, and of their worship, and their freedom, and their liberty.

¹³And it came to pass that before this thirteenth year had passed away, the Nephites were threatened with utter destruction because of this war, which had become exceeding sore.

¹⁴And it came to pass that those Lamanites which had united with the Nephites were numbered among the Nephites. ¹⁵And their curse was taken from them. And their skin became white, like unto the Nephites. ¹⁶And their young men and their daughters became exceeding fair. And they were numbered among the Nephites and were called Nephites. And thus ended the thirteenth year.

¹⁷And it came to pass in the commencement of the fourteenth year, the war between the robbers and the people of Nephi did continue, and did become exceeding

---

a. These lines have been separated to highlight the repetition of the years in which little occurs. Mormon forces his readers to pay attention to the accumulation of the years. The first to make certain that they understood that the signs had appeared 600 years after Lehi left Jerusalem, as prophesied. Also, he counts to 100 years of the reign of the judges. This makes 609 years in the older count, but after arriving at a full 100 years of the reign of the judges, they back date a beginning of a new count from the time of the signs nine years previously.

sore. Nevertheless, the people of Nephi did gain some advantage of the robbers, insomuch that they did drive them back out of their lands—into the mountains and into their secret places. ¹⁸And thus ended the fourteenth year.

And in the fifteenth year, they did come forth again against the people of Nephi. And because of the wickedness of the people of Nephi, and their many contentions, and dissensions, the Gaddianton robbers did gain many advantages over them. ¹⁹And thus ended the fifteenth year. And thus were the people in a state of many afflictions. And the sword of destruction did hang over them, insomuch that they were about to be smitten down by it. And this, because of their iniquity.

Chapter II [3 Nephi 3–5]

[3] ¹And now it came to pass that in the sixteenth year from the coming of Christ, Lachoneas (the Governor of the land) received an epistle from the leader and the Governor of this band of robbers. And these are the words which were written, saying:

²Lachoneas. Most noble and Chief Governor of the land.

Behold, I write this epistle unto you, and do give unto you exceeding great praise because of your firmness, and also the firmness of your people, in maintaining that which ye suppose to be your right and liberty.

Yea, ye do stand well—as if ye were supported by the hand of God in the defense of your liberty, and your property, and your country—or that which ye do call so. ³And it seemeth a pity unto me, most noble Lachoneas, that ye should be so foolish and vain as to suppose that ye can stand against so many brave men which are at my command, which do now (at this time) stand in their arms—and do await with great anxiety for the word: "Go down upon the Nephites and destroy them."

⁴And I, knowing of their unconquerable spirit—having proved them in the field of battle, and knowing of their everlasting hatred towards you (because of their many wrongs which ye have done unto them)—therefore, if they should come down against you they would visit you with utter destruction. ⁵Therefore, I have wrote this epistle, sealing it with mine own hand—feeling for your welfare because of your firmness in that which ye believe to be right, and your noble spirit in the field of battle. ⁶Therefore, I write unto you—desiring that ye would yield up unto this, my people—your cities, your lands, and your possessions—rather than that they should visit you with the sword and that destruction should come upon you (⁷or, in other words)—yield yourselves up unto us and unite with us and become acquainted with our secret works. And become our brethren, that ye may be like unto us—not our slaves but our brethren, and partners of all our substance.

⁸And behold, I swear unto you—if ye will do this, with an oath, ye shall not be destroyed. But, if ye will not do this, I swear unto you, with an oath, that on the morrow month, I will command that my armies shall come down against you. And they shall not stay their hand, and shall spare not—but shall slay you, and shall let fall the sword upon you, yea, even until ye shall become extinct!

⁹And behold. I am Giddianhi and am the Governor of this, the secret society of Gaddianton—and which society and the works thereof I know to be good. And they are of ancient date. And they have been handed down unto us.

¹⁰And I write this epistle unto you, Lachoneus. And I hope that ye will deliver up your lands and your possessions without the shedding of blood, that this, my people, may recover their rights and government which have dissented away from you—because of your wickedness in retaining from them their rights of government. And except ye do this, I will avenge their wrongs.

I am Giddianhi.

¹¹And now it came to pass when Lachoneus received this epistle, he was exceedingly astonished because of the boldness of Giddianhi in demanding the possession of the land of the Nephites—and also of threatening the people, and avenging the wrongs

of those that had received no wrong, save it were they had wronged themselves by dissenting away unto those wicked and abominable robbers.

¹²And now behold, this Lachoneus (the Governor) was a just man and could not be frightened by the demands and the threatenings of a robber. Therefore, he did not hearken to the epistle of Giddianhi, the Governor of the robbers. But he did cause that his people should cry unto the Lord for strength against the time that the robbers should come down against them.

¹³Yea, he sent a proclamation among all the people that they should gather together their women and their children—their flocks and their herds, and all their substance (save it were their land) unto one place. ¹⁴And he caused that fortifications should be built round about them, and the strength thereof should be exceeding great. And he caused that there should be armies both of the Nephites and of the Lamanites (or of all them which were numbered among the Nephites)—should be placed as guards round about to watch them, and to guard them from the robbers day and night.

¹⁵Yea, he said unto them—as the Lord liveth, except ye repent of all your iniquities and cry unto the Lord, that they could in no wise be delivered out of the hands of those Gaddianton robbers. ¹⁶And so great and marvelous were the word and prophecies of Lachoneus that they did cause fear to come upon all the people. And they did exert themselves, in their might, to do according to the words of Lachoneus.

¹⁷And it came to pass that Lachoneus did appoint chief captains over all the armies of the Nephites to command them at the time that the robbers should come down out of the wilderness against them. ¹⁸Now, the chiefest among all the chief captains, and the great commander of all the armies of the Nephites was appointed. And his name was Gidgiddoni.

¹⁹Now, it was the custom among all the Nephites to appoint for their chief captains (save it were in their times of wickedness) someone that had the spirit of revelation and also of prophecy. Therefore, this Gidgiddoni was a great prophet among them. And also was the Chief Judge.

²⁰Now, the people said unto Gidgiddoni: "Pray unto the Lord! And let us go up upon the mountains and into the wilderness, that we may fall upon the robbers and destroy them in their own lands!"

²¹But Gidgiddoni saith unto them: "The Lord forbid. For if we should go up against them, the Lord would deliver us into their hands. Therefore, we will prepare ourselves in the center of our lands. And we will gather all our armies together. And we will not go against them. But we will wait till they shall come against us. Therefore, as the Lord liveth—if we do this, he will deliver them into our hands."

²²And it came to pass in the seventeenth year, in the latter end of the year—the proclamation of Lachoneas had gone forth throughout all the face of the land. And they had taken their horses, and their chariots, and their cattle, and all their flocks, and their herds, and their grain, and all their substance—and did march forth by thousands, and by tens of thousands, until they had all gone forth to the place which had been appointed that they should gather themselves together to defend themselves against their enemies. ²³And the land which was appointed was the land of Zarahemla, and the land which was between the land of Zarahemla and the land Bountiful, yea, the line which was betwixt the land Bountiful and the land Desolation. ²⁴And there were a great many

thousand people (which were called Nephites), which did gather themselves together in this land.

Now, Lachoneus did cause that they should gather themselves together in the land southward, because of the great curse which was upon the land northward. ²⁵And they did fortify themselves against their enemies. And they did dwell in one land, and in one body. And they did fear the words which had been spoken by Lachoneus, insomuch that they did repent of all their sins. And they did put up their prayers unto the Lord, their God, that he would deliver them in the time that their enemies should come down against them to battle.

²⁶And they were exceeding sorrowful because of their enemies. And Gidgiddoni did cause that they should make weapons of war of every kind, that they should be strong with armor, and with shields, and with bucklers, after the manner of his instructions.

[4] ¹And it came to pass that in the latter end of the eighteenth year—those armies of robbers had prepared for battle and began to come down, and to sally forth from the hills, and out of the mountains and the wilderness, and their strongholds, and their secret places—and began to take possession of the lands, both which was in the land south, and which was in the land north, and began to take possession of all the lands which had been deserted by the Nephites—and the cities of which had been left desolate.

²But behold, there was no wild beasts nor game in those lands which had been deserted by the Nephites. And there were no game for the robbers, save it were in the wilderness. ³And the robbers could not exist, save it were in wilderness, for the want of food. For the Nephites had left their lands desolate, and had gathered their flocks, and their herds, and all their substance, and they were in one body. ⁴Therefore, there was no chance for the robbers to plunder, and to obtain food, save it were to come up in open battle against the Nephites.

And the Nephites, being in one body and having so great a number, and having reserved for themselves provisions, and horses, and cattle, and flocks of every kind, that they might subsist for the space of seven years—in the which time they did hope to destroy the robbers from off the face of the land. And thus the eighteenth year did pass away.

⁵And it came to pass in the nineteenth year, Giddianhi found that it was expedient that he should go up to battle against the Nephites. For there was no way that they could subsist, save it were to plunder, and rob, and murder. ⁶And they durst not spread themselves upon the face of the land insomuch that they could raise grain, lest the Nephites should come upon them, and slay them. Therefore, Giddianhi gave commandment unto his armies that in this year they should go up to battle against the Nephites.

⁷And it came to pass that they did come up to battle. And it was in the sixth month. And behold, great and terrible was the day that they did come up to battle. And they were girded about after the manner of robbers. And they had a lamb skin about their loins, and they were dyed in blood, and their heads were shorn, and they had headplates upon them. And great and terrible was the appearance of the armies of Giddianhi, because of their armor, and because of their being dyed in blood.

⁸And it came to pass that the armies of the Nephites, when they saw the appearance of the army of Giddianhi, had all fallen to the earth—and did lift their cries to the Lord, their God, that he would spare them, and deliver them out of the hands of their enemies.

⁹And it came to pass that when the armies of Giddianhi saw this, they began to

shout with a loud voice because of their joy, for they had supposed that the Nephites had fallen with fear because of the terror of their armies. ¹⁰But in this thing they were disappointed. For the Nephites did not fear them—but they did fear their God, and did supplicate him for protection. Therefore, when the armies of Giddianhi did rush upon them, they were prepared to meet them, yea, in the strength of the Lord they did receive them. ¹¹And the battle commenced in this the sixth month. And great and terrible was the battle thereof. Yea, great and terrible was the slaughter thereof, insomuch that there never was known so great a slaughter among all the people of Lehi, since he left Jerusalem. ¹²And notwithstanding the threatenings, and the oaths, which Giddianhi had made—behold, the Nephites did beat them, insomuch that they did fall back from before them.

¹³And it came to pass that Gidgiddoni commanded that his armies should pursue them as far as to the borders of the wilderness—and, that they should not spare any that should fall into their hands by the way. And thus they did pursue them and did slay them, to the borders of the wilderness, even until they had fulfilled the commandment of Gidgiddoni.

¹⁴And it came to pass that Giddianhi, who had stood and fought with boldness, was pursued as he fled. And being weary because of his much fighting, he was overtaken, and slain. And thus was the end of Giddianhi, the robber.

¹⁵And it came to pass that the armies of the Nephites did return again to their place of security.

And it came to pass that this nineteenth year did pass away. And the robbers did not come again to battle, neither did they come in the twentieth year. ¹⁶But in the twenty and first year, they did not come up to battle but they came up on all sides, to lay siege round about the people of Nephi. For they did suppose that if they should cut off the people of Nephi from their lands and should hem them in on every side—and if they should cut them off from all their outward privileges, that they could cause them to yield themselves, according to their wishes.

¹⁷Now, they had appointed unto themselves another leader, whose name was Zemnarihah. Therefore, it was Zemnarihah that did cause that this siege should take place. ¹⁸But behold, this was an advantage unto the Nephites, for it was impossible for the robbers to lay siege sufficiently long to have any affect upon the Nephites because of their much provision, which they had laid up in store—¹⁹and because of the scantiness of provisions among the robbers. For behold, they had nothing save it were meat for their subsistence, which meat they did obtain in the wilderness.

²⁰And it came to pass that the wild game became scarce in the wilderness, insomuch that the robbers were about to perish with hunger. ²¹And the Nephites were continually marching out by day and by night and falling upon their armies, and cutting them off by thousands and by tens of thousands. ²²And thus, it became the desire of the people of Zemnarihah to withdraw from their design because of the great destruction which come upon them by night and by day.

²³And it came to pass that Zemnarihah did give command unto his people that they should withdraw themselves from the siege, and to march into the farthermost parts of the land northward. ²⁴And now, Gidgiddoni, being aware of their design and knowing of their weakness because of the want of food and the great slaughter which had been made among them—therefore, he did send out his armies in the night time,

and did cut off the way of their retreat—and did place his armies in the way of their retreat. ²⁵And this did they do in the night time—and got on their march beyond the robbers, so that on the morrow when the robbers began their march, they were met by the armies of the Nephites, both in their front, and in their rear. ²⁶And the robbers which were on the south were also cut off in their places of retreat. And all these things were done by command of Gidgiddoni. ²⁷And there were many thousands which did yield themselves up prisoners unto the Nephites. And the remainder of them were slain.

²⁸And their leader Zemnarihah was taken and hanged upon a tree, yea, even upon the top thereof, until he was dead. And when they had [hanged[a]] him until he was dead they did fall the tree to the earth—and did cry with a loud voice, saying: ²⁹"May the Lord preserve his people in righteousness, and in holiness of heart!, that they may cause to be fell to the earth all who shall seek to slay them because of power and secret combinations, even as this man hath been fell to the earth!"

³⁰And they did rejoice, and cry again with one voice—saying: "May the God of Abraham, and the God of Isaac, and the God of Jacob, protect this people in righteousness—so long as they shall call on the name of their God for protection."

³¹And it came to pass that they did break forth, all as one, in singing—praising their God for the great thing which he had done for them, in preserving them from falling into the hands of their enemies.

³²Yea, they did cry: "Hosanna to the Most High God!" And they did cry: "Blessed be the name of the Lord God Almighty, the Most High God!" ³³And their hearts were swollen with joy—unto the gushing out of many tears because of the great goodness of God in delivering them out of the hands of their enemies. And they knew it was because of their repentance, and their humility, that they had been delivered from an everlasting destruction.

[5] ¹And now behold, there was not a living soul among all the people of the Nephites which did doubt (in the least thing) in the words of all the holy prophets which had been spoken. For they knew that it must needs be that they must be fulfilled. ²And they knew that it must be expedient that Christ had come because of the many signs which had been given, according to the words of the prophets. And because of the things which had come to pass already, they knew it must needs be that all things should come to pass according to that which had been spoken. ³Therefore, they did forsake all their sins, and their abominations, and their whoredoms, and did serve God with all diligence day and night.

⁴And now it came to pass that when they had taken all the robbers prisoners (insomuch that none did escape which were not slain), they did cast their prisoners into prison, and did cause the word of God to be preached unto them. And, as many as would repent of their sins, and enter into a covenant that they would murder no more—were set at liberty. ⁵But, as many as there were who did not enter into a covenant and who did still continue to have those secret murders in their hearts, yea, as many as were found breathing out threatenings against their brethren—were condemned and punished according to the law. ⁶And thus, they did put an end to all

---

a. The Printer's Manuscript originally had "handed," which clearly should have been "hanged.' Hyrum Smith made that correction superlinearly.

those wicked, and secret, and abominable, combinations—in the which there were so much wickedness and so many murders committed.

⁷And thus had the twenty and second year passed away.

And the twenty and third year also.

And the twenty and fourth.

And the twenty and fifth.

And thus had twenty and five years passed away.

⁸And there had been many things transpired, which (in the eyes of some) would be great and marvelous. Nevertheless, they could not all be written in this book, yea, this book cannot contain even a hundredth part of what was done among so many people in the space of twenty and five years.

>⁹But behold, there are records which do contain all the proceedings of this people. And a more short, but a true account, was given by Nephi. ¹⁰Therefore, I have made my record of these things according to the record of Nephi, which were engraven on the plates which were called the plates of Nephi.

¹¹And behold, I do make the record on plates which I have made with mine own hands. ¹²And behold, I am called Mormon—being called after the land of Mormon, the land in the which Alma did establish the church among this people, yea, the first church which was established among them after their transgression.

¹³Behold, I am a disciple of Jesus Christ, the Son of God. I have been called of him to declare his word among his people, that they might have everlasting life.

¹⁴And it hath become expedient that I (according to the will of God, that the prayer of those which have gone hence, which were the holy ones, should be fulfilled according to their faith)—should make a record of these things which have been done. ¹⁵Yea, a small record of that which hath taken place from the time that Lehi left Jerusalem, even down until the present time. ¹⁶Therefore, I do make my record from the accounts which hath been given by those which were before me, until the commencement of my day. ¹⁷And then do I make a record of the things which I have seen with mine own eyes.

¹⁸And I know the record which I make to be a just, and a true, record. Nevertheless, there are many things which, according to our language, we are not able to write. ¹⁹And now, I make an end of my saying, which is of myself—and proceed to give my account of the things which hath been before me.

²⁰I am Mormon, and a pure descendant of Lehi. I have reason to bless my God and my Savior, Jesus Christ, that he brought our fathers out of the land of Jerusalem (and no one knew it, save it were himself and those which he brought out of that land)—and that he hath given me and my people so much knowledge—unto the salvation of our souls. ²¹Surely he hath blessed the house of Jacob! And hath been merciful unto the seed of Joseph! ²²And inasmuch as the children of Lehi hath kept his commandments, he hath blessed them, and prospered them, according to his word.

²³Yea, and surely shall he again bring a remnant of the seed of Joseph to the knowledge of the Lord, their God! ²⁴And as surely as the Lord liveth will he gather in from the four quarters of the earth, all the remnant of the seed of Jacob, which are scattered abroad upon all the face of the earth. ²⁵And, as he hath covenanted

with all the house of Jacob, even so shall the covenant wherewith he hath covenanted with the house of Jacob be fulfilled in his own due time—unto the restoring all the house of Jacob unto the knowledge of the covenant that he hath covenanted with them. ²⁶And then shall they know their Redeemer, which is Jesus Christ, the Son of God. And then shall they be gathered in from the four quarters of the earth—unto their own lands from whence they have been dispersed.

Yea, as the Lord liveth—so shall it be. Amen.ᵃ<

---

a. Mormon inserts this information at a transition point. In most cases, the use of the year as specific demarcations for the text is a characteristic of the large plates of Nephi. Mormon declares that he is using a smaller record written by Nephi, the son of Nephi. As he mentions this, Mormon thinks on his relationship to his sources, and (much as did Nephi, the son of Lehi) he takes a tangent to explain himself as the editor/creator of this text.

Chapter III [3 Nephi 6–7]

[3] ¹And now it came to pass that the people of the Nephites did all return to their own lands in the twenty and sixth year—every man with his family, his flocks, and his herds, his horses, and his cattle, and all things whatsoever did belong unto them.

²And it came to pass that they had not eaten up all their provisions. Therefore, they did take with them all that they had not devoured of all their grain of every kind, and their gold, and their silver, and all their precious things, and they did return to their own lands, and their possessions—both on the north, and on the south—both on the land northward, and on the land southward.

³And they granted unto those robbers which had entered into a covenant to keep the peace of the land (which were desirous to remain Lamanites), lands according to their numbers, that they might have (with their labors) wherewith to subsist upon. And thus they did establish peace in all the land. ⁴And they began again to prosper and to wax great. And the twenty and sixth, and seventh, years passed away. And there was great order in the land. And they had formed their laws according to equity, and justice.

⁵And now, there was nothing in all the land to hinder the people from prospering continually, except they should fall into transgressions. ⁶And now, it was Gidgiddoni and the Judge Lachoneus, and those which had been appointed leaders, which had established this great peace in the land.

⁷And it came to pass that there were many cities built anew, and there were many old cities repaired. ⁸And there were many highways cast up, and many roads made which led from city to city, and from land to land, and from place to place. ⁹And thus passed away the twenty and eighth year. And the people had continual peace.

¹⁰But it came to pass in the twenty and ninth year, there began to be some disputings among the people. And some were lifted up unto pride and boastings because of their exceeding great riches, yea, even unto great persecutions. ¹¹For there were many merchants in the land, and also many lawyers, and many officers. ¹²And the people began to be distinguished by ranks, according to their riches, and their chance for learning.

Yea, some were ignorant because of their poverty, and others did receive great learning—because of their riches.

¹³Some were lifted up in pride, and others were exceeding humble.

Some did return railing for railing—while others would receive railing, and persecution, and all manner of afflictions, and would not turn, and revile again—but were humble, and penitent before God.

¹⁴And thus there became a great inequality in all the land, insomuch that the church began to be broken up—yea, insomuch that in the thirtieth year, the church was broken up in all the land, save it were among a few of the Lamanites which were converted unto the true faith. And they would not depart from it. For they were firm, and steadfast, and immoveable—willing with all diligence to keep the commands of the Lord.

¹⁵Now, the cause of this iniquity of the people was this—Satan had great power, unto the stirring up of the people to do all manner of iniquity and to the buffeting[a]

---

a. Although the Printer's Manuscript has "buffeting," Skousen suggests that it doesn't make much sense. The original is not extant. The 1830 edition uses the word "puffed," which is more common. Therefore, Skousen suggests that it should be "puffed." It is retained as in the Printer's Manuscript. See Skousen, *Analysis of the Textual Variants*, 5:3284–85.

them up with pride—tempting them to seek for power, and authority, and riches, and the vain things of the world. ¹⁶And thus Satan did lead away the hearts of the people to do all manner of iniquity. Therefore, they had not enjoyed peace but a few years.

¹⁷And thus in the commencement of the thirtieth year, the people having been delivered up for the space of a long time to be carried about by the temptations of the devil (whithersoever he desired to carry them) and to do whatsoever iniquity he desired they should. And thus, in the commencement of this, the thirtieth year—they were in a state of awful wickedness. ¹⁸Now, they did not sin ignorantly, for they knew the will of God concerning them. For it had been taught unto them. Therefore, they did willfully rebel against God.

¹⁹And now, it was in the days of Lachoneus, the son of Lachoneus (for Lachoneus did fill the seat of his father, and did govern the people that year)—²⁰and there began to be men inspired from heaven, and sent forth—standing among the people in all the land—preaching, and testifying boldly, of the sins, and iniquities, of the people, and testifying unto them concerning the redemptions which the Lord would make for his people (or in other words, the resurrection of Christ). And they did testify boldly of his death, and sufferings.

²¹Now, there were many of the people which were exceeding angry because of those which testified of these things. And those which were angry were chiefly the chief judges, and they which had been high priests, and lawyers, yea, all they which were lawyers were angry with those which testified of these things.

²²Now, there was no lawyer nor judge, nor high priest, that could have power to condemn any one to death, save their condemnation was signed by the Governor of the land. ²³Now, there were many of those which testified of the things pertaining to Christ, which testified boldly, which were taken and put to death secretly by the judges, that the knowledge of their death come not unto the Governor of the land until after their death.

²⁴Now behold, this was contrary to the laws of the land, that any man should be put to death except they had power from the Governor of the land. ²⁵Therefore, a complaint came up unto the land of Zarahemla to the Governor of the land against these judges which had condemned the prophets of the Lord unto death—not according to the law.

²⁶Now it came to pass that they were taken and brought up before the Judge to be judged of their crime which they had done, according to the law which had been given by the people.

²⁷Now it came to pass that those judges had many friends and kindreds. And the remainder, yea, even almost all the lawyers and the high priests—did gather themselves together and unite with the kindreds of those judges which were to be tried, according to the law. ²⁸And they did enter into a covenant, one with another, yea, even into that covenant which was given by them of old (which covenant was given, and administered by the devil), to combine against all righteousness. ²⁹Therefore, they did combine against the people of the Lord, and enter into a covenant to destroy them—and to deliver those which were guilty of murder from the grasp of justice (which was about to be administered, according to the law). ³⁰And they did set at defiance the law, and the rights of their country. And they did covenant, one with another, to destroy the Governor and to establish a king over the land, that the land should no more be at liberty, but should be subject unto kings.

Chapter III [3 Nephi 6–7]

[7] ¹Now behold, I will show unto you that they did not establish a king over the land. But, in this same year, yea, the thirtieth year—they did destroy upon the Judgment Seat—yea, did murder the Chief Judge of the land. ²And the people were divided one against another. And they did separate, one from another, into tribes—every man according to his family, and his kindred, and his friends. And thus, they did destroy the government of the land. ³And every tribe did appoint a chief, or a leader over them. And thus they became tribes and leaders of tribes. ⁴Now behold, there were no man among them, save he had much family, and many kindreds, and friends. Therefore, their tribes became exceeding great.

⁵Now, all this was done. And there was no wars, as yet, among them. And all this iniquity had come upon the people because they did yield themselves unto the power of Satan. ⁶And the regulations of the government was destroyed because of the secret combination of the friends, and the kindreds, of them which murdered the prophets. ⁷And they did cause a great contention in the land, insomuch that the more righteous part of the people (although they were nearly all become wicked), yea, there were but few righteous men among them.ª ⁸And thus, six years had not passed away since the more part of the people had turned from their righteousness—like the dog to his vomit, or like the sow to her wallowing in the mire.ᵇ

⁹Now, this secret combination, which had brought so great iniquity upon the people, did gather themselves together—and did place at their head a man whom they did call Jacob. ¹⁰And they did call him their king. Therefore, he became a king over this wicked band. And he was one of the chiefest which had given his voice against the prophets which testified of Jesus.

¹¹And it came to pass that they were not so strong in numbers as the tribes of the people which were united together—save it were their leaders did establish their laws, every one, according to his tribe. Nevertheless, they were enemies, notwithstanding they were not a righteous people. Yet, they were united in the hatred of those who had entered into a covenant to destroy the government. ¹²Therefore, Jacob, seeing that their enemies were more numerous than they—he, being the king of the band, therefore he commanded his people that they should take their flight into the northernmost part of the land, and there build up, unto themselves, a kingdom, until they were joined by dissenters. For he flattered them that there would be many dissenters. And they become sufficiently strong to contend with the tribes of the people. And they did so. ¹³And so speedy was their march that it could not be impeded until they had gone forth, out of the reach of the people. And thus ended the thirtieth year. And thus were the affairs of the people of Nephi.

¹⁴And it came to pass in the thirty and first year, that they were divided into tribes, every man according to his family, kindred, and friends. Nevertheless, they had come to an agreement that they would not go to war one with another. But they were not united as to their laws and their manner of government. For they were established according to the minds of them which was their chiefs and their leaders. But they did establish very strict laws, that one tribe should not trespass against another, insomuch

---

a. This sentence does not resolve the verb at the beginning. It shifts in the middle, and the following sentence continues the meaning that it became.

b. See 2 Peter 2:22: "But it is happened unto them according to the true proverb, The dog is turned to his own vomit again; and the sow that was washed to her wallowing in the mire."

that in some degree, they had peace in the land. Nevertheless, their hearts were turned from the Lord, their God. And they did stone the prophets and did cast them out from among them.

[15]And it came to pass that Nephi, having been visited by angels, and also the voice of the Lord—therefore, having seen angels, and being eye-witness, and having had power given unto him that he might know concerning the ministry of Christ—and also being eye-witness to their quick return from righteousness unto their wickedness and also abominations—[16]therefore, being grieved for the hardness of their hearts, and the blindness of their minds—went forth among them (in that same year) and began to testify boldly—repentance, and remission of sins through faith on the Lord, Jesus Christ. [17]And he did minister many things unto them. And all of them cannot be written. And a part of them would not suffice. Therefore, they are not written in this book. And Nephi did minister with power and with great authority.

[18]And it came to pass that they were angry with him, even because he had greater power than they. For it were not possible that they could disbelieve his words. For so great was his faith on the Lord, Jesus Christ, that angels did minister unto him daily. [19]And in the name of Jesus did he cast out devils, and unclean spirits. And even his brother did he raise from the dead after he had been stoned and suffered death by the people. [20]And the people saw it, and did witness of it, and were angry with him because of his power. And he did also do many more miracles in the sight of the people, in the name of Jesus.

[21]And it came to pass that the thirty and first year did pass away. And there were but few which were converted unto the Lord. But as many as were converted, did truly signify unto the people that they had been visited by the power and spirit of God, which was in Jesus Christ—in whom they believed. [22]And as many as had devils cast out from them, and were healed of their sicknesses and their infirmities, did truly manifest unto the people that they had been wrought upon by the spirit of God—and had been healed. And they did show forth signs also, and did do some miracles among the people.

[23]And it came to pass that thus passed away the thirty and second year also. And Nephi did cry unto the people in the commencement of the thirty and third year. And he did preach unto them repentance and remissions of sins.

[24]Now, I would have you remember also, that there were none which were brought unto repentance who were not baptized with water. [25]Therefore, there were ordained of Nephi, men, unto this ministry, that all such as should come unto them should be baptized with water. And this, as a witness and a testimony—before God, and unto the people, that they had repented and received a remission of their sins. [26]And there were many in the commencement of this year that were baptized unto repentance. And thus the more part of the year did pass away.

Chapter IV [3 Nephi 8–10]

[8] ¹And now it came to pass that according to our record—

>and we know our record to be true, for behold it was a just man which did keep the record. For he truly did many miracles in the name of Jesus. And there was not any man which could do a miracle in the name of Jesus, save he were cleansed, every whit, from his iniquity.ᵃ<

²And now it came to pass (if there was no mistake made by this man in the reckoning of our time), the thirty and third year had passed away. ³And the people began to look with great earnestness for the sign which had been given by the prophet Samuel, the Lamanite, yea, for the time that there should be darkness for the space of three days over the face of the land. ⁴And there began to be great doubtings and disputations among the people—notwithstanding so many signs had been given.

⁵And it came to pass that in the thirty and fourth year, in the first month, in the fourth day of the month, there arose a great storm—such an one as never had been known in all the land. ⁶And there was also a great and terrible tempest. And there was terrible thunder, insomuch that it did shake the whole earth as if it was about to divide asunder. ⁷And there was exceeding sharp lightnings—such as never had been known in all the land.

⁸And the city of Zarahemla did take fire.

⁹And the city of Moroni did sink into the depths of the sea, and the inhabitants thereof were drowned.

¹⁰And the earth was carried up upon the city of Moronihah, that in the place of the city thereof there became a great mountain.

¹¹And there were a great and terrible destruction in the land southward.

¹²But behold, there were a more great and terrible destruction in the land northward.

For behold, the whole face of the land was changed because of the tempests, and the whirlwinds, and the thunderings, and the lightnings, and the exceeding great quakingᵇ of the whole earth.ᶜ

¹³And the highways were broken up, and the level roads were spoiled, and many smooth places became rough.

¹⁴And many great and notable cities were sunk.

And many were burned.

And many were shook till the buildings thereof had fallen to the earth—and the inhabitants thereof were slain, and the places were left desolate.

¹⁵And there were some cities which remained, but the damage thereof was exceeding great.

And there were many in them which were slain.

---

a. This appears to be Mormon's aside about the truth of the record. He begins to speak of the record and starts over in verse 2. It is Mormon's testimony to the truthfulness of the record he will use for his information on the coming of Christ to the people in Bountiful.

b. Uses language from Revelation 8:5: "And there were voices, and thunderings, and lightnings, and an earthquake."

c. Verse 12a is the completement of verse 11. Verse 12b is a new thought. The destruction of the whole face of the land was not meant to describe only the land northward, as confirmed by verse 17 below.

¹⁶And there were some which were carried away in the whirlwind. And whither they went, no man knoweth, save they know that they were carried away.

¹⁷And the face of the whole earth became deformed because of the tempests, and the thunderings, and the lightnings, and the quaking of the earth.

¹⁸And behold, the rocks were rent in twain, yea, they were broken up upon the face of the whole earth, insomuch that they were found in broken fragments, and in seams, and in cracks, upon all the face of the land.

¹⁹And it came to pass that when the thunderings, and the lightnings, and the storm, and the tempest, and the quakings of the earth[a] did cease (>for behold, they did last for about the space of three hours—and it was said by some that the time was greater—nevertheless, all these great and terrible things were done in about the space of three hours[b]<),—and then behold, there was darkness upon the face of the land.

²⁰And it came to pass that there was thick darkness upon the face of all the land, insomuch that the inhabitants thereof (which had [not[c]] fallen) could feel the vapor of darkness. ²¹And there could be no light—because of the darkness. Neither candles, neither torches, neither could there be fire kindled with their fine and exceeding dry wood—so that there could not be any light at all. ²²And there was not any light seen—neither fire, nor glimmer, neither the sun, nor the moon, nor the stars. For so great were the mists of darkness which were upon the face of the land.

²³And it came to pass that it did last for the space of three days that there was no light seen. And there was great mourning, and howling, and weeping, among all the people continually. Yea, great were the mournings of the people because of the darkness and the great destruction which had come upon them.

²⁴And in one place they were heard to cry, saying: "O, that we had repented before this great and terrible day! And then would our brethren have been spared and they would not have been burned in that great city Zarahemla!"

²⁵And in another place, they were heard to cry and mourn, saying: "O, that we had repented before this great and terrible day, and had not killed and stoned the prophets, and cast them out! Then would our mothers, and our fair daughters, and our children, have been spared and not have been buried up in that great city Moronihah!"

And thus were the howling of the people great and terrible.

[9] ¹And it came to pass that there was a voice heard among all the inhabitants of the earth—upon all the face of this land—crying:

²Wo, wo, wo, unto this people.

Wo unto the inhabitants of the whole earth, except they shall repent. For the devil laugheth, and his angels rejoice because of the slain of the fair sons and daughters of my people. And it is because of their iniquity and their abominations that they are fallen.

³Behold, that great city Zarahemla have I burned with fire, and the inhabitants thereof.

---

a. Uses language from Revelation 8:5: "And there were voices, and thunderings, and lightnings, and an earthquake."

b. An interesting aside that suggests that there were different accounts in Mormon's source.

c. Added superlinearly by Hyrum Smith.

Chapter IV [3 Nephi 8–10]

⁴And behold, that great city Moroni have I caused to be sunk in the depths of the sea, and the inhabitants thereof to be drowned.

⁵And behold that great city Moronihah have I covered with earth, and the inhabitants thereof—to hide their iniquities, and their abominations, from before my face, that the blood of the prophets and of the saints shall not come up any more unto me against them.ª

⁶And behold, the city of Gilgal have I caused to be sunk, and the inhabitants thereof to be buried up in the depths of the earth.

⁷Yea, and the city of Onihah and the inhabitants thereof—and the city of Mocum and the inhabitants thereof—and the city of Jerusalem and the inhabitants thereof—and waters have I caused to come up in the stead thereof, to hide their wickedness and their abominations from before my face, that the blood of the prophets and the saints shall not come up any more unto me against them.ᵇ

⁸And behold, the city of Gadiandi and the city of Gadiomnah, and the city of Jacob, and the city of Gimgimno—all these have I caused to be sunk, and made hills and valleys in the places thereof. And the inhabitants thereof have I buried up in the depths of the earth, to hide their wickedness and abominations from before my face, that the blood of the prophets and the saints shall not come up any more unto me against them.ᶜ

⁹And behold, that great city Jacob-Ugathᵈ (which was inhabited by the people of the king ofᵉ Jacob) have I caused to be burned with fire because of their sins and their wickedness, which was above all the wickedness of the whole earth—because of their secret murders and combinations. For it was they that did destroy the peace of my people and the government of the land. Therefore, I did cause them to be burned, to destroy them from before my face, that the blood of the prophets and the saints should not come up to unto me any more against them.ᶠ

¹⁰And behold, the city of Laman, and the city of Josh, and the city of Gad, and the city of Kishcumen—have I caused to be burned with fire, and the inhabitants thereof—because of their wickedness in casting out the prophets, and stoning them, which I did send to declare unto them concerning their wickedness, and their abominations. ¹¹And because they did cast them all out, that there were none righteous among them—I did send down fire, and destroy them, that their wickedness, and abominations, might be hid from before my face, that the blood of the prophets, and the saints (which I sent among them)—might not cry unto

---

a. Uses language from Revelation 18:24: "And in her was found the blood of prophets, and of saints, and of all that were slain upon the earth."

b. Uses language from Revelation 18:24: "And in her was found the blood of prophets, and of saints, and of all that were slain upon the earth."

c. Uses language from Revelation 18:24: "And in her was found the blood of prophets, and of saints, and of all that were slain upon the earth."

d. Retained as it appears in the Printer's Manuscripts. It is typically rendered "Jacobugath."

e. The unnecessary "of" was removed in the 1920 edition. Skousen elected to remove it for his *The Book of Mormon: The Earliest Text* (New Haven, CT: Yale Univesity Press, 2009), 589.

f. Uses language from Revelation 18:24: "And in her was found the blood of prophets, and of saints, and of all that were slain upon the earth."

me from the ground against them.[a] [12]And many great destructions have I caused to come upon this land, and upon this people—because of their wickedness, and their abominations.

[13]O, all ye that are spared because ye were more righteous than they! Will ye not now return unto me, and repent of your sins and be converted, that I may heal you? [14]Yea, verily I say unto you: If ye will come unto me, ye shall have eternal life.

Behold, mine arm of mercy is extended towards you. And whosoever will come, him will I receive. And blessed are they which cometh unto me!

[15]Behold, I am Jesus Christ, the Son of God. I created the heavens and the earth, and all things that in them is.[b] I was with the Father from the beginning.[c] I am in the Father, and the Father in me.[d] And in me hath the Father glorified his name.[e] [16]I came unto my own, and my own received me not.[f] And the scriptures concerning my coming are fulfilled. [17]And as many as have received me, to them have I given to become the sons of God—and even so will I to as many as shall believe on my name.[g] For behold, by me redemption cometh. And in me is the law of Moses fulfilled. [18]I am the light, and the life of the world.[h] I am Alpha and Omega, the beginning and the end.[i]

[19]And ye shall offer up unto me no more the shedding of blood. Yea, your sacrifices, and your burnt offerings shall be done away. For I will [accept[j]] none of your sacrifices and your burnt offerings. [20]And ye shall offer for a sacrifice unto me a broken heart and a contrite spirit.[k] And whoso cometh unto me with a broken heart and a contrite spirit,[l] him will I baptize with fire and with the Holy Ghost, even as the Lamanites because of their faith in me at the time of their conversion were baptized with fire and with the Holy Ghost—and they knew it not.

[21]Behold, I have come unto the world to bring redemption unto the world, to save the world from sin. [22]Therefore, whoso repenteth and cometh unto me as a little child—him will I receive. For of such is the kingdom of God. Behold, for such I have laid down my life, and have taken it up again. Therefore, repent, and come unto me ye ends of the earth, and be saved!

[10] [1]And now behold, it came to pass that all the people of the land did hear these

---

a. Uses language from Revelation 18:24: "And in her was found the blood of prophets, and of saints, and of all that were slain upon the earth."

b. See John 1:3: "All things were made by him; and without him was not any thing made that was made."

c. John 1:2: "The same was in the beginning with God."

d. John 14:11: "Believe me that I am in the Father, and the Father in me."

e. Alludes to John 12:28: "Father, glorify thy name. Then came there a voice from heaven, saying, I have both glorified it, and will glorify it again."

f. See John 1:11: "He came unto his own, and his own received him not."

g. See John 1:12: "But as many as received him, to them gave he power to become the sons of God, even to them that believe on his name."

h. See John 8:12: "Then spake Jesus again unto them, saying, I am the light of the world."

i. See Revelation 22:13: "I am Alpha and Omega, the beginning and the end, the first and the last."

j. The Printer's Manuscript has "except," which was clearly intended to be its homophone, "accept."

k. See Psalm 34:18: "The Lord is nigh unto them that are of a broken heart; and saveth such as be of a contrite spirit."

l. See Psalm 34:18: "The Lord is nigh unto them that are of a broken heart; and saveth such as be of a contrite spirit."

sayings and did witness of it. And after these sayings, there was silence in the land for the space of many hours. ²For so great was the astonishment of the people that they did cease lamenting, and howling, for the loss of their kindreds (which had been slain). Therefore, there was silence in all the land for the space of many hours.

³And it came to pass that there came a voice again unto the people. And all the people did hear, and did witness of it, saying:

⁴O ye people of these great cities which have fallen, which are a descendant of Jacob, yea, which are of the house of Israel! O ye people of the house of Israel!

How oft have I gathered you as a hen gathereth her chickens under her wings, and have nourished you? ⁵And again, how oft would I have gathered you, as a hen gathereth her chickens under her wings?ª Yea, O ye people of the house of Israel which have fallen!

Yea, O ye people of the house of Israel, ye that dwell at Jerusalem as ye that have fallen! Yea, [howᵇ] oft would I have gathered you as a hen gathereth her chickens, and ye would not!ᶜ

⁶O ye house of Israel whom I have spared! How oft will I gather you as a hen gathereth her chickens under her wingsᵈ—if ye will repent and return unto me, with full purpose of heart. ⁷But if not, O house of Israel, the place of your dwellings shall become desolate until the time of the fulfilling of the covenant to your fathers.

⁸And now it came to pass that after the people had heard these words—behold they began to weep, and howl again—because of the loss of their kindreds, and friends.

⁹And it came to pass that thus did the three days pass away.

And it was in the morning.

And the darkness dispersed from off the face of the land.

And the earth did cease to tremble.

And the rocks did cease to rend.

And the dreadful groanings did cease.

And all the tumultuous noises did pass away.

¹⁰And the earth did cleave together again, that it stood.

And the mourning, and the weeping, and the wailing of the people (which were spared alive) did cease.

And their mourning was turned unto into joy, and their lamentations into the praise and the thanksgiving unto the Lord, Jesus Christ. their Redeemer. ¹¹And thus far were the scriptures fulfilled, which had been spoken by the prophets.

¹²And it was the more righteous part of the people which were saved.

And it was they which received the prophets and stoned them not.

And it was they which had not shed the blood of the saints which were spared.

¹³And they were spared, and were not sunk and buried up in the earth.

And they were not drowned in the depths of the sea.

---

a. See Matthew 23:37: "How often would I have gathered thy children together, even as a hen gathereth her chickens under her wings, and ye would not!"

b. The Printer's Manuscript has "hay." The intended word was surely "how."

c. See Matthew 23:37: "How often would I have gathered thy children together, even as a hen gathereth her chickens under her wings, and ye would not!"

d. See Matthew 23:37: "How often would I have gathered thy children together, even as a hen gathereth her chickens under her wings, and ye would not!"

And they were not burned by fire, neither were they fallen upon and crushed to death. And they were not carried away in the whirlwind. Neither were they overpowered by the vapors of smoke and of darkness.

>¹⁴And now, whoso readeth—let him understand. He that hath the scriptures—let him search them, and see and behold if all these deaths, and destructions by fire, and by smoke, and by tempests, and by whirlwinds, and by the opening of the earth to receive them, and all these things—is not unto the fulfilling of the prophecies of many of the holy prophets.

¹⁵Behold, I say unto you, yea, many have testified of these things at the coming of Christ and were slain because they testified of these things! ¹⁶Yea, the prophet Zenos did testify of these things. And also Zenock spake concerning these things, because they testified particular concerning us, which is the remnant of their seed.

¹⁷Behold, our father Jacob also testified concerning a remnant of the seed of Joseph. And behold! Are not we a remnant of the seed of Joseph? And these things, which testifies of us, are they not written upon the plates of Brass which our father Lehi brought out of Jerusalem?

¹⁸And it came to pass that in the ending of the thirty and fourth year, behold, I will show unto you that the people of Nephi (which were spared) and also they which had had been called Lamanites (which had been spared) did have great favors shown unto them and great blessings poured out upon their heads, insomuch that soon after the ascension of Christ into heaven he did truly manifest himself unto them—¹⁹showing his body unto them and ministering unto them. And an account of his ministry shall be given hereafter. Therefore, for this time I make an end of my sayings. ᵃ<

---

a. Mormon inserts his admonition to his readers, explaining what they should understand from what was written. He also previews the section to come where Christ appears.

Chapter V [3 Nephi 11–13:24]

[11] *Jesus Christ showeth himself unto the people of Nephi as the multitude were gathered together in the land Bountiful and did minister unto them. And on this wise did he show himself unto them.*[a]

¹And now it came to pass that there were a great multitude gathered together of the people of Nephi round about the temple which was in the land Bountiful. And they were marveling and wondering one with another—and were showing one to another the great and marvelous change which had taken place. ²And they were also conversing about this Jesus Christ, of which the sign had been given concerning his death.

³And it came to pass that while they were thus conversing, one with another, they heard a voice—as if it came out of heaven.

And they cast their eyes round about, for they understood not the voice which they heard.

And it was not a harsh voice.

Neither was it a loud voice.

Nevertheless—and notwithstanding it being a small voice—it did pierce them that did hear to the center, insomuch that there were no part of their frame that it did not cause to quake.

Yea, it did pierce them to the very soul, and did cause their hearts to burn.

⁴And it came to pass that again they heard the voice, and they understood it not.

⁵And again, the third time they did hear the voice—and did open their ears to hear it. And their eyes were towards the sound thereof. And they did look steadfastly towards heaven, from whence the sound came.

⁶And behold, the third time, they did understand the voice which they heard. And it saith unto them: ⁷"Behold my beloved Son, in whom I am well pleased—in whom I have glorified my name! Hear ye him!"[b]

⁸And it came to pass as they understood, they cast their eyes up again towards heaven. And behold, they saw a man descending out of heaven—and he was clothed in a white robe.

And he came down and stood in the midst of them.

And the eyes of the whole multitude was turned upon him.

And they durst not open their mouths, even one to another—and wist not what it meant. For they thought it was an angel that had appeared unto them.

⁹And it came to pass that he stretched forth his hand, and spake unto the people, saying:

¹⁰Behold! I am Jesus Christ of which the prophets testified that should come into the world. ¹¹And behold! I am the light, and the life of the world.[c] And I have

---

a. This chapter heading is different from Mormon's standard procedure. Typically, Mormon uses the chapter heading to introduce a secondary source. He has already indicated that in 3 Nephi 5:9. In this case, he creates the header to let his readers understand the importance of the information to come. Mormon is switching from the Nephite history leading to Christ's appearance in Bountiful to what occurred during that visit.

b. See Matthew 17:5: "While he yet spake, behold, a bright cloud overshadowed them: and behold a voice out of the cloud, which said, This is my beloved Son, in whom I am well pleased; hear ye him."

c. See John 8:12: "Then spake Jesus again unto them, saying, I am the light of the world."

drank out of that bitter cup which the Father hath given me,[a] and have glorified the Father—in taking upon me the sins of the world—in the which I have suffered the will of the Father in all things from the beginning.

¹²And it came to pass that when Jesus had spake these words the whole multitude fell to the earth. For they remembered that it had been prophesied among them, that Christ should show himself unto them after his ascension into heaven.

¹³And it came to pass that the Lord spake unto them, saying:

¹⁴Arise! And come forth unto me, that ye may thrust your hands into my side, and also that ye may feel the prints of the nails in my hands, and in my feet, that ye may know that I am the God of Israel, and the God of the whole earth—and have been slain for the sins of the world.[b]

¹⁵And it came to pass that the multitude went forth and did thrust their hands into his side, and did feel the prints of the nails in his hands, and in his feet. And this they did do—going forth one by one, until they had all gone forth, and did see with their eyes, and did feel with their hands—and did know of a surety, and did bear record that it was he of whom it was written by the prophets that should come.

¹⁶And it came to pass that when they had all gone forth and had witnessed for themselves—they did cry out with one accord, saying: ¹⁷"Hosanna! Blessed be the name of the Most High God!" And they did fall down at the feet of Jesus and did worship him.

¹⁸And it came to pass that he spake unto Nephi (for Nephi was among the multitude)—and commanded him that he should come forth. ¹⁹And Nephi arose, and went forth, and bowed himself before the Lord. And he did kiss his feet. ²⁰And the Lord commanded him that he should arise. And he arose—and stood before him. ²¹And the Lord said unto him: "I give unto you power, that ye shall baptize this people when I am again ascended into heaven."

²²And again, the Lord called others, and said unto them likewise. And he gave unto them power to baptize. And he saith unto them:

On this wise shall ye baptize, and there shall be no disputations among you. ²³Verily, I say unto you, that whosoever repenteth of his sins—through your words—and desireth to be baptized in my name—on this wise shall ye baptize them: Behold, ye shall go down, and stand in the water. And in my name shall ye baptize them.

²⁴And now behold, these are the words which ye shall say, calling them by name—saying: ²⁵"Having authority given me of Jesus Christ, I baptize you in the name of the Father, and of the Son, and of the Holy Ghost. Amen."[c]

²⁶And then shall ye immerse them in the water and come forth again out of the water. ²⁷And after this manner shall ye baptize in my name. For behold, verily

---

a. Allusion to John 18:11: "Then said Jesus unto Peter, Put up thy sword into the sheath: the cup which my Father hath given me, shall I not drink it?"

b. Uses language from John 20:26: "Then saith he to Thomas, Reach hither thy finger, and behold my hands; and reach hither thy hand, and thrust it into my side: and be not faithless, but believing."

c. See Matthew 28:19: "Go ye therefore, and teach all nations, baptizing them in the name of the Father, and of the Son, and of the Holy Ghost."

Chapter V [3 Nephi 11–13:24]

I say unto you that the Father and the Son and the Holy Ghost, are one. And I am in the Father and the Father in me. And the Father and I are one.[a]

²⁸And, according as I have commanded you, thus shall ye baptize. And there shall be no disputations among you (as there hath hitherto been)—neither shall there be disputations among you concerning the points of my doctrine as there hath hitherto been.[b] ²⁹For verily, verily, I say unto you: He that hath the spirit of contention is not of me—but is of the devil, which is the father of contention. And he stirreth up the hearts of men, to contend with anger, one with another. ³⁰Behold, this is not my doctrine, to stir up the hearts of men with anger one against another. But this is my doctrine, that such things should be done away.

³¹Behold. Verily, verily, I say unto you: I will declare unto you my doctrine. ³²And this is my doctrine. And it is the doctrine which the Father hath given unto me. And I bear record of the Father, and the Father beareth record of me, and the Holy Ghost beareth record of the Father and me. And I bear record that the Father commandeth all men, everywhere, to repent, and believe in me. ³³And whoso believeth in me and is baptized, the same shall be saved. And they are they which shall inherit the kingdom of God. ³⁴And whoso believeth not in me, and is not baptized, shall be damned.[c] ³⁵And verily, verily, I say unto you, that this is my doctrine. And I bear record of it from the Father.

And whoso believeth in me, believeth in the Father also, and unto him will the Father bear record of me. For he will visit him with fire, and with the Holy Ghost. ³⁶And thus will the Father bear record of me. And the Holy Ghost will bear record unto him of the Father, and me. For the Father and I, and the Holy Ghost, are one.

³⁷And again, I say unto you: Ye must repent, and become as a little child, and be baptized in my name—or ye can in no wise receive these things.

³⁸And again, I say unto you: Ye must repent, and be baptized in my name, and become as a little child—or ye can in no wise inherit the kingdom of God.

³⁹Verily, verily, I say unto you that this is my doctrine. And whoso buildeth upon this, buildeth upon my rock.[d] And the gates of hell shall not prevail against them.[e] ⁴⁰And whoso shall declare more or less than this, and establisheth it for my doctrine—the same cometh of evil and is not built upon my rock, but he buildeth upon a sandy foundation.[f] And the gates of hell standeth open to receive such, when the floods come, and the winds beat upon them. ⁴¹Therefore, go forth unto this people and declare the words which I have spoken unto the ends of the earth.

---

a. See 1 John 5:7: "For there are three that bear record in heaven, the Father, the Word, and the Holy Ghost: and these three are one." Also, John 14:11: "Believe me that I am in the Father, and the Father in me."

b. Much of this sentence is written above the line with cross-outs. The Printer's Manuscript also has a double "you you." This edition accepts the reading in Royal Skousen, *The Book of Mormon: The Earliest Text* (New Haven, CT: Yale Univesity Press, 2009), 595, which also is how it appears in modern editions.

c. For verses 33–34, see Mark 16:16: "He that believeth and is baptized shall be saved; but he that believeth not shall be damned."

d. Language echoes Matthew 7:24: "Therefore whosoever heareth these sayings of mine, and doeth them, I will liken him unto a wise man, which built his house upon a rock."

e. Language reprises Matthew 16:18: "And I say also unto thee, That thou art Peter, and upon this rock I will build my church; and the gates of hell shall not prevail against it."

f. See Matthew 7:24–27.

[12] ¹And it came to pass that when Jesus had spake these words unto Nephi, and to those which had been called (now the number of them which had been called, and received power and authority to baptize—were twelve)—and behold, he stretched forth his hand unto the multitude, and cried unto them, saying:

Blessed are ye, if ye shall give heed unto the words of these twelve, which I have chosen from among you, to minister unto you and to be your servants.[a] And unto them I have given power that they may baptize you with water. And after that ye are baptized with water—behold, I will baptize you with fire and with the Holy Ghost.[b] Therefore, blessed are ye if ye shall believe in me and be baptized—after that ye have seen me and know that I am.

²And again, more blessed are they which shall believe in your words, because that ye shall testify that ye have seen me, and that ye know that I am. Yea, blessed are they which shall believe in your words, and come down into the depths of humility, and be baptized.[c] For they shall be visited with fire, and with the Holy Ghost—and shall receive a remission of their sins.

[**Compare Matthew 5:3–6:24**]

³**Yea**, blessed are the poor in spirit **which cometh unto me**! For theirs is the kingdom of heaven.

⁴**And again**, blessed are **all** they that mourn! For they shall be comforted.

⁵**And** blessed are the meek! For they shall inherit the earth.

⁶**And** blessed **are** all they which do hunger and thirst after righteousness! For they shall be filled with the Holy Ghost.

⁷**And** blessed are the merciful! For they shall obtain mercy.

⁸**And** blessed are **all** the pure in heart! For they shall see God.

⁹**And** blessed are **all** the peacemakers! For they shall be called the children of God.

¹⁰**And** blessed are all they which are persecuted for **my name's** sake! For theirs is the kingdom of heaven.

¹¹**And** blessed are ye, when men shall revile you, and persecute you, and shall say all manner of evil against you—falsely—for my sake. ¹²**For ye shall have great joy** and be exceeding glad! For great **shall be** your reward in heaven. For so persecuted they the prophets which were before you.

¹³**Verily, verily, I say unto you:** I give unto you to be the salt of the earth. But, if the salt **shall lose its** savor, wherewith shall **the earth** be salted? **The salt shall be** thenceforth good for nothing but to be cast out, and to be trodden under foot of men.

¹⁴**Verily, verily, I say unto you,** I give unto you to be the light of **this people**. A city that is set on a hill cannot be hid. ¹⁵**Behold**, do men light a candle and put it under a bushel? **Nay**, but on a candlestick—and it giveth light to all that are in the house. ¹⁶**Therefore**, let your light so shine before **this people** that they may see your good works and glorify your Father, which is in heaven.

---

a. Allusion to Matthew 23:11.

b. Uses language from Matthew 3:11: "I indeed baptize you with water unto repentance. . . . [H]e shall baptize you with the Holy Ghost, and with fire."

c. Echoes John 20:29. "Jesus saith unto him, Thomas, because thou hast seen me, thou hast believed: blessed are they that have not seen, and yet have believed."

¹⁷Think not that I am come to destroy the law or the prophets! I am not come to destroy, but to fulfil. ¹⁸For verily I say unto you [ᵃ]: One jot **nor** one tittle **hath not passed away** from the law. **But in me it hath** all **been fulfilled.**

¹⁹And behold, I have given unto you the law and the commandments of my Father—that ye shall believe in me, and that ye shall repent of your sins, and come unto me with a broken heart and a contrite spirit.ᵇ Behold, ye have the commandments before you. And the law is fulfilled. ²⁰Therefore, come unto me and be ye saved. For verily, I say unto you, that except **ye shall keep my commandments which I have commanded you at this time,** ye shall in no case enter into the kingdom of heaven.ᶜ

²¹Ye have heard that it **hath been** said by them of old time (**and it is also written before you**) that thou shalt not kill. And whosoever shall kill shall be in danger of the judgment **of God**. ²²But I say unto you, that whosoever is angry with his brother shall be in danger of **his** judgment. And whosoever shall say to his brother, raca! shall be in danger of the council. And whosoever shall say, thou fool! shall be in danger of hellfire. ²³Therefore, **if ye shall come unto me, or shall desire to come unto me**, and rememberest that thy brother hath aught against thee—²⁴go thy way **unto thy brother and** first be reconciled to thy brother. And then **come unto me with full purpose of heart and I will receive you.**ᵈ

²⁵Agree with thine adversary quickly, while thou art in the way with him, lest at any time **he shall get thee**, and thou **shalt** be cast into prison. ²⁶Verily, I say unto thee, thou shalt by no means come out thence until thou hast paid the uttermost **senine. And while ye are in prison, can ye pay even one senine? Verily, verily, I say unto you: Nay!**

²⁷**Behold, it is written by** them of old time, **that** thou shalt not commit adultery. ²⁸But I say unto you, that whosoever looketh on a woman, to lust after her, hath committed adultery already in his heart.

²⁹**Behold, I give unto you a commandment—that ye suffer none of these things to enter into your heart.** ³⁰**For it is better that ye should deny yourselves of these things (wherein ye will take up your cross) than that** ye should be cast into hell.ᵉ

³¹It hath been **written that** whosoever shall put away his wife, let him give her a writing of divorcement. ³²**Verily, verily,** I say unto you, that whosoever shall put away his wife, saving for the cause of fornication, causeth her to commit adultery. And **whoso** shall marry her who is divorced, committeth adultery.

³³**And again, it is written:** Thou shalt not forswear thyself, but shalt perform unto the Lord thine oaths. ³⁴But verily, I say unto you: Swear not at all. Neither by

---

a. Omits "till heaven and earth pass."

b. See Psalm 34:18: "The Lord is nigh unto them that are of a broken heart; and saveth such as be of a contrite spirit."

c. Matthew 5:20 reads: "For I say unto you, That except your righteousness shall exceed the righteousness of the scribes and Pharisees, ye shall in no case enter into the kingdom of heaven."

d. Matthew 5:24 reads: "Leave there thy gift before the altar, and go thy way; first be reconciled to thy brother, and then come and offer thy gift."

e. Matthew 5:29 reads: "And if thy right eye offend thee, pluck it out, and cast it from thee: for it is profitable for thee that one of thy members should perish, and not that thy whole body should be cast into hell."

heaven, for it is God's throne. ³⁵Nor by the earth. For it is his footstool.ᵃ ³⁶Neither shalt thou swear by thy head, because thou canst not make one hair **black or white**. ³⁷But let your communication be, yea, yea—nay, nay.ᵇ For whatsoever **cometh of** more than these are evil.ᶜ

³⁸**And behold**, it **is written**—an eye for an eye, and a tooth for a tooth. ³⁹But I say unto you, that ye **shall not resist** evil. But whosoever shall smite thee on thy right cheek, turn to him the other also.

⁴⁰And if any man will sue thee at the law and take away thy coat—let him have thy cloak also.

⁴¹And whosoever shall compel thee to go a mile—go with him twain.

⁴²Give to him that asketh thee, and to him that would borrow of thee turn **thou not** away.

⁴³**And behold**, it **is written also**, that thou shalt love thy neighbor and hate thine enemy. ⁴⁴But **behold**, I say unto you: Love your enemies! Bless them that curse you. Do good to them that hate you. And pray for them which despitefully use you and persecute you—⁴⁵that ye may be the children of your heavenly Father (which is in heaven). For he maketh his sun to rise on the evil and on the good [ᵈ].ᵉ ⁴⁶**Therefore, those things which were of old time (which were under the law)—in me are all fulfilled.** ⁴⁷**Old things are done away, and all things have become new.**ᶠ

⁴⁸Therefore, I would that ye should be perfect, even as I, or your Father which is in heaven, is perfect.

[Compare Matthew 6:1–24]

[13] ¹Verily, verily, **I say that I would that ye should do alms unto the poor. But** take heed that ye do not your alms before men, to be seen of them. Otherwise, ye have no reward of your Father which is in heaven. ²Therefore, when **ye shall do your** alms, do not sound a trumpet before you, as will hypocrites do in the synagogues and in the streets, that they may have glory of men. Verily, I say unto you: They have their reward.

³But, when thou doest alms let not thy left hand know what thy right hand doeth ⁴that thine alms may be in secret. And thy Father, which seeth in secret himself, shall reward thee openly.

⁵And when thou prayest, thou shalt not **do** as the hypocrites. For they love to pray, standing in the synagogues and in the corners of the streets, that they may be seen of men. Verily, I say unto you: They have their reward. ⁶But thou, when thou prayest, enter into thy closet. And when thou hast shut thy door, pray to thy Father (which is in secret). And thy Father (which seeth in secret) shall reward thee openly.

---

a. Allusion to Isaiah 66:1.

b. This phrase was initially missing in the Printer's Manuscript and added by Hyrum Smith, likely from proofreading.

c. Matthew 5:37 reads: "But let your communication be, Yea, yea; Nay, nay: for whatsoever is more than these cometh of evil."

d. Omits "and sendeth rain on the just an on the unjust."

e. Matthew 4:46–47 reads: "For if ye love them which love you, what reward have ye? do not even the publicans the same? And if ye salute your brethren only, what do ye more than others? do not even the publicans so?"

f. See 2 Corinthians 5:17: "old things are passed away; behold, all things are become new."

Chapter V [3 Nephi 11–13:24]

⁷But when ye pray, use not vain repetitions as the heathen [ᵃ]. For they think that they shall be heard for their much speaking. ⁸Be not ye, therefore, like unto them. For your Father knoweth what things ye have need of before ye ask him.

⁹After this manner, therefore, pray ye:

> Our Father, which art in heaven,
>> hallowed be thy name.
>
> ¹⁰Thy will be done in earth
>> as it is in heaven.
>
> ¹¹And forgive us our debts,
>> as we forgive our debtors.
>
> ¹²And lead us not into temptation,
>> but deliver us from evil.
>
> ¹³For thine is the kingdom,
>> and the power,
>> and the glory,
>> forever.
>
> Amen.

¹⁴For, if ye forgive men their trespasses, your heavenly Father will also forgive you. ¹⁵But if ye forgive not men their trespasses—neither will your Father forgive your trespasses.

¹⁶Moreover, when ye fast, be not as the hypocrites, of a sad countenance. For they disfigure their faces that they may appear unto men to fast. Verily I say unto you: They have their reward. ¹⁷But thou, when though fasteth, anoint thy head and wash thy face, ¹⁸that thou appear not unto men to fast—but unto thy Father (which is in secret). And thy Father (which seeth in secret) shall reward thee openly.

¹⁹Lay not up for yourselves treasures upon earth, where moth and rust doth corrupt, and thieves break through and steal. ²⁰But lay up for yourselves treasures in heaven, where neither moth nor rust doth corrupt, and where thieves do not break through, nor steal. ²¹For where your treasure is—there will your heart be also.

²²The light of the body is the eye. If, therefore, thine eye be single, thy whole body shall be full of light. ²³But if thine eye be evil, thy whole body shall be full of darkness. If, therefore, the light that is in thee be darkness—how great is that darkness!

²⁴No man can serve two masters—or, either he will hate the one and love the other—or else he will hold to the one, and despise the other. Ye cannot serve God and Mammon.

---

a. Omits "do," which is in italics.

Chapter VI [3 Nephi 13:25–14:27]

[13 continued]

[Compare Matthew 6:25–31]

²⁵And now it came to pass that when Jesus had spoken these words, he looked upon the twelve whom he had chosen, and saith unto them:

Remember the words which I have spoken. For behold, ye are they which I have chosen to minister unto this people. Therefore, I say unto you: Take no thought for your life, what ye shall eat, or what ye shall drink—nor yet for your body, what ye shall put on. Is not the life more than meat, and the body than raiment? ²⁶Behold the fowls of the air! For they sow not, neither do they reap, nor gather into barns. Yet your heavenly Father feedeth them. Are ye not much better than they? ²⁷Which of you, by taking thought, can add one cubit unto his stature? ²⁸And why take ye thought for raiment? Consider the lilies of the field—how they grow. They toil not, neither do they spin. ²⁹And yet I say unto you, that even Solomon in all his glory was not arrayed like one of these. ³⁰Wherefore, if God so clothe the grass of the field (which today is, and tomorrow is cast into the oven), **even so** will he clothe you, if ye are not of little faith. ³¹Therefore, take no thought—saying: What shall we eat? Or what shall we drink? Or wherewithal shall we be clothed? [a] ³²For your heavenly Father knoweth that ye have need of all these things. ³³But, seek ye first the kingdom of God, and his righteousness. And all these things shall be added unto you. ³⁴Take, therefore, no thought for the morrow. For the morrow shall take thought for the things of itself. Sufficient **is** the day, **unto** the evil thereof.

[Compare Matthew 7:1–27]

[14] ¹And now it came to pass that when Jesus had spoken these words, he turned again to the multitude. And he did open his mouth unto them again, saying:

Verily, verily, I say unto you: Judge not, that ye be not judged! ²For with what judgment ye judge, ye shall be judged. And with what measure ye mete, it shall be measured to you again. ³And why beholdest thou the mote that is in thy brother's eye, but considerest not the beam that is in thine own eye? ⁴Or how wilt thou say to thy brother—let me pull out the mote out of thine eye, and behold, a beam is in thine own eye? ⁵Thou hypocrite! First cast out the beam out of thine own eye, and then shalt thou see clearly to cast out the mote out of thy brother's eye.

⁶Give not that which is holy unto the dogs. Neither cast ye your pearls before swine, lest they trample them under their feet, and turn again, and rend you.

⁷Ask, and it shall be given unto you. Seek, and ye shall find. Knock, and it shall be opened unto you. ⁸For everyone that asketh, receiveth. And he that seeketh, findeth. And to him that knocketh, it shall be opened.

⁹Or what man is there of you, whom if his son ask bread, will he give him a stone? ¹⁰Or if he ask a fish, will he give him a serpent? ¹¹If ye, then, being evil, know how to give good gifts unto your children, how much more shall your Father,

---

a. Omits "For after all these things do the Gentiles seek."

Chapter VI [3 Nephi 13:25–14:27]

which is in heaven, give good things to them that ask him. ¹²Therefore, all things whatsoever ye would that men should do to you—do ye even so to them. For this is the law and the prophets.

¹³Enter ye in at the strait gate. For wide is the gate, and broad is the way, that leadeth to destruction. And many there be which go in thereat. ¹⁴Because strait is the gate and narrow is the way which leadeth unto life. And few there be that find it.[a]

¹⁵Beware of false prophets which come to you in sheep's clothing—but inwardly they are ravening wolves! ¹⁶Ye shall know them by their fruits. Do men gather grapes of thorns, or figs of thistles? ¹⁷Even so, every good tree bringeth forth good fruit. But a corrupt tree bringeth forth evil fruit. ¹⁸A good tree cannot bring forth evil fruit—neither a corrupt tree bring forth good fruit. ¹⁹Every tree that bringeth not forth good fruit, is hewn down, and cast into the fire. ²⁰Wherefore, by their fruits ye shall know them.

²¹Not everyone that saith unto me—Lord! Lord!—shall enter into the kingdom of heaven—but he that doeth the will of my Father, which is in heaven. ²²Many will say to me, in that day: Lord! Lord, have we not prophesied in thy name? And in thy name have cast out devils? And in thy name done many wonderful works? ²³And then will I profess unto them—I never knew you. Depart from me, ye that work iniquity. ²⁴Therefore, whoso heareth these sayings of mine, and doeth them, I will liken him unto a wise man which built his house upon a rock. ²⁵And the rain descended, and the floods came, and the winds blew, and beat upon that house. And it fell not, for it was founded upon a rock.

²⁶And everyone that heareth these sayings of mine, and doeth them not, shall be likened unto a foolish man, which built his house upon the sand. ²⁷And the rain descended, and the floods came, and the winds blew, and beat upon that house—and it fell. And great was the fall of it.

---

a. See Matthew 7:14: "Because strait is the gate, and narrow is the way, which leadeth unto life, and few there be that find it."

Chapter VII [3 Nephi 15–16]

[15] ¹And it now it came to pass that when Jesus had ended these sayings, he cast his eyes round about on the multitude, and saith unto them:

Behold, ye have heard the things which I have taught before I ascended to my Father. Therefore, whoso remembereth these sayings of mine, and doeth them—him will I raise up at the last day.

²And it came to pass that when Jesus had said these words, he perceived that there were some among them which marveled and wondered—what he would, concerning the law of Moses. For they understood not the saying that old things had passed away, and that all things had become new. ³And he saith unto them:

Marvel not that I said unto you, that old things had passed away, and that all things had become new.

⁴Behold, I say unto you, that the law is fulfilled that was given unto Moses.

⁵Behold, I am he that gave the law. And I am he which covenanted with my people, Israel. Therefore, the law, in me is fulfilled. For I have come to fulfil the law. Therefore, it hath an end.

⁶Behold, I do not destroy the prophets For as many as have not been fulfilled in me—verily, I say unto you shall all be fulfilled. ⁷And because I said unto you that old things hath passed away, I do not destroy that which hath been spoken concerning things which is to come. ⁸For behold, the covenants which I have made with my people is not all fulfilled—but the law which was given unto Moses hath an end in me.

⁹Behold, I am the law and the light! Look unto me, and endure to the end,ᵃ and ye shall live! For unto him that endureth to the endᵇ will I give eternal life.

¹⁰Behold, I have given unto you the commandments. Therefore, keep my commandments. And this is the law and the prophets. For they truly testified of me.

¹¹And now it came to pass that when Jesus had spoken these words, he said unto those twelve whom he had chosen:

¹²Ye are my disciples. And ye are a light unto this people, which are a remnant of the house of Joseph. ¹³And behold, this is the land of your inheritance, and the Father hath given it unto you. ¹⁴And not at any time hath the Father given me commandment that I should tell it unto your brethren at Jerusalem, ¹⁵neither at any time hath the Father given me commandment that I should tell unto them concerning the other tribes of the house of Israel, which the Father hath led away out of the land.

¹⁶This much did the Father command me, that I should tell unto them ¹⁷that other sheep I have which are not of this fold. Them also I must bring. And they shall hear my voice. And there shall be one fold, and one shepherd.ᶜ

¹⁸And now, because of stiffneckedness and unbelief, they understood not my

---

a. The phrase "endure to the end" occurs in Matthew 24:13.

b. See Matthew 10:22: "he that endureth to the end shall be saved."

c. See John 10:16: "And other sheep I have, which are not of this fold: them also I must bring, and they shall hear my voice; and there shall be one fold, and one shepherd."

word. Therefore, I was commanded to say no more of the Father concerning this thing, unto them. ¹⁹But verily, I say unto you, that the Father hath commanded me, and I tell it unto you, that ye were separated from among them because of their iniquity. Therefore, it is because of their iniquity that they know not of you.

²⁰And verily, I say unto you again, that the other tribes hath the Father separated from them. And it is because of their iniquity that they know not of them. ²¹And verily, I say unto you, that ye are they of which I said—other sheep I have, which are not of this fold. Them also I must bring. And they shall hear my voice, and there shall be one fold and one shepherd.[a] ²²And they understood me not. For they supposed it had been the Gentiles. For they understood not that the Gentiles should be converted through their preaching.

²³And they understood me not, that I said they shall hear my voice. And they understood me not, that the Gentiles should not, at any time, hear my voice—that I should not at manifest myself unto them, save it were by the Holy Ghost. ²⁴But behold, ye have both heard my voice, and seen me. And ye are my sheep. And ye are numbered among them which the Father hath given me.

[16] ¹And verily, verily, I say unto you, that I have other sheep which are not of this land—neither of the land of Jerusalem—neither in any parts of that land round about whither I have been to minister. ²For they of which I speak, are they which have not as yet heard my voice—neither have I at any time manifested myself unto them. ³But, I have received a commandment of the Father that I shall go unto them. And that they shall hear my voice. And shall be numbered among my sheep, that there may be one fold and one shepherd.[b] Therefore, I go to show myself unto them.

⁴And I command you, that ye shall write these sayings after that I am gone, that if it so be that my people at Jerusalem (they which have seen me, and been with me in my ministry) do not ask the Father in my name, that they may receive a knowledge of you by the Holy Ghost, and also of the other tribes which they know not of, that these sayings which ye shall write shall be kept and shall be manifested unto the Gentiles, that through the fulness of the Gentiles the remnant of their seed (which shall be scattered forth upon the face of the earth, because of their unbelief)—may be brought in, or may be brought to a knowledge of me, their Redeemer. ⁵And then will I gather them in from the four quarters of the earth. And then will I fulfil the covenant which the Father hath made unto all the people of the house of Israel. ⁶And blessed are the Gentiles because of their belief in me, in and of the Holy Ghost, which witness unto them of me, and of the Father.

⁷Behold, because of their belief in me (saith the Father) and because of the unbelief of you, O house of Israel—in the latter day shall the truth come unto the Gentiles, that the fulness of these things shall be made known unto them. ⁸But wo (saith the Father) unto the unbelieving of the Gentiles! For notwithstanding that they have come forth upon the face of this land, and have scattered my people (which are of the house of Israel—and my people which are of the house of

---

a. See John 10:16: "And other sheep I have, which are not of this fold: them also I must bring, and they shall hear my voice; and there shall be one fold, and one shepherd."

b. See John 10:16: "And other sheep I have, which are not of this fold: them also I must bring, and they shall hear my voice; and there shall be one fold, and one shepherd."

Israel have been cast out from among them, and have been trodden under feet by them—⁹and because of the mercies of the Father unto the Gentiles, and also the judgments of the Father upon my people, which are of the house of Israel)—verily, verily, I say unto you, that after all this, and I have caused my people which are of the house of Israel to be smitten, and to be afflicted, and to be slain, and to be cast out from among them, and to become hated by them, and to become a hiss and a byword[a] among them.[b]

¹⁰And thus commandeth the Father that I should say unto you—at that day, when the Gentiles shall sin against my Gospel, and shall reject the fulness of my Gospel, and shall be lifted up in the pride of their hearts above all nations, and above all the people of the whole earth, and shall be filled with all manner of lyings, and of deceits, and of mischiefs, and all manner of hypocrisy, and murders, and priestcrafts, and whoredoms, and of secret abominations—and if they shall do all these things—and shall reject the fulness of my Gospel—behold (saith the Father)—I will bring the fulness of my Gospel from among them.

¹¹And then will I remember my covenant which I have made unto my people, O house of Israel. And I will bring my gospel unto them. ¹²And I will show unto thee, O house of Israel, that the Gentiles shall not have power over you. ¹³But I will remember my covenant unto you, O house of Israel. And ye shall come unto the knowledge of the fulness of my gospel.

But if the Gentiles will repent and return unto me (saith the Father)—behold, they shall be numbered among my people, O house of Israel. ¹⁴And I will not suffer my people (which are of the house of Israel) to go through among them and tread them down (saith the Father).[c]

¹⁵But, if they will not return unto me, and hearken unto my voice, I will suffer them, yea, I will suffer my people, O house of Israel, that they shall go through among them, and shall tread them down. And they shall be as salt that hath lost its savor (which is thenceforth good for nothing, but to be cast out, and to be trodden under foot of my people).[d]

O house of Israel! ¹⁶Verily, verily, I say unto you—thus hath the Father commanded me, that I should give unto this people this land for their inheritance—¹⁷and when[e] the words of the prophet Isaiah shall be fulfilled, which saith:

---

a. Perhaps a reference to Deuteronomy 28:30: "And thou shalt become an astonishment, a proverb, and a byword, among all nations whither the Lord shall lead thee."

b. The numerous clauses, beginning with the first that has been placed in parentheses, create too much distance from the beginning of the sentence. Thus, verse 10 is the repetitive resumption to return to the original idea. It is also possible, however, that "after all this, and I have caused" could be read "after all things, therefore I have caused." That would allow the sentence to be complete and is possibly the intended meaning.

c. Using language and imagery from Micah 5:8: "And the remnant of Jacob shall be among the Gentiles in the midst of many people as a lion among the beasts of the forest, as a young lion among the flocks of sheep: who, if he go through, both treadeth down, and teareth in pieces, and none can deliver."

d. See Matthew 5:13: "Ye are the salt of the earth: but if the salt have lost his savour, wherewith shall it be salted? it is thenceforth good for nothing, but to be cast out, and to be trodden under foot of men."

e. The word "when" was in the Printer's Manuscript and printed editions up until the 1920 edition, when the editors changed it to "then." The change removed an incomplete sentence. Skousen, *Analysis of the Textual Variants:* 5:3409. Skousen appears to agree with the change. However, it may misunderstand the intent. The point has been to say that this land would be given to the Nephites.

¹⁸"Thy watchmen shall lift up the voice—
   with the voice together, shall they sing!
For they shall see eye to eye
   when the Lord shall bring again Zion.
¹⁹Break forth into joy!
   Sing together, ye waste places of Jerusalem!
For the Lord hath comforted his people.
   He hath redeemed Jerusalem.
²⁰The Lord hath made bare his holy arm
   in the eyes of all the nations.
And all the ends of the earth
   shall see the salvation of God."ᵃ

Although that was the foundational promise, this reiteration appears to exist in the future, when "the Lord hath made bare his holy arm in the eyes of all nations." In that future context, the word "when" would be more appropriate. It would be another case where the "and" is added where another word would have been better—in this case it might have been better left out entirely.

a. Quoting Isaiah 52:9–10.

Chapter VIII [3 Nephi 17–18]

[17] ¹Behold, now it came to pass that when Jesus had spoken these words, he looked round about again on the multitude, and he saith unto them:

Behold, my time is at hand. ²I perceive that ye are weak, that ye cannot understand all my words which I am commanded of the Father to speak unto you at this time. ³Therefore, go ye unto your homes and ponder upon the things which I have said. And ask of the Father, in my name, that ye may understand. And prepare your minds for the morrow. And I come unto you again, ⁴but now I go unto the Father—and also to show myself unto the lost tribes of Israel. For they are not lost unto the Father. For he knoweth whither he hath taken them.

⁵And it came to pass that when Jesus had thus spoken, he cast his eyes round about again on the multitude. And behold, they were in tears—and did look steadfastly upon him, as if they would ask him to tarry a little longer with them. ⁶And he saith unto them:

Behold, my bowels is filled with compassion towards you. ⁷Have ye any that are sick among you? Bring them hither. Have ye any that are lame, or blind, or halt, or maimed, or leprous, or that are withered, or that are deaf, or that are afflicted in any manner? Bring them hither and I will heal them, for I have compassion upon you. My bowels is filled with mercy, ⁸for I perceive that ye desire that I should show unto you what I have done unto your brethren at Jerusalem. For I see that your faith is sufficient that I should heal you.

⁹And it came to pass that when he had thus spoken—all the multitude, with one accord, did go forth with their sick, and their afflicted, and their lame, and with their blind, and with their dumb, and with all they that were afflicted in any manner. And he did heal them—every one—as they were brought forth unto him. ¹⁰And they did all (both they which had been healed, and they which were whole)—did bow down at his feet and did worship him. And as many as could come [fore[a]] the multitude did kiss his feet insomuch that they did bathe his feet with their tears.

¹¹And it came to pass that he commanded that their little children should be brought. ¹²So they brought their little children and sat them down upon the ground round about him. And Jesus stood in the midst. And the multitude gave way, till they had all been brought unto him.

¹³And it came to pass that when they had all been brought, and Jesus stood in the midst—he commanded the multitude that they should kneel down upon the ground.

¹⁴And it came to pass that when they had knelt upon the ground, Jesus groaned within himself, and saith: "Father. I am troubled because of the wickedness of the people of the house of Israel."

---

a. Skousen has "for" where the Printer's Manuscript has "fore." He notes that it is a problematic reading. Skousen, *Analysis of the Textual Variants*, 5:3415. This edition keeps the word as in the Printer's Manuscript under the assumption that it is a colloquial version of "before," which might have been "fore" (as in "come to the fore"). This changes the meaning slightly, though not significantly. This is the first time that "fore" appears in the text. That is the spelling used all other places where it should instead be "for." The punctuation in the current LDS edition leaves a difficult reading: "and as many as could come for the multitude did kiss his feet." That would appear to have the meaning of "because the multitude." The reading in this edition suggests that it means "in front of the multitude."

Chapter VIII [3 Nephi 17–18]

¹⁵And when he had said these words, he himself also knelt upon the earth. And behold, he prayed unto the Father. And the things which he prayed cannot be written. And the multitude did bear record (which heard him). ¹⁶And after this manner do they bear record—the eye hath never seen, neither hath the ear heard before,ᵃ so great and marvelous things as we saw and heard Jesus speak unto the Father. ¹⁷And no tongue cannot speak. Neither can there be written by any man. Neither can the hearts of men conceive so great and marvelous things as we both saw and heard Jesus speak. And no one can conceive of the joy which filled our souls at the time we heard him pray for us, unto the Father.

¹⁹And it came to pass that when Jesus had made an end of praying unto the Father, he arose. But so great was the joy of the multitude that they were overcome.

¹⁹And it came to pass that Jesus spake unto them and bade them arise. ²⁰And they arose from the earth. And he saith unto them: "Blessed are ye because of your faith. And now behold, my joy is full." ²¹And when he had said these words, he wept. And the multitude bear record of it.

And he took their little children, one by one, and blessed them—and prayed unto the Father for them. ²²And when he had done this, he wept again.

²³And he spake unto the multitude, and saith unto them: "Behold your little ones!"

²⁴And as they looked to behold, they cast their eyes towards heaven and they saw the heavens open. And they saw angels descending out of heaven, as it were in the midst of fire. And they came down and encircled those little ones about. And they were encircled about with fire. And the angels did minister unto them. ²⁵And the multitude did see, and hear, and bear record. And they know that their record is true. For they—all of them—did see, and hear, every man for himself. And they were in number about two thousand and five hundred souls. And they did consist of men, women, and children.

[18] ¹And it came to pass that Jesus commanded his disciples that they should bring forth some bread and wine unto him. ²And while they were gone for bread and wine, he commanded the multitude that they should sit themselves down upon the earth.

³And when the disciples had come with bread and wine—he took of the bread, and brake and blessed it. And he gave unto the disciples and commanded that they should eat. ⁵And when they had eat and were filled, he commanded that they should give unto the multitude. And when the multitude had eaten and were filled, he saith unto the disciples:

> Behold, there shall one be ordained among you, and to him will I give power that he shall brake bread and bless it, and give it unto the people of my church—unto all they which shall believe and be baptized in my name. ⁶And this shall ye always observe to do, even as I have done, even as I have broken bread and blessed it and gave it unto you. ⁷And this shall ye do in remembrance of my body, which I have shown unto you. And it shall be a testimony unto the Father that ye do always remember me. And if ye do always remember me, ye shall have my spirit to be with you.

⁸And it came to pass that when he had said these words, he commanded his disciples that they should take of the wine of the cup and drink of it, and that they should also give unto the multitude, that they might drink of it.

---

a. See 1 Corinthians 2:9: "But as it is written, Eye hath not seen, nor ear heard."

⁹And it came to pass that they did so, and did drink of it and were filled. And they gave unto the multitude. And they did drink and they were filled. ¹⁰And when the disciples had done this, Jesus saith unto them:

Blessed are ye for this thing, which ye have done. For this is fulfilling my commandments. And this doth witness unto the Father, that ye are willing to do that which I have commanded you. ¹¹And this shall ye always do, unto those who repent and are baptized in my name. And ye shall do it in remembrance of my blood which I have shed for you, that ye may witness unto the Father that ye do always remember me. And if ye do always remember me, ye shall have my spirit to be with you.

¹²And I give unto you a commandment, that ye shall do these things. And if ye shall always do these things, blessed are ye. For ye are built upon my rock.[a] ¹³But whoso among you shall do more or less than these, are not built upon my rock—but are built upon a sandy foundation.[b] And when the rain descends, and the floods come, and the winds blow, and beat upon them—they shall fall. And the gates of hell is already open to receive them. ¹⁴Therefore, blessed are ye if ye shall keep my commandments which the Father hath commanded me that I should give unto you.

¹⁵Verily, verily, I say unto you: Ye must watch and pray always, lest ye be tempted by the devil and ye are led away captive by him. ¹⁶And, as I have prayed among you, even so shall ye pray in my church, among my people which do repent and are baptized in my name. Behold, I am the light. I have set an example before you.

¹⁷And it came to pass that when Jesus had spake these words unto his disciples, he turned again unto the multitude, and saith unto them:

¹⁸Behold! Verily, verily, I say unto you: Ye must watch, and pray always, lest ye enter into temptation. For Satan desireth to have you, that he may sift you as wheat. ¹⁹Therefore, ye must always pray unto the Father, in my name. ²⁰And whatsoever ye shall ask the Father in my name (which is right), believing that ye shall receive—and behold, it shall be given unto you. ²¹Pray in your families unto the Father, always in my name, that your wives and your children may be blessed.

²²And behold, ye shall meet together oft. And ye shall not forbid any man from coming unto you when ye shall meet together. But suffer them that they may come unto you and forbid them not. ²³But ye shall pray for them and shall not cast them out.

And if it so be that they come unto you oft, ye shall pray for them, unto the Father, in my name. ²⁴Therefore, hold up your light, that it may shine unto the world. Behold, I am the light which ye shall hold up. That which ye have seen me do—behold, ye see that I have prayed unto the Father (and ye all have witnessed)—²⁵and ye see that I have commanded that none of you should go away, but rather have commanded that ye should come unto me that ye might feel, and see—even so shall ye do unto the world. And whosoever breaketh this commandment suffereth himself to be led into temptation.

---

a. Language reprises Matthew 16:18: "And I say also unto thee, That thou art Peter, and upon this rock I will build my church; and the gates of hell shall not prevail against it."
b. See Matthew 7:24–27.

Chapter VIII [3 Nephi 17–18]

²⁶And now it came to pass that when Jesus had spoken these words, he turned his eyes again upon the disciples (whom he had chosen), and saith unto them:

²⁷Behold, verily, verily, I say unto you: I give unto you another commandment and then I must go unto my Father, that I may fulfil other commandments which he hath given me. ²⁹And now behold, this is the commandment which I give unto you, that ye shall not suffer any one knowingly to partake of my flesh and blood unworthily when ye shall minister it. For whoso eateth and drinketh my flesh and blood unworthily, eateth and drinketh damnation to his soul.ᵃ Therefore, if ye know that a man is unworthy to eat and drink of my flesh and blood—ye shall forbid him. ³⁰Nevertheless, ye shall not cast him out from among you. But ye shall minister unto him, and shall pray for him unto the Father, in my name. And if it so be that he repenteth and is baptized in my name—then shall ye receive him and shall minister unto him of my flesh and blood.

³¹But if he repenteth not, he shall not be numbered among my people, that he may not destroy my people. For behold, I know my sheep, and they are numbered. ³²Nevertheless, ye shall not cast him out of your synagogues, or your places of worship. For unto such ye shall continue to minister. For ye know not but what they will return and come unto me willᵇ full purpose of heart—and I shall heal them.

And ye shall be the means of bringing salvation unto them. ³³Therefore, keep these sayings which I have commanded you, that ye come not under condemnation. For wo unto him whom the Father condemneth!

³⁴And I give you these commandments because of the disputations which hath been among you before-times. And blessed are ye if ye have no disputations among you.

³⁵And now I go unto the Father, because it is expedient that I should go unto the Father for your sakes.

³⁶And it came to pass that when Jesus had made an end of these sayings, he touched (with his hand) the disciples whom he had chosen, one by one, even until he had touched them all—and spake unto them as he touched them. ³⁷And the multitude heard not the words which he spake. Therefore, they did not bear record. But the disciples bear record that he gave them power to give the Holy Ghost. And I will show unto you hereafter that this record is true.

³⁸And it came to pass that when Jesus had touched them all, there came a cloud and overshadowed the multitude, that they could not see Jesus. ³⁹And while they were overshadowed, he departed from them and ascended into heaven. And the disciples saw and did bear record that he ascended again into heaven.

---

a. See 1 Corinthians 11:29: "For he that eateth and drinketh unworthily, eateth and drinketh damnation to himself, not discerning the Lord's body."

b. The Printer's Manuscript has "will," which appears to be an obvious error. It should have been "with."

Chapter IX [3 Nephi 19–21:21]

[19] ¹And now it came to pass that when Jesus had ascended into heaven, the multitude did disperse. And every man did take his wife and his children, and did return to his own home. ²And it was noised abroad among the people—immediately, before it was yet dark, that the multitude had seen Jesus and that he had ministered unto them, and that he would also show himself on the morrow unto the multitude. ³Yea, and even all the night it was noised abroad concerning Jesus. And insomuch did they send forth unto the people, that there were many, yea, an exceeding great number, did labor exceedingly all that night that they might be on the morrow in the place where Jesus should show himself unto the multitude.

⁴And it came to pass that on the morrow, when the multitude was gathered together, behold, Nephi and his brother (whom he had raised from the dead—whose name was Timothy), and also his son (whose name was Jonas), and also Mathoni, and Mathonihah (his brother), and Kumen, and Kumenonki,ᵃ and Jeremiah, and Shemnon, and Jonas, and Zedekiah, and Isaiah—(now these were the names of the disciples whom Jesus had chosen)—and it came to pass that they went forth and stood in the midst of the multitude.ᵇ

⁵And behold, the multitude was so great that they did cause that they should be separated into twelve bodies. ⁶And the twelve did teach the multitude. But behold, they did cause that the multitude should kneel down upon the face of the earth and should pray unto the Father—in the name of Jesus. ⁷And the disciples did pray unto the Father also, in the name of Jesus.

And it came to pass that they arose and ministered unto the people. ⁸And when they had ministered them same words which Jesus had spoken (nothing varying from the words which Jesus had spoken), behold, they knelt again and prayed to the Father in the name of Jesus. ⁹And they did pray for that which they most desired. And they desired that the Holy Ghost should be given unto them. ¹⁰And when they had thus prayed, they went down unto the water's edge. And the multitude followed them.

¹¹And it came to pass that Nephi went down into the water and was baptized. ¹²And he came up out of the water and began to baptize. And he did baptize all they whom Jesus had chosen.

¹³And it came to pass when they were all baptized and had come up out of the water—the Holy Ghost did fall upon them. And they were filled with the Holy Ghost, and with fire. ¹⁴And behold, they were encircled about as if it were fire. And it came down from heaven. And the multitude did witness it, and do bear record. And angels did come down out of heaven and did minister unto them.

¹⁵And it came to pass that while angels were ministering unto the disciples, behold, Jesus came and stood in the midst and ministered unto them.

¹⁶And it came to pass that he spake unto the multitude and commanded them that

---

a. The Printer's Manuscript has Kumenonki, and it has been retained, even though printed editions have Kumenonhi. Skousen notes that Oliver Cowdery's "h" and "k" were similar and led to the confusion. In this text, Cowdery made several corrections, and the typesetter selected Kumenonhi, doubtless modeling it on the other names ending in -hi. Skousen, *Analysis of the Textual Variants*, 6:3436.

b. An incomplete sentence. The list of names separated the sentence too far from the beginning verb. The second "and it came to pass" is formatted as a repetitive resumption intended to restart the original sentence.

Chapter IX [3 Nephi 19–21:21]

they should kneel down again upon the earth, and also that his disciples should kneel down upon the earth.

¹⁷And it came to pass that when they had all knelt down upon the earth, he commanded his disciples that they should pray. ¹⁸And behold, they began to pray. And they did pray unto Jesus—calling him their Lord, and their God.

¹⁹And it came to pass that Jesus departed out of the midst of them, and went a little way off from them, and bowed himself to the earth. And he saith:

²⁰Father, I thank thee that thou hast given the Holy Ghost unto these, whom I have chosen And it is because of their belief in me that I have chosen them out of the world.

²¹Father, I pray thee, that thou wilt give the Holy Ghost unto all them that shall believe in their words.

²²Father, thou hast given them the Holy Ghost because they believed in me. And thou seest that they believe in me because thou hearest them. And they pray unto me. And they pray unto me because I am with them.

²³And now Father, I pray unto thee for them, and also for all they which shall believe on their words, that they may believe in me, that I may be in them as thou, Father, art in me—that we may be one.^a

²⁴And it came to pass that when Jesus had thus prayed unto the Father, he came unto his disciples. And behold, they did still continue, without ceasing, to pray unto him. And they did not multiply many words, for it was given unto them what they should pray. And they were filled with desire.

²⁵And it came to pass that Jesus beheld them as they did pray unto him. And his countenance did smile upon them. And the light of his countenance did shine upon them. And behold, they were as white as the countenance, and also the garments, of Jesus. And behold, the whiteness thereof did exceed the whiteness—yea, even there could be nothing upon earth so white as the whiteness thereof.

²⁶And Jesus saith unto them: "Pray on!" Nevertheless, they did not cease to pray. ²⁷And he turned from them again, and went a little way off, and bowed himself to the earth. And he prayed again unto the Father, saying:

²⁸Father, I thank thee that thou hast purified these, which I have chosen, because of their faith. And I pray for them, and also for them which shall believe on their words, that they may be purified in me through faith on their words, even as they are purified in me.

²⁹Father, I pray not for the world, but for them which thou hast given unto me out of the world^b because of their faith, that they may be purified in me, that I may be in them as thou, Father, art in me—that we may be one,^c that I may be glorified in them.

³⁰And it came to pass that when Jesus had spake these words, he came again unto his disciples. And behold, they did pray steadfastly, without ceasing, unto him. And he did smile upon them again. And behold, they were white, even as Jesus.

³¹And it came to pass that he went again a little way off and prayed unto the Father.

---

a. See John 17:22: "that they may be one, even as we are one."
b. See John 17:9: "I pray for them: I pray not for the world, but for them which thou hast given me."
c. See John 17:22: "that they may be one, even as we are one."

³²And tongue cannot speak the words which he prayed—neither can be written by man the words which he prayed. ³³And the multitude did hear, and do [bear^a] record. And their hearts were open. And they did understand, in their hearts, the words which he prayed. ³⁴Nevertheless, so great and marvelous were the words which he prayed that they cannot be written—neither can they be uttered by man.

³⁵And it came to pass that when Jesus had made an end of praying, he came again to the disciples and saith unto them:

> So great faith have I never seen among all the Jews. Wherefore, I could not show unto them so great miracles because of their unbelief. ³⁶Verily, I say unto you: There are none of them that have seen so great things as ye have seen, neither have they heard so great things as ye have heard.

[20] ¹And it came to pass that he commanded the multitude that they should cease to pray, and also his disciples. ²And he commanded them that they should not cease to pray in their hearts. And he commanded them that they should arise and stand up upon their feet. And they arose up and stood up on their feet.

³And it came to pass that he broke bread again, and blessed it, and gave to the disciples to eat. ⁴And when they had eat, he commanded them that they should break bread and give unto the multitude. ⁵And when they had given unto the multitude, he also gave them wine to drink. And commanded them that they should give unto the multitude. ⁶Now, there had been no bread, neither wine, brought by the disciples. Neither by the multitude. ⁷But he truly gave unto them bread to eat, and also wine to drink.

⁸And he saith unto them:

> He that eateth this bread, eateth of my body, to their soul.
> And he that drinketh of this wine, drinketh of my blood, to their soul.
> And their soul shall never hunger, nor thirst—but shall be filled.

⁹Now, when the multitude had all eat and drank—behold, they were filled with the spirit. And they did cry out with one voice and gave glory to Jesus, whom they both saw and heard.

¹⁰And it came to pass that when they had all given glory unto Jesus, he saith unto them:

> Behold, now I finish the commandment which the Father hath commanded me concerning this people, which are a remnant of the house of Israel.

¹¹Ye remember that I spake unto you and said that when the words of Isaiah should be fulfilled (behold, they are written—ye have them before you, therefore search them)—¹²and verily, verily, I say unto you that when they shall be fulfilled—then is the fulfilling of the covenant which the Father hath made unto his people, O house of Israel.^b ¹³And then shall the remnants (which shall be scattered abroad upon the face of the earth) be gathered in—from the east, and from the west, and from the south, and from the north. And they shall be brought to the knowledge of the Lord, their God, who hath redeemed them.

¹⁴And the Father hath commanded me that I should give unto you this land for

---

a. The Printer's Manuscript had "their," which was corrected in proofreading.
b. Verse 12 is the repetitive resumption to return to the original thought of the sentence.

your [inheritance[a]]. ¹⁵And I say unto you that if the Gentiles do not repent—after the blessings which they shall receive, after that they have scattered my people—

[Compare Micah 5:8–9]

¹⁶**then shall ye (which are** a remnant **of the house** of Jacob)—
go forth among **them.**
And **ye shall be** in the midst of **them, which shall be many.**
And **ye shall be among them** as a lion among the beasts of the forest,
and as a young lion among the flocks of sheep,
who, if he goeth through—both treadeth down, and teareth in pieces.
And none can deliver.
¹⁷Thy hand shall be lifted up upon their adversaries.
And all their enemies shall be cut off.

[Compare Micah 4:12–13]

¹⁸**And I will** gather **my people together,**
as a man gathereth his sheaves into the floor.
¹⁹**For I will make my people**
(with whom the Father hath covenanted),
yea, I will make **thy** horn iron,
and I will make thy hoofs brass.
And thou shalt beat in pieces many people.
And I will consecrate their gain unto the Lord,
and their substance unto the Lord of the whole earth.
And behold, I am he which doeth it.

²⁰And it shall come to pass (saith the Father), that the sword of my justice shall hang over them at that day. And except they repent, it shall fall upon them (saith the Father), yea, even upon all the nations of the Gentiles.

²¹And it shall come to pass that I will establish my people, O house of Israel. ²²And behold, this people will I establish in this land—unto the fulfilling of the covenant which I made with your Father, Jacob. And it shall be a new Jerusalem. And the powers of heaven shall be in the midst of this people, yea, even I will be in the midst of you.

²³Behold, I am in the he of whom Moses spake, saying: "A [prophet[b]] shall the Lord your God raise up unto you, of your brethren, like unto me. Him shall ye hear in all things, whatsover he shall say unto you. And it shall come to pass that every soul which will not hear that prophet shall be cut off from among the people."

²⁴Verily I say unto you, yea, and all the prophets from Samuel and those that follow after, as many as have spoken—have testified of me.[c] ²⁵And behold, ye are the children of the prophets. And ye are of the house of Israel. And ye are of the

---

a. The Printer's Manuscript has "inheritage," which might have meant "heritage," or "inheritance." "Inheritance" was selected based on similar passages. It is "inheritance" in printed versions.

b. The Printer's Manuscript has "people." Hyrum Smith corrected it to "prophet," which is correct, as this quotes Deuteronomy 18:15. While the quotation originates in Deuteronomy, the version quoted is from Acts 3:22, 7:37.

c. See Acts 3:24: "Yea, and all the prophets from Samuel and those that follow after, as many as have spoken, have likewise foretold of these days."

covenant which the Father made with your fathers, saying unto Abraham—and in thy seed shall all the kindreds of the earth be blessed[a]—²⁶the Father having raised me up unto you first, and sent me to bless you—in turning away every one of you from his iniquities. And this, because ye are the children of the covenant.[b]

²⁷And after that ye were blessed—then fulfilleth the Father the covenant which he made with Abraham, saying: In thy seed shall all the kindreds of the earth be blessed,[c] unto the pouring out of the Holy Ghost through me upon the Gentiles, which blessing upon the Gentiles shall make them mighty above all—unto the scattering of my people, O house of Israel.

²⁸And they shall be a scourge unto the people of this land. Nevertheless, when they shall have received the fullness of my gospel—then, if they shall harden their hearts against me, I will return their iniquities upon their own heads (saith the Father). ²⁹And I will remember the covenant which I have made with my people. And I have covenanted with them, that I would gather them together in mine own due time, that I would give unto them again the land of their fathers for their inheritance, which is the land of Jerusalem, which is the promised land unto them forever (saith the Father).

³⁰And it shall come to pass that the time cometh when the fullness of my gospel be preached unto them. ³¹And they shall believe in me, that I am Jesus Christ, the Son of God—and shall pray unto the Father in my name.

[Compare Isaiah 52:8–10]

³²**Then shall their** watchmen lift up **their** voice,
   and with the voice together shall they sing.
   For they shall see eye to eye.
³³**Then will the Father gather them together again,**
   and give unto them Jerusalem for the land of their inheritance.
³⁴**Then shall they** break forth into joy.
Sing together ye waste places of Jerusalem!
   For the Father hath comforted his people.
He hath redeemed Jerusalem.
³⁵The Father hath made bare his holy arm
   in the eyes of all the nations.
And all the ends of the earth
   shall see the salvation of **the Father**.[d]
   And the Father and I are one.[e]

---

a. See Acts 3:25: "Ye are the children of the prophets, and of the covenant which God made with our fathers, saying unto Abraham, And in thy seed shall all the kindreds of the earth be blessed." Acts is quoting Genesis 22:18: "And in thy seed shall all the nations of the earth be blessed; because thou hast obeyed my voice."

b. Verses 24–26 loosely quote Acts 3:24–26.

c. See Acts 3:25: "Ye are the children of the prophets, and of the covenant which God made with our fathers, saying unto Abraham, And in thy seed shall all the kindreds of the earth be blessed." Acts is quoting Genesis 22:18: "And in thy seed shall all the nations of the earth be blessed; because thou hast obeyed my voice."

d. See Isaiah 52:10: "The Lord hath made bare his holy arm in the eyes of all the nations; and all the ends of the earth shall see the salvation of our God."

e. See John 10:30: "I and my Father are one."

Chapter IX [3 Nephi 19–21:21]

[Compare Isaiah 52: 1–3]

³⁶And then shall be brought to pass that which is written:

"**Awake, awake again! And** put on thy strength, O Zion!
   Put on thy beautiful garments, O Jerusalem, the holy city.
For henceforth there shall no more come into thee
   the uncircumcised
   and the unclean.
³⁷Shake thyself from the dust!
   Arise. [ᵃ] Sit down, O Jerusalem.
Loose thyself from the bands of thy neck,
   O captive daughter of Zion.
³⁸For thus saith the Lord:
"Ye have sold yourselves for naught.
And ye shall be redeemed without money."

[Compare Isaiah 52: 6–7]

³⁹**Verily, verily, I say unto you that** my people shall know my name.
   Yea, in that day they shall know that I am he that doth speak. [ᵇ]
⁴⁰**And then shall they say:**
"How beautiful upon the mountains
   are the feet of him that bringeth good tidings **unto them**
that publisheth peace,
   that bringeth good tidings **unto them** of good,
that publisheth salvation,
   that saith unto Zion: Thy God reigneth!'"

[Compare Isaiah 52:11–15]

⁴¹And then shall a cry go forth—
"Depart ye! Depart ye! Go ye out from thence.
   Touch **not that which** is unclean.
Go ye out of the midst of her.
   Be ye clean that bear the vessels of the Lord!
⁴²For ye shall not go out with haste, nor go by flight.
   For the Lord will go before you.
   And the God of Israel **shall** be your rearward."

"⁴³Behold, my servant shall deal prudently.
   He shall be exalted, and extolled, and be very high.
⁴⁴As many were astonished at thee–
   his visage was so marred more than any man,
   and his form more than the sons of men.
⁴⁵So shall he sprinkle many nations.
   The kings shall shut their mouths at him.

---

a. Omits "and," which is in italics.
b. Omits "behold it is I."

For that which had [ª] been told them, shall they see.
And that which they had not heard, shall they consider."

⁴⁶Verily, verily, I say unto you: All these things shall surely come, even as the Father hath commanded me. And then shall this covenant, which the Father hath covenanted with his people, be fulfilled. And then shall Jerusalem be inhabited again with my people. And it shall be the land of their inheritance.

[21] ¹And verily I say unto you, I give unto you a sign—that ye may know the time when these things shall be about to take place, that I shall gather in from their long dispersion, my people, O house of Israel, and shall establish again among them, my Zion. ²And behold, this is the thing which I will give unto you for a sign, for verily I say unto you, that when these things (which I [declareᵇ] unto you, and which I shall [declareᶜ] unto you hereafter, of myself—and by the power of the Holy Ghost, which shall be given unto you of the Father)—shall be made known unto the Gentiles, that they may know concerning this people, which are a remnant of the house of Jacob—and concerning this, my people, which shall be scattered by them.

³Verily, verily, I say unto you: When these things shall be made known unto them of the Father, and shall come forth of the Father from them unto you (⁴for it is wisdom in the Father that they should be established in this land and be set up as a free people by the power of the Father), that these might come forth from them, unto a remnant of your seed, that the covenant of the Father may be fulfilled which he hath covenanted with his people, O house of Israel.ᵈ ⁵Therefore, when these works, and the work which shall be wrought among you hereafter, shall come forth from the Gentiles unto your seed (which shall dwindle in unbelief because of iniquity)—⁶for thus it behoveth the Father that it should come forth from the Gentiles, that he may show forth his power unto the Gentiles for this cause, that the Gentiles (if they will not harden their hearts), that they may repent and come unto me, and be baptized in my name, and know of the true points of my doctrine, that they may be numbered among my people, O house of Israel.ᵉ

⁷And when these things come to pass that thy seed shall begin to know these things, it shall be a sign unto them that they may know that the work of the Father hath already commenced, unto the fulfilling of the covenant which he hath made unto the people which are of the house of Israel. ⁸And when that day shall come, it shall come to pass that kings shall shut their mouths. For that which had not been told them—shall they see. And that which they had not heard—shall they

---

a. Omits "not." This may have been a copy error. The "not" is required to parallel the "not" in the next phrase.

b. The Printer's Manuscript had "deliver," which Hyrum Smith changed to "declare," both here and later in this verse. The Original Manuscript is not extant here, but Hyrum's edits usually make a sentence read correctly and perhaps in accordance with the Original.

c. Hyrum Smith also changed "deliver" to "declare" at this point.

d. This sentence uses repetitive resumption to recover from the long clause that creates the distance from the original idea.

e. This is an incomplete sentence. The "when" at the beginning is never resolved.

consider.ᵃ ⁹For, in that day, for my sake, shall the Father work a work (which shall be a great, and a marvelous work) among them.ᵇ

And there shall be among them which will not believe it, although a man shall declare it unto them. ¹⁰But behold, the life of my servant shall be in my hand. Therefore, they shall not hurt him, although he shall be marred because of them.ᶜ Yet, I will heal him. For I will show unto him them that my wisdom is greater than the cunning of the devil. ¹¹Therefore, it shall come to pass that whosoever will not believe in my words (which am Jesus Christ, which the Father shall cause him to bring forth unto the Gentiles, and shall give unto him power, that he shall bring them forth unto the Gentiles)—it shall be done, even as Moses said—"they shall be cut off from among my people", which are of the covenant.

[Compare Micah 5:8–15]

¹²**And my people, which are** a remnant of Jacob,
> shall be among the Gentiles,

yea, in the midst of **them**—as a lion among the beasts of the forest—
> as a young lion among the flocks of sheep—

who, if he go through, both treadeth down, and teareth in pieces.
> And none can deliver.

¹³**Their** hand shall be lifted up upon **their** adversaries,
> and all their enemies shall be cut off.

¹⁴**Yea, wo be unto the Gentiles, except they repent!**
"For it shall come to pass in that day" (saith the **Father**),
"that I will cut off thy horses out of the midst of thee.
> And I will destroy thy chariots.

¹⁵And I will cut off the cities of thy land
> and throw down all thy strongholds.

¹⁶And I will cut off witchcrafts out of thy hand.
> And thou shalt have no more soothsayers.

¹⁷Thy graven images **I will also** cut off,
> and thy standing images out of the midst of thee.
> And thou shalt no more worship the **works** of thy hands.

¹⁸And I will pluck up thy groves out of the midst of thee—
> so will I destroy thy cities."

¹⁹**And it shall come to pass**
> that all lyings,
> and deceivings,
> and envyings,
> and strife,
> and priestcraft,

---

a. See Isaiah 52:15: "the kings shall shut their mouths at him: for that which had not been told them shall they see; and that which they had not heard shall they consider." Recently quoted in 3 Nephi 20:45.

b. Acts 13:41: "Behold, ye despisers, and wonder, and perish: for I work a work in your days, a work which ye shall in no wise believe, though a man declare it unto you."

c. See Isaiah 52:14: "As many were astonied at thee; his visage was so marred more than any man, and his form more than the sons of men." Recently quoted in 3 Nephi 20:44.

and whoredoms,
shall be done away.
²⁰"For it shall come to pass" (saith the Father),
"that at that day, whosoever will not repent
and come unto my beloved Son—
them will I cut off from among my people, O house of Israel!ᵃ
²¹And I will execute vengeance and fury **upon them,
even as** upon the heathen—such as they have not heard.

---

a. Verses 19–20 are added into the Micah quotation. Verse 21 quotes Micah 5:15.

Chapter X [3 Nephi 21:22–23:13]

[**21 continued**] ²²But if they will repent, and hearken unto my words and harden not their hearts, I will establish my church among them. And they shall come in unto the covenant and be numbered among this, the remnant of Jacob—unto whom I have given this land for their inheritance. ²³And they shall assist my people, the remnant of Jacob (and also as many of the house of Israel as shall come), that they may build a city, which shall be called the New Jerusalem. ²⁴And then shall they assist my people that they may be gathered in which are scattered upon all the face of the land—in unto the New Jerusalem.

²⁵And then shall the powers of heaven come down among them. And I also will be in the midst. ²⁶And then shall the work of the Father commence at that day, even when this gospel shall be preached among the remnant of this people. Verily I say unto you: At that day shall the work of the Father commence among all the dispersed of my people, yea, even the tribes which have been lost, which the Father hath led away out of Jerusalem.

²⁸Yea, the work shall commence among all the dispersed of my people (with the Father), to prepare the way whereby they may come unto me, that they may call on the Father, in my name. Yea, and then shall the work commence (with the Father) among all nations in preparing the way. Whereby, his people may be gathered home to the land of their inheritance. ²⁹And they shall go out from all nations.

> And "they shall not go out in haste, nor go by flight.
> For I will go before them (saith the Father).
> And I will be their rearward."[a]

[**22**] ¹And then shall that which is written come to pass:

[Compare Isaiah 54:1–17]

> "Sing O barren!—thou that didst not bear.
>   Break forth into singing and cry aloud,
>   thou that didst not travail with child.
> For more are the children of the desolate
>   than the children of the married wife" (saith the Lord).
> ²Enlarge the place of thy tent
>   and let them stretch forth the curtain of thy habitations.
>   Spare not! Lengthen thy cords and strengthen thy stakes.
> ³For thou shalt break forth on the right hand, and on the left,
>   and thy seed shall inherit the Gentiles,
>   and make the desolate cities to be inhabited.
>
> ⁴Fear not! For thou shalt not be ashamed.
>   Neither be thou confounded.
>   For thou shalt not be put to shame.
> For thou shalt forget the shame of thy youth,
>   and shalt not remember the reproach of thy widowhood any more.

---

a. Quotes Isaiah 52:11, recently quoted as well in 3 Nephi 20:41.

⁵For thy maker, [ᵃ] thy husband, the Lord of Hosts is his name!
  And thy Redeemer, the Holy One of Israel,
  the God of the whole earth, shall he be called.
⁶For the Lord hath called thee as a woman forsaken, and grieved in spirit,
  and a wife of youth (when thou wast refused). Saith thy God:
⁷"For a small moment have I forsaken thee.
  But with great mercies will I gather thee.
⁸In a little wrath, I hid my face from thee for a moment.
  But with everlasting kindness will I have mercy on thee"
(saith the Lord, thy Redeemer).

⁹"For this [ᵇ], the waters of Noah unto me.
  For as I have sworn that the waters of Noah
  should no more go over the earth,
so have I sworn
  that I would not be wroth with thee.
¹⁰For the mountains shall depart, and the hills be removed.
  But my kindness shall not depart from thee.
Neither shall the covenant of my peace be removed,"
  saith the Lord that hath mercy on thee.

¹¹"O thou afflicted, tossed with tempests,
  and not comforted!
Behold, I will lay thy stones with fair colors,
  and lay thy foundations with sapphires.
¹²And I will make thy windows of agates,
  and thy gates of carbuncles.
And all thy borders of pleasant stones.
¹³And all thy children shall be taught of the Lord.
  And great shall be the peace of thy children.
¹⁴In righteousness shalt thou be established.
  Thou shalt be far from oppression, for thou shalt not fear—
  and from terror, for it shall not come near thee.

¹⁵Behold, they shall surely gather together **against thee**, [ᶜ] not by me.
  Whosoever shall gather together against thee shall fall, for thy sake.
  ¹⁶Behold, I have created the smith that bloweth the coals in the fire
  and that bringeth forth an instrument for his work.
  And I have created the waster, to destroy.
¹⁷No weapon that is formed against thee shall prosper.
  And every tongue that shall **revile** against thee in judgment,
  thou shalt condemn.
This is the heritage of the servants of the Lord.
  And their righteousness is of me," saith the Lord.

---

a. Omits "is," which is in italics.
b. Omits "is as," which is in italics.
c. Omits "but," which is in italics.

CHAPTER X [3 NEPHI 21:22–23:13]

[23] ¹And now behold, I say unto you, that ye had ought to search these things. Yea, a commandment I give unto you, that ye search these things diligently. For great is the words of Isaiah. ²For surely he spake as touching all things concerning my people, which are of the house of Israel. Therefore, it must needs be that he must speak to also to the Gentiles. ³And all things that he spake hath been, and shall be, even according to the words which he spake. ⁴Therefore, give heed to my words.

Write the things which I have told you. And, according to the time and the will of the Father, [they shall[a]] go forth unto the Gentiles. ⁵And whosoever will hearken unto my words, and repenteth, and is baptized, the same shall be saved.

Search the prophets! For many there be that testify of these things.

⁶And now it came to pass that when Jesus had said these words, he saith unto them again (after he had expounded all the scriptures unto them, which they had received)—he saith unto them: "Behold! Other scriptures I would that ye should write, that ye have not." ⁷And it came to pass that he saith unto Nephi: "Bring forth the records which ye have kept."

⁸And when Nephi had brought forth the records, and laid them before him, and he cast his eyes upon them, and saith: ⁹"Verily I say unto you: I commanded my servant Samuel the Lamanite, that he should testified testify unto this people that at the day that the Father should glorify his name in me, that there were many saints which should arise from the dead, and should appear unto many, and should minister unto them."

And he saith unto them: "Were it not so?"

¹⁰And his disciples answered him, and said: "Yea, Lord. Samuel did prophesy according to thy words. And they were all fulfilled."

¹¹And Jesus saith unto them: "How be it that ye have not written this thing: That many saints did arise, and appear unto many, and did minister unto them?"

¹²And it came to pass that Nephi remembered that this thing had not been written.

¹³And it came to pass that Jesus commanded that it should be written. Therefore, it was written, according as he commanded.

---

a. Inserted above the line.

Chapter XI [3 Nephi 23:14–26:5]

[**23 continued**] ¹⁴And now it came to pass that when Jesus had expounded all the scriptures in one (which they had written), he commanded them that they should teach the things which he had expounded unto them.

[**24**] ¹And it came to pass that he commanded them that they should write the words which the Father had given unto Malachi, which he should tell unto them.

And it came to pass that after they were written, he expounded them. And these are the words which he did tell unto them, saying:

Thus said the Father unto Malachi:

[Compare Malachi 3]

"Behold, I will send my messenger, and he shall prepare the way before me. And the Lord, whom ye seek, shall suddenly come to his temple, even the messenger of the covenant, whom ye delight in.

Behold, he shall come, saith the Lord of Hosts—²but who may abide the of day of his coming? And who shall stand when he appeareth? For he is like a refiner's fire, and like fullers' soap. ³And he shall sit as a refiner and purifier of silver. And he shall purify the sons of Levi, and purge them as gold and silver, that they may offer unto the Lord an offering in righteousness. ⁴Then shall the offering of Judah and Jerusalem be pleasant unto the Lord as in the days of old, and as in former years.

⁵And I will come near to you to judgment. And I will be a swift witness against the sorcerers, and against the adulterers, and against false swearers, and against those that oppress the hireling in his wages, the widow, and the fatherless, and that turn aside the stranger, and fear not me (saith the Lord of Hosts). ⁶For I am the Lord. I change not. Therefore, ye sons of Jacob are not consumed. ⁷Even from the days of your fathers, ye are gone away from mine ordinances and have not kept them.

Return unto me, and I will return unto you (saith the Lord of Hosts)."

But ye said: "Wherein shall we return?"

⁸"Will a man rob God? Yet ye have robbed me."

But ye **say**: "Wherein have we robed thee?"

"In tithes and offerings. ⁹Ye are cursed with a curse. For ye have robbed me, even this whole nation! ¹⁰Bring ye all the tithes into the storehouse, that there may be meat in my house! And prove me now herewith" (saith the Lord of Hosts)—"if I will not open you the windows of heaven and pour you out a blessing that there shall not be room enough to receive it.

¹¹And I will rebuke the devourer for your sakes. He shall not destroy the fruits of your ground, neither shall your vine cast her fruit (before the time) in the field (saith the Lord of Hosts). ¹²And all nations shall call you blessed. For ye shall be a delightsome land" (saith the Lord of Hosts).

¹³"Your words have been stout against me" (saith Lord). Yet ye say: "What have we spoken against thee?"

¹⁴Ye have said: "It is vain to serve God. And, what doth it profit that we have kept his ordinances, and that we have walked mournfully before the Lord of Hosts? ¹⁵And now, we call the proud happy. Yea, they that work wickedness are set up. Yea, them that tempt God are even delivered!"

¹⁶Then they that feared the Lord spake often, one to another. And the Lord hearkened and heard. And a book of remembrance was written before him. For them that feared the Lord, and that thought upon his name. ¹⁷And they shall be mine (saith the Lord of Hosts) in that day when I make up my jewels. And I will spare them, as a man spareth his own son, that saveth him. ¹⁸Then shall ye return and discern between the righteous, and the wicked—between him that serveth God, and him that serveth him not.

[Compare Malachi 4]

[25] ¹For behold, the day cometh that [ᵃ] shall burn as an oven. And all the proud, yea, and all that do wickedly shall be stubble. And the day that cometh shall burn them up (saith the Lord of Hosts), that it shall leave them neither root nor branch. ²But unto you that fear my name shall the son[b] of righteousness arise with healing in his wings.

And ye shall go forth and grow up as calves of the stall. ³And ye shall tread down the wicked. For they shall be ashes under the soles of your feet in the day that I shall do this (saith the Lord of Hosts).

⁴Remember ye the law of Moses (my servant), which I commanded unto him in Horeb for all Israel, with the statutes and judgments.

⁵Behold, I will send you Elijah the prophet before the coming of the great and dreadful day of the Lord. ⁶And he shall turn the heart of the fathers to the children, and the heart of the children to their fathers, lest I come and smite the earth with a curse.

[26] ¹And now it came to pass that when Jesus had told these things, he expounded them unto the multitude. And he did expound all things unto them, both great and small. ²And he saith: These scriptures, which ye had not with you, the Father commanded that I should give unto you. For it was wisdom in Him that they should be given unto future generations.

³And he did expound all things, even from the beginning until the time that he should come in his glory, yea, even all things which should come upon the face of the earth, even until the elements should melts with fervent heat[c], and the earth should be wrapped together as a scroll,[d] and the heaven and the earth should pass away. And ⁴even unto the great, and last day—when all people and all kindreds, and all nations, and tongues, shall stand before God, to be judged of their works—whether they be good, or whether they be evil. ⁵If they be good, to the resurrection of everlasting life. And if they be evil, to the resurrection of damnation, being on a parallel, the one on the one hand, and the other on the other hand—according to the mercy, and the justice, and the holiness, which is in Christ, which was before the world began.

---

a. Malachi 4:1 has "that." The word is missing in the Printer's Manuscript. It was not italicized and therefore that was not the reason it was left out. It was simply an oversight.

b. Malachi 4:2 has "sun" instead of "son." This homophone was simply written as it was heard, and it was not corrected because it made sense in the context of Christ.

c. See 2 Peter 3:12: "Looking for and hasting unto the coming of the day of God, wherein the heavens being on fire shall be dissolved, and the elements shall melt with fervent heat?"

d. See Isaiah 34:4: "And all the host of heaven shall be dissolved, and the heavens shall be rolled together as a scroll."

Chapter XII [3 Nephi 26:6–27:22]

>[26] ⁶And now, there cannot be written in this book even an hundredth part of the things which Jesus did truly teach unto the people. ⁷But behold, the plates of Nephi do contain the more part of the things which he taught the people. ⁸And these things have I written which are a lesser part of the things which he taught the people. And I have wrote them to the intent they may be brought again unto this people from the Gentiles, according to the words which Jesus hath spoken.

⁹And when they shall have received this (which is expedient that they should have first, to try their faith)—and if it should so be that they shall believe these things, then shall the greater things be made manifest unto them. ¹⁰And if it so be that they will not believe these things, then shall the greater things be withheld from them—unto their condemnation.

¹¹Behold, I were about to write them all, which were engraven upon the plates of Nephi—but the Lord forbid it, saying: "I will try the faith of my people." ¹²Therefore I, Mormon, do write the things which have been commanded me of the Lord.

And now I, Mormon, make an end of my sayings and proceed to write the things which have been commanded me. ¹³Therefore, I would that ye should behold that the Lord truly did teach the people for the space of three days. And after, that he did show himself unto them oft, and did break bread oft, and bless it, and give it unto them.ᵃ<

¹⁴And it came to pass that he did teach and minister unto the children of the multitude (of whom hath been spoken), and he did loose their tongues. And they did speak unto their fathers great and marvelous things, even greater than he had revealed unto the people and loosed their tongues that they could utter.ᵇ

¹⁵And it came to pass that after he ascended into heaven (the second time that he showed himself unto them) and gone unto the Father—after having healed all their sick, and their lame, and opened the eyes of the blind, and unstopped the ears of the deaf, and even had done all manner of cures among them, and raised a man from the dead, and had shown forth his power unto them, and had ascended unto the Father—¹⁶behold, it came to pass on the morrow that the multitude gathered themselves together,ᶜ and they both saw and heard these children, yea, even babes—did open their mouths, and utter marvelous things. And the things which they did utter were forbidden that there should not any man write them.

---

a. Mormon inserts a reference to his task. He provides information about the large plates as well as the smaller record from which he took this information. He explicitly closes the aside by noting that he makes an end of his sayings.

b. This sentence repeats the idea of loosed tongues from the previous sentence. The two similar phrases are so close together that they might be redundant. As the compositor added punctuation, there is a semi-colon between "the people; and loosed." That punctuation makes it appear that the loosed tongues belong to the children. I have chosen to remove the semi-colon and try to make sense of the idea by supposing that both the children and "the people" had their tongues loosed, but that what the children were able to say was greater.

c. The repeated "and it came to pass" is an intentional recovery from the multiple clauses and moves from the idea that Christ ascended on one day and came back the next.

¹⁷And it came to pass that the disciples (whom Jesus had chosen) began from that time forth to baptize and to teach as many as did come unto them. And, as many as were baptized in the name of Jesus, were filled with the Holy Ghost. ¹⁸And many of them saw and heard unspeakable things, which are not lawful to be written.[a] ¹⁹And they taught and did minister, one to another. And they had all things common among them,[b] every man dealing justly, one with another.

²⁰And it came to pass that they did do all things, even as Jesus had commanded them. ²¹And they which were baptized in the name of Jesus were called the church of Christ.

[27] ¹And it came to pass that as the disciples of Jesus were journeying and were preaching the things which they had both heard and seen, and were baptizing in the name of Jesus—it came to pass that the disciples were gathered together[c] and were united in mighty prayer, and fasting. ²And Jesus again showed himself unto them. For they were praying unto the Father in his name. And Jesus came, and stood in the midst of them, and saith unto them: "What will ye, that I shall give unto you?"

³And they saith unto him: "Lord, we will that thou wouldst tell us the name whereby we shall call this church. For there are disputations among the people concerning this matter."

⁴And the Lord said unto them:

> Verily, verily, I say unto you: Why is it that the people should murmur and dispute because of this thing? ⁵Have they not read the scriptures which saith, "Ye must take upon you the name of Christ," which is my name. For by this name shall ye be called at the last day. ⁶And whoso taketh upon him my name and endureth to the end, the same shall be saved at the last day.[d] ⁷Therefore, whatsoever ye shall do, ye shall do it in my name. Therefore, ye shall call the church in my name.
>
> And ye shall call upon the Father in my name, that he will bless the church for my sake. ⁸And how be it my church, save it be called in my name? For if a church be called in Moses' name—then it be Moses' church. Or, if it be called in the name of a man—then it be the church of a man. But if it be called in my name, then it is my church—if it so be that they are built upon my gospel.
>
> ⁹Verily I say unto you that ye are built upon my gospel. Therefore, ye shall call whatsoever things ye do call in my name. Therefore, if ye call upon the Father for the church—if it be in my name, the Father will hear you. ¹⁰And if it so be that the church is built upon my gospel, then will the Father show forth his own works in it. ¹¹But, if it be not built upon my gospel, and is built upon the works of [men[e]] (or upon the works of the devil)—verily I say unto you, they have joy in their works for a season. And by and by the end cometh, and they are hewn down, and cast into the fire from whence there is no return. ¹²For their works do follow them. For, it is because of their works that they are hewn down. Therefore, remember the things that I have told you.

---

a. See 2 Corinthians 12:4: "How that he was caught up into paradise, and heard unspeakable words, which it is not lawful for a man to utter."

b. See Acts 2:44: "and had all things common."

c. Another case of sentence-level repetitive resumption.

d. See Matthew 10:22: "he that endureth to the end shall be saved."

e. The Printer's Manuscript has "man." Hyrum Smith changed this to "men."

¹³Behold, I have given unto you my gospel. And this is the gospel which I have given unto you—that I came into the world to do the will of my Father, because my Father sent me. ¹⁴And my Father sent me that I might be lifted up upon the cross. And after that [I[a]] had been lifted up upon the cross, I might draw all men unto me,[b] that as I have been lifted up by men, even so should men be lifted up by the Father, to stand before [me[c]], to be judged of their works (whether they be good, or whether they be evil). ¹⁵And for this cause have I been lifted up. Therefore, according to the power of the Father, I will draw all men unto me, that they may be judged according to their works.

¹⁶And it shall come to pass that whoso repenteth, and is baptized in my name, shall be filled. ¹⁷And if he endureth to the end,[d] behold, him will I hold guiltless before my Father at that day when I shall stand to judge the world. And he that endureth not unto the end—the same is he that is also hewn down and cast into the fire (from whence they can no more return)—because of the justice of the Father.

¹⁸And this is the word which he hath given unto the children of men. And for this cause he fulfilleth the words which he hath given, and he lieth not, but fulfilleth all his words. ¹⁹And no unclean thing can enter into his kingdom.[e] Therefore, nothing entereth into his rest save it be those who have washed their garments in my blood, because of their faith and the repentance of all their sins, and their faithfulness unto the end.

²⁰Now, this is the commandment: Repent all ye ends of the earth!—and come unto me and be baptized in my name, that ye may be sanctified by the reception of the Holy Ghost, that ye may stand spotless before me at the last day.

²¹Verily, verily, I say unto you: This is my gospel. And ye know the thing that ye must do in my church. For the works which ye have seen me do, that shall ye also do. For that which ye have seen me do, even that shall ye do. ²²Therefore, if ye do these things, blessed are ye. For ye shall be lifted up at the last day.

---

a. The Printer's Manuscript had "he." It was caught in proofreading and changed to "I."
b. See John 12:32: "And I, if I be lifted up from the earth, will draw all men unto me."
c. Hyrum Smith added this above the line.
d. See Matthew 10:22: "he that endureth to the end shall be saved."
e. Perhaps a reference to 2 Chronicles 23:19: "And he set the porters at the gates of the house of the Lord, that none which was unclean in any thing should enter in." Although this verse specifically refers to the temple rather than to the kingdom, I suggest that they are symbolically parallel.

Chapter XIII [3 Nephi 27:23–29:9]

[27] ²³Write the things which ye have seen and heard, save it be those which are forbidden. ²⁴Write the [works^a] of this people, which shall be even as hath been written of that which hath been. ²⁵For behold, out of the books which have been written (and which shall be written) shall this people be judged.^b For by them shall their works be known unto men. ²⁶And behold, all things are written by the Father. Therefore, out of the books which shall be written—shall the world be judged.^c

²⁷And know ye that ye shall be judges of this people, according to the judgment which I shall give unto you, which shall be just. Therefore, what manner of men had ye ought to be? Verily I say unto you, even as I am.

²⁸And now I go unto the Father. And verily I say unto you: Whatsoever things ye shall ask the Father, in my name, it shall be given unto you. ²⁹Therefore, ask and ye shall receive, knock and it shall be opened unto you. For he that asketh, receiveth, and unto him that knocketh, it shall be opened.^d

³⁰And now behold, my joy is great, even unto fullness, because of you and also this generation. Yea, and even the Father rejoiceth, and also all the holy angels, because of you and this generation. For none of them are lost. ³¹Behold, I would that you should understand. For I mean them which are now alive of this generation—and none of them are lost. And in them, I have fullness of joy.

³²But behold, it sorroweth me because of the fourth generation from this generation, for they are led away captive by him, even as was the Son of Perdition. For they will sell me for silver, and for gold, and for that which moth doth corrupt, and which thieves can break through, and steal. And in that day will I visit them, even in turning their works upon their own heads.

³³And it came to pass that when Jesus had ended these sayings, he saith unto his disciples: "Enter ye in at the strait gate. For strait is the gate, and narrow is the way, that leads to life. And few there be that find it.^e But wide is the gate, and broad the way, which leads to death. And many there be that traveleth therein, until the night cometh wherein no man can work."

[28] ¹And it came to pass when Jesus had said these words, he spake unto his disciples, one by one, saying unto them: "What is it that ye desire of me, after that I am gone to the Father?"

²And they all spake, save it were three, saying: "We desire that after we have lived

---

a. The Printer's Manuscript had "words." Hyrum Smith crossed it out and replaced it with "works." It seems that Hyrum was editing against the Original Manuscript, since "words" would be perfectly acceptable.

b. Uses language from Revelation 20:12: "And I saw the dead, small and great, stand before God; and the books were opened: and another book was opened, which is the book of life: and the dead were judged out of those things which were written in the books, according to their works."

c. Uses language from Revelation 20:12: "And I saw the dead, small and great, stand before God; and the books were opened: and another book was opened, which is the book of life: and the dead were judged out of those things which were written in the books, according to their works."

d. See 3 Nephi 13:7–8, as well as Matthew 7:7: "Ask, and it shall be given you; seek, and ye shall find; knock, and it shall be opened unto you."

e. See Matthew 7:14: "Because strait is the gate, and narrow is the way, which leadeth unto life, and few there be that find it."

unto the age of man, that our ministry (wherein thou hast called us) may have an end, that we may speedily come unto thee in thy kingdom.

³And he saith unto them: "Blessed are ye, because ye desire this thing of me. Therefore, after that ye are seventy and two years old, ye shall come unto me in my kingdom. And with me, ye shall find rest."

⁴And when he had spake unto them, he turned himself unto the three and said unto them: "What will ye, that I should do unto you when I am gone unto the Father?"

⁵And they sorrowed in their hearts, for they durst not speak unto him the thing which they desired. ⁶And he saith unto them:

Behold, I know your thoughts. And ye have desired the thing which John, my beloved (which was with me in my ministry, before that I was lifted up by the Jews) desired of me. ⁷Therefore, more blessed are ye. For ye shall never taste of death. But ye shall live to behold all the doings of the Father unto the children of men, even until all things shall be fulfilled (according to the will of the Father) when I shall come in my glory, with the powers of heaven.

⁸And ye shall never endure the pains of death. But when I shall come in my glory, ye shall be changed in the twinkling of an eye from mortality to immortality.ᵃ And then shall ye be blessed in the kingdom of my Father. ⁹And again, you shall not have pain while ye shall dwell in the flesh, neither sorrow, save it be for the sins of the world.

And all this will I do because of the thing which you have desired of me. For ye have desired that ye might bring the souls of men unto me, while the world shall stand. ¹⁰And for this cause—ye shall have fullness of joy. And ye shall sit down in the kingdom of my Father. Yea, your joy shall be full, even as the Father hath given me fullness of joy. And ye shall be even as I am. And I am even as the Father. And the Father and I are one. ¹¹And the Holy Ghost beareth record of the Father and me. And the Father giveth the Holy Ghost unto the children of men because of me.

¹²And it came to pass that when Jesus had spake these words, he touched every one of them with his finger, save it were the three which were to tarry. And then he departed. ¹³And behold, the heavens were opened and they [were]ᵇ caught up into heaven, and saw and heard unspeakable things.ᶜ ¹⁴And it was forbidden them that they should utter—neither was it given unto them power that they could utter the things which they saw and heard. ¹⁵And whether they were in the body or out of the body, they could not tell.ᵈ For it did seem unto them like a transfiguration of them, that they were changed from this body of flesh into an immortal state, that they could behold the things of God.

¹⁶But it came to pass that they did again minister upon the face of the earth. Nevertheless, they did not minister of the things which they had heard and seen because of the commandment which was given them in heaven.

---

a. Uses language from 1 Corinthians 15:51–52: "Behold, I shew you a mystery; We shall not all sleep, but we shall all be changed, In a moment, in the twinkling of an eye, at the last trump: for the trumpet shall sound, and the dead shall be raised incorruptible, and we shall be changed."

b. Added during proofreading.

c. Uses language from 2 Corinthains 12:4: "How that he was caught up into paradise, and heard unspeakable words, which it is not lawful for a man to utter."

d. See 2 Corinthians 12:2: "I knew a man in Christ above fourteen years ago, (whether in the body, I cannot tell; or whether out of the body, I cannot tell: God knoweth;) such an one caught up to the third heaven."

Chapter XIII [3 Nephi 27:23–29:9]

>¹⁷And now, whether they were mortal, or immortal, from the day of their transfiguration—I know not. ¹⁸But this much I know. According to the record which hath been given, they did go forth upon the face of the land and did minister unto all the people—uniting as many to the church as would believe in their preaching—baptizing them. And as many as were baptized, did receive the Holy Ghost.

¹⁹And they were cast into prison by them who did not belong to the church. And the prisons could not hold them. For they were rent in twain. ²⁰And they were cast down into the earth. But they did smite the earth with the words of God, insomuch that by his power they were delivered out of the depths of the earth. And therefore, they could not dig pits sufficiently to hold them. ²¹And thrice they were cast into a furnace and received no harm. ²²And twice were they cast into a den of wild beasts. And behold, they did play with the beasts as a child with a suckling lamb, and received no harm.

²³And it came to pass that thus they did go forth among all the people of Nephi and did preach the gospel of Christ unto all people upon the face of the land. And they were converted unto the Lord and were united unto the church of Christ. And thus, the people of that generation were blessed, according to the word of Jesus.

²⁴And now I, Mormon, make an end of speaking concerning these things for a time. ²⁶Behold, I were about to write the names of those who were never to taste of death, but the Lord forbade. Therefore, I write them not. For they are hid from the world. ²⁷But behold, I have seen them. And they have ministered unto me. And behold, they will be among the Gentiles, and the Gentiles knoweth them not. ²⁸They will also be among the Jews, and the Jews shall know them not.

²⁹And it shall come to pass, when the Lord seeth fit in his wisdom, that they shall minister unto all the scattered tribes of Israel and unto all nations, kindreds, tongues, and people—and shall bring out of them, unto Jesus, many souls, that their desire may be fulfilled—and also because of the convincing power of God which is in them.

³⁰And they are as the angels of God. And if they shall pray unto the Father in the name of Jesus, they can show themselves unto whatsoever man it seemeth them good. ³¹Therefore, great and marvelous works shall be wrought by them before the great and coming day, when all people must surely stand before the Judgment Seat of Christ. ³²Yea, even among the gentiles shall there be a great and marvelous work wrought by them before that judgment day.

³³And if ye had all the scriptures which gives an account of all the marvelous works of Christ, ye would (according to the words of Christ) know that these things must surely come. ³⁴And wo be unto him that will not hearken unto the words of Jesus and also to them which he hath chosen and sent among them! For whoso receiveth not the words of Jesus and the words of them which he hath sent, receiveth not him. And therefore, he will not receive them at the last day. ³⁴And it would be better for them if they had not been born. For, do ye suppose that ye can get rid of the justice of an offended God (who hath been trampled under feet of men), that thereby salvation might come?

³⁶And now behold, as I spake concerning them whom the Lord had chosen, yea, even three which were caught up into the heavens, that I knew not whether they were cleansed from mortality to immortality. ³⁷But behold, since I wrote, I

have enquired of the Lord. And he hath made it manifest unto me that there must needs be a change wrought upon their bodies, or else needs be that they must taste of death. ³⁸Therefore, that they might not taste of death, there was a change wrought upon their bodies, that they might not suffer pain, nor sorrow save it were for the sins of the world.

³⁹Now, this change was not equal to that which should take place at the last day. But, there was a change wrought upon them, insomuch that Satan could have no power over them, that he could not tempt them. And they were sanctified in the flesh, that they were holy—and that the powers of the earth could not hold them. ⁴⁰And in this state they were to remain, until the judgment day of Christ. And at that day, they were to receive a greater change, and to be received into the kingdom of the Father to go no more out, but to dwell with God eternally in the heavens.

[29] ¹And now behold I say unto you, that when the Lord shall see fit (in his wisdom) that these sayings shall come unto the gentiles (according to his word)—then ye may know that the covenant which the Father hath made with the children of Israel (concerning their restoration to the lands of their inheritance) is already beginning to be fulfilled. ²And ye may know that the words of the Lord (which have been spoken by the holy prophets) shall all be fulfilled.

And ye need not say that the Lord delays his coming unto the children of Israel. ³And ye need not imagine in your hearts that the words which have been spoken are vain. For behold, the Lord will remember his covenant which he hath made unto his people of the house of Israel. ⁴And when ye shall see these sayings coming forth among you—then ye need not any longer spurn at the doings of the Lord. For the sword of his justice is in his right hand.

And behold, at that day, if ye shall spurn at his doings—he will cause it, that it shall soon overtake you.

⁵Wo unto him that spurneth at the doings of the Lord!
Yea, wo unto him that shall deny the Christ and his works!
⁶Yea, wo unto him that shall deny the revelations of the Lord, and that shall say the Lord no longer worketh by revelations, or by prophecy, or by gifts, or by tongues, or by healings, or by the power of the Holy Ghost!
⁷Yea, and wo unto him that shall say, at that day, that there can be no miracle wrought by Jesus Christ—for to get gain. For he that doeth this shall become likes unto the son of perdition, for whom there was no mercy (according the words of Christ).

⁸Yea, and ye need not any longer hiss, nor spurn, nor make game of the Jews—nor of any of the remnant of the house of Israel! For behold, the Lord remembereth his covenant unto them. And he will do unto them according to that which he hath sworn. ⁹Therefore, ye need not suppose that ye can turn the right hand of the Lord unto the left, that he may not execute judgment unto the fulfilling of the covenant which he hath made unto the house of Israel.ᵃ<

---

a. As Mormon closes 3 Nephi he has moved to an explanation of the ministry of the three Nephites. His final testimony is about the future redemption of Israel in which the three will participate. Without specifically emphasizing it, Mormon understands that Jesus will be the reason for the future redemption.

Chapter XIV [3 Nephi 30]

¹Hearken O ye gentiles—and hear the words of Jesus Christ, the Son of the living God!, which he hath commanded me that I should speak concerning you. For behold, he commandeth me that I should write, saying:

>²Turn, all ye gentiles, from your wicked ways!
>>And repent of your evil doings—
>>of your lyings,
>>and deceivings,
>>and your whoredoms,
>>and of your secret abominations,
>>and your idolatries,
>>and of your murders,
>>and your priestcrafts,
>>and your envyings,
>>and your strifes,
>
>and from all your wickedness and abominations—
>and come unto me, and be baptized in my name,
>>that ye may receive a remission of your sins,
>
>and be filled with the Holy Ghost,
>>that ye may be numbered with my people,
>>which are of the house of Israel.

The Book of Nephi
(Which is the Son of Nephi),
One of the Disciples of Jesus Christ

Chapter I [4 Nephi 1]

An account of the people of Nephi, according to his record.

[1] ¹And it came to pass that the thirty and fourth year passed away, and also the thirty and fifth. And behold, the disciples of Jesus had formed a church of Christ in all the lands round about. And as many as did come unto them, and did truly repent of their sins, were baptized in the name of Jesus. And they did also receive the Holy Ghost.

²And it came to pass in the thirty and sixth year, the people were all converted unto the Lord, upon all the face of the land—both Nephites and Lamanites. And there was no contentions, and disputations, among them. And every man did deal justly, one with another. ³And they had all things common among them.[a] Therefore, there were not rich and poor, bond and free[b]—but they were all made free, and partakers of the heavenly gift.[c]

⁴And it came to pass that the thirty and seventh year passed away also. And there still continued to be peace in the land. ⁵And there were great and marvelous works wrought by the disciples of Jesus, insomuch that they did heal the sick, and raise the dead, and cause the lame to walk, and the blind to receive their sight, and the deaf to hear. And all manner of miracles did they work among the children of men. And in nothing did they work miracles, save it were in the name of Jesus.

⁶And thus did the thirty and eighth year pass away.

And also the thirty and ninth.

And the forty and first.

And the forty and second.

Yea, even until forty and nine years had passed away.

And also the fifty and first.

And the fifty and second.

Yea, and even until fifty and nine years had passed away.

⁷And the Lord did prosper them exceedingly in the land, yea, insomuch that they did build cities again where there had been cities burned. ⁸Yea, even that great city Zarahemla did they cause to be built again. ⁹But there were many cities which had been sunk and waters came up in the stead thereof. Therefore, these cities could not be renewed.

¹⁰And now behold, it came to pass that the people of Nephi did wax strong, and did multiply exceeding fast, and became an exceeding fair and delightsome people. ¹¹And they were married, and given in marriage, and were blessed according to the

---

a. See Acts 2:44: "And all that believed were together, and had all things common."

b. See Galatians 3:28: "There is neither Jew nor Greek, there is neither bond nor free, there is neither male nor female: for ye are all one in Christ Jesus."

c. The phrase "the heavenly gift" is found in Hebrews 6:4.

multitude of the promises which the Lord had made unto them. ¹²And they did not walk any more after the performances and ordinances of the law of Moses. But they did walk after the commandments which they had received from their Lord, and their God—continuing in fasting, and prayer, and in meeting together oft—both to pray and to hear the word of the Lord.

¹³And it came to pass that there was no contention among all the people in all the land. But there were mighty miracles wrought among the disciples of Jesus.

¹⁴And it came to pass that the seventy and first year passed away.

And also the seventy and second year.

Yea, and in fine, until the seventy and ninth year too had passed away.

Yea, even an hundred years had passed away. And the disciples of Jesus (whom he had chosen) had all gone to the paradise of God, save it were the three which should tarry. And there were other disciples ordained in their stead. And also many of that generation which had passed away.

¹⁵And it came to pass that there was no contention in the land, because of the love of God which did dwell in the hearts of the people. ¹⁶And there were no envyings, nor strifes, nor tumults, nor whoredoms, nor lyings, nor murders, nor no manner of lasciviousness. And surely there could not be a happier people among all the people which had been created by the hand of God.

¹⁷There were no robbers nor no murderers, neither were there Lamanites nor no manner of -ites. But they were in one the children of Christ, and heirs to the kingdom of God. ¹⁸And how blessed were they! For the Lord did bless them in all their doings, yea, even they were blesse, and prospered, until an hundred and ten years had passed away. And the first generation from Christ had passed away. And there was no contention in all the land.

¹⁹And it came to pass that Nephi (he that kept the last record—and he kept it upon the plates of Nephi) died. And his son Amos kept the record in his stead. And he kept it upon the plates of Nephi also. ²⁰And he kept it eighty and four years. And there was still peace in the land, save it were a small part of the people which had revolted from the church, and took upon them the name of Lamanites. Therefore, there began to be Lamanites again in the land.

²¹And it came to pass that Amos died also. And it was an hundred and ninety and four years from the coming of Christ. And his son, Amos, kept the record in his stead. And he also kept it upon the plates of Nephi. And it was also written in the book of Nephi, which is this book.

²²And it came to pass that two hundred years had passed away. And the second generation had also all passed away, save it were a few.

> ²³And now I, Mormon, would that ye should know that the people had multiplied, insomuch that they were spread upon all the face of the land—and that they had become exceeding rich, because of their prosperity in Christ.[a]<

²⁴And now, in this two hundred and first year there began to be among them—those which were lifted up in pride (such as the wearing of costly apparel, and all man-

---

a. Mormon briefly steps into the fore. This typically signals Mormon's message to future readers that there is something important that should not be missed. Here is where he makes the division between the pax Christiana and the coming Nephite decline.

ner of fine pearls, and of the fine things of the world). ²⁵And from that time forth, they did have their goods and their substance no more common among them. ²⁶And they began to be divided into classes. And they began to build up churches unto themselves, to get gain—and began to deny the true church of Christ.

²⁷And it came to pass that when two hundred and ten years had passed away, there were many churches in the land. Yea, there were churches which professed to know the Christ, and yet they did deny the more part of his gospel, insomuch that they did receive all manner of wickedness and did administer that which was sacred unto him to whom it had been forbidden (because of unworthiness). ²⁸And this church did multiply exceedingly because of iniquity, and because of the power of Satan, which did get hold upon their hearts.

²⁹And again, there was another church which denied the Christ. And they did persecute the true church of Christ because of their humility and their belief in Christ. And they did despise them, because of the many miracles which were wrought among them. ³⁰Therefore, they did exercise power and authority over the disciples of Jesus which did tarry with them. And they did cast them into prison. But by the power of the word of God (which was in them), the prisons were rent in twain. And they went forth— doing mighty miracles among them. ³¹Nevertheless and notwithstanding all these miracles, the people did harden their hearts and did seek to kill them, even as the Jews at Jerusalem sought to kill Jesus (according to his word).

³²And they did cast them into furnaces of fire—and they came forth receiving no harm. ³³And they also cast them into dens of wild beasts—and they did play with the wild beasts, even as a child with a lamb And they did come forth from among them, receiving no harm. ³⁴Nevertheless, the people did harden their hearts. For they were led by many priests and false prophets to build up many churches and to do all manner of iniquity. And they did smite upon the people of Jesus. But the people of Jesus did not smite again. And thus, they did dwindle in unbelief and wickedness, from year to year, even until two hundred and thirty years had passed away.

³⁵And now it came to pass in this year, yea, in the two hundred and thirty and first year—there were a great division among the people.

³⁶And it came to pass that in this year, there arose a people which was called the Nephites. And they were true believers in Christ. And among them there were they which was called by the Lamanites—Jacobites, and Josephites, and Zoramites. ³⁷Therefore, the true believers in Christ and the true worshipers of Christ (among whom were the three disciples of Jesus, which should tarry) were called Nephites, and Jacobites, and Josephites, and Zoramites.

³⁸And it came to pass that they which rejected the gospel were called Lamanites, and Lemuelites, and Ishmaelites. And they did not dwindle in unbelief—but they did willfully rebel against the gospel of Christ. And they did teach their children that they should not believe (even as their fathers from the beginning did dwindle). ³⁹And it was because of the wickedness and abominations of their fathers, even as it was in the beginning. And they were taught to hate the children of God, even as the Lamanites were taught to hate the children of Nephites from the beginning.

⁴⁰And it came to pass that two hundred and forty and four years had passed away. And thus were the affairs of the people. And the more wicked part of the people did wax strong and became exceeding more numerous than were the people of God. ⁴¹And they

did still continue to build up churches to themselves, and adorn them with all manner of precious things. And thus did two hundred and fifty years pass away, and also two hundred and sixty years.

⁴²And it came to pass that the wicked part of the people began again to build up the secret oaths and combinations of Gaddianton. ⁴³And also, the people which were called the people of Nephi began to be proud in their hearts because of their exceeding riches—and became vain, like unto their brethren the Lamanites. ⁴⁴And from this time the disciples began to sorrow for the sins of the world.

⁴⁵And it came to pass that when three hundred years had passed away, both the people of Nephi and the Lamanites had become exceeding wicked—one like unto another.

⁴⁶And it came to pass that the robbers of Gaddianton did spread over all the face of the land. And there were none that were righteous save it were the disciples of Jesus. And gold and silver did they lay up in store, in abundance—and did traffic in all manner of traffic.

⁴⁷And it came to pass that after three hundred and five years had passed away (and the people did still remain in wickedness), and Amos died.[a] And his brother, Ammoron, did keep the record in his stead.

⁴⁸And it came to pass that when three hundred and twenty years had passed away, Ammoron (being constrained by the Holy Ghost) did hide up the records which were sacred, yea, even all the sacred records which had been handed down from generation to generation which were sacred, even until the three hundred and twentieth year from the coming of Christ—⁴⁹and [b] did hide them up unto the Lord, that they might come again unto the remnant of the house of Jacob, according to the prophesies and the promises of the Lord.

And thus is the end of the records of Ammoron.

---

a. Another sentence where "after three hundred and five years" is followed by "and" rather than "then."

b. Skousen suggests that "he" was inadvertently left out. See Skousen, *Analysis of the Textual Variants*, 6: 3580–81. It appears in this location beginning with the 1830 printed edition.

The Book of Mormon

Chapter I [Mormon 1–3]

[1] ¹*And now I, Mormon, make a record of the things which I have both seen and heard, and call it the book of Mormon.*ᵃ

²And about the time that Ammoron hid up the records unto the Lord, he came unto me, I being about ten years of age. And I began to be learned somewhat after the manner of the learning of my people. And Ammoron saith unto me:

> I perceive that thou art a sober child and art quick to observe. ³Therefore, when ye are about twenty and four years old, I would that ye should remember the things that ye have observed concerning this people.
>
> And when ye are of that age, go to the land of Antum, unto a hill (which shall be called Shim) and there have I deposited (unto the Lord) all the sacred engravings concerning this people.
>
> ⁴And behold, ye shall take the plates of Nephi unto yourself. And the remainder shall ye leave in the place where they are. And ye shall engrave upon the plates of Nephi all the things that ye have observed concerning this people.

⁵And I, Mormon, being a descendant of Nephi (and my father's name was Mormon)—and I remembered the things which Ammoron commanded me.ᵇ

⁶And it came to pass that I (being eleven years old) was carried by my father into the land southward, even to the land of Zarahemla—⁷the whole face of the land havingᶜ become covered with buildings, and the people were as numerous, almost, as it were the sands of the sea.

⁸And it came to pass that in this year there began to be a war between the Nephites—

>which consisted of the Nephites, and the Jacobites, and the Josephites, and the Zoramites. And this war was between the Nephites and the Lamanites, and the Lemuelites, and the Ishmaelites. ⁹Now, the Lamanites, and the Lemuelites, and the Ishmaelites, were called Lamanites. And the two parties were Nephites and Lamanites.ᵈ<

---

a. This is not obviously a chapter header, but it appears to function that way. It is a description of the source and the general contents, without the event descriptions of other book headers. Nevertheless, Mormon may have been writing this book soon after 4 Nephi, which ended with Ammoron. This suggests that verse 2, which begins with Ammoron, is a continuation of the history from the previous book but now fully part of Mormon's experience. It may also parallel the last line of the header to 1 Nephi, which has been moved to a book header: "This is according to the account of Nephi. Or, in other words, I, Nephi, wrote this record." Mormon makes a similar statement in Words of Mormon 1:1, though it is clearly integrated into the text rather than a standalone designation at that point.

b. Although the "being a descendant" is not resolved as expected, the "and" functions as the resolution. This has happened several times throughout the text where the conjunction "and" appears to take the place of "therefore," or some other linkage that would better fulfill modern expectations for the sentence.

c. Changed to "had" in the 1920 edition, continuing to the current edition. The change was made to make the traditional punctuation make more sense.

d. Verse 10 uses repetitive resumption to recover from the inserted explanation.

¹⁰And it came to pass that the war began to be among them in the borders of Zarahemla, by the waters of Sidon.

¹¹And it came to pass that the Nephites had gathered together a great number of men, even to exceed the number of thirty thousand.

And it came to pass that they did have, in this same year, a number of battles in the which the Nephites did beat the Lamanites—and did slay many of them.

¹²And it came to pass that the Lamanites withdrew their design. And there was peace settled in the land. And peace did remain for the [space^a] of about four years, that there was no bloodshed. ¹³But wickedness did prevail upon the face of the whole land, insomuch that the Lord did take away his beloved disciples. And the work of miracles and of healings did cease because of the iniquity of the people. ¹⁴And there were no gifts from the Lord. And the Holy Ghost did not come upon any—because of their wickedness and unbelief.

¹⁵And I, being fifteen years of age (and being somewhat of a sober mind)—therefore, I was visited of the Lord, —and tasted, and knew, of the goodness of Jesus. ¹⁶And I did endeavor to preach unto the people, but my mouth was shut—and I were forbidden that I should preach unto them. For behold, they had willfully rebelled against their God. And the beloved disciples were taken away out of the land because of their iniquity. ¹⁷But I did remain among them. But I were forbidden that I should preach unto them because of the hardness of their hearts.

And because of the hardness of their heart, the land was cursed for their sake. ¹⁸And these Gaddianton robbers (which were among the Lamanites) did infest the land, insomuch that the inhabitants thereof began to hide up their treasures in the earth. And they became slippery (because the Lord had cursed the land), that they could not hold them, nor retain them again.

¹⁹And it came to pass that there were sorceries, and witchcrafts, and magics. And the power of the evil one was wrought upon all the face of the land, even unto the fulfilling of all the words of Abinadi, and also Samuel the Lamanite.

[2] ¹And it came to pass in that same year there began to be a war again between the Nephites and the Lamanites. And, notwithstanding I being young—was large in stature. Therefore, the people of Nephi appointed me that I should be their leader (or the leader of their armies). ²Therefore, it came to pass that in my sixteenth year, I did go forth at the head of an army of the Nephites, against the Lamanites. Therefore, three hundred and twenty-six years had passed away.

³And it came to pass that in the three hundred and twenty and seventh year, the Lamanites did come upon us with exceeding great power, insomuch that they did frighten my armies. Therefore, they would not fight. And they began to retreat towards the north countries.

⁴And it came to pass that we did come to the city of Angolah, and we did take possession of the city and make preparations to defend ourselves against the Lamanites.

And it came to pass that we did fortify the city with our mights. But, notwithstanding all our fortifications, the Lamanites did come upon us and did drive us out of the city. ⁵And they did also drive us forth out of the land of David. ⁶And we marched forth, and came to the land of Joshua, which was in the borders west, by the seashore.

---

a. The Printer's Manuscript has "pace," which must have been a transcription error for "space."

⁷And it came to pass that we did gather in our people as fast as it were possible, that we might get them together in one body. ⁸But behold, the land was filled with robbers and with Lamanites. And notwithstanding the great destruction which hung over my people, they did not repent of their evil doings. Therefore, there was blood and carnage spread throughout all the face of the land—both on the part of the Nephites and also on the part of the Lamanites. And it was one complete revolution throughout all the face of the land.

⁹And now, the Lamanites had a king, and his name was Aaron. And he came against us with an army of forty and four thousand. And behold, I withstood him with forty and two thousand.

And it came to pass that I beat him with my army, that he fled before me. And behold, all this was done—and three hundred and thirty years had passed away.

¹⁰And it came to pass that the Nephites began to repent of their iniquities and began to cry (even as had been prophesied by Samuel the prophet). For behold, no man could keep that which was his own—for the thieves, and the robbers, and the murderers, and the magic art, and the witchcraft, which was in the land. ¹¹Thus, there began to be a mourning and a lamentation in all the land because of these things, and more especially among the people of Nephites.

¹²And it came to pass that when I, Mormon, saw their lamentations, and their mourning, and their sorrowing, before the Lord—my heart did begin to rejoice within me, knowing the mercies and the long suffering of the Lord—therefore supposing that he would be merciful unto them, that they would again become a righteous people. ¹³But behold, this (my joy) was vain. For their sorrowing was not unto repentance because of the goodness of God, but it was rather the sorrowing of the damned—because the Lord would not always suffer them to take happiness in sin. ¹⁴And they did not come unto Jesus with broken hearts and contrite spirits,ᵃ but they did curse God and wish to die. Nevertheless, they would struggle with the sword for their lives.

¹⁵And it came to pass that my sorrow did return unto me again. And I saw that the day of grace was passed with them—both temporally and spiritually.

> For I saw thousands of them hewn down in open rebellion against their God. And heaped up as dung upon the face of the land.ᵇ

And thus, three hundred and forty and four years had passed away.

¹⁶And it came to pass that in the three hundred and forty and fifth year, the Nephites did begin to flee before the Lamanites. And they were pursued until they came even to the land of Jashon before it were possible to stop them in their retreat. ¹⁷And now, the city of Jashon was near the land where Ammoron had deposited the records unto the Lord, that they might not be destroyed.

> And behold, I had gone (according to the words of Ammoron) and taken the plates of Nephi, and did make a record (according to the words of Ammoron). ¹⁸And upon the plates of Nephi, I did make a full account of all the wickedness and abominations. But upon these plates I did forbear to make a full account of

---

a. See Psalm 34:18: "The Lord is nigh unto them that are of a broken heart; and saveth such as be of a contrite spirit."

b. There is a nice reversed parallel between "hewn down" and "heaped up." This is a parallel of general competence rather than intentional parallelism.

their wickedness and abominations. For behold, a continual scene of wickedness and abominations has been before mine eyes—ever since I have been sufficient to behold the ways of man. ¹⁹And wo is me because of their wickedness! For my heart has been filled with sorrow because of their wickedness, all my days. Nevertheless, I know that I shall be lifted up at the last day.[a]<

²⁰And it came to pass that in this year the people of Nephi again were hunted and driven.

And it came to pass that we were driven forth until we had come northward, to the land which was called Shem.

²¹And it came to pass that we did fortify the city of Shem. And we did gather in our people as much as it were possible, that perhaps we might save them from destruction.

²²And it came to pass in the three hundred and forty and sixth year, they began to come upon us again.

²³And it came to pass that I did speak unto my people and did urge them with great energy that they would stand boldly before the Lamanites, and fight for their wives, and their children, and their houses, and their homes. ²⁴And my words did arouse them (somewhat) to vigor, insomuch that they did not flee from before the Lamanites but did stand with boldness against them.

²⁵And it came to pass that we did contend with an army of thirty thousand against an army of fifty thousand.

²⁶And it came to pass that we did stand before them with such firmness, that they did flee from before us.

And it came to pass that when they had fled, we did pursue them with our armies and did meet them again and did beat them. Nevertheless, the strength of the Lord was not with us. Yea, we were left to ourselves, that the spirit of the Lord did not abide in us. Therefore we had become weak, like unto our brethren. ²⁷And my heart did sorrow because of this the great calamity of my people—because of their wickedness, and their abominations. But behold, we did go forth against the Lamanites and the robbers of Gaddianton until we had again taken possession of the lands of our inheritance. And the three hundred and forty and ninth year had passed away.

²⁸And in the three hundred and fiftieth year we made a treaty with the Lamanites and the robbers of Gaddianton, in the which we did get the lands of our inheritance divided. ²⁹And the Lamanites did give unto us the land northward, yea, even to the narrow passage which led into the land southward. And we did give unto the Lamanites all the land southward.

[3] ¹And it came to pass that the Lamanites did not come to battle again until ten years more had passed away. And behold, I had employed my people (the Nephites) in preparing their lands and their arms against the time of battle.

²And it came to pass that the Lord did say unto me: "Cry unto this people: Repent ye! And come unto me! And be ye baptized. And build up again my church. And ye shall be spared!" ³And I did cry unto this people. But it was in vain. And they did not

---

a. This is an aside that refers to an earlier time. Using the dates that would be current to this point in his text, Mormon would be older than the twenty-four years when he was to have obtained the plates. Thus, he inserts this aside because he never confirmed that he took the plates of Nephi. Here he discusses what he wrote on those plates, in contrast to what he is writing on the current set (which will be given to Moroni and eventually to Joseph Smith).

realize that it was the Lord that had spared them and granted unto them a chance for repentance. And behold, they did harden their hearts against the Lord, their God.

⁴And it came to pass that after this tenth year had passed away (making, in the whole, three hundred and sixty years from the coming of Christ), and the king of the of the Lamanites sent an epistle unto me, which gave unto me to know that they were preparing to come again to battle against us.

⁵And it came to pass that I did cause my people that they should gather themselves together at the land Desolation, to a city which was in the borders by the narrow pass, which led into the land southward. ⁶And there we did place our armies that we might stop the armies of the Lamanites, that they might not get possession of any of our lands. Therefore, we did fortify against them with all our force.

⁷And it came to pass that in the three hundred and sixty and first year the Lamanites did come down to the city of Desolation to battle against us.

And it came to pass that in that year we did beat them, insomuch that they did return to their own lands again. ⁸And in the three hundred and sixty and second year they did come down again to battle. And we did beat them again and did slay a great number of them. And their dead was cast into the sea.

⁹And now, because of this great thing which my people (the Nephites) had done—they began to boast in their own strength and began to swear before the heavens that they would avenge themselves of the blood of their brethren, which had been slain by their enemies. ¹⁰And they did swear by the heavens, and also by the throne of God, that they would go up to battle against their enemies and would cut them off from the face of the land.

¹¹And it came to pass that I, Mormon, did utterly refuse, from this time forth, to be a commander and a leader of this people—because of their wickedness and abomination. ¹²Behold, I had led them, notwithstanding their wickedness. I had led them many times to battle. And I had loved them (according to the love of God which was in me) with all my heart. And my soul had been poured out in prayer unto my God all the day long for them. Nevertheless, it was without faith—because of the hardness of their hearts.

¹³And thrice have I delivered them out of the hands of their enemies. And they repented not of their sins. ¹⁴And when they had sworn by all that had been forbidden them by our Lord and Savior, Jesus Christ, that they would go up unto their enemies to battle and avenge themselves of the blood of their brethren—behold, the voice of the Lord came unto me, saying: ¹⁷"Vengeance is mine. And I will repay.ᵃ And because this people repented not after that I had delivered them—behold, they shall be cut off from the face of the earth."

And it came to pass that I utterly refused to go up against mine enemies. And I did, even as the Lord had commanded me.

>And I did stand as an idle witness, to manifest unto the world the things which I saw, and heard, according to the manifestations of the Spirit, which had testified of things to come. Therefore, I write unto you, Gentiles, and also unto you, house of Israel—when the work shall commence, that ye shall be about to prepare to return to the land of your inheritance. ¹⁸Yea behold, I write unto all

---

a. See Deuteronomy 32:35: "To me belongeth vengeance, and recompence." It is rephrased in Romans 12:19: "Vengeance is mine; I will repay, saith the Lord."

the ends of the earth, yea, unto you twelve tribes of Israel, which shall be judged according to your works by the twelve whom Jesus chose to be his disciples in the land of Jerusalem.

¹⁹And I write also unto the remnant of this people, which shall also be judged by the twelve whom Jesus chose in this land. And they shall be judged by the other twelve, whom Jesus chose in the land of Jerusalem. ²⁰And these things do the spirit manifest unto me. Therefore, I write unto you all. And for this cause I write unto you, that ye may know that ye must all stand before the Judgment Seat of Christ, yea, every soul which belongs to the whole human family of Adam. And ye must stand to be judged of your works—whether they be good or evil. ²¹And also, that ye may believe the gospel of Jesus Christ, which ye shall have among you. And also, that the Jews, the covenant people of the Lord, shall have other witness (besides that which they saw and heard) that Jesus, whom they slew, was the very Christ and the very God.

²²And I would that I could persuade all ye ends of the earth to repent and prepare to stand before the Judgment Seat of Christ.[a]<

---

a. The conceptual distance between Mormon the historian and Mormon the theologian is here even shorter than in his edited text. All of these are his own experiences. Grant Hardy points out that Mormon addresses a future audience at the end of the three original chapters of his own small book. Thus, he has created a chapter that has a set of examples, and then Mormon proclaims a moral lesson to the future audience. See *The Book of Mormon: Maxwell Institute Study Edition* (Provo, UT: Neal A. Maxwell Institute, 2018), 525n1.

Chapter II [Mormon 4–5]

[4] ¹And now it came to pass that in the three hundred and sixty and third year, the Nephites did go up with their armies to battle against the Lamanites—out of the land of Desolation.

²And it come to pass that the armies of the Nephites were driven back again to the land of Desolation. And while they were yet weary, a fresh army of the Lamanites did come upon them. And they had a sore battle, insomuch that the Lamanites did take possession of the city Desolation, and did slay many of the Nephites, and did take many prisoners. ³And the remainder did flee and join the inhabitants of the city Teancum.

>Now, the city Teancum lay in the borders by the seashore. And it was also near the city Desolation. ⁴And it was because that the armies of the Nephites went up unto the Lamanites that they began to be smitten. For, were it not for that, the Lamanites could have had no power over them. ⁵But behold, the judgments of God will overtake the wicked. And it is by the wicked that the wicked are punished. For it is the wicked that stireth up the hearts of the children of men unto bloodshed.ª<

⁶And it came to pass that the Lamanites did make preparation to come against the city Teancum.

⁷And it came to pass in the three hundred and sixty and fourth year, the Lamanites did come against the city Teancum, that they might take possession of the city Teancum also.

⁸And it came to pass that they were repulsed and driven back by the Nephites. And when the Nephites saw that they had driven the Lamanites, they did again boast of their own strength. And they went forth in their own might and took possession again of the city Desolation.

⁹And now, all these things had been done. And there had been thousands slain on both sides—both the Nephites and the Lamanites.

¹⁰And it came to pass that the three hundred and sixty and sixth year had passed away. And the Lamanites came again upon the Nephites to battle. And yet, the Nephites repented not of the evil which they had done but persisted in their wickedness continually. ¹¹And it is impossible for the tongue to describe, or for man to write, a perfect description of the horrible scene of the blood, and carnage, which was among the people—both of the Nephites and of the Lamanites. And every heart was hardened, so that they delighted in the shedding of blood continually. ¹²And there never had been so great wickedness among all the children of Lehi—nor even among all the house of Israel (according to the words of the Lord), as were among this people.

¹³And it came to pass that the Lamanites did take possession of the city Desolation. And this, because their number did exceed the number of the Nephites. ¹⁴And they did also march forward against the city Teancum, and did drive the inhabitants forth out of her, and did take many prisoners of women, and of children—and did offer them up as sacrifices unto their idol gods.

---

a. The aside begins with simple geographic information to allow the future reader to understand the history. Mormon is so close to the events that he cannot help but editorialize about the reasons that the Nephites found themselves in such dire straits. He declares that it was because the Nephites initiated the conflict. This is contrary to the commandment from Alma 43:46: "Inasmuch as ye are not guilty of the first offense, neither the second, ye shall not suffer yourselves to be slain by the hands of your enemies."

¹⁵And it came to pass that in the three hundred and sixty and seventh year, the Nephites—being angry because the Lamanites had sacrificed their women and their children—that they did go against the Lamanites with exceeding great anger, insomuch that they did beat again the Lamanites and drive them out of their lands. ¹⁶And the Lamanites did not come again against the Nephites until the three hundred and seventy and fifth year. ¹⁷And in this year, they did come down against the Nephites with all their powers. And they were not numbered, because of the greatness of their number. ¹⁸And from this time forth did the Nephites gain no power over the Lamanites, but began to be swept off by them, even as a dew before the sun.

¹⁹And it came to pass that the Lamanites did come down against the city Desolation. And there was an exceeding sore battle fought in the land Desolation, in the which they did beat the Nephites. ²⁰And they fled again from before them, and they came to the city Boaz. And there they did stand against the Lamanites with exceeding boldness, insomuch that the Lamanites did not beat them, until they had come again the second time. ²¹And when they had come the second time, the Nephites were driven and slaughtered with an exceeding great slaughter. Their women, and their children were again sacrificed unto idols.

²²And it came to pass that the Nephites did again flee from before them, taking all the inhabitants with them—both in towns and villages.

²³And now, I Mormon, seeing that the Lamanites were about to overthrow the land—therefore I did go to the hill Shim, and did take up all the records which Ammoron had hid up unto the Lord.

[5] ¹And it came to pass that I did go forth among the Nephites and did repent of the oath which I had made, that I would no more assist them. And they gave me command again of their armies, for they looked upon me as though I could deliver them from their afflictions. ²But behold, I was without hopes, for I knew the judgments of the Lord which should come upon them. For they repented not of their iniquities but did struggle for their lives without calling upon that being who had created them.

³And it came to pass that the Lamanites did come against us as we had fled to the city of Jordan. But behold, they were driven back that they did not take the city at that time.

⁴And it came to pass that they came against us again. And we did maintain the city. And there were also other cities which were maintained by the Nephites, which strongholds did cut them off, that they could not get into the country which lay before us, to destroy the inhabitants of our land.

⁵But it came to pass that whatsoever lands we had passed by (and the inhabitants thereof were not gathered in), were destroyed by the Lamanites. And their towns, and villages, and cities, were burned with fire. And thus, the three hundred and seventy and nine years passed away.

⁶And it came to pass that in the three hundred and eightieth year the Lamanites did come again against us to battle. And we did stand against them boldly—but it was all in vain. For so great were their numbers that they did tread the people of the Nephites under their feet.

⁷And it came to pass that we did again take to flight. And they whose flight were swifter than the Lamanites did escape. And they whose flight did not exceed the Lamanites were swept down and destroyed.

>⁸And now behold, I, Mormon, do not desire to harrow up the souls of men in casting before them such an awful scene of blood, and carnage, as was laid before mine eyes. But I, knowing that these things must be made known, and that all things which are hid must be revealed upon the housetop—⁹and also, that a knowledge of these things must come unto the remnant of these people and also unto the Gentiles (which the Lord hath said should scatter this people—and this people should be counted as naught among them)—therefore, I write a small abridgement—daring not to give a full account of the things which I have seen because of the commandment which I have received. And also, that ye might not have to great sorrow because of the wickedness of this people.

¹⁰And now behold, this I speak unto their seed, and also to the Gentiles (which hath care for the house of Israel), that realize, and know, from whence their blessings come. ¹¹For I know that such will sorrow for the calamity of the house of Israel. Yea, they will sorrow for the destruction of this people. They will sorrow that this people had not repented that they might have been clasped in the arms of Jesus.

¹²Now, these things are written unto the remnant of the house of Jacob. And they are written after this manner because it is known of God that wickedness will not bring them forth unto them. And they are to be hid up unto the Lord, that they may come forth in his own due time. ¹³And this is the commandment which I have received. And behold, they shall come forth (according to the commandment of the Lord) when he shall see fit in his wisdom.

¹⁴And behold, they shall go unto the unbelieving of the Jews. And for this intent, shall they go—that they may be persuaded that Jesus is the Christ, the Son of the living God, that the Father may bring about (through his most beloved) his great and eternal purpose in the restoring the Jews (or all the house of Israel) to the land of their inheritance, which the Lord, their God hath given them—unto the fulfilling of his covenant. ¹⁵And also that the seed of this people may more fully believe his gospel, which shall go forth unto them from the Gentiles. For this people shall be scattered, and shall become a dark, a filthy, and a loathsome people—beyond the description of that which ever hath been amongst us, yea, even that which hath been among the Lamanites. And this, because of their unbelief and idolatry. ¹⁶For behold, the Spirit of the Lord hath already ceased to strive with their fathers. And they are without Christ, and God, in the world. And they are driven about as chaff before the wind.[a]

¹⁷They were once a delightsome people, and they had Christ for their shepherd. Yea, they were led even by God the Father. ¹⁸But now behold, they are led about by Satan, even as chaff is driven before the wind,[b] or as a vessel is tossed about upon the waves, without sail, or anchor, or without any thing wherewith to steer her. And even as she is—so are they.

¹⁹And behold, the Lord hath reserved their blessing (which they might have received in the land) for the Gentiles which shall possess the land. ²⁰But behold, it shall come to pass that they shall be driven, and scattered, by the Gentiles. And after that they have been driven, and scattered, by the Gentiles—behold, then will

---

a. See Psalm 35:5: "Let them be as chaff before the wind."
b. See Psalm 35:5: "Let them be as chaff before the wind."

the Lord remember the covenant which he made unto Abraham, and unto all the house of Israel. ²¹And also, the Lord will remember the prayers of the righteous, which hath been put up unto him for them. ²²And then, O ye Gentiles, how can ye stand before the power of God, except ye shall repent, and turn from your evil ways?

²³Know ye not that ye are in the hands of God? Know ye not he hath all power, and at his great command the earth shall be rolled together as a scroll[a]? ²⁴Therefore, repent ye! And humble yourselves before him, lest he shall come out in justice against you,

> lest a remnant of the seed of Jacob
> shall go forth among you as a lion,
> and tear you in pieces,
> and there is none to deliver.[b,c]<

---

a. See Isaiah 34:4.

b. The final phrase echoes Micah 5:8.

c. The scene of destruction is sad, and Mormon wants to turn his future readers from that sadness to the reason why he writes of it. Thus, he steps out of narration and into exposition of what will happen in the future. Without being clear, he assumes that his record will be part of what the Gentiles bring to the remnant of his people, which he includes with the Lamanites. The beginning of the next chapter confirms that this is an interruption of the narrative.

Chapter III [Mormon 6–7]

[6] ¹And now, I finish my record concerning the destruction of my people, the Nephites.[a]

And it came to pass that we did march forth before the Lamanites. ²And I, Mormon, wrote an epistle unto the king of the Lamanites, and desired of him that he would grant unto us that we might gather together our people unto the land of Cumorah, by a hill which was called Cumorah. And there we would give them battle.

³And it came to pass that the king of the Lamanites did grant unto me the thing which I desired.

⁴And it came to pass that we did march forth to the land of Cumorah. And we did pitch our tents round about the hill Cumorah. And it was in a land of many waters, rivers, and fountains. And here we had hope to gain advantage over the Lamanites. ⁵And when three hundred and eighty and four years had passed away, we had gathered in all the remainder of our people unto the land Cumorah.

⁶And it came to pass that when we had gathered in all our people in one to the land of Cumorah, behold—I, Mormon, began to be old. And knowing it to be the last struggle of my people, and having been commanded of the Lord that I should not suffer that the records which had been handed down by our fathers (which were sacred) to fall into the hands of the Lamanites (for the Lamanites would destroy them)—therefore, I made this record out of the plates of Nephi, and hid up in the hill Cumorah all the records which had been entrusted to me by the hand of the Lord, save it were these few plates, which I gave unto my son, Moroni.

⁷And it came to pass that my people, with their wives, and their children—did now behold the armies of the Lamanites marching towards them. And, with that awful fear of death which fills the breasts of all the wicked—did they await to receive them.

⁸And it came to pass that they came to battle against us. And every soul was filled with terror because of the greatness of their numbers.

⁹And it came to pass that they did fall upon my people with the sword, and with the bow, and with the arrow, and with the axe, and with all manner of weapons of war.

¹⁰And it came to pass that my men were hewn down, yea, or even my ten thousand (which were with me). And I fell wounded in the midst. And they passed by me, that they did not put an end to my life. ¹¹And when they had gone through, and hewn down all my people, save it twenty and four of us (among whom was my son, Moroni)—and we (having survived the dead of our people) did behold on the morrow, when the Lamanites had returned unto their camps, from the top of the hill Cumorah—the ten thousand of my people which were hewn down, being led in the front by me.

¹²And we also beheld the ten thousands of my people which were led by my son, Moroni.

¹³And behold, the ten thousand of Gidgiddonah had fallen, and he also in the midst.

¹⁴And Lamah had fallen with his ten thousand.

And Gilgal had fallen with his ten thousand.

And Limhah had fallen with his ten thousand.

---

a. This introduction indicates that Mormon understands that the ending of the previous chapter was an insertion into the historical narrative. Thus, he must return and "finish my record."

And Jeneum[a] had fallen with his ten thousand.

And Cumenihah, and Moronihah, and Antionum, and Shiblom, and Shem, and Josh—had fallen with their ten thousand each.

[15] And it came to pass that there were ten more which did fall by the sword—with their ten thousand each. Yea, even all my people (save it were those twenty and four, which were with me, and also a few which had escaped into the south countries, and a few which had deserted over into unto the Lamanites)—had fallen. And their flesh and bones and blood lay upon the face of the earth—being left by the hands of those who slew them, to molder upon the land, and to crumble, and to return to their mother earth.

[16] And my soul was rent with anguish because of the slain of my people. And I cried:

> [17] O ye fair ones!
>> How could ye have departed from the ways of the Lord?
>
> O ye fair ones!
>> How could ye have rejected that Jesus—
>> who stood with open arms to receive you?
>
> [18] Behold, if ye had not done this, ye would not have fallen.
> But behold, ye are fallen, and I mourn your loss!
>
> [19] O ye fair sons and daughters,
>> ye fathers and mothers,
>> ye husbands and wives.
>
> Ye fair ones!
>> How is it that ye could have fallen?
>
> [20] But behold, ye are gone.
>> And my sorrows cannot bring your return.

[21] And the day soon cometh that your mortal must put on immortality, and these bodies (which are now moldering in corruption) must soon become incorruptible bodies.[b] And then ye must stand before the Judgment Seat of Christ, to be judged according to your works. And if it so be that ye are righteous, then are ye blessed with your fathers which have gone before you.

[22] O that ye had repented before that this great destruction had come upon you! But behold, ye are gone. And the Father, yea, the Eternal Father of Heaven—knoweth your state. And he doeth with you according to his justice and mercy.

[7] [1] And now behold, I would speak somewhat unto the remnant of this people which are spared (if it so be that God may give unto them my words), that they may know of the things of their fathers. Yea, I speak unto you, ye remnant of the house of Israel! And this is the words which I speak:

[2] Know ye, that ye are of the house of Israel!

[3] Know ye, that ye must come unto repentance, or ye cannot be saved!

[4] Know ye, that ye must lay down your weapons of war and delight no more in the shedding of blood, and take them not again save it be that God shall command you.

[5] Know ye, that ye must come to the knowledge of your fathers, and repent of all

---

a. This name has had two of the vowels overwritten. It could be read Jeneum, Joneum, or Jonoun. Since it is not clear, the current spelling is retained.

b. See 1 Corinthians 15:53: "For this corruptible must put on incorruption, and this mortal must put on immortality."

your sins, and iniquities, and believe in Jesus Christ—that he is the Son of God and that he was slain by the Jews. And by the power of the Father, he hath risen again. Whereby, he hath gained the victory over the grave. And also, in him is the sting of death swallowed up. ⁶And he bringeth to pass the resurrection of the dead whereby man must be raised to stand before his Judgment Seat.

⁷And he hath brought to pass the redemption of the world—whereby he that is found guiltless before him (at the judgment day) hath it given unto them to dwell in the presence of God in his kingdom, to sing ceaseless praises with the choirs above, unto the Father, and unto the Son, and unto the Holy Ghost, which is one God[a]—in a state of happiness, which hath no end. ⁸Therefore, repent! And be baptized in the name of Jesus. And lay hold upon the gospel of Christ, which shall be set before you—not only in the records, but also in the record which shall come unto the Gentiles, from the Jews (which records shall come from the Gentiles unto you).

⁹For behold—this is written for the intent that ye may believe that—and if ye believe that, ye will believe this also. And if ye believe this—ye will know concerning your fathers, and also the marvelous works which were wrought by the power of God among them. ¹⁰And ye will also know that ye are a remnant of the seed of Jacob. Therefore, ye are numbered among the people of the first covenant. And if it so be that ye believe in Christ, and are baptized—first with water, then with fire and with the Holy Ghost, following the example of our Savior (according to that which he hath commanded us)—it shall be well with you in the day of judgment. Amen.

---

a. See 1 John 5:7: "For there are three that bear record in heaven, the Father, the Word, and the Holy Ghost: and these three are one."

Chapter IV [Mormon 8–9]

[8] ¹Behold I, Moroni, do finish the record of my father, Mormon. Behold, I have but few things to write, which things I have been commanded of my father.

²And now it came to pass that after the great and tremendous battle at Cumorah—behold, the Nephites which had escaped into the country southward were hunted by the Lamanites until they were all destroyed. ³And my father also was killed by them. And I, even I, remaineth alone to write the sad tale of the destruction of my people. But behold, they are gone. And I fulfill the commandment of my father. And whether they will slay me, I know not. ⁴Therefore, I will write, and hide up the records in the earth. And whither I go, it mattereth not.

⁵Behold, my father hath made this record. And he hath written the intent thereof. And behold, I would write it also, if I had room upon the plates—but I have not. And ore I have none. For I am alone. My father hath been slain in battle—and all my kinsfolks. And I have not friends, nor whither to go. And how long the Lord will suffer that I may live, I know not.

⁶Behold, four hundred years have passed since the coming of our Lord and Savior. ⁷And behold, the Lamanites have hunted my people (the Nephites) down from city to city, and from place to place, even until they are no more. And great has been their fall. Yea, great and marvelous is the destruction of my people, the Nephites. ⁸And behold, it is the hand of the Lord which hath done it.

And behold also, the Lamanites are at war one with another. And the whole face of this land is one continual round of murders and bloodshed. And no one knoweth the end of the war.

⁹And now behold, I say no more concerning them. For there are none, save it be Lamanites and robbers that do exist upon the face of the land. ¹⁰And there are none that do know the true God, save it be the disciples of Jesus which did tarry in the land until the wickedness of the people were so great that the Lord would not suffer them to remain with the people. And whither[a] they be upon the face of the land no man knoweth. ¹¹But behold, my father and I have seen them, and they have ministered unto us.

¹²And whoso receiveth this record and shall not condemn it because of the imperfections which are in it, the same shall know of greater things than these.

Behold, I am Moroni. And were it possible, I would make all things known unto you. ¹³Behold, I make an end of speaking concerning this people. I am the son of Mormon. And my father was a descendant of Nephi. ¹⁴And I am the same which hide up this record unto the Lord (the plates thereof are of no worth) because of the commandment of the Lord. For he truly saith that none shall have them to get gain. But the record thereof is of great worth. And whoso shall bring it to light—him will the Lord bless. ¹⁵For no one can have power to bring it to light, save it be given him of God. For God will that it shall be done with an eye single to his glory—or the welfare of the ancient and long-dispersed covenant people of the Lord.

¹⁶And blessed be him that shall bring this thing to light. For it shall be brought

---

a. The Printer's Manuscript reads "whither," as indicated. However, Oliver Cowdery frequently mixed up "whither" and "whether." The 1830 edition has "whether," and that has remained in the text. Skousen argues that "whither" was likely intended. Skousen, *Analysis of Textual Variants*, 6:3655–56.

out of darkness unto light according to the word of God. Yea, it shall be brought out of the earth. And it shall shine forth out of darkness and come unto the knowledge of the people. And it shall be done by the power of God.

¹⁷And if there be faults, they be faults of a man. But behold, we know no fault. Nevertheless, God knoweth all things. Therefore, he that condemneth, let him be aware lest he shall be in danger of hellfire. ¹⁸And he that saith, "Show unto me, or ye shall be smitten!"—let him be aware, lest he commandeth that which is forbidden of the Lord. ¹⁹For behold, the same that judgeth rashly shall be judged rashly again. For, according to his works shall his wages be. Therefore, he that smiteth shall be smitten again of the Lord.

²⁰Behold what the scriptures saith, man shall not smite—neither shall he judge. For judgment is mine (saith the Lord), and vengeance is mine also. And I will repay.[a] ²¹And he that shall breathe out wrath and strifes against the work of the Lord, and against the covenant people of the Lord (which is the house of Israel), and shall say: "We will destroy the work of the Lord. And the Lord will not remember his covenant, which he hath made unto the house of Israel"—the same is in danger to be hewn down and cast into the fire. ²²For the eternal purposes of the Lord shall roll on until all his promises shall be fulfilled.

²³Search the prophecies of Isaiah! Behold, I cannot write them. Yea behold, I say unto you that those saints which have gone before me (which have possessed this land) shall cry, yea, even from the dust will they cry unto the Lord. And, as the Lord liveth, he will remember the covenant which he hath made with them.

²⁴And he knoweth their prayers, that they were in behalf of their brethren. And he knoweth their faith. For in his name could they remove mountains. And in his name could they cause the earth to shake. And by the power of his word did they cause prisons to tumble to the earth, yea, even the fiery furnace could not harm them—neither wild beasts, nor poison serpents—because of the power of his word.

²⁵And behold, their prayers were also in behalf of him that the Lord should suffer to bring these things forth. ²⁶And no one need not say they shall not come. For they surely shall. For the Lord hath spoken it. For out of the earth shall they come, by the hand of the Lord. And none can stay it.

²⁷And it shall come in a day when it shall be said that miracles are done away. And it shall come, even as if one should speak from the dead. And it shall come in a day when the blood of saints shall cry unto the Lord because of secret combinations and the works of darkness.

²⁸Yea, it shall come in a day when the power of God shall be denied and churches become defiled—and shall be lifted up in the pride of their hearts, yea, even in a day when leaders of churches (and teachers), in the pride of their hearts, even to the envying of them who belong to their church.[b]

²⁹Yea, it shall come in a day when there shall be heard of fires, and tempests, and vapors of smoke in foreign lands.[c] ³⁰And there shall also be heard of wars and rumors of wars[d]—and earthquakes in divers places.

---

a. See Romans 12:19: "Vengeance is mine; I will repay, saith the Lord."

b. Incomplete sentence. The "even in a day when the leaders of churches" requires some verb to complete it. That verb is missing.

c. See similar language in Acts 2:19 and Joel 2:30.

d. Uses language from Matthew 24:6: "And ye shall hear of wars and rumours of wars."

³¹Yea, it shall come in a day when there shall be great pollutions upon the face of the earth. There shall be murders, and robbing, and lying, and deceivings, and whoredoms, and all manner of abominations—when there shall be many which will say: "Do this! Or, do that! And it mattereth not. For the Lord will uphold such at the last day." But wo unto such! For they are in the gall of bitterness and in the bonds of iniquity.

³²Yea, it shall come in a day when there shall be churches built up that shall say: "Come unto me, and for your money you shall be forgiven of your sins."

³³O ye wicked and perverse generation—and stiffnecked people! Why have ye built up churches unto yourselves to get gain? Why have ye transfigured the holy word of God, that ye might bring damnation upon your souls?

³⁴Behold! Look ye unto the revelations of God! For behold, the time cometh, at that day, when all these things must be fulfilled. Behold, the Lord hath shown unto me great and marvelous things concerning that which must shortly come at that day when these things shall come forth among you.

³⁵Behold, I speak unto you as if ye were present—and yet ye are not. But behold, Jesus Christ hath shown you unto me. And I know your doing. ³⁶And I know that ye do walk in the pride of your hearts. And there are none, save a few only, which do not lift themselves up in the pride of their hearts, unto the wearing of very fine apparel—unto envying, and strife, and malice, and persecutions, and all manner of iniquity. And your churches, yea, even every one, have become polluted because of the pride of your hearts. ³⁷For behold, ye do love money, and your substances, and your fine apparel, and the adorning of your churches—more than ye love the poor, and needy—the sick, and the afflicted.

³⁸O ye pollutions! Ye hypocrites! Ye teachers which sell yourselves for that which will canker!

Why have ye polluted the holy church of God?

Why are ye ashamed to take upon you the name of Christ?

Why do you not think that greater is the value of an endless happiness than that misery which never dies because of the praise of the world?

³⁹Why do ye adorn yourselves with that which hath no life, and yet suffer the hungry, and the needy, and the naked, and the sick, and the afflicted, to pass by you—and notice them not?

⁴⁰Yea, why do ye build up your secret abominations to get gain—and cause that widows should mourn before the Lord—and also orphans to mourn before the Lord—and also the blood of their fathers, and their husbands, to cry unto the Lord from the ground, for vengeance upon your heads?

⁴¹Behold! The sword of vengeance hangeth over you! And the time soon cometh that he avengeth the blood of the saints upon you. For he will not suffer their cries any longer.

[9] ¹And now I speak also concerning those who do not believe in Christ. ²Behold, will ye believe in the day of your visitation—behold, when the Lord shall come? Yea, even that great day when the earth shall be rolled together as a scroll[a] and the elements shall melt with fervent heat.[b] Yea, in that great day when ye shall be brought to stand

---

a. See Isaiah 34:4: "And all the host of heaven shall be dissolved, and the heavens shall be rolled together as a scroll."

b. See 2 Peter 3:12: "Looking for and hasting unto the coming of the day of God, wherein the heavens being on fire shall be dissolved, and the elements shall melt with fervent heat?"

before the Lamb of God[a]—then will ye say that there is no God? ³Then will ye longer deny the Christ? Or can ye behold the Lamb of God[b]?

Do ye suppose that ye shall dwell with him, under a consciousness of your guilt?

Do ye suppose that ye could be happy to dwell with that Holy Being when your souls are racked with a consciousness of your guilt, that ye have ever abused his laws?

⁴Behold I say unto you that ye would be more miserable to dwell with a holy and a just God, under a consciousness of your filthiness before him, than ye would to dwell with the damned souls in hell! ⁵For behold, when ye shall be brought to see your nakedness before God, and also the glory of God, and the holiness of Jesus Christ—it will kindle a flame of anguishable[c] fire upon you.

⁶O then, ye unbelieving! Turn ye unto the Lord! Cry mightily unto the Father in the name of the Jesus, that perhaps ye may be found spotless—pure, fair, and white—having been cleansed by the blood of the Lamb at that great and last day!

⁷And again, I speak unto you who deny the revelations of God and say that they are done away, that there is no revelations, nor prophecies, nor gifts, nor healing, nor speaking with tongues, and the interpretations of tongues. ⁸Behold, I say unto you: He that denieth these things knoweth not the gospel of Christ. Yea, they have not read the scriptures—if so, they do not understand them. ⁹For do we not read that God is the same yesterday, today, and forever[d], and in him there is no variableness, neither shadow of changing?

¹⁰And now, if ye have imagined up unto yourselves a God which doth vary, and in him there is a shadow of changing—then have ye imagined up unto yourselves a God which is not a God of miracles!

¹¹But behold, I will show you a God of miracles, even the God of Abraham, and the God of Isaac, and the God of Jacob! And it is that same God which created the heavens and the earth and all things that in them is. ¹²Behold, he created Adam. And by Adam came the fall of man. And because of the fall of man came Jesus Christ, even the Father and the Son. And because of Jesus Christ came the redemption of man. ¹³And because of the redemption of man (which came by Jesus Christ) they are brought back into the presence of the Lord.

Yea, this is wherein all men are redeemed—because the death of Christ bringeth to pass the resurrection, which bringeth to pass a redemption from an endless sleep (from which sleep all men shall be awoke by the power of God) when the trump shall sound. And they shall come forth, both small and great. And all shall stand before his bar—being redeemed, and loosed from this eternal bond of death, which death is a temporal death. ¹⁴And then cometh the judgment of the Holy One upon them. And then cometh the time that he that is filthy shall be filthy still. And he that is righteous shall be righteous still. He that is happy shall be happy still. And he that is unhappy shall be unhappy still.[e]

---

a. The phrase "Lamb of God" is from John 1:29.

b. The phrase "Lamb of God" is from John 1:29.

c. Changed to "unquenchable" for the 1830 edition. It is plausible that this was the intention. It has been left as it appears in the Printer's Manuscript.

d. See Hebrews 13:8.

e. Uses language from Revelation 22:11: "He that is unjust, let him be unjust still: and he which is filthy, let him be filthy still: and he that is righteous, let him be righteous still: and he that is holy, let him be holy still."

¹⁵And now, O all ye that have imagined up unto yourselves a God which can do no miracles! I would ask of you—have all these things [passed[a]] of which I have spoken? Has the end come yet? Behold. I say unto you: Nay! And God has not ceased to be a God of miracles. ¹⁶Behold, are not the things that God hath wrought marvelous in our eyes? Yea, and who can comprehend the marvelous works of God? ¹⁷Who shall say that it was not a miracle, that by his word the heavens and the earth should be? And by the power of his word man was created of the dust of the earth? And by has the power of his word hath miracles been wrought? ¹⁸And who shall say that Jesus Christ did not do many mighty miracles? And there was many mighty miracles wrought by the hands of the Apostles. ¹⁹And if there was miracles wrought—then why has God ceased to be a God of miracles—and yet be an unchangeable being?

And behold, I say unto you, he changeth not! If so—he would cease to be God. And he ceaseth not to be God. And is a God of miracles! ²⁰And the reason why he ceaseth to do miracles among the children of men is because that they dwindle in unbelief and depart from the right way, and know not the God in whom they should trust. ²¹Behold, I say unto you, that whoso believeth in Christ, doubting nothing—whatsoever he shall ask the Father in the name of Christ, it shall be granted them. And this promise is unto all, even unto the ends of the earth. ²²For behold, thus saith Jesus Christ, the Son of God, unto his disciples which should tarry, yea, and also to all his disciples in the hearing of the multitude—

> Go ye into all the world and preach the gospel to every creature! ²³And he that believeth and is baptized shall be saved. But he that believeth not—shall be damned.
>
> ²⁴And these signs shall follow them that believe. In my name shall they cast out devils. They shall speak with new tongues. They shall take up serpents. And if they drink any deadly thing—it shall not hurt them. They shall lay hands on the sick, and they shall recover.[b] ²⁵And whosoever shall believe in my name, doubting nothing, unto him will I confirm all my words, even unto the ends of the earth.[c]

²⁶And now behold! Who can stand stand against the works of the Lord?!
Who can deny his sayings?
Who will rise up against the almighty power of the Lord?
Who will despise the works of the Lord?
Who will despise the children of Christ?
Behold, all ye that are despisers of the works of the Lord! For ye shall wonder—and perish!

²⁷O then, despise not! And wonder not! But hearken unto the words of the Lord. And ask the Father, in the name of Jesus, for what things soever ye shall stand in need.

Doubt not! But be believing! And begin as in times of old and come unto the Lord with all your hearts—and work out your own salvation, with fear, and trembling before him.[d]

²⁸Be wise in the days of your probation! Strip yourselves of all uncleanness! Ask not

---

a. The Printer's Manuscript has "past," but the intent appears to suggest that it should be the homophone "passed."

b. The last phrase of verse 22 through verse 24 use language from Mark 16: 15–18,

c. All but the last sentence quotes Mark 16:15–18.

d. See Philippians 2:12: "work out your own salvation with fear and trembling."

that ye may consume it on your lusts,[a] but ask with a firmness unshaken—that ye will yield to no temptation, but that ye will serve the true, and living God.

[29]See that ye are not baptized unworthily.

See that ye partake not of the sacrament of Christ unworthily. But see that ye do all things in worthiness. And do it in the name of Jesus Christ, the Son of the living God.

And if ye do this and endure to the end[b]—ye will in no wise be cast out.

[30]Behold! I speak unto you as though I spake from the dead. For I know that ye shall have my words. [31]Condemn me not because of mine imperfection—neither my father because of his imperfection—neither them which have written before him. But rather, give thanks unto God that he hath made manifest unto you our imperfections, that ye may learn to be more wise than that which we have been.

[32]And now behold, we have written this record according to our knowledge—in the characters which are called among us, the reformed Egyptian—being handed down, and altered by us, according to our manner of speech. [33]And if our plates had been sufficiently large, we should have written in the Hebrew. But the Hebrew hath been altered by us also. And if we could have written in the Hebrew—behold, ye would have had none imperfections in our record. [34]But the Lord knoweth the things which we have written, and also, that none other people knoweth our language. And because that none other people knoweth our language, therefore, he hath prepared means for the interpretation thereof.

[35]And these things are written that we may rid our garments of the blood of our brethren (which have dwindled in unbelief). [36]And behold, these things which we have desired concerning our brethren, yea, even their restoration to the knowledge of Christ—is according to the prayers of all the saints, which have dwelt in the land.

[37]And may the Lord Jesus Christ grant that their prayers may be answered, according to their faith. And may God the Father remember the covenant which he hath made with the house of Israel. And may he bless them forever, through faith on the name of Jesus Christ. Amen.

---

a. Uses language from James 4:3: "Ye ask, and receive not, because ye ask amiss, that ye may consume *it* upon your lusts."

b. The phrase "endure to the end" occurs in Matthew 24:13.

The Book of Ether

Chapter I [Ether 1–4]

[1] ¹And now I, Moroni, proceed to give an account of those ancient inhabitants which were destroyed by the hand of the Lord upon the face of this north country. ²And I take mine account from the twenty and four plates, which were found by the people of Limhi, which is called the book of Ether.[a]

³And, as I suppose that the first part of this record (which speaketh concerning the creation of the world, and also of Adam, and an account from that time even to the great tower, and whatsoever things transpired among the children of men until that time) is had among the Jews, ⁴therefore, I do not write those things which transpired from the days of Adam until that time. But they are had upon the plates. And whoso findeth them, the same will have power that he may get the full account. ⁵But behold, I give not the full account—but a part of the account I give, from the tower down until they were destroyed. ⁶And on this wise do I give the account.[b]

He that wrote this record was Ether.
And he was a descendant of Coriantor.[c]
⁷And Coriantor was the son of Moron.
⁸And Moron was the son of Ethem.
⁹And Ethem was the son of Ahah.
¹⁰And Ahah was the son of Seth.
¹¹And Seth was the son of Shiblon.
¹²And Shiblon was the son of Com.
¹³And Com was the son of Coriantum.
¹⁴And Coriantum was the son of Amnigaddah.
¹⁵And Amnigaddah was the son of Aaron.
¹⁶And Aaron was a descendant of Heth,
who was the son of Hearthom.[d]
¹⁷And Hearthom was the son of Lib.
¹⁸And Lib was the son of Kish.
¹⁹And Kish was the son of Corom.
²⁰And Corom was the son of Levi.
²¹And Levi was the son of Kim.
²²And Kim was the son of Morianton.

---

a. Verses 1 and 2 fulfil the function of a book header, but they are not written in that form. Indeed, they make more sense as they have been listed—as the beginning of the chapter.

b. Moroni continues to give the identifying characteristics of what he intends to write. The information about the creation of the tower is not given because it was part of the record, but simply noted because Moroni intended to skip it. Verse 1 to the first sentence of verse 6 are basically his identifying colophon.

c. Ether 11:23 confirms that Ether was the son of Coriantor. Therefore, they are listed as though it were a son/father part of the list.

d. Although we have "descendant" in verse 16, Ether 10:30–31 indicates that Hearthom "begat Heth." For that reason, they are listed in the same form as the rest of this list.

²³And Morianton was a descendant of Riplakish.ᵃ

²⁴And Riplakish was the son of Shez.

²⁵And Shez was the son of Heth.

²⁶And Heth was the son of Com.

²⁷And Com was the son of Coriantum.

²⁸And Coriantum was the son of Emer.

²⁹And Emer was the son of Omer.

³⁰And Omer was the son of Shule.

³¹And Shule was the son of Kib.

³²And Kib was the son of Orihah.

Which was the son of Jared.

³³Which Jared came forth, with his brother, and their families (with some others and their families) from the great tower at the time the Lord confounded the language of the people and swore in his wrath that they should be scattered upon all the face of the earth. And according to the word of the Lord, the people were scattered.

³⁴And the brother of Jared, being a large and a mighty man and being a man highly favored of the Lord.ᵇ For Jared his brother said unto him: "Cry unto the Lord, that he will not confound us that we may not understand our words."

³⁵And it came to pass that the brother of Jared did cry unto the Lord. And the Lord had compassion upon Jared. Therefore, he did not confound the language of Jared. And Jared and his brother were not confounded.

³⁶Then Jared said unto his brother: "Cry again unto the Lord, and it may be that he will turn away his anger from them which are our friends, that he confound not their language."

³⁷And it came to pass that the brother of Jared did cry unto the Lord, and the Lord had compassion upon their friends, and their families also, that they were not confounded.

³⁸And it came to pass that Jared spake again unto his brother, saying: "Go, and inquire of the Lord—[whetherᶜ] he will drive us out of the land. And if he will drive us out of the land, cry unto him whither shall we go. And who knoweth but the Lord will carry us forth into a land which is choice above all the earth? And if it so be—let us be faithful unto the Lord that we may receive it for our inheritance."

³⁹And it came to pass that the brother of Jared did cry unto the Lord, according to that which had been spoken by the mouth of Jared.

⁴⁰And it came to pass that the Lord did hear the brother of Jared and had compassion upon him. And said unto him: ⁴¹"Go to, and gather together thy flocks, both male and female of every kind, also of the seed of the earth of every kind—and thy family and also Jared thy brother and his family, and also thy friends and their families, and the friends of Jared and their families. ⁴²And when thou hast done this, thou shalt go at the head of them, down into the valley which is northward. And there will I meet thee. And I will go before thee into a land which is choice above all the land of the earth.

---

a. Ether 10:9 repeats that Morianton was "a descendant of Riplakish." It also indicates "after the space of many years," allowing for more than one generation although possibly not requiring it.

b. An incomplete sentence that does not resolved the verb "being." It could work if connected to the next sentence and the word "for" were read as "therefore."

c. The Printer's Manuscript has "whither," which does not fit the full context of the sentence. It is most likely a spelling error for "whether," as it appears in modern editions.

⁴³And there will I bless thee and thy seed—and raise up unto me of thy seed (and the seed of thy brother and they which shall go with thee) a great nation. And there shall be none greater than the nation which I will raise up unto me of thy seed upon all the face of the earth. And this I will do unto thee because of this long time which ye have cried unto me.

[2] ¹And it came to pass that Jared and his brother and their families, and also the friends of Jared and his brother and their families—went down into the valley which was northward (>and the name of the valley was Nimrod being called after the mighty hunter^a<) with their flocks which they had gathered together—male and female of every kind. ²And they did also lay snares and catch fowls of the air. And they did also prepare a vessel in the which they did carry with them the fish of the waters. ³And they did also carry with them deseret (>which by interpretation is a honeybee^b<). And thus they did carry with them swarms of bees and all manner of that which was upon the face of the land—seeds of every kind.

⁴And it came to pass that when they had came down into the valley of Nimrod, the Lord came down and talked with the brother of Jared. And he was in a cloud. And the brother of Jared saw him not.

⁵And it came to pass that the Lord commanded them that they should go forth into the wilderness, yea, into that quarter where there never had man been.

And it came to pass that the Lord did go before them and did talk with them (as he stood in a cloud^c) and gave directions whither they should travel.

⁶And it came to pass that they did travel in the wilderness and did build barges in the which they did cross many waters, being directed continually by the hand of the Lord. ⁷And the Lord would not suffer that they should stop beyond the sea in the wilderness. But he would that they should come forth, even unto the land of promise (which was choice above all other lands), which the Lord God had preserved for a righteous people. ⁸And he had sworn in his wrath, unto the brother of Jared, that whoso should possess this land of promise—from that time henceforth and forever—should serve him (the true, and only God) or they should be swept off when the fulness of his wrath should come upon them.

>⁹And now, we can behold the decrees of God concerning this land, that it is a land of promise, and whatsoever nation shall possess it shall serve God or they shall be swept off when the fulness of his wrath shall come upon them. And the fulness of his wrath cometh upon them when they are ripened in iniquity. ¹⁰For behold, this is a land which is choice above all other lands. Wherefore, he that doth possess it, shall serve God or shall be swept off. For it is the everlasting decrees of God. And it is not until the fulness of iniquity among the children of the land that they are swept off.

¹¹And this cometh unto you, O ye Gentiles, that ye may know the decrees of God, that ye may repent and not continue in your iniquities, until the fulness be

---

a. Moroni adds this information. Perhaps it was on the plates, but it is also possible he knew it from the brass plates. In any case, it would not have been part of the source narrative and is thus seen as an aside. The information is found in Genesis 10:8–9.

b. The source narrative required no such explanation. This is Moroni's insertion.

c. See Exodus 34:5: "And the Lord descended in the cloud, and stood with him there, and proclaimed the name of the Lord."

come, that ye may not bring down the fulness of the wrath of God upon you, as the inhabitants of the land hath hitherto done. ¹²Behold, this is a choice land. And whatsoever nation shall possess it, shall be free from bondage, and from captivity, and from all other nations under heaven—if they will but serve the God of the land, which is Jesus Christ, which hath been manifested by the things which we have written.ᵃ<

¹³And now, I proceed with my record.

For behold, it came to pass that the Lord did bring Jared and his brethren forth, even to that great sea which divideth the lands. And as they came to the sea, they pitched their tents. And they called the name of the place Moriancumer. And they dwelt in tents—and dwelt in tents upon the seashore for the space of four years.

¹⁴And it came to pass at the end of the four years that the Lord came again unto the brother of Jared, and stood in a cloud and talked with him. And for the space of three hours did the Lord talk with the brother of Jared—and chastened him because he remembered not to call upon the name of the Lord. ¹⁵And the brother of Jared repented him of the evil which he had done and did call upon the name of the Lord for his brethren, which were with him.

And the Lord said unto him: "I will forgive thee and thy brethren of their sins—but thou shalt not sin any more. For ye shall remember that my spirit will not always strive with man. Wherefore, if ye will sin until ye are fully ripe, ye shall be cut off from the presence of the Lord.ᵇ And this is my thoughts upon the land which I shall give you for your inheritance. For it shall be a land of choiceᶜ above all other lands."

¹⁶And the Lord said: "Go to work! And build after the manner of barges which ye have hitherto built."

And it came to pass that the brother of Jared did go to work (and also his brethren) and built barges after the manner which they had built (according to the instructions of the Lord). And they were small, and they were light upon the water, even like unto the lightness of a fowl upon the water. ¹⁷And they were built after a manner that they were exceeding tight, even that they would hold water like unto a dish. And the bottom there thereof was tight like unto a dish, and the sides thereof was tight like unto a dish, and the ends thereof were peaked. And the top thereof was tight like unto a dish. And the length thereof was the length of a tree. And the door thereof, when it was shut, was tight like unto a dish.

¹⁸And it came to pass that the brother of Jared cried unto the Lord, saying: "O Lord! I have performed the work which thou hast commanded me, and I have made the barges according as thou hast directed me. ¹⁹And behold, O Lord, in them there is no

---

a. The promise of the land was foundational for the Nephites just as it was for the Jaredites. At this point, Moroni is painfully aware that God would exercise the negative part of the promise. Therefore, he uses the initiation of the promise to the Jaredites to transfer it to the Gentiles who will come. That this is an interruption is confirmed with the next sentence that has Moroni saying that he will return to his narrative about the Jaredites.

b. The phrase "cut off from my presence" is found in Leviticus 22:3.

c. "Land of choice" is the way it appears in the Printer's Manuscript. Skousen notes that the compositor changed it to the more standard "land choice." Skousen accepts the compositor's correction as the preferred reading. Skousen, *Analysis of Textual Variants,* 6:3746–48. The idea that it would be a "land of choice" nevertheless might emphasize the responsibility of those in the land to follow God.

light. Whither shall we steer? And also, we shall perish, for in them we cannot breathe, save it is the air which is in them. Therefore, we shall perish."

²⁰And the Lord said unto the brother of Jared: "Behold, thou shalt make a hole in the top thereof, and also in the bottom thereof. And when thou shalt suffer for air—thou shalt unstop the hole thereof, and receive air. And if it so be that the water come in upon thee, behold, ye shall stop the hole thereof, that ye may not perish in the flood."

²¹And it came to pass that the brother of Jared did so, according as the Lord had commanded. ²²And he cried again unto the Lord, saying: "O Lord! Behold, I have done, even as thou hast commanded me. And I have prepared the vessels for my people. And behold, there is no light in them. Behold, O Lord! Wilt thou suffer that we shall cross this great water in darkness?"

²³And the Lord said unto the brother of Jared:

> What will ye that I should do, that ye may have light in your vessels? For behold, ye cannot have windows, for they will be dashed in pieces. Neither shall ye take fire with you, for ye shall not go by the light of fire. ²⁴For behold, ye shall be as a whale in the midst of the sea. For the mountain waves shall dash upon you. Nevertheless, I will bring you up again out of the depths of the sea. For the winds have gone forth out of my mouth, and also and the rains, and the floods, have I sent forth. ²⁵And behold, I prepare you against these things. For how be it ye cannot cross this great deep—save I prepare you against the waves of the sea, and the winds which have gone forth, and the floods which shall come. Therefore, what will ye, that I should prepare for you, that ye may have light when ye are swallowed up in the depths of the sea?

[3] ¹And it came to pass that the brother of Jared—ᵃ Now, the number of the vessels which had been prepared was eight. Therefore, the brother of Jared went forth unto the mount (>which they called the mount Shelem, because of its exceeding heightᵇ<)—and did molten out of a rock, sixteen small stones. And they were white and clear, even as transparent glass. And he did carry them in his hands up on the top of the mount and cried again unto the Lord, saying:

> ²O Lord! Thou hast said that we must be encompassed about by the floods. Now behold, O Lord, and do not be angry with thy servant because of his weakness before thee. For we know that thou art holy and dwellest in the heavens, and that we are unworthy before thee. Because of the fall our natures have become evil continually. Nevertheless, O Lord, thou hast given us a commandment that we must call upon thee, that from thee we may receive according to our desires.
>
> ³Behold, O Lord! Thou hast smitten us because of our iniquity and hath driven us forth. And for this many years we have been in the wilderness. Nevertheless, thou hast been merciful unto us.
>
> O Lord! Look upon me in pity, and turn away thine anger from this, thy people, and suffer not that they shall go forth across this raging deep in darkness. But, behold these things which I have molten out of the rock!
>
> ⁴And I know, O Lord, that thou hast all power and can do whatsoever thou

---

a. The sentence has no obvious ending. The intent might be fulfilled in "did carry them."

b. Moroni's insertion. The source narrative would not have required the explanation even though it was the reason for the name of the mount.

wilt for the benefit of man. Therefore, touch these stones, O Lord, with thy finger—and prepare them that they may shine forth in darkness. And they shall shine forth unto us in the vessels which we have prepared, that we may have light while we shall cross sea.

⁵Behold, O Lord! Thou canst do this. We know that thou art able to show forth great power, which looks small unto the understanding of men!

⁶And it came to pass that when the brother of Jared had said these words, behold—the Lord stretched forth his hand and touched the stones, one by one, with his finger. And the veil was taken from off the eyes of the brother of Jared and he saw the finger of the Lord! And it was as the finger of a man—like unto flesh and blood. And the brother of Jared fell down before the Lord. For he was struck with fear.

⁷And the Lord saw that the brother of Jared had fallen to the earth. And the Lord said unto him: "Arise! Why hast thou fallen?"

⁸And he saith unto the Lord: "I saw the finger of the Lord. And I feared lest he should smite me. For I knew not that the Lord had flesh and blood."

⁹And the Lord said unto him: "Because of thy faith, thou hast seen that I shall take upon me flesh and blood. And never has man come before me with such exceeding faith as thou hast. For were it so, ye could not have seen my finger. Sawest thou more than this?"

¹⁰And he answered: "Nay! Lord, show thyself unto me!"

¹¹And the Lord said unto him: "Believest thou the words which I shall speak?"

¹²And he answered: "Yea, Lord. I know that thou speakest the truth. For thou art a God of truth and canst not lie."

¹³And when he had said these words, behold, the Lord showed himself unto him, and said:

> Because thou knowest these things—ye are redeemed from the fall. Therefore, ye are brought back into my presence. Therefore, I show myself unto you. ¹⁴Behold, I am he which was prepared from the foundation of the world to redeem my people. Behold, I am Jesus Christ. I am the Father, and the Son. In me shall all mankind have life—and that eternally, even they which shall believe on my name. And they shall become my sons and my daughters.
>
> ¹⁵And never hath I showed myself unto man whom I have created. For never hath man believed in me as thou hast. Seest thou that ye are created after mine own image! Yea, even all men were created in the beginning after mine own image. ¹⁶Behold, this body, which ye now behold—is the body of my Spirit. And man have I created after the body of my spirit. And even as I appear unto thee to be in the spirit—will I appear unto my people in the flesh.
>
> >¹⁷And now as I, Moroni, said—I could not make a full account of these things, which are written. Therefore, it sufficeth me to say that Jesus showed himself unto this man in the spirit, even after the manner, and in the likeness, of the same body, even as he showed himself unto the Nephites. ¹⁸And he ministered unto him even as he ministered unto the Nephites.
>
> And all this, that this man knew that he was God because of the many great works which the Lord had showed unto him. ¹⁹And because of the knowledge of this man, he could not be kept from beholding within the veil.

Chapter I [Ether 1–4]

And he saw the finger of Jesus—which, when he saw, he fell with fear. For he knew that it was the finger of the Lord. And he had faith no longer. For he knew, nothing doubting. ²⁰Wherefore, having this perfect knowledge of God, he could not be kept from beholding within the veil. Therefore, he saw Jesus, and he did minister unto him.[a]<

²¹And it came to pass that the Lord said unto the brother of Jared:

Behold! Thou shalt not suffer these things (which ye have seen and heard) to go forth unto the world until the time cometh that I shall glorify my name in the flesh. Wherefore, ye shall treasure up the things which ye have seen and heard—and show it to no man. ²²And behold, when ye shall come unto me, ye shall write them, and shall seal them up, that no one can interpret them. For ye shall write them in a language that they cannot be read.

²³And behold, these two stones will I give unto thee. And ye shall seal them up also with the things which ye shall write. ²⁴For behold, the language which ye shall write—I have confounded. Wherefore, I will cause (in mine own due time) that these stones shall magnify to the eyes of men these things which ye shall write.

²⁵And when the Lord had said these words, the Lord showed unto the brother of Jared all the inhabitants of the earth which had been, and also all that would be. And the Lord withheld them not from his sight, even unto the ends of the earth. ²⁶For the Lord had said unto him in times before that, if he would believe in him that he could show unto him all things—it should be shown unto him. Therefore, the Lord could not withhold anything from him. For he knew that the Lord could show him all things.

²⁷And the Lord said unto him: "Write these things and seal them up. And I will show them in mine own due time unto the children of men."

²⁸And it came to pass that the Lord commanded him that he should seal up the two stones which he had received and show them not until the Lord should show them unto the children of men.

[4] ¹And the Lord commanded the brother of Jared to go down out of the mount, from the presence of the Lord and write the things which he had seen.[b]

>And they were forbidden to come unto the children of men until after that he should be lifted up upon the cross. And for this cause did king Benjamin[c] keep them, that they should not come unto the world until after Christ should show

---

a. As did Mormon, Moroni discusses his creation process. In this case, he notes that he cannot write everything and proceeds to finish the description. This becomes an opportunity to explain the theology behind the appearance of Yahweh (Jehovah) to the brother of Jared, something that would not have been on the plates of Ether.

b. Most of chapter 4 is an aside. Chapters 4 and 5 are inserted and not part of the Jaredite story. Since Moroni began a new chapter, the first sentence is considered as the beginning of the next phase of the story, with the aside beginning with the next sentence. That isn't clear, but it appears that Moroni had not planned the insertion, and it was triggered by Moroni's explanation of his relation to the story to be told.

c. In the 1847 and subsequent editions, Benjamin has been changed to Mosiah. The change makes more historical sense as the Jaredite records were never in Benjamin's possession. This same change was made to Mosiah 21:28, which also originally had Benjamin, but was changed to Mosiah. This may suggest that Moroni got the information from his father's record and it was a repetition of that "error" rather than a confirmation that it should have been Benjamin.

himself unto his people. ²And after that Christ truly had showed himself unto his people—he commanded that they should be made manifest.

³And now, after that they have all dwindled in unbelief and there is none save it be the Lamanites (and they have rejected the gospel of Christ)—therefore, I am commanded that I should hide them up again in the earth. ⁴Behold, I have written upon these plates the very things which the brother of Jared saw. And there never was greater things made manifest than that which was made manifest unto the brother of Jared. ⁵Wherefore, the Lord hath commanded me to write them. And I have wrote them. And he commanded me that I should seal them up. And he also hath commanded that I should seal up the interpretation thereof. Wherefore, I have sealed up the interpreters, according to the commandment of the Lord. ⁶For the Lord saith unto me:

> They shall not go forth unto the Gentiles until the day that they shall repent of their iniquity and become clean before the Lord. ⁷And in that day that they shall exercise faith in me (saith the Lord), even as the brother of Jared did, that they may become sanctified in me—then will I manifest unto them the things which the brother of Jared saw, even to the unfolding unto them all my revelations (saith Jesus Christ, the Son of God—the Father of the heavens and of the earth, and all things that in them is).
>
> ⁸And he that will contend against the word of the Lord—let him be accursed! And he that shall deny these things—let him be accursed! For unto them will I show no greater things (saith Jesus Christ). For I am he which speaketh. ⁹And at my command, the heavens are opened and are shut. And at my word the earth shall shake! And at my command the inhabitants thereof shall pass away, even so as by fire! ¹⁰And he that believeth not my words, believeth not my disciples.
>
> And if it so be that I do not speak—judge ye! For ye shall know that it is I that speaketh, at the last day. ¹¹But he that believeth these things (which I have spoken)—him will I visit with the manifestations of my spirit. And he shall know, and bear record. For, because of my spirit, he shall know that these things are true. For it persuadeth men to do good. ¹²And whatsoever thing persuadeth men to do good is of me. For good cometh of none save it be of me. And I am the same that leadeth men to all good.
>
> He that will not believe my words, will not believe me, that I am. And he that will not believe me, will not believe the Father (which sent me). For behold, I am the Father. I am the light, and the life, and the truth, of the world.[a]
>
> ¹³Come unto me, O ye Gentiles! And I will show unto you the greater things, the knowledge which is hid up because of unbelief.
>
> ¹⁴Come unto me, O ye house of Israel! And it shall be made manifest unto you how great things the Father hath laid up for you from the foundation of the world. And it hath not come unto you because of unbelief. ¹⁵Behold, when ye shall rend that veil of unbelief (which doth cause you to remain in your awful state of wickedness and hardness of heart, and blindness of mind)—

---

a. See John 8:12: "Then spake Jesus again unto them, saying, I am the light of the world." Also, John 1:4: "In him was life; and the life was the light of men."

then shall the great and marvelous things which have been hid up from the foundation of the world from you—yea, when ye shall call upon the Father in my name, with a broken heart and a contrite spirit[a]—then shall ye know that the Father hath remembered the covenant which he made unto your fathers, O house of Israel! [16]And then shall my revelations which I have caused to be written by my servant John be unfolded in the eyes of all the people.

Remember! When ye see these things, ye shall know that the time is at hand that they shall be made manifest in very deed. [17]Therefore, when ye shall receive this record, ye may know that the work of the Father has commenced upon all the face of the earth. [18]Therefore, repent all ye ends of the earth! And come unto me, and believe in my gospel, and be baptized in my name. For he that believeth and is baptized, shall be saved. But he that believeth not shall be damned.[b]

And signs shall follow them that believe in my name. [19]And blessed is he that is found faithful unto my name at the last day. For they shall be lifted up to dwell in the kingdom prepared for them from the foundation of the world.[c]

And behold, it is I that hath spoken it! Amen.[d]<

---

a. See Psalm 34:18: "The Lord *is* nigh unto them that are of a broken heart; and saveth such as be of a contrite spirit."

b. See Mark 16:16: "He that believeth and is baptized shall be saved; but he that believeth not shall be damned."

c. See Matthew 25:34: "Come, ye blessed of my Father, inherit the kingdom prepared for you from the foundation of the world."

d. The command to the brother of Jared to seal up his vision leads Moroni to discuss his own commandment to seal up the records and the interpreters. That then leads Moroni to include his command from Yahweh (Jehovah), which obviously was not on the plates of Ether.

Chapter II [Ether 5]

>[5] ¹And now I, Moroni, have written the words which was commanded me, according to my memory.ᵃ And I have told you the things which I have sealed up. Therefore, touch them not—in order that ye may translate. For that thing is forbidden you. Except, by and by, it shall be wisdom in God.

²And behold. Ye may be privileged that ye may show the plates unto those who shall assist to bring forth this work. ³And unto three shall they be shown by the power of God. Wherefore, they shall know of a surety that these things are true.

⁴And in the mouth of three witnesses shall these things be established.ᵇ And the testimony of three, and this work (in the which shall be shown forth the power of God, and also his word) of which the Father, and the Son, and the Holy Ghost beareth record—and all this shall stand as a testimony against the world at the last day.ᶜ ⁵And if it so be that they repent, and come unto the Father, in the name of Jesus, they shall be received into the kingdom of God.

⁶And now, if I have no authority for these things—judge ye! For ye shall know that I have authority when ye shall see me and we shall stand before God, at the last day. Amen.ᵈ<

---

a. This chapter is the continuation of Moroni's aside from the end of the previous chapter, which ended with a testificatory amen. Moroni hadn't finished the aside, so he continues in this short chapter, which again ends with amen.

b. Allusion to Deuteronomy 19:15: "One witness shall not rise up against a man for any iniquity, or for any sin, in any sin that he sinneth: at the mouth of two witnesses, or at the mouth of three witnesses, shall the matter be established."

c. A difficult sentence. It appears that the final "and" is intended as the concluding linkage, similar to other sentences in Mormon's text.

d. Moroni's previous aside was to the future audience. This aside is to an audience of one: Joseph Smith. By this time, Moroni must have had a very clear vision of the man who would be the one to unseal the records Moroni cared for.

Chapter III [Ether 6–8]

[6] ¹And now I, Moroni, proceed to give the record of Jared and his brother.[a]

²For it came to pass (after that the Lord had prepared the stones which the brother of Jared had carried up into the mount), the brother of Jared came down out of the mount. And he did put forth the stones into the vessels which were prepared—one in each end thereof. And behold, they did give light unto the vessels thereof. ³And thus, the Lord caused stones to shine in darkness, to give light unto men, women, and children, that they might not cross the great waters in darkness.

⁴And it came to pass that when they had prepared all manner of food, that thereby they might subsist upon the water—and also food for their flocks, and herds, and whatsoever beast or animal, or fowl, that they should carry with them.

And it came to pass that when they had done all these things, they got aboard of their vessels, or barges, and set forth into the sea—commending themselves unto the Lord, their God.

⁵And it came to pass that the Lord God caused that there should a furious wind blow upon the face of the waters, towards the promised land. And thus, they were tossed upon the waves of the sea, before the wind.

⁶And it came to pass that they were many times buried in the depths of the sea because of the mountain waves which broke upon them, and also the great and terrible tempests which were caused by the fierceness of the wind.

⁷And it came to pass that when they were buried in the deep there was no water that could hurt them—their vessels being tight, like unto a dish. And also, they were tight like unto the ark of Noah.[b] Therefore, when they were encompassed about by many waters, they did cry unto the Lord. And he did bring them forth again upon the top of the waters.

⁸And it came to pass that the wind did never cease to blow towards the promised land, while they were upon the waters.

And thus, they were driven forth before the wind. ⁹And they did sing praises unto the Lord. Yea, the brother of Jared did sing praises unto the Lord. And he did thank, and praise the Lord all the day long. And when the night came, they did not cease to praise the Lord.

¹⁰And thus, they were driven forth. And no monster of the sea could break them, neither whale that could mar them. And they did have light continually—whether it was above the water, or under the water. ¹¹And thus, they were driven forth three hundred and forty and four days upon the water.

¹²And they did land upon the shore of the promised land. And when they had set their feet upon the shores of the promised land, they bowed themselves down upon the face of the land and did humble themselves before the Lord—and did shed tears of joy before the Lord because of the multitude of his tender mercies[c] over them.

¹³And it came to pass that they went forth upon the face of the land and began to till the earth. ¹⁴And Jared had four sons. And they were called Jacom, and Gilgah, and

---

a. This is a clear marker that Moroni understood that he had moved away from the story to be told.

b. It cannot be known if this reference was in the source narrative or if Moroni is making the parallel to Noah's story explicit.

c. The phrase "tender mercies" is found in Psalm 25:6, 40:11, 51:1, 69:16, and others.

Mahah, and Orihah. ¹⁵And the brother of Jared also begat sons and daughters. ¹⁶And the friends of Jared and his brother were in number about twenty and two souls. And they also begat sons and daughters before they came to the promised land. And therefore, they began to be many. ¹⁷And they were taught to walk humbly before the Lord. And they were also taught from on high.

¹⁸And it came to pass that they began to spread upon the face of the land, and to multiply, and to till the earth. And they did wax strong in the land. ¹⁹And the brother of Jared began to be old, and saw that he must soon go down to the grave. Wherefore, he saith unto Jared: "Let us gather together our people, that we may number them, that we may know of them, what they will desire of us—before we go down to our graves."

²⁰And accordingly, the people were gathered together. Now, the number of the sons and the daughters of the brother of Jared were twenty and two souls. And the number of the sons and daughters of Jared were twelve, he having four sons.

²¹And it came to pass that they did number their people. And after that they had numbered them, they did desired of them the things which they would that they should do before they went down to their graves.

²²And it came to pass that the people desired of them that they should anoint one of their sons to be a king over them. ²³And now behold, this was grievous unto them. But the brother of Jared said unto them: "Surely this thing leadeth into captivity."

²⁴But Jared said unto his brother: "Suffer them, that they may have a king."

And therefore he said unto them: "Choose ye out from among our sons, a king, even whom ye will."

²⁵And it came to pass that they chose, even the first born of the brother of Jared. And his name was Pagag.

And it came to pass that he refused and would not be their king. And the people would that his father should constrain him. But his father would not. And he commanded them that they should [ᵃ] constrain no man to be their king.

²⁶And it came to pass that they chose all the brothers of Pagag. And they would not.

²⁷And it came to pass that neither would the sons of Jared, even all save it were one. And Orihah, he was anointed to be king over the people. ²⁸And he began to reign. And the people began to prosper. And they became exceeding rich.

²⁹And it came to pass that Jared died, and his brother also.

³⁰And it came to pass that Orihah did walk humbly before the Lord and did remember how great things the Lord had done for his father, and also taught his people how great things the Lord had done for their fathers.

[7] ¹And it came to pass that Orihah did execute judgment upon the land, in righteousness, all his days (whose days were exceeding many). ²And he begat sons and daughters. Yea, he begat thirty and one, among whom were twenty and three sons.

³And it came to pass that he also begat Kib in his old age.

And it came to pass that Kib reigned in his stead.

And Kib begat Corihor. ⁴And when Corihor was thirty and two years old, he rebelled against his father, and went over and dwelt in the land of Nehor. And he begat sons and daughters. And they became exceeding fair. Wherefore, Corihor drew away

---

a. The Printer's Manuscript originally has "not," which was the crossed out. It would have formed a double negative. Skousen suggests that this was a nearly immediate correction Oliver Cowdery made during copying. See Skousen, *Textual Variants*, 6:3779.

Chapter III [Ether 6–8]

many people after him. ⁵And when he had gathered together an army, he came up unto the land of Moron (where the king dwelt) and took him captive, which brought to pass the saying of the brother of Jared that they would be brought into captivity. >⁶Now, the land of Moron (where the king dwelt) was near the land which is called Desolation by the Nephites.ᵃ<

⁷And it came to pass that Kib dwelt in captivity, and his people under Corihor (his son), until he became exceeding old. Nevertheless, Kib begat Shule in his old age, while he was yet in captivity.

⁸And it came to pass that Shule was angry with his brother. And Shule waxed strong and became mighty as to the strength of a man. And he was also mighty in judgment. ⁹Wherefore, he came to the hill Ephraim and he did molten out of the hill—and made swords out of steel for those which he had drew away with him. And after that he had armed them with swords, he returned to the city Nehor and gave battle unto his brother Corihor—by which means he obtained the kingdom, and restored it unto his father Kib.

¹⁰And now, because of the thing which Shule had done, his father bestowed upon him the kingdom. Therefore, he began to reign in the stead of his father.

¹¹And it came to pass that he did execute judgment in righteousness. And he did spread his kingdom upon all the face of the land, for the people had become exceeding numerous.

¹²And it came to pass that Shule also begat many sons and daughters. ¹³And Corihor repented of the many evils which he had done. Wherefore, Shule gave him power in his kingdom.

¹⁴And it came to pass that Corihor had many sons and daughters. And among the sons of Corihor there was one whose name was Noah.

¹⁵And it came to pass that Noah rebelled against Shule, the king, and also his father, Corihor, and drew away Cohor, his brother, and also all his brethren, and many of the people. ¹⁶And he gave battle unto Shule, the king, in the which he did obtain the land of their first inheritance. And he became a king over that part of the land.

¹⁷And it came to pass that he gave battle again unto Shule, the king. And he took Shule, the king, and carried him away captive into Moron.

¹⁸And it came to pass as he was about to put him to death, the sons of Shule crept into the house of Noah by night and slew him, and broke down the door of the prison and brought out their father, and placed him upon his throne in his own kingdom. ¹⁹Wherefore, the son of Noah did build up his kingdom in his stead. Nevertheless, they did not gain power any more over Shule, the king. And the people which were under the reign of Shule, the king, did prosper exceedingly and wax great. ²⁰And the country was divided. And there was two kingdoms—the kingdom of Shule, and the kingdom of Cohor, the son of Noah. ²¹And Cohor, the son of Noah, caused that his people should give battle unto Shule—in the which Shule did beat them, and did slay Cohor.

²²And now, Cohor had a son which was called Nimrod. And Nimrod gave up the kingdom of Cohor unto Shule. And he did gain favor in the eyes of Shule. Wherefore,

---

a. Moroni inserts geographical information that would be useful to a future reader, as long as that reader was familiar with Nephite geography. It is not clear how Moroni gained the information about how the lands corresponded.

Shule did bestow great favors upon him, in the which he did do (in the kingdom of Shule) according to his desires.

²³And also, in the reign of Shule, there came prophets among the people (which were sent from the Lord) prophesying, that the wickedness and idolatry of the people was bringing a curse upon the land—in the which they should be destroyed if they did not repent.

²⁴And it came to pass that the people did revile against the prophets and did mock them.

And it came to pass that King Shule did execute judgment against all those who did revile against the prophets. ²⁵And he did execute a law throughout all the land which gave power unto the prophets, that they should go whithersoever they would. And by this cause, the people were brought unto repentance. ²⁶And because the people did repent of their iniquities and idolatries, the Lord did spare them. And they began to prosper again in the land.

And it came to pass that Shule begat sons and daughters in his old age. ²⁷And there was no more wars in the days of Shule. And he remembered the great things that the Lord had done for his fathers in bringing them across the great deep into the promised land. Wherefore, he did execute judgment in righteousness all his days.

[8] ¹And it came to pass that he begat Omer. And Omer reigned in his stead. And Omer begat Jared, and Jared begat sons and daughters. ²And Jared rebelled against his father, and came and dwelt in the land of Heth.

And it came to pass that he did flatter much people, because of his cunning words, until he had gained the half of the kingdom. ³And when he had gained the half of the kingdom, he gave battle unto his father. And he did carry away his father into captivity and did make them serve in captivity.

⁴And now, in the days of the reign of Omer (he was in captivity the half of his days)—and it came to pass that he begat sons and daughters, among whom were Esrom and Coriantumr. ⁵And they were exceeding angry because of the doings of Jared, their brother, insomuch that they did raise an army, and gave battle unto Jared.

And it came to pass that they did give battle unto him by night.

⁶And it came to pass that when they had slew the army of Jared, they were about to slay him also—and he pled with them that they would not slay him, and he would give up the kingdom unto his father.

And it came to pass that they did grant unto him his life.

⁷And now, Jared became exceeding sorrowful because of the loss of the kingdom. For he had set his heart upon the kingdom, and upon the glory of the world. ⁸Now, the daughter of Jared (being exceeding expert, and seeing the sorrow of her father) thought to devise a plan whereby she could redeem the kingdom unto her father. ⁹Now, the daughter of Jared was exceeding fair.

And it came to pass that she did talk with her father, and saith unto him:

> Whereby hath my father so much sorrow? Hath he not read the record, which our fathers brought across the great deep? Behold, is there not an account concerning them of old, that they (by their secret plans) did obtain kingdoms and great glory? ¹⁰And now, therefore, let my father send for Akish, the son of Kimnor. And behold, I am fair. And I will dance before him and I will please him, that he will

Chapter III [Ether 6–8]

desire me to wife. Wherefore, if he shall desire of thee that ye shall give (unto him) me to wife, then shall ye say: I will give her, if ye will bring unto me the head of my father, the king.

¹¹And now, Omer was a friend to Akish. Wherefore, when Jared had sent for Akish, the daughter of Jared danced before him, that she pleased him, insomuch that he desired her to wife.

And it came to pass that he said unto Jared: "Give her unto me to wife."

¹²And Jared said unto him: "I will give her unto you, if ye will bring unto me the head of my father, the king.

¹³And it came to pass that Akish gathered in unto the house of Jared all his kinsfolks, and saith unto them: "Will ye swear unto me that ye will be faithful unto me in the thing which I shall desire of you?"

¹⁴And it came to pass that they all swear unto him by the God of heaven, and also by the heavens, and also by the earth, and by their heads, that whoso should vary from the assistance which Akish desired, should lose his head. And whoso should divulge whatsoever thing Akish made known unto them, the same should lose his life.

¹⁵And it came to pass that thus they did agree with Akish. And Akish did administer unto them the oaths which was given by them of old who also sought power (which had been handed down even from Cain, who was a murderer from the beginning). ¹⁶And they were kept up by the power of the devil, to administer these oaths unto the people, to keep them in darkness, to help such as sought to gain power—and to murder, and to plunder, and to lie, and to commit all manner of wickedness and whoredoms. ¹⁷And it was the daughter of Jared which put it into his heart to search up these things of old. And Jared put it into the heart of Akish. Wherefore, Akish administered it unto his kindreds, and friends—leading them away by fair promises to do whatsoever thing he desired.

¹⁸And it came to pass that they formed a secret combination, even as they of old—

>which combination is a most abominable, and wicked, above all, in the sight of God. ¹⁹For the Lord worketh not in secret combinations, neither doth he will that man should shed blood, but in all things hath forbidden it from the beginning of man.

²⁰And now I, Moroni, do not write the manner of their oaths, and combinations. For it hath been made known unto me that they are had among all people, and they are had among the Lamanites. ²¹And they have caused the destruction of this people of which I am now speaking—and also the destruction of the people of Nephi.

²²And whatsoever nation shall uphold such secret combinations to get power, and gain until they shall spread over the nation—behold, they shall be destroyed. For the Lord will not suffer that the blood of his saints, which shall be shed by them, shall always cry unto him from the ground for vengeance upon them—and yet he avengeth them not. ²³Wherefore, O ye Gentiles! It is wisdom in God that these things should be shown unto you, that thereby ye may repent of your sins, and suffer not that these murderous combinations shall get above you, which are built up to get power, and gain—and the work, yea, even the work of destruction come upon you.

Yea, even the sword of the justice of the Eternal God shall fall upon you, to your overthrow and destruction, if ye shall suffer these things to be. ²⁴Wherefore, the Lord commandeth you, when ye shall see these things come among you, that ye shall awake to a sense of your awful situation because of this secret combination which shall be among you, or wo be unto it, because of the blood of them which have been slain. For they cry from the dust for vengeance upon it, and also upon those who build it up.

²⁵For it cometh to pass that whoso buildeth it up—seeketh to overthrow the freedom of all lands, nations, and countries. And it bringeth to pass the destruction of all people, for it is built up by the devil, which is the father of all lies, even that same liar which beguiled our first parents. Yea, even that same liar which hath caused man to commit murder from the beginning, which hath hardened the hearts of men that they have murdered the prophets, and stoned them, and cast them out from the beginning. ²⁶Wherefore I, Moroni, am commanded to write these things, that evil may be done away, and that the time may come that Satan may have no power upon the hearts of the children of men, but that they may be persuaded to do good continually, that they may come unto the fountain of all righteousness and be saved.ᵃ<

---

a. This insertion highlights both the message that Moroni believes is most important in this section of the record of Ether as well as the message his father took from the record. The idea that secret combinations destroy nations began here and became Mormon's leit motif as he told the story of the destruction of the Nephites. Moroni confirms that this is an insertion when he states in the first verse of the next chapter that he is returning to his narration.

Chapter IV [Ether 9–11]

[9] ¹And now I, Moroni, proceed with my record.ᵃ

Therefore, behold, it came to pass that because of the secret combinations of Akish and his friends—behold, they did overthrow the kingdom of Omer. ²Nevertheless, the Lord was merciful unto Omer, and also to his sons, and to his daughters, which were not, or which did not, seek his destruction.ᵇ ³And the Lord warned Omer in a dream that he should depart out of the land. Wherefore, Omer departed out of the land with his family, and traveled many days—and came over and passed by >the hill of Shim—and came over by the place where the Nephites were destroyedᶜ<—and from thence eastward—and came to a place (which was called Ablom) by the seashore. And there he pitched his tent (and also his sons and his daughters, and all his household, save it were Jared and his family).

⁴And it came to pass that Jared was anointed king over the people by the hand of wickedness. And he gave unto Akish his daughter to wife.

⁵And it came to pass that Akish sought the life of his father-in-law. And he applied unto those whom he had sworn by the oath of the ancients. And they obtained the head of his father-in-law as he sat upon his throne giving audience to his people—⁶for so great had been the spreading of this wicked, and secret society that it had corrupted the hearts of all the people. Therefore, Jared was murdered upon his throne. And Akish reigned in his stead.

⁷And it came to pass that Akish began to be jealous of his son. Therefore, he shut him up in prison, and kept him upon a little (or no) food, until he had suffered death. ⁸And now the brother of him that suffered death (and his name was Nimrah) and heᵈ was angry with his father because of that which his father had done unto his brother.

⁹And it came to pass that Nimrah gathered together a small number of men and fled out of the land—and came over and dwelt with Omer.

¹⁰And it came to pass that Akish begat other sons, and they won the hearts of the people, notwithstanding they had sworn unto him to do all manner of iniquity, according to that which he desired. ¹¹Now, the people of Akish were desirous for gain, even as Akish was desirous for power. Wherefore, the sons of Akish did offer them money, by the which means they drew away the more part of the people after them. ¹²And there began to be a war between the sons of Akish and Akish, which lasted for the space of many years, yea, unto the destruction of nearly all the people of the kingdom, yea, even all save it were thirty souls and they which fled with the house of Omer. ¹³Wherefore, Omer was restored again to the land of his inheritance.

¹⁵And it came to pass that Omer began to be old. Nevertheless, in his old age he begat Emer. And he anointed Emer to be king, to reign in his stead. And after that he

---

a. Moroni recognized that he had diverged from the Jaredite story and declares that he returns to it.

b. In 1837, Joseph Smith removed "which were not, or." That phrase is a use of the corrective "or" and indicates that a correction was made. The quick correction, and the clearly incorrect direction that "were not" was indicating, suggests that this is a correction that was made during the dictation rather than something that was written on the plates.

c. Moroni continues to give directions according to Nephite geographic indicators.

d. The compositor crossed out the "and he" in preparation for the printed edition. The reading in the Printer's Manuscript is confirmed in the Original Manuscript and therefore retained in this text. It is a similar construction to other sentences. Skousen, *Textual Variants,* 6:3798.

had anointed Emer to be king, he saw peace in the land for the space of two years. And he died, having seen exceeding many days which were full of sorrow.

And it came to pass that Emer did reign in his stead and did fill the steps of his father.[a] [16]And the Lord began again to take the curse from off the land. And the house of Emer did prosper exceedingly under the reign of Emer. And in the space of sixty and two years they had become exceeding strong, insomuch that they became exceeding rich—

>[17]having all manner of fruit, and of grain, and of silks, and of fine linen, and of gold, and of silver, and of precious things. [18]And also, all manner of cattle of oxen and cows, and of sheep, and of swine, and of goats, and also many other kind of animals which were useful for the food of man. [19]And they also had horses, and asses. And there were elephants, and cureloms, and cumoms, all of which were useful unto man—and more especially the elephants, and cureloms, and cumoms. [20]And thus, the Lord did pour out his blessings upon this land, which was choice above all other lands. And he commanded that whoso should possess the land should possess it unto the Lord—or they should be destroyed when they were ripened in iniquity. For upon such, saith the Lord: "I will pour out the fulness of my wrath."[b]<

[21]And Emer did execute judgment in righteousness all his days. And he begat many sons, and daughters. And he begat Coriantum, [22]and he anointed Coriantum to reign in his stead. And after that he had anointed Coriantum to reign in his stead, he lived four years. And he saw peace in the land, yea, and he even saw the son of righteousness[c] and did rejoice, and glory in his day. And he died in peace.

[23]And it came to pass that Coriantum did walk in the steps of his father, and did build many mighty cities and did administer that which was good unto his people in all his days.

And it came to pass that he had no children, even until he was exceeding old.

[24]And it came to pass that his wife died, being an hundred and two years old.

And it came to pass that Coriantum took to wife (in his old age) a young maid, and begat sons and daughters. Wherefore, he lived until he was an hundred and forty and two years old.

[25]And it came to pass that he begat Com. And Com reigned in his stead. And he reigned forty and nine years, and he begat Heth. And he also begat other sons and daughters. [26]And the people had spread again over all the face of the land. And there began again to be an exceeding great wickedness upon the face of the land. And Heth began to embrace the secret plans again (of old) to destroy his father.

[27]And it came to pass that he did dethrone his father, for he slew him with his own sword. And he did reign in his stead. [28]And there came prophets in the land again, crying repentance unto them—that they must prepare the way of the Lord or there should come a curse upon the face of the land, yea, even there should be a great famine, in the which they should be destroyed if they did not repent. [29]But the people believed not the

---

a. The phrase is as it appears in the Printer's Manuscript and published editions. However, it seems to be incorrectly stating a metaphor that is correctly given in Ether 8:23: "did walk in the steps of his father."

b. Moroni inserts his emphasis on the promise of the land. It was mentioned at the beginning of his edited book of Ether, and Moroni will emphasize the theme at times. Moroni saw this promise as a tie creating the parallel between the Jaredites and the Nephites.

c. Malachi 4:2 has the phrase "sun of righteousness" which is referenced as "son of righteousness" here and in 2 Nephi 26:9.

words of the prophets, but they cast them out—and some of them they cast into pits and left them to perish.

And it came to pass that they done all these things, according to the commandment of the king, Heth.

³⁰And it came to pass that there began to be a great dearth upon the land. And the inhabitants began to be destroyed exceeding fast because of the dearth, for there was no rain upon the face of the earth. ³¹And there came forth poisonous serpents also upon the face of the land, and did poison many people.

³²And it came to pass that their flocks began to flee before the poisonous serpents towards the land southward (>which was called by the Nephites Zarahemla<).

³³And it came to pass that there were many of them which did perish by the way. Nevertheless, there were some which fled into the land southward.

And it came to pass that the Lord did cause the serpents, that they should pursue them no more, but that they should hedge up the way,ª that they people could not pass, that whoso should attempt to pass might fall by the poisonous serpents.

³⁴And it came to pass that the people did follow the course of the beasts and did devour the carcasses of them which fell by the way, until they had devoured them all. Now, when the people saw that they must perish, they began to repent of their iniquities and cry unto the Lord.

³⁵And it came to pass that when they had humbled themselves sufficiently before the Lord, the Lord did send rain upon the face of the earth. And the people began to revive again. And there began to be fruit in the north countries and in all the countries round about. And the Lord did show forth his power unto them in preserving them from famine.

[10] ¹And it came to pass that Shez (>which was a descendant of Heth, for Heth had perished by the famine, and all his household save it were Shezᵇ<)—wherefore, Shez began to build up again a broken people.

²And it came to pass that Shez did remember the destructions of his fathers. And he did build up a righteous kingdom. For he remembered what the Lord had done in bringing Jared and his brother across the deep. And he did walk in the ways of the Lord. And he begat sons and daughters. ³And his eldest son, whose name was Shez, did rebel against him. Nevertheless, Shez was smitten by the hand of a robber because of his exceeding riches, which brought peace again unto his father.

⁴And it came to pass that his father did build up many cities upon the face of the land. And the people began again to spread over all the face of the land. And Shez did live to an exceeding old age and he begat Riplakish. And he died. And Riplakish reigned in his stead.

⁵And it came to pass that Riplakish did not do that which was right in the sight of the Lord, for he did have many wives and concubines and did lay that upon men's shoulders which was grievous to be born, yea, he did tax them with heavy taxes. And with the taxes he did build many spacious buildings. ⁶And he did erect him an exceeding beautiful throne. And he did build many prisons. And whosoever would not be subject unto taxes, he did cast into prison. And whosoever were not able to pay taxes, he did cast into prison. And he did cause that they should labor continually for their support. And whoso refused to labor, he did cause to be put to death. ⁷Wherefore, he

---

a. The phrase "hedge up the way" occur in Hosea 2:6.

b. Moroni realized that he hadn't given enough of the story and quickly adds the basic background.

did obtain all his fine work. Yea, even his fine gold he did cause to be refined in prison. And all manner of fine workmanship he did cause to be wrought in prison.

And it came to pass that he did afflict the people with his whoredoms and abominations. ⁸And when he had reigned for the space of forty and two years, the people did raised up in rebellion against him. And there began to be war again in the land, insomuch that Riplakish was killed, and his descendants were driven out of the land.

⁹And it came to pass that after the space of many years, Morianton (he, being a descendant of Riplakish) gathered together an army of outcasts and went forth and gave battle unto the people. And he gained power over many cities. And the war became exceeding sore and did last for the space of many years. And he did gain power over all the land and did establish himself king over all the land. ¹⁰And, after that he had established himself king, he did ease the burden of the people—in the which he did gain favor in the eyes of the people. And they did anoint him to be their king. ¹¹And he did do justice unto the people, but not unto himself, because of his many whoredoms. Wherefore, he was cut off from the presence of the Lord.[a]

¹²And it came to pass that Morianton built up many cities. And the people became exceeding rich under his reign, both in buildings, and in gold, and in silver, and in raising grain, and in flocks and herds, and such things which had been restored unto them. ¹³And Morianton did live to an exceeding great age, and then he begat Kim. And Kim did reign in the stead of his father. And he did reign eight years, and his father died.

And it came to pass that Kim did not reign in righteousness. Wherefore, he was not favored of the Lord. ¹⁴And his brother did raise up in rebellion against him, in the which he did bring him into captivity. And he did remain in captivity all his days. And he begat sons and daughters in captivity. And in his old age he begat Levi. And he died.

¹⁵And it came to pass that Levi did serve in captivity (after the death of his father) for the space of forty and two years. And he did make war against the king of the land, in the which he did obtain unto himself the kingdom. ¹⁶And after that he had obtained unto himself the kingdom, he did that which was right in the sight of the Lord. And the people did prosper in the land. And he did live to a good old age, and begat sons and daughters. And he also begat Corom, whom he anointed king in his stead.

¹⁷And it came to pass that Corom did that which was good in the sight of the Lord all his days. And he begat many sons and daughters. And after that he had seen many days, he did pass away, even like unto the rest of the earth. And Kish reigned in his stead.

¹⁸And it came to pass that Kish passed away also, and Lib reigned in his stead.

¹⁹And it came to pass that Lib also did that which was good in the sight of the Lord. And in the days of Lib, the poisonous serpents were destroyed. Wherefore, they did go into the land southward to hunt food for the people of the land, for the land was covered with animals of the forest. And Lib also, himself, became a great hunter. ²⁰And they built a great city by the narrow neck of land—by the place where the sea divides the land. ²¹And they did preserve the land southward for a wilderness, to get game.

>And the whole face of the land northward was covered with inhabitants.

²²And they were exceeding industrious. And they did buy and sell and traffic, one with another, that they might get gain. ²³And they did work in all manner of ore. And they did make gold, and silver, and iron, and brass, and all manner of metals.

---

a. The phrase "cut off from my presence" is found in Leviticus 22:3.

And they did dig it out of the earth. Wherefore, they did cast up mighty heaps of earth, for to get ore of gold, and of silver, and of iron, and of copper.

And they did work all manner of fine work. ²⁴And they did have silks, and fine twined linen. And they did work all manner of cloth that they might clothe themselves from their nakedness.

²⁵And they did make all manner of tools to till the earth, both to plow, and to sow, to reap, and to hoe—and also to thrash. ²⁶And they did make all manner of tools, in the which they did work their beasts. ²⁷And they did make all manner of weapons of war. And they did work all manner of work of exceeding [curious[a]] workmanship. ²⁸And never could be a people more blessed than were they. And more prospered by the hand of the Lord. And they were in a land that was choice above all lands. For the Lord had spoken it.[b]<

²⁹And it came to pass that Lib did live many years, and begat sons and daughters. And he also begat Hearthom.

³⁰And it came to pass that Hearthom reigned in the stead of his father. And when Hearthom had reigned twenty and four years, behold the kingdom was taken away from him. And he served many years in captivity, yea, even all the remainder of his days. ³¹And he begat Heth. And Heth lived in captivity all his days. And Heth begat Aaron, and Aaron dwelt in captivity all his days. And he begat Amnigaddah. And Amnigaddah also dwelt in captivity all his days. And he begat Coriantum. And Coriantum dwelt in captivity all his days. And he begat Com.

³²And it came to pass that Com drew away the half of the kingdom. And he reigned over the half of the kingdom forty and two years. And he went to battle against the king, Amgid. And they fought for the space of many years, in the which Com gained power over Amgid, and obtained power over the remainder of the kingdom.

³³And in the days of Com there began to be robbers in the land. And they adopted the old plans and administered oaths after the manner of the ancients—and sought again to destroy the kingdom. ³⁴Now, Com did fight against them much. Nevertheless, he did not prevail against them.

[11] ¹And there came also in the days of Com many prophets, and prophesied of the destruction of that great people, except they should repent and turn unto the Lord, and forsake their murders and wickedness.

²And it came to pass that the prophets were rejected by the people. And they fled unto Com for protection, for the people sought to destroy them. ³And they prophesied unto Com many things. And he was blessed in all the remainder of his days. ⁴And he lived to a good old age and begat Shiblom. And Shiblom reigned in his stead. And the brother of Shiblom rebelled against him. And there began to be an exceeding great war in all the land.

⁵And it came to pass that the brother of Shiblom did cause that all the prophets which prophesied of the destruction of the people should be put to death. ⁶And there was great calamity in all the land, for they had testified that a great curse should come upon the land, and also upon the people—and that there should be a great destruc-

---

a. Added above the line, apparently by Hyrum Smith. The word fits, and other changes he made would appear to be corrections against the Original Manuscript, which is not extant at this point. Therefore, his change has been added.

b. These verses are similar in intent to Ether 9:17–20, where Moroni similarly lists evidence of how the Lord fulfills the promise of the land.

tion among such an one as never had been upon the face of the earth. And their bones should become as heaps of earth upon the face of the land, except they should repent of their wickedness. [7]And they hearkened not unto the voice of the Lord because of their wicked combinations. Wherefore, there began to be wars [and[a]] contentions, in all the land—and also many famines and pestilences, insomuch that there was a great destruction, such an one as never had been known upon the face of the earth.

And all this came to pass in the days of Shiblom. [8]And the people began to repent of their iniquity. And inasmuch as they did, the Lord did have mercy on them.

[9]And it came to pass that Shiblom was slain, and Seth was brought into captivity. And he did dwell in captivity all his days.

[10]And it came to pass that Ahah his son did obtain the kingdom. And he did reign over the people all his days, and he did do all manner of iniquity in his days, in the which he did cause the shedding of much blood. And few were his days. [11]And Ethem, being a descendant of Ahah, did obtain the kingdom. And he also did do that which was wicked in his days.

[12]And it came to pass in the days of Ethem there came many prophets, and prophesied again unto the people. Yea, they did prophesy that the Lord would utterly destroy them from off the face of the earth, except they repented of their iniquities.

[13]And it came to pass that the people hardened their hearts and would not hearken unto their words. And the prophets mourned and withdrew from among the people.

[14]And it came to pass that Ethem did execute judgment in wickedness all his days. And he begat Moron.

And it came to pass that Moron did reign in his stead. And Moron did do that which was wicked before the Lord.

[15]And it came to pass that there arose a rebellion among the people because of that secret combination which was built up to get power, and gain. And there arose a mighty man among them (in iniquity),[b] and gave battle unto Moron—in the which he did overthrow the half of the kingdom. And he did maintain the half of the kingdom for many years.

[16]And it came to pass that Moron did overthrow him and did obtain the kingdom again.

[17]And it came to pass that there arose another mighty man and he was a descendant of the brother of Jared.

[18]And it came to pass that he did overthrow Moron and obtain the kingdom. Wherefore, Moron dwelt in captivity all the remainder of his days. And he begat Coriantor.

[19]And it came to pass that Coriantor dwelt in captivity all his days. [20]And in the days of Coriantor there also came many prophets—and prophesied of great and marvelous things, and cried repentance unto the people—and except they should repent, the Lord God would execute judgment against them, to their utter destruction. [21]And that the Lord God would send (or bring forth) an other people to possess the land (by his power) after the manner which he brought their fathers. [22]And they did reject all the words of the prophets because of their secret society and wicked abominations.

[23]And it came to pass that Coriantor begat Ether. And he died, having dwelt in captivity all his days.

---

a. Ampersand written above the line during editing.

b. It seems the meaning is intended as: "There arose a mighty man among them ([mighty] in iniquity)."

Chapter V [Ether 12]

[12] ¹And it came to pass that the days of Ether was in the days of Coriantumr. And Coriantumr was king over all the land. ²And Ether was a prophet of the Lord. Wherefore, Ether came forth in the days of Coriantumr and began to prophesy unto the people. For he could not be constrained—because of the spirit of the Lord which was in him. ³For he did cry from the morning, even until the going down of the sun—exhorting the people to believe in God unto repentance, lest they should be destroyed—saying unto them that by faith all things are fulfilled. ⁴Wherefore, whoso believeth in God might (with surety) hope for a better world (yea, even a place at the right hand of God) which hope cometh of faith—maketh an anchor to the souls of men—which would make them sure, and steadfast, always abounding in good works, being led to glorify God.[a]

⁵And it came to pass that Ether did prophesy great and marvelous things unto the people—which they did not believe because they saw them not.

>⁶And now I, Moroni, would speak somewhat concerning these things. I would show unto the world that faith is things which are hoped for and not seen.[b] Wherefore, dispute not because ye see not. For ye receive no witness—not until after the trial of your faith. ⁷For it was by faith that Christ showed himself unto our fathers, after that he had risen from the dead. And he showed [not[c]] himself unto them until after they had faith in him. Wherefore, it must needs be that some had faith in him. For he showed himself not unto the world ⁸but because of the faith of men.[d]

He has shown himself unto the world and glorified the name of the Father, and prepared a way that thereby others might be partakers of the heavenly gift,[e] that they might hope for those things which they have not seen. ⁹Wherefore, ye may also have hope and be partakers of the gift—if ye will but have faith.

¹⁰Behold, it was by faith that they of old were called, after the holy order of God. ¹¹Wherefore, by faith was the law of Moses given. But, in the gift of his Son hath God prepared a more excellent way.[f] And it is by faith that it hath been fulfilled. ¹²For, if there be no faith among the children of men—God can do no miracle among them. Wherefore, he showed not himself until after their faith.

¹³Behold, it was the faith of Alma and Amulek that caused the prison to tumble to the earth.

---

a. See Hebrews 6:19: "Which hope we have as an anchor of the soul, both sure and steadfast, and which entereth into that within the veil."

b. Echoes language from Hebrews 11:1: "Now faith is the substance of things hoped for, the evidence of things not seen."

c. The Printer's Manuscript had "and he showed himself not unto them." Hyrum Smith moved the "not" by writing it above the line in the current location and drawing a line through the original "not."

d. Royal Skousen, with Stanford Carmack, *The History of the Text of the Book of Mormon: Part Five, The King James Quotations in the Book of Mormon* (Provo, Utah: The Foundation for Ancient Research and Mormon Studies, Brigham Young University, 2019), 91—92, argues that "but because" should be read where "but" takes the meaning of "except." His argument is convincing and therefore this phrase has been punctuated according to that meaning.

e. The phrase "the heavenly gift" is found in Hebrews 6:4.

f. The phrase "a more excellent way" occurs in 1 Corinthians 12:31.

¹⁴Behold, it was the faith of Nephi and Lehi that wrought the change upon the Lamanites, that they were baptized with fire and with the Holy Ghost.

¹⁵Behold, it was the faith of Ammon and his brethren which wrought so great a miracle among the Lamanites.

¹⁶Yea, and even all they which wrought miracles, wrought them by faith—even those which were before Christ and also them which were after. ¹⁷And it was by faith that the three disciples obtained a promise that they should not taste of death. And they obtained not the promise until after their faith. ¹⁸And neither at any time hath any wrought miracles, until after their faith. Wherefore, they first believed in the Son of God. ¹⁹And there were many whose faith was so exceeding strong, even before Christ came, which could not be kept from within the veil—but truly saw with their eyes the things which they had beheld with an eye of faith. And they were glad.

²⁰And behold, we have seen in this record, that one of these was the brother of Jared. For, so great was his faith in God, that when God put forth his finger he could not hide it from the sight of the brother of Jared because of his word, which he had spoken unto him, which word he had obtained by faith. ²¹And after that the brother of Jared had beheld the finger of the Lord (because of the promise, which the brother of Jared had obtained by faith), the Lord could not withhold anything from his sight. Wherefore, he showed him all things. For he could no longer be kept without the veil.

²²And it is by faith that my fathers have obtained the promise that these things should come unto their brethren, through the Gentiles. Therefore, the Lord hath commanded me, yea, even Jesus Christ. ²³And I said unto him:

> Lord! The Gentiles will mock at these things because of our weakness in writing. For Lord, thou hast made us mighty in word, by faith, whereunto thou hast not made us mighty in writing. For thou hast made all this this people that they could speak much because of the Holy Ghost, which thou hast given them. ²⁴And thou hast made us that we could write but little because of the awkwardness of our hands. Behold, thou hast not made us mighty in writing like unto the brother of Jared! For thou madest him that the things which he wrote were mighty, even as thou art—unto the overpowering of man to read them. ²⁵Thou hast also made our words powerful and great, even that we cannot write them. Wherefore, when we write, we behold our weakness, and stumble—because of the placing of our words. And I fear, lest the Gentiles shall mock at our words.

²⁶And when I had said this, the Lord spake unto me, saying:

> Fools mock—but they shall mourn. And my grace is sufficient for the meek, that they shall take no advantage of weakness. ²⁷And if men come unto me, I will show unto them their weakness. I give unto men weakness that they may be humble. And my grace is sufficient for all men that humble themselves before me. For if they humble themselves before me and have faith in me—then will I make weak things become strong unto them.[a]

---

a. Verses 26–27 use language and concepts from 2 Corinthians 12:9–10: "And he said unto me, My

Chapter V [Ether 12]

²⁸Behold, I will show unto the Gentiles their weakness. And I will show unto them that faith, hope, and charity[a], bringeth unto me (the fountain of all righteousness).

²⁹And I, Moroni (having heard these words) was comforted, and said:

O Lord! Thy righteous will be done. For I know that thou workest unto the children of men, according to their faith. ³⁰For the brother of Jared said unto the mountain Zerin—remove! And it was removed. And if he had not had faith, it would not have moved. Wherefore, thou workest after that men have faith. ³¹For thus did thou manifest thyself unto thy disciples. For after that they had faith, and did speak in thy name, thou didst show thyself unto them in great power.

³²And I also rememberest that thou hast said that thou hast prepared a house for man, yea, even among the mansions of thy Father—in the which man might have a more excellent hope.[b] Wherefore, man must hope, or he cannot receive an inheritance in the place which thou hast prepared.

³³And again, I remember that thou hast said that thou hast loved the world, even unto the laying down of thy life for the world, that thou mightest take it again to prepare a place for the children of men.[c]

³⁴And now, I know that this love which thou hast had for the children of men is charity. Wherefore, except men shall have charity, they cannot inherit that place which thou hast prepared in the mansions of thy Father. ³⁵Wherefore, I know by this thing (which thou hast said), that if the Gentiles have not charity (because of our weakness), that thou wilt prove them and take away their talent, yea, even that which they have received—and give unto them which shall have more abundantly.[d]

³⁶And it came to pass that I prayed unto the Lord that he would give unto the Gentiles grace, that they might have charity.

³⁷And it came to pass that the Lord said unto me:

If they have not charity, it mattereth not unto thee. Thou hast been faithful. Wherefore, thy garments shall be made clean. And because thou hast seen thy weakness, thou shalt be made strong, even unto the setting down in the place which I have prepared in the mansions of my Father.

³⁸And now I, Moroni, bid farewell unto the Gentiles. Yea, and also unto

---

grace is sufficient for thee: for my strength is made perfect in weakness. Most gladly therefore will I rather glory in my infirmities, that the power of Christ may rest upon me. Therefore I take pleasure in infirmities, in reproaches, in necessities, in persecutions, in distresses for Christ's sake: for when I am weak, then am I strong."

a. Faith, hope, and charity echo 1 Corinthians 13:13: "And now abideth faith, hope, charity, these three; but the greatest of these *is* charity."

b. Echoes language from John 14:2: "In my Father's house are many mansions: if it were not so, I would have told you. I go to prepare a place for you."

c. Echoes language from John 3:16: "For God so loved the world, that he gave his only begotten Son, that whosoever believeth in him should not perish, but have everlasting life."

d. Echoes language from Matthew 25:28–29: "Take therefore the talent from him, and give it unto him which hath ten talents. For unto every one that hath shall be given, and he shall have abundance: but from him that hath not shall be taken away even that which he hath."

my brethren, whom I love, until we shall meet before the Judgment Seat of Christ, where all men shall know that my garments are not spotted with your blood. [39]And then shall ye know that I have seen Jesus, and that he hath talked with me face to face—and that he told me, in plain humility, even as a man telleth another in mine own language, concerning these things. [40]And only a few have I written, because of my weakness in writing.

[41]And now, I would commend you to seek this Jesus, of whom the prophets and apostles have written, that the grace of God, the Father, and also the Lord Jesus Christ, and the Holy Ghost (which beareth record of them)—may be, and abide in you—forever. Amen.[a]<

---

a. Moroni has wandered far from his text. Ether 13:1 recognizes that he is returning to the story. This aside is interesting because it is so personal. In it we see Moroni grappling with his own task and responsibility far beyond simply writing the Jaredite story.

Chapter VI Ether [13–15]

[13] ¹And now I, Moroni, proceed to finish my record concerning the destruction of the people of which I have been writing.

²For behold, they rejected all the words of Ether. For he truly told them of all things from the beginning of man, and how that after the waters had receded from off the face of this land it became a choice land above all other lands—a chosen land of the Lord. Wherefore, the Lord would have that all men should serve him (which dwelt upon the face thereof)—³and that it was the place of the New Jerusalem (which should come down out of heaven) and the holy sanctuary of the Lord.

⁴Behold, Ether saw the days of Christ, and he spake concerning a New Jerusalem upon this land. ⁵And he spake also, concerning the house of Israel and the Jerusalem from whence Lehi should come. After that it should be destroyed, it should be built up again, &ᵃ holy city unto the Lord. Wherefore, it could not be a New Jerusalem, for it had been in a time of old. But it should be built up again and become a holy city of the Lord. And it should be built up unto the house of Israel.

⁶And, that a New Jerusalem should be built up upon this land—unto the remnant of the seed of Joseph. For the which things there has been a type. ⁷For, as Joseph brought his father down into the land of Egypt, even so he died there. Wherefore, the Lord brought a remnant of the seed of Joseph out of the land of Jerusalem that he might be merciful unto the seed of Joseph, that they should perish not (even as he was merciful unto the father of Joseph, that he should perish not). ⁸Wherefore, the remnant of the house of Joseph shall be built up upon this land. And it shall be a land of their inheritance. And they shall build up a holy city unto the Lord like unto the Jerusalem of old. And they shall no more be confounded, until the end come when the earth shall pass away ⁹and there shall be a new heaven and a new earth. And they shall be like unto the old, save the old have passed away. And all things have become new.ᵇ

¹⁰And then cometh the New Jerusalem.ᶜ And blessed are they which dwell therein. For it is they whose garments are white through the blood of the Lamb.ᵈ And they are they which are numbered among the remnant of the seed of Joseph, which were of the house of Israel.

¹¹And then also cometh the Jerusalem of old, and the inhabitants thereof. Blessed are they! For they have been washed in the blood of the Lamb. And they are they which were scattered, and gathered in from the four quarters of the earth, and from the north countries, and are partakers of the fulfilling of the covenant which God made with their father, Abraham. ¹²And when these things come—bringethᵉ to pass the scripture which

---

a. Although this edition typically replaces & with "and" throughout the text, it is left here because it was probably a misheard "an." *Printer's Manuscript of the Book of Mormon*, 3:377.

b. See Revelation 21:1: "And I saw a new heaven and a new earth: for the first heaven and the first earth were passed away; and there was no more sea." Also, 2 Corinthians 5:17: "Therefore if any man *be* in Christ, *he is* a new creature: old things are passed away; behold, all things are become new."

c. The New Jerusalem is mentioned in Revelation 21:2: "And I John saw the holy city, new Jerusalem, coming down from God out of heaven."

d. See Revelation 7:14: "These are they which came out of great tribulation, and have washed their robes, and made them white in the blood of the Lamb."

e. Skousen examines the suggestion that there is a missing "it," where it would be "come, it bringeth to pass." As there is no specific evidence for this, Skousen leaves the text as it is. See Skousen, *Analysis of*

saith: "There are they which were first, which shall be last! And there are they which were last, which shall be first!"ᵃ

¹³And I was about to write more, but I am forbidden. But great and marvelous were the prophecies of Ether. But they esteemed him as naught and cast him out. And he hid himself in the cavity of a rock by day. And by night, he went forth, viewing the things which should come upon the people. ¹⁴And as he dwelt in the cavity of a rock, he made the remainder of this record, viewing the destruction which came upon the people by night.

¹⁵And it came to pass that in that same year which he was cast out from among the people, there began to be a great war among the people. For there were many which rose up who were mighty men—and sought to destroy Coriantumr by their secret plans of wickedness (of which hath been spoken). ¹⁶And now Coriantumr, having studied (himself) in all the arts of war and all the cunning of the world–wherefore, he gave battle unto them which sought to destroy him. ¹⁷But he repented not—neither his fair sons nor daughters, neither the fair sons and daughters of Cohor, neither the fair sons and daughters of Corihor. And in fine, there was none of the fair sons and daughters upon the face of the whole earth which repented of their sins. ¹⁸Wherefore, it came to pass that in the first year that Ether dwelt in the cavity of a rock there was many people which was slain by the sword—those secret combinations fighting against Coriantumr, that they might obtain the kingdom.

¹⁹And it came to pass that the sons of Coriantumr fought much and bled much. ²⁰And in the second year, the word of the Lord came unto Ether, that he should go and prophesy unto Coriantumr, that if he would repent (and all his household), the Lord would give unto him his kingdom and spare the people. ²¹Otherwise, they should be destroyed—and all his household (save it were himself). And he should only live to see the fulfilling of the prophecies which had been spoken concerning an other people receiving the land for their inheritance. And Coriantumr should receive a burial by them. And every soul should be destroyed, save it were Coriantumr.

²³And it came to pass that Coriantumr repented not—neither his household, neither the people. And the wars did cease not. And they sought to kill Ether. But he fled from before them and hid again in the cavity of the rock.

And it came to pass that there arose up Shared. And he also gave battle unto Coriantumr. And he did beat him, insomuch that in the third year, he did bring him into captivity. ²⁴And the sons of Coriantumr, in the fourth year, did beat Shared and did obtain the kingdom again unto their father.

²⁵Now, there began to be a war upon all the face of the land—every man with his band, fighting for that which he desired. ²⁶And there was robbers—in fine, all manner of wickedness upon all the face of the land.

²⁷And it came to pass that Coriantumr was exceeding angry with Shared. And he

---

the *Textual Variants*, 6:3845. Another possibility is that there was a slip in writing where "come to pass" and "bringeth to pass" were mixed up and the error was not caught. That type of error has happened before but was typically caught early. In those cases, it is the first word that is typically crossed out. The compositor punctuated it with a comma (come, bringeth). This edition uses a similar solution but has an em dash to indicate a longer pause. The intent appears to accommodate both verbs, and there are things to come, and those "bringeth to pass" the scripture (or fulfill the scripture).

a. The allusion is to Mark 10:31 and Luke 13:30.

Chapter VI [Ether 13–15]

went against him with his armies to battle. And they did meet in great anger. And they did meet in the valley of Gilgal. And the battle became exceeding sore.

²⁸And it came to pass that Shared fought against him for the space of three days.

And it came to pass that Coriantumr beat him, and pursued him until he had came to the plains of Heshlon.

²⁹And it came to pass that Shared gave him battle again upon the plains. And behold, he did beat Coriantumr and drove him back again to the valley of Gilgal. ³⁰And Coriantumr gave Shared battle again in the valley of Gilgal, in the which he beat Shared and slew him. ³¹And Shared wounded Coriantumr in his thigh, that he did not go to battle again for the space of two years—in the which time, all the people upon all the face of the land were a-shedding blood. And there was none to constrain them.

>[14] ¹And now, there began to be a great curse upon the land because of the iniquity of the people—in the which, if a man should lay his tool, or his sword, upon the shelf, or upon the place whither he would keep it—and behold, upon the morrow he could not find it, so great was the curse upon the land. ²Wherefore, every man did cleave unto that which was his own with his hands–and would not borrow neither would he lend. And every man kept the hilt of his sword thereof in his right hand in the defense of his property and his own life, and they of his wives and children.ᵃ<

³And now, after the space of two years and after the death of Shared, behold, there arose the brother of Shared. And he gave battle unto Coriantumr, in the which Coriantumr did beat him and did pursue him to the wilderness of Akish.

⁴And it came to pass that the brother of Shared did give battle unto him in the wilderness of Akish. And the battle became exceeding sore. And many thousands fell by the sword.

⁵And it came to pass that Coriantumr did lay siege to the wilderness. And the brother of Shared did march forth out of the wilderness, by night, and slew a part of the army of Coriantumr as they were drunken. ⁶And he came forth to the land of Moron and placed himself upon the throne of Coriantumr.

⁷And it came to pass that Coriantumr dwelt with his army in the wilderness for the space of two years, in the which he did receive great strength to his army. ⁸Now, the brother of Shared (whose name was Gilead) also received great strength to his army because of secret combinations.

⁹And it came to pass that his High Priest murdered him as he sat upon his throne.

¹⁰And it came to pass that one of the secret combinations murdered him in a secret pass and obtained unto himself the kingdom. And his name was Lib. And Lib was a man of great stature—more than any other man among all the people.

¹¹And it came to pass that in the first year of Lib, Coriantumr came up unto the land of Moron and gave battle unto Lib.

¹²And it came to pass that he fought with Lib—in the which Lib did smite upon his arm, that he was wounded. Nevertheless, the army of Coriantumr did press forward upon Lib, that he fled to the borders upon the seashore.

---

a. Moroni inserts information that describes how bad things became. The theme of the curse on the land so that one could not keep ones goods reflects similar ideas from Helaman 13:33–35 and Mormon 1:17–18.

¹³And it came to pass that Coriantumr pursued him. And Lib gave battle unto him upon the seashore.

¹⁴And it came to pass that Lib did smite the army of Coriantumr, that they fled again to the wilderness of Akish.

¹⁵And it came to pass that Lib did pursue him until he came to the plains of Agosh. And Coriantumr had taken all the people with him as he fled before Lib—in that quarter of the land whither he fled. ¹⁶And when he had came to the plains of Agosh, he gave battle unto Lib. And he smote upon him until he died. Nevertheless, the brother of Lib did come against Coriantumr in the stead thereof. And the battle became exceeding sore—in the which Coriantumr fled again before the army of the brother of Lib.

¹⁷Now, the name of the brother of Lib was called Shiz.

And it came to pass that Shiz pursued after Coriantumr, and he did overthrow many cities. And he did slay both women and children, and he did burn the cities thereof. ¹⁸And there went a fear of Shiz throughout all the land, yea, a cry went forth throughout the land: "Who can stand before the army of Shiz! Behold, he sweepeth the earth before him!"

¹⁹And it came to pass that the people began to flock together in armies throughout all the face of the land. ²⁰And they were divided. And a part of them fled to the army of Shiz, and a part of them fled to the army of Coriantumr. ²¹And so great and lasting had been the war, and so long had been the scene of bloodshed and carnage, that the whole face of the land was covered with the bodies of the dead. ²²And so swift and speedy was the war that there was none left to bury the dead. But they did march forth from the shedding of blood to the shedding of blood—leaving the bodies of both men, women, and children, strewed upon the face of the land—to become a prey to the worms of the flesh. ²³And the scent thereof went forth upon the face of the land, even upon all the face of the land. Wherefore, the people became troubled by day and by night because of the scent thereof. ²⁴Nevertheless, Shiz did not cease to pursue Coriantumr. For he had sworn to avenge himself upon Coriantumr of the blood of his brother (which had been slain) and the word of the Lord which came to Ether, that Coriantumr should not fall by the sword.[a]

>²⁵And thus, we see that the Lord did visit them in the fulness of his wrath. And their wickedness and abominations had prepared a way for their everlasting destruction.[b]<

²⁶And it came to pass that Shiz did pursue Coriantumr eastward, even to the borders by the seashore. And there he gave battle unto Shiz for the space of three days. ²⁷And so terrible was the destruction among the armies of Shiz that the people began to be frightened and began to flee before the armies of Coriantumr. And they fled to the land of Corihor and swept off the inhabitants before them—all they that would not join them. ²⁸And they pitched their tents in the valley of Corihor. And Coriantumr pitched his tents in the valley of Shurr.

---

a. The final phrase, beginning "and the word of the Lord which came to Ether," is hard to see as a continuation of Shiz's desire to avenge the death of his brother. It makes some grammatical sense here as otherwise the "which came to Ether" would be out of place. This is the compositor's solution and appears to be the best option even if it doesn't fully make sense.

b. Moroni provides the moral in a "thus we see statement."

Now, the valley of Shurr was near the hill Comron.[a] Wherefore, Coriantumr did gather his armies together upon the hill Comron, and did sound a trumpet unto the armies of Shiz to invite them forth to battle.

²⁹And it came to pass that they came forth—but were driven again.

And they came the second time, and they were driven again the second time.

And it came to pass that they came again the third time, and the battle became exceeding sore.

³⁰And it came to pass that Shiz smote upon Coriantumr, that he gave him many deep wounds. And Coriantumr, having lost his blood, fainted—and was carried away as though he were dead.

³⁰Now, the loss of men, women, and children, on both sides were so great that Shiz commanded his people that they should not pursue the armies of Coriantumr. Wherefore, they returned to their camp.

[15] ¹And it came to pass that when Coriantumr had recovered of his wounds, he began to remember the words which Ether had spoken unto him. ²He saw that there had been slain by the sword—already nearly two millions of his people. And he began to sorrow in his heart. Yea, there had been slain two millions of mighty men, and also their wives, and their children. ³He began to repent of the evil which he had done. He began to remember the words which had been spoken by the mouth of all the prophets.[b] And he saw them—that they were fulfilled thus far, every whit. And his soul mourned and refused to be comforted.

⁴And it came to pass that he wrote an epistle unto Shiz, desiring him that he would spare the people—and he would give up the kingdom for the sake of the lives of the people.

⁵And it came to pass that when Shiz had received his epistle, he wrote an epistle unto Coriantumr, that if he would give himself up that he might slay him with his own sword, that he would spare the lives of the people.

⁶And it came to pass that the people repented not of their iniquity. And the people of Coriantumr were stirred up to anger against the people of Shiz. And the people of Shiz were stirred up to anger against the people of Coriantumr. Wherefore, the people of Shiz did give battle unto the people of Coriantumr. ⁷And when Coriantumr saw that he was about to fall, he fled again before the people of Shiz.

⁸And it came to pass that he came to the waters of Ripliancum (>which, by interpretation, is large—or to exceed all[c]<). Wherefore, when they came to these waters, they pitched their tents. And Shiz also pitched his tents near unto them. And therefore, on the morrow they did come to battle.

⁹And it came to pass that they fought an exceeding sore battle—in the which Coriantumr was wounded again, and he fainted with the loss of blood.

¹⁰And it came to pass that the armies of Coriantumr did press upon the armies of

---

a. The Printer's Manuscript had Comron as retained, in both locations in the manuscript. The compositor set them as Comnor in the 1830 edition, and that spelling has been retained since. Skousen, *Analysis of Textual Variants*, 6:3874–75.

b. See Acts 3:21: "Whom the heaven must receive until the times of restitution of all things, which God hath spoken by the mouth of all his holy prophets since the world began."

c. This makes most sense as Moroni's explanation rather than anything original to Ether's record.

Shiz, that they beat them, that they caused them to flee before them. And they did flee southward and did pitch their tents in a place which was called Ogath.

[11]And it came to pass that the army of Coriantumr did pitch their tents by the hill Ramah (>and it was that same hill where my father, Mormon, did hide up the records unto the Lord, which were sacred[a]<).

[12]And it came to pass that they did gather together all the people upon all the face of the land which had not been slain (save it were Ether).

[13]And it came to pass that Ether did behold all the doings of the people. And he beheld that the people which were for Coriantumr were gathered together to the army of Coriantumr, and the people which were for Shiz were gathered together to the army of Shiz. [14]Wherefore, they were for the space of four years gathering together the people, that they might get all which were upon the face of the land, and that they might receive all the strength which it were possible that they could receive.

[15]And it came to pass that when they were all gathered together, every one to the army which he would (with their wives, and their children)—both men, women, and children being armed with weapons of war, having shields, and breast plates, and head plates, and being clothed after the manner of war. And they did march forth, one against another, to battle. And they fought all that day—and conquered not.

[16]And it came to pass that when it was night they were weary, and retired to their camps. And after that they had retired to their camps, they took up a howling and a lamentation for the loss of the slain of their people. And so great were their cries, their howlings, and lamentations, that it did rend the air exceedingly.

[17]And it came to pass that on the morrow they did go again to battle. And great and terrible was that day. Nevertheless, they conquered not. And when the night came again, they did rend the air with their cries, and their howlings, and their mournings, for the loss of the slain of their people.

[18]And it came to pass that Coriantumr wrote again an epistle unto Shiz, desiring that he would not come again to battle—but that he would take the kingdom and spare the lives of the people.

[19]But behold, the Spirit of the Lord had ceased striving with them, and Satan had full power over the hearts of the people. For they were given up unto the hardness of their hearts and the blindness of their minds, that they might be destroyed. Wherefore, they went again to battle.

[20]And it came to pass that they fought all that day. And when the night came, they slept upon their swords. [21]And on the morrow they fought, even until the night came. [22]And when the night came they were drunken with anger, even as a man which is drunken with wine.

And they slept again upon their swords. [22]And on the morrow they fought again. And when the night came they had all fallen by the sword, save it were fifty and two of the people of Coriantumr, and sixty and nine of the people of Shiz.

[24]And it came to pass that they slept upon their swords that night. And on the morrow they fought again. And they contended in their mights with their swords and with their shields all that day. [25]And when the night came, there was thirty and two of

---

a. Moroni identifies Ramah as the hill he knew as Cumorah, although it would have had to have been through a prophetic understanding as it could not have come from the plates of Ether unless there was some obvious distinctive feature that has remained unmentioned.

Chapter VI [Ether 13–15]

the people of Shiz, and twenty and seven of the people of Coriantumr.

²⁶And it came to pass that they ate, and slept, and prepared for death on the morrow. And they were large, and mighty men (as to the strength of men).

²⁷And it came to pass that they fought for the space of three hours. And they fainted with the loss of blood.

²⁸And it came to pass that when the men of Coriantumr had received sufficient strength that they could walk, they were about to flee for their lives. But behold, Shiz arose, and also his men. And he swore in his wrath that he would slay Coriantumr, or he would perish by the sword. ²⁹Wherefore, he did pursue them. And on the morrow he did overtake them. And they fought again with the sword.

And it came to pass that when they had all fallen by the sword (save it were Coriantumr and Shiz), behold, Shiz had fainted with loss of blood.

³⁰And it came to pass that when Coriantumr had leaned upon his sword, that he rested a little—and he smote off the head of Shiz.

³¹And it came to pass that after he had smote off the head of Shiz, that Shiz raised upon his hands, and fell. And after that he had struggled for breath, he died.

³²And it came to pass that Coriantumr fell to the earth and became as if he had no life.

³³And the Lord spake unto Ether and said unto him: "Go forth!"

And he went forth and beheld the words of the Lord had all been fulfilled. And he finished his record. And the hundredth part I have not written. And he had hid them in a manner that the people of Limhi did find them.

³⁴Now, the last words which are written by Ether are these: "Whether the Lord will that I be translated, or that I suffer the will of the Lord in the flesh, it mattereth not—if it so be that I am saved in the kingdom of God. Amen."

The Book of Moroni

Chapter I [Moroni 1]

[1] ¹*Now I, Moroni, after having made an end of abridging the account of the people of Jared, I had supposed to not have written more. But I have not as yet perished. And I make not myself known to the Lamanites, lest they should destroy me.* ²*For behold, their wars are exceeding fierce among themselves.*

And because of their hatred, they put to death every Nephite that will not deny the Christ. ³*And I, Moroni, will not deny the Christ! Wherefore, I wander whithersoever I can for the safety of mine own life.* ⁴*Wherefore, I write a few more things contrary to that which I had supposed, for I had supposed not to have written any more. But I write a few more things that perhaps they may be of worth unto my brethren, the Lamanites, in some future day, according to the will of the Lord.*[a]

---

a. Chapters in the book of Moroni are labeled as such in the Printer's Manuscript. However, their diffuse nature suggests that the book is composed according to a very different logic than others in the Book of Mormon. Rather than any specific plan, the organization is basically: "But I have not as yet perished . . . wherefore, I write a few more things." Although set as a chapter, this is really an introduction, as it is closer in function to a book header.

Chapter II [Moroni 2]

[2] ¹ *The words of Christ, which he spake unto his disciples (the twelve whom he had chosen) as he laid his hands upon their them.*ᵃ

²And he called them by name, saying:

Ye shall call on the Father in my name in mighty prayer. And after that ye have done this, ye shall have power that on him whom ye shall lay your hands, ye shall give the Holy Ghost. And in my name shall ye give it. For thus do mine apostles.

³Now, Christ spake these words unto them at the time of his first appearing. And the multitude heard it not—but the disciples heard it. And on as many as they laid their hands, fell the Holy Ghost.

---

a. Moroni's first sentence is clearly descriptive. It is set as a chapter heading, understanding that Moroni uses this as a title rather than an indicator of a change in source.

Chapter III [Moroni 3]

[3] ¹*The manner which the disciples (which were called the elders of the church) ordained priests and teachers.*

²After they had prayed unto the Father in the name of Christ, they laid their hands upon them, and said:

³In the name of Jesus Christ, I ordain you to be a priest (or if he be a teacher, I ordain you to be a teacher), to preach repentance and remission of sins through Jesus Christ, by the endurance of faith on his name, to the end. Amen.

⁴And after this manner did they ordain priests and teachers, according to the gifts and callings of God unto men. And they ordained them by the power of the Holy Ghost, which was in them.

Chapter IV [Moroni 4]

[4] ¹ *The manner of their elders and priests administering the flesh and blood of Christ unto the church. And they administered it according to the commandments of Christ. Wherefore, we know that the manner to be true. And the elder or priest did minister it.*

²And they did kneel down with the church, and pray to the Father in the name of Christ, saying:

³O God, the Eternal Father. We ask thee in the name of thy Son, Jesus Christ, to bless and sanctify this bread to the souls of all those who partake of it—that they may eat in remembrance of the body of thy Son. And witness unto thee, O God the Eternal Father, that they are willing to take upon them the name of thy Son- and always remember him, and keep his commandments (which he hath given them), that they may always have his spirit to be with them. Amen.

Chapter V [Moroni 5]

[5] ¹ *The manner of administering the wine.*

Behold, they took the cup, and said:

²O God, the Eternal Father, we ask thee in the name of thy Son, Jesus Christ, to bless and sanctify this wine to the souls of all those who drink of it—that they may do it in remembrance of the blood of thy Son, which was shed for them, that they may witness unto thee, O God, the Eternal Father, that they do always remember him, that they may have his Spirit to be with them. Amen.

Chapter VI [Moroni 6]

[6] ¹*And now, I speak concerning baptism.*

Behold, elders, priests, and teachers were baptized. And they were not baptized, save they brought forth fruit meet that they were worthy of it. ²Neither did they receive any unto baptism, save they came forth with a broken heart and a contrite spirit,[a] and witnessed unto the church that they truly repented of all their sins. ³And none were received unto baptism, save they took upon them the name of Christ, having a determination to serve him unto the end.

⁴And after that they had been received unto baptism and were wrought upon and cleansed by the power of the Holy Ghost—they were numbered among the people of the church of Christ. And their names were taken, that they might be remembered, and nourished by the good word of God—to keep them in the right way, to keep them continually watchful unto prayer—relying alone upon the merits of Christ, who was the author and the finisher of their faith.[b]

⁵And the church did meet together oft to fast, and to pray, and to speak one with another concerning the welfare of their souls. ⁶And they did meet together oft to partake of bread and wine in remembrance of the Lord Jesus. ⁷And they were strict to observe that there should be no iniquity among them.

And whoso was found to commit iniquity (and three witnesses of the church did condemn them before the elders)—and if they repented not and confessed not—their names were blotted out and they were not numbered among the people of Christ. ⁸But, as oft as they repented and sought forgiveness, with real intent, they were forgiven.

⁹And their meetings were conducted by the church after the manner of the workings of the Spirit and by the power of the Holy Ghost. For, as the power of the Holy Ghost led them—whether to preach, or exhort, or to pray, or to supplicate, or to sing, even so it was done.

---

a. See Psalm 34:18: "The Lord is nigh unto them that are of a broken heart; and saveth such as be of a contrite spirit."

b. See Hebrews 12:2: "Looking unto Jesus the author and finisher of our faith."

Chapter VII [Moroni 7]

[7] ¹*And now, I Moroni, write a few of the words of my father Mormon, which he spake concerning faith, hope, and charity.*ᵃ *For after this manner did he speak unto the people as he taught them in the synagogue, which they had built for the place of worship.*

²And now I, Mormon, speak unto you, my beloved brethren. And it is by the grace of God the Father, and our Lord Jesus Christ, and his Holy Will—because of the gift of his calling unto me, that I am permitted to speak unto you at this time. ³Wherefore, I would speak unto you that are of the church, that are the peaceable followers of Christ, and that have obtained a sufficient hope by which ye can enter into the rest of the Lord from this time hence forth until ye shall rest with him in heaven.

⁴And now, my brethren, I judge these things of you because of your peaceable walk with the children of men. ⁵For I remember the word of God, which saith: By their works ye shall know them.ᵇ For, if their works be good, then they are good also.ᶜ

⁶For behold, God hath said: A man (being evil) cannot do that which is good. For if he offereth a gift or prayeth unto God, except he shall do it with real intent—it profiteth him nothing. ⁷For behold, it is not counted unto him for righteousness.ᵈ ⁸For behold, if a man (being evil) giveth a gift—he doeth it grudgingly. Wherefore, it is counted unto him the same as if he had retained the gift. Wherefore, he is counted evil before God.

⁹And likewise also is it counted evil unto a man if he shall pray, and not with real intent of heart. Yea, and it profiteth him nothing, for God receiveth none such. ¹⁰Wherefore, a man (being evil) cannot do that which is good—neither will he give a good gift. ¹¹For behold, a bitter fountain cannot bring forth good water—neither can a good fountain bring forth bitter water. Wherefore, a man (being the servant of the devil) cannot follow Christ. And if he follow Christ—he cannot be a servant of the devil. ¹²Wherefore, all things which are good cometh of God. And that which is evil cometh of the devil. For the devil is an enemy unto God and fighteth against him continually, and inviteth and enticeth to sin—and to do that which is evil continually. ¹³But behold, that which is of God inviteth and enticeth to do good continually. Wherefore, every thing which inviteth and enticeth to do good and to love God, and to serve him—is inspired of God. ¹⁴Wherefore, take heed, my beloved brethren, that ye do not judge that which is evil to be of God—or that which is good and of God, to be of the devil. ¹⁵For behold, my brethren, it is given unto you to judge, that ye may know good from evil.

And the way to judge is as plain, that ye may know with a perfect knowledge, as the day light is from the dark night. ¹⁶For behold, the spirit of Christ is given to every man,ᵉ that they may know good from evil. Wherefore, I show unto you the way to judge. For

---

a. Faith, hope, and charity echo 1 Corinthians 13:13: "And now abideth faith, hope, charity, these three; but the greatest of these *is* charity."

b. Possible reference to Proverbs 20:11: "Even a child is known by his doings, whether his work be pure, and whether it be right."

c. Possible reference to Ecclesiastes 12:14: "For God shall bring every work into judgment, with every secret thing, whether it be good, or whether it be evil."

d. Uses language from Romans 4:3: "Abraham believed God, and it was counted unto him for righteousness."

e. See 1 Corinthains 12:7: "But the manifestation of the Spirit is given to every man to profit withal."

everything which inviteth to do good and to persuade to believe in Christ—is sent forth by the power and gift of Christ. Wherefore, ye may know with a perfect knowledge it is of God. ¹⁷But whatsoever thing persuadeth men to do evil and believe not in Christ, and deny him, and serve not God—then ye may know with a perfect knowledge it is of the devil. For after this manner doth the devil work. For he persuadeth no man to do good—no not one. Neither doth his angels. Neither doth they which subject themselves unto him.

¹⁸And now, my brethren, seeing that ye know the light by which ye may judge (which light is the light of Christ)—see that ye do not judge wrongfully. For, with that same judgment which ye judge—ye shall also be judged.[a] ¹⁹Wherefore, I beseech of you, brethren, that ye should search diligently in the light of Christ, that ye may know good from evil. And if ye will lay hold upon every good thing and condemn it not—ye certainly will be a child of Christ.

²⁰And now, my brethren, how is it possible that ye can lay hold upon every good thing? ²¹And now, I come to that faith of which I said I would speak. And I will tell you the way whereby ye may lay hold on every good thing. ²²For behold, God, knowing all things being from everlasting to everlasting—behold, he sent angels to minister unto the children of men, to make manifest concerning the coming of Christ. And in Christ there should come every good thing. ²³And God also declared unto prophets, by his own mouth, that Christ should come.

²⁴And behold, there were diverse ways that he did manifest things unto the children of men, which were good. And all things which are good cometh of Christ—otherwise, men were fallen and there could no good thing come unto them. ²⁵Wherefore, by the ministering of angels, and by every word which proceeded forth out of the mouth of God, men began to exercise faith in Christ. And thus, by faith they did lay hold upon every good thing. And thus it was, until the coming of Christ.

²⁶And after that he come, men also were saved by faith in his name. And by faith they become the sons of God. And as suredly as Christ liveth, he spake these words unto our fathers, saying: "Whatsoever thing ye shall ask the Father, in my name, which is good—in faith, believing that ye shall receive—behold it shall be done unto you."[b] ²⁷Wherefore, my beloved brethren, hath miracles ceased because that Christ hath ascended into heaven, and hath sit down on the right hand of God, to claim of the Father his rights of mercy (which he hath upon the children of men)? ²⁸For, he hath answered the ends of the law. And he claimeth all those that hath faith in him. And they that have faith in him will cleave unto every good thing. Wherefore, he advocateth the cause of the children of men. And he dwelleth eternally in the heavens. ²⁹And because that he hath done this, my beloved brethren, hath miracles ceased?

Behold, I say unto you nay! Neither hath angels ceased to minister unto the children of men. ³⁰For behold, they are subject unto him, to minister according to the word of his command—showing themselves unto them of strong faith, and a firm mind—in every form of Godliness. ³¹And the office of their ministry is to call men unto repentance and to fulfil (and to do) the work of the covenants of the Father (which he hath

---

a. See Matthew 7:2: "For with what judgment ye judge, ye shall be judged: and with what measure ye mete, it shall be measured to you again."

b. Internal reference to 3 Nephi 18:20. See also John 14:13: "And whatsoever ye shall ask in my name, that will I do, that the Father may be glorified in the Son."

Chapter VII [Moroni 7]

made unto the children of men), to prepare the way among the children of men by declaring the word of Christ unto [the chosen[a]] vessels of the Lord, that they may bear testimony of him. [32]And, by so doing, the Lord God prepareth the way that the residue [of men[b]] may have faith in Christ, that the Holy Ghost may have place in their hearts (according to the power thereof).

And after this manner bringeth to pass the Father the covenants which he hath made unto the children of men. [33]And Christ hath said: "If ye will have faith in me, ye shall have power to do whatsoever thing is expedient in me." [34]And he hath said: "Repent, all ye ends of the earth! And come unto me, and be baptized in my name, and have faith in me, that ye may be saved."

[35]And now, my beloved brethren, if this be the case, that these things are true (which I have spoken unto you)—and God will show unto you, with power, and great glory (at the last day) that they are true—and if they are true, hath the day of miracles ceased?

[36]Or hath angels ceased to appear unto the children of men?

Or hath he withheld the power of the Holy Ghost from them?

Or will he, so long as time shall last—or the earth shall stand?

Or there shall be one man upon the face thereof to be saved?

[37]Behold, I say unto you nay! For it is by faith that miracles are wrought. And it is by faith that angels appear and minister unto men. Wherefore, if these things have ceased—wo be unto the children of men, for it is because of unbelief—and all is vain! [38]For no man can be saved (according to the words of Christ), save they shall have faith in his name. Wherefore, if these things have ceased—then has faith ceased also. And awful is the state of man! For they are as though there had been no redemption made.

[39]But behold, my beloved brethren, I judge better things of you. For I judge that ye have faith in Christ because of your meekness. For if ye have not faith in him, then ye are not fit to be numbered among the people of his church.

[40]And again, my beloved brethren, I would speak unto you concerning hope. How is it that ye can attain unto faith, save ye shall have hope? [41]And what is it that ye shall hope for?

Behold, I say unto you, that ye shall have hope, through the atonement of Christ and the power of his resurrection, to be raised unto life eternal. And this, because of your faith in him, according to the promise. [42]Wherefore, if a man have faith, he must needs have hope. For without faith there cannot be any hope.

[43]And again, behold, I say unto you, that he cannot have faith and hope save he shall be meek and lowly of heart. [44]If so, his faith and hope is vain. For none is acceptable before God save the meek and lowly of heart. And if a man be meek and lowly in heart, and confess by the power of the Holy Ghost that Jesus is the Christ—he must needs have charity.[c] For if he have not charity, he is nothing. Wherefore, he must needs have charity. [45]And charity suffereth long, and is kind, and envieth not, and is not puffed up, seeketh not her own, is not easily provoked, thinketh no evil, and rejoi-

---

a. The printer's manuscript originally had "unto them vessels." It appears that Hyrum Smith made the change to "unto the chosen vessels." I have used his emendation as it typically makes sense and may have come from checking against the original.

b. Hyrum Smith's insertion. Nothing was replaced.

c. Moroni expounds on faith, hope, and charity, which echo 1 Corinthians 13:13: "And now abideth faith, hope, charity, these three; but the greatest of these is charity."

ceth not in iniquity—but rejoiceth in the truth, beareth all things, believeth all things, hopeth all things, endureth all things.[a] ⁴⁶Wherefore, my beloved brethren, if ye have not charity, ye are nothing. For charity never faileth.[b] Wherefore, cleave unto charity, which is the greatest of all. For all things must fail. ⁴⁷But charity is the pure love of Christ and it endureth forever. And whoso is found possessed of it at the last day—it shall be well with them. ⁴⁸Wherefore, my beloved brethren, pray unto the Father with all the energy of heart, that ye may be filled with this love (which he hath bestowed upon all who are true followers of his Son, Jesus Christ), that ye may become the sons of God,[c] that when he shall appear, we shall be like him. For we shall see him as he is,[d] that we may have this hope, that we may be purified even as he is pure.[e] Amen.

---

a. See 1 Corinthians 13:4–7: "Charity suffereth long, and is kind; charity envieth not; charity vaunteth not itself, is not puffed up, Doth not behave itself unseemly, seeketh not her own, is not easily provoked, thinketh no evil; Rejoiceth not in iniquity, but rejoiceth in the truth; Beareth all things, believeth all things, hopeth all things, endureth all things."

b. See 1 Corinthians 13:8: "Charity never faileth: but whether there be prophecies, they shall fail; whether there be tongues, they shall cease; whether there be knowledge, it shall vanish away."

c. The phrase "sons of God" appears in 1 John 3:1. The quotation from 1 John 3:2 that follows makes this the likely source for the phrase in this instance.

d. See 1 John 3:2: "Beloved, now are we the sons of God, and it doth not yet appear what we shall be: but we know that, when he shall appear, we shall be like him; for we shall see him as he is."

e. See 1 John 3:3: "And every man that hath this hope in him purifieth himself, even as he is pure."

Chapter VIII [Moroni 8]

[8] ¹*An epistle of my father Mormon. Written to me, Moroni. And it was written unto me soon after my calling to the ministry. And on this wise did he write unto me, saying:*

²My beloved son, Moroni. I rejoice exceedingly that your Lord, Jesus Christ, hath been mindful of you and hath called you to his ministry, and to his holy work. ³I am mindful of you always in my prayers—continually praying unto God, the Father, in the name of his holy child Jesus,[a] that he, through his infinite goodness and grace, will keep you—through the endurance of faith on his name to the end.

⁴And now, my son. I speak unto you concerning that which grieveth me exceedingly. For it grieveth me that there should disputations rise among you. ⁵For if I have learned the truth, there has been disputations among you concerning the [baptism[b]] of your little children.

⁶And now, my son, I desire that ye should labor [diligently[c]] that this gross error should be removed from among you. For, for this intent I have written this epistle. ⁷For immediately after I had learned these things of you, I inquired of the Lord concerning the matter. And the word of the Lord came to me, by the power of the Holy Ghost, saying:

⁸Listen to the words of Christ, your Redeemer—your Lord and your God! Behold, I came into the world—not to call the righteous, but sinners to repentance.[d] The whole need no physician, but they that are sick.[e] Wherefore, little children are whole, for they are not capable of committing sin. Wherefore, the curse of Adam is taken from them in me, that it hath no power over them. And the law of circumcision is done away in me.

⁹And after this manner did the Holy Ghost manifest the word of God unto me. Wherefore, my beloved son, I know that it is solemn mockery before God that ye should baptize little children. ¹⁰Behold, I say unto you that this thing shall ye teach—repentance and baptism unto they which are accountable, and capable of committing sin. Yea, teach parents that they must repent and be baptized, and humble themselves as their little children—and they shall all be saved with their little children. ¹¹And their little children need no repentance, neither baptism.

Behold, baptism is unto repentance, to the fulfilling the commandments unto the remission of sins. ¹²But little children are alive in Christ, even from the foundation of the world. If not so, God is a partial God, and also a changeable God, and a respecter to persons.[f] For, how many little children have died without baptism? ¹³Wherefore, if little children could not be saved without baptism—these must have gone to an endless hell.

¹⁴Behold, I say unto you that he that supposeth that little children needeth baptism is in the gall of bitterness, and in the bonds of iniquity. For he hath neither faith, hope, nor charity[g]—wherefore, should he be cut off while in the thought. He must go down to

---

a. The phrase "thy holy child Jesus" is found in Acts 4:30.
b. Hyrum Smith changed "baptizing" to "baptism."
c. Hyrum Smith changed "exceedingly" to "diligently."
d. See Matthew 9:13: "I am not come to call the righteous, but sinners to repentance."
e. See Matthew 9: 12: "They that be whole need not a physician, but they that are sick."
f. The phrase "no respecter of persons" is found in Acts 10:34.
g. Faith, hope, and charity echo 1 Corinthians 13:13: "And now abideth faith, hope, charity, these

hell! ¹⁵For awful is the wickedness to suppose that God saveth one child because of baptism, and the other must perish because he hath no baptism. ¹⁶Wo be unto him that shall pervert the way of the Lord after this manner! For they shall perish, except they repent.

Behold, I speak with boldness, having authority from God. And I fear not what man can do. For perfect love casteth out all fear.[a] ¹⁷And I am filled with charity, which is everlasting love. Wherefore, all children are alike unto me. Wherefore, I love little children with a perfect love. And they are all alike and partakers of salvation. ¹⁸For I know that God is not a partial God, neither a changeable being. But he is unchangeable, from all eternity to all eternity.

¹⁹Little children cannot repent. Wherefore, it is awful wickedness to deny the pure mercies of God unto them. For they are all alive in him because of his mercy. ²⁰And he that saith that little children needeth baptism, denieth the mercies of Christ and setteth at naught the atonement of him—and the power of his redemption. ²¹Wo unto such! For they are in danger of death, hell, and an endless torment!

I speak it boldly! God hath commanded me listen unto them and give heed—or they stand against you at the Judgment Seat of Christ. ²²For behold that all little children are alive in Christ—and also all they that are without the law. For the power of redemption cometh on all they that have no law. Wherefore, he that is not condemned (or he that is under no condemnation) cannot repent! And unto such, baptism availeth nothing. ²³But it is mockery before God—denying the mercies of Christ and the power of his Holy Spirit, and putting trust in dead works.

²⁴Behold my son, this thing had not ought to be! For repentance is unto them that are under condemnation and under the curse of a broken law. ²⁵And the firstfruits of repentance is baptism. And baptism cometh by faith unto the fulfilling the commandments. And the fulfilling the commandments bringeth remission of sins, ²⁶and the remission of sins bringeth meekness and lowliness of heart. And because of meekness and lowliness of heart, cometh the visitation of the Holy Ghost, which comforter filleth with hope and perfect love, which love endureth by diligence, unto prayer, until the end shall come when all the saints shall dwell with God.

²⁷Behold, my son. I write unto you again, if I go not out soon against the Lamanites.

Behold, the pride of this nation (or the [people[b]] of the Nephites) hath proved their destruction, except they should repent. ²⁸Pray for them, my son, that repentance may come unto them. But behold, I fear lest the spirit hath ceased striving with them.[c] And in this part of the land, they are also seeking to put down all power and authority which cometh from God. And they are denying the Holy Ghost. ²⁹And after rejecting so great a knowledge, my son, they must perish soon—unto the fulfilling of the prophecies, which was spoken by the prophets, as well as the words of our Savior himself.

³⁰Farewell my son, until I shall write unto you—or shall meet you again. Amen.

---

three; but the greatest of these is charity."

  a. See 1 John 4:18: "There is no fear in love; but perfect love casteth out fear."
  b. Hyrum Smith changed "pride" to "people."
  c. The idea that the spirit of God would not always strive with man comes from Genesis 6:3: "And the Lord said, My spirit shall not always strive with man."

Chapter IX [Moroni 9]

[9] *The second epistle of Mormon to his son Moroni.*

¹My beloved son. I write unto you again, that ye may know that I am yet alive. But I write somewhat that which is grievous. ²For behold, I have had a sore battle with the Lamanites in the which we did not conquer. And Archeantus has fallen by the sword, and also Luram, and [Emron^a]. Yea, and we have lost a great number of our choice men.

³And now behold, my son, I fear lest the Lamanites shall destroy this people. For they do not repent. And Satan stireth them up continually to anger, one with another. ⁴Behold, I am laboring with them continually. And when I speak the word of God with sharpness—they tremble, and anger against me. And when I use no sharpness—they harden their hearts against it. Wherefore, I fear lest the spirit of the Lord hath ceased striving with them. ⁵For so exceedingly do they anger that it seemeth me that they have no fear of death. And they have lost their love, one towards another. And they thirst after blood, and revenge continually.

⁶And now, my beloved son, notwithstanding their hardness, let us labor diligently! For if we should cease to labor, we should be brought under condemnation. For we have a labor to perform, whilst in this tabernacle of clay, that we may conquer the enemy of all righteousness, and rest our souls in the kingdom of God.

⁷And now, I write somewhat concerning the sufferings of this people. For, according to the knowledge which I have received from Amoron—behold, the Lamanites have many prisoners, which they took from the tower of Sherrizah. And there were men, women, and children. ⁸And the husbands and fathers of those women and children they have slain. And they feed the women upon the flesh of their husbands—and the children upon the flesh of their fathers. And no water, save a little, do they give unto them.

⁹And notwithstanding this great abomination of the Lamanites, it doth not exceed that of our people in Moriantum. For behold, many of the daughters of the Lamanites have they taken prisoners. And, after depriving them of that which was most dear and precious above all things (which is chastity and virtue), ¹⁰and after that they had [done^b] this thing—they did murder them in a most cruel manner, torturing their bodies even unto death. And after that they have done this, they devour their flesh like unto wild beasts—because of the hardness of their hearts. And they do it for a token of bravery.

¹¹O my beloved son! How can a people like this, that are without civilization— ¹²and only a few years have passed away, and they were a civil, and a delightsome people?^c ¹⁴But O, my son! How can a people like this, whose delight is in so much abomination—how can we expect that God will stay his hand in judgment against us?

¹⁵Behold, my heart cries: Wo unto this people! Come out in judgment, O God, and hide their sins, and wickedness, and abominations from before thy face!

¹⁶And again, my son, there are many widows and their daughters which remain in Sherrizah. And that part of the provisions which the Lamanites did not carry away, behold, the army of Zenephi has carried away—and left them to wander whithersoever they can, for food. And many old women do faint by the way and die. ¹⁷And the army which

---

a. The Printer's Manuscript had Emer, which Hyrum Smith changed to Emron.
b. The Printer's Manuscript had "none," which is clearly incorrect. Hyrum Smith changed it to "done."
c. This is an awkward sentence that is not completely resolved.

is with me is weak. And the armies of the Lamanites are betwixt Sherrizah and me. And as many as have fled to the army of Aaron, have fallen victims to their awful brutality.

¹⁸O the depravity of my people! They are without order, and without mercy.

Behold, I am but a man, and I have but the strength of a man, and I cannot any longer enforce my commands. ¹⁹And they have become strong in their perversion. And they are alike brutal, sparing none, neither old nor young. And they delight in every thing, save that which is good. And the sufferings of our women and our children upon all the face of this land doth exceed every thing. Yea, tongue cannot tell—neither can it be written.

²⁰And now my son, I dwell no longer upon this horrible scene. Behold, thou knowest the wickedness of this people. Thou knowest that they are without principle, and past feeling—and their wickedness doth exceed that of the Lamanites.

²¹Behold, my son—I cannot recommend them unto God, lest he should smite me. ²²But behold, my son, I recommend thee unto God. And I trust in Christ that thou wilt be saved. And I pray unto God that he would spare thy life, to witness the return of his people unto him—or their utter destruction. For I know that they must perish, except they repent and return unto him. ²³And if they perish, it will be like unto the Jaredites—because of the willfulness of their hearts, seeking for blood and revenge.

²⁴And if it so be that they perish, we know that many of our brethren have dissented over unto the Lamanites, and many more will also dissent over unto them. Wherefore, write somewhat a few things, if thou art spared and I should perish, and not see thee. But I trust that I may see thee soon. For I have sacred records that I would deliver up unto thee, my son.

²⁵Be faithful in Christ. And may not the things which I have written grieve thee, to weigh thee down unto death. But may Christ lift thee up. And may his sufferings, and death, and the showing his body unto our fathers, and his mercy, and long suffering, and the hope of his glory, and of eternal life—rest in your mind forever. ²⁶And may the grace of God the Father (whose throne is high in the heavens) and our Lord Jesus Christ (who sitteth on the right hand of his power, until all things shall become subject unto him), be, and abide with you forever. Amen.

Chapter X [Moroni 10]

[10] ¹*Now I, Moroni, write somewhat as seemeth me good. And I write unto my brethren, the Lamanites. And I would that they should know that more than four hundred and twenty [years*ᵃ*] has passed away since the sign was given of the coming of Christ.* ²*And I seal up these records—after that I have spoken a few words, by way of exhortation [unto you*ᵇ*].*

³Behold, I would exhort you that when ye shall read these things (if it be wisdom in God that ye should read them), that ye would remember how merciful the Lord hath been unto the children of men from the creation of Adam, even down until the time that ye shall receive these things—and ponder it in your hearts. ⁴And when ye shall receive these things, I would exhort you that ye would ask God, the Eternal Father, in the name of Christ, if these things are not true. And if ye shall ask with a sincere heart, with real intent, having faith in Christ—and he will manifest the truth of it unto you, by the power of the Holy Ghost. ⁵And by the power of the Holy Ghost ye may know the truth of all things. ⁶And whatsoever thing is good—is just and true. Wherefore, nothing that is good denieth the Christ, but acknowledgeth that he is. ⁷And ye may know that he is—by the power of the Holy Ghost. Wherefore, I would exhort you that ye deny not the power of God. For he worketh by power, according to the faith of the children of men—the same today, and tomorrow, and forever.

⁸And again, [Iᶜ] exhort you, my brethren, that ye deny not the gifts of God. For they are many. And they come from the same God. And there are different ways that these gifts are administered, but it is the same God which worketh, all in all. And they are given by the manifestations of the spirit of God unto men, to profit them.ᵈ

[References 1 Corinthians 12:8–11]

⁹For behold, to one is given by the spirit of God, that he may teach the word of wisdom,

¹⁰and to another, that he may teach the word of knowledge, by the same spirit—

¹¹and to another, exceeding great faith—

and to another the gifts of healing, by the same spirit.

¹²And again to another, that he may work mighty miracles.

¹³And again to another, that he may prophesy concerning all things.

¹⁴And again to another, the beholding of angels, and ministering spirits.

¹⁵And again to another, all kinds of tongues.

¹⁶And again to another, the interpretation of languages, and of diversᵉ kinds of tongues.

---

a. Missing in the Printer's Manuscript. Hyrum Smith added.
b. Missing in the Printer's Manuscript. Hyrum Smith added.
c. Missing in the Printer's Manuscript. Hyrum Smith added.
d. Echoes 1 Corinthians 13:3–7: "And though I bestow all my goods to feed the poor, and though I give my body to be burned, and have not charity, it profiteth me nothing. Charity suffereth long, and is kind; charity envieth not; charity vaunteth not itself, is not puffed up, Doth not behave itself unseemly, seeketh not her own, is not easily provoked, thinketh no evil; Rejoiceth not in iniquity, but rejoiceth in the truth; Beareth all things, believeth all things, hopeth all things, endureth all things."
e. Archaic form, not to be confused with "diverse." Instead it means "several."

¹⁷And all these gifts comes by the spirit of Christ. And they come unto every man, severally, according as he will.

¹⁸And I would exhort you, my beloved, brethren, that ye remember that every good gift cometh of Christ. ¹⁹And I would exhort you, my beloved brethren, that ye remember that he is the same yesterday, today, and forever[a], and that all these gifts (of which I have spoken, which are spiritual) never will be done away, even as long as the world shall stand—only according to the unbelief of the children of men. ²⁰Wherefore, there must be faith. And if there must be faith, there must also be hope. And if there must be hope, there must also be charity.[b] ²¹And except ye have charity, ye can in no wise be saved in the kingdom of God. Neither can ye be saved in the kingdom of God if ye have not faith—neither can ye if ye have not hope. ²²And if ye have no hope, ye must needs be in despair. And despair cometh because of iniquity. ²³And Christ truly said unto our fathers: "If ye have faith, ye can do all things, which is expedient unto me."

²⁴And now, I speak unto all the ends of the earth—that, if the day cometh that the power and gifts of God shall be done away among you, it shall be because of unbelief. ²⁵And wo be unto the children of men, if this be the case! For there shall be none that doeth good among you—no not one.[c] For if there be one among you that doeth good, he shall work by the power and gifts of God. ²⁶And wo unto them which shall do these things away, and die. For they die in their sins, and they cannot be saved in the kingdom of God. And I speak it according to the words of Christ. And I lie not.

²⁷And I exhort you to remember these things. For the time speedily cometh that ye shall know that I lie not! For ye shall see me at the bar of God. And the Lord God will say unto you: "Did I not declare my words unto you (which was written by this man)—like as one crying from the dead, yea, even as one speaking out of the dust?"[d]

²⁸I declare these things, unto the fulfilling of the prophecies. And behold, they shall proceed forth out of the mouth of the everlasting God. And his word shall hiss forth, [from[e]] generation to generation. ²⁹And God shall show unto you that that which I have written is true.

³⁰And again, I would exhort you that ye would come unto Christ and lay hold upon every good gift. And touch not the evil gift, nor the unclean thing.

³¹And awake, and arise from the dust,[f] O [Jerusalem[g]]!
Yea, and put on thy beautiful garments, O daughter of Zion.[h]

---

a. See Hebrews 13:8: "Jesus Christ the same yesterday, and to day, and for ever."

b. See 1 Corinthians 13:13: "And now abideth faith, hope, charity, these three; but the greatest of these is charity."

c. See Psalm 14:3: "there is none that doeth good, no, not one."

d. See Isaiah 29:4: "And thou shalt be brought down, and shalt speak out of the ground, and thy speech shall be low out of the dust, and thy voice shall be, as of one that hath a familiar spirit, out of the ground, and thy speech shall whisper out of the dust."

e. Missing in the Printer's Manuscript. Hyrum Smith added.

f. Echoes 2 Nephi 1:14, where Lehi uses this phrase.

g. The Printer's Manuscript had "daughter of Zion." Hyrum Smith made the change.

h. Reprising language from Isaiah 52:1–2: "Awake, awake; put on thy strength, O Zion; put on thy beautiful garments, O Jerusalem, the holy city: for henceforth there shall no more come into thee the uncircumcised and the unclean. Shake thyself from the dust; arise, and sit down, O Jerusalem: loose thyself from the bands of thy neck, O captive daughter of Zion."

> And strengthen thy stakes,[a]
>> and enlarge thy borders forever,
> that thou mayest no more be confounded,[b]
> that the covenants of the Eternal Father
>> (which he hath made unto thee, O house of Israel)
>> may be fulfilled.

[32] Yea, come unto Christ and be perfected in him. And deny yourselves of all ungodliness. And if ye shall deny yourselves of all ungodliness, and love God with all your might, mind, and strength—then is his grace sufficient for you[c]—that by his grace ye may be perfect in Christ. And if by the grace of God ye are perfect in Christ, ye can in no wise deny the power of God.

[33] And again, if ye (by the grace of God) are perfect in Christ and deny not his power—then are ye sanctified in Christ (by the grace of God) through the shedding of the blood of Christ (which is in the covenant of the Father) unto the remission of your sins, that ye become holy—without spot.

[34] And now, I bid unto all, farewell! I soon go to rest in the paradise of God until my spirit and body shall again reunite and I am brought forth triumphant through the air to meet you before the pleasing bar of the great Jehovah, the Eternal Judge of both quick and dead.[d] Amen.

The End.[e]

---

a. Language from Isaiah 54:2: "Enlarge the place of thy tent, and let them stretch forth the curtains of thine habitations: spare not, lengthen thy cords, and strengthen thy stakes."

b. The phrase "neither be thou confounded" occurs in Isaiah 54:4.

c. Uses language from 2 Corinthians 12:9: "And he said unto me, My grace is sufficient for thee."

d. The phrase "the quick and the dead" is found in Acts 10:42.

e. Skousen suggests that this was an unnecessary addition by a scribe. The text itself would have ended with "amen." Skousen, *Analysis of the Textual Variants*, 6:3962. The use of the testificatory "amen" forces the end of chapters, and it only makes sense that it would also signify an end to the Moroni's writing. Therefore, "the end" should be seen as a scribal addition, per Skousen's suggestion.

The Small Plates of Nephi

The Words of Mormon

Chapter I [Words of Mormon 1]

¹And now I, Mormon, being about to deliver up the record which I have been making into the hands of my son, Moroni—behold, I have witnessed almost all the destruction of my people the Nephites. ²And it is many hundred years after the coming of Christ that I deliver these records into the hands of my son. And it supposeth me that he will witness the entire destruction of my people. But may God grant that he may survive them, that he may write somewhat concerning them, and somewhat concerning Christ—that perhaps someday it may profit them.

³And now, I speak somewhat concerning that which I have written. For after that I had made an abridgment from the plates of Nephi down to the reign of this King Benjamin (of which Amaleki spake), I searched among the records which had been delivered into my hands and I found these plates, which contained this small account of the prophets from Jacob down to the reign of this King Benjamin. And also many of the words of Nephi. ⁴And the things which are upon these plates, pleasing me because of the prophesies of the coming of Christ and my fathers, knowing that many of them have been fulfilled.ᵃ And yea, and I also know that as many things as have been prophesied concerning us down to this day has been fulfilled. And as many as go beyond this day must surely come to pass. ⁵Wherefore, I chose these things to finish my record upon them, which remainder of my record I shall take from the plates of Nephi. And I cannot write a hundredth part of the things of my people. ⁶But behold, I shall take these plates, which contain these prophesyings and revelations, and put them with the remainder of my record. For they are choice unto me. And I know they will be choice unto my brethren. ⁷And I do this for a wise purpose. For thus it whispereth me according to the workings of the Spirit of the Lord, which is in me.

And now, I do not know all things. But the Lord knoweth all things which is to come. Wherefore, he worketh in me to do according to his will. ⁸And my prayer to God is concerning my brethren, that they may once again come to the knowledge of God—yea, the redemption of Christ, that they may once again be a delightsome people.

⁹And now I, Mormon, proceed to finish out my record, which I take from the plates of Nephi. And I make it according to the knowledge and the understanding which God hath given me. ¹⁰Wherefore, it came to pass that after Amaleki had delivered up these plates into the hands of King Benjamin, he took them, and put them with the other plates, which contained records which had been handed down by the kings from generation to generation until the days of King Benjamin. ¹¹And they were handed down from King Benjamin from generation to generation until they have fallen into my hands.

And I, Mormon, pray to God, that they may be preserved from this time hence forth. And I know that they will be preserved. For there are great things written upon them—out of which my people and their brethren shall be judged at the great and last day, according to the word of God which is written.

---

a. Incomplete sentence.

>¹²And now, concerning this King Benjamin. He had somewhat contentions among his own people.

¹³And it came to pass also that the armies of the Lamanites came down out of the land of Nephi to battle against his people. But behold, King Benjamin gathered together his armies and he did stand against them. And he did fight with the strength of his own arm, with the sword of Laban. ¹⁴And in the strength of the Lord they did contend against their enemies until they had slain many thousand of the Lamanites.

And it came to pass that they did contend against the Lamanites until they had driven them out of all the lands of their inheritance.

¹⁵And it came to pass that after there had been false Christs (and their mouths had been shut and they punished according to their crimes),[a] ¹⁶and after there had been false prophets, and false preachers, and teachers, among the people (and all these having been punished according to their crimes), and after there having been much contentions and many dissensions away unto the Lamanites—behold, it came to pass that King Benjamin (with the assistance of the holy prophets which were among his people, ¹⁷for behold, King Benjamin was a holy man and he did reign over his people in righteousness—and there were many holy men in the land, and they did speak the word of God with power, and with authority—and they did use much sharpness because of the stiff-neckedness of the people)—¹⁸wherefore, with the help of these, King Benjamin, by laboring with all the might of his body and the faculty of his whole soul, and also the prophets—wherefore, they did once more establish peace in the land.<[b]

---

a. Verses 15–18 are a single sentence. It is difficult to parse due to the numerous asides.

b. This is blocked as an aside. Mormon has discussed the small plates being given to Benjamin, and enters tangential information about Benjamin.

The Book of Nephi:
His Reign and Ministry[a]

An account of Lehi and his wife Sariah, and his four sons—being called (beginning at the eldest) Laman, Lemuel, Sam, and Nephi.

The Lord warns Lehi to depart out of the land of Jerusalem because he prophesieth unto the people concerning their iniquity, and they seek to destroy his life. He taketh three days journey into the wilderness with his family.

Nephi taketh his brethren and returns to the land of Jerusalem after the record of the Jews. The account of their sufferings.

They take the daughters of Ishmael to wife. They take their families and depart into the wilderness. Their sufferings and afflictions in the wilderness. The course of their travels.

They come to the large waters. Nephi's brethren rebelleth against him. He confoundeth them and buildeth a ship. They call the place Bountiful.

They cross the large waters into the promised land, etcetera.[b]

Chapter I [1 Nephi 1–5]

This is according to the account of Nephi. Or, in other words, I, Nephi, wrote this record.[c]

[1] ¹I, Nephi, having been born of goodly parents, therefore I was taught somewhat in all the learning of my father. And having seen many afflictions in the course of my days—nevertheless having been highly favored of the Lord in all my days, yea, having had a great knowledge of the goodness and the mysteries of God[d]—therefore I make a record of my proceedings in my days. ²Yea, I make a record in the language of my father, which consists of the learning of the Jews and the language of the Egyptians. ³And I know that the record which I make to be true. And I make it with mine own hand. And I make it according to my knowledge.

⁴For it came to pass in the commencement of the first year of the reign of Zedekiah, King of Judah, >my father, Lehi, having dwelt at Jerusalem in all his days[e]<—and in

---

a. Beginning with the 1830 edition, the phrase "his reign and ministry" has been set as a subtitle. This edition places it as part of the title, reflecting the reason why Nephi wrote this second record after the one on the large plates.

b. The Printer's Manuscript does not make a separation between the synopsis and the text proper. This was a decision the compositor made. Other synoptic book headers have similar characteristics to this one. They are in third person and provide a very short preview of what will come in the book.

c. The Printer's Manuscript does not give any indication of where the synoptic header ends and the narrative begins. The compositor made the decision to include this sentence with the synoptic header, probably to avoid the apparent duplication. This edition considers it as more of a title and declaration of authorship, with the next sentence beginning the story proper. It is best seen as a chapter header, declaring the source from which this record is taken—that is, Nephi's record and memory.

One of the corroborating factors for this change is that the synoptic header (here and in all other synoptic headers) is written in third person, but this sentence is clearly first person. Having the two different voices in the same synoptic header is otherwise unattested.

d. The phrase "mystery of God" appears in 1 Corinthians 4:1, Colossians 2:2, and Revelation 10:7.

e. This is a difficult sentence in that the parenthetical phrase has interrupted the flow of the

that same year[a] there came many prophets, prophesying unto the people that they must repent or that great city Jerusalem must be destroyed. ⁵Wherefore, it came to pass that my father Lehi (as he went forth) prayed unto the Lord, yea even with all his heart, in behalf of his people.

⁶And it came to pass as he prayed unto the Lord, there came a pillar of fire and dwelt upon a rock before him. And he saw and heard much. And because of the things which he saw and heard he did quake and tremble exceedingly.

⁷And it came to pass that he returned to his own house at Jerusalem. And he cast himself upon his bed, being overcome with the Spirit and the things which he had seen. ⁸And being thus overcome with the Spirit, he was carried away in a vision, even that he saw the heavens open. And he thought he saw God sitting upon his throne, surrounded with numberless concourses of angels in the attitude of singing and praising their God.

⁹And it came to pass that he saw one descending out of the midst of heaven. And he beheld that his luster was above that of the sun at noonday. ¹⁰And he also saw twelve others following him. And their brightness did exceed that of the stars in the firmament. ¹¹And they came down and went forth upon the face of the earth. And the first came and stood before my father and gave unto him a book. And bade him that he should read it.

¹²And it came to pass that as he read he was filled with the spirit of the Lord. ¹³And he read, saying: "Wo, wo unto Jerusalem! For I have seen thine abominations." Yea, and many things did my father read concerning Jerusalem, that it should be destroyed. And the inhabitants thereof—many should perish by the sword. And many should be carried away captive into Babylon.

And it came to pass that when my father had read and saw many great and marvelous things, he did exclaim many things unto the Lord, such as:

> Great and marvelous are thy works,
>   O Lord God Almighty!
> Thy throne is high in the heavens,
>   and thy power and goodness and mercy
>   is over all the in habitants of the earth.
> And because thou art merciful,
>   thou wilt not suffer those who come unto thee
>   that they shall perish.[b]

¹⁵And after this manner was the language of my father, in the praising of his God. For his soul did rejoice, and his whole heart was filled because of the things which he had seen, yea, which the Lord had shown unto him.

>¹⁶And now, I, Nephi, do not make a full account of the things which my father hath written. For he hath written many things which he saw in visions and

---

sentence. The resumption of the meaning uses "and" rather than "that." This is an example of repetitive resumption on a sentence level. The phrase "in that same year" is the repetition that recovers from the parenthetical interruption.

a. Repetitive resumption after the insertion.

b. These appear to be separate examples rather than a cohesive statement. If Nephi is quoting from memory, they are the more memorable lines. If he is consulting a text, he is selecting exclamations that probably began a larger theological discussion. That type of discourse is seen later, where a general statement leads to more detailed analysis.

in dreams. And he also hath written may things which he prophesied, and spake, unto his children, which I shall not make a full account. ¹⁷But I shall make an account of my proceedings in my days.

Behold, I make an abridgment of the record of my father upon plates which I have made with mine own hands. Wherefore, after that I have abridged the record of my father, then will I make an account of mine own life.ᵃ<

¹⁸Therefore, I would that ye should know that after the Lord had shown so many marvelous things unto my father, Lehi (yea, concerning the destruction of Jerusalem), behold he went forth among the people and began to prophesy and to declare unto them concerning the things which he had both seen and heard.

¹⁹And it came to pass that the Jews did mock him because of the things which he testified of them. For he truly testified of their wickedness and their abominations. And he testified that the things which he saw and heard, and also the things which he read in the book, manifested plainly of the coming of a Messiah. And also the redemption of the world.

²⁰And when the Jews heard these things they were angry with him. Yea, even as with the prophets of old whom they had cast out, and stoned, and slain. And they also sought his life, that they might take it away. But behold, I, Nephi, will show unto you that the tender merciesᵇ of the Lord is over all them whom he hath chosen because of their faith, to make them mighty, even unto the power of deliverance.

[2] ¹For behold, it came to pass that the Lord spake unto my father, yea, even in a dream, and saith unto him: "Blessed art thou Lehi, because of the things which thou hast done. And because thou hast been faithful and declared unto this people the things which I commanded thee, behold, they seek to take away thy life."

²And it came to pass that the Lord commanded my father, even in a dream, that he should take his family and depart into the wilderness.

³And it came to pass that he was obedient unto the word of the Lord. Wherefore, he did as the Lord commanded him.

⁴And it came to pass that he departed into the wilderness. And he left his house and the land of his inheritance, and his gold, and his silver, and his precious things—and took nothing with him save it were his family, and provisions, and tents. And he departed into the wilderness.

⁵And he came down by the borders near the shore of the Red Sea. And he traveled in the wilderness in the borders which was nearer the Red Sea. And he did travel in the wilderness with his family, which consisted of my mother Sariah, and my elder brethren, which were Laman, Lemuel, and Sam.

⁶And it came to pass that when he had traveled three days in the wilderness, he pitched his tent in a valley beside a river of water.

⁷And it came to pass that he built an altar of stones.ᶜ And he made an offering unto the Lord. And gave thanks unto the Lord our God.

---

a. The indented text (verses 16–17) is an aside. This is the first of several asides where Nephi speaks of the process of creating his records. In this case, Nephi explains that while this book is declared to be a record of Nephi's reign and ministry, he finds that he must begin with his father's story. After the explanation about the construction of the text, Nephi returns to his planned text in verse 19.

b. The phrase "tender mercies" is found in Psalm 145:1.

c. The commandment to build altars of stone is found in Deuteronomy 27:5–7: "And there shalt thou

⁸And it came to pass that he called the name of the river Laman. And it emptied into the Red Sea. And the valley was in the borders near the mouth thereof.

⁹And when my father saw that the waters of the river emptied into the fountain of the Red Sea, he spake unto Laman, saying: "O that thou mightest be like unto this river, continually running into the fountain of all righteousness!"

¹⁰And he also spake unto Lemuel: "O that thou mightest be like unto this valley, firm and steadfast, and immoveable in keeping the commandments of the Lord!"

¹¹Now, this he spake because of the stiffneckedness of Laman and Lemuel. For behold, they did murmur in many things against their father, because that he was a visionary man and that he had led them out of the land of Jerusalem—to leave the land of their inheritance, and their gold, and their silver, and their precious things, and to perish in the wilderness. And this they said he had done because of the foolish imaginations of his heart.

¹²And thus Laman and Lemuel (being the eldest) did murmur against their father. And they did murmur because they knew not the dealings of that God who had created them. ¹³Neither did they believe that Jerusalem, that great city, could be destroyed according to the words of the prophets. And they were like unto the Jews which were at Jerusalem which sought to take away the life of my father.

¹⁴And it came to pass that my father did speak unto them (in the valley of Lemuel) with power (being filled with the Spirit) until their frames did shake before him. And he did confound them, that they durst not utter against him. Wherefore, they did do as he commanded them. ¹⁵And my father dwelt in a tent.[a]

¹⁶And it came to pass that I, Nephi, being exceeding young (nevertheless being large in stature) and also having great desires to know of the mysteries of God,[b] wherefore I did cry unto the Lord. And behold he did visit me and did soften my heart that I did believe all the words which had been spoken by my father. Wherefore, I did not rebel against him like unto my brothers.

¹⁷And I spake unto Sam, making known unto him the things which the Lord had manifested unto me by his Holy Spirit. And it came to pass that he believed in my words.[c]

¹⁸But behold, Laman and Lemuel would not hearken unto my words. And being grieved because of the hardness of their hearts, I cried unto the Lord for them.

¹⁹And it came to pass that the Lord spake unto me, saying:

---

build an altar unto the Lord thy God, an altar of stones: thou shalt not lift up any iron tool upon them. Thou shalt build the altar of the Lord thy God of whole stones: and thou shalt offer burnt offerings thereon unto the Lord thy God: And thou shalt offer peace offerings, and shalt eat there, and rejoice before the Lord thy God."

a. Nephi repeats the idea of his father dwelling in a tent in 1 Nephi 2:15, 9:1, and 10:16. None of these verses really say anything about why it was important to note that he dwelt in a tent, but the phrases appear to mark a transition between narrative units. A similar phrase, "tent of my father" occurs in 1 Nephi 3:1, 5:7, 7:22, and 15:1. In this verse the intent of the "my father dwelt in a tent" is to shift the focus from Laman and Lemuel to Nephi. The narrative function of his father's tent is more fully discussed in Chapter 6 of *Engraven Upon Plates*.

b. The phrase "mystery of God" appears in 1 Corinthians 4:1, Colossians 2:2, and Revelation 10:7.

c. Although "and it came to pass" is usually used as a paragraph marker (and might be in this case), this edition has elected to keep the information about Sam in the same paragraph and let the next paragraph be the contrast with Laman and Lemuel.

Chapter I [1 Nephi 1–5]

Blessed art thou Nephi, because of thy faith. For thou hast sought me diligently, with lowliness of heart.

²⁰And inasmuch as ye shall keep my commandments ye shall prosper, and shall be led to a land of promise. Yea, even a land which I have prepared for you. Yea, a land which is choice above all other lands.

²¹And inasmuch as thy brethren shall rebel against thee, they shall be cut off from the presence of the Lord.[a]

²²And inasmuch as thou shalt keep my commandments, thou shalt be made a ruler and a teacher over thy brethren.

²³For behold, in that day that they shall rebel against me, I will curse them, even with a sore curse. And they shall have no power over thy seed—except they shall rebel against me also. ²⁵And, if it so be that they rebel against me, they shall be a scourge unto thy seed, to stir them up in the ways of remembrance.

[3] ¹And it came to pass that I, Nephi, returned from speaking with the Lord to the tent of my father.

²And it came to pass that he spake unto me, saying:

Behold I have dreamed a dream—in the which the Lord hath commanded me that thou and thy brethren shall return to Jerusalem. ³For behold, Laban hath the record of the Jews, and also a genealogy of my forefathers. And they are engraven upon plates of brass. ⁴Wherefore, the Lord hath commanded me that thou and thy brothers should go unto the house of Laban and seek the records, and bring them down hither into the wilderness.

⁵And now behold, thy brothers murmur—saying it is a hard thing which I have required of them. But behold, I have not required it of them. But it is a commandment of the Lord. ⁶Therefore, go, my son. And thou shalt be favored of the Lord because thou hast not murmured.

⁷And it came to pass that I, Nephi, said unto my father: "I will go and do the things which the Lord hath commanded. For I know that the Lord giveth no commandments unto the children of men, save he shall prepare a way for them that they may accomplish the thing which he commandeth them."

⁸And it came to pass that when my father had heard these words, he was exceeding glad. For he knew that I had been blessed of the Lord.

⁹And I Nephi, and my brethren, took our journey in the wilderness (with our tents) to go up to the land of Jerusalem.

¹⁰And it came to pass that when we had come up to the land of Jerusalem, I and my brethren did consult one with another. ¹¹And we cast lots—which of us should go in unto the house of Laban.

And it came to pass that the lot fell upon Laman. And Laman went in unto the house of Laban, and he talked with him as he sat in his house. ¹²And he desired of Laban the records, which were engraven upon the plates of brass, which contained the genealogy of my father.

¹³And behold, it came to pass that Laban was angry and thrust him out from his presence. And he would not that he should have the records. Wherefore, he said unto

---

a. The phrase "cut off from my presence" is found in Leviticus 22:3.

him: "Behold, thou art a robber! And I will slay thee!" ¹⁴But Laman fled out of his presence, and told the things which Laban had done—unto us. And we began to be exceeding sorrowful. And my brethren were about to return unto my father in the wilderness.

¹⁵But behold, I said unto them that:

> As the Lord liveth and as we live!ᵃ We will not go down unto our father in the wilderness until we have accomplished the thing which the Lord hath commanded us. ¹⁶Wherefore, let us be faithful in keeping the commandments of the Lord. Therefore, let us go down to the land of our father's inheritance. For behold, he left gold and silver, and all manner of riches.
>
> And all this he hath done because of the commandments of the Lord. ¹⁷For he, knowing that Jerusalem must be destroyed because of the wickedness of the people (¹⁸for behold, they have rejected the words of the prophets), wherefore, if my father should dwell in the land after that he had been commanded to flee out of the land, behold, he would also perish.ᵇ Wherefore, it must needs be that he flee out of the land.
>
> ¹⁹And behold, it is wisdom in God that we should obtain these records, that we might preserve unto our children the language of our fathers. ²⁰And also that we may preserve unto them the words which have been spoken by the mouth of all the holy prophets (which have been delivered unto them by the spirit and power of God) since the world began, even down unto this present time.ᶜ

²¹And it came to pass that after this manner of language did I persuade my brethren—thatᵈ they might be faithful in keeping the commandments of the Lord God.

²²And it came to pass that we went down to the land of our inheritance. And we did gather together our gold, and our silver, and our precious things. ²³And after that we had gathered these things together, we went up again unto the house of Laban.

²⁴And it came to pass that we went in unto Laban, and desired him that he would give unto us the records which were engraven upon the plates of brass. For which we would give unto him our gold, and our silver, and all our precious things.

²⁵And it came to pass that when Laban saw our property, that it was exceeding great, he did lust after it, insomuch that he thrust us out and sent his servants to slay us, that he might obtain our property.

²⁶And it came to pass that we did flee before the servants of Laban. And we were obliged to leave behind our property. And it fell into the hands of Laban.

²⁷And it came to pass that we fled into the wilderness. And the servants of Laban did not overtake us. And we hid ourselves in the cavity of a rock.

²⁸And it came to pass that Laman was angry with me, and also with my father—

---

a. The oath is similar to a common one from the Old Testament: "As the Lord liveth, and as they soul liveth." See 1 Samuel 20:3, 25:26; 2 Kings 2:2,4,6, 4:30. The oath "As the Lord liveth" is more common both in the Old Testament and in the Book of Mormon.

b. There is no simple formatting that will make this a complete sentence. The culprit is "knowing." Skousen, *Analysis of the Textual Variants,* 1:90, notes: "For the 1840 edition, Joseph Smith (presumably) edited the present participle "knowing" to the past tense "knew." This change eliminates what appears to be a dependent participial clause."

c. See Acts 3:21: "Whom the heaven must receive until the times of restitution of all things, which God hath spoken by the mouth of all his holy prophets since the world began."

d. A more modern sentence would have "so that."

and also was Lemuel (for he hearkened unto the words of Laman). Wherefore, Laman and Lemuel did speak many hard words unto us, their younger brothers. And they did smite us, even with a rod.

²⁹And it came to pass as they smote us with a rod, behold, an angel of the Lord came and stood before them. And he spake unto them, saying: "Why do ye smite your younger brothers with a rod? Know ye not that the Lord hath chosen him to be a ruler over you—and this, because of your iniquities? Behold, thou shalt go up to Jerusalem again. And the Lord will deliver Laban into your hands."

³⁰And after that the angel had spake unto us, he departed. ³¹And after that the angel had departed, Laman and Lemuel again began to murmur, saying: "How is it possible that the Lord will deliver Laban into our hands? Behold, he is a mighty man, and he can command fifty. Yea, even he can slay fifty—then why not us?"

[4] ¹And it came to pass that I spake unto my brethren, saying:

> Let us go up again unto Jerusalem. And let us be faithful in keeping the commandments of the Lord. For behold, he is mightier than all the earth—then why not mightier than Laban and his fifty—yea, or even than his tens of thousands? ²Therefore, let us go up.
>
> Let us be strong like unto Moses. For he truly spake unto the waters of the Red Sea and they divided hither and thither. And our fathers came through out of captivity on dry ground. And the armies of pharaoh did follow and were drowned in the waters of the Red Sea.ᵃ
>
> ³Now behold, ye know that this is true. And ye also know that an angel hath spoken unto you. Wherefore can ye doubt?
>
> Let us go up. The Lord is able to deliver us, even as our fathers—and to destroy Laban, even as the Egyptians.

⁴Now, when I had spoken these words, they was yet wroth and did still continue to murmur. Nevertheless, they did follow me up until we came without the walls of Jerusalem. ⁵And it was by night. And I caused that they should hide themselves without the walls. And after that they had hid themselves, I, Nephi, crept in into the city and went forth towards the house of Laban.

⁶And I was led by the Spirit, not knowing beforehand the things which I should do. ⁷Nevertheless, I went forth. And as I came near unto the house of Laban, I beheld a man. And he had fallen to the earth before me, for he was drunken with wine. ⁸And when I came to him, I found that it was Laban.

⁹And I beheld his sword and I drew it forth from the sheath thereof. And the hilt thereof was of pure gold. And the workmanship thereof was exceeding fine. And I saw that the blade thereof was of the most precious steel.

¹⁰And it came to pass that I was constrained by the Spirit, that I should kill Laban. But I said in my heart: "Never at any time have I shed the blood of man." And I shrunk—and would that I might not slay him.

¹¹And the Spirit saith unto me again: "Behold, the Lord hath delivered him into thy hands."

Yea, and I also knew that he had sought to take away mine own life. Yea, and he

---

a. This refers to the story told in Exodus 14.

would not hearken unto the commandments of the Lord. And he also had taken away our property.

¹²And it came to pass that the Spirit said unto me again: "Slay him, for the Lord hath delivered him into thy hands. ¹³Behold, the Lord slayeth the wicked to bring forth his righteous purposes. It is better that one man should perish than that a nation should dwindle and perish in unbelief."[a]

¹⁴And now, when I, Nephi, had heard these words, I remembered the words of the Lord, which he spake unto me in the wilderness, saying that: "Inasmuch as thy seed shall keep my commandments, they shall prosper in the land of promise." ¹⁵Yea, and I also thought that they could not keep the commandments of the Lord according to the law of Moses, save they should have the law. ¹⁶And I also knew that the law was engraven upon the plates of brass.

¹⁷And again, I knew that the Lord had delivered Laban into my hands for this cause, that I might obtain the records according to his commandments. ¹⁸Therefore, I did obey the voice of the Spirit, and took Laban by the hair of the head, and I smote off his head with his own sword.

¹⁹And after that I had smote off his head with his own sword, I took the garments of Laban and put them upon mine own body, yea, even every whit. And I did gird on his armor about my loins. ²⁰And after that I had done this, I went forth unto the treasury of Laban.

And as I went forth towards the treasury of Laban, behold, I saw the servant of Laban which had the keys of the treasury. And I commanded him in the voice of Laban that he should go with me into the treasury. ²¹And he, supposing me to be his master Laban (for he beheld the garments and also the sword girted about my loins)— ²²and he spake unto me concerning the elders of the Jews, he knowing that his master Laban had been out by night among them.[b]

²³And I spake unto him as if it had been Laban. ²⁴And I also spake unto him that I should carry the engravings which were upon the plates of brass to my elder brethren, which were without the walls. ²⁵And I also bade him that he should follow me.

²⁶And he, supposing that I spake of the brethren of the church and that I was truly that Laban (whom I had slew[c]), wherefore, he did follow me. ²⁷And he spake unto me many times concerning the elders of the Jews, as I went forth unto my brethren, which were without the walls.

²⁸And it came to pass that when Laman saw me, he was exceedingly frightened (and also Lemuel and Sam). And they fled from before my presence, for they supposed it was Laban and that he had slain me and had sought to take away their lives also.

²⁹And it came to pass that I called after them, and they did hear me. Wherefore, they did cease to flee from my presence.

---

a. See John 11:50: "Nor consider that it is expedient for us, that one man should die for the people, and that the whole nation perish not."

b. This sentence gets lost after the parenthetical phrase. It is an incomplete sentence. This was changed in the 1830 edition to: "And he *supposed* me to be his master, Laban, for he beheld the garments and also the sword girded about my loins." The change in tense was the easiest way to make the sentence complete. Skousen, *Analysis of Textual Variants*, 1:112.

c. Oliver Cowdery changed "had slew" to "had slain" in the Printer's Manuscript. Skousen, *Analysis of the Textual Variants*, 1:112. This edition has elected to retain it, as it will appear in other locations where Cowdery did not change it.

Chapter I [1 Nephi 1–5]

³⁰And it came to pass that when the servant of Laban beheld my brethren he began to tremble, and was about to flee from before me and return to the city of Jerusalem.

³¹And now I, Nephi, being a man of large stature (and also having received much strength of the Lord), therefore I did seize upon the servant of Laban and held him that he should not flee.

³²And it came to pass that I spake with him, that if he would hearken unto my words, as the Lord liveth and as I live[a]—even so, that if he would hearken unto our words, we would spare his life. ³³And I spake unto him, even with an oath, that he need not fear—that he should be a free man like unto us, if he would go down in the wilderness with us. ³⁴And I also spake unto him, saying: "Surely the Lord hath commanded us to do this thing, and shall we not be diligent in keeping the commandments of the Lord?[b] Therefore, if thou wilt go down into the wilderness to my father, thou shalt have place with us."

³⁵And it came to pass that Zoram did take courage at the words which I spake. >Now Zoram was the name of the servant[c]<. And he promised that he would go down into the wilderness unto our father. And he also made an oath unto us that he would tarry with us from that time forth. ³⁶Now, we were desirous that he should tarry with us for this cause, that the Jews might not know concerning our flight unto into the wilderness—lest they should pursue us and destroy us.

³⁷And it came to pass that when Zoram had made an oath unto us, our fears did cease concerning him.

³⁸And it came to pass that we took the plates of brass, and the servant of Laban—and departed into the wilderness, and journeyed unto the tent of our father.

[5] ¹And it came to pass that after we had came down into the wilderness unto our father, behold, he was filled with joy. And also, my mother Sariah was exceeding glad, ²for she truly had mourned because of us. For she had supposed that we had perished in the wilderness. And she also had complained against my father, telling him that he was a visionary man, saying: "Behold, thou hast led us forth from the land of our inheritance. And my sons are no more. And we perish in the wilderness." ³And after this manner of language had my mother complained against my father.

⁴And it had came to pass that my father spake unto her, saying:

> I know that I am a visionary man. For if I had not seen the things of God in a vision I should not have known the goodness of God, but had tarried at Jerusalem and had perished with my brethren.
>
> ⁵But behold, I have obtained a land of promise, in the which things I do rejoice. Yea, and I know that the Lord will deliver my sons out of the hands of Laban and bring them down again unto us in the wilderness.

⁶And after this manner of language did my father Lehi, comfort my mother Sariah, concerning us—while we journeyed in the wilderness, up to the land of Jerusalem to obtain the record of the Jews.

---

a. The oath is similar to a common one from the Old Testament: "As the Lord liveth, and as they soul liveth." See 1 Samuel 20:3, 25:26; 2 Kings 2:2,4,6, 4:30. The oath "As the Lord liveth" is more common both in the Old Testament and in the Book of Mormon.

b. Perhaps alluding to Deuteronomy 6:17: "Ye shall diligently keep the commandments of the Lord your God, and his testimonies, and his statutes, which he hath commanded thee.

c. This is an aside where Nephi realized that he had not yet named Zoram.

⁷And when we had returned to the tent of my father—behold, their joy was full. And my mother was comforted. ⁸And she spake, saying: "Now I know of a surety that the Lord hath commanded my husband to flee into the wilderness. Yea, and I also know of a surety that the Lord hath protected my sons, and delivered them out of the hands of Laban, and gave them power whereby they could accomplish the thing which the Lord hath commanded them." And after this manner of language did she speak.

⁹And it came to pass that they did rejoice exceedingly and did offer sacrifice and burnt offerings unto the Lord. And they gave thanks unto the God of Israel. ¹⁰And after that they had given thanks unto the God of Israel, my father, Lehi, took the records which were engraven upon the plates of brass and he did search them from the beginning.

¹¹And he beheld that they did contain the five books of Moses, which gave an account of the creation of the world.

And also, of Adam and Eve, which was our first parents—¹²and also, a record of the Jews from the beginning, even down to the commencement of the reign of Zedekiah, King of Judah—¹³and also, the prophesies of the holy prophets from the beginning, even down to the commencement of the reign of Zedekiah—and also, many prophesies which have been spoken by the mouth of Jeremiah.

¹⁴And it came to pass that my father, Lehi, also found upon the plates of brass a genealogy of his fathers. Wherefore, he knew that he was a descendant of Joseph, yea, even that Joseph which was the son of Jacob, which was sold into Egypt, and which was preserved by the hand of the Lord that he might preserve his father, Jacob, and all his household from perishing with famine. ¹⁵And they were also led out of captivity, and out of the land of Egypt, by that same God who had preserved them. ¹⁶And thus my father, Lehi, did discover the genealogy of his fathers.

> And Laban also was a descendant of Joseph. Wherefore, he and his fathers had kept the records.ᵃ<

¹⁷And now, when my father saw all these things, he was filled with the Spirit, and began to prophesy concerning his seed—¹⁸that these plates of brass should go forth unto all nations, kindreds, tongues, and people, which were of his seed. ¹⁹Wherefore, he said that these plates of brass should never perish. Neither should they be dimmed any more by time. And he prophesied many things concerning his seed.

²⁰And it came to pass that thus far, I and my father had kept the commandments wherewith the Lord had commanded us. ²¹And we had obtained the record which the Lord had commanded us, and searched them, and found that they were desirable, yea, even of great worth unto us, insomuch that we could preserve the commandments of the Lord unto our children. ²²Wherefore, it was wisdom in the Lord that we should carry them with us as we journeyed in the wilderness, towards the land of promise.

---

a. This sentence has the feel of Nephi inserting information that was important but not necessarily part of the discussion at the time.

Chapter II [1 Nephi 6–9]

[6] ¹And now I, Nephi, do not give the genealogy of my fathers in this part of my record. Neither at any time shall I give it after upon these plates which I am writing, for it is given in the record which has been kept by my father. Wherefore, I do not write it in this work, ²for it sufficeth me to say that we are a descendant of Joseph.

> ³And it mattereth not to me that I am particular to give to give a full account of all the things of my father. For they cannot be written upon these plates, for I desire the room that I may write of the things of God. ⁴For the fullness of mine intent is that I may persuade men to come unto the God of Abraham, and the God of Isaac, and the God of Jacob—and be saved. ⁵Wherefore, the things which are pleasing unto the world I do not write, but the things which are pleasing unto God, and unto them which are not of the world. ⁶Wherefore, I shall give commandment unto my seed that they shall not occupy these plates with things which are not of worth unto the children of men.[a] <

[7] ¹And now I would that ye might know that after my father Lehi had made an end of prophesying concerning his seed, it came to pass that the Lord spake unto him again, saying that it was not mete for him, Lehi, that he should take his family into the wilderness alone—but that his sons should take daughters to wife that they might raise up seed unto the Lord in the land of promise.

²And it came to pass that the Lord commanded him that I, Nephi, and my brethren should again return unto the land of Jerusalem and bring down Ishmael and his family into the wilderness.

³And it came to pass that I, Nephi, did again (with my brethren) go forth into the wilderness, to go up to Jerusalem.

⁴And it came to pass that we went up unto the house of Ishmael. And we did gain favor in the sight of Ishmael, insomuch that we did speak unto him the words of the Lord.

⁵And it came to pass that the Lord did soften the heart of Ishmael, and also his household[b], insomuch that they took their journey with us down into the wilderness to the tent of our father.

⁶And it came to pass that as we journeyed in the wilderness, behold, Laman and Lemuel, and two of the daughters of Ishmael, and the two sons of Ishmael, and their families—did rebel against us. Yea, against I, Nephi, and Sam, and their father Ishmael, and his wife, and his three other daughters.

⁷And it came to pass [that[c]] in the which rebellion, they were desirous to return unto the land of Jerusalem. ⁸And now I, Nephi, being grieved for the hardness of their

---

a. The indented text (verses 3–6) is an aside. Orson Pratt must have noticed that this text didn't easily fit into the overall plan of the chapter, as he created a chapter break between this aside and what we now have as chapter 7. Verses 1 and 2 are suggested as the beginning of the chapter, followed by the aside, then a return to the planned text in the modern chapter 7, verse 1.

b. The Original Manuscript has the nonsensical "hole hole." Skousen has suggested an emendation of "whole household." The mention of "all the house of Ishmael" in verse 22 supports the idea that the intent is to describe the whole household. See Skousen, *Analysis of the Textual Variants*, 1:142–43.

c. The word "that" is added from the Original Manuscript. A copying error removed it from the Printer's Manuscript. Skousen, *Analysis of the Textual Variants*, 1:144.

hearts, therefore I spake unto them saying (yea, even unto Laman and unto Lemuel):

Behold, thou art mine elder brethren. And how is it that ye are so hard in your hearts, and so blind in your minds that ye have need that I, your younger brother, should speak unto you—yea, and set an example for you?

⁹How is it that ye have not hearkened unto the word of the Lord?

¹⁰How is it that ye have forgotten that ye have seen an angel of the Lord?

¹¹Yea, and how is it that ye have forgot how great things the Lord hath done for us in delivering us out of the hands of Laban, and also that we should obtain the record?

¹²Yea, and how is it that ye have forgotten that the Lord is able to do all things according to his will for the children of men, if it so be that they exercise faith in him? Wherefore, let us be faithful in him. ¹³And if it so be that we are faithful in him, we shall obtain the land of promise.

And ye shall know at some future period that the word of the Lord shall be fulfilled concerning the destruction of Jerusalem. For all things which the Lord hath spoken concerning the destruction of Jerusalem must be fulfilled. ¹⁴For behold, the spirit of the Lord ceaseth soon to strive with them.ª For behold, they have rejected the prophets and Jeremiah have they cast into prison. And they have sought to take away the life of my father, insomuch that they have driven him out of the land.

¹⁵Now behold, I say unto you, that if ye will return unto Jerusalem, ye shall also perish with them. And now, if ye have choice, go up to the land and remember the words which I speak unto you, that if ye go ye will also perish. For thus the spirit of the Lord constraineth me that I should speak.

¹⁶And it came to pass that when I, Nephi, had spoken these words unto my brethren they were angry with me.

And it came to pass that they did lay their hands upon me, for behold, they were exceeding wroth. And they did bind me with cords, for they sought to take away my life, that they might leave me in the wilderness to be devoured by wild beasts. ¹⁷But it came to pass that I prayed unto the Lord, saying: "O Lord, according to my faith which is in thee, wilt thou deliver me from the hands of my brethren? Yea, even give me strength that I may burst these bands with which I am bound."

¹⁸And it came to pass that when I had said these words, behold the bands were loosed from off my hands and feet, and I stood before my brethren. And I spake unto them again.

¹⁹And it came to pass that they were angry with me again, and sought to lay hands upon me. But behold, one of the daughters of Ishmael (yea, and also her mother and one of the sons of Ishmael) did plead with my brethren insomuch that they did soften their hearts. And they did cease striving to take away my life.

²⁰And it came to pass that they were sorrowful because of their wickedness, insomuch that they did bow down before me and did plead with me that I would forgive them of the thing that they had done against me.

²¹And it came to pass that I did frankly forgive them all that they had done. And I did exhort them that they would pray unto the Lord, their God, for forgiveness.

And it came to pass that they did so. And after that they had done praying unto the Lord, we did again travel on our journey toward the tent of our father.

---

a. See Genesis 6:3: "And the Lord said, My spirit shall not always strive with man."

Chapter II [1 Nephi 6–9]

²²And it came to pass that we did come down unto the tent of our father. And after that I and my brethren (and all the house of Ishmael) had come down unto the tent of my father, they did give thanks unto the Lord, their God. And they did offer sacrifice and burnt offerings unto him.

[8] ¹And it came to pass that we had gathered together all manner of seeds of every kind, both of grain of every kind, and also of the seeds of fruits of every kind.

²And it came to pass that while my father tarried in the wilderness, he spake unto us, saying:

Behold, I have dreamed a dream, or in other words, I have seen a vision. ³And behold, because of the thing which I have seen, I have reason to rejoice in the Lord because of Nephi, and also of Sam. For I have reason to suppose that they, and also many of their seed, will be saved.

⁴But behold, Laman and Lemuel—I fear exceedingly because of you. For behold, methought I saw a dark and dreary wilderness.

⁵And it came to pass that I saw a man, and he was dressed in a white robe. And he came and stood before me.

⁶And it came to pass that he spake unto me and bade me follow him.

⁷And it came to pass that as I followed him, I beheld myself—that I was in a dark and dreary waste. ⁸And after that I had traveled for the space of many hours in darkness, I began to pray unto the Lord that he would have mercy on me, according to the multitude of his tender mercies.ᵃ

⁹And it came to pass that after I had prayed unto the Lord, I beheld a large and spacious field.

¹⁰And it came to pass that I beheld a tree whose fruit was desirable to make one happy.

¹¹And it came to pass that I did go forth and partook of the fruit thereof. And I beheld that it was most sweet, above all that I ever had before tasted. Yea, and I beheld that the fruit thereof was white, to exceed all the whiteness that I had ever seen. ¹²And as I partook of the fruit thereof, it filled my soul with exceeding great joy. Wherefore, I began to be desirous that my family should partake of it also. For I knew that it was desirous above all other fruit.

¹³And as I cast my eyes round about (that perhaps I might discover my family also), I beheld a river of water. And it ran along, and it was near the tree of which I was partaking the fruit. ¹⁴And I looked to behold from whence it came, and I saw the head thereof a little way off. And at the head thereof, I beheld your mother Sariah, and Sam, and Nephi. And they stood as if they knew not whither they should go.

¹⁵And it came to pass that I beckoned unto them. And I also did say unto them, with a loud voice, that they should come unto me and partake of the fruit which was desirable above all other fruit.

¹⁶And it came to pass that they did come unto me and partake of the fruit also.

¹⁷And it came to pass that I was desirous that Laman and Lemuel should come and partake of the fruit also. Wherefore, I cast mine eyes towards the head of the river, that perhaps I might see them.

---

a. The phrase "tender mercies" is found in Psalm 25:6, 40:11, 51:1, 69:16, and others.

¹⁸And it came to pass that I saw them, but they would not come unto me [and partake of the fruit[a]].

¹⁹And I beheld a rod of iron. And it extended along the bank of the river, and led to the tree by which I stood. ²⁰And I also beheld a strait and narrow path, which came along by the rod of iron, even to the tree by which I stood. And it also led by the head of the fountain unto a large and spacious field, as if it had been a world. ²¹And I saw numberless concourses of people, many of whom were pressing forward, that they might obtain the path which led unto the tree by which I stood.

²²And it came to pass that they did come forth and commence in the path which led to the tree.

²³And it came to pass that there arose a mist of darkness, yea, even an exceeding great mist of darkness, insomuch that they which had commenced in the path did lose their way, that they wandered off and were lost.

²⁴And it came to pass that I beheld others pressing forward. And they came forth and caught hold of the end of the rod of iron. And they did press forward through the mists of darkness, clinging to the rod of iron, even until they did come forth and partake of the fruit of the tree.

²⁵And after that they had partook of the fruit of the tree, they did cast their eyes about, as if they were ashamed.

²⁶And I also cast my eyes round about, and [beheld[b]] (on the other side of the river of water) a great and spacious building. And it stood as it were in the air high above the earth. ²⁷And it was filled with people, both old and young, both male and female. And their manner of dress was exceeding fine. And they were in the attitude of mocking and pointing their fingers towards those which had came [up[c]] and were partaking of the fruit. ²⁸And after that they had tasted of the fruit, they were ashamed because of those that were a scoffing at them. And they fell away into forbidden paths, and were lost.

²⁹And now I, Nephi, do not speak all the words of my father. ³⁰But (to be short in writing), behold, he saw other multitudes pressing forward. And they came and caught hold of the end of the rod of iron. And they did press their way forward continually, holding fast to the rod of iron until they came forth and fell down, and partook of the fruit of the tree. ³¹And he also saw other multitudes [pressing[d]] their way towards that great and spacious building.

³²And it came to pass that many were drowned in the depths of the fountain. And

---

a. Skousen, *Analysis of the Textual Variants*, 1:174: "Here is an example of how Joseph Smith, in his editing for the 1840 edition, used the original manuscript to restore phrases that had been accidentally dropped during the earlier transmission of the text. In this case, Oliver Cowdery omitted the conjoined predicate 'and partake of the fruit' when copying from [the Original Manuscript] into [the Printer's Manuscript]."

b. Skousen, *Analysis of the Textual Variants*, 1:184: "In his copying from [the Original Manuscript] to [the Printer's Manuscript], Oliver Cowdery replaced 'beheld' with 'behold,' which the 1830 typesetter corrected."

c. The phrase "had came at" is in the Printer's Manuscript, rendered "had come at" in the current edition. Skousen, *Analysis of the Textual Variants*, 1:184: "The original manuscript definitely reads *up* rather than *at*. The *u* was partially overwritten, which permitted it to be interpreted as an *a*."

d. The Printer's Manuscript has "feeling," which has been retained in subsequent editions. Skousen, *Analysis of the Textual Variants*, 1:187, notes that it should be "pressing," based on both the original manuscript and the lack of any similar use of "feeling their way."

many were lost from his view—wandering in strange roads. ³³And great was the multitude that did enter into that strange building. And after that they did enter into that building, they did point the finger of scorn at me and those that were partaking of the fruit also. But we heeded them not[a] ³⁴(these are the words of my father). For as many as heeded them had fallen away.

³⁵And Laman and Lemuel partook not of the fruit (saith my father).[b]

³⁶And it came to pass that after my father had spoken all the words of his dream (or vision), which were many, he said unto us (because of these things which he saw in a vision) he exceedingly feared for Laman and Lemuel. Yea, he feared lest they should be cast off from the presence of the Lord. ³⁷And he did exhort them, then, with all the feeling of a tender parent, that they would hearken to his words—in that perhaps the Lord would be merciful to them and not cast them off. Yea, my father did preach unto them. ³⁸And after that he had preached unto them, and also prophesied unto them of many things, he bade them to keep the commandments of the Lord. And he did cease speaking unto them.

[9] ¹And all these things did my father see, and hear, and speak, as he dwelt in a tent in the valley of Lemuel—and also a great many more things which cannot be written upon these plates.[c]

> ²And now, as I have spoken concerning these plates—behold, they are not the plates upon which I make a full account of the history of my people. For the plates upon which I make a full account of my people I have given the name of Nephi. Wherefore, they are called the plates of Nephi (after mine own name).

And these plates also are called the plates of Nephi. ³Nevertheless, I have received a commandment of the Lord that I should make these plates for the special purpose that there should be an account engraven of the ministry of my people. ⁴And upon the other plates should be engraven an account of the reign of the kings and the wars and contentions of my people. Wherefore, these plates are for the more part of the ministry, and the other plates are for the more part of the reign of the kings, and the wars, and contentions, of my people.

⁵Wherefore, the Lord hath commanded me to make these plates for a wise purpose in him, which purpose I know not. ⁹But the Lord knoweth all things from the beginning. Wherefore, he prepareth a way to accomplish all his works among the children of men. For behold, he hath all power unto the fulfilling of all his words. And thus it is, Amen.<

---

a. This section appears to be Nephi's summary. Thus, when we see "they did point the finger of scorn at me, and those that were partaking of the fruit also," we should understand that the "me" is Nephi. Nephi recorded that his father had seem him partaking, and this refers to that part of his father's vision.

b. Parentheses are used to parallel the use in the previous sentence as well as to highlight what may have been an intended parallel, indicating what their father said of each of these groups.

c. This verse was intended to be the final verse of chapter II. The use of "dwelt in a tent" marks subdivisions in the story Nephi relates in 1 Nephi. Verses 2 through 9 are an aside that was triggered by the phrase "which cannot be written upon these plates." The mention of "these plates" occasioned an aside to explain what "these plates" meant.

Chapter III [1 Nephi 10–14]

> [10] ¹And now I, Nephi, proceed to give an account upon these plates of my proceedings and my reign and ministry. Wherefore, to proceed with mine account, I must speak somewhat of the things of my father, and also of my brethren.ᵃ<

²For behold, it came to pass that after my father had made an end of speaking the words of his dream (and also of exhorting them to all diligence), he spake unto them concerning the Jews—³how that after they were destroyed (yea, even that great city Jerusalem and that many were carried away captive into Babylon) that, according to the own due time of the Lord, they should return again. Yea, even be brought back out of captivity.

And after they are brought back out of captivity to possess again the land of their inheritance—ᵇ ⁴Yea, even six hundred years from the time that my father left Jerusalem, a prophet would the Lord God raise up among the Jews. Yea, even a Messiah. Or, in other words, a Savior of the world.

⁵And he also spake concerning the prophets, how great a number had testified of these things concerning this Messiah (of which he had spoken), or this Redeemer of the world. ⁶Wherefore, all mankind was in a lost and in a fallen state, and ever would be, save they should rely on this Redeemer.

⁷And he spake also concerning a prophet which should come before the Messiah to prepare the way of the Lord. ⁸Yea, even he should go forth, and cry in the wilderness: "Prepare ye the way of the Lord! And make his paths strait! For there standeth one among you whom ye know not, and he is mightier than I—whose shoe's latchet I am not worthy to unloose."ᶜ And much spake my father concerning this thing.

⁹And my father saith that he should baptize in Bethabara beyond Jordan. And he also spake that he should baptize with water. Yea, even that he should baptize the Messiah with water. ¹⁰And after that he had baptized the Messiah with water he should behold and bear record that he had baptized the Lamb of Godᵈ, which should take away the sins of the world.

¹¹And it came to pass that after my father had spoken these words, he spake unto my brethren concerning the gospel, which should be preached among the Jews. And also concerning the dwindling of the Jews in unbelief. And, after that they had slain the

---

a. Nephi had not intended to end the chapter where it did. The end was required by the testificatory amen. (Details for this type of chapter ending are discussed in Chapter 6 of *Engraven Upon Plates*. To return to his story, Nephi picked up the theme of the plates and what he intended for them. He noted that while he is telling his own story, it first required that he finish with his father's story.

b. This has been left as an incomplete sentence, although it is technically complete. The problem is that based on the way the sentence is constructed, it would seem that the Messiah would come six hundred years after the Jews returned to Jerusalem. That is not correct, and the correct timing is in the final phrase. By separating them, it decreases any confusion about the timing.

c. The ultimate reference here is: "The voice of him that crieth in the wilderness, Prepare ye the way of the Lord, make straight in the desert a highway for our God" (Isaiah 40:3). However, that text was picked up in Matthew 3:3, Mark 1:3, and Luke 3:4, and it was placed in the context of John the Baptist. It is that New Testament context that the "shoe's latchet" is a part of. See Mark 1:7, Luke 3:16, and John 1:27. Verse 9 suggests that John 1:27–28 is the actual source.

d. The phrase "Lamb of God" is from John 1:29.

Messiah (which should come), and after that he had been slain—he should rise from the dead and should make himself manifest by the Holy Ghost unto the Gentiles.

¹²Yea, even my father spake much concerning the Gentiles, and also concerning the house of Israel, that they should be compared like unto an olive tree, whose branches should be broken off and should be scattered upon all the face of the earth.[a] ¹³Wherefore, he said it must needs be that we should be led with one accord into the land of promise, unto the fulfilling of the word of the Lord that we should be scattered upon all the face of the earth.

¹⁴And after that the house of Israel should be scattered, they should be gathered together again, or in fine, that after the Gentiles had received the fullness of the gospel, the natural branches of the olive tree (or the remnants of the house of Israel) should be grafted in[b] (or come to the knowledge of the true Messiah, their Lord and their Redeemer). ¹⁵And after this manner of language did my father prophesy and speak unto my brethren. And also many more things which I do not write in this book. For I have written as many of them as were expedient for me in mine other book. ¹⁶And all these things of which I have spoken, was done as my father dwelt in a tent in the valley of Lemuel.

¹⁷And it came to pass that after I, Nephi, having heard all the words of my father concerning the things which he saw in a vision (and also the things which he spake by the power of the Holy Ghost, which power he received by faith on the Son of God, and the Son of God was the Messiah which should come).[c]

And it came to pass that I, Nephi, was desirous also that I might see, and hear, and know of these things, by the power of the Holy Ghost >(which is the gift of God unto all those who diligently seek him, as well in times of old as in the time that he should manifest himself unto the children of men. ¹⁸For he is the same yesterday, today, and forever[d]).[e]

>And the way is prepared [for all men[f]] from the foundation of the world, if it so be that they repent and come unto him. ¹⁹For he that diligently seeketh shall find, and the mysteries of God[g] shall be unfolded unto them by the power of the Holy Ghost—as well in this time as in times of old, and as well in times of old as in times to come. Wherefore, the course of the Lord is one eternal round. ²⁰Therefore, remember, O man, for all thy doings thou shalt be brought into judgment. ²¹Wherefore, if ye have sought to do wickedly in the days of your probation, then ye are found unclean before the Judgment Seat of God. And no unclean thing can dwell with

---

a. Language has similarities to Romans 11:16–20.

b. Echoes language from Romans 11:21–24.

c. As with other cases with "having," the verb tense grammatically requires a concluding verb that is not present. In this case, the text in parentheses was expanding on what Lehi had said, and that thread of thought led to the concluding idea that the Son of God was the Messiah which should come. That is important information, but it isn't the intent from the beginning of the sentence. That intent is picked up with the "and it came to pass." The intent was to introduce what Lehi saw in a vision, and then move to Nephi's desire to see the same thing.

d. See Hebrews 13:8.

e. This aside begins with the extrapolation of the information on the Holy Ghost. The mention that it is God's gift led to the discussion of God.

f. Restored from the Original Manuscript per Skousen, *Analysis of the Textual Variants*, 1:209.

g. The phrase "mystery of God" appears in 1 Corinthians 4:1, Colossians 2:2, and Revelation 10:7.

God.[a] Wherefore, ye must be cast off forever. ²²And the Holy Ghost giveth authority that I should speak these things and deny them not.[b]<

[11] ¹For it came to pass that after I had desired to know the things that my father had seen (and believing that the Lord was able to make them known unto me), wherefore, as I sat pondering in mine heart I was caught away in the spirit of the Lord—yea, into an exceeding high mountain which I never had before seen, and upon which I never had before sat my foot.

²And the spirit saith unto me, "Behold, what desirest thou?"

³And I saith: "I desire to behold the things which my father saw."

⁴And the spirit saith unto me: "Believest thou that thy father saw the tree of which he hath spoken?"

⁵And I said: "Yea, thou knowest that I believe all the words of my father."

⁶And when I had spake these words, the spirit cried with a loud voice, saying:

> Hosanna to the Lord, the Most High God! For he is God over all the earth, yea, even above all. And blessed art thou, Nephi, because thou believest in the Son of the Most High God. Wherefore, thou shalt behold the things which thou hast desired.
>
> ⁷And behold, this thing shall be given unto thee for a sign, that after thou hast beheld the tree which bore the fruit (which thy father tasted), thou shalt also behold a man descending out of heaven. And him shall ye witness. And after that ye have witnessed him, ye shall bear record that it is the Son of God.

⁸And it came to pass that the spirit saith unto me: "Look."

And I looked, and beheld a tree. And it was like unto the tree which my father had seen. And the beauty thereof was far beyond, yea, exceeding of all beauty. And the whiteness thereof did exceed the whiteness of the driven snow.

⁹And it came to pass that after that I had seen the tree, I said unto the spirit: "I behold thou hast shown unto me the tree which is [most[c]] precious above all."

¹⁰And he saith unto me: "What desirest thou?"

¹¹And I said unto him: "To know the interpretation thereof."

> For I spake unto him as a man speaketh. For I beheld that he was in the form of a man. Yet nevertheless, I knew that it was the spirit of the Lord. And he spake unto me as a man speaketh with another.[d]<

¹²And it came to pass that he said unto me: "Look."

And I looked as if to look upon him and I saw him not, for he had gone from before my presence.

¹³And it came to pass that I looked—and beheld the great city Jerusalem, and also other cities. And I beheld the city of Nazareth. And in the city of Nazareth, I beheld a virgin. And she was exceeding fair and white.

---

a. Some of the themes appear in Ephesians 5:5: "For this ye know, that no whoremonger, nor unclean person, nor covetous man, who is an idolater, hath any inheritance in the kingdom of Christ and of God."

b. This is an aside marked by the repetitive resumption of the idea that Nephi wanted to know about his father's dream/vision. It was triggered by the mention of the Holy Ghost and turns to a description of the function of the Holy Ghost, which is tangential to the planned text.

c. Restored from the Original Manuscript per Skousen, *Analysis of the Textual Variants*, 1:226.

d. This is a very short aside. Although it is marked with the repetitive resumption of speaking as a man speaketh, it is an aside that deviates from the dialogue characterizing the rest of this section.

Chapter III [1 Nephi 10–14]

¹⁴And it came to pass that I saw the heavens open. And an angel came down and stood before me.

And he saith unto me: "Nephi, what beholdest thou?"

¹⁵And I saith unto him: "A virgin most beautiful and fair, above all other virgins."

¹⁶And he saith unto me: "Knowest thou the condescension of God?"

¹⁷And I said unto him: "I know that he loveth his children. Nevertheless, I do not know the meaning of all things."

¹⁸And he said unto me: "Behold, the virgin which thou seest is the mother of God, after the manner of the flesh."

¹⁹And it came to pass that I beheld that she was carried away in the spirit. And after that she had been carried away in the spirit for the space of a time, the angel spake unto me saying: "Look."

²⁰And I looked—and beheld the virgin again, bearing a child in her arms.

²¹And the angel said unto me: "Behold the Lamb of God![a] Yea, even the Eternal Father. Knowest thou the meaning of the tree which thy father saw?"

²²And I answered him, saying: "Yea, it is the love of God, which shedeth itself abroad in the hearts of the children of men.[b] Wherefore, it is the most desirable above all things."

²³And he spake unto me, saying: "Yea, and the most joyous to the soul!"

²⁴And after that he had said these words, he said unto me: "Look."

And I looked—and I beheld the Son of God, a-going forth among the children of men. And I saw many fall down at his feet and worship him.

²⁵And it came to pass that I beheld that the rod of iron (which my father had seen), was the word of God, which led to the fountain of living waters (or to the tree of life), which waters are a representation of the love of God. And I also beheld that the tree of life was a representation of the love of God.

²⁶And the angel said unto me again: "Look! And behold the condescension of God."

²⁷And I looked—and beheld the Redeemer of the world, of which my father had spoken. And I also beheld the prophet, which should prepare the way before him. And the Lamb of God[c] went forth and was baptized of him. And after that he was baptized, I beheld the heavens open, and the Holy Ghost come down out of heaven, and abode upon him in the form of a dove.[d]

²⁸And I beheld that he went forth, ministering unto the people in power, and great glory. And the multitudes were gathered together to hear him.

And I beheld that they cast him out from among them.

²⁹And I also beheld twelve others following him.

And it came to pass that they were carried away in the spirit from before my face, that I saw them not.

³⁰And it came to pass that the angel spake unto me again, saying: "Look."

And I looked—and I beheld the heavens open again. And I saw angels descending upon the children of men. And they did minister unto them.

---

a. The phrase "Lamb of God" is from John 1:29.

b. See Romans 5:5: "And hope maketh not ashamed; because the love of God is shed abroad in our hearts by the Holy Ghost which is given unto us."

c. The phrase "Lamb of God" is from John 1:29.

d. Referencing John 1:32: "And John bare record, saying, I saw the Spirit descending from heaven like a dove, and it abode upon him."

³¹And he spake unto me again, saying: "Look."

And I looked—and I beheld the Lamb of God[a] going forth among the children of men. And I beheld multitudes of people which were sick, and which were afflicted of all manner of diseases, and with devils, and unclean spirits. And the angel spake and showed all these things unto me. And they were healed by the power of the Lamb of God.[b] And the devils and the unclean spirits were cast out.

³²And it came to pass that the angel spake unto me again, saying: "Look."

And I looked—and beheld the Lamb of God[c], that he was taken by the people. Yea, the everlasting God was judged of the world. And I saw, and bear record.

³³And I, Nephi, saw that he was lifted up upon the cross and slain for the sins of the world.

³⁴And after that he was slain, I saw the multitudes of the earth, that they were gathered together to fight against the apostles of the Lamb (for thus were the twelve called by the angel of the Lord). ³⁵And the multitude of the earth was gathered together. And I beheld that they were in a large and a spacious building, like unto the building which my father saw.

And the angel of the Lord spake unto me again, saying: "Behold the world and the wisdom thereof! Yea, behold, the house of Israel hath gathered together to fight against the twelve apostles of the Lamb."

³⁶And it came to pass that I saw and bear record that the great and spacious building was the pride of the world. And [the fall[d]] thereof was exceeding great.

And the angel of the Lord spake unto me again, saying: "Thus shall be the destruction of all nations, kindreds, tongues, and people that shall fight against the twelve apostles of the Lamb."

[12] ¹And it came to pass that the angel said unto me: "Look, and behold thy seed. And also the seed of thy brethren."

And I looked—and beheld the land of promise. And I beheld multitudes of people, yea, even as it were in number as many as the sand of the sea.

²And it came to pass that I beheld multitudes gathered together to battle one against the other. And I beheld wars and rumors of wars[e], and great slaughters with the sword among my people.

³And it came to pass that I beheld many generations pass away after the manner of wars and contentions in the land. And I beheld many cities, yea, even that I did not number them.

⁴And it came to pass that I saw a mist of darkness on the face of the land of promise.

And I saw lightnings.

And I heard thunderings, and earthquakes, and all manner of tumultuous noises.

And I saw the earth, and the rocks, that they rent.

And I saw mountains tumbling into pieces.

And I saw the plains of the earth, that they were broken up.

---

a. The phrase "Lamb of God" is from John 1:29.

b. The phrase "Lamb of God" is from John 1:29.

c. The phrase "Lamb of God" is from John 1:29.

d. The Printer's Manuscript and subsequent printed editions have "it fell, and the fall," but the Original Manuscript has only "and the fall." See Skousen, *Analysis of the Textual Variants*, 1:237–38.

e. Uses language from Matthew 24:6: "And ye shall hear of wars and rumours of wars."

CHAPTER III [1 NEPHI 10–14]

And I saw many cities, that they were sunk.
And I saw many, that they were burned with fire.
And I saw many, that they did tumble to the earth, because of the quaking thereof.

⁵And it came to pass that after I saw these things, I saw the vapor of darkness, that it passed from off the face of the earth.

And behold, I saw [the] multitudes which had [not^a] fallen because of the great and terrible judgments of the Lord.

⁶And I saw the heavens open, and the Lamb of God^b descending out of heaven. And he came down and showed himself unto them.

⁷And I also saw, and bear record, that the Holy Ghost fell upon twelve others. And they were ordained of God, and chosen.

⁸And the angel spake unto me, saying: "Behold the twelve disciples of the Lamb, which are chosen to minister unto thy seed." ⁹And he saith unto me: "Thou remembereth the twelve apostles of the Lamb? Behold, they are they which shall judge the twelve tribes of Israel. Wherefore, the twelve ministers of thy seed shall be judged of them, for ye are of the house of Israel. ¹⁰And these twelve ministers which thou beholdest shall judge thy seed. And behold, they are righteous forever. For, because of their faith in the Lamb of God^c, their garments are made white in his blood."

¹¹And the angel saith unto me: "Look."

And I looked—and beheld three generations did pass away in righteousness. And their garments were white, like even like unto the Lamb of God^d.

And the angel said unto me: "These are made white in the blood of the Lamb because of their faith in him."

¹²And I, Nephi, also saw many of the fourth generation which did pass away in righteousness.

¹³And it came to pass that I saw the multitudes of the earth gathered together.

¹⁴And the angel said unto me: "Behold thy seed and also the seed of thy brethren."

¹⁵And it came to pass that I looked—and beheld the people of my seed gathered together in multitudes against the seed of my brethren. And they were gathered together to battle.

¹⁶And the angel spake unto me, saying:

Behold the fountain of filthy water (which thy father saw), yea, even the river of which he spake. And the depths thereof are the depths of hell. ¹⁷And the mists of darkness are the temptations of the devil, which blindeth the eyes and hardeneth the hearts of the children of men, and leadeth them away into broad roads—that they may perish and are lost.

¹⁸And the large and spacious building which thy father saw is vain imaginations and the pride of the children of men. And a great and a terrible gulf divideth

---

a. Insertions in brackets were in the Original Manuscript but were not copied to the Printer's Manuscript. Skousen, *Analysis of the Textual Variants*, 1:248. While the inserted "not" is in the current edition, the inserted "the" before "multitudes" is not.

b. The phrase "Lamb of God" is from John 1:29.

c. The phrase "Lamb of God" is from John 1:29.

d. The phrase "Lamb of God" is from John 1:29.

them, yea, even the [sword[a]] of the justice of the Eternal God and Jesus Christ[b] —which is the Lamb of God[c] of whom the Holy Ghost beareth record from the beginning of the world until this time, and from this time hence forth and forever.

[19]And while the angel spoke these words, I beheld—and saw that the seed of my brethren did contend against my seed, according to the word of the angel. And because of the pride of my seed and the temptations of the devil, I beheld that the seed of my brethren did overpower the people of my seed.

[20]And it came to pass that I beheld—and saw the people of the seed of my brethren, that they had overcome my seed. And they went forth in multitudes upon the face of the land. [21]And I saw them gathered together in multitudes. And I saw wars and rumors of wars[d] among them. And in wars and rumors of wars[e], I saw many generations pass away.

[22]And the angel said unto me: "Behold, these shall dwindle in unbelief."

[23]And it came to pass that I beheld that, after they had dwindled in unbelief, they became a dark, and loathsome, and a filthy people—full of idleness and all manner of abominations.

[13] [1]And it came to pass that the angel spake unto me, saying: "Look."

And I looked—and beheld many nations and kingdoms.

[2]And the angel saith unto me: "What beholdest thou?"

And I said: "I behold many nations and kingdoms."

[3]And he saith unto me: "These are the nations and kingdoms of the Gentiles."

[4]And it came to pass that I saw among the nations of the Gentiles the foundation of a great church.

[5]And the angel said unto me: "Behold the foundation of a church (which is most abominable above all other churches) which slayeth the saints of God. Yea, and tortureth them, and bindeth them down, and yoketh them with a yoke of iron, and bringeth them down into captivity."

[6]And it came to pass that I beheld this great and abominable church. And I saw the devil, that he was the founder of it. [7]And I also saw gold, and silver, and silks, and scarlets, and fine twined linen, and all manner of precious clothing. And I saw many harlots.

[8]And the angel spake unto me, saying: "Behold the gold and the silver, and the silks and the scarlets, and the fine twined linen and the precious clothing[f], and harlots[g]—are

---

a. The Printer's Manuscript has "word," but the Original Manuscript reads "sword." Skousen, *Analysis of the Textual Variants*, 1:258.

b. This sentence is difficult because it expects that the "sword of justice" is the clarification of what creates the terrible gulf dividing the children of men. That "sword of justice" belongs to the Eternal God and Jesus Christ. The "and" between Eternal God and Jesus Christ makes it appear that there are two entities. However, in other passages (most famously in the Title Page), the Eternal God is Jesus Christ. See also 2 Ne. 26:12: "Jesus is the Christ, the Eternal God." For these reasons, the two designations are kept together to attempt to ameliorate any possible confusion.

c. The phrase "Lamb of God" is from John 1:29.

d. Uses language from Matthew 24:6: "And ye shall hear of wars and rumours of wars."

e. Uses language from Matthew 24:6: "And ye shall hear of wars and rumours of wars."

f. Echoes language from Revelation 18:12 "The merchandise of gold, and silver, and precious stones, and of pearls, and fine linen, and purple, and silk, and scarlet."

g. These are intentional pairings (gold/silver, silks/scarlets, fine-twined linen/precious clothing), hence the lack of commas in the pairs.

Chapter III [1 Nephi 10–14]

the desires of this great and abominable church. ⁹And also, for the praise of the world do they destroy the saints of God and bring them down into captivity."

¹⁰And it came to pass that I looked—and beheld many waters. And they divided the Gentiles from the seed of my brethren.

¹¹And it came to pass that the angel saith unto me: "Behold. The wrath of God is upon the seed of thy brethren."

¹²And I looked—and beheld a man among the Gentiles (which was separated from the seed of my brethren by the many waters). And I beheld the spirit of God, that it came down and and wrought upon the man. And he went forth upon the many waters, even unto the seed of my brethren (which were in the promised land).

¹³And it came to pass that I beheld the spirit of God, that it wrought upon other Gentiles. And they went forth out of captivity upon the many waters.

¹⁴And it came to pass that I beheld many multitudes of the Gentiles upon the land of promise. And I beheld the wrath of God, that it was upon the seed of my brethren. And they were scattered before the Gentiles. And they were smitten.

¹⁵And I beheld the spirit of the Lord, that it was upon the Gentiles, that they did prosper and obtain the land for their inheritance. And I beheld that they were white and exceeding fair, and beautiful like unto my people (before that they were slain).

¹⁶And it came to pass that I, Nephi, beheld that the Gentiles (which had gone forth out of captivity) did humble themselves before the Lord. And the power of the Lord was with them. ¹⁷And I beheld that their mother Gentiles was, with them, gathered together upon the waters, and upon the land also—to battle against them. ¹⁸And I beheld that the power of God was with them. And also that the wrath of God was upon all them that were gathered together against them to battle. ¹⁹And I, Nephi, beheld that the Gentiles (which had gone out of captivity) were delivered by the power of God out of the hands of all other nations.

²⁰And it came to pass that I, Nephi, beheld that they did prosper in the land. And I beheld a book, and it was carried forth among them.

²¹And the angel saith unto me: "Knowest thou the meaning of the book?"

²²And I [saith:ᵃ] "I know not."

²³And he saith unto me: "Behold, it proceedeth out of the mouth of a Jew."

And I, Nephi, beheld it.

And he saith unto me: "The book which thou beholdest is a record of the Jews, which contains the covenants of the Lord (which he hath made unto the house of Israel). And it also containeth many of the prophesies of the holy prophets. And it is a record, like unto the engravings which are upon the plates of brass, save there are not so many. Nevertheless, they contain the covenants of the Lord which he hath made unto the house of Israel. Wherefore, they are of great worth unto the Gentiles."

²⁴And the angel of the Lord said unto me:

> Thou hast beheld that the book proceeded forth from the mouth of a Jew. And when it proceeded forth from the mouth of a Jew, it contained the [fullnessᵇ]

---

a. Oliver Cowdery added "unto him" in the Printer's Manuscript, but it is not present in the Original Manuscript. It has been removed here. See Skousen, *Analysis of the Textual Variants,* 1:272.

b. The Printer's Manuscript has "planeness," but the Original Manuscript has "fullness," hence it is restored here. See Skousen, *Analysis of the Textual Variants,* 1:275.

of the gospel of the Lord[a], of whom the twelve apostles bear record. And they bear record, according to the truth (which is in the Lamb of God[b]). [5]Wherefore, these things go forth from the Jews in purity unto the Gentiles, according to the truth which is in God.

[26]And after that they go forth by the hand of the twelve apostles of the Lamb (from the Jews unto the Gentiles), behold, after this, thou seest the foundation of a great and abominable church (which is the most abominable, above all other churches). For behold, they have taken away from the gospel of the Lamb many parts which are plain and most precious. And also many covenants of the Lord have they taken away. [27]And all this have they done, that they might pervert the right ways of the Lord—that they might blind the eyes and harden the hearts of the children of men. [28]Wherefore, thou seest that after the book hath gone forth through the hands of the great and abominable church, that there are many plain and precious things taken away from the book, which is the book of the Lamb of God[c].

[29]And after that these plain and [most[d]] precious things were taken away, it goeth forth unto all the nations of the Gentiles. And after it goeth forth unto all the nations of the Gentiles, yea, even across the many waters (which thou hast seen with the Gentiles, which have gone forth out of captivity)—and thou seest, because of the many plain and precious things which have been taken out of the book (which were plain unto the understanding of the children of men, according to the plainness which is in the Lamb of God[e])—and because of these things which are taken away out of the Gospel of the Lamb, an exceeding great many do stumble, yea, insomuch that Satan hath great power over them.[f]

[30]Nevertheless, thou beholdest that the Gentiles which have gone forth out of captivity, and have been lifted up by the power of God above all other nations upon the face of the land (which is choice above all other lands, which is the land which the Lord God hath covenanted with thy father that his seed should have for the land of their inheritance)[g]— Wherefore, thou seest that the Lord God will not suffer that the Gentiles will utterly destroy the mixture of thy seed which is among thy brethren.

[31]Neither will he suffer that the Gentiles shall destroy the seed of thy brethren. [32]Neither will the Lord God suffer that the Gentiles shall forever remain in that awful state of woundedness (which thou beholdest that they are in, because of the plain and most precious parts of the Gospel of the Lamb, which hath been kept

---

a. The Original Manuscript has "land," which is clearly incorrect. Although the Printer's Manuscript changes it to a logical "Lord," Skousen emends this to "Lamb." He notes that there are four subsequent occurrences of "gospel of the Lamb," making this most likely the correct reading.

b. The phrase "Lamb of God" is from John 1:29.

c. The phrase "Lamb of God" is from John 1:29.

d. Added from the Original Manuscript, per Skousen, *Analysis of the Textual Variants,* 1:283.

e. The phrase "Lamb of God" is from John 1:29.

f. This very long sentence is created because internal clauses require the use of repetitive resumption—twice—to complete the whole idea.

g. This is an incomplete sentence. It might see a type of resolution if the next sentence were added (beginning with "wherefore"), but it would remain a difficult and incomplete idea. Also, "wherefore" typically begins a sentence. The number of clauses is the reason for the incompletion, and particularly the aside marked with parentheses.

CHAPTER III [1 NEPHI 10–14]

back by that abominable church, whose formation thou hast seen). ³³Wherefore, saith the Lamb of God[a]: "I will be merciful unto the Gentiles, unto the visiting of the remnant of the house of Israel in great judgment."

³⁴And it came to pass that the angel of the Lord spake unto me, saying:

³⁵Behold, saith the Lamb of God[b]: After that I have visited the remnant of the house of Israel (and this remnant of which I speak is the seed of thy father)[c], wherefore, after that I have visited them in judgment, and smitten them by the hand of the Gentiles, and after that the Gentiles do stumble exceedingly because of the most plain and precious parts of the gospel of the Lamb, which hath been kept back by that abominable church (which is the mother of harlots, saith the Lamb).[d] Wherefore, I will be merciful unto the Gentiles in that day (saith the Lamb), insomuch that I will bring forth unto them, in mine own power, much of my gospel, which shall be plain and precious (saith the Lamb). For behold (saith the Lamb), I will manifest myself unto thy seed, that they shall write many things which I shall minister unto them, which shall be plain and precious.

And after that thy seed shall be destroyed and dwindle in unbelief (and also the seed of thy brethren), behold, these things shall be hid up—to come forth unto the Gentiles by the gift and power of the Lamb. ³⁶And in them shall be written my gospel (saith the Lamb), and my rock, and my salvation.

³⁷And blessed are they which shall seek to bring forth my Zion at that day. For they shall have the gift and the power of the Holy Ghost. And if they endure unto the end they shall be lifted up at the last day, and shall be saved in the everlasting kingdom of the Lamb. Yea, whoso shall publish peace, that shall publish tidings of great joy—how beautiful upon the mountains shall they be!

³⁸And it came to pass that I beheld the remnant of the seed of my brethren, and also the book of the Lamb of God[e] which had proceeded forth from the mouth of the Jew. And I beheld that it came forth from the Gentiles unto the remnant of the seed of my brethren. ³⁹And after it had come forth unto them, I beheld other books which came forth by the power of the Lamb (from the Gentiles) unto them—unto the convincing of the Gentiles and the remnant of the seed of my brethren and also to the Jews which were scattered upon all the face of the earth—that the records of the prophets and of the twelve apostles of the Lamb are true.

⁴⁰And the angel spake unto me, saying:

These last records, which thou hast seen among the Gentiles, shall establish the truth of the first (which is of the twelve apostles of the Lamb), and shall make known the plain and precious things which have been taken away from them—and shall make known unto all kindreds, tongues, and people that the Lamb of God[f] is

---

a. The phrase "Lamb of God" is from John 1:29.

b. The phrase "Lamb of God" is from John 1:29.

c. This aside (marked with parentheses) has interrupted the flow of the sentence and left it incomplete. The attempt to correct this has a repetition of visiting with judgement.

d. Another incomplete sentence. It has been left without resolution, beginning the next sentence with "Wherefore," which typically begins sentences.

e. The phrase "Lamb of God" is from John 1:29.

f. The phrase "Lamb of God" is from John 1:29.

the Eternal Father, and the Savior of the world. And that all men must come unto him or they cannot be saved. ⁴¹And they must come, according to the words which shall be established by the mouth of the Lamb. And the words of the Lamb shall be made known in the records of thy seed as well as in the records of the twelve apostles of the Lamb. Wherefore, they both shall be established in one.

For there is one God, and one shepherd, over all the earth. ⁴¹And the time cometh that he shall manifest himself unto all nations, both unto the Jews and also unto the Gentiles. And after that he hath manifested himself unto the Jews and also unto the Gentiles, then he shall manifest himself unto the Gentiles and also unto the Jews. And the last shall be first, and the first shall be last.[a]

[14] ¹And it shall come to pass that if the Gentiles shall hearken unto the Lamb of God[b] in that day, that he shall manifest himself unto them in word and also in power, in very deed—unto the taking away of their stumbling blocks, ²if it so be that they harden not their hearts against the Lamb.[c]

And if it so be that they harden not their hearts against the Lamb of God[d], they shall be numbered among the seed of thy father. Yea, they shall be numbered among the house of Israel. And they shall be a blessed people upon the promised land forever. They shall be no more brought down into captivity. And the house of Israel shall no more be confounded.

³And that great pit, which hath been digged for them by that great and abominable church (which was founded by the devil and his children, that he might lead away the souls of men down to hell), yea, that great pit which hath been digged for the destruction of men—shall be filled by those who digged it, unto their utter destruction (saith the Lamb of God[e])—not the destruction of the soul, save it be the casting of it into that hell which hath no end. ⁴For behold, this is according to the captivity of the devil, and also according to the justice of God upon all those who will work wickedness and abomination before him.

⁵And it came to pass that the angel spake unto me, Nephi, saying:

Thou hast beheld that if the Gentiles repent, it shall be well with them. And thou also knowest concerning the covenants of the Lord unto the house of Israel. And thou also hast heard that whoso repenteth not must perish. ⁶Therefore, wo be unto the Gentiles, if it so be that they harden their hearts against the Lamb of God[f]! ⁷For the time cometh (saith the Lamb of God[g]) that I will work a great and a marvelous work among the children of men[h]—a work which shall be everlasting—either on the one hand or on the other, either to the convincing of them unto peace and life eternal, or unto the deliverance of them to the hardness of their hearts and

---

a. The allusion of "last shall be first" is to Mark 10:31 and Luke 13:30.

b. The phrase "Lamb of God" is from John 1:29.

c. The versification does not match with the modern text because Joseph Smith removed some of this text and made other small modifications in the 1837 edition.

d. The phrase "Lamb of God" is from John 1:29.

e. The phrase "Lamb of God" is from John 1:29.

f. The phrase "Lamb of God" is from John 1:29.

g. The phrase "Lamb of God" is from John 1:29.

h. Reference to Isaiah 29:14: "Therefore, behold, I will proceed to do a marvellous work among this people, even a marvellous work and a wonder."

Chapter III [1 Nephi 10–14]

the blindness of their minds—unto their being brought down into captivity and also unto destruction, both temporally and spiritually, according to the captivity of the devil of which I have spoken.

⁸And it came to pass that when the angel had spoken these words, he saith unto me: "Remember thou the covenants of the Father unto the house of Israel?"

I saith unto him: "Yea."

⁹And it came to pass that he saith unto me, "Look, and behold that great and abominable church, which is the mother of abominations[a], whose [foundation[b]] is the devil."

¹⁰And he saith unto me: "Behold, there is save it be two churches. The one is the church of the Lamb of God[c], and the other is the church of the devil. Wherefore, whoso belongeth not to the church of the Lamb of God[d] belongeth to that great church, which is the mother of abominations. And she is the whore of all the earth."

¹¹And it came to pass that I looked—and beheld the whore of all the earth. And she sat upon many waters[e], and she had dominion over all the earth, among all nations, kindreds, tongues, and people[f].

¹²And it came to pass that I beheld the church of the Lamb of God[g]. And its numbers were few, because of the wickedness and abominations of the whore which sat upon many waters. Nevertheless, I beheld that the church of the Lamb, which were the saints of God, were also upon all the face of the earth. And their dominion upon the face of the earth were small because of the wickedness of the great whore which I saw.

¹³And it came to pass that I beheld that the great mother of abominations did gather together in multitudes upon the face of all the earth, among all the nations of the Gentiles, to fight against the Lamb of God[h].

¹⁴And it came to pass that I, Nephi, beheld the power of the Lamb of the God[i], that it descended upon the saints of the church of the Lamb, and upon the covenant people of the Lord (which were scattered upon all the face of the earth). And they were armed with righteousness, and with the power of God, in great glory.

¹⁵And it came to pass that I beheld that the wrath of God was poured out upon the great and abominable church, insomuch that there were wars and rumors of wars[j] among all the nations and kindreds of the earth.

¹⁶And as there began to be wars and rumors of wars[k] among all the nations which belonged to the mother of abominations, the angel spake unto me, saying:

---

a. See Revelation 17:5: "And upon her forehead *was* a name written, Mystery, Babylon the Great, the Mother of Harlots and Abominations of the Earth."

b. This edition has restored "foundation" from the Original Manuscript, per Skousen, *Analysis of the Textual Variants*, 1:306.

c. The phrase "Lamb of God" is from John 1:29.

d. The phrase "Lamb of God" is from John 1:29.

e. Uses language from Revelation 17:1: "I will shew unto thee the judgment of the great whore that sitteth upon many waters."

f. Compare Revelation 17:15: "The waters which thou sawest, where the whore sitteth, are peoples, and multitudes, and nations, and tongues."

g. The phrase "Lamb of God" is from John 1:29.

h. The phrase "Lamb of God" is from John 1:29.

i. The phrase "Lamb of God" is from John 1:29.

j. Uses language from Matthew 24:6: "And ye shall hear of wars and rumours of wars."

k. Uses language from Matthew 24:6: "And ye shall hear of wars and rumours of wars."

Behold! The wrath of God is upon the mother of harlots. And behold, thou seest all these things. ¹⁷And when the day cometh that the wrath of God is poured out upon the mother of harlots (which is the great and abominable church of all the earth, whose founder is the devil), then at that day, the work of the Father shall commence in preparing the way for the fulfilling of his covenants which he hath made to his people, which are of the house of Israel.

¹⁸And it came to pass that the angel spake unto me, saying: "Look."
¹⁹And I looked—and beheld a man. And he was dressed in a white robe.
²⁰And the angel said unto me:

Behold one of the twelve apostles of the Lamb. ²¹Behold, he shall see, and write, the remainder of these things, yea, and also many things which have been. ²²And he shall also write concerning the end of the world. ²³Wherefore, the things which he shall write are just and true.

And behold, they are written in the book which thou beheld proceeding out of the mouth of the Jew. And at the time they proceeded out of the mouth of the Jew (or at the time the book proceeded out of the mouth of the Jew) the things which were written were plain and pure, and most precious, and easy to the understanding of all men.

²⁴And behold, the things which this apostle of the Lamb shall write are many things which thou hast seen. And behold the remainder shalt thou see. ²⁵But the things which thou shalt see hereafter, thou shalt not write. For the Lord God hath ordained the apostle of the Lamb of God[a], that he should write them, ²⁶And also others which have been. To them hath he shown all things. And they have written them. And they are sealed up to come forth in their purity (according to the truth which is in the Lamb in the own due time of the Lord) unto the house of Israel.

²⁷And I, Nephi, heard, and bear record, that the name of the apostle of the Lamb was John, according to the word of the angel.

²⁸And behold, I, Nephi, am forbidden that I should write the remainder of the things which I saw [b]. Wherefore, the things which I have written sufficeth me. And I have not written but a small part of the things which I saw. ²⁹And I bear record that I saw the things which my father saw. And the angel of the Lord did make them known unto me.

³⁰And now, I make an end of speaking concerning the things which I saw while I was carried away in the Spirit. And if all the things which I saw are not written, the things which I have written are true. And thus it is, Amen.

---

a. The phrase "Lamb of God" is from John 1:29.
b. Oliver Cowdery added "and heard" at the end of the sentence. Removed to conform to the Original Manuscript. Skousen, *Analysis of the Textual Variants*, 1:310.

Chapter IV [1 Nephi 15]

[15] ¹And it came to pass that after I, Nephi, had been carried away in the spirit, and seen all these things, I returned to the tent of my father.ᵃ

²And it came to pass that I beheld my brethren, and they were disputing one with another concerning the things which my father had spoken unto them. ³For he truly spake many great things unto them, which was hard to be understood, save a man should enquire of the Lord. And they, being hard in their hearts—therefore they did not look unto the Lord as they had ought.

⁴And now I, Nephi, was grieved because of the hardness of their hearts. And also because of the things which I had seen and knew they must unavoidably come to pass because of the great wickedness of the children of men.

⁵And it came to pass that I was overcome because of my afflictions. For I considered that mine afflictions were great above all because of the destruction of my people. For I had beheld their fall.

⁶And it came to pass that after I had received strength, I spake unto my brethren, desiring to know of them the cause of their disputations. ⁷And they said: "Behold, we cannot understand the words of which our father hath spoken, concerning the natural branches of the olive tree, and also concerning the Gentiles.ᵇ"

⁸And I said unto them: "Have ye enquired of the Lord?"

⁹And they said unto me: "We have not. For the Lord maketh no such thing known unto us."

¹⁰Behold, I said unto them:

> How is it that ye do not keep the commandments of the Lord? How is it that ye will perish because of the hardness of your hearts? ¹¹Do ye not remember the things which the Lord hath said?: "If ye will not harden your hearts, and ask me in faith, believing that ye shall receive (with diligence in keeping my commandments), surely these things shall be made known unto you.ᶜ"
>
> ¹²Behold, I say unto you that the house of Israel was compared unto an olive tree by the spirit of the Lord (which was in our [fatherᵈ]). And behold, and are we not broken off from the house of Israel? And are we not a branch of the house of Israel?
>
> ¹³And now the thing which our father meaneth concerning the grafting in of the natural branches through the fullness of the Gentiles, is that: in the latter days, when our seed shall have dwindled in unbelief (yea, for the space of many years) and many generations after that the Messiah hath manifested himself in body unto the children of men—then shall the fullness of the gospel of the Messiah come unto the Gentiles, and from the Gentiles unto the remnant of our seed.

---

a. The testificatory amen of the previous chapter created an end to the chapter, but it is a logical end. However, the presence of this internal marker of an action at the "tent of my father" raises the question (at least) as to whether Nephi's original conception of his chapters would have had a break at this point. It is possible that the testimony at the end of the previous chapter was an addition, and this verse would have been internal to a chapter rather than the first verse of a chapter.

b. Echoes language from Romans 11:21–24.

c. Echoes Matthew 21:22: "And all things, whatsoever ye shall ask in prayer, believing, ye shall receive."

d. Restored the Original Manuscript's "father," which was made plural in the Printer's Manuscript "fathers." Skousen, *Analysis of the Textual Variants*, 1:318.

¹⁴And at that day shall the remnant of our seed know that they are of the house of Israel and that they are the covenant people of the Lord. And then shall they know, and come to the knowledge of, their forefathers—and also to the knowledge of the gospel of their Redeemer, which was ministered unto their fathers by him. Wherefore, they shall come to the knowledge of their Redeemer and the very points of his doctrine, that may know how to come unto him and be saved.

¹⁵And then at that day will they not rejoice and give praise unto their everlasting God, their rock and their salvation?[a]

Yea, at that day will they not receive strength and nourishment from the true vine?[b]

Yea, will they not come unto the true fold of God?

¹⁶Behold, I say unto you yea, they shall be [numbered[c]] again among the house of Israel. They shall be gathered, grafted in (being a natural branch of the olive tree), into the true olive tree.[d] ¹⁷And this is what our father meaneth.

And he meaneth that it will not come to pass until after that they are scattered by the Gentiles. And he meaneth that it shall come by way of the Gentiles, that the Lord may show his power unto the Gentiles for the very cause that he shall be rejected of the Jews (or of the house of Israel). ¹⁸Wherefore, our father hath not spoken of our seed alone, but also of all the house of Israel, pointing to the covenant which should be fulfilled in the latter days, which covenant the Lord made to our father Abraham, saying: "In thy seed shall all the kindreds of the earth be blessed.[e]"

¹⁹And it came to pass that I, Nephi, spake much unto them concerning these things. Yea, I spake unto them concerning the restoration of the Jews in the latter days. ²⁰And I did rehearse unto them the words of Isaiah, which spake concerning the restoration of the Jews (or of the house of Israel). And after that they were restored, they should no more be confounded, neither should they be scattered again.

²¹And it came to pass that I did speak many words unto my brethren, that they were pacified and did humble themselves before the Lord.

And it came to pass that they did speak unto me again, saying: "What meaneth the thing which of our father saw in a dream? What meaneth the tree, which he saw?"

²²And I said unto them: "It was a representation of the tree of life."

²³And they said unto me: "What meaneth the rod of iron, which our father saw that led to the tree?"

²⁴And I said unto them, that: "It was the word of God. And whoso would hearken unto the word of God, and would hold fast unto it, they would never perish. Neither

---

a. See Psalm 62:2: "He only is my rock and my salvation."

b. Echoes language from John 1:15: "I am the true vine, and my Father is the husbandman."

c. The Original Manuscript reads "numbered," as restored here. The Printer's Manuscript has "remembered," which influenced subsequent editions, including the current. Skousen, *Analysis of the Textual Variants*, 1:321.

d. Echoes language from Romans 11:21–24.

e. See Acts 3:25: "Ye are the children of the prophets, and of the covenant which God made with our fathers, saying unto Abraham, And in thy seed shall all the kindreds of the earth be blessed." Acts is quoting Genesis 22:18: "And in thy seed shall all the nations of the earth be blessed; because thou hast obeyed my voice."

Chapter IV [1 Nephi 15]

could the temptations and the fiery darts of the adversary[a] overpower them unto blindness to lead them away to destruction." ²⁵Wherefore I, Nephi, did exhort them to give heed unto the word of the Lord. Yea, I did exhort them with all the energies of my soul, and with all the faculty which I possessed, that they would give heed to the word of God and remember to keep his commandments always, in all things.

²⁶And they said unto me: "What meaneth the river of water which our father saw?"

²⁷And I said unto them, that: "The water which my father saw was filthiness, and so much was his mind swallowed up in other things that he beheld not the filthiness of the water."

²⁸And I said unto them, that: "It was an awful gulf which separateth the wicked from the tree of life, and also from the saints of God."

²⁹And I said unto them, that: "It was a representation of that awful hell, which the angel said unto me was prepared for the wicked."

³⁰And I said unto them, that: "Our father also saw that the justice of God did also divide the wicked from the righteous. And the brightness thereof was like unto the brightness of a flaming fire, which ascendeth up unto God, forever and ever, and hath no end."

³¹And they said unto me: "Doth this thing mean the torment of the body in the days of probation, or doth it mean the final state of the soul after the death of the temporal [body[b]], or doth it speak of the things which are temporal?"

³²And it came to pass that I said unto them, that:

> It was a representation of things both temporal and spiritual, for the day should come that they must be judged of their works, yea, even the works which were done by the temporal body in their days of probation. ³³Wherefore, if they should die in their wickedness, they must be cast off also as to the things which are spiritual, which are pertaining to righteousness. Wherefore, they must be brought to stand before God, to be judged of their work.
>
> And if their works have been filthiness, they must needs be filthy. And if they be filthy, it must needs be that they cannot dwell in the kingdom of God (if so, the kingdom of God must be filthy also).
>
> ³⁴But behold, I say unto you the kingdom of God is not filthy. And there cannot any unclean thing enter into the kingdom of God.[c] Wherefore, there must needs be a place of filthiness prepared for that which is filthy. And there is a place prepared, yea, even that awful hell of which I have spoken. And the devil is the [preparator[d]] of it. Wherefore, the final state of the souls of men is to dwell in the

---

a. Echoes language from Ephesians 6:16: "Ye shall be able to quench all the fiery darts of the wicked."

b. The Printer's Manuscript has "baby," which is clearly in error. Skousen, *Analysis of the Textual Variants*, has no listing for this change, but teh passage reads "body" in the 1830 edition.

c. Perhaps a reference to 2 Chronicles 23:19, although this verse specifically refers to the temple rather than to the kingdom: "And he set the porters at the gates of the house of the Lord, that none which was unclean in any thing should enter in."

d. Skousen suggests the Original Manuscript might have had "proprietor." In *Analysis of the Textual Variants*, 1:330–31, he notes:

> Oliver Cowdery was not able to figure out the word scribe 2 wrote down in [the Original Manuscript] to describe the devil's connection with hell. Oliver interpreted the word as *preparator*. The 1830 compositor set this word. In his editing for the 1837 edition, Joseph Smith did not like the word *preparator*. He first thought of *father* as a possible replacement and wrote it above the line,

kingdom of God, or to be cast out because of that justice of which I have spoken. ³⁵Wherefore, the wicked are [separated[a]] from the righteous and also from that tree of life whose fruit is most precious and most desirable [of[b]] all other fruits. Yea, and it is the greatest of all the gifts of God.

And thus I spake unto my brethren. Amen.

---

after crossing out *preparator*. Joseph then changed his mind and replaced *father* with *foundation*. In selecting this word, he was probably influenced by the earlier passages in 1 Nephi 13–14 which he had recently edited so that Satan would be the foundation (rather than the founder) of the great and abominable church. The 1981 edition restored the earlier *preparator*.

a. The Printer's Manuscript and all printed editions read "rejected." The Original Manuscript has "separated," which is restored here. Skousen, *Analysis of the Textual Variants*, 1:334.

b. The Printer's Manuscript and all printed editions have "above." The Original Manuscript has "of," which is restored here. Skousen, *Analysis of the Textual Variants*, 1:334.

Chapter V [1 Nephi 16–19:21]

[16] ¹And now it came to pass that after I, Nephi, had made an end of speaking to my brethren, behold they said unto me: "Thou hast declared unto us hard things, more than that which we are able to bear."

²And it came to pass that I said unto them that:

> I knew that I had spoken hard things against the wicked, according to the truth. And the righteous have I justified. And testified that they should be lifted up at the last day. Wherefore, the guilty taketh the truth to be hard, for it cutteth them to the very center.
>
> ³And now my brethren, if ye were righteous, and were willing to hearken to the truth, and give heed unto to it—that ye might walk uprightly before God, then ye would not murmur because of the truth, and say: "Thou speakest hard things against us."

⁴And it came to pass that I, Nephi, did exhort my brethren with all diligence to keep the commandments of the Lord.

⁵And it came to pass that they did humble themselves before the Lord, insomuch that I had joy and great hopes of them, that they would walk in the paths of righteousness.[a]

⁶Now, all these things were said and done as my father dwelt in a tent in the valley which he called Lemuel.

⁷And it came to pass that I, Nephi, took one of the daughters of Ishmael to wife. And also my brethren took of the daughters of Ishmael to wife. And also Zoram took the elder daughter of Ishmael to wife. ⁸And thus my father had fulfilled all the commandments of the Lord which had been given unto him. And also I, Nephi, had been blessed of the Lord exceedingly.

⁹And it came to pass that the voice of the Lord spake unto my father by night and commanded him that on the morrow he should take his journey into the wilderness.

¹⁰And it came to pass that as my father arose in the morning, and went forth to the tent door (and to his great astonishment) he beheld upon the ground a round ball of curious workmanship. And it was of fine brass. And within the ball was two spindles. And the one pointed the way whither we should go into the wilderness.

¹¹And it came to pass that we did gather together whatsoever things we should carry into the wilderness. And all the remainder of our provisions which the Lord had given unto us. And we did take seed of every kind that we might carry into the wilderness.

¹²And it came to pass that we did take our tents and departed into the wilderness, across the river Laman.

¹³And it came to pass that we traveled for the space of four days, nearly a south-southeast direction. And we did pitch our tents again. And we did call the name of the place Shazer.

¹⁴And it came to pass that we did take our bows, and our arrows, and go forth into the wilderness to slay food for our families. And after that we had slain food for our families, we did return again to our families in the wilderness to the place of Shazer.

---

a. See Psalm 23:3: "He restoreth my soul: he leadeth me in the paths of righteousness for his name's sake."

And we did go forth again in the wilderness, following the same direction, keeping in the most fertile parts of the wilderness, which was in the borders near the Red Sea.

¹⁵And it came to pass that we did travel for the space of many days, slaying food by the way with our bows and our arrows, and our stones, and our slings. ¹⁶And we did follow the directions of the ball, which led us in the more fertile parts of the wilderness. ¹⁷And after that we had traveled for the space of many days, we did pitch our tents for the space of a time, that we might again rest ourselves and obtain food for our families.

¹⁸And it came to pass that as I, Nephi, went forth to slay food, behold, I did break my bow, which was made of fine steel. And after that I did break my bow, behold, my brethren were angry with me because of the loss of my bow, for we did obtain no food.

¹⁹And it came to pass that we did return, without food, to our families. And being much fatigued because of their journeying, they did suffer much for the want of food.

²⁰And it came to pass that Laman, and Lemuel, and the sons of Ishmael, did begin to murmur exceedingly because of their sufferings and afflictions in the wilderness. And also my father began to murmur against the Lord, his God. Yea, and they were all exceeding sorrowful, even that they did murmur against the Lord.

²¹Now it came to pass that I, Nephi, having been afflicted (with my brethren) because of the loss of my bow >(and their bows having lost their springs[a])<, it began to be exceeding difficult, yea, insomuch that we could obtain no food.

²²And it came to pass that I, Nephi, did speak much unto my brethren because that they had hardened their hearts again, even unto complaining against the Lord, their God.

²³And it came to pass that I, Nephi, did make out of wood, a bow. And out of a strait stick, an arrow. Wherefore, I did arm myself with a bow and an arrow, with a sling and with stones. And I said unto my father: "Whither shall I go to obtain food."

²⁴And it came to pass that he did enquire of the Lord, for they had humbled themselves because of my words, for I did say many things unto them in the energy of my soul.

²⁵And it came to pass that the voice of the Lord came unto my father. And he was truly chastened because of his murmuring against the Lord, insomuch that he was brought down into the depths of sorrow.

²⁶And it came to pass that the voice of the Lord said unto him: "Look upon the ball and behold the things which are written."

²⁷And it came to pass that when my father beheld the things which were written upon the ball, he did fear and tremble exceedingly, and also my brethren, and the sons of Ishmael, and our wives.

²⁸And it came to pass that I, Nephi, beheld that the pointers which were in the ball, that they did work according to the faith and diligence and heed which we did give unto them. ²⁹And there was also written upon them a new writing (which was plain to be read), which did give us understanding concerning the ways of the Lord.

And it was written (and changed from time to time) according to the faith and diligence which we gave unto it. And thus, we see that by small means the Lord can bring about great things.

---

a. The text in parentheses appears to be an insertion. Nephi apparently realized that he had only mentioned the loss of his bow, which would have left his brothers' bows available. He lets his readers know that it was serious because their bows had already become non-functional: they had "lost their springs."

Chapter V [1 Nephi 16–19:21]

³⁰And it came to pass that I, Nephi, did go forth up into the top of the mountain, according to the directions which was given upon the ball.

³¹And it came to pass that I did slay wild beasts, insomuch that I did obtain food for our families.

³²And it came to pass that I did return to our tents bearing the beasts which I had slain. And now, when they beheld that I had obtained food, how great was their joy!

And it came to pass that they did humble themselves before the Lord and did give thanks unto him.

³³And it came to pass that we did again take our journey, traveling nearly the same course as in the beginning. And after that we had traveled for the space of many days we did pitch our tents again, that we might tarry for the space of a time.

³⁴And it came to pass that Ishmael died and was buried in the place which was called Nahom.

³⁵And it came to pass that the daughters of Ishmael did mourn exceedingly because of the loss of their father and because of their afflictions in the wilderness. ³⁶And they did murmur against my father because that he had brought them out of the land of Jerusalem, saying: "Our father is dead. Yea, and we have wandered much in the wilderness. And we have suffered much afflictions, hunger, thirst, and fatigue. And after all these sufferings, we must perish in the wilderness with hunger." And thus they did murmur against my father, and also against me. And they were desirous to return again to Jerusalem.

³⁷And Laman saith unto Lemuel, and also unto the sons of Ishmael:

> Behold, let us slay our father, and also our brother Nephi, who hath taken it upon him to be our ruler and our teacher (who are his elder brethren). ³⁸Now, he saith that the Lord hath talked with him, and also that angels hath ministered unto him. But behold, we know that he lieth unto us.
>
> And he telleth us these things, and he worketh many things by his cunning arts, that he may deceive our eyes—thinking, perhaps, that he may lead us away into some strange wilderness. And after that he hath led us away, he hath thought to make himself a king and a ruler over us, that he may do with us according to his will and pleasure.

And after this manner did my brother Laman stir up their hearts to anger.

³⁹And it came to pass that the Lord was with us, yea, even the voice of the Lord came, and did speak many words unto them, and did chasten them exceedingly. And after that they were chastened by the voice of the Lord, they did turn away their anger and did repent of their sins, insomuch that the Lord did bless us again with food, that we did not perish.

[17] ¹And it came to pass that we did again take our journey in the wilderness. And we did travel nearly eastward from that time forth. And we did travel and wade through much afflictions in the wilderness. And our women bare children in the wilderness. ²And so great was the blessings of the Lord upon us that while we did live upon raw meat in the wilderness, our women did give plenty of suck for their children and were strong, yea, even like unto the men. And they began to bear their journeyings without murmuring. ³And thus we see that the commandments of God must be fulfilled. And if it so be that the children of men keep the commandments of God, he doth nourish

them and strengthen them, and provide [ways and[a]] means whereby they can accomplish the thing which he hath commanded them. Wherefore, he did provide [ways and[b]] means for us while we did sojourn in the wilderness. ⁴And we did sojourn for the space of many years, yea, even eight years in the wilderness.

⁵And we did come to the land which we called Bountiful, because of its much fruit and also wild honey. And all these things were prepared of the Lord that we might not perish. And we beheld the sea, which we called Irreantum (which being interpreted, is many waters).

⁶And it came to pass that we did pitch our tents by the seashore. And notwithstanding we had suffered many afflictions and much difficulty (yea, even so much that we cannot write them all), we was exceedingly rejoiced when we came to the sea shore. And we called the place Bountiful, because of its much fruit.[c]

⁷And it came to pass that after I, Nephi, had been in the land Bountiful for the space of many days, the voice of the Lord came unto me, saying: "Arise, and get thee into the mountain."

And it came to pass that I arose and went up into the mountain and cried unto the Lord.

⁸And it came to pass that the Lord spake unto me, saying: "Thou shalt construct a ship after the manner which I shall show thee, that I may carry thy people across these waters."

⁹And I saith: "Lord, whither shall I go that I may find ore to molten, that I may make tools to construct the ship after the manner which thou has shown unto me?"

¹⁰And it came to pass that the Lord told me whither I should go to find ore, that I might make tools.

¹¹And it came to pass that I, Nephi, did make bellows (wherewith to blow the fire) of the skins of beasts. And after that I had made bellows (that I might have wherewith to blow the fire), I did smite two stones together that I might make fire. ¹²For the Lord had not hitherto suffered that we should make much fire as we journeyed in the wilderness. For he saith:

> I will make that thy food shall become sweet, that ye cook it not. ¹³And I will also be your light in the wilderness.[d] And I will prepare the way before you, if it so be that ye shall keep my commandments. Wherefore, inasmuch as ye shall keep my commandments, ye shall be led towards the promised land. And ye shall know that it is by me that ye are led.

¹⁴Yea, and the Lord said also, that: "After ye have arriven to the promised land, ye shall know that I, the Lord, am God, and that I, the Lord, did deliver you from destruction. Yea, that I did bring you out of the land of Jerusalem." ¹⁵Wherefore I, Nephi, did strive to keep the commandments of the Lord. And I did exhort my brethren to faithfulness, and diligence.

---

a. Restored from the Original Manuscript. Skousen, *Analysis of the Textual Variants*, 1:350–51.

b. Restored from the Original Manuscript. Skousen, *Analysis of the Textual Variants*, 1:350–51.

c. "Called the place bountiful, because of its much fruit," duplicates the beginning of verse 5. Such a repetition can mean that it is a repetitive resumption. However, this does not qualify and the material between the repetitions is part of the logical explanation. This is simply a repetition. It cannot be discerned if it was intentional or simply accidental. It does not appear to have any poetic function.

d. Allusion to Exodus 13:21: "And the Lord went before them by day in a pillar of a cloud, to lead them the way; and by night in a pillar of fire, to give them light; to go by day and night."

¹⁶And it came to pass that I did make tools of the ore which I did molten out of the rock. ¹⁷And when my brethren saw that I was about to build a ship, they began to murmur against me, saying: "Our brother is a fool, for he thinketh that he can build a ship. Yea, and he also thinketh that he can cross these great waters."

¹⁸And thus my brethren did complain against me and were desirous that they might not labor, for they did not believe that I could build a ship. Neither would they believe that I were instructed of the Lord.

¹⁹And now it came to pass that I, Nephi, was exceeding sorrowful because of the hardness of their hearts. And now when they saw that I began to be sorrowful, they were glad in their hearts, insomuch that they did rejoice over me, saying:

> We knew that ye could not construct a ship, for we knew that ye were lacking in judgment. Wherefore, thou canst not accomplish so great a work. ²⁰And thou art like unto our father—lead away by the foolish imaginations of his heart. Yea, he hath led us out of the land of Jerusalem. And we have wandered in the wilderness for these many years. And our women have toiled, being big with child. And they have born children in the wilderness and suffered all things (save it were death). And it would have been better that they had died before they came out of Jerusalem than to have suffered these afflictions.
>
> ²¹Behold, these many years we have suffered in the wilderness, which time we might have enjoyed our possessions and the land of our inheritance. Yea, and we might have been happy.
>
> ²²And we know that the people, which were in the land of Jerusalem, were a righteous people. For they keep the statutes and the judgments of the Lord, and all his commandments according to the law of Moses. Wherefore we know that they are a righteous people. And our father hath judged them and hath led us away because we would hearken unto his words. Yea, and our brother is like unto him.

And after this manner of language did my brethren murmur and complain against us. ²³And it came to pass that I, Nephi, spake unto them, saying:

> Do ye believe that our fathers, which were the children of Israel, would have been led away out of the hands of the Egyptians if they had not hearkened unto the words of the Lord? ²⁴Yea, do ye suppose that they would have been led out of bondage if the Lord had not commanded Moses that he should lead them out of bondage?
>
> ²⁵Now, ye know that the children of Israel were in bondage. And ye know that they were laiden with tasks which were grievous to be born. Wherefore, ye know that it must needs be a good thing for them that they should be brought out of bondage.
>
> ²⁶Now, ye know that Moses was commanded of the Lord to do that great work. And ye know that by his word the waters of the Red Sea was divided hither and thither, and they passed through on dry ground. ²⁷But ye know that the Egyptians were drowned in the Red Sea, which were the armies of Pharaoh.ᵃ
>
> ²⁸And ye also know that they were fed with manna in the wilderness. ²⁹Yea, and ye also know that Moses, by his word (according to the power of God which

---

a. Refers to the story as told in Exodus 14 and 15.

was in him) smote the rock. And there came forth water, that the children of Israel might quench their thirst.[a]

³⁰And notwithstanding they being led (the Lord, their God, their Redeemer, going before them—leading them by day, and giving light unto them by night,[b] and doing all things for them which was expedient for man to receive), they hardened their hearts, and blinded their minds, and reviled against Moses and against the true and living God.

³¹And it came to pass that according to his word, he did destroy them. And according to his word, he did lead them. And according to his word, he did do all things for them. And there was not anything done, save it were by his word. ³²And after they had crossed the river Jordan, he did make them mighty unto the driving out the children of the land. Yea, unto the scattering them to destruction.

³³And now, do ye suppose that the children of this land, which were in the land of promise (which were driven out by our fathers), do ye suppose that they were righteous? Behold, I say unto you, nay. ³⁴Do ye suppose that our fathers would have been more choice than they, if they had been righteous? I say unto you, nay. ³⁵Behold, the Lord esteemeth all flesh in one. He that is righteous is favored of God. But behold, this people had rejected every word of God. And they were ripe in iniquity. And the fullness of the wrath of God was upon them. And the Lord did curse the land against them and bless it unto our fathers. Yea, he did curse it against them, unto their destruction. And he did bless it unto our fathers, unto their obtaining power over it.

³⁶Behold, the Lord hath created the earth that it should be inhabited. And he hath created his children that they should possess it. ³⁷And he raiseth up a righteous nation and destroyeth the nations of the wicked. ³⁸And he leadeth away the righteous into precious lands, and the wicked he destroyeth and curseth the land unto them, for their sakes.

³⁹He ruleth high in the heavens, for it is his throne. And this earth is his footstool.[c] ⁴⁰And he loveth them which will have him to be their God. Behold, he loved our fathers and he covenanted with them, yea, even Abraham, Isaac, and Jacob. And he remembered the covenants which he had made. Wherefore, he did bring them out of the land of Egypt.

⁴¹And he did straiten them in the wilderness with his rod, for they hardened their hearts, even as ye have. And the Lord straitened them because of their iniquity. He sent [flying fiery[d]] serpents among them. And after they were bitten he prepared a way that they might be healed.[e] And the labor which they had to perform were to look. And because of the simpleness of the way, or the easiness of it, there were many which perished. ⁴²And they did harden their hearts from time

---

a. Refers to the story as told in Exodus 17.
b. Alludes to Exodus 13:21.
c. Alludes to Isaiah 66:1.
d. This is a restoration of the Original Manuscript's order of the two words, echoing the fiery flying serpent in Isaiah 14:29 and 30:6. They are reversed in the Printer's Manuscript. Skousen, *Analysis of the Textual Variants*, 1:369.
e. Story in Numbers 21:6–9.

to time. And they did revile against Moses, and also against God. Nevertheless, ye know that they were led forth by his matchless power into the land of promise.

⁴³And now, after all these things, the time has come that they have become wicked, yea, nearly unto ripeness. And I know not but they are, at this day, about to be destroyed. For I know that the day must surely come that they must be destroyed, save a few only which shall be led away into captivity. ⁴⁴Wherefore, the Lord commanded my father that he should depart into the wilderness.

And the Jews also sought to take away his life. Yea, and ye also have sought to take away his life. Wherefore, ye are murderers in your hearts. And ye are like unto they. ⁴⁵Ye are swift to do iniquity, but slow to remember the Lord, your God. Ye have seen an angel and he spake unto you. Yea, ye have heard his voice from time to time, and he hath spoken unto you in a still small voice, but ye were past feeling—that ye could not feel his words. Wherefore, he hath spoken unto you like unto the voice of thunder, which did cause the earth to shake as if it were to divide asunder.

⁴⁶And ye also know that by the power of his almighty word he can cause the earth that it shall pass away. Yea, and ye know that by his word he can cause that rough places be made smooth and smooth places shall be broken up.ª O then, why is it that ye can be so hard in your hearts?

⁴⁷Behold, my soul is rent with anguish because of you, and my heart is pained. I fear lest ye shall be cast off forever. Behold, I am full of the spirit of God, insomuch as if my frame had no strength.

⁴⁸And now it came to pass that when I had spoken these words they were angry with me, and were desirous to throw me into the depths of the sea. And as they came forth to lay their hands upon me, I spake unto them, saying:

In the name of the Almighty God, I command you that ye touch me not! For I am filled with the power of God, even unto the consuming of my flesh. And whoso shall lay their hands upon me shall wither, even as a dried weed. And he shall be as naught before the power of God. For God shall smite him.

⁴⁹And it came to pass that I, Nephi, saith unto them that they should murmur no more against their father. Neither should they withhold their labor from me. For God had commanded me that I should build a ship. ⁵⁰And I saith unto them:

If God had commanded me to do all things, I could do it. If he should command me that I should say unto this water be thou earth, it should be earth. And if I should say it, it would be done. ⁵¹And now, if the Lord hath such great power and hath wrought so many miracles among the children of men, how is it that he cannot instruct me that I should build a ship?

⁵²And it came to pass that I, Nephi, said many things unto my brethren, insomuch that they were confounded and could not contend against me. Neither durst they lay their hands upon me, nor touch me with their fingers, even for the space of many days.

---

a. May be an allusion to Isaiah 40:4: "Every valley shall be exalted, and every mountain and hill shall be made low: and the crooked shall be made straight, and the rough places plain." The allusion is not very precise. It is also possible that it is Nephi's reworking of that allusion based on his vision of the destructions that will accompany the Savior's coming to Bountiful.

Now, they durst not do this, least they should wither before me, so powerful was the spirit of God. And thus it had wrought upon them.

⁵³And it came to pass that the Lord said unto me: "Stretch forth thine hand again unto thy brethren and they shall not wither before thee, but I will shock them," saith the Lord. "And this will I do that they may know that I am the Lord, their God."

⁵⁴And it came to pass that I stretched forth my hand unto my brethren and they did not wither before me. But the Lord did shake them, even according to the word which he had spoken.

⁵⁵And now they said: "We know of a surety that the Lord is with thee. For we know that it is the power of the Lord that hath shaken us."

And they fell down before me and were about to worship me. But I would not suffer them, saying: "I am thy brother. Yea, even thy younger brother. Wherefore, worship the Lord thy God. And honor thy father and thy mother that thy days may be long in the land which the Lord thy God shall give thee."ᵃ

[18] ¹And it came to pass that they did worship the Lord, and did go forth with me. And we did work timbers of curious workmanship. And the Lord did show me, from time to time, after what manner I should work the timbers of the ship. ²Now I, Nephi, did not work the timbers after the manner which was learned by men. Neither did build the ship after the manner of man. But I did build it after the manner which the Lord had shown unto me. Wherefore, it was not after the manner of men.

³And I, Nephi, did go into the mount oft. And I did pray oft unto the Lord. Wherefore, the Lord showed unto me great things.

⁴And it came to pass [thatᵇ] after I had finished the ship, according to the word of the Lord, my brethren beheld that it was good and that the workmanship thereof was exceeding fine. Wherefore, they did humble themselves again before the Lord.

⁵And it came to pass that the voice of the Lord came unto my father that we should arise and go down into the ship.

⁶And it came to pass that on the morrow, after that we had prepared all things (much fruits and meat from the wilderness, and honey in abundance, and provisions according to that which the Lord had commanded us), we did go down into the ship with all our loading, and our seeds, and whatsoever thing we had brought with us, every one according to his age. Wherefore, we did all go down into the ship, with our wives, and our children.

⁷And now, my father had begat two sons in the wilderness. The [elderᶜ] was called Jacob, and the younger, Joseph.

⁸And it came to pass that after we had all gone down into the ship, and had taken with us our provisions, and things which had been commanded us—we did put forth into the sea and were driven forth before the wind towards the promised land.

⁹And after that we had been driven forth before the wind for the space of many days, behold—my brethren, and the sons of Ishmael (and also their wives), began

---

a. See Exodus 20:12: "Honour thy father and thy mother: that thy days may be long upon the land which the Lord thy God giveth thee."

b. The transcript indicates that the word begins with "t," but there is a blob of ink covering the remainder of the word. The word "that" has been restored based on other occasions of that construction.

c. Restored from the Original Manuscript. The Printer's Manuscript "has eldest." Skousen, *Analysis of the Textual Variants*, 1:383.

Chapter V [1 Nephi 16–19:21]

to make themselves merry, insomuch that they began to dance, and to sing, and to speak with much rudeness. Yea, even that they did forget by what power they had been brought thither. Yea, they were lifted up unto exceeding rudeness.

¹⁰And I, Nephi, began to fear exceedingly (least the Lord should be angry with us, and smite us because of our iniquity), that we should be swallowed up in the depths of the sea. Wherefore I, Nephi, began to speak to them with much soberness. But behold, they were angry with me, saying: "We will not that our younger brother shall be a ruler over us."

¹¹And it came to pass that Laman and Lemuel did take me, and bind me with cords. And they did treat me with much harshness. Nevertheless, the Lord did suffer it, that he might show forth his power unto the fulfilling of his word which he hath spoken concerning the wicked.

¹²And it came to pass that after they had bound me, insomuch that I could not move, the compass (which had been prepared of the Lord) did cease to work. ¹³Wherefore, they knew not whither they should steer the ship, insomuch that there arose a great storm, yea, a great and terrible tempest. And we were driven back upon the waters for the space of three days. And they began to be frightened exceedingly, least they should be drowned in the sea. Nevertheless, they did loose me not. ¹⁴And on the fourth day which we had been driven back, the tempest began to be exceeding sore.

¹⁵And it came to pass that we were about to be swallowed up in the depths of the sea. And after that we had been driven back upon the waters for the space of four days, my brethren began to see that the judgments of God was upon them and that they perish, save that they should repent of their iniquities. Wherefore, they came unto me, and loosed the bands which was upon my wrists. And behold, they had much swollen exceedingly. And also mine ankles were much swollen. And great was the soreness thereof. ¹⁶Nevertheless, I did look unto my God, and I did praise him all the day long. And I did not murmur against the Lord because of mine afflictions.

¹⁷Now my father, Lehi, had said many things unto them, and also unto the sons of Ishmael. But behold, they did breathe out much threatening against anyone that should speak for me. And my parents, being stricken in years, and having suffered much grief (because of their children), they were brought down, yea, even upon their sick beds. ¹⁸Because of their grief, and much sorrow, and the iniquity of my brethren, they were brought near, even to be carried out of this time to meet their God. Yea, their gray hairs were about to be brought down, to lie low in the dust. Yea, even they were near to be cast, [with sorrow[a]], into a watery grave.

¹⁹And Jacob and Joseph also, being young, having need of much nourishment, were grieved because of the afflictions of their mother—and also my wife, with her tears and prayers, and also my children, did not soften their hearts of my brethren that they would loose me. ²⁰And there was nothing, save it were the power of God which threatened them with destruction, could soften their hearts. Wherefore, when they saw that they were about to be swallowed up in the depths of the sea, they repented of the thing which they had done, insomuch that they loosed me.

²¹And it came to pass that after they had loosed me, behold, I took the compass. And it did work whither I desired it.

---

a. Restored per the Original Manuscript. This phrase was lost when Oliver Cowdery copied from the Original to the Printer's Manuscript. Skousen, *Analysis of the Textual Variants*, 1:393.

And it came to pass that I prayed unto the Lord. And after that I had prayed, the winds did cease. And the storm did cease. And there was a great calm.

²²And it came to pass that I, Nephi, did guide the ship, that we sailed again towards the promised land.

²³And it came to pass that after we had sailed for the space of many days, we did arrive to the promised land. And we went forth upon the land and did pitch our tents. And we did call it the promised land.

²⁴And it came to pass that we did begin to till the earth. And we began to plant seeds. Yea, we did put all our seeds into the earth which we had brought from the land of Jerusalem.

And it came to pass that they did grow exceedingly. Wherefore, we were blessed in abundance.

²⁵And it came to pass that we did find upon the land of promise, as we journeyed in the wilderness, that there were was beasts in the forests of every kind—both the cow and the ox, and the ass and the horse, and the goat and the wild goat, and all manner of wild animals which were for the use of men. And we did find all manner of ore—both of gold and of silver, and of copper.

> [19] ¹And it came to pass that the Lord commanded me, wherefore, I did make plates of ore that I might engraven upon them the record of my people.[a] And upon the plates which I made, I did engraven the record of my father, and also our journeyings in the wilderness. And the prophesies of my father and also many of mine own prophesies have I engraven upon them.

²And I knew not at that time when I made them that I should be commanded of the Lord to make these plates. Wherefore, the record of my father, and the genealogy of his forefathers, and the more part of all our proceedings in the wilderness, are engraven upon those [first[b]] plates of which I have spoken. Wherefore, the things which transpired before that I made these plates are, of a truth, more particularly made mention upon the first plates.

³And after that I made these plates by way of commandment, I, Nephi, received a commandment that the ministry and the prophesies (the more plain and precious parts of them) should be written upon these plates—and that the things which were written should be kept for the instruction of my people, which should possess the land—and also for other wise purposes, which purposes are known unto the Lord. ⁴Wherefore, I, Nephi, did make a record upon the other plates which gives an account (or which gives a greater account) of the wars, and contentions, and destructions of my people. And this have I done, and commanded my people that they should do after that I was gone—and that these plates should be handed down from one generation to another, or from one prophet to another,

---

a. The mention of finding ore led to Nephi's aside about his making plates and their purpose. That discussion led Nephi to reflect on his purpose in writing. The remainder of the book of 1 Nephi could have been set as an aside. It was not part of the planned text. The nature of 1 Nephi's story (and the logic of the division into two books) suggests that the arrival in the promised land was the planned end of his text. From here to the end of the book is extemporaneous sermonizing, eventually couched as a lecture to his brothers. That may have been a literary addition rather than the historical recollection of an event.

b. Restored per the Original Manuscript (also restored in the 1981 edition). Skousen, *Analysis of the Textual Variants*, 1:401.

Chapter V [1 Nephi 16–19:21]

until further commandments of the Lord. ⁵And an account of my making these plates shall be given hereafter.

And then behold, I proceeded according to that which I have spoken.[a] And this I do that the more sacred things may be kept for the knowledge of my people. ⁶Nevertheless, I do not write anything upon plates, save it be that I think it be sacred.

And now, if I do err, even did they err of old. Not that I would excuse myself because of other men. But, because of the weakness which is in me (according to the flesh) I would excuse myself. ⁷For the things which some men esteem to be of great worth, both to the body and soul, others set at naught, and trample under their feet. Yea, even the very God of Israel do men trample under their feet. I say trample under their feet, but I would speak in other words. They do set him at naught, and hearken not to the voice of his councils.

⁸And behold, he cometh (according to the words of the angel), in six hundred years from the time my father left Jerusalem. ⁹And the world (because of their iniquity) shall judge him to be a thing of naught. Wherefore, they scourge him, and he suffereth it. And they smite him, and he suffereth it. Yea, they spit upon him, and he suffereth it—because of his loving kindness, and his long suffering towards the children of men.

¹⁰And the God of our fathers (which were led out of Egypt out of bondage, and also were preserved in the wilderness by him), yea, the God of Abraham, and of Isaac, and the God of Jacob—yieldeth himself (according to the words of the angel) as a man into the hands of wicked men to be lifted up (according to the words of Zenock), and to be crucified (according to the words of Neum), and to be buried in a sepulcher (according to the words of Zenos, which he spake concerning the three days of darkness which should be a sign given of his death unto them who should inhabit the Isles of the Sea—more especially given unto them which are of the house of Israel).

¹¹For thus spake the prophet: "The Lord God surely shall visit all the house of Israel at that day, some with his voice (because of their righteousness unto their great joy and salvation), and others with the thunderings and the lightnings[b] of his power—by tempest, by fire, and by smoke, and vapor of darkness, and by the opening of the earth, and by mountains which shall be carried up." ¹²And all these things must surely come, saith the prophet Zenos. And the rocks of the earth must rend. And because of the groanings of the earth, many of the kings of the isles of the sea shall be wrought upon by the spirit of God to exclaim: "The God of nature suffers!"

¹³And as for they which are at Jerusalem (saith the prophet) shall be scourged by all people (saith the prophet) because they crucify the God of Israel, and turned their hearts aside—rejecting signs, and wonders, and power, and glory, of the God of Israel. ¹⁴And because they turned their hearts aside, saith the prophet, and have

---

a. The mention of the ore triggered the mention of creating the plates. Having written that, Nephi's discussion of the small plates triggered his thinking on why he was writing them. This leads to the discussion that finishes the chapter. All of this is an aside, but this section is marked as a second aside because it does not return to the original intent but rather from the previous aside.

b. Uses language from Revelation 8:5: "And there were voices, and thunderings, and lightnings, and an earthquake."

despised the Holy One of Israel, they shall wander in the flesh. And perish. And become a hiss and a by word. And be hated among all nations.

¹⁵Nevertheless, when that day cometh, saith the prophet, that they no more turn aside their hearts against the Holy One of Israel, then will he remember the covenants which he made to their fathers. ¹⁶Yea, then will he remember the isles of the sea, yea, and "all the people which are of the house of Israel will I gather in," saith the Lord (according to the words of the prophets Zenos), "from the four quarters of the earth." ¹⁷"Yea, and "all the earth shall see the salvation of the Lord,"ᵃ saith the prophet. Every nation, kindred, tongue, and people shall be blessed.ᵇ

¹⁸And I, Nephi, have written these things unto my people that perhaps I might persuade them that they would remember the Lord, their Redeemer. ¹⁹Wherefore, I speak unto all the house of Israel, if it so be that they should obtain these things. ²⁰For behold, I have workings in the spirit which doth weary me (even that all my joints are weak) for they which are at Jerusalem. For had not the Lord been merciful, to show unto me concerning them, even as he had prophets of old. ²¹For he surely did show unto prophets of old, all things concerning them.ᶜ And also, he did show unto many, concerning us. Wherefore, it must needs be that we know concerning them, for they are written upon the plates of brass.<

---

a. See Isaiah 52:10: "The Lord hath made bare his holy arm in the eyes of all the nations; and all the ends of the earth shall see the salvation of our God."

b. See Revelation 14:6: "And I saw another angel fly in the midst of heaven, having the everlasting gospel to preach unto them that dwell on the earth, and to every nation, and kindred, and tongue, and people."

c. This is an incomplete sentence. It cannot be made complete through punctuation.

Chapter VI [1 Nephi 19:22–21:26]

²²Now it came to pass that I, Nephi, did teach my brethren these things.ᵃ

And it came to pass that I did read many things to them, which were engraven upon the plates of brass, that they might know concerning the doings of the Lord in other lands, among people of old. ²³And I did read many things unto them which were [in the booksᵇ] of Moses. But, that I might more fully persuade them to believe in the Lord, their Redeemer—wherefore, I did read unto them that which was written by the prophet Isaiah. For I did liken all scriptures unto us, that it might be for our profit and learning. ²⁴Wherefore, I spake unto them, saying:

Hear ye the words of the prophet, ye which are a remnant of the house of Israel, a branch which have been broken off.

Hear ye the words of the prophet, which was written unto all the house of Israel, and liken it unto yourselves—that ye may have hope (as well as your brethren from whom ye have been broken off).

For after this manner hath the prophet written:

[20, compare Isaiah 48]

¹**Hearken, and** hear this, O house of Jacob,
   which are called by the name of Israel,
and are come forth out of the waters of Judah;
   which swear by the name of the Lord,
      and make mention of the God of Israel,
   yet, they swear not in truth, nor in righteousness.
²**Nevertheless,** they call themselves of the holy city,
   but they do not stay themselves upon the God of Israel,
   which is the Lord of Hosts. Yea, the Lord of Hosts is his name.

³**Behold,** I have declared the former things from the beginning.
   And they went forth out of my mouth. And I showed them.
   I did **show** them suddenly.
⁴**And I did it** because I knew that thou art obstinate,
   and thy neck was an iron sinew, and thy brow brass.
⁵**And** I have even from the beginning declared to thee.
   Before it came to pass, I showed them thee.
And I showed them, for fear least thou shouldst say:

---

a. It is probable that the original chapters VI and VII were not part of the original planned text. The planned text would have ended with the modern chapter 18 (included in chapter V). The longer aside that ends chapter 19 led Nephi to desire to say more. The addition of texts on Isaiah and their explication are couched as teaching his brethren, but there is no textual lead-in to that teaching. There are no questions asked as previously done to couch Nephi's explanations within the story. Nephi is clearly in awe of the Savior and therefore expounds more about him. Because this aside covers multiple chapters, it is not marked up as an aside.

b. Skousen, *Analysis of the Textual Variants*, 1:421. "The original text seems to have read 'which were in the books of Moses', but this ended up being copied in [the Printer's Manuscript] as 'which were written in the book of Moses". The 1981 LDS edition restored the plural "books," but the intrusive "written" has been maintained in all editions.

"Mine idol hath done them.
And my graven image,
and my molten image,
hath commanded them."

⁶Thou hast **seen and heard** all this.
And will **ye not** declare **them?**
And that I have showed thee new things from this time,
even hidden things. And thou didst not know them.
⁷They are created now (and not from the beginning),
even before the day when thou heardest them not
they were declared unto thee—
least thou shouldst say: "Behold, I knew them."
⁸Yea, **and** thou heardest not.
Yea, thou knewest not.
Yea, from that time, thine ear was not opened.
For I knew that thou wouldst deal very treacherously,
and wast called a transgressor from thy womb.
⁹**Nevertheless,** for my [name's[a]] sake will I defer mine anger.
And for my praise will I refrain from thee,
that I cut thee not off.
¹⁰**For** behold, I have refined thee.
I have chosen thee in the furnace of affliction.
¹¹For mine own sake, **yea,** for mine own sake will I do **this.**
For [**how should I**[b]] **suffer** my name to be polluted?
And I will not give my glory unto another.

¹²Hearken unto me, O Jacob, and Israel, my called!
For I am he.
And I am the first, **and** I [c] am also the last.
¹³Mine hand hath also laid the foundations of the earth.
And my right hand hath spanned the heavens.
And I called unto them, **and** they stand up together.
¹⁴All ye! Assemble yourselves and hear!
Which among them hath declared these things **unto them?**
The Lord hath loved him—
yea, and he will fulfil his word which he hath declared by them.
And he will do his pleasure on Babylon,
and his arm shall **come upon** the Chaldeans.
¹⁵**Also, saith the Lord:** "I, the Lord, **yea,** I have spoken.
Yea, I have called him **to declare.**
I have brought him, and he shall make his way prosperous.
¹⁶Come ye near unto me!
I have not spoken in secret from the beginning.

---

a. The Printer's Manuscript has "name." The possessive is restored from the King James Version.
b. Restored per the Original Manuscript. Skousen, *Analysis of the Textual Variants,* 1:432–34
c. Omits "also," which is in italics.

Chapter VI [1 Nephi 19:22–21:26]

From the time that it was **declared, have I spoken."**[a]
And the Lord God and his spirit hath sent me.
¹⁷And thus saith the Lord thy Redeemer the Holy One of Israel:
   "I have sent him."
The Lord thy God, which teacheth thee to profit,
   which leadeth thee by the way thou shouldst go,
   hath done it.

¹⁸O that thou hadst hearkened to my commandments!
   Then had thy peace been as a river,
   and thy righteousness as the waves of the sea.
¹⁹Thy seed also had been as the sand.
   The offspring of thy bowels like the gravel thereof.
His name should not have been cut off,
   nor destroyed from before me.
²⁰Go ye forth of Babylon.
   Flee ye from the Chaldeans.
With a voice of singing, declare ye. Tell this.
   Utter to the end of the earth. Say ye:
   "The Lord hath redeemed his servant Jacob!"
²¹And they thirsted not [b].
   He led them through the deserts.
He caused the waters to flow out of the rock for them.
   He **cleaved** the rock also, and the waters gushed out.
²²**And notwithstanding, he hath done all this—and greater also.**
   "There is no peace," saith the Lord, "unto the wicked."

[21, compare Isaiah 49]

¹And again—
Hearken, O ye house of Israel!
   All ye that are broken off, and are driven out
   because of the wickedness of the pastors of my people.
**Yea, all ye that are broken off, that are scattered abroad,
which are of my people. O house of Israel!**
Listen, O isles, unto me!
And hearken ye people from far!

The Lord hath called me from the womb,
   from the bowels of my mother hath he made mention of my name.
²And he hath made my mouth like a sharp sword.
   In the shadow of his hand hath he hid me—
   and made me a polished shaft.
   In his quiver, hath he hid me—
³and said unto me: "**You** art my servant, O Israel,
   in whom I will be glorified."

---

a. Replaces "from the time that it was, there am I" (Isaiah 48:16).
b. Omits "when," which is in italics.

⁴Then I said: "I have labored in vain.
   I have spent my strength for naught, and in vain.
[ᵃ] Surely my judgment is with the Lord,
   and my work with my God."

⁵And now, saith the Lord that formed me from the womb—
   that I should be his servant, to bring Jacob again to him.
Though Israel be not gathered,
   yet shall I be glorious in the eyes of the Lord.
   And my God shall be my strength.

⁶And he said:
"It is a light thing that thou shouldst be my servant,
   to raise up the tribes of Jacob,
   and to restore the preserved of Israel.
I will also give thee for a light to the Gentiles,
   that thou mayest be my salvation unto the **ends** of the earth."

⁷Thus saith the Lord, the Redeemer of Israel, [ᵇ] his Holy One,
   to him whom man despiseth,
   to him whom the **nations** abhoreth,
   to servant of rulers.
"Kings shall see and arise.
   Princes also shall worship,
   because of the Lord that is faithful.[ᶜ]"

⁸Thus saith the Lord:
"In an acceptable time have I heard thee, **O isles of the sea.**
   And in a day of salvation have I helped thee.
And I will preserve thee and give thee **my servant,**
   for a covenant of the people
to establish the earth,
   to cause to inherit the desolate heritages,
⁹that thou mayest say to the prisoners: 'Go forth,'—
   to them that **sit** in darkness, "show yourselves."
They shall feed in the ways,
   and their pastures shall be in all high places.
¹⁰They shall not hunger, nor thirst.
   Neither shall the heat, nor **the** sun, smite them.
For he that hath mercy on them, shall lead them.
   Even by the springs of waters shall he guide them.
¹¹And I will make all my mountains a way,
   and my high ways shall be exalted.
¹²**And then, O house of Israel,**
   behold, these shall come from far—

---

a. Omits "yet," which is in italics.
b. Omits "and," which is in italics.
c. Omits "and the Holy One of Israel, and he shall choose thee."

Chapter VI [1 Nephi 19:22–21:26]

and lo, these from the north and from the west,
    and these from the land of Sinim.

¹³Sing, O heavens! And be joyful, O earth!
    For the feet of them which are in the east shall be established.
And break forth into singing, O mountains!
    For they shall be smitten no more.
For the Lord hath comforted his people,
    and will have mercy upon his afflicted.

¹⁴But **behold**, Zion **hath** said:
"The Lord hath forsaken me,
    and my Lord hath forgotten me."
But he will show that he hath not.

¹⁵"**For** can a woman forget her sucking child,
    that she should not have compassion on the son of her womb?
Yea, they may forget,
    yet will I not forget thee, **O house of Israel.**
¹⁶Behold, I have graven thee upon the palms of my hands.
    Thy walls are continually before me.
¹⁷Thy children shall make haste **against** thy destroyers,
    and they that made thee waste, shall go forth of thee.
¹⁸Lift up thine eyes round about and behold—
    all these gather themselves together.
    And **they shall** come to thee."
"**And** as I live," saith the Lord,
    "thou shalt surely clothe thee with them all, as with an ornament,
    and bind them on [a], **even** as a bride [b].

¹⁹For thy waste, and thy desolate places,
    and the land of thy destruction,
shall even now be too narrow, by reason of the inhabitants.
    And they that swallowed thee up, shall be far away.
²⁰The children which thou shalt have,
    after thou hast lost the other,
shall again in thine ears say:
    'The place is too strait for me.
    Give place to me that I may dwell.'

²¹Then shalt thou say in thine heart:
'Who hath begotten me these,
    seeing I have lost my children,
    and am desolate—a captive,
    and removing to and fro?

---

a. Omits "thee," which is in italics.
b. Omits "doeth," which is in italics.

And who hath brought up these?
>Behold, I was left alone.
>These—where **have** they been?'

²²Thus saith the Lord God:
"Behold, I will lift up mine hand to the Gentiles,
>and set up my standard to the people.
And they shall bring thy sons in their arms,
>and thy daughters shall be carried upon their shoulders.
²³And kings shall be thy nursing fathers,
>and their queens thy nursing mothers.
They shall bow down to thee, with their face towards the earth,
>and lick up the dust of thy feet.
And thou shalt know that I am the Lord.
>For they shall not be ashamed that wait for me.

²⁴**For** shall the prey be taken from the mighty,
>or the lawful captive delivered?
²⁵But thus saith the Lord:
"Even the captive of the mighty shall be taken away.
>And the prey of the terrible shall be delivered.
For I will contend with him that contendeth with thee.
>And I will save thy children.
²⁶And I will feed them that oppress thee with their own flesh.
>They shall be drunken with their own blood, as with sweet wine.
And all flesh shall know that I the Lord, am thy Savior, and thy Redeemer,
>the Mighty One of Jacob.

Chapter VII [1 Nephi 22]

[22] ¹And now it came to pass that after I, Nephi—after that I had read these things which were engraven upon the plates of brass, my brethren came unto me, and said unto me: "What mean these things which ye have read? Behold, are they to be understood according to things which are spiritual, which shall come to pass according to the spirit, and not the flesh?"

²And I, Nephi, saith unto them:

Behold, they were made manifest unto the prophet, by the voice of the spirit. For by the spirit are all things made known unto the prophets, which shall come upon the children of men, according to the flesh. ³Wherefore, the things of which I have read are things pertaining to things both temporal and spiritual.

For it appears that the house of Israel, sooner or later, will be scattered upon all the face of the earth, and also among all nations. ⁴And [behold[a]], there are many which are already lost from the knowledge of they which are at Jerusalem. Yea, the more part of all the tribes have been led away, and they are scattered to and fro upon the isles of the sea. And whither they are, none of us knoweth, save that we know that they have been led away.

⁵And since that they have been led away, these things have been prophesied concerning them—and also concerning all they which shall hereafter be scattered, and be confounded, because of the Holy One of Israel. For against him will they harden their hearts. Wherefore, they shall be scattered among all nations, and shall be hated by all men. ⁶Nevertheless, after that they have been nursed by the Gentiles and the Lord hath lifted up his hand upon the Gentiles (and set them up for a standard)—and their children shall be carried in their arms.[b] And their daughters shall be carried upon their shoulders.[c]

Behold, these things (of which are spoken) are temporal. For thus is the covenants of the Lord with our fathers. ⁷And it meaneth us in the days to come. And also all our brethren which are of the house of Israel. And it meaneth that the time cometh that after all the house of Israel have been scattered and confounded, that the Lord God will raise up a mighty nation among the Gentiles, yea, even upon the face of this land. ⁸And by them shall our seed be scattered.

And after that our seed is scattered, the Lord God will proceed to do a marvelous work[d] among the Gentiles, which shall be of great worth unto our seed. Wherefore, it is likened unto the being nourished by the Gentiles, and being carried in their arms, and upon their shoulders. ⁹And it shall also be of worth unto the Gentiles. And not only unto the Gentiles, but unto all the house of Israel—unto the making known of the covenants of the Father of heaven unto Abraham, saying: "In thy seed shall all the kindreds of the earth be blessed.[e]"

---

a. Restored per the Original Manuscript. Skousen, *Analysis of the Textual Variants*, 1:456.

b. The "and" in "and their children" should be read with the meaning "then." Thus, "then their children shall be carried in their arms."

c. Referencing the previously quoted Isaiah 49:22.

d. Reference to Isaiah 29:14: "Therefore, behold, I will proceed to do a marvellous work among this people, *even* a marvellous work and a wonder."

e. See Acts 3:25: "Ye are the children of the prophets, and of the covenant which God made with

¹⁰And I would, my brethren, that ye should know that all the kindreds of the earth cannot be blessed, unless he shall make bare his arm in the eyes of the nations. ¹¹Wherefore, the Lord God will proceed to make bare his arm in the eyes of all the nations[a] in bringing about his covenants and his Gospel, unto them (they which are of the house of Israel). ¹²Wherefore, he will bring them again out of captivity. And they shall be gathered together to the lands of their [first[b]] inheritance. And they shall be brought out of obscurity, and out of darkness. And they shall know that the Lord is their Savior, and their Redeemer, the Mighty One of Israel.

¹³And the blood of that great and abominable church (which is the whore of all the earth) shall turn upon their own heads. For they shall war among themselves, and the sword of their own hands shall fall upon their own heads. And they shall be drunken with their own blood.[c] ¹⁴And every nation which shall war against thee, O house of Israel, shall be turned one against another. And they shall fall into the pit which they digged to ensnare the people of the Lord. And all which fight against Zion shall be destroyed. And that great whore, which hath perverted the right ways of the Lord, yea, that great and abominable church[d]—shall tumble to the dust. And great shall be the fall of it.

¹⁵For behold saith the prophet, that the time cometh speedily, that Satan shall have no more power over the hearts of the children of men. ¹⁶For the day soon cometh, that all the proud (and they which do wickedly) shall be as stubble.[e] And the day cometh, that they must be burned. For the time soon cometh, that the fulness of the wrath of God shall be poured out upon all the children of men. For he will not suffer that the wicked shall destroy the righteous. ¹⁷Wherefore, he will preserve the righteous by his power (even if it so be that the fullness of his wrath must come), and the righteous be preserved even unto the destruction of their enemies by fire. Wherefore, the righteous need not fear. For thus saith the prophet: "They shall be saved, even if it so be as by fire."

¹⁸Behold my brethren, I say unto you that these things must shortly come, yea, even blood, and fire, and vapor of smoke—must come (and it must needs be upon the face of this earth).[f] And it cometh unto men according to the flesh, if it so be that they will harden their hearts against the Holy One of Israel.

¹⁹For behold, the righteous shall not perish. For the time surely must come, that all they which fight against Zion shall be cut off. ²⁰And the Lord will surely prepare a way for his people, unto the fulfilling of the words of Moses, which he spake, saying: "A prophet shall the Lord your God raise up unto you, like unto me. Him shall ye hear in all things whatsoever he shall say unto you.[g] And it shall come

---

our fathers, saying unto Abraham, And in thy seed shall all the kindreds of the earth be blessed." Acts is quoting Genesis 22:18: "And in thy seed shall all the nations of the earth be blessed; because thou hast obeyed my voice."

   a. Quotes Isaiah 52:10: "The Lord hath made bare his holy arm in the eyes of all the nations."
   b. Restored from the Original Manuscript. Skousen, *Analysis of the Textual Variants*, 1:462.
   c. Quotes Isaiah 49:26: "And they shall be drunken with their own blood."
   d. Echoes language from 1 Nephi 14:10–11 and from Revelation 17:1, 5.
   e. See Malachi 4:1: "For, behold, the day cometh, that shall burn as an oven; and all the proud, yea, and all that do wickedly, shall be stubble."
   f. See similar language in Acts 2:19 and Joel 2:30.
   g. These two sentences quote Acts 3:22, 7:37.

Chapter VII [1 Nephi 22]

to pass that all they which will not hear that prophet, shall be cut off from among the people."

²¹And now I, Nephi, declare unto you that this prophet of whom Moses spake was the Holy One of Israel. Wherefore, he shall execute judgment in righteousness. ²²And the righteous need not fear, for it is they which shall not be confounded. But it is the kingdom of the devil which shall be built up among the children of men (which kingdom is established among them which are in the flesh, ²³for the time speedily shall come that all churches which are built up to get gain, and all they which are built up to get power over the flesh, and they which are built up to become popular in the eyes of the world, and they which seek the lusts of the flesh, and the things of the world, and to do all manner of iniquity)—yea in fine, all they which belong to the kingdom of the devil—it is they which need fear, and tremble, and quake.ᵃ It is they which must be brought low in the dust. It is they which must be consumed as stubble.ᵇ And this is according to the words of the prophet.

²⁴And the time cometh speedily, that the righteous must be led up as calves of the stall,ᶜ and the Holy One of Israel must reign in dominion, and might, and power, and great glory. ²⁵And he gathereth his children from the four quarters of the earth. And he numbereth his sheep, and they know him. And there shall be one fold, and one Shepherd.ᵈ And he shall feed his sheep. And in him they shall find pasture.

²⁶And because of the righteousness of his people, Satan hath no power. Wherefore, he cannot be loosed for the space of many years. For he hath no power over the hearts of the people. For they dwell in righteousness. And the Holy One of Israel reigneth.

²⁷And now behold, I, Nephi, say unto you that all these things must come according to the flesh.

²⁸But behold, all nations, kindreds, tongues, and people, shall dwell safely in the Holy One of Israel, if it so be that they will repent.

²⁹And now, I, Nephi, make an end, for I durst not speak further (as yet) concerning these things. ³⁰Wherefore, my brethren, I would that ye should consider that the things which have been written upon the plates of brass are true—and they testify that a man must be obedient to the commandments of God. ³¹Wherefore, ye need not suppose that I, and my father, are the only ones which have testified, and also taught them. Wherefore, if ye shall be obedient to the commandments, and endure to the end,ᵉ ye shall be saved at the last day. And thus it is, Amen.

---

a. The text in parentheses is a long insertion that allows the meaning to drift. It is recovered to finish the reverse parallel between "righteous need not fear" and "it is kingdom of the devil—it is they which need fear."

b. See Malachi 4:1: "For, behold, the day cometh, that shall burn as an oven; and all the proud, yea, and all that do wickedly, shall be stubble."

c. See Malachi 4:2: "And ye shall go forth, and grow up as calves of the stall."

d. See John 10:16: "And other sheep I have, which are not of this fold: them also I must bring, and they shall hear my voice; and there shall be one fold, and one shepherd."

e. See Matthew 10:22: "he that endureth to the end shall be saved."

The Book of Nephi

An account of the death of Lehi. Nephi's brethren rebelleth against him. The Lord warns Nephi to depart into the wilderness, etc. His journeyings in the wilderness, etc.

Chapter I [2 Nephi 1–2]

[1] ¹And now it came to pass after I, Nephi, had made an end of teaching my brethren, our father, Lehi, also spake many things unto them, [and rehearsed unto them[a]] how great things the Lord had done for them,[b] in bringing them out of the land of Jerusalem. ²And he spake unto them concerning their rebellions upon the waters, and the mercies of God in sparing their lives, that they were not swallowed up in the sea. ³And he also spake unto them concerning the land of promise, which they had obtained— how merciful the Lord had been in warning us that we should flee out of the land of Jerusalem.

⁴For behold, saith he:

> I have seen a vision, in the which I know that Jerusalem is destroyed. And had we remained in Jerusalem, we should also have perished. ⁵But (said he), notwithstanding our afflictions, we have obtained a land of promise—and a land which is choice above all other lands—a land which the Lord God hath [consecrated[c]] with me should be a land for the inheritance of my seed. Yea, the Lord hath [consecrated[d]] this land unto me (and to my children) forever—and also all they which should be led out of other countries by the hand of the Lord. ⁶Wherefore, I, Lehi, prophesy (according to the workings of the spirit, which is in me) that there shall be none come into this land save they should be brought by the hand of the Lord. ⁷Wherefore, this land is consecrated unto him whom he shall bring. And if it so be that they shall serve him, according to the commandments which he hath given, it shall be a land of liberty unto them. Wherefore, they shall never be brought down into captivity. If so, it shall be because of iniquity. For if iniquity shall abound, cursed shall be the land for their sakes. But unto the righteous it shall be blessed forever.

> ⁸And behold, it is wisdom that this land should be kept, as yet, from the knowledge of other nations. For behold, many nations would overrun [this[e]] land, that there would be no place for an inheritance. ⁹Wherefore, I, Lehi, have obtained a promise that inasmuch as they which the Lord God shall bring out of the land of Jerusalem, shall keep his commandments, they shall prosper upon the face of

---

    a. "When copying from [the Original manuscript] to [the Printer's manuscript], Oliver Cowdery accidentally skipped the conjoined predicate 'and rehearsed unto them', probably because his eye skipped from the preceding 'unto them' to the following one as he copied the text." Skousen, *Analysis of the Textual Variants*, 1:475.

    b. Uses language from Mark 5:19.

    c. Restored from the Original Manuscript. The printer's manuscript has "covenanted."

    d. Restored from the Original Manuscript. Skousen, *Analysis of the Textual Variants*, 1:476–77.

    e. Restored from the Original Manuscript. Skousen, *Analysis of the Textual Variants*, 1:480.

this land. And they shall be kept from all other nations, that they may possess this land unto themselves. And if it so be that they shall keep his commandments, they shall be blessed upon the face of this land. And there shall be none to molest them, nor to take away the land of their inheritance. And they shall dwell safely, forever.

¹⁰But behold, when the time cometh that they shall dwindle in unbelief after that they have received so great blessings from the hand of the Lord (having a knowledge of the creation of the earth, and all men—knowing the great and marvelous works of the Lord from the creation of the world—having power given them to do all things by faith—having all the commandments from the beginning—and having been brought by his infinite goodness into this precious land of promise), behold, I say, if the day shall come that they will reject the Holy One of Israel, the true Messiah, their Redeemer and their God—behold, the judgments of him that is just shall rest upon them.[a] ¹¹Yea, he will bring other nations unto them, and he will give unto them power. And he will take away from them the lands of their possessions. And he will cause them to be scattered and smitten. ¹²Yea, as one generation passeth to another, there shall be bloodsheds, and great visitations among them. Wherefore, my sons, I would that ye would remember, yea, I would that ye would hearken unto my words.

¹³O that ye would awake! Awake from a deep sleep,

yea, even from the sleep of hell, and shake off the awful chains by which ye are bound, which are the chains which bind the children of men that they are carried away captive, down to the eternal gulf of misery and wo.

¹⁴Awake! And arise from the dust!

And hear the words of a trembling parent, whose limbs ye must soon lay down in the cold and silent grave (from whence no traveler can return).

A few more days, and I go the way of all the earth.[b] ¹⁵But behold, the Lord hath redeemed my soul from hell. I have beheld his glory and am encircled about eternally in the arms of his love.

¹⁶And I desire that ye should remember to observe the statutes, and the judgments, of the Lord. Behold, this hath been the anxiety of my soul from the beginning. ¹⁷My heart hath been weighed down with sorrow, from time to time, for I have feared—lest, for the hardness of your hearts, the Lord your God, should come out in the fulness of his wrath upon you, that ye be cut off and destroyed forever. ¹⁸Or, that a cursing should come upon you for the space of many generations and ye are visited by sword, and by famine, and are hated, and are led according to the will and captivity of the devil.

¹⁹O my sons!

That these things might not come upon you!

But, that ye might be a choice, and a favored people of the Lord!

But behold, his will be done, for his ways are righteousness forever. ²⁰And he hath said that:

---

a. This long sentence is a combination of a sentence fragment that recovers by using repetitive resumption. The idea that "they shall dwindle in unbelief" is paralleled by "if the day shall come that they will reject the Holy One of Israel." The simple idea, without all of the internal clauses is that those who dwindle in unbelief will have "the judgments" of God leveled against them.

b. See 1 Kings 2:2: "I go the way of all the earth."

Chapter I [2 Nephi 1–2]

"Inasmuch as ye shall keep my commandments,
    ye shall prosper in the land.
But, inasmuch as ye will not keep [his[a]] commandments
    ye shall be cut off from [his[b]] presence."[c]

²¹And now, that my soul might have joy in you, and that my heart might leave this world with gladness because of you, that I might not be brought down with grief and sorrow to the grave—

Arise from the dust my sons!
    And be men!
    And be determined in one mind, and in one heart—
united in all things,
    that ye may not come down into captivity,
    ²²that ye may not be cursed with a sore cursing—
    and also that ye may not incur the displeasure of a just God upon you—
        unto the destruction,
        yea, the eternal destruction of both soul and body.

²³Awake my sons!
    Put on the armor of righteousness![d]
    Shake off the chains with which ye are bound.
        And come forth out of obscurity.
        And arise from the dust!

²⁴Rebel no more against your brother, whose views have been glorious. And who hath kept the commandments from the time we left Jerusalem. And who hath been an instrument in the hands of God in bringing us forth into the land of promise. For were it not for him, we must have perished with hunger in the wilderness. Nevertheless, ye sought to take away his life. Yea, and he hath suffered much sorrow because of you. ²⁵And I exceedingly fear and tremble because of you, lest he shall suffer again. For behold, ye have accused him that he sought power and authority over you. But I know that he hath not sought for power nor authority over you, but he hath sought the glory of God and your own eternal welfare.

²⁶And ye have murmured because he hath been plain unto you. Ye say that he hath used sharpness. Ye say that he hath been angry with you. But behold, his sharpness was the sharpness of the power of the word of God, which was in him. And that which ye call anger was the truth, according to that which is in God (which he could not constrain), manifesting boldly concerning your iniquities. ²⁷And it must needs be that the power of God must be with him, even unto his commanding you that ye must obey. But behold, it was not him, but it was the spirit of the Lord (which was in him) which opened his mouth to utterance, that he could not shut it.

²⁸And now, my son Laman, and also Lemuel, and Sam, and also my sons,

---

    a. Restored from the Original Manuscript. The Printer's Manuscript has "my." While "my" makes it more logical as a quotation from God, the original was a reference to God's words rather than an intended verbatim quotation.
    b. Restored from the Original Manuscript. The Printer's Manuscript has "my."
    c. The phrase "cut off from my presence" is found in Leviticus 22:3.
    d. Uses language from 2 Corinthians 6:7.

which are the sons of Ishmael—behold, if ye will hearken unto the voice of Nephi, ye shall not perish. And if ye will hearken unto him, I leave unto you a blessing. Yea, even my first blessing. ²⁷But, if ye will not hearken unto him, I take away my first blessing. Yea, even my blessing. And it shall rest upon him.

³⁰And now, Zoram, I speak unto you. Behold, thou art the servant of Laban. Nevertheless, thou hast been brought out of the land of Jerusalem. And I know that thou art a true friend unto my son, Nephi, forever. ³¹Wherefore, because thou hast been faithful, thy seed shall be blessed with his seed—that they dwell (in prosperity) long upon the face of this land. And nothing, save it shall be iniquity among them shall harm or disturb their prosperity upon the face of this land, forever. ³²Wherefore, if ye shall keep the commandments of the Lord, the Lord hath consecrated this land for the security of thy seed with the seed of my son.

[2] ¹And now, Jacob, I speak unto you. Thou art my first born in the days of my tribulation in the wilderness. And behold, in thy childhood thou hast suffered afflictions, and much sorrow, because of the rudeness of thy brethren. ²Nevertheless, Jacob (my first born in the wilderness), thou knowest the greatness of God. And he shall consecrate thine afflictions for thy gain. ³Wherefore, thy soul shall be blessed. And thou shalt dwell safely with thy brother, Nephi. And thy days shall be spent in the service of thy God. Wherefore, I know that thou art redeemed. because of the righteousness of thy Redeemer. For thou hast beheld that in the fullness of time he cometh to bring salvation unto men.

⁴And thou hast beheld, in thy youth, his glory. Wherefore, thou art blessed even as they unto whom he shall minister in the flesh. For the spirit is the same yesterday, today, and forever.ᵃ And the way is prepared from the fall of man. And salvation is free. ⁵And men are instructed sufficiently that they know good from evil. And the law is given unto men. And by the law no flesh is justified, or, by the law men are cut off.ᵇ Yea, by the temporal law they were cut off. And also by the spiritual law, they perish from that which is good and become miserable forever. ⁶Wherefore, redemption cometh in and through the holy Messiah. For he is full of grace and truth.ᶜ

⁷Behold, he offereth himself a sacrifice for sin, to answer the ends of the law unto all those which have a broken heart and a contrite spirit.ᵈ And unto none else can the ends of the law be answered. ⁸Wherefore, how great the importance to make these things known unto the inhabitants of the earth, that they may know that there is no flesh that can dwell in the presence of God save it be through the merits, and mercy, and grace, of the holy Messiah, which layeth down his life (according to the flesh) and taketh it again by the power of the spirit—that he may bring to pass the resurrection of the dead, being the first that should rise.

---

a. See Hebrews 13:8.

b. See Romans 3:20: "Therefore by the deeds of the law there shall no flesh be justified in his sight: for by the law *is* the knowledge of sin."

c. See John 1:14 for the phrase "full of grace and truth."

d. See Psalm 34:18: "The Lord is nigh unto them that are of a broken heart; and saveth such as be of a contrite spirit."

Chapter I [2 Nephi 1–2]

⁹Wherefore, he is the firstfruits unto God,ᵃ inasmuch as he shall make intersession for all the children of men. And they that believe in him shall be saved.

¹⁰And because of the intersession for all, all men cometh unto God. Wherefore, they stand in the presence of him, to be judged of him according to the truth and holiness which is in him. Wherefore, the ends of the law which the Holy One hath given unto the inflicting of the punishment which is affixed (which punishment that is affixed is in opposition to that of the happiness, which is affixed) to answer the ends of the atonement.ᵇ

¹¹For it must needs be that there is an opposition in all things. If not so, my first born in the wilderness, righteousness could not be brought to pass—neither wickedness, neither holiness nor misery, neither good nor bad. Wherefore, all things must needs be a compound in one. Wherefore, if it should be one body, it must needs remain as dead—having no life neither death, nor corruption nor incorruption,ᶜ happiness nor misery, neither sense nor insensibility. ¹²Wherefore, it must needs have been created for a thing of naught. Wherefore, there would have been no purpose in the end of its creation. Wherefore, this thing must needs destroy the wisdom of God and his eternal purposes, and also the power, and the mercy, and the justice, of God.

¹³And if ye shall say there is no law, ye shall also say there is no sin. And if ye shall say there is no sin, ye shall also say there is no righteousness. And if there be no righteousness, there be no happiness. And if there be no righteousness nor happiness, there be no punishment, nor misery. And if these things are not—there is no God. And if there is no God, we are not, neither the earth. For there could have been no creation of things, neither to act nor to be acted upon. Wherefore, all things must have vanished away.

¹⁴And now, my son, I speak unto you these things for your profit and learning. For there is a God. And he hath created all things, both the heavens and the earth, and all things that in them is—both things to act and things to be acted upon. ¹⁵And, to bring about his eternal purposes in the end of man (after that he had created our first parents, and the beasts of the field, and the fowls of the air, and in fine, all things which are created) it must needs be that there was an opposition—even the forbidden fruit in opposition to the tree of life, the one being sweet and the other bitter. ¹⁶Wherefore, the Lord God gave unto man that he should act for himself. Wherefore, man could not act for himself save it should be that he were enticed by the one or the other.

¹⁷And I, Lehi (according to the things which I have read), must needs suppose that an angel of God (according to that which is written) had fallen from heaven. Wherefore, he became a devil, having sought that which was evil before God. ¹⁸And because that he had fallen from heaven and had became miserable forever (and he sought also the misery of all mankind), wherefore, he saith unto Eve (yea,

---

a. See Revelation 14:4 for the phrase "firstfruits unto God."

b. This sentence is difficult to parse. As it is here, there is a missing "is" before the final clause. The original intent was "the ends of the law which the Holy One hath given unto the inflicting of the punishment which is affixed, [is] to answer the ends of the atonement." The phrases in parentheses interrupted the flow and caused the missing verb before the conclusion.

c. See 1 Corinthians 15:54 for the use of "corruption and incorruption."

even that old serpent which is the devil,[a] which is the father of all lies)—wherefore, he saith: "Partake of the forbidden fruit, and ye shall not die. But ye shall be as God, knowing good and evil."[b]

[19] And after that Adam and Eve had partaken of the forbidden fruit, they were driven out from the garden of Eden to till the earth. [20] And they have brought forth children, yea, even the family of all the earth. [21] And the days of the children of men were prolonged, according to the will of God, that they might repent while in the flesh. Wherefore, their state became a state of probation. And their time was lengthened, according to the commandments which the Lord God gave unto the children of men. For he gave commandment that all men must repent. For he showed unto all men that they were lost because of the transgression of their parents.

[22] And now, behold, if Adam had not transgressed, he would not have fallen, but he would have remained in the Garden of Eden. And all things which were created, must have remained in the same state which they were after that they were created. And they must have remained forever and had no end. [23] And they would have had no children. Wherefore, they would have remained in a state of innocence. Having no joy for they knew no misery. Doing no good for they knew no sin.

[24] But behold, all things have been done in the wisdom of him who knoweth all things. [25] Adam fell that men might be. And men are that they might have joy. [26] And the Messiah cometh in the fullness of time that he might redeem the children of men from the fall. And because that they are redeemed from the fall, they have become free forever. Knowing good from evil. To act for themselves and not to be acted upon (save it be by the punishment of the law at the great and last day, according to the commandments which God hath given). [27] Wherefore, men are free according to the flesh. And all things are given them which is expedient unto man. And they are free to choose liberty and eternal life through the great mediator of all men, or to choose captivity and death, according to the captivity and power of the devil—for he seeketh that all men might be miserable like unto himself.

[28] And now, my sons, I would that ye should look to the great mediator and hearken unto his great commandments and be faithful unto his words—and chose eternal life (according to the will of his Holy Spirit)—[29] and not chose eternal death (according to the will of the flesh and the evil which is therein—which giveth the spirit of the devil power to captivate, to bring you down to hell that he may reign over you in his own kingdom).

[30] I have spoken these few words unto you, all my sons, in the last days of my probation. And I have chosen the good part,[c] according to the words of the prophet. And I have none other object save it be the everlasting welfare of your souls. Amen.

---

a. See Revelation 20:2 for the phrase "that old serpent, which is the Devil."
b. The "wherefore" serves to return to the original intent of the sentence.
c. See Luke 10:42 for the phrase "chosen the good part."

Chapter II [2 Nephi 3]

[3] ¹And now, I speak unto you, Joseph, my last born. Thou wast born in the wilderness of mine afflictions. Yea, in the days of my greatest sorrow did thy mother bear thee. ²And may the Lord consecrate also unto thee this land (which is a most precious land) for thine inheritance, and the inheritance of thy seed (with thy brethren), for thy security forever–if it so be that ye shall keep the commandments of the Holy One of Israel.

³And now, Joseph, my last born, whom I have brought out of the wilderness of mine afflictions, may the Lord bless thee forever. For thy seed shall not utterly be destroyed. ⁴For behold, thou art the fruit of my loins. And I am a descendant of Joseph which was carried captive into Egypt. And great was the covenants of the Lord which he made unto Joseph. ⁵Wherefore, Joseph truly saw our day and he obtained a promise of the Lord, that out of the fruit of his loins the Lord God would raise up a righteous branch unto the house of Israel—not the Messiah, but a branch which was to be broken off (nevertheless to be remembered in the covenants of the Lord)—that the Messiah should be made manifest unto them in the latter days, in the spirit of power, unto the bringing of them out of darkness unto light.ᵃ Yea, out of hidden darkness and out of captivity unto freedom.

⁶For Joseph truly testified, saying: "A seer shall the Lord my God raise up, which shall be a choice seer unto the fruit of my loins." ⁷Yea, Joseph truly said:

> Thus saith the Lord unto me: a choice seer will I raise up out of the fruit of thy loins. And he shall be esteemed highly among the fruit of thy loins. ⁸And unto him will I give commandment that he shall do a work for the fruit of thy loins (his brethren) which shall be of great worth unto them, even to the bringing of them to the knowledge of the covenants which I have made with thy fathers.
>
> And I will give unto him a commandment that he shall do none other work, save the work which I shall command him. And I will make him great in mine eyes, for he shall do my work. ⁹And he shall be great, like unto Moses (whom I have said I would raise up unto you), to deliver my people, O house of Israel. ¹⁰And Moses will I raise up to deliver thy people out of the land of Egypt. ¹¹But a seer will I raise up out of the fruit of thy loins.
>
> And unto him will I give power to bring forth my word unto the seed of thy loins. Not to the bringing forth my word only (saith the Lord), but to the convincing them of my word (which shall have already gone forth among them). ¹²Wherefore, the fruit of my loins shall write. And the fruit of the loins of Judah shall write. And that which shall be written by the fruit of thy loins, and also that which shall be written by the fruit of the loins of Judah, shall grow together—unto the confounded confounding of false doctrines, and laying down of contentions, and establishing peace among the fruit of thy loins,

---

a. This is an awkward sentence. It would have been better to have been two sentences, with "the Messiah should" beginning the second sentence (and leaving out "that"). The original intent of the sentence was to establish the branch broken off as the remnant of Joseph. The declaration that it was not the Messiah led to the discussion of the Messiah.

and bringing them to the knowledge of their fathers in the latter days, and also to the knowledge of my covenants (saith the Lord). ¹³And out of weakness, he shall be made strong in that day when my work shall commence among all my people, unto the restoring thee, O house of Israel (saith the Lord).

¹⁴And thus prophesied Joseph, saying:

Behold, that seer will the Lord bless. And they that seek to destroy him shall be confounded. For this promise (of which I have obtained of the Lord) of the fruit of thy loins, shall be fulfilled.ᵃ Behold, I am sure of the fulfilling of this promise. ¹⁵And his name shall be called after me. And it shall be after the name of his father. And he shall be like unto me. For the thing which the Lord shall bring forth by his hand, by the power of the Lord, shall bring my people unto salvation.

¹⁶Yea, thus prophesied Joseph:

I am sure of this thing, even as I am sure of the promise of Moses. For the Lord hath said unto me: "I will preserve thy seed forever." ¹⁷And the Lord hath said: "I will raise up a Moses, and I will give power unto him in a rod. And I will give judgment unto him in writing, yet I will not loose his tongue that he shall speak much. For I will not make him mighty in speaking, but I will write unto him my law, by the finger of mine own hand. And I will make one a spokesman for him."

¹⁸And the Lord said unto me also: I will raise up unto the fruit of thy loins, and I will make one for him, a spokesman. And I, behold I, will give unto him that he shall write the writing of the fruit of thy loins—unto the fruit of thy loins. And the spokesman of thy loins shall declare it. ¹⁹And the words which he shall write shall be the words which is expedient, in my wisdom, should go forth unto the fruit of thy loins. And it shall be as if the fruit of thy loins had cried unto them from the dust.ᵇ For I know their faith.

²⁰And they shall cry from the dust,ᶜ yea, even repentance unto their brethren, even that after many generations have gone by them. And it shall come to pass that their cry shall go, even according to the simpleness of their words. ²¹Because of their faith, their words shall proceed forth out of my mouth unto their brethren (which are the fruit of thy loins). And the weakness of their words will I make strong in their faith, unto the remembering of my covenant which I made unto thy fathers.

²²And now behold, my son Joseph, after this manner did my father of old prophesy. ²³Wherefore, because of this covenant, thou art blessed. For thy seed shall not be destroyed. For they shall hearken unto the words of the book. ²⁴And

---

a. This is a difficult sentence. This edition posits the main clause as "For this promise ... of the fruit of thy loins, shall be fulfilled." The construction of "promise of the fruit of thy loins" is a little awkward and might be modernized to "promise to (or for) the fruit of thy loins."

b. See Isaiah 29:4: "And thou shalt be brought down, and shalt speak out of the ground, and thy speech shall be low out of the dust."

c. See Isaiah 29:4: "And thou shalt be brought down, and shalt speak out of the ground, and thy speech shall be low out of the dust."

there shall raise up one mighty among them, which shall do much good (both in word and in deed)—being an instrument in the hands of God—with exceeding faith to work mighty wonders, and do that thing which is great in the sight of God, unto the bringing to pass much restoration unto the house of Israel and unto the seed of thy brethren.

²⁵And now, blessed art thou Joseph. Behold, thou art little. Wherefore, hearken unto the words of thy brother, Nephi, and it shall be done unto thee, even according to the words which I have spoken. Remember the words of thy dying father. Amen.

Chapter III [2 Nephi 4]

[4] ¹And now, I, Nephi, speak concerning the prophesies of which my father hath spoken concerning Joseph who was carried into Egypt. ²For behold, he truly prophesied concerning all his seed. And the prophesies which he wrote—there are not many greater. And he prophesied concerning us, and our future generations. And they are written upon the plates of brass.

³Wherefore, after my father had made an end of speaking concerning the prophesies of Joseph, he called the children of Laman, his sons and his daughters, and saith unto them[a]:

Behold, my sons and my daughters (which are the sons and the daughters of my first born), I would that ye should give ear unto my words. ⁴For the Lord God hath said: "That inasmuch as ye shall keep my commandments, ye shall prosper in the land. And inasmuch as ye will not keep my commandments, ye shall be cut off from my presence."[b]

⁵But behold, my sons and my daughters, I cannot go down to my grave, save I should leave a blessing upon you.

For behold, I know that if ye are brought up in the right way that ye should go, ye will not depart from it.[c] ⁶Wherefore, if ye are cursed, behold, I leave my blessing upon you, that the cursing may be taken from you and be answered upon the heads of your parents. ⁷Wherefore, because of my blessing, the Lord God will not suffer that ye shall perish. Wherefore, he will be merciful unto you and unto your seed forever.

⁸And it came to pass that after my father had made an end of speaking to the sons and daughters of Laman, he caused that the sons and daughters of Lemuel be to be brought before him. ⁹And he spake unto them, saying:

Behold my sons and my daughters (which are the sons and the daughters of my second son), behold, I leave unto you the same blessing which I left unto the sons and daughters of Laman. Wherefore, thou shalt not utterly be destroyed. But in the end, thy seed shall be blessed.

¹⁰And it came to pass that when my father had made an end of speaking unto them, behold, it came to pass that he spake unto the sons of Ishmael, yea, and even all his household. ¹¹And after that he had made an end of speaking unto them, he spake unto Sam, saying:

---

a. This edition typically keeps clauses beginning with "wherefore" in the paragraph that leads to them. In most cases, the "wherefore" refers to the previous content. (See, for example, verses 6 and 7 below.) In this case, however, "wherever" does not fit that function. It seems out of place. Nephi makes an end of Lehi's blessings to his sons and now turns to the next generation. This is a different topic and has nothing to do with the prophesies Joseph of Egypt had given. For this reason, it is a new paragraph, simply noting that "wherefore" is functionally out of place.

b. The phrase "cut off from my presence" is found in Leviticus 22:3.

c. See Proverbs 22:6: "Train up a child in the way he should go: and when he is old, he will not depart from it."

Chapter III [2 Nephi 4]

Blessed art thou, and thy seed. For thou shalt inherit the land, like unto thy brother Nephi. And thy seed shall be numbered with his seed. And thou shalt be even like unto thy brother—and thy seed, like unto his seed. And thou shalt be blessed in all thy days.

¹²And it came to pass that after Lehi had spake unto all his household, according to the feelings of his heart, and the spirit of the Lord which was in him—he waxed old. ¹³And it came to pass that he died and was buried.

And it came to pass that not many days after his death, Laman, and Lemuel, and the sons of Ishmael, were angry with me because of the admonitions of the Lord. ¹⁴For I, Nephi, was constrained to speak unto them, according to the word. For I had spake many things unto them (and also my father, before his death), many of which sayings are written upon mine other plates. For a more history-part[a] are written upon mine other plates.

> ¹⁵And upon these I write the things of my soul, and many of the scriptures which are engraven upon the plates of brass.[b] For my soul delighteth in the scriptures. And my heart pondereth them, and writeth them for the learning and the profit of my children.[c]

¹⁶Behold, my soul delighteth in the things of the Lord, and my heart pondereth continually upon the things which I have seen and heard. ¹⁷Nevertheless, notwithstanding the great goodness of the Lord in showing me his great and marvelous works, my heart exclaimeth—O wretched man that I am![d]

Yea, my heart sorroweth, because of mine flesh.

My soul grieveth because of mine iniquity.

¹⁸I am encompassed about because of the temptations, and the sins which doth so easily beset me.

¹⁹And when I desire to rejoice, my heart groaneth because of my sins. Nevertheless, I know in whom I have trusted. ²⁰My God hath been my support.

He hath led me through mine afflictions in the wilderness, and he hath preserved me upon the waters of the great deep.

²¹He hath filled me with his love, even unto the consuming of my flesh.

²²He hath confounded mine enemies, unto the causing of them to quake before me.

²³Behold, he hath heard my cry by day, and he hath given me knowledge by visions in the nighttime.

²⁴And by day, have I waxed bold in mighty prayer before him. Yea, my voice have I sent upon high. And angels came down and ministered unto me. ²⁵And

---

a. Modern editions leave this as "more history part." That is correct, but it is not sufficiently clear. The base phrase would be "the more part" (as in Acts 19:32, 27:12; 1 Nephi 9:4, 19:2, 4, etc.). We might render it "historical part."

b. As with previous insertions that explain the small plates (1 Nephi 9:2–6 and 19:1–18), this mention also generates an aside. In this case, the mention of the plates coincides with Nephi writing of his father's death and continued conflicts with Laman and Lemuel. This leads into the beautiful extemporaneous Psalm of Nephi through the end of this chapter.

c. From this point on the insertion runs to poetic parallels. They are formatted into the more obvious parallels for emphasis. They could easily be made paragraphs, but that might obscure the intentional paralleling.

d. See Romans 7:24 for the phrase "O wretched man that I am."

upon the wings of his spirit hath my body been carried away upon exceeding high mountains. And mine eyes hath beheld great things, yea, even too great for man. Therefore, I was bidden that I should not write them.

²⁶O then, if I have seen so great things—if the Lord (in his condescension unto the children of men) hath visited me in so much mercy—

Why should my heart weep?

And my soul linger in the valley of sorrow?

And my flesh waste away?

And my strength slacken because of mine afflictions?

²⁷And why should I yield to sin because of my flesh?

Yea, why should I give way to temptations, that the evil one have place in my heart, to destroy my peace and afflict my soul?

Why am I angry because of mine enemy?

²⁸Awake my soul! No longer droop in sin!

Rejoice, O my heart! And give place no more for the enemy of my soul!

²⁹Do not anger again because of mine enemies!

Do not slacken my strength because of mine afflictions!

³⁰Rejoice, O my heart! And cry unto the Lord! And say:

O Lord, I will praise thee forever! Yea, my soul will rejoice in thee, my God, and the rock of my salvation.

³¹O Lord, wilt thou redeem my soul?

Wilt thou deliver me out of the hands of mine enemies?

Wilt thou make me that I may shake at the appearance of sin?

³²May the gates of hell be shut continually before me, because that my heart is broken, and my spirit is contrite![a]

O Lord, wilt thou not shut the gates of thy righteousness[b] before me, that I may walk in the path of the low valley, that I may be strict in the [plain[c]] road?

³³O Lord, wilt thou encircle me around in the robe of thy righteousness?[d]

O Lord, wilt thou make a way for mine escape before mine enemies?

Wilt thou make my path strait before me?

Wilt thou not place a stumbling block in my way,[e]

but that thou wouldst clear my way before me.

And hedge not up my way,[f]

but the ways of mine enemy?

³⁴O Lord, I have trusted in thee.

And I will trust in thee forever.

---

a. See Psalm 34:18: "The Lord is nigh unto them that are of a broken heart; and saveth such as be of a contrite spirit."

b. See Psalm 118:19: "Open to me the gates of righteousness: I will go into them, and I will praise the Lord."

c. The Printer's Manuscript has "plane." Given the imprecise spelling, it might be intended to be "a plain road." However, "plane" (as in "smooth") is also a possible reading.

d. The phrase "robe of righteousness" occurs in Isaiah 61:10.

e. See Isaiah 57:14: "And shall say, Cast ye up, cast ye up, prepare the way, take up the stumblingblock out of the way of my people."

f. See Hosea 2:6: "Therefore, behold, I will hedge up thy way with thorns, and make a wall, that she shall not find her paths."

Chapter III [2 Nephi 4]

I will not put my trust in the arm of flesh,
> for I know that cursed is he that puteth his trust in the arm of flesh.[a]
> Yea, cursed is he that puteth his trust in man, or maketh flesh his arm!

³⁵Yea, I know that God will give liberally to him that asketh.[b]

Yea, my God will give me if I ask not amiss.

Therefore, I will lift up my voice unto thee.

I will cry unto thee, my God, the rock of my righteousness!

Behold, my voice shall forever ascend up unto thee—my rock, and mine everlasting God. Amen.<

---

a. See Jeremiah 17:5: "Thus saith the Lord; Cursed be the man that trusteth in man, and maketh flesh his arm, and whose heart departeth from the Lord."

b. See James 1:5 for the phrase "giveth to all men liberally."

Chapter IV [2 Nephi 5]

[5] ¹Behold, it came to pass that I, Nephi, did cry much unto the Lord, my God, because of the anger of my brethren. ²But behold, their anger did increase against me, insomuch that they did seek to take away my life. ³Yea, they did murmur against me, saying:

> Our younger brother thinketh to rule over us. And we have had much trial because of him. Wherefore, now let us slay him, that we may not be afflicted more because of his words. For behold, we will not that he shall be our ruler. For it belongeth unto us (which are the elder brethren) to rule over this people.

⁴Now, I do not write upon these plates all the words which they murmured against me. But it sufficeth me to say that they did seek to take away my life.

⁵And it came to pass that the Lord did warn me, that I, Nephi, should depart from them, and flee into the wilderness—and all they which would go with me. ⁶Wherefore, it came to pass that I, Nephi, did take my family, and also Zoram and his family, and Sam (mine elder brother) and his family, and Jacob and Joseph (my younger brethren), and also my sisters, and all they which would go with me. And all they which would go with me were they which believed in the warnings and the revelations of God. Wherefore, they did hearken unto my words.

⁷And we did take our tents and whatsoever things were possible for us, and did journey in the wilderness for the space of many days. And after that we had journeyed for the space of many days, we did pitch our tents. ⁸And my people would that we should call the name of the place Nephi. Wherefore, we did call it Nephi. ⁹And all they which were with me did take it upon them to call themselves the people of Nephi. ¹⁰And we did observe to keep the judgments, and the statutes, and the commandments, of the Lord in all things (according to the law of Moses). ¹¹And the Lord was with us. And we did prosper exceedingly. For we did sow seed and we did reap again in abundance. And we began to raise flocks, and herds, and animals of every kind.

¹²And I, Nephi, had also brought the records which were engraven upon the plates of brass, and also the ball (or compass), which was prepared for my father by the hand of the Lord, according to that which is written.

¹³And it came to pass that we began to prosper exceedingly, and to multiply in the land.

¹⁴And I, Nephi, did take the sword of Laban—and after the manner of it, did make many swords, lest by any means the people (which were now called Lamanites) should come upon us, and destroy us. For I knew their hatred towards me, and my children, and they which were called my people.

¹⁵And I did teach my people that they should build buildings, and that they should work in all manner of wood, and of iron, and of copper, and of brass, and of steel—and of gold, and of silver, and of precious ores (which were in great abundance). ¹⁶And I, Nephi, did build a temple. And I did construct it after the manner of the temple of Solomon, save it were not built of so many precious things—for they were not to be found upon the land. Wherefore, it could not be built like unto Solomon's temple. But the manner of the construction was like unto the temple of Solomon. And the workmanship thereof was exceeding fine.

Chapter IV [2 Nephi 5]

¹⁷And it came to pass that I, Nephi, did cause my people that they should be industrious. And that they should labor with their hands.

¹⁸And it came to pass that they would that I should be their king. But I, Nephi, was desirous that they should have no king. Nevertheless, I did do for them according to that which was in my power.

>¹⁹And behold, the words of the Lord had been fulfilled unto my brethren, which he spake concerning them, that I should be their ruler, and their teacher. Wherefore, I had been their ruler, and their teacher, according to the commandments of the Lord, until the time that they sought to take away my life. ²⁰Wherefore, the word of the Lord was fulfilled, which he spake unto me, saying that: "Inasmuch as they will not hearken unto thy words, they shall be cut off from the presence of the Lord."ᵃ And behold, they were cut off from his presence. ²¹And he had caused the cursing to come upon them, yea, even a sore cursing, because of their iniquity. For behold, they had hardened their hearts against him that they had become like unto a flint. Wherefore, as they were white and exceeding fair and delightsome—that they might not be enticing unto my people, therefore, the Lord God did cause a skin of blackness to come upon them.

²²And thus saith the Lord God: "I will cause that they shall be loathsome unto thy people, save they shall repent of their iniquities. ²³And cursed shall be the seed of him that mixeth with their seed, for they shall be cursed even with the same cursing."

And the Lord spake it, and it was done.

²⁴And because of their cursing which was upon them, they did become an idle people, full of mischief, and subtlety, and did seek in the wilderness for beasts of prey.

²⁵And the Lord God said unto me: "They shall be a scourge unto thy seed, to stir them up in remembrance of me. And inasmuch as they will not remember me and hearken unto my words, they shall scourge them, even unto destruction."ᵇ<

²⁶And it came to pass that I, Nephi, did consecrate Jacob and Joseph, that they should be priests and teachers,ᶜ over the land of my people.

²⁷And it came to pass that we lived after the manner of happiness. ²⁸And thirty years had passed away from the time we left Jerusalem. ²⁹And I, Nephi, had kept the records (upon my plates) which I had made of my people, thus far.ᵈ

³⁰And it came to pass that the Lord God said unto me: "Make other plates. And thou shalt engraven many things upon them which are good in my sight, for the profit of thy people." ³¹Wherefore I, Nephi, to be obedient to the commandments of the

---

a. The phrase "cut off from my presence" is found in Leviticus 22:3.

b. Nephi has been speaking of his own people. This aside is triggered by what Nephi wrote about being a king. That led him to the problem of ruling over his brothers, and that to their cursing. This is an aside in the intended discussion of the people of Nephi who at this time are separated from the Lamanites.

c. This edition elects to have "priests and teachers," indicating that each of the two brothers fulfilled each function. Perhaps "priests and teachers" were descriptions of responsibilities rather than names of roles. Nevertheless, it is also possible that it should be "priests, and teachers," indicating that each role was separate. The other reading is also possible.

d. Where previous instances of Nephi mentioning the creation of the small plates were insertions, this description comes at the correct time period. Therefore, this is not an insertion but rather a planned part of the historical description.

Lord, went, and made these plates upon which I have engraven these things. ³²And I engravened that which is pleasing unto God.

³³And if my people be pleased with the things of God, they be pleased with mine engravings which are upon these plates. And if my people desire to know the more particular part of the history of my people, they must search mine other plates.

³⁴And it sufficeth me to say that forty years had passed away. And we had already had wars and contentions with our brethren.

Chapter V [2 Nephi 6–8]

[6] ¹*The words of Jacob, the brother of Nephi, which he spake unto the people of Nephi.*ᵃ

²Behold, my beloved brethren, that I, Jacob, having been called of God and ordained after the manner of his holy order, and having been consecrated by my brother, Nephi (unto whom ye look as a king, or a protector, and on whom ye depend for safety)—behold, ye know that I have spoken unto you exceeding many things. ³Nevertheless, I speak unto you again, for I am desirous for the welfare of your souls. Yea, mine anxiety is great for you. And ye yourselves know that it ever has been. For I have exhorted you with all diligence. And I have taught you the words of my father. And I have spoken unto you concerning all things which are written from the creation of the world.

⁴And now behold, I would speak unto you concerning things which are, and which are to come. Wherefore, I will read you the words of Isaiah. And they are the words which my brother hath desired me that I should speak unto you. And I speak them unto you for your sakes, that ye may learn, and glorify, the name of your God.

⁵And now, the words which I shall read are they which Isaiah spake, concerning all the house of Israel. Wherefore, they may be likened unto you, for ye are of the house of Israel. And there are many things which have been spoken by Isaiah which may be likened unto you because that ye are of the house of Israel.

⁶And now, these are the words:

> Thus saith the Lord God: Behold, I will lift up mine hand unto the Gentiles, and set up my standard to the people. And they shall bring thy sons in their arms, and thy daughters shall be carried upon their shoulders. ⁷And kings shall be thy nursing fathers. And their queens thy nursing mothers. They shall bow down to thee with their faces towards the earth, and lick up the dust of thy feet. And thou shalt know that I am the Lord. For they shall not be ashamed that wait for me.ᵇ

⁸And now, I, Jacob, would speak somewhat concerning these words. For behold, the Lord hath shown me that they which were at Jerusalem (from whence we came) have been slain and carried away captive. ⁹Nevertheless, the Lord hath shown unto me that they should return again. And he also hath shown unto me that the Lord God, the Holy One of Israel, should manifest himself unto them in the flesh. And after that he should manifest himself, they should scourge him, and crucify him (according to the words of the angel, which spake it unto me).

¹⁰And after that they have hardened their hearts, and stiffened their necks,ᶜ against the Holy One of Israel, behold, the judgments of the Holy One of Israel shall come upon them. And the day cometh that they shall be smitten and afflicted. ¹⁰Wherefore, after they are driven to and fro (for thus saith the angel), many shall be afflicted in the flesh, and shall not be suffered to perish, because of the prayers of the faithful. Wherefore, they shall be scattered, and smitten, and hated. Nevertheless, the Lord will

---

a. This sentence is set as a chapter header as Grant Hardy suggests in his *The Book of Mormon: Maxwell Institute Study Edition* (Provo, UT: Neal A. Maxwell Institute, 2018), 71.

b. Reference Isaiah 49:22–23.

c. See 2 Chronicles 36:13: "And he also rebelled against king Nebuchadnezzar, who had made him swear by God: but he stiffened his neck, and hardened his heart from turning unto the Lord God of Israel."

be merciful unto them, that when they shall come to the knowledge of their Redeemer, they shall be gathered together again to the lands of their inheritance.

¹²And blessed are the Gentiles, they of whom the prophet hath written. For behold, if it so be that they shall repent, and fight not against Zion, and do not unite themselves to that great and abominable church, they shall be saved. For the Lord God will fulfil his covenants which he hath made unto his children. And for this cause, the prophet hath written these things. ¹³Wherefore, they that fight against Zion and the covenant people of the Lord, shall lick up the dust of their feet. And the people of the Lord shall not be ashamed. For the people of the Lord are they which wait for him. For they still wait for the coming of the Messiah.

¹⁴And behold (according to the words of the prophet) the Messiah will set himself again, the second time, to recover them.[a] Wherefore, he will manifest himself unto them in power and great glory—unto the destruction of their enemies when that day cometh when they shall believe in him. And none will he destroy that believeth in him. ¹⁵And they that believe not in him shall be destroyed both by fire, and by tempest, and by earthquakes, and by bloodsheds, and by pestilence, and by famine. And they shall know that the Lord is God, the Holy One of Israel.

[Compare Isaiah 49: 24–26]

¹⁶For shall the prey be taken from the mighty,
    or the lawful captive delivered?
¹⁷But thus saith the Lord:
"Even the captives of the mighty shall be taken away,
    and the prey of the terrible shall be delivered.
    For the mighty God shall deliver his covenant people."
For thus saith the Lord:
"I will contend with **them** that contendeth with thee [b].
¹⁸And I will feed them that oppress thee with their own flesh.
    And they shall be drunken with their own blood, as with sweet wine.
    And all flesh shall know that I, the Lord, am thy Savior and thy Redeemer,
        the Mighty One of Jacob."[c]

[7, Compare Isaiah 50]

¹Yea, for thus saith the Lord:
"Have I put thee away?
    Or, have I cast thee off forever?"

For thus saith the Lord:
"Where is the bill of your mother's divorcement?
    To whom **have I** put thee away?
    Or, to which of my creditors **have I sold you?**
        Yea, to whom **have I** sold you?
    Behold, for your iniquities have ye sold yourselves.

---

    a. See Isaiah 11:11: "And it shall come to pass in that day, *that* the Lord shall set his hand again the second time to recover the remnant of his people."
    b. Omits "and I will save thy children."
    c. Quoting Isaiah 49:24–26.

And for your transgressions is your mother put away.
²Wherefore, when I come^a, **there was** no man.
   When I called, **yea, there was** none to answer.
   O house of Israel! Is my hand shortened at all, that it cannot redeem?
      Or, have I no power to deliver?
Behold, at my rebuke I dry up the sea.
   I make the^b rivers a wilderness
and their fish to stink, **because the waters are dried up.**
   And **they dieth because** of thirst.
³I clothe the heavens with blackness,
   and I make sackcloth their covering."

⁴The Lord God hath given me the tongue of the learned,
      that I should know how to speak a word in season
      unto thee, O house of Israel. when ye are weary.
He waketh morning by morning.
   He [wakeneth^c] mine ear to hear as the learned.
⁵The Lord God hath [opened^d] mine ear.
   And I was not rebellious.
   Neither turned away back.
⁶I gave my back to the [smiters^e],
   and my cheeks to them that plucked off the hair.
   I hid not my face from shame and spitting.

⁷For the Lord God will help me.
   Therefore shall I not be confounded!
   Therefore have I set my face like a flint!
   And I know that I shall not be ashamed.
⁸**And the Lord** is near. **And he** justifieth me.
Who will contend with me? Let us stand together!
   Who is mine adversary? Let him come near me,
   and I will smite him with the strength of my mouth!
⁹For the Lord God will help me.
And all they which shall condemn me,
   Behold, all they shall wax old as a garment.
   And the moth shall eat them up.

---

   a. Isaiah 50:2 has the past tense, "came," which makes more sense.
   b. A fragment of the Original Manuscript indicates that the dictated text agreed with the King James passage: "I make the rivers a wilderness and their fish to stink." Oliver Cowdery apparently added "their" under the influence of "their fish" in the same sentence. The Original Manuscript follows the King James Bible's "I make the rivers a wilderness." Skousen, *Analysis of Textual Variants*, 1:581.
   c. Restored from the Original Manuscript. The Printer's Manuscript has "waketh." Skousen, *Analysis of the Textual Variants*, 1:584.
   d. Restored from the Original Manuscript. The Printer's Manuscript has "appointed." Skousen, *Analysis of the Textual Variants,* 1:584.
   e. Restored from the Original Manuscript. The Printer's Manuscript has "smiter." Per Isaiah 50:6 and Skousen, *Analysis of the Textual Variants,* 1:584.

¹⁰Who is among you that feareth the Lord,
> that obeyeth the voice of his servant,
> that walketh in darkness, and hath no light? [a]

¹¹Behold all ye that **kindleth** fire,
> that compass yourselves about with sparks!

Walk in the light of your fire
> and in the sparks which ye have kindled!

This shall ye have of mine hand—
> ye shall lie down in sorrow.

[8, Compare Isaiah 51]

¹Hearken to me, ye that follow after righteousness! [b]

²Look unto the rock **from** whence ye are hewn,
> and to the hole of the pit **from** whence ye are digged!

Look unto Abraham, your father,
> and unto Sarah, she that bear you!

For I called him alone, and blessed him [c].

³For the Lord shall comfort Zion.
> He will comfort all her waste places.

And he will make her wilderness like Eden,
> and her desert like the garden of the Lord.

Joy and gladness shall be found therein—
> thanksgiving, and the voice of melody!

⁴Hearken unto me, my beloved people,
> and give ear unto me, O, my Nation!

For a law shall proceed from me.
> And I will make my judgment to rest for a light thing of the people.

⁵My righteousness is near.
> My salvation is gone forth.
> And mine arm shall judge the people.

The isles shall wait upon me.
> And on mine arm shall they trust.

⁶Lift up your eyes to the heavens!
> And look upon the earth beneath!

For the heavens shall vanish away like smoke,
> and the earth shall wax old like a garment.
> And they that dwell therein shall die in like manner.

But my salvation shall be forever!
> And my righteousness shall not be abolished!

⁷Hearken unto me, ye that know righteousness—
> the people in whose heart **I have written** my law!

Fear ye not the reproach of men!
> Neither be ye afraid of their revilings!

---

a. Omits "let him trust I the name of the Lord, and stay upon his God."
b. Omits "ye that seek the Lord."
c. Omits "and increased him."

Chapter V [2 Nephi 6–8]

⁸For the moth shall eat them up like a garment,
    and the worm shall eat them like wool.
But my righteousness shall be forever.
    And my salvation from generation to generation.

⁹Awake! Awake! Put on strength, O arm of the Lord!
    Awake as in the ancient days [a].
¹⁰Art thou not it that hath cut Rahab,
    and wounded the dragon?
Art thou not it which hath dried the sea,
    the waters of the great deep,
that hath made the depths of the sea
    a way for the ransomed to pass over?
¹¹Therefore, the redeemed of the Lord shall return,
    and come with singing unto Zion.
And everlasting joy **and holiness** shall be upon their **heads**.
    And they shall obtain gladness, and joy.
    Sorrow and mourning shall flee away.

¹²**I am he. Yea,** I am he that comforteth you.
Behold, who art thou
    that thou shouldst be afraid of man (which shall die),
    and of the son of man (which shall be made like unto grass)—
¹³and forgetest the Lord, thy maker,
    that hath stretched forth the heavens,
    and laid the foundations of the earth,
    and hast feared continually every day
    because of the fury of the oppressor,
    as if he were ready to destroy.
    And where is the fury of the oppressor?

¹⁴The captive exile hasteneth,
    that he may be loosed,
and that he should not die in the pit,
    nor that his bread should fail.
¹⁵But I am the Lord thy God, [b] whose waves roared.
    The Lord of Hosts is **my** name.
¹⁶And I have put my words in thy mouth,
    and hath covered thee in the shadow of mine hand,
that I may plant the heavens,
    and lay the foundations of the earth—
    and say unto Zion: "Behold, thou art my people."

¹⁷Awake! Awake! Stand up, O Jerusalem,
    which hast drunk (at the hand of the Lord) the cup of his fury.
    Thou hast drunken the dregs of the cup of trembling, wrung out.

---

a. Omits "in the generations of old."
b. Omits "that divided the sea."

¹⁸**And** none to guide her
>among all the sons she hath brought forth,

neither that taketh her by the hand of all the sons she hath brought up.
¹⁹These two **sons** are come unto thee, who shall be sorry for thee—
>thy desolation and destruction,
>and the famine and the sword.

And by whom shall I comfort thee?
²⁰Thy sons have fainted, **save these two**.
>They lie at the head of all the streets, as a wild bull in a net.
>They are full of the fury of the Lord, the rebuke of thy God.

²¹Therefore hear now this, thou afflicted
>and drunken (**and** not with wine).

²²Thus saith thy lord:
>The Lord and thy God pleadeth the cause of [his^a] people.^b

Behold, I have taken out of thine hand the cup of trembling.
>The dregs of the cup of my fury
>thou shalt no more drink it again.

²³But I will put it unto the hand of them that afflict thee,
>[who have^c] said to thy soul—"Bow down that we may go over."

And thou hast laid thy body as the ground
>and as the street, to them that went over.

[Compare Isaiah 52:1–2]

²⁴Awake! Awake! Put on thy strength, O Zion!
>Put on thy beautiful garments, O Jerusalem, the holy city.

For henceforth, there shall no more come into thee
>the uncircumcised and the unclean.

²⁵Shake thyself from the dust!
>Arise! [^d] Sit down, O Jerusalem.

Loose thyself from the bands of thy neck,
>O captive daughter of Zion.

---

a. The word "thy" is in the Printer's Manuscript. It is crossed out and corrected to "his" in heavier ink, indicating that it occurred later, probably during proofreading. The Isaiah passage has "his."

b. The phrase "the lord the Lord" appears awkward. This is due to the use of "Lord" to replace the tetragrammaton. The intent in Isaiah would have been "the ruler, YHWH." This sentence was made more difficult by the removal of the italicized "that" after "thy God." Isaiah makes more sense with "they God that pleadeth." The word "and" replaced the italicized "that."

c. The Printer's Manuscript has a corrected word that is difficult to read. This edition follows Skousen, *Analysis of the Textual Variants,* 1:608, where he notes: "Contextually the original reading of the printer's manuscript ('which **I said** to thy soul') does not make much sense since quite obviously it is Israel's afflicters, not the Lord, who said 'bow down that we may go over'." The word "have" is written above the line.

d. Omits "and," which is in italics.

Chapter VI [2 Nephi 9]

[9] ¹And now, my beloved brethren, I have read these things that ye might know concerning the covenants of the Lord—that he hath covenanted with all the house of Israel. ²That he hath spoken unto the Jews by the mouth of his holy prophets, even from the beginning down from generation to generation[a], until the time cometh that they shall be restored to the true church and fold of God—when they shall be gathered home to the lands of their inheritance and shall be established in all their lands of promise.

³Behold my beloved brethren, I speak unto you these things that ye may rejoice, and lift up your heads forever, because of the blessings which the Lord God shall bestow upon your children. ⁴For I know that thou hast searched much (many of you) to know of things to come. Wherefore, I know that ye know that our flesh must waste away and die. Nevertheless, in our bodies we shall see God.

⁵Yea, and I know that ye know that in the body he shall show himself unto they at Jerusalem (from whence we came). For it is expedient that it should be among them. For it behoveth the great Creator that he suffereth himself to become subject unto man in the flesh and die for all men, that all men might become subject unto him. ⁶For, as death hath passed upon all men[b] (to fulfil the merciful plan of the great Creator), there must needs be a power of resurrection.

And the resurrection must needs come unto man, by reason of the fall. And the fall came by reason of transgression. And because man became fallen, they were cut off from the presence of the Lord.[c] ⁷Wherefore, it must needs be an infinite atonement. Save it should be an infinite atonement, this corruption could not put on incorruption.[d] Wherefore, the first judgment which came upon man, must needs have remained to an endless duration. And if so, this flesh must have laid down to rot, and to crumble to its mother earth. to rise no more.

⁸O, the wisdom of God! His mercy, and grace! For behold, if the flesh should rise no more, our spirits must become subject to that angel which fell from before the presence of the Eternal God (and became the devil), to rise no more. ⁹And our spirits must have become like unto him. And we become devils, angels to a devil—to be shut out from the presence of our God and to remain with the father of lies—in misery like unto himself. Yea, to that being who beguiled our first parents, who transformeth himself nigh unto an angel of light,[e] and stireth up the children of men unto secret combinations of murder and all manner of secret works of darkness.

¹⁰O, how great the goodness of our God—who prepareth a way for our escape from the grasp of this awful monster! Yea, that monster death and hell (which I call the death of the body and also the death of the spirit). ¹¹And because of the way of deliverance of our God, the Holy One of Israel, this death of which I have spoken (which is the temporal) shall deliver up its dead (which death is the grave).

¹²And this death of which I have spoken (which is the spiritual death), shall deliver

---

a. See Acts 3:21: "Whom the heaven must receive until the times of restitution of all things, which God hath spoken by the mouth of all his holy prophets since the world began."
b. See Romans 5:12 for the phrase "death passed upon all men."
c. The phrase "cut off from my presence" is found in Leviticus 22:3.
d. See 1 Corinthians 15:54.
e. See 2 Corinthians 11:14: "And no marvel; for Satan himself is transformed into an angel of light."

up its dead (which spiritual death is hell). Wherefore, death and hell must deliver up its dead. And hell must deliver up its captive spirits. And the grave must deliver up its captive bodies.[a] And the bodies and the spirits of men will be restored one to the other. And it is by the power of the resurrection of the Holy One of Israel.

[13]O, how great the plan of our God! For on the other hand, the paradise of God must deliver up the spirits of the righteous, and the grave deliver up the body of the righteous. And the spirit and the body is restored to itself again. And all men become incorruptible and immortal. And they are living souls, having a perfect knowledge like unto us in the flesh, save it be that our knowledge shall be perfect. [14]Wherefore, we shall have a perfect knowledge of all our guilt, and our uncleanness, and our nakedness. And the righteous shall have a perfect knowledge of their enjoyment, and their righteousness—being clothed with purity. Yea, even with the robe of righteousness.

[15]And it shall come to pass that when all men shall have passed from this first death unto life (insomuch as they have become immortal), they must appear before the Judgment Seat of the Holy One of Israel. And then cometh the judgment. And then must they be judged, according to the holy judgment of God.[b] [16]And assuredly (as the Lord liveth, for the Lord God hath spoken it, and it is his Eternal word which cannot pass away), that they which are righteous, shall be righteous still. And they which are filthy, shall be filthy still.[c] Wherefore, they which are filthy are the devil and his angels. And they shall go away into everlasting fire, prepared for them. And their torment is a lake of fire and brimstone,[d] whose flames ascendeth up forever and ever,[e] and hath no end.

[17]O, the greatness and the justice of our God! For he executeth all his words. And they have gone forth out of his mouth. And his law must be fulfilled. [18]But behold the righteous! The saints of the Holy One of Israel! They which have believed in the Holy One of Israel. They which have endured the crosses of the world, and despised the shame of it. They shall inherit the kingdom of God—which was prepared for them from the foundation of the world.[f] And their joy shall be full, forever.

[19]O, the greatness of the mercy of our God, the Holy One of Israel! For he delivereth his saints from that awful monster (the devil, and death, and hell, and that lake of fire and brimstone,[g] which is endless torment).

[20]O, how great the holiness of our God! For he knoweth all things. And there is not any thing, save he know it. [21]And he cometh into the world, that he may save all men, if they will hearken unto his voice. For behold, he suffereth the pains of all men, yea, the pains of every living creature, both men, women, and children, which belong to the family of Adam. [22]And he suffereth this, that the resurrection might pass upon all men—that all might stand before him at the great and judgment day. [23]And he com-

---

a. See Revelation 20:13: "And the sea gave up the dead which were in it; and death and hell delivered up the dead which were in them: and they were judged every man according to their works."

b. See 2 Corinthians 5:10: "For we must all appear before the judgment seat of Christ; that every one may receive the things done in his body, according to that he hath done, whether it be good or bad."

c. See Revelation 22:11: "He that is unjust, let him be unjust still: and he which is filthy, let him be filthy still: and he that is righteous, let him be righteous still: and he that is holy, let him be holy still."

d. See Revelation 20:14: "And death and hell were cast into the lake of fire. This is the second death."

e. See Revelation 14:11: "And the smoke of their torment ascendeth up for ever and ever."

f. See Matthew 25:34: "Come, ye blessed of my Father, inherit the kingdom prepared for you from the foundation of the world."

g. See Revelation 20:14: "And death and hell were cast into the lake of fire. This is the second death."

Chapter VI [2 Nephi 9]

mandeth all men that they must repent and be baptized in his name, having perfect faith in the Holy One of Israel—or they cannot be saved in the kingdom of God.

²⁴And if they will not repent, and believe in his name, and be baptized in his name, and endure to the end[a]—they must be damned. For the Lord God, the Holy One of Israel, hath spoken it. ²⁵Wherefore, he hath given a law. And where there is no law given, there is no punishment. And where there is no punishment, there is no condemnation. And where there is no condemnation, the mercies of the Holy One of Israel hath claim upon them because of the atonement. For they are delivered by the power of him. ²⁶For the atonement satisfieth the demands of his justice upon all those who hath not the law given to them, that they are delivered from that awful monster (death, and hell, and the devil, and the lake of fire and brimstone,[b] which is endless torment), and they are restored to that God who gave them breath (which is the Holy One of Israel).

²⁷But wo unto him that hath the law given. Yea, that hath all the commandments of God (like unto us) and that transgresseth them, and that wasteth the days of his probation. For awful is his state.

²⁸O, that cunning plan of the evil one. O, the vainness and the frailties, and the foolishness of men. When they are learned they think they are wise, and they hearken not unto the councils of God. For they set it aside, supposing they know of themselves. Wherefore, their wisdom is foolishness. And it profiteth them not. Wherefore, they shall perish. ²⁹But to be learned is good, if it so be that they hearken unto the councils of God.

³⁰But wo unto the rich, which are rich as to the things of the world. For because that they are rich, they despise the poor. And they persecute the meek. And their hearts are upon their treasures. Wherefore, their treasure is their god. And behold, their treasure shall perish with them also.

³¹And wo unto the deaf that will not hear.
For they shall perish.
³²Wo unto the blind that will not see.
For they shall perish also.
³³Wo unto the uncircumcised of heart.
For a knowledge of their iniquities shall smite them at the last day.
³⁴Wo unto the liar.
For he shall be thrust down to hell.
³⁵Wo unto the murderer (who deliberately killeth).
For he shall die.
³⁶Wo unto them who commit whoredoms.
For they shall be thrust down to hell.
³⁷Yea, wo unto they that worship idols.
For the devil of all devils delighteth in them.
³⁸And, in fine, wo unto all they that die in their sins.
For they shall return to God, and behold his face, and remain in their sins.

³⁹O, my beloved brethren, remember the awfulness in transgressing against that Holy God. And also, the awfulness of yielding to the enticings of that cunning one.

---

a. The phrase "endure to the end" occurs in Matthew 24:13.
b. See Revelation 20:14: "And death and hell were cast into the lake of fire. This is the second death."

Remember—to be carnally minded is death. And to be spiritually minded is life eternal.[a]

⁴⁰O, my beloved brethren, give ear to my words! Remember the greatness of the Holy One of Israel! Do not say that I have spoken hard things against you. For if ye do, ye will revile against the truth. For I have spoken the words of your Maker. I know that the words of truth are hard against all uncleanness. But the righteous fear it not, for they love the truth and are not shaken.

⁴¹O then, my beloved brethren, come unto the Lord, the Holy One! Remember that his paths are righteousness! Behold, the way for man is narrow, but it lieth in a [straight[b]] course before him. And the keeper of the gate is the Holy One of Israel. And he employeth no servant there. And there is none other way, save it be by the gate. For he cannot be deceived. For the Lord God is his name.

⁴²And whoso knocketh to him, will he open.[c] And the wise, and the learned, and they that are rich (which are puffed up because of their learning, and their wisdom, and their riches), yea, they are they whom he despiseth. And—save they shall cast these things away and consider themselves fools before God, and come down in the depths of humility—he will not open unto them. ⁴³But the things of the wise and the prudent shall be hid from them forever—yea, that happiness which is prepared for the saints.

⁴⁴O, my beloved brethren, remember my words! Behold, I take off my garments, and I shake them before you. I pray the God of my salvation, that he view me with his all-searching eye. Wherefore, ye shall know at the last day, when all men shall be judged of their works, that the God of Israel did witness that I shook your iniquities from my soul. And that I stand with brightness before him—and am rid of your blood.

⁴⁵O, my beloved brethren, turn away from your sins! Shake off the chains of him that would bind you fast! Come unto that God, who is the rock of your salvation. ⁴⁶Prepare your souls for that glorious day, when justice shall be administered unto the righteous, even the day of judgment—that ye may not shrink with awful fear. That ye may not remember your awful guilt, in perfectness, and be constrained to exclaim: "Holy, holy, are thy judgments O Lord God Almighty! But I know my guilt. I transgressed thy law, and my transgressions are mine. And the devil hath obtained me, that I am a prey to his awful misery."

⁴⁷But behold, my brethren, is it expedient that I should awake you to an awful reality of these things. Would I harrow up your souls, if your minds were pure? Would I be plain unto you (according to the plainness of the truth), if ye were freed from sin?

⁴⁸Behold, if ye were holy, I would speak unto you of holiness. But, as ye are not holy, and ye look upon me as a teacher, it must needs be expedient that I teach you the consequences of sin.

⁴⁹Behold, my soul abhoreth sin, and my heart delighteth in righteousness. And I will praise the holy name of my God.

---

a. Compare Romans 8:6: "For to be carnally minded is death; but to be spiritually minded is life and peace."

b. The Printer's Manuscript has "strait." The Original Manuscript is not extant here, and the issue of "strait/straight" appears in multiple locations. In this case, the logic of the sentence suggests that "straight" is meant as a complement to "narrow." It would be superfluous to have "narrow" then "strait." See Skousen, *Analysis of the Textual Variants*, 1:632, for a longer discussion.

c. See Matthew 7:7: "Ask, and it shall be given you; seek, and ye shall find; knock, and it shall be opened unto you."

Chapter VI [2 Nephi 9]

⁵⁰**Come, my brethren**, every one that thirsteth!
    Come ye to the waters!
And he that hath no money,
    come, buy and eat!
Yea, come buy wine and milk
    without money and without price.
⁵¹Wherefore, do not spend money for that which is **of no worth**,
    nor your labor for that which **cannot satisfy**.
Hearken diligently unto me
    and remember the words which I have spoken,
and come unto the Holy One of Israel—
    and feast upon that which perisheth not,
    neither can be corrupted—
and let your soul delight in fatness.[a]

⁵²Behold, my beloved brethren, remember the words of your God. Pray unto him continually by day and give thanks unto his Holy Name by night. Let your hearts rejoice! ⁵³And behold, how great the covenants of the Lord! And how great his condescensions unto the children of men! And because of his greatness, and his grace and mercy, he hath promised unto us that our seed shall not utterly be destroyed (according to the flesh), but that he would preserve them. And in future generations they shall become a righteous branch unto the house of Israel.

⁵⁴And now, my brethren, I would speak unto you more. But on the morrow I will declare unto you the remainder of my words. Amen.

---

a. Verses 50 and 51 paraphrase Isaiah 5:1–2.

Chapter VII [2 Nephi 10]

[10] ¹And now, I, Jacob, speak unto you again, my beloved brethren, concerning this righteous branch (of which I have spoken). ²For behold, the promises which we have obtained are promises unto us (according to the flesh). Wherefore, as it hath been shown unto me that many of our children shall perish in the flesh because of unbelief—nevertheless, God will be merciful unto many. And our children shall be restored, that they may come to that which will give them the true knowledge of their Redeemer. ³Wherefore, as I said unto you, it must needs be expedient that Christ (for in the last night the angel spake unto me that this should be his name)—that he should come among the Jews, among they which are the more wicked part of the world. And they shall crucify him, for it behoveth our God.

And there is none other nation on earth that would crucify their God. ⁴For should the mighty miracles be wrought among other nations, they would repent, and know that he be their God. ⁵But because of priestcrafts and iniquities, they at Jerusalem will stiffen their necks against him, that he be crucified. ⁶Wherefore, because of their iniquities—destructions, famines, pestilences, and bloodsheds, shall come upon them. And they which shall not be destroyed, shall be scattered among all nations.

⁷But behold, thus saith the Lord God:

When the day cometh that they shall believe in me, that I am Christ—then have I covenanted with their fathers that they shall be restored in the flesh upon the earth, unto the lands of their inheritance.

⁸And it shall come to pass that they shall be gathered in from their long dispersion—from the isles of the sea, and from the four parts of the earth. And the nations of the Gentiles shall be great in the eyes of me (saith God), in carrying them forth to the lands of their inheritance.

⁹Yea, the kings of the Gentiles shall be nursing fathers unto them, and their queens shall become nursing mothers. Wherefore, the promises of the Lord is great unto the Gentiles. For he hath spoken it. And who can dispute?

¹⁰But behold:

This land (saith God) shall be a land of thine inheritance. And the Gentiles shall be blessed upon the land. ¹¹And this land shall be a land of liberty unto the Gentiles. And there shall be no kings upon the land which shall raise up unto the Gentiles. ¹²And I will fortify this land against all other nations. ¹³And he that fighteth against Zion shall perish (saith God). ¹⁴For he that raiseth up a king against me shall perish. For I the Lord, the king of heaven, will be their king.

And I will be a light unto them forever that hear my words. ¹⁵Wherefore, for this cause, that my covenants may be fulfilled (which I have made unto the children of men), that I will do unto them (while they are in the flesh). I must needs destroy the secret works of darkness, and of murders, and of abominations. ¹⁶Wherefore, he that fighteth against Zion (both Jew and Gentile, both bond and free, both male and female) shall perish.[a] For they are they which are the whore of

---

a. See Galatians 3:28: "There is neither Jew nor Greek, there is neither bond nor free, there is neither male nor female: for ye are all one in Christ Jesus."

all the earth. For they which are not for me, are against me (saith our God). ¹⁷For I will fulfil my promises (which I have made unto the children of men), that I will do unto them while they are in the flesh.

¹⁸Wherefore, my beloved brethren, thus saith our God:

I will afflict thy seed by the hand of the Gentiles. Nevertheless, I will soften the hearts of the Gentiles, that they shall be like unto a father to them. Wherefore, the Gentiles shall be blessed and numbered among the house of Israel. ¹⁹Wherefore, I will consecrate this land unto thy seed (and they which shall be numbered among thy seed) forever—for the land of their inheritance. For it is a choice land (saith God unto me) above all other lands. Wherefore, I will have all men that dwell thereon—that they shall worship me (saith God).

²⁰And now, my beloved brethren, seeing that our merciful God hath given us so great knowledge concerning these things, let us remember him, and lay aside our sins, and not hang down our heads. For we are not cast off. Nevertheless, we have been driven out of the land of our inheritance, but we have been led to a better land. For the Lord hath made the sea our path. And we are upon an isle of the sea. ²¹But great is the promises of the Lord unto they which are upon the isles of the sea. Wherefore, as it saith isles, there must needs be more than this. And they are inhabited also by our brethren. ²²For behold, the Lord God hath led away (from time to time) from the house of Israel, according to his will and pleasure.

And now behold, the Lord remembereth all they which have been broken off. Wherefore, he remembereth us also. ²³Therefore, cheer up your hearts, and remember that ye are free to act for yourselves, to choose this way of everlasting death or the way of eternal life. ²⁴Wherefore, my beloved brethren, reconcile yourselves to the will of God, and not to the will of the devil and the flesh.

And remember that after ye are reconciled unto God, that it is only in and through the grace of God that ye are saved. ²⁵Wherefore, my[a] God raise you from death by the power of the resurrection, and also from everlasting death by the power of the atonement—that ye may be received into the eternal kingdom of God, that ye may praise him through grace divine. Amen.

---

a. The Printer's Manuscript has "my," but the 1830 edition has "may." The Original Manuscript is not extant at this point, but "may" is the better reading. Skousen has no information on the change.

Chapter VIII [2 Nephi 11–15]

[11] ¹And now, Jacob spake many more things to my people at that time. Nevertheless, only these things have I caused to be written. For the things which I have written sufficeth me.

²And now I, Nephi, write more of the words of Isaiah, for my soul delighteth in his words. For I will liken his words unto my people. And I will send them forth unto all my children. For he verily saw my Redeemer, even as I have seen him. ³And my brother Jacob also hath seen him, as I have seen him. Wherefore, I will send their words forth unto my children to prove unto them that my words are true. Wherefore, "By the words of three (God hath said), I will establish my word." Nevertheless, God sendeth more witnesses, and he proveth all his words.

⁴Behold, my soul delighteth in proving unto my people the truth of the coming of Christ. For, for this end hath the law of Moses been given. And all things which have been given of God (from the beginning of the world) unto man, are the type-ifying[a] of him.

⁵And also, my soul delighteth in the covenants of the Lord which he hath made to our fathers. Yea, my soul delighteth in his grace, and his justice, and power, and mercy—in the great and eternal plan of deliverance from death.

⁶And my soul delighteth in proving unto my people that save Christ should come, all men must perish. ⁷For if there be no Christ, there be no God. And if there be no God, we are not. For there could have been no creation. But there is a God. And he is Christ. And he cometh in the fullness of his own time.

⁸And now, I write some of the words of Isaiah, that whoso of my people which shall see these words, may lift up their hearts and rejoice for all men.

Now, these are the words. And ye may liken them unto you, and unto all men.

[12, compare Isaiah 2]

¹The word that Isaiah, the son of Amoz, saw concerning Judah and Jerusalem.

²And it shall come to pass in the last days—
when[b] the mountain of the Lord's house
    shall be established in the top of the mountains
and shall be exalted above the hills.
    And all nations shall flow unto it.
³And many people shall go, and say:
    "Come ye. And let us go up to the mountain of the Lord,
    to the house of the God of Jacob.
And he will teach us of his ways
    and we will walk in his paths."
For out of Zion shall go forth the law,

---

a. This is spelled "typefying" in the Printer's Manuscript. This has been changed to the modern spelling in current editions: "typifying." This edition elects a different way to spell this, as the pronunciation of typify has lost the immediate connection to a type.

b. Isaiah 2:2 has "that," which makes more sense. The insertion of "when" creates an incomplete sentence. The word "that" is in italics and was probably excised for that reason. Because the events are declared to occur "in the last days," that future date probably influenced the substituted word "when."

Chapter VIII [2 Nephi 11–15]

and the word of the Lord from Jerusalem.
⁴And he shall judge among the nations
    and shall rebuke many people.
And they shall beat their swords into plowshares,
    and their spears into pruninghooks.
Nation shall not lift up sword against nation,
    neither shall they learn war anymore.

⁵O, house of Jacob! Come ye!
    And let us walk in the light of the Lord.
Yea, come! For ye have all gone astray,
    every one, to his wicked ways.
⁶Therefore, O Lord, thou hast forsaken thy people,
    the house of Jacob,
because they be replenished from the east,
    and **hearken unto** soothsayers like the Philistines.
And they please themselves in the children of strangers.
⁷Their land also is full of silver and gold.
    Neither is there any end of their treasures.
Their land is also full of horses.
    Neither is there any end of their chariots.
⁸Their land also is full of idols.
    They worship the work of their own hands,
    that which their own fingers have made.
¹⁰And the mean men boweth down
    and the great man humbleth himself **not**.
    Therefore, forgive **him** not.
O, ye wicked ones! Enter into the rock
    and hide thee in the dust.
For the fear of the Lord
    and the glory of his majesty, **shall smite thee!**
¹¹**And it shall come to pass that**
    the lofty looks of man shall be humbled
    and the haughtiness of men shall be bowed down.
And the Lord alone shall be exalted in that day.

¹²For the day of the Lord of Hosts **soon cometh upon all nations.**
    Yea, upon every one.
Yea, upon the proud and lofty,
    and upon every one which is lifted up.
    And he shall be brought low.[a]
¹³Yea, and **the day of the Lord shall** come upon all the cedars of Lebanon,
    for they are high and lifted up—
    and upon all the oaks of Bashan,

---

    a. This verse from Isaiah 2:12 is more extensively reworked after the italicized words were removed. The King James Version reads: "For the day of the Lord of hosts *shall be* upon every *one that is* proud and lofty, and upon every *one that is* lifted up; and he shall be brought low."

¹⁴and upon all the high mountains,
    and upon all the hills,
and upon all the nations which are lifted up—
    and upon every people,
¹⁵and upon every high tower,
    and upon every fenced wall,
and upon all the ships of the sea,
    ¹⁶and upon all the ships of Tarshish,
    and upon all the pleasant pictures—
¹⁷And the loftiness of man shall be bowed down.
    And the haughtiness of men shall be made low.
    And the Lord alone shall be exalted in that day.
¹⁸And the idols he shall utterly abolish.

¹⁹And they shall go into the holes of the rocks,
    and into the caves of the earth.
For the fear of the Lord **shall come upon them**,
    and the glory of his majesty **shall smite them**,
    when he ariseth to shake terribly the earth.
²⁰In that day a man shall cast his idols of silver
    and his idols of gold
(which **he hath** made [ᵃ] for himself to worship)
    to the moles, and to the bats,
²¹to go into the clefts of the rocks,
    and into the tops of the ragged rocks.
For the fear of the Lord **shall come upon them**,
    and the **majesty of his glory shall smite them**,
when he ariseth to shake terribly the earth.
²²Cease ye from man, whose breath is in his nostrils. For wherein is he to be accounted of?

[13, compare Isaiah 3]

¹For behold, the Lord, the Lord of Hosts,
    doth take away from Jerusalem and from Judah,
the stay and the staff,
    the whole staff of bread
    and the whole stay of water.
²**And** the mighty man, and the man of war,
    the judge, and the prophet,
and the prudent, and the ancient,
    ³the captain of fifty, and the honorable man,
and the counsellor, and the cunning artificer,
    and the eloquent orator—
⁴and I will give children **unto them** to be their princes.
    And babes shall rule over them.

---

a. Omits "each one," which is in italics.

Chapter VIII [2 Nephi 11–15]

⁵And the people shall be oppressed, every one by another—
and every one by his neighbor.
The child shall behave himself proudly against the ancient,
and the base against the honorable.

⁶When a man shall take hold of his brother (of the house of his father)
and shall say: "Thou hast clothing, be thou our ruler,
and let not this ruin **come** under thy hand."
⁷In that day, shall he swear, saying: "I will not be a healer.
For in my house **there** is neither bread nor clothing.
Make me not a ruler of the people."
⁸For Jerusalem is ruined
and Judah is fallen
because their **tongues** and their doings **have been** against the Lord,
to provoke the eyes of his glory.
⁹The show of their countenance doth witness against them,
and **doth** declare their sin **to be even** as Sodom.
And they cannot hide it.[a]
Wo unto their **souls**!
For they have rewarded evil unto themselves.
¹⁰Say **unto** the righteous that it **is** well with **them**!
For they shall eat the fruit of their doings.
¹¹Wo unto the wicked, **for they shall perish!**
For the reward of **their** hands shall be **upon them**.
¹²**And** my people children are their oppressors.
And women rule over them.
O my people, they which lead thee cause thee to err,
and destroy the way of thy paths.

¹³The Lord standeth up to plead,
and standeth to judge the people.
¹⁴The Lord will enter into judgment
with the ancients of his people, and the princes thereof:
"For ye have eaten up the vineyard
and the spoil of the poor [b] your houses.
¹⁵What mean ye? [c] "Ye beat my people to pieces,
and grind the faces of the poor,"
saith the Lord God of Hosts.

¹⁶Moreover, the Lord saith:
"Because the daughters of Zion are haughty,
and walk with stretched forth necks and wanton eyes,
walking and mincing as they go,

---

a. Replaces "they hide *it* not."
b. This verse in Isaiah has "is in your houses." The italicized "is in" was removed and no attempt was made to restore the meaning. Skousen, *Analysis of Textual Variants*, 2:670.
c. Omits "that," which is in italics.

and making a tinkling with their feet."
¹⁷Therefore, the Lord will smite with a scab
> the crown of the head of the daughters of Zion.
> And the Lord will discover their secret parts.

¹⁸In that day, the Lord will take away
> the bravery of [ᵃ] tinkling ornaments [ᵇ],
> and cauls,
> and [ᶜ] round tires (like the moon)—
> ¹⁹the chains,
> and the bracelets,
> and the mufflers—
> ²⁰the bonnets,
> and the ornaments of the legs,
> and the headbands,
> and the tablets,
> and the earrings—
> ²¹the rings,
> and nose jewels,
> ²²the changeable suits of apparel—
> and the mantles,
> and the wimples,
> and the crisping pins—
> ²³the glasses,
> and the fine linen,
> and hoods, and the veils.

²⁴And it shall all come to pass,
[ᵈ] instead of sweet smell, there shall be stink—
> and instead of a girdle, a rent—
and instead of well-set hair, baldness—
> and instead of a stomacher, a girding of sack cloth—
> [ᵉ] burning instead of beauty.

²⁵Thy men shall fall by the sword
> and thy mighty in the war.
²⁶And her gates shall lament and mourn.
> And she **shall be** desolate
> and shall sit upon the ground.

[14, compare Isaiah 4]

¹And in that day, seven women shall take hold of one man, saying:
> "We will eat our own bread

---

a. Omits "their," which is in italics.
b. Omits "about their feet," which is in italics.
c. Omits "their," which is in italics.
d. Omits "that," which is in italics.
e. Omits "and," which is in italics.

Chapter VIII [2 Nephi 11–15]

and wear our own apparel.
Only let us be called by thy name
to take away our reproach."

²In that day shall the branch of the Lord be beautiful—
and glorious the fruit of the earth [ᵃ],
and excellent and comely to them that are escaped of Israel.
³And it shall come to pass, **them that are** left in Zion,
and [ᵇ] remaineth in Jerusalem,
shall be called holy—
every one that is written among the living in Jerusalem,
⁴when the Lord shall have washed away the filth of the daughters of Zion,
and shall have purged the blood of Jerusalem
from the midst thereof by the spirit of judgment,
and by the spirit of burning.
⁵And the Lord will create upon every dwelling place of mount Zion
(and upon her assemblies)—
a cloud and smoke by day,
and the shining of a flaming fire by night.
For upon all, the glory of Zion shall be a defense.
⁶And there shall be a tabernacle for a shadow in the daytime (from the heat),
and for a place of refuge,
and a [covertᶜ] from storm and from rain.

[15, compare Isaiah 5]

¹And then will I sing to my well-beloved a song of my beloved, touching his vineyard.

My well-beloved hath a vineyard
in a very fruitful hill.
²And he fenced it
and gathered out the stones thereof,
and planted it with the choicest vine,
and built a tower in the midst of it.
And also made a winepress therein.
And he looked, that it should bring forth grapes.
And it brought forth wild grapes.

³And now, O inhabitants of Jerusalem, and men of Judah!
Judge, I pray you, betwixt me and my vineyard.
⁴What could have been done more to my vineyard,
that I have not done in it?
Wherefore, when I looked, that it should bring forth grapes,
it **brought** forth wild grapes.

---

a. Omits "shall be," which is in italics.
b. Omits "he that," which is in italics.
c. Restored from the King James Bible. The Printer's Manuscript has "covet," which appears to be an unintentional misspelling.

⁵And now, go to. I will tell you what I will do to my vineyard.
I will take away the hedge thereof,
    and it shall be eaten up.
And **I will** break down the wall thereof,
    and it shall be trodden down.
⁶And I will lay it waste.
    It shall not be pruned, nor digged,
    but there shall come up briers and thorns.
I will also command the clouds that they rain no rain upon it.

⁷For the vineyard of the Lord of Hosts is the house of Israel,
    and the men of Judah his pleasant plant.
And he looked for judgment, and behold—oppression.
    For righteousness, but behold—a cry.

⁸Wo unto them that join house to house [a]
    till there can be no place,
        that they may be placed alone in the midst of the earth!
⁹In mine ears (saith the Lord of Hosts),
    of a truth, many houses shall be desolate,
    and great and fair cities without inhabitant.
¹⁰Yea, ten acres of vineyard shall yield one bath,
    and the seed of a homer shall yield an ephah!

¹¹Wo unto them that rise up early in the morning
    that they may follow strong drink—
that continue until night,
    and wine inflame them!
¹²And the harp, and the viol,
    the tabret, and pipe, and wine are in their feasts—
but they regard not the work of the Lord.
    Neither consider the operation of his hands.
¹³Therefore, my people are gone into captivity
    because they have no knowledge.
And their honorable men are famished,
    and their multitude dried up with thirst.
¹⁴Therefore, hell hath enlarged herself
    and opened her mouth without measure.
And their glory, and their multitude, and their pomp,
    and he that rejoiceth, shall descend into it.
¹⁵And the mean man shall be brought down.
    And the mighty man shall be humbled.
    And the eyes of the lofty shall be humbled.
¹⁶But the Lord of Hosts shall be exalted in judgment.
    And God (that is holy) shall be sanctified in righteousness.
¹⁷Then shall the lambs feed after their manner.

---

a. Omits "that lay field to field."

Chapter VIII [2 Nephi 11–15]

And the waste places of the fat ones shall strangers eat.
¹⁸Wo unto them that draw iniquity with cords of vanity,
    and sin as it were with a cart rope—
¹⁹that say: "Let him make speed! [ª] Hasten his work,
    that we may see it!
And let the counsel of the holy one of Israel draw nigh, and come,
    that we may know it!"
²⁰Wo unto them that call evil good, and good evil—
    that put darkness for light, and light for darkness—
    that put bitter for sweet, and sweet for bitter.
²¹Wo unto **the** wise in their own eyes,
    and prudent in their own sight!
²²Wo unto **the** mighty to drink wine,
    and men of strength to mingle strong drink,
which justify the wicked for reward
    and take away the righteousness of the righteous from him.

²³Therefore, as the fire devoureth the stubble
    and the flame consumeth the chaff,
their root shall be rottenness.
    And their blossom shall go up as dust
because they have cast away the law of Lord of hosts
    and despised the word of the holy one of Israel.
²⁵Therefore is the anger of the Lord kindled against his people.
    And he hath stretched forth his hand against them,
and hath smitten them. And the hills did tremble,
    and their carcasses were torn in the midst of the streets.
For all this his anger is not turned away,
    but his hand stretched out still.

²⁶And he will lift up an ensign to the nations from far,
    and will hiss unto them from the end of the earth.
    And behold, they shall come with speed swiftly.
None shall be weary, nor stumble among them.
    ²⁷None shall slumber, nor sleep.
Neither shall the girdle of their loins be loosed,
    nor the latchet of their shoes be broken.
²⁸Whose arrows **shall be** sharp
    and all their bows bent.
And their horses' hoofs shall be counted like flint,
    and their wheels like a whirlwind.
Their roaring [ᵇ] like a lion.
    ²⁹They shall roar like young lions.
Yea, they shall roar,

---

a. Omits "and," which is in italics.
b. Omits "shall be," which is in italics.

  and lay hold of the prey,
 and shall carry away safe.
  And none shall deliver [a].
³⁰And in that day, they shall roar against them
  like the roaring of the sea.
And if **they** look unto the land behold darkness and sorrow.
  And the light is darkened in the heavens thereof.

---

a. Omits "it," which is in italics.

Chapter IX [2 Nephi 16–22]

[16, compare Isaiah 6]

¹In the year that King Uzziah died,
I saw, also, the Lord sitting upon a throne,
> high and lifted up.
> And his train filled the temple.

²Above it stood the seraphims.ᵃ
> Each one had six wings.
> With twain he covered his face,
> and with twain he covered his feet,
> and with twain he did fly.

³And one cried unto another, and said:
> "Holy, holy, holy is the Lord of Hosts!
> The whole earth is full of his glory!"

⁴And the posts of the door moved at the voice of him that cried.
> And the house was filled with smoke.

⁵Then said I: "Wo [ᵇ] me! For I [am undone because Iᶜ]
> [ᵈ] a man of unclean lips,
> and I dwell in the midst of a people of unclean lips.

For mine eyes have seen the King, the Lord of Hosts!"

⁶Then flew one of the seraphims unto me,
> having a live coal in his hand,
> which he had taken with the tongs from off the alter.

⁷And he laid [ᵉ] upon my mouth, and said:
> "Lo, this hath touched thy lips,
> and thine iniquity is taken away,
> and thy sin purged."

⁸And also I heard the voice of the Lord saying: "Whom shall I send?"
> And: "Who will go for us?"

Then **I said**: "Here I [ᶠ], send me!"

---

    a. "The original Book of Mormon text uses the double plural 'seraphims,' just as in the King James Bible. In Hebrew, the *-im* ending makes 'seraph' plural. But for English speakers, 'seraphim' doesn't seem plural, thus the tendency to add *-s* to the Hebrew plural 'seraphim' to form a double plural, 'seraphims.'" Skousen, *Analysis of the Textual Variants*, 2:693–94.

    b. Skousen notes that the KJV has "wo *is* me," and "the Book of Mormon text frequently omits the lining verb "be" when it is italicized in the King James Bible." Skousen, *Analysis of the Textual Variants*, 2:692. Joseph Smith wrote "unto me" as a superscript correction.

    c. Accidentally omitted while copying from the Original to the Printer's Manuscript. Oliver Cowdery made the correction, probably during proofreading. Skousen, *Analysis the Textual Variants*, 2:693.

    d. Omits "am," which is in italics.

    e. Omits "it," which is in italics.

    f. Omits "am," which is italics.

⁹And he said:
Go and tell this people,
"Hear ye indeed!" But they understand not.
    And: "See ye indeed!" But they **perceived** not.
¹⁰Make the heart of this people fat,
    and make their ears heavy,
    and shut their eyes—
lest they see with their eyes,
    and hear with their ears,
    and understand with their heart,
and convert and be healed.

¹¹Then said I: "Lord how long?"

And **he said:**
"Until the cities be wasted without inhabitant,
    and the houses without man,
    and the land be utterly desolate,
¹²and the Lord have removed men far away.
    For there **shall** be a great forsaking in the midst of the land.
¹³But yet, in it **there** shall be a tenth.
    And **they** shall return,
    and shall be eaten as a teil-tree,
    and as an oak (whose substance is in them when they cast their leaves).
So the holy seed shall be the substance thereof."

[17, compare Isaiah 7]

¹And it came to pass in the days of Ahaz (the son of Jotham, the son of
    Uzziah, king of Judah),
    and Rezin [ᵃ] (king of Syria)
    and Pekah (the son of Remaliah, king of Israel),
    went up towards Jerusalem to war against it
    but could not prevail against it.

²And it was told the house of David, saying:
"Syria is confederate with Ephraim."
    And his heart was moved.
    And the heart of his people,
    as the trees of the wood
    are moved with the wind.

³Then said the Lord unto Isaiah:
Go forth now to meet Ahaz,
    thou and Shear-Jashub (thy son)
    at the end of the conduit of the upper pool
    in the highway of the fuller's field.

---

a. Omits "the." It is not in italics.

⁶And say unto him:
"Take heed and be quiet.
    Fear not,
       neither be feint-hearted.
For the two tails of these smoking firebrands
    (for the fierce anger of Rezin with Syria
    and of the son of Remaliah),
    because Syria, Ephraim,
    and the son of Remaliah,
    have taken evil counsel against thee,
saying: 'Let us go up against Judah, and vex it.
    And let and us make a breach therein for us,
    and set a king in the midst of it, yea, the son of Tabeal.'"

⁷Thus saith the Lord God:
"It shall not stand.
    Neither shall it come to pass.
⁸For the head of Syria is Damascus.
    And the head of Damascus, [a]Rezin.
And within three score and five years,
    shall Ephraim be broken, that it be not a people.
⁹And the head of Ephraim is Samaria,
    and the head of Samaria is Remaliah's son.
If ye will not believe,
    surely ye shall not be established."

¹⁰Moreover, the Lord spake again unto Ahaz saying:
"¹¹Ask thee a sign of the Lord thy God.
    Ask [b] either in the **depths**,
    of or in the **heights** above."

¹²But Ahaz said:
    "I will not ask,
    neither will I tempt the Lord."

¹³And he said:
Hear ye now, O house of David!
    Is it a small thing for you to weary men.
    But will ye weary my God also?
¹⁴Therefore the Lord himself shall give you a sign.
    Behold, a virgin shall conceive,
    and **shall** bear a son,
    and shall call his name Immanuel.
¹⁵Butter and honey shall he eat,

---

    a. The King James Bible has "it" in italics. It may have been removed due to the italics, but that explanation is weak given the other phrases that also have the italicized "is" ("head of Syria *is* Damascus"; "head of Ephraim *is* Samaria;" "head of Samaria *is* Ramaliah's son"). It may have been an inadvertent error, either in the dictation or the copying.

    b. Omits "it," which is in italics.

that he may know to refuse the evil,
and to choose the good. ¹
⁶For, before the child shall know to refuse the evil,
and chose the good,
the land that thou abhorest
shall be forsaken of both her kings.
¹⁷The Lord shall bring upon thee,
and upon thy people,
and upon thy father's house,
days that have not come from the day that Ephraim departed from Judah,
[ᵃ] the king of Assyria.

¹⁸And it shall come to pass in that day, that the Lord shall hiss
for the fly that is in the uttermost part [ᵇ] of Egypt,
and for the bee that is in the land of Assyria.
¹⁹And they shall come and shall rest, all of them,
in the desolate valleys,
and in the holes of the rocks,
and upon all thorns,
and upon all bushes.
²⁰In the same day, shall the Lord shave with a razor
(that is hired [ᶜ] by them beyond the river, by the king of Assyria)
the head and the hair of the feet.
And it shall also consume the beard.
²¹And it shall come to pass that in that day,
[ᵈ] a man shall nourish a young cow, and two sheep.
²²And it shall come to pass for the abundance of milk [ᵉ] they shall give,
he shall eat butter.
For butter and honey shall everyone eat that is left in the land.
²³And it shall come to pass in that day,
[ᶠ] every place shall be, where there were a thousand vines,
thatᵍ a thousand silverlings, **which** shall be for briars and thorns.
²⁴With arrows and with bows shall men come thither,
because all the land shall become briars and thorns.
²⁵And [ʰ] all hills that shall be digged with the mattock,

---

a. Omits "even," which is in italics.
b. Omits "of the rivers."
c. Omits "namely," which is in italics.
d. Omits "that," which is in italics.
e. Omits "that," which is in italics.
f. Omits "that," which is in italics.
g. "The original reading of the printer's manuscript ('that a thousand silverlings') seems impossible. The 1830 compositor corrected the printer's manuscript by changing it to "at," to agree with the King James text." Skousen suggests that it may have been Oliver Cowdery misunderstanding the oral "vines at" for "vines that." Skousen, *Analysis of Textual Variants*, 2:717.
h. Omits "on," which is in italics.

there shall not come thither the fear of briars and thorns.
But it shall be for the sending forth of oxen
    and the treading of lesser cattle.

[18, compare Isaiah 8]

¹Moreover, the Lord said unto me:

"Take thee a great roll,
    and write in it with a man's pen,
    concerning Maher-shalal-hash-baz."
²And I took unto me faithful witnesses to record—
    Uriah the Priest and Zechariah the son of Jeberechiah.
³And I went unto the prophetess,
    and she conceived,
    and bear a son.

Then said the Lord to me:

"Call his name Maher-shalal-hash-baz.
⁴For behold, the child shall not have knowledge
    to cry 'my father,'
    and 'my mother,'
before the riches of Damascus
    and the spoil of Samaria
    shall be taken away before the king of Assyria."

⁵The Lord spake also unto me again, saying:

⁶"For as much as this people refuseth
    the waters of Shiloah (that go softly)
and rejoice in Rezin
    and Remeliah's son—
⁷now therefore behold,
the Lord bringeth up upon them
    the waters of the river, strong and many—
    even the king of Assyria and all his glory.
And he shall come up over all his channels
    and go over all his banks.
⁸And he shall pass through Judah.
    He shall overflow, and go [over[a]].
    He shall reach even to the neck.
And the stretching out of his wings
    shall fill the breadth of thy land, O Immanuel.

⁹Associate yourselves, O ye people,
    and ye shall be broken in pieces.
And give ear, all ye of far countries!

---

a. The printer's manuscript has "ever." Isaiah 8:8 reads "over" rather than "ever." "Ever" was an error that was not caught at the time but was corrected for the 1830 edition, perhaps by the compositor. Skousen does not comment on this.

> Gird yourselves, and ye shall be broken in pieces!
> Gird yourselves, and ye shall be broken in pieces!
> ¹⁰Take counsel together, and it shall come to naught.
> > Speak the word, and it shall not stand!
> > For God is with us."

¹¹For the Lord spake thus to me with a strong hand,
> and instructed me
> > that I should not walk in the way of this people,
> > saying:

¹²"Say ye not 'A confederacy'
> to all **to whom** this people shall say, 'A confederacy.'
Neither fear ye their fear,
> nor be afraid.
¹³Sanctify the Lord of Hosts himself.
> And let him be your fear.
> And let him be your dread.
¹⁴And he shall be for a sanctuary.
> But for a stone of stumbling
and for a rock of offence to both the houses of Israel.
> For a gin and a snare to the inhabitants of Jerusalem.
¹⁵And many among them shall stumble and fall,
> and be broken,
> and be snared,
> and be taken.
¹⁶Bind up the testimony.
> Seal the law among my disciples.
¹⁷And I will wait upon the Lord,
> that hideth his face from the house of Jacob.
> And I will look for him.
¹⁸Behold, I, and the children whom the Lord hath given me,
> are for signs and for wonders in Israel
> from the Lord of Hosts, which dwelleth in mount Zion.

¹⁹And when they shall say unto you:

"Seek unto them that have familiar spirits,
> and unto wizards that peep and mutter," —
should not a people seek unto their God
> for the living to hear from the dead,
> > ²⁰to the law and to the testimony?
And if they speak not according to this word,
> it is because there is no light in them.
> > ²¹And they shall pass through it,
> > hardly bestead and hungry.

Chapter IX [2 Nephi 16–22]

And it shall come to pass that when they shall be hungry,
> they shall fret themselves,
> and curse their king and their God,
> and look upward.

²²And they shall look unto the earth,
> and behold trouble and darkness, dimness of anguish,
> and [ᵃ] shall be driven to darkness.

[19, compare Isaiah 9]

¹Nevertheless, the dimness shall not be such as was in her vexation,
> when at the first he lightly afflicted the land of Zebulon,
> and the land of Naphtali,

and afterward did more grievously afflict [ᵇ]
> (by the way of the red Sea)
> beyond Jordan,
> in Galilee of the nations.

²The people that walked in darkness
> have seen a great light.

They that dwell in the land of the shadow of death—
> upon them hath the light shined.

³Thou hast multiplied the nation
> and [ᶜ] increased the joy.

They joy before thee, according to the joy in harvest,
> and as men rejoice when they divide the spoil.

⁴For thou hast broken the yoke of his burden,
> and the staff of his shoulder,
> the rod of his oppressor [ᵈ].

⁵For every battle of the warrior [ᵉ] with confused noise
> and garments rolled in blood.

But this shall be with burning,
> and fuel of fire.

⁶For unto us a child is born.
> Unto us, a son is given.
> And the government shall be upon his shoulder,

and his name shall be called
> Wonderful, Counsellor,
> the Mighty God,
> the Everlasting Father,
> the Prince of Peace.

⁷Of the increase of [ᶠ] government and peace

---

a. Omits "they," which is in italics.
b. Omits "her," which is in italics."
c. Omits "not." It is not in italics.
d. Omits "as in the day of Midian."
e. Omits "is," which is in italics.
f. Omits "he," which is in italics.

> **there is** no end
> upon the throne of David,
> > and upon his kingdom—to order it,
> and to establish it with judgment,
> > and with justice from henceforth, even forever.
> The zeal of the Lord of Hosts will perform this.
>
> ⁸The Lord sent his word unto Jacob,
> > and it hath lighted upon Israel.
> ⁹And all the people shall know
> > (even Ephraim and the **inhabitants** of Samaria)
> that say in the pride
> > and the stoutness of heart:
> ¹⁰"The bricks are fallen down,
> > but we will build with hewn stones.
> The sycamores are cut down,
> > but we will change them into cedars.
> ¹¹Therefore, the Lord shall set up the adversaries of Rezin against him,
> > and join his enemies together—
> ¹²the Syrians before, and the Philistines behind.
> > And they shall devour Israel with open mouth.
> For all this his anger is not turned away,
> > but his hand [ª] stretched out still.
> ¹³For the people turneth not unto him that smiteth them,
> > neither do they [seekᵇ] the Lord of Hosts.
> ¹⁴Therefore **will the Lord** cut off from Israel,
> > head and tail,
> > branch and rush,
> > in one day.
> ¹⁵The ancient [ᶜ]—he is the head.
> > And the prophet that teacheth lies—he is the tail.
> ¹⁶For the leaders of this people cause them to err.
> > And they that are led of them are destroyed.
> ¹⁷Therefore, the Lord shall have no joy in their young men,
> > neither shall have mercy on their fatherless and widows.
> For every one **of them** is a hypocrite, and an evil doer.
> > And every mouth speaketh folly.
> For all this, his anger is not turned away.
> > But his hand [ᵈ] stretched out still.
> ¹⁸For wickedness burneth as the fire.
> > It shall devour the briars and thorns

---

a. Omits "is," which is in italics.

b. Restored from Isaiah 9:13. Oliver Cowdery added it, apparently upon proofreading. *Printer's Manuscript of the Book of Mormon*, 1:169.

c. Omits "and honourable."

d. Omits "is," which is in italics.

Chapter IX [2 Nephi 16–22]

and shall kindle in the thickets of the forests.
    And they shall mount up, like the lifting up of smoke.
[19]Through the wrath of the Lord of Hosts is the land darkened,
    and the people shall be as the fuel of the fire.
No man shall spare his brother.
[20]And he shall snatch on the right hand, and be hungry.
    And he shall eat on the left hand, and they shall not be satisfied.
    They shall eat, every man, the flesh of his own arm.
[21]Manasseh, Ephraim, and Ephraim, Manasseh—
    [a] they together shall be against Judah.
For all this, his anger is not turned away,
    but his hand [b] stretched out still.

[20, compare Isaiah 10]

[1]Wo unto them that decree unrighteous decrees,
    and that write grievousness which they have prescribed
[2]to turn aside the needy from judgment,
    and to take away the right from the poor of my people—
that widows may be their prey,
    and that they may rob the fatherless.
[3]And what will ye do in the day of visitation,
    and in the desolation, which shall come from far?
To whom will ye flee for help?
    And where will ye leave your glory?
[4]Without me, they shall bow down under the prisoners,
    and they shall fall under the slain.
For all this, his anger is not turned away,
    but his hand [c] stretched out still.

[5]O Assyrian! The rod of mine anger
    and the staff in their hand, is **their** indignation.
[6]I will send him against a hypocritical nation.
    And against the people of my wrath,
will I give him a charge to take the spoil and to take the prey.
    And to tread them down like the mire of the streets.
[7]Howbeit he meaneth not,
    so neither doth his heart think so,
but in his heart it is to destroy
    and cut off nations, not a few.
[8]For he saith:
"Are not my princes altogether kings?
    [9]Is not Calno as Carchemish?
    Is not Hamath as Arpad?

---

a. Omits "and," which is in italics.
b. Omits "is," which is in italics.
c. Omits "is,' which is in italics.

Is not Samaria as Damascus?"
¹⁰As my hand hath **founded** the kingdoms of the idols
(and whose graven images [ᵃ] them of Jerusalem and of Samaria)
¹¹shall I not (as I have done unto Samaria and her idols)
so do to Jerusalem and to her idols?

¹²Wherefore, it shall come to pass that
when the Lord hath performed his whole work
upon mount Zion
and upon Jerusalem,
I will punish the fruit of the stout heart
of the king of Assyria
and the glory of his high looks.

¹³For he saith:
"By the strength of my hand **and by my wisdom**,ᵇ
I have done **these things**.
For I am prudent,
and I have **moved** the **borders** of the people,
and have robbed their treasures.
And I have put down the inhabitants, like a valiant man.
¹⁴And my hand hath found as a nest, the riches of the people.
And as one gathereth eggs that are left,
have I gathered all the earth.
And there was none that moved the wing,
or opened the mouth, or peeped."

¹⁵Shall the axe boast itself against him that heweth therewith?
[ᶜ] Shall the saw magnify itself against him that shaketh it,
as if the rod should shake itself against them that lift it up.
Or, as if the staff should lift up itself, as if it were no wood.
¹⁶Therefore shall the Lord, the Lord of Hosts,
send among his fat ones, leanness.
And under his glory, he shall kindle a burning,
like the burning of a fire.
¹⁷And the light of Israel shall be for a fire,
and his Holy One for a flame—
and shall burn and **shall** devour
his thorns and his briars in one day—
¹⁸and shall consume the glory of his forest,
and of his fruitful field, both soul and body.
And they shall be as when a standard bearer feinteth.

---

a. The verb "did excel" is missing in the printer's manuscript. The compositor consulted Isaiah for the replacement and wrote it above. See Skousen, *Analysis of the Textual Variants*, 2:750.

b. Relocated in the sentence. "For he saith, By the strength of my hand I have done *it*, **and by my wisdom**; for I am prudent," (Isaiah 10:13). The italicized words "have" and "it" were removed and caused a reformation of the sentence.

c. Omits "or," which is in italics.

¹⁹And the rest of the trees of his forest shall be few,
> that a child may write them.

²⁰And it shall come to pass in that day,
> that the remnant of Israel
>> (and such as are escaped of the house of Jacob)

shall no more again stay upon him that smote them,
> but shall stay upon the Lord,
>> the Holy One of Israel, in truth.

²¹The remnant shall return,
> **yea**, even the remnant of Jacob,
> unto the mighty God.

²²For, though thy people Israel be as the sand of the sea,
> yet a remnant of them shall return.

The consumption decreed
> shall overflow with righteousness.

²³For the Lord God of hosts shall make a consumption,
> even determined in [ᵃ] all the land.

²⁴Therefore, thus saith the Lord God of hosts:

"O my people that dwellest in Zion!
> Be not afraid of the Assyrian!

He shall smite thee with a rod
> and shall lift up his staff against thee
> after the manner of Egypt.

²⁵For yet a very little while, and the indignation shall cease,
> and mine anger in their destruction.

²⁶And the Lord of Hosts shall stir up a scourge for him,
> according to the slaughter of Midian at the rock of Oreb.

And as his rod was upon the sea,
> so shall he lift it up after the manner of Egypt.

²⁷And it shall come to pass in that day
that his burden shall be taken away from off thy shoulder,
> and his yoke from off thy neck.

And the yoke shall be destroyed
> because of the anointing.

²⁸He is come to Aiath. He is passed to Migron.
> At Mishmash, he hath laid up his carriages.

²⁹They are gone over the passage.
> They have taken up their lodging at Geba.
> **Ramath** is afraid. Gibeah of Saul is fled.

³⁰Lift up the voice, O daughter of Gallim!
> Cause it to be heard unto Laish, O poor Anathoth!

³¹Madmenah is removed.
> The inhabitants of Gebim gather themselves to flee.

---

a. Omits "in the midst."

³²As yet shall he remain at Nob that day.
    He shall shake his hand
against the mount of the daughter of Zion,
    the hill of Jerusalem.

³³Behold, the Lord, the Lord of Hosts,
    shall lop the bough with terror.
And the high ones of stature shall be hewn down.
    And the haughty shall be humbled.
³⁴And he shall cut down the thickets of the forests with iron.
    And Lebanon shall fall by a mighty one.

[21, compare Isaiah 11]

¹And there shall come forth a rod out of the stem of Jesse,
    and a branch shall grow out of his roots.
²And the spirit of the Lord shall rest upon him—
    the spirit of wisdom and understanding,
    the spirit of counsel and might,
    the spirit of knowledge and of the fear of the Lord—
³and shall make him[a] of quick understanding
    in the fear of the Lord.
And he shall not judge after the sight of his eyes,
    neither reprove after the hearing of his ears.
⁴But with righteousness shall he judge the poor.
    And reprove with equity for the meek of the earth.
And he shall smite the earth with the rod of his mouth,
    and with the breath of his lips shall he slay the wicked.
⁵And righteousness shall be the girdle of his loins
    and faithfulness the girdle of his reins.

⁶The wolf also shall dwell with the lamb.
    And the leopard shall lie down with the kid,
    and the calf, and the young lion, and the fatling together.
And a little child shall lead them.
⁷And the cow and the bear shall feed.
    Their young ones shall lie down together.
And the lion shall eat straw like the ox.
⁸And the sucking child shall play on the hole of the asp.
    And the weaned child shall put his hand on the cockatrice's den.

⁹They shall not hurt nor destroy in all my holy mountain.
    For the earth shall be full of the knowledge of the Lord,
    as the waters cover the sea.

---

a. The printer's manuscript had "and *he* shall *not* make him of quick understanding in the fear of the Lord." Oliver crossed out the "he" and "not." It now reads in accordance with Isaiah 11:3. Skousen, *Analysis of the Textual Variants*, 2:765.

Chapter IX [2 Nephi 16–22]

¹⁰And in that day, there shall be a root of Jesse
    which shall stand for an ensign of the people.
To it shall the Gentiles seek.
    And his rest shall be glorious.

¹¹And it shall come to pass in that day,
    that the Lord shall set his hand again the second time
    to recover the remnant of his people,
    which shall be left from Assyria,
    and from Egypt,
    and from Pathros,
    and from Cush,
    and from Elam,
    and from Shinar,
    and from Hamath,
    and from the Islands of the sea.

¹²And he shall set up an ensign for the nations,
    and shall assemble the outcasts of Israel,
    and gather together the dispersed of Judah
    from the four corners of the earth.

¹³The envy of Ephraim **also** shall depart,
    and the adversaries of Judah shall be cut off.
Ephraim shall not envy Judah.
    And Judah shall not vex Ephraim.

¹⁴But they shall fly upon the shoulders of the Philistines towards the west.
    They shall spoil them of the east together.
They shall lay their hand upon Edom, and Moab,
    and the children of Ammon shall obey them.

¹⁵And the Lord shall utterly destroy
    the tongue of the Egyptian Sea.
And with his mighty wind
    he shall shake his hand over the river,
and shall smite it in the seven streams,
    and make men go over dryshod.

¹⁶And there shall be a highway for the remnant of his people
    (which shall be left from Assyria),
    like as it was to Israel
    in the day that he came up out of the land of Egypt.

[22, compare Isaiah 12]

¹And in that day, thou shalt say:

"O Lord! I will praise thee.
    Though thou wast angry with me,
thine anger is turned away.
    And thou comfortedst me.

²Behold, God is my salvation!

> I [will^a] trust, and not be afraid.
> For the Lord Jehovah is my strength, and my song.
> He also is become my salvation.
> ³Therefore, with joy shall ye draw water out of the wells of salvation.
>
> ⁴And in that day shall ye say:
> "Praise the Lord! Call upon his name!
> Declare his doings among the people!
> Make mention that his name is exalted!
> ⁵Sing unto the Lord, for he hath done excellent things!
> This is known in all the earth.
> ⁶Cry out, and shout, thou inhabitant of Zion!
> For great is the Holy One of Israel in the midst of thee."

---

a. This was added later, perhaps during proofreading.

Chapter X [2 Nephi 23–24]

[23, compare Isaiah 13]

¹The burden of Babylon, which Isaiah (the son of Amoz) did see:

²Lift ye up a banner upon the high mountain!
    Exalt the voice unto them!
Shake the hand,
    that they may go into the gates of the nobles.
³I have commanded my sanctified ones.
    I have also called my mighty ones,
    for mine anger **is not upon** them that rejoice in my highness.

⁴The noise of **the** multitude in the mountains,
    like as of a great people,
a tumultuous noise of the kingdoms
    of nations gathered together—
    the Lord of Hosts mustereth the **hosts** of the battle.
⁵They come from a far country,
    from the end of heaven,
yea, the Lord and the weapons of his indignation—
    to destroy the whole land.

⁶Howl ye! For the day of the Lord is at hand!
    It shall come as a destruction from the Almighty.
⁷Therefore shall all hands be feint.
    Every man's heart shall melt,
⁸and they shall be afraid.
    Pangs and sorrows shall take hold of them.[a]
They shall be amazed one at another.
    Their faces shall be as flames.

⁹Behold! The day of the Lord cometh,
    cruel both with wrath and fierce anger,
to lay the land desolate.
    And he shall destroy the sinners thereof out of it.
¹⁰For the stars of heaven, and the constellations thereof,
    shall not give their light.
The sun shall be darkened in his going forth,
    and the moon shall not cause her light to shine.
¹¹And I will punish the world for [b] evil,
    and the wicked for their iniquity.
I will cause the arrogancy of the proud to cease
    and will lay **down** the haughtiness of the terrible.

---

    a. Omits "They shall be in pain as a woman that travaileth." Skousen, *Analysis of the Textual Variants*, 2:767, suggests that the phrase might have been inadvertently missed in copying from the Original to the Printer's Manuscript.

    b. Omits "their," which is in italics.

¹²I will make a man more precious than fine gold,
>even a man than the golden wedge of Ophir.
¹³Therefore, I will shake the heavens.
>And the earth shall remove out of her place
in the wrath of the Lord of Hosts,
>and in the day of his fierce anger.
¹⁴And it shall be as the chased roe,
>and as a sheep that no man taketh up.
They shall, every man, turn to his own people,
>and flee every one into his own land.
¹⁵Every one that is proud shall be thrust through.
>**Yea**, and everyone that is joined **to the wicked** shall fall by the sword.
¹⁶Their children also shall be dashed to pieces before their eyes.
>Their houses shall be spoiled, and their wives ravished.
¹⁷Behold, I will stir up the Medes against them,
>which shall not regard silver and [a] gold
>**nor** they shall not delight in it.
¹⁸Their bows **shall also** dash the young men to pieces.
>And they shall have no pity on the fruit of the womb.
>Their **eyes** shall not spare children.
¹⁹And Babylon, the glory of kingdoms,
>the beauty of the Chaldees' excellency,
>shall be as when God overthrew Sodom and Gomorrah.
²⁰It shall never be inhabited,
>neither shall it be dwelt in, from generation to generation.
>Neither shall the Arabian pitch tent there,
>neither shall the shepherds make their fold there.
²¹But wild beasts of the desert shall lie there.
>And their houses shall be full of doleful creatures,
and owls shall dwell there,
>and satyrs shall dance there.
²²And the wild beasts of the islands shall cry in their desolate houses,
>and dragons in their pleasant palaces.
And her time is near to come,
>and her **day** shall not be prolonged.
For I will destroy her speedily.
>Yea, for I will be merciful unto my people,
>but the wicked shall perish!

---

a. Isaiah 13:17 reads: "Behold, I will stir up the Medes against them, which shall not regard silver; and *as for* gold, they shall not delight in it." It appears that the elimination of the "as for" (in italics in the KJV), influenced the insertion of "nor." The deletion and resolution are inferior in meaning to the original.

Chapter X [2 Nephi 23–24]

[24, compare Isaiah 14]

¹For the Lord will have mercy on Jacob,
    and will yet chose Israel,
    and set them in their own land.
And the strangers shall be joined with them,
    and they shall cleave to the house of Jacob.
²And the people shall take them,
and bring them to their place,
    yea, from far, unto the ends of the earth.
    And they shall return to their lands of promise.
And the house of Israel shall possess them.
    And the land of the Lord **shall be** for servants and handmaids.
And they shall take them captives, **unto whom they were captives.**[a]
    And they shall rule over their oppressors.
³And it shall come to pass in that day, that the Lord shall give thee rest
    from thy sorrows,
    and from thy fear,
and from the hard bondage wherein thou wast made to serve.

⁴And it shall come to pass in that day, that thou shalt take up this proverb against the king of Babylon, and say:

"How hath the oppressor ceased,
    the golden city ceased!"
⁵The Lord hath broken the staff of the wicked,
    [b] the **scepters** of the rulers.
⁶He who smote the people in wrath with a continual stroke,
    he that ruled the nations in anger,
    is persecuted. And none hindereth.
⁷The whole earth is at rest, and is quiet.
    They break forth into singing.
⁸Yea, the fir trees rejoice at thee.
    And **also** the cedars of Lebanon, saying:
"Since thou art laid down,
    no feller is come up against us."
⁹Hell from beneath is moved for thee,
    to meet thee at thy coming.
It stireth up the dead for thee.
    Even all the chief ones of the earth,
it hath raised up from their thrones
    all the kings of the nations.
¹⁰All they shall speak, and say unto thee:
    "Art thou also become weak as we?

---

    a. The King James Version has the phrase "whose captives they were." The change appears to make better sense of the sentence.
    b. Omits "and," which is in italics.

Art thou become like unto us?"
¹¹Thy pomp is brought down to the grave.
  The noise of thy viols **is not heard**.
The worm is spread under thee,
  and the worms cover thee.

¹²How art thou fallen from heaven,
  O Lucifer, son of the Morning!
Art thou cut down to the ground,
  which did weaken the nations?
¹³For thou hast said in thy heart,
    ¹⁴"I will ascend into heaven.
    I will exalt my throne above the stars of God.
    I will sit also upon the mount of the congregation in the sides of the
    north. I will ascend above the heights of the clouds.
    I will be like the Most High."
¹⁵Yet thou shalt be brought down to hell,
  to the sides of the pit.

¹⁶They that see thee, shall narrowly look upon thee
  and **shall** consider thee, **and shall say**:
"Is this the man that made the earth to tremble?
    That did shake kingdoms?
      ¹⁷**And** made the world as a wilderness?
      And destroyed the cities thereof?
      And opened not the house of his prisoners?"
¹⁸All the kings of the nations,
    yea, all of them, lie in glory.
    Every one **of them** in his own house.
¹⁹But thou art cast out of thy grave
    like an abominable branch
and [ᵃ] the **remnant** of those that are slain,
    thrust through with a sword,
    that go down to the stones of the pit
    as a carcass trodden under feet.
²⁰Thou shalt not be joined with them in burial
    because thou hast destroyed thy land
    and slain thy people.

The seed of evil doers
  shall never be renowned.
²¹Prepare slaughter for his children,
    for the iniquities of their fathers—
that they do not rise, nor possess the land,
    nor fill the face of the world with cities.

---

a. Omits "as," which is in italics.

Chapter X [2 Nephi 23–24]

²²"For I will raise up against them" (saith the Lord of Hosts)
"and cut off from Babylon
the name,
and remnant,
and son,
and nephew (saith the Lord).
²³I will also make it a possession for the bittern and pools of water.
    And I will sweep it with the besom of destruction"
(saith the Lord of Hosts).

²⁴The Lord of Hosts hath sworn, saying:
"Surely as I have thought,
    so shall it come to pass.
And as I have purposed,
    so shall it stand—
that I will **bring** the Assyrian in my land
    and upon my mountains tread him under foot.
Then shall his yoke depart from off them,
    and his burden depart from off their shoulders."

²⁶This is the purpose that is purposed upon the whole earth,
    and this is the hand that is stretched out upon all nations.
²⁷For the Lord of Hosts hath purposed,
    and who shall disannul [a]?
And his hand [b] stretched out.
    And who shall turn it back?

²⁸In the year that King Ahaz died was this burden.

²⁹Rejoice not thou, whole Palestina,
    because the rod of him that smote thee is broken.
For out of the serpent's root shall come forth a cockatrice,
    and his fruit shall be a fiery flying serpent.
³⁰And the first born of the poor shall feed,
    and the needy shall lie down in safety.
And I will kill thy root with famine,
    and he shall slay thy remnant.

³¹Howl O gate! Cry, O city!
    Thou, whole Palestina, art dissolved,
for there shall come from the north a smoke,
    and none shall be alone in his appointed times.
³²What shall [c] then answer the messengers of the **nations**?
    That the Lord hath founded Zion,
    and the poor of his people shall trust in it.

---

a. Omits "it," which is in italics
b. Omits "is," which is in italics.
c. Omits "one," which is in italics.

Chapter XI [2 Nephi 25–27]

[25] ¹Now, I Nephi, do speak somewhat concerning the words which I have written, which have been spoken by the mouth of Isaiah. For behold Isaiah spake many things which were hard for many of my people to understand, for they know not concerning the manner of prophesying among the Jews. ²For I, Nephi, have not taught them many things concerning the manner of the Jews. For their works were works of darkness, and their doings were doings of abomination. ³Wherefore, I write unto my people, unto all they that shall receive hereafter these things which I write, that they may know the judgments of God—that they come upon all nations, according to the word which he hath spoken. ⁴Wherefore, hearken O my people (which are of the house of Israel)! And give ear to my words![a] For, because that the words of Isaiah are not plain unto you—nevertheless they are plain unto all they that are filled with the spirit of prophesy.

But I give unto you a prophesy, according to the spirit which is in me. Wherefore, I shall prophesy, according to the plainness which hath been with me from the time that I came out from Jerusalem with my father.

For behold, my soul delighteth in plainness unto my people, that they may learn. ⁵Yea, and my soul delighteth in the words of Isaiah, for I came out from Jerusalem. And mine eyes hath beheld the things of the Jews. And I know that the Jews do understand the things of the prophets. And there is none other people that understand the things which were spoken unto the Jews like unto them—save it be that they are taught after the manner of the things of the Jews. ⁶But behold, I, Nephi, have not taught my children after the manner of the Jews.

⁷But behold, I, of myself, have dwelt at Jerusalem. ⁸Wherefore, I know concerning the regions round about. And I have made mention unto my children concerning the judgments of God, which hath come to pass among the Jews unto my children, according to all that which Isaiah hath spoken. And I do not write them. But behold, I proceed with mine own prophesy, according to my plainness—in the which I know that no man can err. Nevertheless, in the days that the prophesies of Isaiah shall be fulfilled, men shall know of a surety—at the times when they shall come to pass. Wherefore, they are of worth unto the children of men. And he that supposeth that they are not, unto them will I speak particularly, and confine the words unto mine own people. For I know that they shall be of great worth unto them in the last days. For in that day shall they understand them. Wherefore, for their good have I written them.

⁹And as one generation hath been destroyed among the Jews because of iniquity, even so have they been destroyed from generation to generation, according to their iniquities. And never hath any of them been destroyed, save it were foretold them by the prophets of the Lord. ¹⁰Wherefore, it hath been told them concerning the destruction which should come upon them immediately after my father left Jerusalem. Nevertheless, they hardened their hearts. And according to my prophesy, they have been destroyed, save it be those which are carried away captive into Babylon.

¹¹And now, this I speak because of the spirit which is in me. And notwithstanding that they have been carried away, they shall return again and possess the land of Jerusalem. Wherefore, they shall be restored again to the lands of their inheritance.

---

a. Uses language from Isaiah 51:4: "Hearken unto me, my people; and give ear unto me, O my nation."

CHAPTER XI [2 NEPHI 25–27]

¹²But behold, they shall have wars, and rumors of wars. And when the day cometh that the Only Begotten of the Father, yea, even the Father of Heaven and of Earth, shall manifest himself unto them in the flesh—behold, they will reject him because of [their iniquities[a]], and the hardness of their hearts, and the stiffness of their necks. ¹³Behold, they will crucify him. And after that he is laid in a sepulcher for the space of three days, he shall rise from the dead with healing in his wings.[b] And all [they who[c]] shall believe on his name shall be saved in the kingdom of God. Wherefore, my soul delighteth to prophesy concerning him. For I have seen his day. And my heart doth magnify his holy name. ¹⁴And behold it shall come to pass that after the Messiah hath risen from the dead, and hath manifested himself unto his people, unto as many as will believe on his name—behold, Jerusalem shall be destroyed again. For wo unto them that fight against God and the people of his church! ¹⁵Wherefore, the Jews shall be scattered among all nations. Yea, and also Babylon shall be destroyed. Wherefore, the Jews shall be scattered by other nations. ¹⁶And after that they have been scattered, and the Lord God hath scourged them by other nations for the space of many generations (yea, even down from generation to generation) until they shall be persuaded to believe in Christ the Son of God, and the atonement (which is infinite for all mankind)—and when that day shall come, that they shall believe in Christ, and worship the Father in his name, with pure hearts and clean hands,[d] and look not forward any more for another Messiah. And then at that time, the day will come that it must needs be expedient that they should believe these things.

¹⁷And the Lord will set his hand again the second time to restore his people from their lost and fallen state.[e] Wherefore, he will proceed to do a marvelous work and a wonder among the children of men.[f] ¹⁸Wherefore, he shall bring forth his words unto them, which words shall judge them at the last day. For they shall be given them for the purpose of convincing them of the true Messiah (who was rejected by them), and unto the convincing of them that they need not look forward any more for a Messiah to come. For there should not any come, save it should be a false Messiah which should deceive the people. For there is save one Messiah spoken of by the prophets. And that Messiah is he which should be rejected of the Jews.

¹⁹For according to the words of the prophets, the Messiah cometh in six hundred years from the time that my father left Jerusalem. And, according to the words of the prophets (and also the word of the angel of God), his name should be Jesus Christ, the Son of God.

²⁰And now, my brethren, I have spoken plain that ye cannot err. And as the Lord

---

a. The Printer's Manuscript had the word "priestscrafts," but was soon changed to "their iniquities," suggesting a copy error from the Original Manuscript (not extant at this point). Skousen, *Analysis of the Textual Variants* 2:814.

b. The phrase "with healing in his wings" is from Malachi 4:2.

c. The later cross-out makes it difficult to read, but "they who" is probable. Joseph Smith later changed it to "those who." See *Printer's Manuscript of the Book of Mormon*, 181.

d. The phrase "pure hearts and clean hands" alludes to Psalm 24:4: "He that hath clean hands, and a pure heart; who hath not lifted up his soul unto vanity, nor sworn deceitfully."

e. See Isaiah 11:11: "And it shall come to pass in that day, that the Lord shall set his hand again the second time to recover the remnant of his people."

f. Reference to Isaiah 29:14: "Therefore, behold, I will proceed to do a marvellous work among this people, even a marvellous work and a wonder."

God liveth that brought Israel up out of the land of Egypt, and gave unto Moses power that he should heal the nations after they had been bitten by the poisonous serpents (if they would cast their eyes unto the serpent which he did raise up before them)[a]—and also give him power that he should smite the rock and the water should come forth[b]—yea, behold, I say unto you that as these things are true. And as the Lord God liveth, there is none other name given under heaven save it be this Jesus Christ[c] (of which I have spoken) whereby man can be saved. [21]Wherefore, for this cause hath the Lord God promised unto me that these things which I write shall be kept, and preserved, and handed down unto my seed from generation to generation, that the promise may be fulfilled unto Joseph that his seed should never perish as long as the earth should stand. [22]Wherefore, these things shall go from generation to generation as long as the earth shall stand, and they shall go according to the will and pleasure of God.

And the nations which shall possess them, shall be judged of them, according to the words which are written. [23]For we labor diligently to write, to persuade our children, and also our brethren, to believe in Christ and to be reconciled to God. For we know that it is by grace that we are saved, after all that we can do. [24]And notwithstanding we believe in Christ, we keep the law of Moses. And look forward with steadfastness unto Christ until the law shall be fulfilled. [25]For, for this end was the law given. Wherefore, the law hath become dead unto us, and we are made alive in Christ because of our faith. Yet, we keep the law because of the commandments.

[26]And we talk of Christ. We rejoice in Christ. We preach of Christ. We prophesy of Christ. And we write, according to our prophesies, that our children my know to what source to they may look for a remission of their sins. [27]Wherefore, we speak concerning the law, that our children may know the deadness of the law. And they (by knowing the deadness of the law) may look forward unto that life which is in Christ, and know for what end the law was given. And after that the law is fulfilled in Christ, that they need not harden their hearts against him when the law had ought to be done away.

[28]And now behold, my people, ye are a stiffnecked people. Wherefore, I have spoken plain unto you, that ye cannot misunderstand. And the words which I have spoken shall as a testimony against you. For they are sufficient to teach any man the right way. For the right way is to believe in Christ and deny him not. For by denying him, ye also deny the prophets and the law.

[29]And now behold, I say unto you that the right way is to believe in Christ and deny him not. And Christ is the Holy One of Israel. Wherefore, ye must bow down before him, and worship him with all your might, mind, and strength, and your whole soul. And if ye do this, ye shall in no wise be cast out. [30]And inasmuch as it shall be expedient, ye must keep the performances and ordinances of God until the law shall be fulfilled which was given unto Moses.

[26] [1]And after that Christ shall have risen from the dead, he shall show himself unto you, my children and my beloved brethren. And the words which he shall speak unto you shall be the law which ye shall do.

[2]For behold, I say unto you that I have beheld that many generations shall pass

---

a. Story in Numbers 21:6–9.

b. Story in Exodus 17:6.

c. See Acts 4:12: "Neither is there salvation in any other: for there is none other name under heaven given among men, whereby we must be saved."

Chapter XI [2 Nephi 25–27]

away, and there shall be great wars and contentions among my people. ³And after that the Messiah shall come, there shall be signs given unto my people of his birth. And also of his death and resurrection. And great and terrible shall that day be unto the wicked, for they shall perish. And they perish because they cast out the prophets and the saints, and stone them and slay them. Wherefore, the cry of the blood of the saints shall ascend up to God from the ground against them. ⁴Wherefore, all they that are proud and that do wickedly—the day that cometh shall burn them up, saith the Lord of Hosts, for they shall be as stubble.ᵃ

⁵And they that kill the prophets and the saints—the depths of the earth shall swallow them up, saith the Lord of Hosts. And mountains shall cover them, and whirlwinds shall carry them away. And buildings shall fall upon them, and crush them to pieces, and grind them to powder. ⁶And they shall be visited with thunderings, and lightnings, and earthquakesᵇ, and all manner of destructions. For the fire of the anger of the Lord shall be kindled against them, and they shall be as stubble. And the day that cometh shall consume them, saith the Lord of Hosts.

⁷O the pain and the anguish of my soul for the loss of the slain of my people! For I, Nephi, hath seen it, and it well nigh consumeth me before the presence of the Lord. But I must cry unto my God: "Thy ways are just!"

⁸But behold, the righteous that hearken unto the words of the prophets and destroy them not—but look forward unto Christ with steadfastness for the signs which are given (notwithstanding all persecutions). Behold, they are they which shall not perish. ⁹But the son of righteousnessᶜ shall appear unto them, and he shall heal them. And they shall have peace with him until three generations shall have passed away (and many of the fourth generation shall have passed away)ᵈ in righteousness. ¹⁰And when these things shall have passed away, a speedy destruction cometh unto my people. For, notwithstanding the pains of my soul, I have seen it. Wherefore, I know that it shall come to pass.

And they sell themselves for naught.ᵉ For, for the reward of their pride and their foolishness they shall reap destruction. For because they yieldeth unto the devil and chose works of darkness rather than light, therefore they must go down to hell. ¹¹For the spirit of the Lord will not always strive with man.ᶠ And when the spirit ceaseth to strive with man, then cometh speedy destruction. And this grieveth my soul.

¹²And as I spake concerning the convincing of the Jews that Jesus is the very Christ, it must needs be that the Gentiles be convinced also that Jesus is the Christ, the Eternal God, ¹³and that he manifesteth himself unto all they that believe in him, by the power of

---

a. See Malachi 4:1: "For, behold, the day cometh, that shall burn as an oven; and all the proud, yea, and all that do wickedly, shall be stubble."

b. Uses language from Revelation 8:5: "And there were voices, and thunderings, and lightnings, and an earthquake."

c. Malachi 4:2 has the phrase "sun of righteousness," which is referenced as "son of righteousness" here and in Ether 9:22.

d. The parentheses are in the Printer's Manuscript. There isn't a particular reason for them, but there are so few punctuation marks that they have been retained her. See *Printer's Manuscript of the Book of Mormon*, 184–85. At least the opening parenthesis appears to have been added after the text rather than written as a part of the dictation. The parentheses were not reproduced in the 1830 edition.

e. See Isaiah 52:3: "For thus saith the Lord, Ye have sold yourselves for nought."

f. See Genesis 6:3: "And the Lord said, My spirit shall not always strive with man."

the Holy Ghost. Yea, unto every nation, kindred, tongue, and people[a]—working mighty miracles, signs, and wonders among the children of men, according to their faith.

[14]But behold, I prophesy unto you concerning the last days, concerning the days when the Lord God shall bring these things forth unto the children of men. [15]After that my seed and the seed of my brethren shall have dwindled in unbelief, and shall have been smitten by the Gentiles—yea, after that the Lord God shall have camped against them round about, and shall have laid siege against them with a mount, and raised forts against them[b]—and after that they shall have been brought down low in the dust, even that they are not—yet, the words of the righteous shall be written. And the prayers of the faithful shall be heard.

And all they which have dwindled in unbelief shall not be forgotten. [16]For they which shall be destroyed shall speak unto them out of the ground. And their speech shall be low out of the dust. And their voice shall be as one that hath a familiar spirit.[c] For the Lord God will give unto him power, that he may whisper concerning them, even as it were out of the ground. And their speech shall whisper out of the dust. [17]For thus saith the Lord God: "They shall write the things which shall be done among them. And they shall be written and sealed up in a book. And they that have dwindled in unbelief shall not have them. For they seek to destroy the things of God." [18]Wherefore, as they which have been destroyed have been destroyed speedily, and the multitudes of their terrible ones shall be as chaff that passeth away. Yea, thus saith the Lord God: "It shall be at an instant—suddenly.[d]"

[19]And it shall come to pass that they which have dwindled in unbelief shall be smitten by the hand of the Gentiles. [20]And the Gentiles are lifted up in the pride of their eyes and have stumbled (because of the greatness of their stumbling block), that they have built up many churches. Nevertheless, they put down the power and the miracles of God, and preach up unto themselves their own wisdom and their own learning, that they may get gain, and grind upon the face of the poor.[e]

[21]And there are many churches built up, which causeth envyings and strifes, and malice. [22]And there are also secret combinations, even as in times of old (according to the combinations of the devil). For he is the founder of all these things. Yea, the founder of murder and works of darkness. Yea, and he leadeth them by the neck with a flaxen cord until he bindeth them with his strong cords forever.

[23]For behold my beloved brethren, I say unto you that the Lord God worketh not in darkness. [24]He doeth not any thing, save it be for the benefit of the world. For he loveth the world, even that he layeth down his own life—that he may draw all men unto him.[f] Wherefore, he commandeth none that they shall not partake of his salvation.

---

a. See Revelation 14:6: "And I saw another angel fly in the midst of heaven, having the everlasting gospel to preach unto them that dwell on the earth, and to every nation, and kindred, and tongue, and people."

b. See Isaiah 29:3: "And I will camp against thee round about, and will lay siege against thee with a mount, and I will raise forts against thee."

c. See Isaiah 29:4: "And thou shalt be brought down, and shalt speak out of the ground, and thy speech shall be low out of the dust, and thy voice shall be, as of one that hath a familiar spirit, out of the ground, and thy speech shall whisper out of the dust."

d. See Isaiah 29:5: "Moreover the multitude of thy strangers shall be like small dust, and the multitude of the terrible ones shall be as chaff that passeth away: yea, it shall be at an instant suddenly."

e. The phrase "grind the faces of the poor" is found in Isaiah 3:15.

f. Uses language from John 3:16: "For God so loved the world, that he gave his only begotten Son,

Chapter XI [2 Nephi 25–27]

²⁵Behold, doth he cry unto any saying: "Depart from me!"?

Behold, I say unto you, nay! But he saith: "Come unto me all ye ends of the earth! Buy milk and honey without money, and without price."ᵃ

²⁶Behold, hath he commanded any, that they should depart out of the synagogues, or out of the houses of worship?

Behold, I say unto you, nay!

²⁷Hath he commanded any, that they should not partake of his salvation?

Behold, I say unto you, nay! But he hath given it free for all men, and he hath commanded his people, that they should persuade all men unto repentance.

²⁸Behold, hath the Lord commanded any, that they should not partake of his goodness?

Behold, I say unto you, nay! But all men are privileged—the one like unto the other, and none are forbidden.

²⁹He commandeth that there shall be no priestcrafts. For behold, priestcrafts are that men preach, and set themselves up for a light unto the world, that they may get gain and praise of the world. But they seek not the welfare of Zion.

³⁰Behold, the Lord hath forbidden this thing. Wherefore, the Lord God hath given a commandment that all men should have charity, which charity is love. And except they should have charity, they were nothing. Wherefore, if they should have charity, they would not suffer the laborer in Zion to perish. ³¹But the laborer in Zion shall labor for Zion. For, if they labor for money—they shall perish.

And again, the Lord God hath commanded:

that men should not murder,

that they should not lie,

that they should not steal,

that they should not take the name of the Lord, their God, in vain,

that they should not envy,

that they should not have malice,

that they should not contend one with another,

that they should not commit whoredoms.

And that they should [notᵇ] do none of these things. For whoso doeth them shall perish. ³³For none of these iniquities come of the Lord, for he doeth that which is good among the children of men.

And he doeth nothing, save it be plain unto the children of men. And he inviteth them all to come unto him and partake of his goodness. And he denieth none that come unto him—black and white, bond and free, male and female.ᶜ And he remembereth the heathen. And all are alike unto God, both Jew and Gentile.

---

that whosoever believeth in him should not perish, but have everlasting life."

a. See Isaiah 55:1: "Ho, every one that thirsteth, come ye to the waters, and he that hath no money; come ye, buy, and eat; yea, come, buy wine and milk without money and without price."

b. The word "not" was crossed out in the Printer's Manuscript, apparently by the compositor. It prevented a double negative. Skousen, *Analysis of the Textual Variants*, 2:839. Although it should be removed (and was), it is preserved because it was an error left in the text when it was sent to the compositor. Skousen, 2:840, also indicates: "It is possible that the five cases where the earliest sources support the multiple negative could be due to dialectal interference during the early transmission of the text."

c. See Galatians 3:28: "There is neither Jew nor Greek, there is neither bond nor free, there is neither male nor female: for ye are all one in Christ Jesus."

[27] ¹But behold, in the last days (or in the days of the Gentiles), yea behold, all the nations of the Gentiles, and also the Jews (both they which shall come upon this land and they which shall be upon other lands, yea, even upon all the lands of the earth), behold, they will be drunken with iniquity, and all manner of abominations.ᵃ

²**And when that day shall come,**
they shall be visited with the Lord of Hosts,
with thunder and with earthquake,
> and with a great noise,
> and with storm
> and tempest,
> and **with** the flame of devouring fire.

³And all the nations that fight against Zion, and that distress her,
> shall be as a dream of a night vision.

Yea, it shall be **unto them** even as unto a hungry man **which** dreameth.
> And behold, he eateth, but he awaketh and his soul is empty.

Or **like unto** a thirsty man, **which** dreameth.
> And behold he drinketh, but he awaketh and behold he is faint,
> and his soul hath appetite.

Yea, even so shall the multitude of all the nations be
> that fight against mount Zion.

⁴**For, behold all ye that do iniquity!**
Stay yourselves, and wonder!
> **For ye shall** cry out, and cry.

Yea, ye shall be drunken. But not with wine.
> **Ye shall** stagger. But not with strong drink.

⁵For **behold**, the Lord hath poured out upon you the spirit of deep sleep.
> **For behold, ye** have closed your eyes,

and ye have rejected the prophets and your rulers.
> **And** the seers hath he covered **because of your iniquity.**ᵇ

⁶And it shall come to pass that the Lord God shall bring forth unto you the words of a book. And [ᶜ] shall be the words of them which have slumbered. ⁷And behold, the book shall be sealed.ᵈ And in the book shall be a revelation from God, from the beginning of the world to the ending thereof. ⁸Wherefore, because of the things which are sealed up, the things which are sealed shall not be delivered in the day of the wickedness and abominations of the people. Wherefore, the book shall be kept from them. ⁹But the book shall be delivered unto a man. And he shall deliver the words of the book, which are the words of they which have slumbered in the dust. And he shall deliver these

---

a. This sentence wanders, and the second "behold" is a repetitive resumption to get it back on track.
b. Verses 2–5 quote Isaiah 29:6–10.
c. The word "they" was added for the 1830 edition. Skousen suggests that the supralinear addition of "they" on the Printer's Manuscript may have been in the compositor's hand. It is clearly required to complete the sentence. Skousen *Analysis of the Textual Variants*, 2:849.
d. Reprising Isaiah 29:11: "And the vision of all is become unto you as the words of a book that is sealed, which men deliver to one that is learned, saying, Read this, I pray thee: and he saith, I cannot; for it is sealed."

Chapter XI [2 Nephi 25–27]

words unto another. ¹⁰But the words which are sealed, he shall not deliver. Neither shall he deliver the book. For the book shall be sealed by the power of God. And the revelation which was sealed shall be kept in the book until the own due time of the Lord, that they may come forth. For behold, they reveal all things from the foundation of the world unto the end thereof.[a]

¹¹And the day cometh, that the words of the book which were sealed shall be read upon the house tops. And they shall be read by the power of Christ. And all things shall be revealed unto the children of men which ever hath been among the children of men, and which ever will be, even unto the end of the earth. ¹²Wherefore, at that day when the book shall be delivered unto the man of whom I have spoken, the book shall be hid from the eyes of the world, that eyes of none shall behold it, save it be that three witnesses shall behold it by the power of God (besides him to whom the book shall be delivered). And they shall testify to the truth of the book, and the things therein. ¹³And there is none other which shall view it, save it be a few, according to the will of God, to bear testimony of his word unto the children of men.

For the Lord God hath said that the words of the faithful should speak as if it were from the dead. ¹⁴Wherefore, the Lord God will proceed to bring forth the words of the book. And in the mouth of as many witnesses as seemeth him good will he establish his word. And wo be unto him that rejecteth the word of God!

¹⁵But behold, it shall come to pass that the Lord God shall say unto him to whom he shall deliver the book: "Take these words which are not sealed and deliver them to another, that he may show them unto the learned,[b]" saying: "Read this I pray thee." And the learned will say: "Bring hither the book, and I will read them."

¹⁶And now, because of the glory of the world (and to get gain) will they say this. And not for the glory of God. ¹⁷And the man shall say: "I cannot bring the book, for it is sealed.[c]"

¹⁸Then shall the learned say: "I cannot read it." ¹⁹Wherefore, it shall come to pass that the Lord God will deliver again the book, and the words thereof, to him that is not learned. And the man that is not learned shall say: "I am not learned.[d]" ²⁰Then shall the Lord God say unto him: "The learned shall not read them, for they have rejected them. And I am able to do mine own work. Wherefore, thou shalt read the words which I shall give unto thee.

²¹Touch not the things which are sealed, for I will bring them forth in mine own due time. For, I will show unto the children of men that I am able to do mine own work. ²²Wherefore, when thou hast read the words which I have commanded thee, and obtained the witnesses which I have promised unto thee, then shalt thou seal up the

---

a. This paragraph appears to be bounded with the beginning phrase: "from the beginning of the world to the ending thereof," and the concluding: "all things from the foundation of the world unto the end thereof."

b. Reprising Isaiah 29:11: "And the vision of all is become unto you as the words of a book that is sealed, which men deliver to one that is learned, saying, Read this, I pray thee: and he saith, I cannot; for it is sealed."

c. Reprising Isaiah 29:11: "And the vision of all is become unto you as the words of a book that is sealed, which men deliver to one that is learned, saying, Read this, I pray thee: and he saith, I cannot; for it is sealed."

d. Reprising Isaiah 29: 12: "And the book is delivered to him that is not learned, saying, Read this, I pray thee: and he saith, I am not learned."

book [again[a]] and hide it up unto me, that I may preserve the words which the thou hast not read until I shall see fit in mine own wisdom to reveal all things unto the children of men.

[23]For behold, I am God. And I am a God of miracles. And I will show unto the world that I am the same yesterday, today, and forever.[b] And I work not among the children of men, save it be according to their faith.

[24]And again, it shall come to pass that the Lord shall say unto him that shall read the words that shall be delivered him:

> [25]"For as much as this people draw near **unto** me with their mouth,
>> and with them their lips do honor me,
>
> but have removed their heart far from me—
>> and their fear towards me is taught by the precept of men—
>
> [26]therefore, I will proceed to do a marvelous work among this people,
>> **yea**, a marvelous work and a wonder.
>
> For, the wisdom of their wise **and learned** shall perish,
>> and the understanding of their prudent [[c]] shall be hid.
>
> [27]**And** wo unto them that seek deep to hide their counsel from the Lord,
>> and their works are in the dark.
>
>> And they say: "Who seeth us, and who knoweth us?"
>
> **And they also say:** "Surely your turning of things upside down
>> shall be esteemed as the potters clay."
>
> **But behold, I will show unto them, saith the Lord of Hosts,**
>> **that I know all their works.**
>
> For shall the work say of him that made it:
>> "He made me not."
>
> Or shall the thing framed say of him that framed it:
>> "He had no understanding?"
>
> [28]**But behold, saith the Lord of Hosts:**
> **"I will show unto the children of men**
>> **that** it is **not** yet a very little while,
>
> and Lebanon shall be turned into a fruitful field.
>> And the fruitful field shall be esteemed as a forest."
>
> [29]And in that day shall the deaf hear the words of the book,
>> and the eyes of the blind shall see out of obscurity,
>> and out of darkness.
>
> [30]**And** the meek also shall increase,
>> **and** their joy **shall be** in the Lord.

---

a. A later insertion from Oliver Cowdery in the Printer's Manuscript, perhaps during proofreading. In this case, it restores a word present in Isaiah. In a later, similar, example on the same page, it is no longer from a time where Isaiah is quoted and therefore more likely to have been upon proofreading. Skousen, *Analysis of the Textual Variants*, 2:854, notes both possibilities and suggests a restoration from Isaiah. He had apparently not yet seen the second example on that page, which is a similar insertion, but upon which he did not comment.

b. See Hebrews 13:8.

c. Omits "men," which is in italics.

And the poor among men shall rejoice in the Holy One of Israel.
 ³¹**For assuredly, as the Lord liveth,**
they shall see that the terrible one is brought to naught,
 and the scorner is consumed.
 And all that watch for iniquity are cut off.
³²**And they** that make a man an offender for a word
 and lay a snare for him that reproveth in the gate,
 and turn aside the just for a thing of naught.
³³Therefore, thus saith the Lord (who redeemed Abraham) concerning
 the house of Jacob:
"Jacob shall not now be ashamed.
 Neither shall his face now wax pale.
³⁴But, when he seeth his children,
 the work of my hands
 in the midst of him,
they shall sanctify my name
 and sanctify the Holy One of Jacob,
 and shall fear the God of Israel.
³⁵They also that erred in spirit shall come to understanding.
 And they that murmured shall learn doctrine."ᵃ

---

a. Verses 25–35 quote Isaiah 29:13–35.

Chapter XII [2 Nephi 28–30]

[28] ¹And now behold, my brethren, I have spoken unto you according as the spirit hath constrained me. Wherefore, I know that they must surely come to pass. ²And the things which shall be written out of the book shall be of great [worth^a] unto the children of men, and especially unto our seed which are a remnant of the house of Israel.

³For it shall come to pass in that day, that the churches which are built up (and not unto the Lord), when the one shall say unto the other: "Behold, I am the Lord's!" And the other shall say: "I am the Lord's!" And thus shall every one say that hath built up churches (and not unto the Lord). ⁴And they shall contend one with another. And their priests shall contend one with another. And they shall teach with their learning, and deny the Holy Ghost (which giveth utterance). ⁵And they deny the power of God, the Holy One of Israel.

And they say unto the people:

> Hearken unto us and hear ye our precept! For behold, there is no God today. For the Lord and the Redeemer hath done his work. And he hath given his power unto men. ⁶Behold, hearken ye unto my precept! If they shall say there is a miracle wrought by the hand of the Lord, believe it not! For this day he is not a God of miracles. He hath done his work.

⁷Yea, and there shall be many which shall say:

> Eat, drink, and be merry!^b For tomorrow we die!^c And it shall be well with us.

⁸And there shall also be many which shall say:

> Eat, drink, and be merry!^d Nevertheless, fear God! He will justify in committing a little sin. Yea, lie a little. Take the advantage of one because of his words. Dig a pit for thy neighbor. There is no harm [in this^e]. And do all these things, for tomorrow we die.^f And if it so be that we are guilty, God will beat us with a few stripes.^g And at last we shall be saved in the kingdom of God.

⁹Yea, and there shall be many which shall teach after this manner—false and vain and foolish doctrines—and shall be puffed up in their hearts and shall seek deep to hide

---

a. A later insertion by Oliver Cowdery. The word is required and makes most sense as a copying error that was corrected upon proofreading. Skousen has no comment for this superscripted word. The phrase to "be of great worth" is found in 1 Nephi 13:23, 19:7, 22:8; 2 Nephi 3:7, 25:8; Alma 11:25 ("are of great worth"); Mormon 8:14 ("is of great worth:—the context is the record). These strongly confirm that it is intended here in 2 Ne. 28:2.

b. See Luke 12:19: "Soul, thou hast much goods laid up for many years; take thine ease, eat, drink, and be merry."

c. See 1 Corinthains 15:32: "let us eat and drink; for to morrow we die."

d. See Luke 12:19: "Soul, thou hast much goods laid up for many years; take thine ease, eat, drink, and be merry."

e. Oliver Cowdery originally skipped "in this" when copying from the Original Manuscript. His first correction was to add "in doing these things," possibly influenced by "do all these things," which follows. His final correction is what has been accepted in the current text. See Skousen, *Analysis of the Textual Variants*, 2:863.

f. See 1 Corinthains 15:32: "let us eat and drink; for to morrow we die."

g. See Luke 12:48: "But he that knew not, and did commit things worthy of stripes, shall be beaten with few stripes."

their counsels from the Lord.[a] And their works shall be in the dark. ¹⁰And the blood of the Saints shall cry from the ground against them.

¹¹Yea, they have all gone out of the way.[b] They have become corrupted ¹²because of pride, and because of false teachers, and false doctrines. Their churches have become corrupted. And their churches are lifted up because of pride. They are puffed up. ¹³They rob the poor because of their fine sanctuaries.[c] They rob the poor because of their fine clothing. And they persecute the meek and the poor in heart because, in their pride, they are puffed up. ¹⁴They wear stiff necks, and high heads. And yea, and because of pride, and wickedness, and abominations, and whoredoms, they have all gone astray (save it be a few which are the humble followers of Christ). Nevertheless, they are led, that in many instances they do err because they are taught by the precepts of men.[d]

¹⁵O, the wise and the learned, and the rich that are puffed up in the pride of their hearts, and all they that preach false doctrines, and all they that commit whoredoms, and pervert the right way of the Lord! Wo! Wo, wo be unto them, saith the Lord God Almighty! For they shall be thrust down to hell! ¹⁶Wo unto them that turn aside the just for a thing of naught,[e] and revile against that which is good, and say that it is of no worth! For the day shall come that the Lord God will speedily visit the inhabitants of the earth. And in that day that they are fully ripe in iniquity, they shall perish.

¹⁷But behold, if the inhabitants of the earth shall repent of their wickedness and abominations, they shall not be destroyed (saith the Lord of Hosts).

¹⁸But behold, that great and abominable church, the whore of all the earth, must tumble to the earth. And great must be the fall [thereof][f]! ¹⁹For the kingdom of the devil must shake. And they which belong to it must needs be stirred up unto repentance, or the devil will grasp them with his everlasting chains, and they be stirred up to anger, and perish.

²⁰For behold, at that day shall he rage in the hearts of the children of men and stir them up to anger against that which is good. ²¹And others will he pacify, and lull them away into carnal security, that they will say: "All is well in Zion! Yea, Zion prospereth! All is well!" And thus the devil cheateth their souls, and leadeth them away carefully down to hell.

²²And behold, others he flatereth away, and telleth them there is no hell. And he saith unto them: "I am no devil, for there is none." And thus he whispereth in their ears until he grasps them with his awful chains, from whence there is no deliverance. ²³Yea, they are grasped with death and hell—and death and hell, and the devil, and all that have been seized therewith, must stand before the throne of God and be judged according to their works—from whence they must go into the place prepared for them, even a lake of fire and brimstone[g] (which is endless torment).

---

a. See Isaiah 29:15: "Woe unto them that seek deep to hide their counsel from the Lord, and their works are in the dark, and they say, Who seeth us? and who knoweth us?"

b. See Romans 3:12: "They are all gone out of the way, they are together become unprofitable."

c. The "because of" here is in the sense of "in order to have." The poor are not the ones with the fine sanctuaries nor clothing. They are robbed to create those things for the churches which are puffed up.

d. See Isaiah 29:13: "and their fear toward me is taught by the precept of men."

e. See Isaiah 29:21: "and turn aside the just for a thing of nought."

f. The word "thereof" is Oliver Cowdery's later insertion. This is probably a proofreading correction. Skousen, *Analysis of the Textual Variants*, 2:872.

g. See Revelation 20:14: "And death and hell were cast into the lake of fire. This is the second death."

²⁴Therefore, wo be unto him that is at ease in Zion!

²⁵Wo be unto him that crieth: "All is well!"ᵃ

²⁶Yea, wo be unto him that hearkeneth unto the precepts of men,ᵇ and denyeth the power of God, and the gift of the Holy Ghost!

²⁷Yea, wo be unto him that saith: "We have received, and we need no more!"

²⁸And in fine, wo unto all they that tremble, and are angry because of the truth of God! For behold, he that is built upon the rock receiveth it with gladness. And he that is built upon a sandy foundation trembleth, lest he shall fall.ᶜ

²⁹Wo be unto him that shall say: "We have received the word of God, and we need no more of the word of God! For we have enough!" ³⁰For behold, thus saith the Lord God: "I will give unto the children of men line upon line, and precept upon precept, here a little and there a little.ᵈ And blessed are they that hearken unto my precepts and lend an ear unto my counsel. For they shall learn wisdom. For unto him that receiveth, I will give more. And them that shall say we have enough, from them shall be taken away even that which they have.

³¹Cursed is he that puteth his trust in man, or maketh flesh his arm, or shall hearken unto the precepts of men, save their precepts shall be given by the power of the Holy Ghost.

³²Wo be unto the Gentiles (saith the Lord God of Hosts), for notwithstanding I shall lengthen our out mine arm unto them from day to day, they will deny me. Nevertheless, I will be merciful unto them (saith the Lord God), if they will repent, and come unto me. For mine arm is lengthened out all the day long (saith the Lord God of Hosts).

[29] ¹But behold, there shall be many at that day (when I shall proceed to do a marvelous work among themᵉ), that I may remember my covenants (which I have made unto the children of men), that I may set my hand again, the second time, to recover my people (which are of the house of Israel).ᶠ ²And also that I may remember the promises which I have made unto thee, Nephi (and also unto thy father), that I would remember your seed, and that the words of your seed should proceed forth out of my mouth unto your seed. And my words shall hiss forth unto the ends of the earth for a standard unto my people (which are of the house of Israel).ᵍ ³And because my words shall hiss forth, many of the Gentiles shall say: "A Bible! A Bible! We have got a Bible, and there cannot be any more Bible!"

⁴But thus saith the Lord God:

---

a. There is no introduction to declare that this is God speaking until verse 32. At that point the speaker is in first person. With that understanding, the beginning of the modern chapter 29 (which is a continuation of Nephi's original chapter) should also be seen in the context of a quotation.

b. See Isaiah 29:13: "and their fear toward me is taught by the precept of men."

c. See Matthew 7:24–27.

d. See Isaiah 28:10: "For precept must be upon precept, precept upon precept; line upon line, line upon line; here a little, and there a little."

e. Reference to Isaiah 29:14: "Therefore, behold, I will proceed to do a marvellous work among this people, *even* a marvellous work and a wonder."

f. See Isaiah 11:11: "And it shall come to pass in that day, that the Lord shall set his hand again the second time to recover the remnant of his people."

g. See Isaiah 5:26: "And he will lift up an ensign to the nations from far, and will hiss unto them from the end of the earth: and, behold, they shall come with speed swiftly."

CHAPTER XII [2 NEPHI 28–30] 543

O fools! They shall have a Bible. And it shall proceed forth from the Jews, mine ancient covenant people. And what thank they the Jews for the Bible which they receive from them? Yea, what do the Gentiles mean? Do they remember the [travails[a]], and the labors, and the pains of the Jews, and their diligence unto me in bringing forth salvation unto the Gentiles?

[5]O ye Gentiles! Have ye remembered the Jews, mine ancient covenant people? Nay, but ye have cursed them, and have hated them, and have not sought to recover them. But behold, I will return all these things upon your own heads. For I, the Lord, hath not forgotten my people.

[6]Thou fool, that shall say "a Bible, we have got a Bible and we need no more Bible." Have ye obtained a Bible save it were by the Jews? [7]Know ye not that there are more nations than one? Know ye not that I, the Lord your God, have created all men and that I remember they which are upon the isles of the sea, and that I rule in the heavens above and in the earth beneath, and I bring forth my word unto the children of men, yea, even upon all the nations of the earth? [8]Wherefore[b] murmur ye because that ye shall receive more of my word?

Know ye not that the testimony of two nations is a witness unto you that I am God, that I remember one nation like unto another? Wherefore, I speak the same words unto one nation like unto another. And when the two nations shall run together, the testimony of the two nations shall run together also. [9]And I do this that I may prove unto many that I am the same yesterday, today, and forever.[c] And that I speak forth my words according to mine own pleasure.

And because that I have spoken one word, ye need not suppose that I cannot speak another. For my work is not yet finished, neither shall it be, until the end of man. Neither from that time, henceforth and forever. [10]Wherefore, because that ye have a Bible, ye need not suppose that it contains all my words. Neither need ye suppose that I have not caused more to be written. [11]For I command all men, both in the east and in the west, and in the north and in the south, and in the islands of the sea, that they shall write the words which I speak unto them. For out of the books which shall be written I will judge the world[d]—every man according to their works, according to that which is written.

[12]For behold, I shall speak unto the Jews—and they shall write it.

And I shall also speak unto the Nephites—and they shall write it.

And I shall also speak unto the other tribes of the house of Israel which I have led away—and they shall write it.

And I shall also speak unto all the nations of the earth—and they shall write it.

[13]And it shall come to pass that the Jews shall have the words of the Nephites,

---

a. The word in the Printer's Manuscript is "travels." Travails not only fits the context better, but Skousen notes that in other cases where the intended word is "travails," the scribe also wrote "travels." It is "travails" in the modern edition, though it remained "travels" in 1830. Skousen, *Analysis of the Textual Variants*, 2:881.

b. Most of the time "wherefore" is used as an indicator of the result of the logic of the argument preceding it. In this case, however, it is in the older sense of "why."

c. See Hebrews 13:8.

d. Uses language from Revelation 20:12: "And I saw the dead, small and great, stand before God; and the books were opened: and another book was opened, which is the book of life: and the dead were judged out of those things which were written in the books, according to their works."

and the Nephites shall have the words of the Jews, and the Nephites and the Jews shall have the words of the lost tribes of Israel, and the lost tribes of Israel shall have the words of the Nephites and the Jews.

[14]And it shall come to pass that my people which are of the house of Israel shall be gathered home unto the lands of their possessions. And my word also shall be gathered in one, and I will show unto them that fight against my word, and against my people (which are of the house of Israel), that I am God, and that I covenanted with Abraham that I would remember his seed forever.

[30] [1]And now behold, my beloved brethren, I would speak unto you. For I, Nephi, would not suffer that ye should suppose that ye are more righteous than the Gentiles shall be. For except ye shall keep the commandments of God, ye shall all likewise perish. And because of the words which have been spoken, ye need not suppose that the Gentiles are utterly destroyed.

[2]For behold, I say unto you, as many of the Gentiles will repent are the covenant people of the Lord. And as many of the Jews as will not repent shall be cast off. For the Lord covenanteth with none, save it be with them that repent and believe in his Son, which is the Holy One of Israel.

[3]And now, I would prophesy somewhat more concerning the Jews and the Gentiles. For after the book (of which I have spoken) shall come forth and be written unto the Gentiles, and sealed up again unto the Lord, there shall be many which shall believe the words which are written. And they shall carry them forth unto the remnant of our seed. [4]And then shall the remnant of our seed know concerning us. How that we came out from Jerusalem and that they are a descendant of the Jews. [5]And the Gospel of Jesus Christ shall be declared among them. Wherefore, they shall be restored unto the knowledge of their fathers, and also to the knowledge of Jesus Christ which was had among their fathers.

[6]And then shall they rejoice. For they shall know that it is a blessing unto them from the hand of God. And their scales of darkness shall begin to fall from their eyes,[a] and many generations shall not pass away among them, save they shall be a white and a delightsome people.

[7]And it shall come to pass that the Jews which are scattered also shall begin to believe in Christ. And they shall begin to gather in upon the face of the land. And as many as shall believe in Christ shall also become a delightsome people.

[8]And it shall come to pass that the Lord God shall commence his work among all nations, kindreds, tongues, and people, to bring about the restoration of his people upon the earth.

> [9]**And** with righteousness shall **the Lord God** judge the poor,
>   and reprove with equity for the meek of the earth.
> And he shall smite the earth with the rod of his mouth,
>   and with the breath of his lips shall he slay the wicked.
> [10]**For the time speedily cometh**
>   **that the Lord God shall cause a great division among the people.**
>   **And the wicked will he destroy. And he will spare his people,**

---

a. The combination of "eyes, scales" alludes to Acts 9:18: "And immediately there fell from his eyes as it had been scales: and he received sight forthwith, and arose, and was baptized."

Chapter XII [2 Nephi 28–30]

yea, even if it so be that he must destroy the wicked by fire.
¹¹And righteousness shall be the girdle of his loins,
and faithfulness the girdle of his reins.
¹²**And then shall** the wolf dwell with the lamb,
and the leopard shall lie down with the kid—
and the calf,
and the young lion,
and the fatling together.
And a little child shall lead them.

¹³And the cow and the bear shall feed.
Their young ones shall lie down together.
And the lion shall eat straw like the ox.
¹⁴And the sucking child shall play on the hole of the asp,
and the weaned child shall put his hand on the cockatrice's den.
¹⁵They shall not hurt, nor destroy, in all my holy mountain.
For the earth shall be full of the knowledge of the Lord
as the waters cover the sea.[a]

¹⁶Wherefore, the things of all nations shall be made known. Yea, all things shall be made known unto the children of men. ¹⁷There is nothing which is secret, save it shall be revealed. There is no works of darkness, save it shall be made manifest in the light. And there is nothing which is sealed upon earth, save it shall be loosed. ¹⁸Wherefore, all things which have been revealed unto the children of men shall at that day be revealed. And Satan shall have power over the hearts of the children of men no more, for a long time. And now my beloved brethren, I must make an end of my sayings.

---

a. Verses 9, 11–15 quote Isaiah 11:4–9. Verse 10 is added.

Chapter XIII [2 Nephi 31]

[31] ¹And now, I, Nephi, make an end of my prophesying unto you, my beloved brethren. And I cannot write but a few things which I know must surely come to pass. Neither can I write but a few of the words of my brother Jacob. ²Wherefore, the things which I have written sufficeth me, save it be a few words which I must speak concerning the doctrine of Christ. Wherefore, I shall speak unto you plainly, according to the plainness of my prophesying. ³For my soul delighteth in plainness.

For after this manner doth the Lord God work among the children of men. For the Lord God giveth light unto the understanding. For he speaketh unto men according to their language, unto their understanding. ⁴Wherefore, I would that ye should remember that I have spoken unto you concerning that prophet, which the Lord showed unto me that should baptize the Lamb of God[a], which should take away the sin of the world.

⁵And now, if the Lamb of God[b], he being holy, should have need to be baptized by water to fulfil all righteousness,[c] O then how much more need have we, being unholy, to be baptized, yea, even by water?

⁶And now, I would ask of you, my beloved brethren, wherein the Lamb of God[d] did fulfil all righteousness in being baptized by water? ⁷Know ye not that he was holy? But not withstanding he being holy, he showeth unto the children of men that according to the flesh, he humbleth himself before the Father, and witnesseth unto the Father that he would be obedient unto him in keeping his commandments. ⁸Wherefore, after that he was baptized with water, the Holy Ghost descended upon him in the form of a dove.[e]

⁹And again, it showeth unto the children of men the straitness of the path, and the narrowness of the gate by which they should enter[f]—he having set the example before them. ¹⁰And he saith unto the children of men: "Follow thou me." Wherefore, my beloved brethren, can we follow Jesus save we shall be willing to keep the commandments of the Father?

¹¹And the Father saith: "Repent ye! Repent ye, and be baptized in the name of my beloved son!" ¹²And also the voice of the Son came unto me, saying: "He that is baptized in my name, to him will the Father give the Holy Ghost, like unto me. Wherefore, follow me, and do the things which ye have seen me do." ¹³Wherefore, my beloved brethren, I know that if ye shall follow the Son (with full purpose of heart—acting no hypocrisy and no deception before God—but with real intent, repenting of your sins, witnessing unto the Father that ye are willing to take upon you the name of Christ by baptism, yea, by following your Lord and Savior down into the water according to his word)[g]—behold, then shall ye receive the Holy Ghost. [Yea, then cometh the baptism

---

    a. The phrase "Lamb of God" is from John 1:29.
    b. The phrase "Lamb of God" is from John 1:29.
    c. Alludes to Matthew 3:14–15.
    d. The phrase "Lamb of God" is from John 1:29.
    e. See Luke 3:22: "And the Holy Ghost descended in a bodily shape like a dove upon him."
    f. See Matthew 7:14: "Because strait is the gate, and narrow is the way, which leadeth unto life, and few there be that find it."
    g. This complicated sentence separates the beginning "if" from the eventual "then shall ye receive the Holy Ghost." The phrases in parentheses help a modern reader see how the sentence is finally resolved.

of fire and of the Holy Ghost.^a] And then can ye speak with the tongue of angels, and shout praises unto the Holy One of Israel.

¹⁴But behold, my beloved brethren, thus came the voice of the Son unto me, saying: "After that ye have repented of your sins, and witnessed unto the Father that ye are willing to keep my commandments by the baptism of water, and have received the baptism of fire and of the Holy Ghost, and can speak with a new tongue (yea, even with the tongue of angels)—and after this should deny me, it would have been better for you that ye had not known me."

¹⁵And I heard a voice from the Father, saying: "Yea, the words of my beloved are true and faithful. He that endureth to the end, the same shall be saved.^b"

⁶And now, my beloved brethren, I know by this, that unless a man shall endure to the end^c (in following the example of the Son of the living God) he cannot be saved. ¹⁷Wherefore, do the things which I have told you that I have seen that your Lord and your Redeemer should do. For, for this cause have they been shown unto me, that ye might know the gate by which ye should enter. For the gate by which ye should enter is repentance, and baptism by water. And then cometh a remission of your sins by fire, and by the Holy Ghost. ¹⁸And then are ye in this straight and narrow path which leads to Eternal Life. Yea, ye have entered in by the gate. Ye have done according to the commandments of the Father, and the Son, and ye have received the Holy Ghost (which witness of the Father and the Son) unto the fulfilling of the promise which he hath made, that if ye entered in by the way, ye should receive.

¹⁹And now, my beloved brethren, after that ye have got into this strait and narrow path, I would ask if all is done? Behold, I say unto you, nay. For ye have not come thus far save it were by the word of Christ, with unshaken faith in him, relying wholly upon the merits of him who is mighty to save. ²⁰Wherefore, ye must press forward with a steadfastness in Christ, having a perfect brightness of hope, and a love of God, and of all men. Wherefore, if ye shall press forward, feasting upon the word of Christ, and endure to the end,^d behold thus saith the Father: "Ye shall have eternal life."

²¹And now behold, my beloved brethren, this is the way. And there is none other way, nor name, given under heaven whereby man can be saved in the kingdom of God.

And now behold, this is the doctrine of Christ—and the only, and true doctrine of the Father, and of the Son, and of the Holy Ghost—which is one God, without end. Amen.

---

a. The phrase "Yea, then cometh the Baptism of Fire & the holy Ghost" is inserted. Skousen suggests that it was missed in the copying from the Original to the Printer's Manuscript and restored upon proofreading. Skousen, *Analysis of the Textual Variants*, 2:913.

b. See Matthew 10:22: "he that endureth to the end shall be saved."

c. The phrase "endure to the end" occurs in Matthew 24:13.

d. The phrase "endure to the end" occurs in Matthew 24:13.

Chapter XIV [2 Nephi 32]

[32] ¹And now behold, my beloved brethren, I suppose that ye ponder somewhat in your hearts concerning that which ye should do after that ye have entered in by the way. But behold, why do ye ponder these things in your hearts? ²Do ye not remember that I said unto you, that after that ye have received the Holy Ghost, ye could speak with the tongue of angels?

And now, how could ye speak with the tongue of angels, save it were by the Holy Ghost? ³Angels speak by the power of the Holy Ghost, wherefore they speak the words of Christ. Wherefore I said unto you: Feast upon the words of Christ.[a] For behold, the words of Christ will tell you all things what ye should do. ⁴Wherefore now, after that I have spoken these words, if ye cannot understand them it will be because ye ask not, neither do ye knock.[b] Wherefore, ye are not brought into the light, but must perish in the dark.

⁵For behold, again I say unto you, that if ye will enter in by the way and receive the Holy Ghost, it will show unto you all things what ye should do. ⁶Behold, this is the doctrine of Christ, and there will be no more doctrine given until after that he shall manifest himself unto you in the flesh. And when he shall manifest himself unto you in the flesh, the things which he shall say unto you—shall ye observe to do.

⁷And now, I, Nephi, cannot say more. The spirit stoppeth mine utterance, and I am left to mourn because of the unbelief, and the wickedness, and the ignorance, and the stiffneckedness, of men. For they will not search knowledge, nor understand great knowledge when it is given unto them in plainness, even as plain as word can be.

⁸And now, my beloved brethren, I perceive that ye ponder still in your hearts. And it grieveth me that I must speak concerning this thing, for if ye would hearken unto the spirit which teacheth a man to pray, ye would know that ye must pray. For the evil spirit teacheth not a man to pray, but teacheth him that he must not pray.

⁹But behold, I say unto you that ye must pray always, and not faint,[c] that ye must not perform any thing unto the Lord, save in the first place ye shall pray unto the Father, in the name of Christ, that he will consecrate thy performance unto thee, that thy performance may be for the welfare of thy soul.

---

a. Internal reference to the previous chapter, 2 Nephi 31:20.

b. See Matthew 7:7: "Ask, and it shall be given you; seek, and ye shall find; knock, and it shall be opened unto you."

c. See Luke 18:1: "Men ought always to pray, and not to faint."

Chapter XV [2 Nephi 33]

[33] ¹And now, I, Nephi, cannot write all the things which were taught among my people. Neither am I mighty in writing like unto speaking. For when a man speaketh by the power of the Holy Ghost, the power of the Holy Ghost carrieth it unto the hearts of the children of men.

²But behold, there are many that harden their hearts against the Holy Spirit, that it hath no place in them. Wherefore, they cast many things away which are written, and esteem them as things of naught. ³But I, Nephi, have written what I have written. And I esteem it as of great worth, and especially unto my people. For I pray continually for them by day and mine eyes water my pillow by night because of them.[a]

And I cry unto my God in faith, and I know that he will hear my cry. ⁴And I know that the Lord God will consecrate my prayers for the gain of my people. And the things which I have written in weakness will he make strong unto them, for it persuadeth them to do good. It maketh known unto them of their Fathers, and it speaketh of Jesus, and persuadeth men to believe in him and to endure to the end,[b] which is life eternal. ⁵And it speaketh harsh against sin, according to the plainness of the truth. Wherefore, no man will be angry at the words which I have written save he shall be of the spirit of the devil.

⁶I glory in plainness! I glory in truth! I glory in my Jesus! For he hath redeemed my soul from hell. ⁷I have charity for my people, and great faith in Christ, that I shall meet many souls spotless at his Judgment Seat. ⁸I have charity for the Jew (I say Jew because I mean them from whence I came). ⁹I also have charity for the Gentiles. But behold, for none of these I cannot hope, except they shall be reconciled unto Christ and enter into the narrow gate[c] and walk in the straight[d] path which leads to life—and continue in the path until the end of the day of probation.

¹⁰And now, my beloved brethren, and also Jew, and all ye ends of the earth—hearken unto these words and believe in Christ. And if ye believe not in these words, believe in Christ. And if ye shall believe in Christ, ye will believe in these words. For they are the words of Christ. And he hath given them unto me. And they teach all men that they should do good.

¹¹And if they are not the words of Christ, judge ye. For Christ will show unto you, with power and great glory, that they are his words at the last day. And you and I shall stand face to face before his bar, and ye shall know that I have been commanded of him to write these things, notwithstanding my weakness. ¹²And I pray the Father, in the name of Christ, that many of us, if not all, may be saved in his kingdom at that great and last day.

¹³And now, my beloved brethren, all they which are of the house of Israel, and all ye

---

a. Perhaps an allusion to Psalm 6:6: "I water my couch with my tears."
b. The phrase "endure to the end" occurs in Matthew 24:13.
c. See Matthew 7:14: "Because strait is the gate, and narrow is the way, which leadeth unto life, and few there be that find it."
d. In this example, it appears that the use should be "straight" rather than "strait." It would appear that the homophone was likely understood as straight, even though that is not the meaning of the model verse.

ends of the earth—I speak unto you as the voice of one crying from the dust.[a] Farewell until that great day shall come. ¹⁴And you that will not partake of the goodness of God and respect the words of the Jews, and also my words, and the words which shall proceed forth out of the mouth of the Lamb of God[b], behold, I bid you an everlasting farewell. For these words shall condemn you at the last day. ¹⁵For what I seal on earth shall be brought against you at the judgment bar. For thus hath the Lord commanded me. And I must obey. Amen.

---

a. See Isaiah 29:4: "And thou shalt be brought down, and shalt speak out of the ground, and thy speech shall be low out of the dust."

b. The phrase "Lamb of God" is from John 1:29.

The Book of Jacob, the Brother of Nephi[a]

The words of his preaching unto his brethren. He confoundeth a man who seeketh to overthrow the doctrine of Christ. A few words concerning the history of the people of Nephi.

Chapter I [Jacob 1]

[1] ¹For behold, it came to pass that fifty and five years had passed away from the time Lehi left Jerusalem. Wherefore, Nephi gave me, Jacob, a commandment concerning these plates upon which these things are engraven. ²And he gave me, Jacob, a commandment that I should write upon these plates a few of the things which I considered to be most precious. That I should not touch, save it were lightly, concerning the history of this people (which are called the people of Nephi). ³For he said that the history of his people should be engraven upon his other plates. And that I should preserve these plates. And hand them down unto my seed, from generation to generation. ⁴And if there were preaching which was sacred, or revelation which was great, or prophesying, that I should engraven the heads of them upon these plates—and touch upon them as much as it were possible for Christ's sake, and for the sake of our people. ⁵For because of faith and great anxiety, it truly had been made manifest unto us concerning our people, what things should happen unto them.

⁶And we also had many revelations. And the spirit of much prophesy. Wherefore, we knew of Christ and his kingdom which should come. ⁷Wherefore, we labored diligently among our people that we might persuade them to come unto Christ and partake of the goodness of God, that they might enter into his rest, lest by any means he should swear in his wrath they should not enter in (as in the provocation in the days of temptation, while the children of Israel were in the wilderness).[b] ⁸Wherefore, we would to God that we could persuade all men not to rebel against God, to provoke him to anger[c]—but that all men would believe in Christ, and view his death, and suffer his cross, and bear the shame of the world. Wherefore I, Jacob, take it upon me to fulfil the commandment of my brother Nephi.

⁹Now Nephi began to be old, and he saw that he must soon die. Wherefore, he anointed a man to be a king and a ruler over his people. Now, according to the reigns of the kings (¹⁰the people, having loved Nephi exceedingly—he having been a great protector for them, having wielded the sword of Laban in their defense, and having

---

a. The Printer's Manuscript has "the brother of Nephi" on a separate line. Although this represents the way Oliver Cowdery heard and copied it, the structure of other books suggests that this should have been part of the title. The word "chapter" was added both after the title "The Book of Jacob" and after "the brother of Nephi" on the Printer's Manuscript. *Printer's Manuscript of the Book of Mormon*, 3:208–9.

b. See Psalm 95:8: "Harden not your heart, as in the provocation, and as in the day of temptation in the wilderness." Hebrews 3:8 reprises the psalm: "Harden not your hearts, as in the provocation, in the day of temptation in the wilderness."

c. The phrase "provoke him to anger" is found in Deuteronomy 4:25.

labored in all his days for their welfare)[a]—[11]wherefore, the people were desirous to retain in remembrance his name. And whoso should reign in his stead were called by the people, second Nephi, and third Nephi, etc., according to the reigns of the kings. And thus they were called by the people, let them be of whatsoever name they would.

[12]And it came to pass that Nephi died.

[13]Now, the people which were not Lamanites were Nephites. Nevertheless, they were called Nephites, Jacobites, Josephites, Zoramites, Lamanites, Lemuelites, and Ishmaelites. [14]But I, Jacob, shall not hereafter distinguish them by these names. But I shall call them Lamanites they that seek to destroy the people of Nephi. And they which are friendly to Nephi, I shall call Nephites, or the people of Nephi (according to the reigns of the kings).

[15]And now it came to pass that the people of Nephi, under the reign of the second king, began to grow hard in their hearts and indulge themselves somewhat in wicked practices, such as like unto David of old—desiring many wives and concubines (and also Solomon, his son). [16]Yea, and they also began to search much gold and silver, and began to be lifted up somewhat in pride. [17]Wherefore I, Jacob, gave unto them these words, as I taught them in the temple, having firstly obtained mine errand from the Lord.

[18]For I, Jacob, and my brother Joseph, had been consecrated priests and teachers of this people by the hand of Nephi. [19]And we did magnify our office unto the Lord, taking upon us the responsibility—answering the sins of the people upon our own heads if we did not teach them the word of God with all diligence. Wherefore, by laboring with our mights, their blood might not come upon our garments. Otherwise, their blood would come upon our garments and we would not be found spotless at the last day.

---

a. The phrases in parentheses interrupt the idea of the sentence, which is to explain that the people desired that their kings be called "Nephi."

Chapter II [Jacob 2–3]

[2] ¹ *The words which Jacob, the brother of Nephi, spake unto the people of Nephi after the death of Nephi.*ᵃ

²Now my beloved brethren, I, Jacob, according to the responsibility which I am under to God to magnify mine office with soberness—and that I might rid my garments of your sins—I come up into the temple this day that I might declare unto you the word of God. ³And ye yourselves know that I have hitherto been diligent in the office of my calling. But I, this day, am weighed down with much more desire and anxiety for the welfare of your souls than I have hitherto been.

⁴For behold, as yet, ye have been obedient unto the word of the Lord which I have given unto you. But behold: Hearken ye unto me! And know, that by the help of the all-powerful creator of heaven and earth, I can tell you concerning your thoughts—how that ye are beginning to labor in sin, which sin appeared very abominable unto me. Yea, and abominable unto God. ⁶Yea, and it grieveth my soul, and causeth me to shrink with shame before the presence of my maker, that I must testify unto you concerning the wickedness of your hearts.

⁷And also it grieveth me that I must use so much boldness of speech concerning you, before your wives and your children, many of whose feelings are exceeding tender, and chaste, and delicate, before God, which thing is pleasing unto God. ⁸And it supposeth me that they have come up hither to hear the pleasing word of God. Yea, the word which healeth the wounded soul. ⁹Wherefore, it burdeneth my soul that I should be constrained because of the strict commandment which I have received from God to admonish you, according to your crimes. To enlarge the wounds of those which are already wounded, instead of consoling and healing their wounds (and those which have not been wounded). Instead of feasting upon the pleasing word of God, have daggers placed to pierce their souls and wound their delicate minds.

¹⁰But notwithstanding the greatness of the task, I must do according to the strict commands of God, and tell you concerning your wickedness, and abominations—in the presence of the pure in heart, and the broken heartᵇ—and under the glance of the piercing eye of the Almighty God. ¹¹Wherefore, I must tell you the truth according to the plainness of the word of God.

For behold, as I enquired of the Lord, thus came the word unto me, saying: "Jacob, get thou up into the temple on the morrow, and declare the words which I shall give thee unto this people."

¹²And now behold, my brethren, this is the word which I declare unto you—that many of you have begun to search for gold and for silver, and all manner of precious ores, in the which this land (which is a land of promise unto you, and to your seed) doth abound most plentifully. ¹³And the hand of providence hath smiled upon you

---

a. This is set as a header rather than part of the verse. It appears to be a nearly identical header to the one Grant Hardy identified for 2 Nephi 6 (as formatted in *The Book of Mormon: Maxwell Institute Study Edition* (Provo, UT: Neal A. Maxwell Institute, 2018)). Even though this is Jacob inserting one of his own sermons, the concept of using the chapter header to indicate the inserted source still holds.

b. See Psalm 34:18: "The Lord is nigh unto them that are of a broken heart; and saveth such as be of a contrite spirit."

most pleasingly, that ye have obtained many riches. And because that some of you have obtained more abundantly than that of your brethren, ye are lifted up in the pride of your hearts—and wear stiff necks and high heads because of the costliness of your apparel—and persecute your brethren because that ye suppose that ye are better than they.

¹⁴And now my brethren, do ye suppose that God justifieth you in this thing? Behold, I say unto you nay! But he condemneth you. And if ye persist in these things, his judgments must speedily come unto you.

¹⁵O that he would show you that he can pierce you, and with one glance of his eye he can smite you to the dust!

¹⁶O that he would rid you from this iniquity and abomination!

And O that ye would listen unto the word of his commands, and let not this pride of your hearts destroy your souls!

¹⁷Think of your brethren like to yourselves. And be familiar with all, and free with your substance, that they may be rich like unto you.

¹⁸But before that ye seek for riches, seek ye for the kingdom of God. ¹⁹And after that ye have obtained a hope in Christ, ye shall obtain riches (if ye seek them). And ye will seek them for the intent to do good—to clothe the naked, and to feed the hungry, and to liberate the captive, and administer relief to the sick and the afflicted.

²⁰And now, my brethren, I have spoken unto you concerning pride. And those of you which have afflicted your neighbor and persecuted him because that ye were proud in your hearts of the things which God hath given you, what say ye of it? ²¹Do ye not suppose that such things are abominable unto him who created all things flesh? And the one being is as precious in his sight as the other? And all flesh is of the dust. And for the selfsame end hath he created them, that they should keep his commandments and glorify him forever.

²²And now, I make an end of speaking unto you concerning this pride. And were it not that I must speak unto you concerning a grosser crime, my heart would rejoice exceedingly because of you. ²³But the word of God burdens me because of your grosser crimes.

For behold, thus saith the Lord:

> This people beginneth to wax in iniquity. They understand not the scriptures, for they seek to excuse themselves in committing whoredoms because of the things which are written concerning David and Solomon, his son. ²⁴Behold, David and Solomon truly had many wives and concubines, which thing was abominable before me (saith the Lord).

²⁵Wherefore, thus saith the Lord:

> I have led this people forth out of the land of Jerusalem by the power of mine arm that I might raise up unto me a righteous branch from the fruit of the loins of Joseph. ²⁶Wherefore, I the Lord God will not suffer that this people shall do like unto them of old.

²⁷Wherefore, my brethren, hear me! And hearken to the word of the Lord:

> For there shall not any man among you have save it be one wife. And concubines he shall have none. ²⁸For I, the Lord God, delighteth in the chastity of women. And whoredoms is abomination before me.

Chapter II [Jacob 2–3]

Thus saith the Lord of Hosts:

²⁹Wherefore, this people shall keep my commandments (saith the Lord of Hosts) or cursed be the land for their sakes. ³⁰For if I will (saith the Lord of Hosts) raise up seed unto me, I will command my people. Otherwise, they shall hearken unto these things.

³¹For behold, I the Lord, have seen the sorrow, and heard the mourning, of the daughters of my people in the land of Jerusalem, yea, and in all the lands of my people, because of the wickedness and abominations of their husbands. ³²And I will not suffer (saith the Lord of Hosts), that the cries of the fair daughters of this people (which I have led out of the land of Jerusalem) shall come up unto me against the men of my people (saith the Lord of Hosts). ³³For they shall not lead away captive the daughters of my people, because of their tenderness, save I shall visit them with a sore curse, even unto destruction. For they shall not commit whoredoms like unto they of old (saith the Lord of Hosts).

³⁴And now behold, my brethren. Ye know that these commandments was given to our father Lehi. Wherefore ye have known them before. And ye have come unto great condemnation, for ye have done these things which ye ought not to have done. ³⁵Behold, ye have done greater iniquity than the Lamanites, our brethren. Ye have broken the hearts of your tender wives and lost the confidence of your children, because of your bad examples before them. And the sobbings of their hearts ascendeth up to God against you. And because of the strictness of the word of God, which cometh down against you, many hearts died—pierced with deep wounds.

[3] ¹But behold, I, Jacob, would speak unto you that are pure in heart. Look unto God with firmness of mind—and pray unto him with exceeding faith and he will console you in your afflictions—and he will plead your cause and send down justice upon those who seek your destruction.

²O, all ye that are pure in heart! Lift up your heads! And receive the pleasing word of God! And feast upon his love—for ye may, if your minds are firm, forever.

³But wo! Wo unto you that are not pure in heart, that are filthy this day before God. For except ye shall repent, the land is cursed for your sakes. And the Lamanites (which are not filthy like unto you, nevertheless they are cursed with a sore cursing) shall scourge you, even unto destruction. ⁴And the time speedily cometh that except ye repent, they shall possess the land of your inheritance. And the Lord God will lead away the righteous out from among you.

⁵Behold, the Lamanites, whom ye hate because of their filthiness and the cursings which hath come upon their skins, are more righteous than you. For they have not forgotten the commandments of the Lord, which was given unto our father, that they should have save it were one wife. And concubines they should have none. And there should not be whoredoms committed among them.

⁶And now, this commandment they observe to keep. Wherefore, because of this observance in keeping this commandment, the Lord God will not destroy them, but will be merciful unto them. And one day, they shall become a blessed people.

⁷Behold, their husbands love their wives, and their wives love their husbands. And their husbands and their wives love their children. And their unbelief and their hatred

towards you is because of the iniquity of their fathers. Wherefore, how much better are you than they in the sight of your great Creator?

⁸O my brethren! I fear, that unless ye shall repent of your sins, that their skins will be whiter than yours when ye shall be brought with them before the throne of God. ⁹Wherefore, a commandment I give unto you, which is the word of God, that ye revile no more against them because of the darkness of their skin. Neither shall ye revile against them because of their filthiness. But ye shall remember your own filthiness. And remember that their filthiness came because of their fathers. ¹⁰Wherefore, ye shall remember your children—how that ye have grieved their hearts because of the example that ye have set before them. And also remember that ye may, because of your filthiness, bring your children unto destruction—and their sins be heaped upon your heads at the last day.

¹¹O my brethren! Hearken unto my words! Arouse the faculties of your souls! Shake yourselves, that ye may awake from the slumber of death. And loose yourselves from the pains of hell, that ye may not become angels to the devil—to be cast into that lake of fire and brimstone (which is the second death).[a]

¹²And now, I Jacob, spake many more things unto the people of Nephi, warning them against fornication, and lasciviousness, and every kind of sin—telling them of the awful consequences of them. ¹³And a hundredth part of the proceedings of this people (which now began to be numerous) cannot be written upon these plates. But many of their proceedings are written upon the larger plates—and their wars, and their contentions, and the reigns of their kings. ¹⁴These plates are called the plates of Jacob. And they were made by the hand of Nephi. And I make an end of speaking these words.

---

a. See Revelation 20:14: "And death and hell were cast into the lake of fire. This is the second death."

Chapter III [Jacob 4–5]

[4] ¹Now behold, it came to pass that I, Jacob, having ministered much unto my people in word—ᵃ

> And I cannot write but a little of my words because of the difficulty of engraving our words upon plates. And we know that the things which we write upon plates must remain. ²But whatsoever things we write upon anything, save it be upon plates, must perish and vanish away. But we can write a few words upon plates, which will give our children (and also our beloved brethren) a small degree of knowledge concerning us (or concerning their fathers).ᵇ<

³Now, in this thing we do rejoice. And we labor diligently to engraven these words upon plates, hoping that our beloved brethren and our children will receive them with thankful hearts, and look upon them that they may learn with joy, and not with sorrow, neither with contempt, concerning their first parents. ⁴For, for this intent have we written these things, that they may know that we knew of Christ. And we had a hope of his glory many hundred years before his coming.

And not only we ourselves had a hope of his glory, but also all the holy prophets which were before us. ⁵Behold, they believed in Christ, and worshiped the Father in his name. And also, we worship the Father in his name. And for this intent we keep the law of Moses—it pointing our souls to him. And for this cause, it is sanctified unto us for righteousness—even as it was accounted unto Abraham in the wilderness to be obedient unto the commands of God in offering up his son Isaac, which was a similitude of God and his only begotten son. ⁶Wherefore, we search the prophets. And we have many revelations, and the spirit of prophesy.

And having all these witnesses, we obtain a hope. And our faith becometh unshaken, insomuch that we truly can command in the name of Jesus and the very trees obey us, or the mountains, or the waves of the sea. ⁷Nevertheless, the Lord God showeth us our weakness that we may know that it is by his grace and his great condescensions unto the children of men that we have power to do these things.

⁸Behold, great and marvelous are the works of the Lord. How unsearchable are the depths of the mysteries of him. And it is impossible that man should find out all his ways. And no man knoweth of his ways, save it be revealed unto him. Wherefore brethren, despise not the revelations of God! ⁹For behold, by the power of his word man came upon the face of the earth, which earth was created by the power of his word. Wherefore, if God, being able to speak and the world was and to speak and man was created—O then, why not able to command the earth, or the workmanship of his

---

a. This is a sentence fragment. Jacob's original intent is hijacked by the difficulty of writing on plates, which leads to a discussion of them. Interestingly, this is the very same kind of interruption the mention of the plates did in Nephi's writing. Jacob never recovers whatever he intended to say. The interruption led to a discussion of Christ. That was likely the intent of the chapter although the first sentence fragment gives no real hint.

b. Although this clearly begins as an aside, Jacob's purpose in writing is to speak of Christ and he turns the aside into the discussion of Christ that he had probably intended. Thus, there is no clear return to a narrative. There is no repetitive resumption at this point. Jacob moves to his text as though the interruption had been planned.

hands upon the face of it, according to his will and pleasure? ¹⁰Wherefore brethren, seek not to counsel the Lord, but to take counsel from his hand.

For behold, ye yourselves know that he counseleth in wisdom, and in justice, and in great mercy, over all his works.[a] Wherefore beloved, be reconciled unto him through the atonement of Christ, his only begotten son[b], that ye may obtain a resurrection, according to the power of the resurrection which is in Christ, and be presented as the firstfruits of Christ unto God[c]—having faith, and obtained a good hope of glory in him, before he manifesteth himself in the flesh.

¹²And now beloved, marvel not that I tell you these things. For why not speak of the atonement of Christ, and attain to a perfect knowledge of him, as to attain to the knowledge of a resurrection and the world to come? ¹³Behold my brethren, he that prophesieth—let him prophesy to the understanding of men. For the Spirit speaketh the truth and lieth not. Wherefore, it speaketh of things as they really are, and of things as they really will be. Wherefore, these things are manifested unto us plainly for the salvation of our souls. But behold, we are not witnesses alone in these things, for God also spake them unto prophets of old. ¹⁴But behold, the Jews were a stiff-necked people and they despised the words of plainness: and killed the prophets, and sought for things that they could not understand. Wherefore, because of their blindness, which blindness came by looking beyond the mark, they must needs fall. For God hath taken away his plainness from them and delivered unto them many things which they cannot understand—because they desired it. And because they desired it, God hath done it—that they may stumble.<

¹⁵And now I, Jacob, am led on by the spirit unto prophesying. For I perceive by the workings of the spirit which is in me, that by the stumbling of the Jews they will reject the stone upon which they might build and have safe foundation. ¹⁶But behold, according to the scriptures this stone shall become the great, and the last, and the only sure foundation, upon which the Jews can build.

¹⁷And now my beloved, how is it possible, that these, after having rejected the sure foundation, can ever build upon it—that it may become the head of their corner?[d]

¹⁸Behold, my beloved brethren, I will unfold this mystery unto you (if I do not, by any means, get shaken from my firmness in the spirit, and stumble because of my over anxiety for you).

[5] ¹Behold my brethren, do ye not remember to have read the words of the prophet Zenos, which spake unto the house of Israel, saying:

> ²Hearken, O ye house of Israel, and hear the words of me, a prophet of the Lord! ³For behold, thus saith the Lord:
> I will liken thee, O house of Israel, like unto a tame olive tree, which a man took and nourished in his vineyard. And it grew and waxed old and began to decay.

---

a. Echoes language from Psalm 145:8–9: "The Lord is gracious, and full of compassion; slow to anger, and of great mercy. The Lord is good to all: and his tender mercies are over all his works."

b. The current edition of the Book of Mormon capitalized "Only Begotten Son." While this can be considered a title for Christ, the New Testament usage is a description rather than a title. This edition elects to display it without capitalization.

c. See Revelation 14:4 for the phrase "firstfruits unto God."

d. The end of verse 16 and verse 17 allude to Psalm 118:22: "The stone which the builders refused is become the head stone of the corner."

Chapter III [Jacob 4–5]

⁴And it came to pass that the master of the vineyard went forth, and he saw that his olive tree began to decay. And he saith: "I will prune it, and dig about it, and nourish it, that perhaps it may shoot forth young and tender branches, and it perish not."

⁵And it came to pass that he pruned it, and digged about it, and nourished it, according to his word.

⁶And it came to pass that after many days, it began to put forth, somewhat a little young and tender branches. But behold, the main top thereof began to perish.

⁷And it came to pass that the master of the vineyard saw it. And he saith unto his servant: "It grieveth me that I should lose this tree. Wherefore, go and pluck the branches from a wild olive tree, and bring them hither unto me. And we will pluck off those main branches which are beginning to wither away, and we will cast them into the fire, that they may be burned."

⁸And behold, saith the Lord of the vineyard: "I take away many of these young and tender branches, and I will graft them whithersoever I will, and it mattereth not. That if it so be that the root of this tree will perish, I may preserve the fruit thereof unto myself. Wherefore, I will take these young and tender branches, and I will graft them whithersoever I will. ⁹Take thou the branches of the wild olive tree and graft them in in the stead thereof. And these which I have plucked off, I will cast into the fire and burn them, that they may not cumber the ground of my vineyard."

¹⁰And it came to pass that the servant of the Lord of the vineyard done according to the word of the Lord of the vineyard and grafted in the branches of the wild olive tree.

¹¹And the Lord of the vineyard caused that it should be digged about, and pruned, and nourished, saying unto his servant: "It grieveth me that I should lose this tree. Wherefore, that perhaps I might preserve the roots thereof, that they perish not, that I might preserve them unto myself, I have done this thing. ¹²Wherefore, go thy way. Watch the tree and nourish it according to my words. ¹³And these will I place in the nethermost part of my vineyard, whithersoever I will. It mattereth not unto thee. And I do it that I may preserve unto myself the natural branches of the tree, and also that I may lay up fruit thereof against the season unto myself. For it grieveth me that I should lose this tree and the fruit thereof."

¹⁴And it came to pass that the Lord of the vineyard went his way and hid the natural branches of the tame olive tree in the nethermost parts of the vineyard—some in one, and some in another, according to his will and pleasure.

¹⁵And it came to pass that a long time passed away, and the Lord of the vineyard saith unto his servant: "Come. Let us go down into the vineyard, that we may labor in the vineyard."

¹⁶And it came to pass that the Lord of the vineyard, and also the servant, went down into the vineyard to labor.

And it came to pass that the servant saith unto his master: "Behold! Look here. Behold the tree!"

¹⁷And it came to pass that the Lord of the vineyard looked, and beheld the tree in the which the wild olive branches had been grafted. And it had sprang forth and began to bear fruit. And he beheld that it was good. And the fruit thereof was

like unto the natural fruit. ¹⁸And he saith unto the servant: "Behold, the branches of the wild tree hath taken hold of the moisture of the root thereof, that the root thereof hath brought forth much strength. And because of the much strength of the root thereof, the wild branches hath brought forth tame fruit. Now, if we had not grafted in these branches, the tree thereof would have perished. And now behold, I shall lay up much fruit, which the tree thereof hath brought forth. And the fruit thereof I shall lay up against the season unto mine own self."

¹⁹And it came to pass that the Lord of the vineyard saith unto the servant: "Come. Let us go to the nethermost parts of the vineyard and behold if the natural branches of the tree hath not brought forth much fruit also, that I may lay up of the fruit thereof against the season unto mine own self."

²⁰And it came to pass that they went forth whither the master of the vineyard had hid the natural branches of the tree. And he saith unto the servant: "Behold these!"

And he beheld the first, that it had brought forth much fruit. And he beheld also that it was good. And he saith unto the servant: "Take of the fruit thereof and lay it up against the season, that I may preserve it unto mine own self. For behold, saith he, this long time have I nourished it. And it hath brought forth much fruit."

²¹And it came to pass that the servant saith unto his master: "How comest thou hither to plant this tree, or this branch of the tree? For behold, it was the poorest spot in all the land of thy vineyard?"

²²And the Lord of the vineyard saith unto him: "Counsel me not. I knew that it was a poor spot of ground. Wherefore I said unto thee, I have nourished it this long time. And thou beholdest that it hath brought forth much fruit."

²³And it came to pass that the Lord of the vineyard saith unto his servant: "Look hither! Behold, I have planted another branch of the tree also, and thou knowest that this spot of ground was poorer than the first. But behold the tree! I have nourished it this long time and it hath brought forth much fruit. Therefore, gather it, and lay it up against the season that I may preserve it unto mine own self."

²⁴And it came to pass that the Lord of the vineyard saith again unto his servant: "Look hither, and behold another branch also, which I have planted, behold, that I have nourished also. And it hath brought forth fruit."

²⁵And he saith unto the servant: "Look hither, and behold the last! Behold, this have I planted in a good spot of ground, and I have nourished it this long time. And only a part of the tree hath brought forth tame fruit, and the other part of the tree hath brought forth wild fruit. Behold, I have nourished this tree like unto the others."

²⁶And it came to pass that the Lord of the vineyard saith unto the servant: "Pluck off the branches that have not brought forth good fruit and cast them into the fire."

²⁷But behold the servant saith unto him: "Let us prune it, and dig about it, and nourish it a little longer, that perhaps it may bring forth good fruit unto thee, that thou canst lay it up against the season."

²⁸And it came to pass that the Lord of the vineyard and the servant of the Lord of the vineyard did nourish all the fruit of the vineyard.

²⁹And it came to pass that a long time had passed away. And the Lord of the vineyard saith unto his servant: "Come. Let us go down in the vineyard, that we may labor again in the vineyard. For behold, the time draweth near and the end soon cometh. Wherefore, I must lay up fruit against the season unto mine own self."

³⁰And it came to pass that the Lord of the vineyard and the servant went down into the vineyard. And they came to the tree whose natural branches had been broken off and the wild branches had been grafted in. And behold, all sorts of fruit did cumber the tree.

³¹And it came to pass that the Lord of the vineyard did taste of the fruit, every sort, according to its number. And the Lord of the vineyard saith: "Behold, this long time have we nourished this tree, and I have laid up unto myself against the season much fruit.

³²But behold, this time it hath brought forth much fruit. And there is none of it which is good. And behold, there are all kinds of bad fruit. And it profiteth me nothing, notwithstanding all our labor. And now it grieveth me that I should lose this tree."

³³And the Lord of the vineyard saith unto the servant: "What shall we do unto the tree that I may preserve again good fruit thereof unto mine own self?

³⁴And the servant saith unto his master: "Behold, because thou didst graft in the branches of the wild olive tree, they have nourished the roots, that they are alive, and they have not perished. Wherefore, thou beholdest that they are yet good."

³⁵And it came to pass that the Lord of the vineyard saith unto his servant: "The tree profiteth me nothing, and the roots thereof profiteth me nothing, so long as it shall bring forth evil fruit. ³⁶Nevertheless, I know that the roots are good, and for mine own purpose I have preserved them. And because of their much strength, they have hitherto brought forth from the wild branches good fruit.

³⁷But behold, the wild branches have grew, and have overran the roots thereof. And because that the wild branches have overcome the roots thereof, it hath brought forth much evil fruit. And because that it hath brought forth so much evil fruit, thou beheldest that it begineth to perish. And it will soon become ripened, that it may be cast into the fire, except we should do something for it to preserve it."

³⁸And it came to pass that the Lord of the vineyard saith unto his servant: "Let us go down into the nethermost parts of the vineyard and behold if the natural branches have also brought forth evil fruit."

³⁹And it came to pass that they went down into the nethermost parts of the vineyard.

And it came to pass that they beheld that the fruit of the natural branches had become corrupt also, yea, the first, and the second, and also the last. And they had all become corrupt. ⁴⁰And the wild fruit of the last had overcome that part of the tree which brought forth good fruit, even that the branch had withered away and died.

⁴¹And it came to pass that the Lord of the vineyard wept, and saith unto the servant: "What could I have done more for my vineyard? ⁴²Behold, I knew that all the fruit of the vineyard save it were these had become corrupted. And now these, which have once brought forth good fruit, have also become corrupted. And now all the trees of my vineyard are good for nothing, save it be to be hewn down and cast into the fire."

⁴³"And behold, this last (whose branch hath withered away) I did plant in a good spot of ground. Yea, even that which was choice unto me above all other parts of the land of my vineyard. ⁴⁴And thou beholdest that I also cut down that which cumbered this spot of ground that I might plant this tree in the stead thereof. ⁴⁵And thou beholdest that a part thereof brought forth good fruit. And the part thereof brought forth wild fruit. And because that I plucked not the branches thereof and cast them into the fire, behold they have overcome the good branch, that it hath withered away."

⁴⁶"And now behold, notwithstanding all the care which we have taken of my vineyard, the trees thereof hath become corrupted, that they bring forth no good fruit. And these I have hope to preserve to have laid up fruit thereof against the season unto mine own self."

"But behold, they have become like unto the wild olive tree. And they are of no worth but to be hewn down and cast into the fire. And it grieveth me that I should lose them. ⁴⁷But what could I have done more in my vineyard? Have I slackened mine hand, that I have not nourished it? Nay! I have nourished it, and I have digged it, and I have pruned it, and I have dunged it, and I have stretched forth mine hand almost all the day long. And the end draweth nigh. And it grieveth me that I should hew down all the trees of my vineyard and cast them into the fire, that they should be burned. Who is it that hath corrupted my vineyard?"

⁴⁸And it came to pass that the servant saith unto his master: "Is it not the loftiness of thy vineyard? Hath not the branches thereof overcame the roots which are good? And because that the branches have overcame the roots thereof. For behold, they grew faster than the strength of the roots (thereof taking strength unto themselves). Behold, I say, is not this the cause that the trees of thy vineyard hath become corrupted?"

⁴⁹And it came to pass that the Lord of the vineyard saith unto the servant: "Let us go to, and hew down the trees of the vineyard, and cast them into the fire, that they shall not cumber the ground of my vineyard. For I have done all. What could I have done more for my vineyard?"

⁵⁰But behold, the servant saith unto the Lord of the vineyard: "Spare it a little longer."

⁵¹And the Lord saith: "Yea, I will spare it a little longer. For it grieveth me that I should lose the trees of my vineyard. ⁵²Wherefore, let us take of the branches of these which I have planted in the nethermost parts of my vineyard, and let us graft them into the tree from whence they came. And let us pluck from the tree those branches whose fruit is most bitter, and graft in the natural branches of the tree in the stead thereof. ⁵³And this will I do that the tree may not perish, that perhaps I may preserve unto myself the roots thereof for mine own purpose."

⁵⁴"And behold, the roots of the natural branches of the tree which I planted whithersoever I would, are yet alive. Wherefore, that I may preserve them also, for mine own purpose, I will take of the branches of this tree, and I will graft them in unto them. Yea, I will graft in unto them the branches of their mother tree, that I may preserve the roots also unto mine own self, that when they shall be sufficiently strong, that perhaps they may bring forth good fruit unto me and I may yet have glory in the fruit of my vineyard."

Chapter III [Jacob 4–5]

⁵⁵And it came to pass that they took from the natural tree (which had become wild) and grafted in unto the natural trees (which also had become wild), ⁵⁶and they also took of the natural trees (which had become wild) and grafted into their mother tree. ⁵⁷And the Lord of the vineyard saith unto the servant: "Pluck not the wild branches from the trees, save it be those which are most bitter. And in them ye shall graft, according to that which I have said. ⁵⁸And we will nourish again the trees of the vineyard. And we will trim up the branches thereof. And we will pluck from the trees those branches which are ripened that must perish, and cast them into the fire. ⁵⁹And this I do, that perhaps the roots thereof may take strength, because of their goodness, and because of the change of the branches, that the good may overcome the evil."

⁶⁰"And because that I have preserved the natural branches and the roots thereof, and that I have grafted in the natural branches again into their mother tree, and have preserved the roots of their mother tree, that perhaps the trees of my vineyard may bring forth again good fruit—and that I may have joy again in the fruit of my vineyard, and perhaps that I may rejoice exceedingly—that I have preserved the roots and the branches of the first fruit.ᵃ ⁶¹Wherefore, go to. And call servants, that we may labor diligently with our mights in the vineyard, that we may prepare the way that I may bring forth again the natural fruit, which natural fruit is good and the most precious above all other fruit. ⁶²Wherefore, let us go to and labor with our mights this last time. For behold, the end draweth nigh. And this is for the last time that I shall prune my vineyard. ⁶³Graft in the branches. Begin at the last, that they may be first, and that the first may be last. And dig about the trees, both old and young, the first and the last and the last and the first, that all may be nourished once again for the last time. ⁶⁴Wherefore, dig about them, and prune them, and dung them once more for the last time. For the end draweth nigh."

"And if it so be that these last grafts shall grow and bring forth the natural fruit, then shall ye prepare the way for them, that they may grow. ⁶⁵And as they begin to grow, ye shall clear away the branches which bring forth bitter fruit, according to the strength of the good, and the size thereof. And ye shall not clear away the bad thereof all at once, lest the roots thereof should be too strong for the graft. And the graft thereof shall perish. And I lose the trees of my vineyard. ⁶⁶For it grieveth me that I should lose the trees of my vineyard. Wherefore, ye shall clear away the bad, according as the good shall grow, that the root and the top may be equal in strength, until the good shall overcome the bad, and the bad be hewn down and cast into the fire, that they cumber not the ground of my vineyard. And thus will I sweep away the bad out of my vineyard."

⁶⁷"And the branches of the natural tree will I graft in again into the natural tree. ⁶⁸And the branches of the natural tree will I graft into the natural branches of the natural tree. And thus will I bring them together again, that they shall bring forth the natural fruit. And they shall be one. ⁶⁹And the bad shall be cast away, yea, even out of all the land of my vineyard. For behold, only this once will I prune my vineyard."

⁷⁰And it came to pass that the Lord of the vineyard sent his servant. And the servant went and did as the Lord had commanded him and brought other servants.

---

a. This is an incomplete sentence. The "because" at the beginning of the verse is never completed.

And they were few. ⁷¹And the Lord of the vineyard saith unto them: "Go to, and labor in the vineyard with your mights. For behold, this is the last time that I shall nourish my vineyard. For the end is nigh at hand, and the season speedily cometh. And if ye labor with your mights with me, ye shall have joy in the fruit of which I shall lay up unto myself against the time which will soon come."

⁷²And it came to pass that the servants did go to it, and labor with their mights. And the Lord of the vineyard labored also with them. And they did obey the commandments of the Lord of the vineyard in all things. ⁷³And there began to be the natural fruit again in the vineyard, and the natural branches began to grow and thrive exceedingly. And the wild branches began to be plucked off and to be cast away. And they did keep the root and the top thereof equal, according to the strength thereof.

⁷⁴And thus they labored with all diligence, according to the commandments of the Lord of the vineyard, even until the bad had been cast away out of the vineyard, and the Lord had preserved unto himself, that the trees had become again the natural fruit. And they became like unto one body. And the fruit were equal. And the Lord of the vineyard had preserved unto himself the natural fruit, which was most precious unto him from the beginning.

⁷⁵And it came to pass that when the Lord of the vineyard saw that his fruit was good, and that his vineyard was no more corrupt, he calleth up his servants, and saith unto them: "Behold, for this last time have we nourished my vineyard. And thou beholdest that I have done according to my will, and I have preserved the natural fruit that it is good, even like as it was in the beginning. And blessed art thou. For because that ye have been diligent in laboring with me in my vineyard, and have kept my commandments, and hath brought unto me again the natural fruit, that my vineyard is no more corrupted. And the bad is cast away."

"Behold, ye shall have joy with me because of the fruit of my vineyard. ⁷⁶For behold, for a long time will I lay up of the fruit of my vineyard unto mine own self, against the season which speedily cometh. And for the last time have I nourished my vineyard, and pruned it, and dug about it, and dunged it. Wherefore, I will lay up unto mine own self of the fruit for a long time, according to that which I have spoken.

⁷⁷And when the time cometh that evil fruit shall again come into my vineyard, then will I cause the good and the bad to be gathered. And the good will I preserve unto myself, and the bad will I cast away into its own place. And then cometh the season, and the end. And my vineyard will I cause to be burned with fire."

Chapter IV [Jacob 6]

[6] ¹And now behold my brethren, as I said unto you, that I would prophesy. Behold, this is my prophesy, that the things which this prophet Zenos spake concerning the house of Israel (in the which he likened them unto a tame olive tree) must surely come to pass. ²And in the day that he shall set his hand again the second time to recover his people[a] is the day, yea, even the last time, that the servants of the Lord shall go forth in his power to nourish and prune his vineyard. And after that, the end soon cometh.

³And how blessed are they who have labored diligently in his vineyard!

And how cursed are they which shall be cast out into their own place! And the world shall be burned with fire.

⁴And how merciful is our God unto us!

For he remembereth the house of Israel, both roots and branches. And he stretches forth his hands unto them all the day long. And they are a stiff-necked, and a gainsaying people. But as many as will not harden their hearts shall be saved in the kingdom of God. ⁵Wherefore, my beloved brethren, I beseech of you in words of soberness, that ye would repent and come with full purpose of heart, and cleave unto God as he cleaveth unto you.

And while his arm of mercy is extended towards you in the light of the day, harden not your hearts. ⁶Yea, today, if ye will hear his voice, harden not your hearts![b] For why will ye die?[c] ⁷For behold, after that ye have been nourished by the good word of God all the day long, will ye bring forth evil fruit, that ye must be hewn down and cast into the fire?

⁸Behold, will ye reject these words? Will ye reject the words of the prophets? And will ye reject all the words which have been spoken concerning Christ (after that so many have spoken concerning him)? And deny the good word of Christ? And the power of God? And the gift of the Holy Ghost? And quench the Holy Spirit? And make a mock of the great plan of redemption which hath been laid for you?

⁹Know ye not that if ye will do these things, that the power of the redemption, and the resurrection (which is in Christ), will bring you to stand with shame and awful guilt before the bar of God? ¹⁰And according to the power of justice (for justice cannot be denied), that ye must go away into that lake of fire and brimstone,[d] whose flames are unquenchable, and whose smoke ascendeth up forever and ever,[e] which lake of fire and brimstone[f] is endless torment.

¹¹O then, my beloved brethren, repent ye! And enter ye in at the strait gate. And continue in the way which is narrow until ye shall obtain eternal life. ¹²O be wise! What can I say more?

¹³Finally[g], I bid you farewell, until I shall meet you before the pleasing bar of God, which bar striketh the wicked with awful dread and fear. Amen.

---

a. See Isaiah 11:11: "And it shall come to pass in that day, that the Lord shall set his hand again the second time to recover the remnant of his people."

b. See Psalm 95:7–8: "To day if ye will hear his voice, Harden not your heart."

c. The phrase "why will ye die" occurs in Jeremiah 27:13.

d. See Revelation 20:14: "And death and hell were cast into the lake of fire. This is the second death."

e. See Revelation 14:11: "And the smoke of their torment ascendeth up for ever and ever."

f. See Revelation 20:14: "And death and hell were cast into the lake of fire. This is the second death."

g. The Printer's Manuscript has "finely." This was clearly intended to be finally and is reasonably homophonous. It was later amended to "finally."

Chapter V [Jacob 7]

[7] ¹And now it came to pass that after some years had passed away, there came a man among the people of Nephi whose name was Sherem.

²And it came to pass that he began to preach among the people and to declare unto them that there should be no Christ. And he preached many things which were flattering unto the people. And this he done that he might overthrow the doctrine of Christ. ³And he labored diligently that he might lead away the hearts of the people, insomuch that he did lead away many hearts.

And he, knowing that I, Jacob, had faith in Christ (which should come), wherefore, he sought much opportunity that he might come unto me. ⁴And he was learned, that he had a perfect knowledge of the language of the people. Wherefore, he could use much flattery, and much power of speech, according to the power of the devil.

⁵And he had hope to shake me from the faith, notwithstanding the many revelations, and the many things which I had seen concerning these things. For I truly had seen angels and they had ministered unto me. And also, I had heard the voice of the Lord speaking unto me in very word from time to time. Wherefore, I could not be shaken.

⁶And it came to pass that he came unto me, and on this wise did he speak unto me, saying:

> Brother Jacob! I have sought much opportunity that I might speak unto you. For I have heard, and also know, that thou goest about much preaching that which ye call the gospel, or the doctrine, of Christ. ⁷And ye have led away much of this people, that they pervert the right way of God, and keep not the law of Moses (which is the right way) and convert the law of Moses into the worship of a being which ye say shall come many hundred years hence.
>
> And now behold, I, Sherem, declare unto you that this is blasphemy! For no man knoweth of such things. For he cannot tell of things to come.

And after this manner did Sherem contend against me. ⁸But behold, the Lord God poured in his spirit into my soul, insomuch that I did confound him in all his words. ⁹And I saith unto him: "Deniest thou the Christ, which should come?"

And he saith: "If there should be a Christ, I would not deny him. But I know that there is no Christ. Neither hath been. Nor never will be."

¹⁰And I saith unto him: "Believest thou the scriptures?"

And he saith: "Yea."

¹¹And I saith unto him: "Then ye do not understand them. For they truly testify of Christ. Behold, I say unto you that none of the prophets have written nor prophesied, save they have spoken concerning this Christ. ¹²And this is not all. It hath been made manifest unto me—for I have heard, and seen, and it also hath been made manifest unto me by the power of the Holy Ghost. Wherefore, I know if there should be no atonement made, all mankind must be lost."

¹³And it came to pass that he saith unto me: "Show me a sign by this power of the Holy Ghost, in the which ye know so much."

¹⁴And I said unto him: "What am I, that I should tempt God to show unto thee a sign in the things which thou knowest to be true? Yet thou wilt deny it because thou art of the devil. Nevertheless, not my will be done. But if God shall smite thee, let that be

Chapter V [Jacob 7]

a sign unto thee that he hath power both in heaven and in earth, and also that Christ shall come. And thy will, O Lord, be done, and not mine."

¹⁵And it came to pass that when I, Jacob, had spoken these words, the power of the Lord came upon him, insomuch that he fell to the earth.

And it came to pass that he was nourished for the space of many days.

¹⁶And it came to pass that he saith unto the people: "Gather together on the morrow, for I shall die. Wherefore, I desire to speak unto the people before that I shall die."

¹⁷And it came to pass that on the morrow, that the multitude were gathered together. And he speak plainly unto them, and denied the things which he had taught them, and confessed the Christ, and the power of the Holy Ghost, and the ministering of angels. ¹⁸And he spake plainly unto them, that he had been deceived by the power of the devil. And he spake of hell, and of eternity, and of eternal punishment. ¹⁹And he saith: "I fear, lest I have committed the unpardonable sin. For I have lied unto God. For I denied the Christ, and said that I believed the scriptures. And they truly testify of him. And because that I have thus lied unto God, I greatly fear lest my case shall be awful. But I confess unto God."

²⁰And it came to pass that when he had said these words, he could say no more., And he gave up the ghost. ²¹And when the multitude had witnessed that he spake these things, as he was about to give up the ghost, they were astonished exceedingly, insomuch that the power of God came down upon them, and they were overcome, that they fell to the earth. ²²Now, this thing was pleasing unto me, Jacob. For I had requested it of my Father, which was in heaven. For he had heard my cry, and answered my prayers.

²³And it came to pass that peace, and the love of God, was restored again among the people. And they searched the scriptures and hearkened no more to the words of this wicked man.

²⁴And it came to pass that many means were devised to reclaim and restore the Lamanites to the knowledge of the truth. But it all were vain. For they delighted in wars, and bloodsheds. And they had an eternal hatred against us, their brethren. And they sought, by the power of their arms, to destroy us continually. ²⁵Wherefore, the people of Nephi did fortify against them with their arms, and with all their might—trusting in the God and the rock of their salvation. Wherefore, they became as yet conquerors of their enemies.

²⁶And it came to pass that I, Jacob, began to be old. And the record of this people, being kept on the other plates of Nephi, wherefore, I conclude this record—declaring that I have written according to the best of my knowledge by saying that the time passed away with us. And also our lives passed away, like as it were unto us a dream, we being a lonesome and a solemn people, wanderers cast out from Jerusalem—born in tribulation in a wild wilderness, and hated of our brethren, which caused wars and contentions. Wherefore, we did mourn out our days.

²⁷And I, Jacob, saw that I must soon go down to my grave. Wherefore, I said unto my son Enos: "Take these plates." And I told him the things which my brother, Nephi, had commanded me. And he promised obedience unto the commands.

And I make an end of my writing upon these plates, which writing hath been small. And to the reader, I bid farewell, hoping that many of my brethren may read my words. Brethren, adieu.

The Book of Enos

Chapter I [Enos 1]

[1] ¹Behold, it came to pass that I, Enos, knowing my father, that he was a just man (for he taught me in his language, and also in the nurture and admonition of the Lord,[a] and blessed be the name of my God for it)—²and I will tell you of the wrestle which I had before God before that I received a remission of my sins.

³Behold, I went to hunt beasts in the forest. And the words which I had often heard my father speak concerning eternal life and the joy of the saints—and the words of my father sunk deep into my heart. ⁴And my soul hungered. And I kneeled down before my maker, and I cried unto him in mighty prayer and supplication for mine own soul. And all the day long did I cry unto him. Yea, and when the night came, I did still raise my voice high, that it reached the heavens.

⁵And there came a voice unto me, saying: "Enos, thy sins are forgiven thee. And thou shalt be blessed."

⁶And I, Enos, knew that God could not lie. Wherefore my guilt was swept away. ⁷And I saith: "Lord! How is it done?"

⁸And he saith unto me: "Because of thy faith in Christ, whom thou hast not heard nor seen. And many years passeth away before that he shall manifest himself in the flesh. Wherefore, go to it. Thy faith hath made thee whole.[b]"

⁹Now it came to pass that when I had heard these words, I began to feel a desire for the welfare of my brethren, the Nephites. Wherefore, I did pour out my whole soul unto God for them. ¹⁰And while I was thus struggling in the spirit, behold the voice of the Lord came into my mind again, saying: "I will visit thy brethren according to their diligence in keeping my commandments. I have given unto them this land, and it is a holy land. And I curse it not, save it be for the cause of iniquity. Wherefore, I will visit thy brethren according as I have said. And their transgressions will I bring down with sorrow upon their own heads."

¹¹And after that I, Enos, had heard these words, my faith began to be unshaken in the Lord. And I prayed unto him with many long strugglings for my brethren, the Lamanites.

¹²And it came to pass that after I had prayed and labored with all diligence, the Lord said unto me: "I will grant unto thee according to thy desires, because of thy faith."

¹³And now behold, this was the desire which I desired of him, that if it should so be that my people, the Nephites, should fall into transgression and by any means be destroyed, and the Lamanites should not be destroyed, that the Lord God would preserve a record of my people (the Nephites), even if it so be by the power of his holy arm—that it might be brought forth some future day unto the Lamanites, that perhaps they might be brought unto salvation. ¹⁴For at the present, our struggings were vain in restoring them to the true faith. And they swore in their wrath that if it were possible, they would

---

a. See Ephesians 6:4: "And, ye fathers, provoke not your children to wrath: but bring them up in the nurture and admonition of the Lord."

b. See Mark 10:52: "And Jesus said unto him, Go thy way; thy faith hath made thee whole."

destroy our records, and us, and also all the traditions of our fathers. ¹⁵Wherefore, I (knowing that the Lord God was able to preserve our records), I cried unto him continually. For he had said unto me: "Whatsoever thing ye shall ask in faith, believing that ye shall receive, in the name of Christ, ye shall receive it.ᵃ"

¹⁶And I had faith. And I did cry unto God, that he would preserve the records. And he covenanted with me that he would bring them forth unto the Lamanites in his own due time. ¹⁷And I, Enos, knew that it would be, according to the covenant which he had made. Wherefore, my soul did rest.

¹⁸And the Lord said unto me: "Thy fathers have also required of me this thing. And it shall be done unto them according to their faith. For their faith was like unto thine."

¹⁹And now it came to pass that I, Enos, went about among the people of Nephi, prophesying of things to come, and testifying of the things which I had heard, and seen. ²⁰And I bear record, that the people of Nephi did seek diligently to restore the Lamanites unto the true faith in God. But our labors were vain. Their hatred was fixed, and they were led by their evil nature, that they became wild, and ferocious, and a bloodthirsty people. Full of idolatry and filthiness. Feeding upon beasts of prey. Dwelling in tents. And wandering about in the wilderness with a short skin girded about their loins. And their heads shaven. And their skill was in the bow, and the scimitar, and the axe. And many of them did eat nothing save it was raw meat. And they were continually seeking to destroy us.

²¹And it came to pass that the people of Nephi did till the land, and raise all manner of grain, and of fruit, and flocks of herds, and flocks of all manner of cattle of every kind, and goats, and wild goats, and also much horses.

²²And there were exceeding many prophets among us. And the people were a stiffnecked people, hard to understand.ᵇ ²³And there was nothing, save it was exceeding harshness, preaching, and prophesying of wars, and contentions, and destructions, and continually reminding them of death, and of the duration of eternity, and the judgments and the power of God—and all these things stirring them up continually, to keep them in the fear of the Lord. I say there was nothing short of these things, and exceeding great plainness of speech, would keep them from going down speedily to destruction. And after this manner do I write concerning them.

²⁴And I saw wars between the Nephites and the Lamanites in the course of my days.

²⁵And it came to pass that I began to be old—and an hundred and seventy and nine years had passed away from the time that our father Lehi left Jerusalem. ²⁶And as I saw that I must soon go down to my grave—having been wrought upon by the power of God, that I must preach and prophesy unto this people, and declare the word according to the truth which is in Christ. And I have declared it in all my days, and have rejoiced in it above that of the world. ²⁷And I soon go to the place of my rest, which is with my redeemer. For I know that in him I shall rest. And I rejoice in the day when my mortal shall put on immortality and shall stand before him. Then shall I see his face with pleasure. And he will say unto me: "Come unto me ye blessed. There is a place prepared for you in the mansions of my Father." Amen.

---

a. Echoes Matthew 21:22: "And all things, whatsoever ye shall ask in prayer, believing, ye shall receive."

b. "Hard to understand" with the meaning that they their hearts were hard and therefore could not understand the things of God.

The Book of Jarom

Chapter I [Jarom 1]

¹Now behold—I, Jarom, write a few words according to the commandment of my father, Enos, that our genealogy may be kept. ²And as these plates are small, and as these things are written for the intent of the benefit of our brethren the Lamanites—wherefore, it must needs be that I write a little. But I shall not write the things of my prophesying, nor of my revelations. For what could I write more than my fathers have written? For have not they revealed the plan of salvation? I say unto you, yea. And this sufficeth me.

³Behold, it is expedient that much should be done among this people because of the hardness of their hearts, and the deafness of their ears, and the blindness of their minds, and the stiffness of their necks. Nevertheless, God is exceeding merciful unto them, and hath not as yet swept them off from the face of the land.

⁴And there are many among us which have many revelations, for they are not all stiff-necked. And as many as are not stiff-necked, and have faith, have communion with the Holy Spirit, which maketh manifest unto the children of men, according to their faith.

⁵And now behold, two hundred years had passed away, and the people of Nephi had waxed strong in the land. They had observed to keep the law of Moses. And the Sabbath day holy unto the Lord. And they profaned not. Neither did they blaspheme. And the laws of the land were exceeding strict.

⁶And they were scattered upon much of the face of the land. And the Lamanites also—and they were exceeding more numerous than were they of the Nephites. And they loved murder, and would drink the blood of beasts.

⁷And it came to pass that they came many times against us, the Nephites, to battle. But our kings and our leaders were mighty men in the faith of the Lord, and they taught the people the ways of the Lord. Wherefore, we withstood the Lamanites and swept them away out of our lands—and began to fortify our cities (or whatsoever place of our inheritance). ⁸And we multiplied exceedingly and spread upon the face of the land—and became exceeding rich in gold, and in silver, and in precious things, and in fine workmanship of wood—in buildings and in machinery, and also in iron, and copper, and brass, and steel. Making all manner of tools of every kind to till the ground and weapons of war. Yea, the sharp pointed arrow, and the quiver, and the dart, and the javelin, and all preparations for war. ⁹And thus being prepared to meet the Lamanites, they did not prosper against us. But the word of the Lord was verified, which he spake unto our fathers, saying: "That inasmuch as ye will keep my commandments, ye shall prosper in the land."

¹⁰And it came to pass that the prophets of the Lord did threaten the people of Nephi, according to the word of God, that if they did not keep the commandments, but should fall into transgression, they should be destroyed from off the face of the land. ¹¹Wherefore, the prophets and the priests, and the teachers, did labor diligently. Exhorting with all long-suffering the people to diligence. Teaching the law of Moses,

and the intent for which it was given. Persuading them to look forward unto the Messiah, and believe in him to come as though he already was. And after this manner did they teach them.

¹²And it came to pass that by so doing, they kept them from being destroyed upon the face of the land. For they did prick their hearts with the word continually, stirring them up unto repentance.

¹³And it came to pass that two hundred and thirty and eight years had passed away, after the manner of wars, and contentions, and dissensions for the space of much of the time.

¹⁴And I, [Jarom[a]], do not write more, for the plates are small. But behold, my brethren, ye can go to the other plates of Nephi. For behold, upon them the record of our wars are engraven, according to the writings of the kings (or that which they caused to be written). ¹⁵And I deliver these plates into the hands of my son, Omni, that they may be kept according to the commandments of my fathers.

---

a. The Printer's Manuscript has "Joram."

The Book of Omni

Chapter I [Omni 1]

¹Behold, it came to pass that I, Omni, being commanded by my father, Jarom, that I should write somewhat upon these plates to preserve our genealogy—²wherefore, in my days I would that ye should know that I fought much with the sword to preserve my people, the Nephites, from falling into the hands of their enemies, the Lamanites. But behold, I, of myself, am a wicked man. And I have not kept the statutes and the commandments of the Lord as I ought to have done.

³And it came to pass that two hundred and seventy and six years had passed away. And we had many seasons of peace. And we had many seasons of serious war and bloodshed. Yea, and in fine, two hundred and eighty and two years had passed away. And I had kept these plates according to the commandments of my fathers. And I conferred them upon my son Amaron. And I make an end.

⁴And now I, Amaron, write the things whatsoever I write (which are few) in the book of my father.

⁵Behold, it came to pass that three hundred and twenty years had passed away. And the more wicked part of the Nephites were destroyed. ⁶For the Lord would not suffer (after he had led them out of the land of Jerusalem, and kept and preserved them from falling into the hands of their enemies)—yea, he would not suffer that the words [should not be verified[a]] which he spake unto our fathers, saying that: "Inasmuch as ye will not keep my commandments, ye shall not prosper in the land." ⁷Wherefore, the Lord did visit them in great judgment. Nevertheless, he did spare the righteous, that they should not perish, but did deliver them out of the hands of their enemies.

⁸And it came to pass that I did deliver the plates unto my brother, Chemish.

⁹Now I, Chemish, write what few things I write in the same book with my brother. For behold, I saw the last which he wrote, that he wrote it with his own hand and he wrote it in the day that he delivered them unto me. And after this manner we keep the records. For it is according to the commandments of our fathers. And I make an end.

¹⁰Behold I, Abinadom, I am the son of Chemish. Behold, it came to pass that I saw much war and contention between my people, the Nephites, and the Lamanites. And I, with mine own sword, have taken the lives of many of the Lamanites in the defense of my brethren. ¹¹And behold, the record of this people is engraven upon plates which is had by the kings, according to the generations. And I know of no revelation (save that which has been written) neither prophesy. Wherefore, that which is sufficient is written. And I make an end.

¹²Behold, I am Amaleki, the son of Abinadom. Behold, I will speak unto you somewhat concerning Mosiah, which was made king over the land of Zarahemla. For

---

a. The Printer's Manuscript originally read: "yea he would not suffer that the words [ ] which he spake unto our fathers. " Oliver Cowdery added phrases required to make a complete sentence. See Skousen, *Analysis of the Textual Variants,* 2:1107.

behold, he being warned of the Lord that he should flee out of the land of Nephi—and as many as would hearken unto the voice of the Lord should also depart out of the land with him, into the wilderness.[a]

¹³And it came to pass that he did according as the Lord had commanded him. And they departed out of the land into the wilderness, as many as would hearken unto the voice of the Lord. And they were led by many preachings and prophesyings. And they were admonished continually by the word of God. And they were led by the power of his arm through the wilderness, until they came down into the land, which is called the land of Zarahemla. ¹⁴And they discovered a people which was called the people of Zarahemla.

Now, there was great rejoicing among the people of Zarahemla. And also Zarahemla did rejoice exceedingly because that the Lord had sent the people of Mosiah with the plates of brass, which contained the record of the Jews.

¹⁵Behold, it came to pass that Mosiah discovered that the people of Zarahemla came out from Jerusalem at the time that Zedekiah, king of Judah, was carried away captive into Babylon. ¹⁶And they journeyed in the wilderness and was brought by the hand of the Lord across the great waters, into the land where Mosiah discovered them. And they had dwelt there from that time forth. ¹⁷And at the time that Mosiah discovered them, they had became exceeding numerous. Nevertheless, they had had wars and serious contentions, and had fallen by the sword from time to time. And their language had become corrupted. And they had brought no records with them. And they denied the being of their Creator. Mosiah (nor the people of Mosiah) could not understand them. ¹⁸But it came to pass that Mosiah caused that they should be taught in his language.

¹⁹And it came to pass that after they were taught in the language of Mosiah, Zarahemla gave a genealogy of his fathers, according to his memory. And they are written. But not in these plates.

And it came to pass that the people of Zarahemla and of Mosiah did unite together. And Mosiah was appointed to be their king.

²⁰And it came to pass in the days of Mosiah there was a large stone brought unto him with engravings on it. And he did interpret the engravings by the gift and power of God. ²¹And they gave an account of one Coriantumr and the slain of his people. And Coriantumr was discovered by the people of Zarahemla. And he dwelt with them for the space of nine moons.

²²It also spake a few words concerning his fathers. And his first parents came out from the tower at the time the Lord confounded the language of the people. And the severity of the Lord fell upon them according, to his judgments, which is just. And their bones lay scattered in the land northward.

²³Behold I, Ameleki, was born in the days of Mosiah. And I have lived [to see his death[b]]. And Benjamin his son reigneth in his stead. ²⁴And behold, I have seen in the days of King Benjamin a serious war and much bloodshed between the Nephites and the Lamanites. But behold, the Nephites did obtain much advantage over them, yea, insomuch that King Benjamin did drive them out of the land of Zarahemla.

---

a. This sentence can be seen as complete if the "and as many" is read as "therefore as many," thus completing the "being warned" from the first clause.

b. Oliver Cowdery added this phrase, which was apparently overlooked when copying from the Original to the Printer's Manuscript. Skousen, *Analysis of the Textual Variants*, 2:1116.

^{25}And it came to pass that I began to be old. And having no seed, and knowing King Benjamin to be a just man before the Lord—wherefore, I shall deliver up these plates unto him, exhorting all men to come unto God, the Holy One of Israel—and believe in prophesying, and in revelations, and in the ministering of angels, and in the gift of speaking with tongues, and in the gift of interpreting languages, and in all things which is good. For there is nothing which is good save it comes from God, the Lord. And that which is evil cometh from the devil.

^{26}And now, my beloved brethren, I would that ye should come unto Christ, which is the Holy One of Israel—and partake of his salvation and the power of his redemption. Yea, come unto him, and offer your whole souls as an offering unto him—and continue in fasting and [praying[a]], and endure to the end.[b] And as the Lord liveth, ye will be saved.

^{27}And now I would speak somewhat concerning a certain number which went up into the wilderness, to return to the land of Nephi. For there was a large number which were desirous to possess the land of their inheritance. ^{28}Wherefore, they went up into the wilderness. And their leader, being a strong and a mighty man, and a stiff-necked man, wherefore he caused a contention among them. And they were all slain, save fifty, in the wilderness. And they returned again to the land of Zarahemla.

^{29}And it came to pass that they also took others (to a considerable number) and took their journey again into the wilderness. ^{30}And I, Amaleki, had a brother which also went with them. And I have not since known concerning them. And I am about to lay down in my grave. And these plates are full. And I make an end of my speaking.

---

a. The Printer's Manuscript has "proping."
b. The phrase "endure to the end" occurs in Matthew 24:13.

Also available from
GREG KOFFORD BOOKS

See more Book of Mormon resources at
https://gregkofford.com/collections/bofm

Second Witness: Analytical and Contextual Commentary on the Book of Mormon

Brant A. Gardner

Second Witness, a new six-volume series from Greg Kofford Books, takes a detailed, verse-by-verse look at the Book of Mormon. It marshals the best of modern scholarship and new insights into a consistent picture of the Book of Mormon as a historical document. Taking a faithful but scholarly approach to the text and reading it through the insights of linguistics, anthropology, and ethnohistory, the commentary approaches the text from a variety of perspectives: how it was created, how it relates to history and culture, and what religious insights it provides.

The commentary accepts the best modern scholarship, which focuses on a particular region of Mesoamerica as the most plausible location for the Book of Mormon's setting. For the first time, that location—its peoples, cultures, and historical trends—are used as the backdrop for reading the text. The historical background is not presented as proof, but rather as an explanatory context.

The commentary does not forget Mormon's purpose in writing. It discusses the doctrinal and theological aspects of the text and highlights the way in which Mormon created it to meet his goal of "convincing . . . the Jew and Gentile that Jesus is the Christ, the Eternal God."

Praise for the *Second Witness* series:

"Gardner not only provides a unique tool for understanding the Book of Mormon as an ancient document written by real, living prophets, but he sets a standard for Latter-day Saint thinking and writing about scripture, providing a model for all who follow. . . . No other reference source will prove as thorough and valuable for serious readers of the Book of Mormon."
-Neal A. Maxwell Institute, Brigham Young University

1. 1st Nephi: 978-1-58958-041-1
2. 2nd Nephi–Jacob: 978-1-58958-042-8
3. Enos–Mosiah: 978-1-58958-043-5
4. Alma: 978-1-58958-044-2
5. Helaman–3rd Nephi: 978-1-58958-045-9
6. 4th Nephi–Moroni: 978-1-58958-046-6

The Gift and Power: Translating the Book of Mormon

Brant A. Gardner

Hardcover, ISBN: 978-1-58958-131-9

From Brant A. Gardner, the author of the highly praised *Second Witness* commentaries on the Book of Mormon, comes *The Gift and Power: Translating the Book of Mormon*. In this first book-length treatment of the translation process, Gardner closely examines the accounts surrounding Joseph Smith's translation of the Book of Mormon to answer a wide spectrum of questions about the process, including: Did the Prophet use seerstones common to folk magicians of his time? How did he use them? And, what is the relationship to the golden plates and the printed text?

Approaching the topic in three sections, part 1 examines the stories told about Joseph, folk magic, and the translation. Part 2 examines the available evidence to determine how closely the English text replicates the original plate text. And part 3 seeks to explain how seer stones worked, why they no longer work, and how Joseph Smith could have produced a translation with them.

Traditions of the Fathers: The Book of Mormon as History

Brant A. Gardner

ISBN: 978-1-58958-665-9

**2015 Best Religious Non-fiction Award
by the Association for Mormon Letters**

"In the study of historical texts, context is king. Traditions of the Fathers masterfully contextualizes the diverse peoples of the Book of Mormon as they move, merge, and multiply across the Mesoamerican landscape. More than a simple lens, Gardner's multidisciplinary approach provides readers with illuminating, prismatic views of the Book of Mormon." — Mark Alan Wright, Assistant Professor of Ancient Scripture at Brigham Young University and Associate Editor of the *Journal of Book of Mormon Studies*

"The work he has done is rich, thorough, provocative. Like all Kofford books, this one is attractively produced, easy to hold in the hands and easy on the eyes. But best of all, it's informative, cogent, and altogether worth reading. I recommend it." — Julie J. Nichols, Association for Mormon Letters

Beholding the Tree of Life: A Rabbinic Approach to the Book of Mormon

Bradley J. Kramer

Paperback, ISBN: 978-1-58958-701-4
Hardcover, ISBN: 978-1-58958-702-1

Too often readers approach the Book of Mormon simply as a collection of quotations, an inspired anthology to be scanned quickly and routinely recited. In Beholding the Tree of Life Bradley J. Kramer encourages his readers to slow down, to step back, and to contemplate the literary qualities of the Book of Mormon using interpretive techniques developed by Talmudic and post-Talmudic rabbis. Specifically, Kramer shows how to read the Book of Mormon closely, in levels, paying attention to the details of its expression as well as to its overall connection to the Hebrew Scriptures—all in order to better appreciate the beauty of the Book of Mormon and its limitless capacity to convey divine meaning.

Praise for *Authoring the Old Testament*:

"Latter-day Saints have claimed the Book of Mormon as the keystone of their religion, but it presents itself first and foremost as a Jewish narrative. *Beholding the Tree of Life* is the first book I have seen that attempts to situate the Book of Mormon by paying serious attention to its Jewish literary precedents and ways of reading scripture. It breaks fresh ground in numerous ways that enrich an LDS understanding of the scriptures and that builds bridges to a potential Jewish readership." — Terryl L. Givens, author of *By the Hand of Mormon: The American Scripture that Launched a New World Religion*

"Bradley Kramer has done what someone ought to have done long ago, used the methods of Jewish scripture interpretation to look closely at the Book of Mormon. Kramer has taken the time and put in the effort required to learn those methods from Jewish teachers. He explains what he has learned clearly and carefully. And then he shows us the fruit of that learning by applying it to the Book of Mormon. The results are not only interesting, they are inspiring. This is one of those books that, on reading it, I thought 'I wish I'd written that!'" — James E. Faulconer, author of *The Book of Mormon Made Harder* and *Faith, Philosophy, Scripture*

The Vision of All: Twenty-five Lectures on Isaiah in Nephi's Record

Joseph M. Spencer

Paperback, ISBN: 978-1-58958-632-1
Hardcover, ISBN: 978-1-58958-633-8

In *The Vision of All*, Joseph Spencer draws on the best of biblical and Latter-day Saint scholarship to make sense of the so-called "Isaiah chapters" in the first two books of the Book of Mormon. Arguing that Isaiah lies at the very heart of Nephi's project, Spencer insists on demystifying the writings of Isaiah while nonetheless refusing to pretend that Isaiah is in any way easy to grasp. Presented as a series of down-to-earth lectures, *The Vision of All* outlines a comprehensive answer to the question of why Nephi was interested in Isaiah in the first place. Along the way, the book presents both a general approach to reading Isaiah in the Book of Mormon and a set of specific tactics for making sense of Isaiah's writings. For anyone interested in understanding what Isaiah is doing in the Book of Mormon, this is the place to start.

Praise for *Gathered in One*:

"With this book, Joseph M. Spencer has accomplished a remarkable feat. He has produced a reader-friendly, engaging study of the writings of Isaiah in the Book of Mormon that makes Isaiah accessible without overly-simplifying his theology and message." — Nicholas J. Frederick, Assistant Professor of Ancient Scripture, Brigham Young University, author of *The Bible, Mormon Scripture, and the "Rhetoric of Allusivity"*

"Spencer has produced by far the most helpful examination of the theological significance of Isaiah within the Book of Mormon. . . . In the emerging field of distinctively theological readings of the Book of Mormon, Joseph Spencer has made a major contribution, suggesting that conversations about the Book of Mormon are far from over." — John Christopher Thomas, *Journal of Book of Mormon Studies*

The 1920 Edition of the Book of Mormon: A Centennial Adventure in Latter-day Saint Book History

Richard L. Saunders

Hardcover, ISBN: 978-1-58958-775-5

Members of The Church of Jesus Christ of Latter-day Saints tend to see the Book of Mormon through the lens of personal use, as a single textual and scriptural monolith—*the* Book of Mormon. That is somewhat natural, since we tend to have at hand and in-use, only the copy or version in our language needed to study it for inspiration. In the process, the point tends to get overlooked that while we may accept the text as inspired, the physical embodiment of that text—the Book of Mormon—is a mortal reality. The *Book* of Mormon, while it has a "spirit," also has a mortal "body" (or rather, bodies) existing in space and time. As such, it has a history—and because it comes to us in the form of a book, it also has a book history.

This study is divided into three parts. The first part is a straightforward history of the edition's editing, production, and manufacturing processes. It examines key points in the reprint history of the book, following important factors in the subsequent impressions of the work across nearly thirty years of re-impressions, corrections, transfers, and one new format. The narrative crowded into chapters one through four together leave Part II to catalogue the bibliographic minutia that is the beating heart of analytic book history and which provides entertainment for true-blooded bibliophiles. The details contained in the production and manufacturing contracts and coupled to the typographical evidence explained in Part III, together resolve once and for all the question of what constitutes the 1920 edition and what does not.

Praise for *The 1920 Edition of the Book of Mormon*:

"This is both the definitive history of the 1920 edition of the Book of Mormon and a peek into how decisions were made at the highest levels of Church leadership at the time. A priceless work for bibliophiles and a great read for anyone interested in the history of The Church of Jesus Christ of Latter-day Saints in the twentieth century." — Gregory Seppi, Curator, L. Tom Perry Special Collections, Brigham Young University

The Lost 116 Pages: Reconstructing the Book of Mormon's Missing Stories

Don Bradley

Paperback, ISBN: 978-1-58958-760-1
Hardcover, ISBN: 978-1-58958-040-4

On a summer day in 1828, Book of Mormon scribe and witness Martin Harris was emptying drawers, upending furniture, and ripping apart mattresses as he desperately looked for a stack of papers he had sworn to God to protect. Those pages containing the only copy of the first three months of Joseph Smith's translation of the golden plates were forever lost, and the detailed stories they held forgotten over the ensuing years—until now.

In this highly anticipated work, author Don Bradley presents over a decade of historical and scriptural research to not only tell the story of the lost pages but to reconstruct many of the detailed stories written on them. Questions explored and answered include:

- Was the lost manuscript actually 116 pages?
- How did Mormon's abridgment of this period differ from the accounts in Nephi's small plates?
- Where did the brass plates and Laban's sword come from?
- How did Lehi's family and their descendants live the Law of Moses without the temple and Aaronic priesthood?
- How did the Liahona operate?
- Why is Joseph of Egypt emphasized so much in the Book of Mormon?
- How were the first Nephites similar to the very last?
- What message did God write on the temple wall for Aminadi to translate?
- How did the Jaredite interpreters come into the hands of the Nephite kings?
- Why was King Benjamin so beloved by his people?

Despite the likely demise of those pages to the sands of time, the answers to these questions and many more are now available for the first time in nearly two centuries in *The Lost 116 Pages: Reconstructing the Book of Mormon's Missing Stories.*

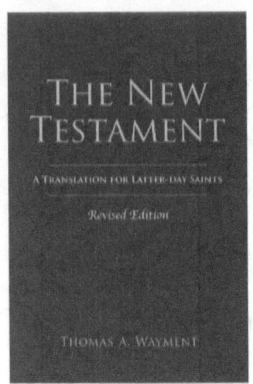

The New Testament: A Translation for Latter-day Saints, Revised Edition

Thomas A. Wayment

Paperback, ISBN: 978-1-58958-786-1

The language of the King James Bible will always be part of the Latter-day Saint cultural fabric in English. It is woven into our hymns, our ordinances, and our scriptural canon, and it has been one of the primary vehicles through which we encounter the word of God. However, when the language of translation becomes too foreign, too distant from the present age, it is time to consider the possibility of another translation. The four-hundred-year-old King James Bible in use by English speaking Latter-day Saints is an artifact of the seventeenth century and is no longer a living and breathing text. The New Testament was written by the marginalized and impoverished; its language is that of common people and not the educated elites.

The New Testament: A Translation for Latter-day Saints is an invitation to engage again the meaning of the text for a new and more diverse English readership by rendering the New Testament into modern language in a way that will help a reader more fully understand the teachings of Jesus, his disciples, and his followers.

This new revised edition is an effort to correct the first edition—in nearly two hundred instances—both in the notes and less frequently in the text. In addition, the introductory material has been expanded to include discussions of the Joseph Smith Translation and on reading scripture, and appendices have been added detailing the many instances in which the language of the New Testament appears in other Latter-day Saint scripture.

Praise for *The New Testament: A Translation for Latter-day Saints*:

"Wayment's volume is uneclipsed by any other available Latter-day Saint presentation of the New Testament." — Philip L. Barlow, *BYU Studies Quarterly*

www.ingramcontent.com/pod-product-compliance
Lightning Source LLC
Chambersburg PA
CBHW020630230426
43665CB00008B/103